D0752933

1996

Community, Identity, and Ideology

Sources for Biblical and Theological Study

General Editor:
David W. Baker
Ashland Theological Seminary

Community, Identity, and Ideology

Social Science Approaches to the Hebrew Bible

edited by

Charles E. Carter
and
Carol L. Meyers

Eisenbrauns
Winona Lake, Indiana
1996

Library of Congress Cataloging-in-Publication Data

Community, identity, and ideology : social science approaches to the Hebrew
    Bible / edited by Charles E. Carter and Carol L. Meyers.
        p.   cm. — (Sources for biblical and theological study ; 6)
    Includes bibliographical references and index.
    ISBN 1-57506-005-1 (cloth : alk. paper)
    1. Bible. O.T.—Social scientific criticism. 2. Bible. O.T.—
Criticism, interpretation, etc. 3. Sociology, Biblical. 4. Palestine—
Social life and customs—To 70 A.D.   I. Carter, Charles E. (Charles
Edward), 1952– . II. Meyers, Carol L. III. Series.
BS1182.6.C66   1996
221.6′7—dc20   96-41505
                                                                    CIP

for Gerhard Lenski
teacher, colleague, friend

CONTENTS

Indexes

SERIES PREFACE

Old Testament scholarship is well served by several recent works which detail, to a greater or lesser extent, the progress made in the study of the Old Testament. Some survey the range of interpretation over long stretches of time, while others concern themselves with a smaller chronological or geographical segment of the field. There are also brief *entrés* into the various subdisciplines of Old Testament study included in the standard introductions as well as in several useful series. All of these provide secondary syntheses of various aspects of Old Testament research. All refer to, and base their discussions upon, various seminal works by Old Testament scholars which have proven pivotal in the development and flourishing of the various aspects of the discipline.

The main avenue into the various areas of Old Testament inquiry, especially for the beginner, has been until now mainly through the filter of these interpreters. Even on a pedagogical level, however, it is beneficial for a student to be able to interact with foundational works firsthand. This contact will not only provide insight into the content of an area, but hopefully will also lead to the sharpening of critical abilities through interaction with various viewpoints. This series seeks to address this need by including not only key, ground-breaking works, but also significant responses to these. This allows the student to appreciate the process of scholarly development through interaction.

The series is also directed toward scholars. In a period of burgeoning knowledge and significant publication in many places and languages around the world, this series will endeavor to make easily accessible significant, but at times hard to find, contributions. Each volume will contain essays, articles, extracts, and the like, presenting in a manageable scope the growth and development of one of a number of different aspects of Old Testament studies. Most volumes will contain previously published material, with synthetic essays by the editor(s) of the individual volume. Some volumes, however, are expected to contain significant, previously unpublished works. To facilitate access to students and scholars, all entries will appear in English and will be newly typeset. If students are excited by the study of Scripture and scholars are encouraged in amicable dialogue, this series would have fulfilled its purpose.

DAVID W. BAKER, *series editor*
Ashland Theological Seminary

Publisher's Note

Articles republished here are reprinted without alteration, except for minor matters of style not affecting meaning. Page numbers of the original publication are marked with double brackets ([[267]], for example). Other editorial notes or supplementations are also marked with double brackets, including editorially-supplied translations of foreign words. Footnotes are numbered consecutively throughout each article, even when the original publication used another system. No attempt has been made to bring transliteration systems into conformity with a single style.

EDITORS' PREFACE

Observations about the social setting of biblical Israel are not new. When the Deuteronomic historian explains the relationship between seers, prophets, and the "man of God" (1 Sam 9:8–10), and when the writer of the Holiness Code explains ritual purity as an expression of Israel's distinctiveness (Lev 20:22 26), they are drawing primitive "sociological" conclusions about their world. Similar attempts to categorize or comment on social structure have been identified in the works of Herodotus, Plato, and the rabbinic sages. Thus, it is not surprising that as sociology and anthropology developed in the wake of the enlightenment, their insights and perspectives should be applied to the study of the Hebrew Bible.

This volume is being produced just over 100 years after the publication of the first comprehensive anthropological study of biblical Israel, W. Robertson Smith's *Lectures on the Religion of the Semites*. In the years following Robertson Smith's work, there appeared several notable studies of Israel's social setting and development, including those by Max Weber and Antonin Causse. Although several biblical scholars subsequently applied concepts from the social sciences to their work, the field of biblical studies continued to be dominated by a "humanities" approach: interests in textual, historical, linguistic, theological, and literary aspects of ancient Israel predominated. In the last thirty years, in large part because of ground-breaking efforts by George Mendenhall and Norman Gottwald, what was once an ancillary part of biblical studies may now be called a new form of biblical criticism, as social science perspectives are systematically applied to more and more of Israel's development and institutions.

This collection of essays seeks to contextualize the history and current state of the social science method and its use in the study of the Hebrew Bible. Yet, as the introductory essay demonstrates, the social sciences represent a wide variety of perspectives and approaches. In this volume, we have adhered to a more limited definition of social science methods, one that is rooted in sociology and anthropology. Many of the essays appeal to archaeology as well as (or sometimes, in preference to) the biblical texts, and all of them apply some type of social theory to the particular practice or institution they analyze. We have not, however, included

xiii

folklore studies, which, while rooted in anthropology in their earliest usage, gradually aligned themselves with literary criticism. Nor have we included any of the few distinctly "psychological" studies of biblical figures. We have attempted to be representative of the diversity of opinion and method in social science approaches and to achieve a balance between studies written from both idealist and materialist perspectives. We have also selected essays that reflect the wider range of viewpoints among biblical scholars about the usefulness of this newer social science criticism.

Part 1 contains what we consider "classic" studies, those that were somehow foundational to the history or development of the method as currently practiced; it contains essays that provide a critical perspective for the social science approach. Part 2 includes significant case studies of the biblical world; it is representative of the major currents within biblical studies: Israel's emergence and early political development as well as Israelite society and institutions.

It is our pleasure to express our gratitude to David Baker, the general editor of the SBTS series, and to James Eisenbraun, its publisher, for inviting us to edit this volume. Their patience and encouragement was important to any success it may enjoy. We are grateful to John Jackson for his careful proofreading of all of the articles. We would also like to thank Beverly Fields for her untiring work and her helpful guidance. This work would not be possible without her efforts.

CHARLES E. CARTER
Seton Hall University

CAROL L. MEYERS
Duke University

On a personal note, this volume reflects my own scholarly development. I entered the graduate program of Duke University in the fall of 1986 as a text-oriented student; for me, the humanities approach, seasoned perhaps with a pinch of archaeology here and there, was the foundation for all substantive study of the Hebrew Bible. However, I had the good fortune to be assigned as Carol Meyers's graduate assistant, and through seeing her applications of the social sciences to the biblical world, I came to view social science methods as essential to understanding ancient Israel's society and interpreting its texts. This in turn led to my fruitful association with sociologist Gerhard Lenski, whose influence on my scholarship is reflected in my introductory article and to whom this volume is dedicated.

Sincere thanks go to Carol Meyers, my colleague David Abalos of the departments of religious studies and sociology at Seton Hall University, and my wife, Elyse, for their helpful comments on my article, all of which improved its style and substance. Finally, I am grateful to my department chair, Prof. Jerry Pire and the administration of Seton Hall University, for granting me a course reduction that allowed me to work on this project.

CHARLES E. CARTER
Seton Hall University

ABBREVIATIONS

General

EB	Early Bronze Age
ET	English Translation
FS	Festschrift
LBA	Late Bronze Age
LXX	Septuagint
MB	Middle Bronze Age
OT	Old Testament

Books and Periodicals

AASOR	Annual of the American Schools of Oriental Research
AcOr	*Acta orientalia*
AJSL	*American Journal of Semitic Languages and Literature*
AJS	*American Journal of Sociology*
ANEP	J. B. Pritchard (ed.), *The Ancient Near East in pictures* (2nd ed.)
ANET	J. B. Pritchard (ed.), *Ancient Near Eastern Texts Relating to the Old Testament* (3d ed.)
AOAT	Alter Orient und Altes Testament
ARM	Archives royales de Mari
AS	Assyriological Studies
ASTI	*Annual of the Swedish Theological Institute*
BA	*Biblical Archaeologist*
BAR Int. Series	British Archaeological Reports, International Series
BASOR	*Bulletin of the American Schools of Oriental Research*
Bib	*Biblica*
BWA(N)T	Beiträge zur Wissenschaft vom Alten (und Neuen) Testament
BZAW	Beihefte zur ZAW
CAH	*Cambridge Ancient History*
CBQ	*Catholic Biblical Quarterly*
CIS	*Corpus inscripttionum semiticarum*
CTA	A. Herdner, *Corpus des tablettes en cunéiformes alphabétiques*
ErIsr	*Eretz-Israel*

FRLANT	Forschungen zur Religion und Literatur des Alten und Neuen Testaments
HibJ	*Hibbert Journal*
HKAT	Handkommentar zum Alten Testament
HSS	Harvard Semitic Studies
HT	*History and Theory*
HTR	*Harvard Theological Review*
HUCA	*Hebrew Union College Annual*
ICC	International Critical Commentary
IDB	G. A. Buttrick (ed.), *Interpreter's Dictionary of the Bible*
IDBS(up)	Supplementary volume to *IDB*
IEJ	*Israel Exploration Journal*
Int	*Interpretation*
JAAR	*Journal of the American Academy of Religion*
JAOS	*Journal of the American Oriental Society*
JBL	*Journal of Biblical Literature*
JCS	*Journal of Cuneiform Studies*
JESHO	*Journal of Economic and Social History of the Orient*
JNES	*Journal of Near Eastern Studies*
JQR(NS)	*Jewish Quarterly Review (New Series)*
JSJ	*Journal for the Study of Judaism*
JSOT	*Journal for the Study of the Old Testament*
JSOTSS	*Journal for the Study of the Old Testament Supplement Series*
JTS	*Journal of Theological Studies*
KAI	H. Donner and W. Röllig, *Kanaanäische und aramäische Inschriften*
MDOG	*Mitteilungen der deutschen Orient-Gesellschaft*
MNDP	Mitteilungen und Nachrichten des Deutschen Palästina-Vereins
Or	*Orientalia*
O(r)A(nt)	*Oriens antiquus*
OS	*Oudtestamentische Studiën*
PEQ	*Palestine Exploration Quarterly*
RAI	Rencontre assyriologique internationale
RB	*Revue biblique*
RHPR	*Revue d'histoire et de philosophie religieuses*
SBAW	Sitzungsberichte der Berliner Akademie der Wissenschaften, Philosophisch-historische Klasse
SBLDS	SBL Dissertation Series
SBLSP	SBL Seminar Papers
SMAW	Sitzungsberichte der münchner Akademie der Wissenschaften, Philosophisch-historische Klasse
SVT	Supplements to Vetus Testamentum (*see* VTSup)
ST	*Studia theologica*
TDNT	G. Kittel and G. Friedrich (eds.), *Theological Dictionary of the New Testament*
VAB	Vorderasiatische Bibliothek

VT	*Vetus Testamentum*
VTS(up)	Vetus Testamentum Supplements
WHJP	World History of the Jewish People
WMANT	Wissenschaftliche Monographien zum Alten und Neuen Testament
ZA	*Zeitschrift für Assyriologie*
ZAW	*Zeitschrift für die Alttestamentliche Wissenschaft*
ZDMG	*Zeitschrift der deutschen morgenländischen Gesellschaft*
ZDPV	*Zeitschrift des deutschen Palästina-Vereins*
ZTK	*Zeitschrift für Theologie und Kirche*

Introduction

A Discipline in Transition:

The Contributions of the Social Sciences to the Study of the Hebrew Bible

CHARLES E. CARTER

A generation ago, biblical scholars spoke confidently of the "assured results of biblical studies." These positions were given sacrosanct status, taken for granted as the foundation for all subsequent study of scripture. Recently, however, many of these consensuses have come under close scrutiny, so that what was once considered "assured" is now often questioned as a legitimate "result." While this has brought a refreshing creative impulse to the field of biblical studies,[1] it is not uncommon for scholars to speak of a "crisis" in both methodology and the direction of the discipline (Sasson 1981; Lemche 1990, reprinted below, pp. 273–86).[2] One may legitimately view these developments as a maturing of the discipline, as an attempt to take the methodologies of previous generations of scholars to new levels of sophistication. One may also see in the newer approaches not only new methodologies but a new set of questions addressed to the biblical texts and the world(s) that produced them.

---

1. Certainly, not all scholars welcome the newer methodologies or results. See I. W. Provan's often contentious and sometimes inaccurate critique of recent attempts to write the history of Israel from a minimalist perspective (1995), and the responses by T. L. Thompson (1995) and P. R. Davies (1995).

2. N. P. Lemche notes: "We find biblical study in a critical situation where nothing is considered definitive, where every single topic seems to be in a state of dissolution and fluidity. I cannot at the moment of writing recollect a single scholarly position of yesterday which has not been called into question" (1990: 75). See "On the Use of 'System Theory,' 'Macro Theories,' and 'Evolutionistic Thinking' in Modern Old Testament Research and Biblical Archaeology" (1990: 75).

In response to some of these methodological shifts, Philip Davies (1992, 1994) has suggested that a combination of literary and sociological approaches holds the most promise for advances in the study of the Hebrew Bible. This approach examines not only the literature and social setting of "Israel"[3] but also the social forces underlying the production of that literature. As Davies puts it, one must distinguish between the "society *behind* the text and the society *within* the text" (1994: 23). He further contends that the sociological study of Israel is necessary in order to place it within its appropriate historical context and in order to free the study of ancient Israel from the theological agenda that has provided the foundation for much of biblical scholarship (Davies 1992; Oden 1987, excerpts reprinted below, pp. 201–29).

The sociological study of the Hebrew Bible has not always been viewed this optimistically. Indeed, the use of social sciences in biblical studies has more often been viewed with great suspicion or simply rejected (Rainey 1987). Compared with the literary, textual, linguistic, or historical approaches, the social sciences seemed less "objective" and more difficult to subject to adequate controls (Halpern 1988).[4] This suspicion prevailed despite fruitful studies of the biblical world by prominent sociologists (Weber 1952, 1988) or biblical scholars with sociological or anthropological interests (Robertson Smith 1889; Causse 1937).

But what exactly is implied in the "social science" study of scripture? What major methodologies does this discipline of study represent; are they complementary or contradictory? How has the discipline contributed to our understanding of the social setting of ancient Israel and the literature it produced? What critiques have been offered of these methods as applied to the Hebrew Bible, and to what degree have these critiques prompted the growth of this newer field of study? In this essay, I

---

3. Using quotation marks around "Israel" is a tacit admission of Davies' observation that the term "Ancient Israel" is a construct that must be carefully defined, as he argues in *In Search of "Ancient Israel"* (1992).

4. Halpern claims: "social-scientific (methods) . . . call on models extrinsic not just to the text, but to the culture as a whole. They apply universal, unhistorical schematics, like those of the natural sciences, yet deal, like the human sciences, in variables (e.g., forms of society) whose components, whose atoms, are never isolated. Such tools cannot usher in a revolution in historical certainty. Their promise, like that of the positivist program of the nineteenth century, is an eschatological one" (Halpern 1988: 5). Although I have cited recent studies that question the value of social science methods, criticisms of the method also date to its early use. Rogerson (1978: 32–35) points to Theodor Nöldeke's critical review of Robertson Smith's *Kinship and Marriage in Early Arabia* (1885). W. F. Albright criticized both Weber and Causse for being overly positivistic and deterministic in their sociological studies of ancient Israel (Kimbrough 1972: 199, 202).

intend to address these major questions and thereby to provide a context from which the works collected in this volume may be better understood.

The Development of the Social Sciences

The social sciences refer to a range of study of humanity and human culture that includes sociology, anthropology, archaeology, economics, psychology, social psychology, and political science, among others (Harris 1968; Rogerson 1978; Wilson 1984; Lenski and Lenski 1987). These various types of the study of humanity and human societies built on the foundation of earlier attempts to categorize and analyze humans and their institutions. Primitive "sociological" observations can be found within the Hebrew Bible itself and in classical and rabbinic sources that reflect on their respective societies (Lenski and Lenski 1985: 24; Wilson 1984: 3, 10ff.).

The enlightenment provided the impetus for the growth of the social sciences and in particular for the emergence of sociology and anthropology as distinct disciplines (Lenski and Lenski 1987: 24–25; Harris 1968). Central to this was the writing of John Locke, particularly his *Essay concerning Human Understanding*, which Harris (1968: 11) calls "the midwife of all those modern behavioral disciplines, including psychology, sociology, and cultural anthropology, which stress the relationship between conditioning environment and human thought and actions." Locke's contentions that experience is the basis for human knowledge and that different experiences cause different perceptions of reality or different cultural patterns and mores were foundational for subsequent sociological and anthropological theory because they provide a basis for the comparative method that is central to the social sciences and because they suggest that there is no true universal truth to which all cultures will automatically adhere. While some of the philosophical foundations for the emergent social sciences may have been laid by Locke, Hobbes, and other enlightenment thinkers, each discipline had its own seminal thinkers and its own trajectory. What unites these divergent disciplines—and what makes them social *sciences*—is the attempt to bring the same rigor of method and observation to their study that the physical sciences demonstrates, particularly as the scientific method was developed and sharpened (Lenski 1988).

Sociology may be defined as the study of human society and its institutions. Auguste Comte is generally regarded as the "founder" of modern sociology, largely because he was the first scholar to use the term regularly (Lenski and Lenski 1987: 25). However, the work of Herbert Spencer was more important for the emerging discipline (Lenski and Lenski 1987: 25; Wilson 1984: 13). Spencer's writings led to an evolutionary perspective that dominated both sociology and anthropology in the late nineteenth and early twentieth centuries. He held that human culture has evolved gradually from "savagery" to various levels of "civilization"[5] and that all cultures, given time, will pass through similar stages (Harris 1968: 80–216; Rogerson 1978: 12–16, 22–45).

Also influential within early sociological theory was Ferdinand Tönnies (1963), from whom two of the major lines of sociological thought flowed.[6] According to A. D. H. Mayes, Tönnies characterized the developments in western Europe from the medieval period to the enlightenment as a "transition from 'community' (*Gemeinschaft*) to 'society' (*Gesellschaft*)" (Mayes 1989: 7ff.; Harris 1968: 192–93). Although he identified these phases of society with particular historical referents, he also viewed them as "ideal types" or sociological models that could be applied to other societies and therefore could be used to describe the phases through which social groups can and do pass. Generally, personal and interpersonal relationships are most important in *Gemeinschaft*—forming a "community of kinship, locality, or mind"—whereas material objects have priority over community for the social relationships within a *Gesellschaft*—which becomes increasingly rational, "a complex network of legal and moral relations" (Mayes 1989: 8).

Both Weber and Durkheim applied Tönnies' concepts to their own study of society. Weber was interested in the prior processes that led to the formation of each type, processes he referred to as the *Vergemeinschaftung*, or 'forming of community', and *Vergesellschaftung*, or 'forming of society' (Mayes 1989: 9). Durkheim suggested that social groups develop from "mechanical" to "organic" solidarities. "Mechanical solidarity" is more simple in its structure; it is characterized by a communality of experience, emotions, and outlook, and has little, if any, social differentiation or stratification. "Organic solidarity" is more complex; it is founded less on kinship ties and/or a common experience than on the contribution each individual makes to the whole (Mayes 1989: 9–10) and is marked by a clear division of labor, or status-differentiation (Harris 1968: 466–76).

---

5. One should note that *civilization* was generally defined in Eurocentric terms and that this perspective, at least in the nineteenth century, was directly related to theories of racial superiority and ultimately to outright racism. However, although in the nineteenth century the evolutionary perspective was racially motivated—often used to justify slavery—racial determinism and evolutionary views of culture are not always related. Harris shows that many early social scientists rejected racial determinism while adhering to an evolutionary viewpoint (1968: 80–141).

6. I am indebted to the helpful work by Mayes, *The Old Testament in Sociological Perspective* (1989), for this insight and much of the discussion that follows.

Karl Marx was more concerned with class divisions and the inter-relationship between the political and economic spheres. His massive *Das Kapital* was initially considered an economic and political treatise but has subsequently influenced both sociology and anthropology. Like Durkheim, Marx observed that as societies grow in complexity, social differentiation—or the division of labor—generally follows. Durkheim saw in the division of labor a creative impulse that preserved social order. However, Marx concluded that class struggle leads to disunity and eventually to open conflict; this is inevitable because the upper classes always seek to exploit the lower classes through extracting surplus from them (Harris 1968: 476). As the gap between the classes widens, the lower classes revolt, and a new society emerges. Further, Marx was interested in the relationship between the material and the ideational realms and held that ideology—indeed virtually all of culture—can be explained by one's material context.

If sociology is defined as the study of human society and its institutions, anthropology may be defined broadly as the study of humans and human culture. Typically the discipline is divided into two separate spheres: (1) physical anthropology—the study of human origins and development from our earliest hominid ancestors to modernity, and (2) cultural or social anthropology—the study of the various aspects of human culture. The former is more concerned with the biological study of humanity, whereas the latter is more interested in the development of culture and its artifacts. Archaeology is a central element of both physical and cultural anthropology; additionally, linguistics and ethnology are fundamental components of cultural anthropology (Rogerson 1978: 9).[7]

The history of anthropology can be conveniently divided into three major periods (Rogerson 1978: 11–21, following Evans-Pritchard 1951). The first period (eighteenth through mid–nineteenth centuries), like that of sociology, was tied to enlightenment philosophy and the notion of continuity in human nature. During the second period, anthropologists developed a greater interest in primitive societies along with an evolutionary perspective and, by using the comparative method, placed the study of human cultures on a more solid footing. A corollary of the evolutionary perspective was the notion of survivals, the idea that primitive beliefs and practices inevitably survived when cultures gradually became more civilized. Survivals, generally found in the form of superstitions

---

7. Rogerson notes that American and British anthropological traditions have particular nomenclature for their disciplines. While American anthropologists prefer the terms *physical* and *cultural* anthropology, British anthropologists prefer to speak of *physical* and *social* anthropology (Rogerson 1978: 10).

within the lower classes, were thought to reflect a time when an entire society held them (Rogerson 1978: 23).[8] These surviving beliefs or customs confirmed the notion of cultural evolution and were used in reconstructing ancient societies.

The third phase of anthropological history began in the 1930s and 1940s and is marked by a commitment to controlled fieldwork and a functionalist approach (Rogerson 1978: 16).[9] These concerns led to a greater emphasis on the components of cultures and their interrelationships, a more direct observation of these cultures or institutions, and a descriptive rather than value-oriented approach. Complementing these developments was the rise of the "new archaeology" (Dever 1988) and "ethnoarchaeology," both of which have impacted biblical studies. The "new archaeology" is interested in the complex interrelationships that are reflected in the archaeological record and seeks to place the various artifacts of human culture within their wider social context. Ethnoarchaeology is a form of problem-oriented study that combines archaeology with ethnography. It emerged as a means of reconstructing prehistoric societies through finding analogs with living societies of the same or similar types but has more recently been applied to historical societies for which the archaeological or written records are deficient (Carter 1991: 31–42; 1997).

Models of Societies and Cultures

One of the functions of social science theory is to provide interpretive frameworks, or heuristic models, from which to evaluate human societies, cultural traditions, and social settings (Malina 1982: 231–32; Lenski 1988). These frameworks allow us to abstract these social patterns and behaviors and to identify common as well as distinctive elements in various societies. Comparisons are made over time, geographic regions, particular patterns of organization, and other factors. This general approach, which characterizes macrosociology, is intentionally *cross-cultural* and *comparative* in nature, interested in the *historical* development of particular cultural patterns, and is *macroorganizational* (interested in the study of societies as entire units, rather than the study of their component parts in isolation) in its perspective (Lenski and Lenski 1987: 3–4, 27–51).[10]

8. This notion was popularized by E. B. Tylor, considered by Douglas (1966: 14) to be the founder of folklore studies.

9. See below, pp. 9–10, for a discussion of the structural-functional approach within the social sciences.

10. The most influential of the early sociologists, Weber, Durkheim, and Marx, all studied societies from the macrosociological perspective. It is only in this century that sociology—particularly American sociology—has focused more on the component parts of society and taken on a more decidedly ahistorical perspective.

Within basic anthropological and sociological theory, there are several different ways of grouping the most important elements or characteristics of societies. Some perspectives emphasize the forces or conflicts that lead to social change, while others emphasize the relative stasis within a society, based upon the structure and function of its institutions (conflict versus structural-functional traditions); some emphasize the particular modes of subsistence that characterize a society, whereas others emphasize the particular economic relationships within that society (subsistence strategies versus mode of production); and some emphasize the importance of ideology, while others see ideology as a function of material realities within the culture (cultural idealism versus cultural materialism). These perspectives are sometimes used alone as the primary means of examining societies; sometimes two or more approaches are used in complementary fashion. Gottwald (1979), for example, combines a structural-functional perspective with a cultural materialist orientation.

Conflict versus Structural-Functional Traditions

The conflict tradition seeks to identify and analyze relationships among social groups that compete with one another for priority and influence (Mayes 1989: 6). It examines the ways in which these competing groups assert their influence, how they protect themselves against the interests of others, how they relate to the established order (either by supporting it when it supports their purposes or by opposing it when tension exists between the group and the social order's interests), and how balance is achieved in this constant social flux. Ultimately the conflict tradition suggests that social systems achieve balance through systems of constraint; that is, they impose a certain level of order on the various groups that constitute the society (Malina 1982: 234–35). The structural-functional tradition, however, emphasizes the essential unity of societies, a unity that emerges as different groups arrive at a sense of balance through consensus (Malina 1982: 233–34). This perspective emerged from the French structuralist movement and gradually replaced Spencer's deterministic approach to social evolution that had dominated both sociology and anthropology in the nineteenth century (Lenski and Lenski 1987: 25; Harris 1968: 468–74, 514–28). The structural-functional approach identifies and analyzes the basic structures of a given society and examines their interrelationships; it is further interested in how the component parts of a society (its institutions, structures, beliefs, and so on) function within the wider society (Malina 1982: 234; Lenski and Lenski 1987: 25). While change can and must occur in all societies, it is measured and ordered, so that "non-adaptive social change is regarded as deviance" (Malina 1982: 234).

Broadly speaking, Weber's work may be placed within the context of the conflict tradition, and the structural-functional tradition may be traced to Durkheim. Studies that examine Israelite society and institutions from the conflict tradition would include Mendenhall's peasant revolt theory of Israelite origins (1962); Hanson's theory of social upheaval and the rise of the apocalyptic tradition in the early postexilic period (1975); and Lang's study on the growth of monotheism (1983). Gottwald's *Tribes of Yahweh* (1979) and Wilson's *Prophecy and Society in Ancient Israel* (1980) are written from a structural-functional perspective.

Subsistence Strategies versus Mode of Production

One of the major ways of categorizing social types identifies them according to the major technology employed by that society to survive in its particular environment. The result is a taxonomy of societies ranging from simple to complex, including hunting and gathering societies, simple and advanced horticultural societies, simple and advanced agrarian societies, simple and advanced herding societies, fishing societies, maritime societies, and industrial societies (Lenski and Lenski 1987: 78ff.). The advantages of this system of classification are that the basic societal types can be compared and contrasted with themselves and with each other and that general patterns that exist within a society of a particular type can be clearly identified. This perspective also observes that differences in social structure are based on differences in technology and differences in environment (Lenski and Lenski 1987: 82). Horticultural societies cultivate plants—distinguishing them from hunting and gathering societies that forage to secure food and other resources—but do so with digging sticks and hoes—distinguishing them from agrarian cultures, which use the plow. Simple and complex agrarian societies are distinguished by the metal used for their tools and weapons: simple agrarian societies typically use copper and bronze tools, whereas complex ones primarily use iron tools and weapons. When a group possesses the same technology as, for example, the complex agrarian society but inhabits an ecologically marginal area, it may adapt by concentrating on animal husbandry, thereby adopting a herding subsistence strategy. Applied to the study of ancient "Israel," we see that the shift from a simple to a complex agrarian society roughly parallels the rise of the state (see Frick 1985). This is predictable as technological improvements in both tools and weapons allow for an increase in surplus, which generally leads to increased stratification and specialization. Yet not all Israelites relied entirely on an agrarian subsistence strategy: some specialized in herding; others—perhaps most—supplemented agriculture with flocks and herds for a mixed subsistence strategy (Hopkins 1985; 1987, reprinted below, pp. 471–88).

While subsistence technology provides a basis for examining the basic structures of a given culture, some would question whether it tells the entire economic story. A more apt approach for them would be Marx's notion of the political economy: the interrelationship between the political and economic spheres. This is best analyzed by a society's mode of production, the "combination of the *material forces* of *production* (including human physical and mental powers) and the *social relations of production*" (Gottwald 1993a: 147). Marx maintained that societies evolve from a classless, egalitarian society to a class-based, oppressive capitalist society. He identified five steps in this cultural evolution: (1) a classless primitive society, (2) a slave-based society, (3) a feudal society, (4) modern capitalist society; (5) the future classless society (Gottwald 1993a: 150). In accounting for non-Western cultural development, Marx also identified the so-called Asiatic mode of production (AMP): this mode of production exists when there is no private ownership of land, where there is a self-sufficient village based economy and a highly centralized state (Gottwald 1993a: 153).

When these categories are applied to the study of early Israel, one sees a transition from a communitarian to a tributary (Gottwald's term for AMP) to a slave-based mode of production (Gottwald 1992). A "communitarian mode of production" typified earliest Israel (1250–1020 B.C.E.). The (extended) family was the basic unit of production, and the primary subsistence mode was agricultural, supplemented by herding. It was organized as a loose confederation of tribes with a Yahwistic perspective that protected the rights of the populace through an egalitarian ideology. The second phase was marked by the rise and fall of the monarchy (1020–586 B.C.E.) and a "native tributary mode of production." As the monarchy emerged, so did a twofold means of extracting surplus (tribute) from the peasants: taxation and a debt cycle. Taxation was both in-kind extraction of resources and conscription of labor for state projects. The debt cycle involved the extension of credit to those who worked land from those who held or supervised land for the state, and led to an indebtedness of the peasantry that was usually "perpetual and irreversible" (Gottwald 1992: 84).

After the fall of both the Northern and Southern Kingdoms, what Gottwald calls the colonial period begins (roughly 586 B.C.E.–63 B.C.E.), marked by a "foreign tributary mode of production." During this time, tribute continues to be extracted but goes primarily to the foreign overlords or the local aristocracy. During the Roman period (63 B.C.E.–74 C.E.),[11] the mode of production shifts entirely to one that is "slave-based."

11. Gottwald ends his treatment of the "Sociology of Israel" with the destruction of Jerusalem and the end of the revolt against Rome, although clearly the Roman period extends well beyond 74 C.E. Note that I have supplied the dates for Gottwald's four modes of production by inference.

Idealist versus Materialist Perspectives

A different approach to the study of the societies addresses the relationship between ideologies that humans produce and the material contexts
in which these ideologies are created. These two streams within sociology
and anthropology are often considered to be mutually exclusive; thus
Weber is considered to be an "idealist" who wrote to counteract the "materialist" perspective of Marx. However, such a reading obscures the fact
that Weber often found material explanations for many social ideas and
phenomena (Mayes 1988, reprinted below, pp. 258–72; 1989: 19; Gerth
and Mills 1947: 47ff.).

The issue is perhaps best understood as one of the degree of
influence of both ideology and material realities on human culture. For
those in the cultural idealist stream,[12] the primary interest is in the way in
which ideologies shape societies or groups and their actions. The history
of human culture and societies is therefore written around the history of
the ideas and ideologies they develop. For those approaching society
from the cultural materialist position, ideologies are equally powerful
but are explained by the physical, economic, and material realities in
which the society is embedded (Harris 1968, 1980). These ideas may function in ways that seem odd or even incoherent from an outsider's perspective, but when seen in the material context from which they arose,
they make perfect sense.

A study of the Israelite dietary laws, particularly the taboo on con-
suming pig flesh, demonstrates the two approaches. Writing from the
perspective of cultural idealism, Mary Douglas (1966, excerpts reprinted
below, pp. 119–34) sees the dietary laws as part of a larger ideational
construct intended to provide boundaries in ancient Israelite society. In
her interpretation, the Israelites observed a basic order in the world;
animals that conformed to these basic patterns maintained this order
and were therefore acceptable, or clean. Animals that did not conform
to these basic categories were considered unclean: since uncleanness introduced disorder, these animals were to be avoided.

Marvin Harris (1974; 1985, excerpts reprinted below, pp. 135–51)
suggests that the pig was considered unclean because it competes with
humans for the same resources. Ruminants, such as sheep, cows, and
goats, consume food that humans discard (hay, straw, stubble) or find
inedible (leaves or high-cellulose plants). The pig cannot survive on a

---

12. Malina (1982: 235–36) considers the term *materialism* unhelpful and identifies as
the "symbolic" model what I am calling "cultural idealism"; the "symbolic" model views society or social movements according to the symbols that they produce or that provide a
sense of coherence to the group or society.

high-cellulose diet but thrives on a diet of foods such as wheat, soybeans, maize, and other tubers, all of which humans need for their own survival. The competition for resources and the relatively marginal economic gains made raising pigs considerably more expensive than raising rumiants. This physical reality in turn led to an ideology that discouraged the raising and consumption of pigs by categorizing them as unclean.

Social Science Applications to the Hebrew Bible: W. Robertson Smith to Martin Noth

By far, the most influential of the early scholars to apply the social sciences to the Hebrew Bible was W. Robertson Smith. Robertson Smith, who may be considered the founder of social anthropology (Douglas 1966: 13), wrote exhaustively about Semitic life and culture. His *Kinship and Marriage in Early Arabia* (1885) became "the model for all subsequent analyses of acephalous, segmentary systems of descent and social organization" (Beidelman 1974: 24). But his best known and perhaps most important work is his *Lectures on the Religion of the Semites—First Series: The Fundamental Institutions*, delivered in October 1888 and March 1889 (excerpts reprinted below, pp. 43–64). The second and third series of lectures followed in March of 1890, and December of 1891, but were only recently rediscovered in 1991, and published in 1995.[13]

Many of Robertson Smith's ideas have been subsequently abandoned or even disproved by anthropologists or biblical scholars, yet his approach to the social data and the questions he brought to the biblical texts from a social perspective have had a lasting impact. Like his contemporaries, his outlook was decidedly evolutionary and comparative; thus, Semitic culture and religion were thought to have passed through a primitive, matrilineal, and totemic phase in which a social and religious relationship (or communion) was established between the group and its god through eating the totem animal that represented the deity (Beidelman 1974: 35–38; Rogerson 1978: 24–26). Although this was a less important aspect of his analysis, the notion of totemism was to have wide-ranging effects on subsequent social scientists and was taken over uncritically by Durkheim, Frazer, and Freud (Beidelman 1974: 35–38). More important, however, was his view of sacrifice and its role within Israelite culture. Robertson Smith suggested that the main function of sacrifice was to promote both social unity and the communion between the social group and its patron deity. In its earliest form, sacrifice was a joyous, spontaneous act

---

13. W. R. Smith, *Lectures on the Religion of the Semites—Second and Third Series* (1995). I have not consulted these latter lectures in my treatment of Robertson Smith's work.

that strengthened social unity within the kinship group. As cultures advanced, sacrifice in turn became more ritualistic and had only tributary significance (Beidelman 1974: 53–57; Robertson Smith 1889: 236–43). This history of the evolution of sacrifice has been widely criticized. However, Robertson Smith's basic question—what is the role of sacrifice in the social community?—remains valid. It thus forms the basis for the sociology of religion as subsequently developed by Durkheim who, like Smith, saw sacrifice as basic to social order and community (Douglas 1966: 19ff.). Durkheim followed Robertson Smith's evolutionary conclusions in another way, by suggesting that primitive culture is marked by a belief in magic, while true religion is marked by an ethical and moral perspective (Beidelman 1974: 61–62; Douglas 1966: 18–20).[14]

Robertson Smith's work is noteworthy in two other important ways: in his commitment to ethnographic fieldwork and in his recognition of material influences on ideology and ritual. Unlike most of his contemporaries, he engaged in first-hand observation of the Arab culture, which he believed maintained "survivals" of older Semitic religious patterns. He traveled to the Middle East on four occasions (Beidelman 1974: 27–28), and he mentions the importance of ethnographic study in the introduction to *Lectures on the Religion of the Semites* (1889: 5ff.). His work also demonstrates a sensitivity to the influences that material conditions have on subsequent ideology. He suggested that rituals typically have materialistic origins and meanings: "a ritual must always remain materialistic, even if its materialism is disguised under the cloak of mysticism."[15] Thus, he saw ritual and sacrifice within the context of the entire social setting and "regarded the institutional matrix as the source of religious ideas" (Harris 1974: 208).

Although the earliest use of social science study of ancient Israel and the Hebrew Bible is found in European scholarship, at the beginning of this century it would find fertile ground in the United States in the work of Louis Wallis (1907, 1912, 1935, 1945). Wallis saw in Israelite history a conflict between urban and rural cultures, with the rural culture representing the ideals of Yahwism, and the urban cultures representing the social elite, first from Canaanite and then from stratified Israelite culture. Thus, "the distinctive religious ideas of the Bible are not a *cause* but an *effect* of the struggle of interests that agitated the history" (Wallis 1907: 539). This view of a protracted cultural and class struggle is later devel-

14. Frazer, Robertson Smith's protégé, took his mentor's approach one step further, suggesting a unitary evolution from magic to religion to science. Frazer's widespread influence on anthropology, folklore studies, and theology are seen in a negative light by Beidelman (1974 throughout, but especially pp. 47ff., 58); Douglas (1966: 10–28); Harris (1968: 204–5); and Rogerson (1978: 47–54, 72–73).

15. W. Robertson Smith 1889: 437, cited by Beidelman 1974: 56–57.

oped by both Mendenhall (1962) and Gottwald (1979) in their own sociologies of biblical Israel. Equally important is the sharp distinction that Wallis draws between the theological and sociological study of the Bible and its culture. He insists on seeing "elements common to the general process of social evolution" within Israel's history (Wallis 1907: 532) and suggests that the sociological study of the Bible will yield a more complete understanding of Israelite culture.

Max Weber's *Ancient Judaism* (1952, excerpts translated and reprinted below, pp. 65–94) has had the most direct impact on biblical scholarship of any sociological study of ancient Israel. Writing as an "outsider," Weber confessed his doubts regarding the significance of his own work, noting that he entertained "but modest hopes of contributing anything essentially new to the discussion" and suggesting that his major contribution would be "some of the sociological viewpoints and questions which we address to the data" (1952: n. 1 and pp. 425–27). Instead, biblical scholars have expanded and developed several of his observations, including the social importance of the covenant (Mendenhall 1962, 1973; Noth 1960; Cross 1973), the social context of prophecy (Wilson 1980), the structure of Israelite social groups (Noth 1960; Gottwald 1979: 237–92; Stager 1985), the social setting of the Levites (Gottwald 1979: 695–96), the development of sectarianism (Talmon 1987), the "routinization" of authority, which progresses from "charismatic" to "rational" as society develops (Malamat 1973), and the various "ideal types" or models that he applied to Israel. Despite its significance, it is important to note that Weber's initial foray into the study of the Hebrew Bible reflects his larger interest in the development of capitalism in Western society. The question that he frames at the beginning of his study is, in retrospect, the wrong question with which to open the study of ancient Israel: "Why did the Jews become a 'pariah' people?" As Causse would later note, by asking this question, Weber is retrojecting a modern category or notion that characterized Jewish experience in the medieval and enlightenment periods onto the biblical period (Kimbrough 1972: 200; Mayes 1989: 80).

The French biblical scholar Antonin Causse applied the structural-functional perspective to the biblical world (Mayes 1989: 78ff.; Kimbrough 1972, 1978) in a series of works (1922; 1929; 1934, excerpts reprinted below, pp. 95–118; 1937), the most important of which is *Du group ethnique à la communauté religieuse: Le problème sociologique de la religion d'Israël* (1937). Fundamental to Causse's understanding of antiquity—and in particular Israelite culture and religion—were Durkheim's notion of the "group mentality" and Lévy-Bruhl's categorization of human development from a collective prelogical mentality to an empirical-logical, and finally to a logical mentality characterized by individualism (Kimbrough 1972: 198–202; Mayes 1989: 80ff.).

Causse saw in ancient Israel a society that was originally unified around family, clan, and tribal patterns. After the settlement in Palestine, these patterns shifted, with territorial groupings gradually replacing kinship ties. During this time period, an "organic solidarity" formed the basis of social and religious unity, with little or no concept of the individual. As the monarchy emerged, many of the older, traditional institutions were further undermined, villages gradually became dependent upon the cities, and class differentiation became more apparent (Kimbrough 1972: 200; Mayes 1989: 81). This distinction formed the basis of the prophetic call for social justice, a call that was echoed in the Psalter and its juxtaposition of the poor and the wicked (Causse 1922; Kimbrough 1972: 200). The prophetic movement at the same time idealized the ancient past of Israel and espoused a righteousness that led to a moral and ethical individualism (Kimbrough 1972: 201), one that found expression in the deuteronomic reform (Mayes 1989: 82; Causse 1937). This shift to individualism was completed in the postexilic period, in which the community of Israel was formed around its religious rather than its ethnic identity. During this period, the older symbols were once again reinterpreted in the restoration prophecies of Second Isaiah, the apocalyptic traditions, Ezekiel's visions of a new community (specifically Ezekiel 40–48), and the ritual program of the Priestly legislator (Causse 1934, 1937). The shift to individualism was completed with the rise of sects within the Judaism of the fifth and fourth centuries, a universalism found in the wisdom texts, a "missionary spirit," and a conception of community based on "faithfulness to the religious tradition and zeal for the torah" (Mayes 1989: 85–86).

The cultural and social setting of ancient Israel continued to be an important element in the study of the Hebrew Bible in the early twentieth century. The studies of Gustav Dalman on the lifeways of Palestinian culture can be broadly considered ethnographic and still provide scholars with valuable information for comparison in the reconstruction of Israelite culture (1928). Pedersen analyzed the significance of the covenant and the development of Israelite institutions (1920); de Vaux's study (1965) of ancient Israelite religion and social institutions is less directly anthropological but still examines the development of these institutions as represented within the Hebrew Bible itself and in the context of other ancient Near Eastern societies. Folklore studies, which emerged from the field of anthropology, subsequently found its rightful place within literary criticism (Rogerson 1978: 66ff.) through the work of Gunkel (1917), Mowinckel (1921), and later, Gaster (1950). Albrecht Alt applied Weber's notion of the ideal type to his study of cities (1930) and followed Robertson Smith's methodology by using Arab culture as a source for parallels in his studies of Israelite religion (Alt 1929). Noth followed Weber's notion of the social significance of the covenant as he developed his theory of an Israelite amphictyony (Noth 1930, 1960). Noth derived this heuristic model from classical studies where six and twelve tribe amphictyonies are known in Greek, Italian (Noth 1960: 88), and Etruscan societies (Gottwald 1979: 345). He suggested that the covenant between Israel and Yahweh bound the tribes together, with one central cult-shrine—located initially at Shechem but then moving to Bethel, Gilgal, and finally Shiloh—functioning as the religious center. This model gradually came to represent the consensus reconstruction of premonarchic Israel (Miller 1985: 13ff.; Bright 1981: 162ff.). However, his understanding of the amphictyony itself and his application of the model to Israel have been shown to be faulty on literary, historical, and sociological grounds (Gottwald 1979: 348–57; Mayes 1989: 60–61).

W. F. Albright's contribution to the field of biblical studies (1946, 1957, 1974)—particularly within American and Israeli scholarship—cannot be overstated. It is largely through his influence that archaeology developed as a distinct discipline within biblical studies, a tradition that continued through G. Ernest Wright (King 1983). Although Albright was well acquainted with the studies of Max Weber and Antonin Causse, he tended to view Israel's history against its ancient Near Eastern archaeological, linguistic, and historical context rather than within its sociological or anthropological setting. It would be left for G. Ernest Wright and his students, such as William Dever (1988, 1993), Eric Meyers (Meyers and Meyers 1989) and Lawrence Stager (1985), to incorporate broader social science perspectives within Syro-Palestinian archaeology.

After Alt and Noth, the use of the social sciences within biblical studies sharply declined. The discipline was dominated on the one hand by a comparative linguistic, literary, and historical approach to Israelite history and on the other hand by a theological orientation that was typically Protestant in nature. Any study of Israelite emergence or its institutions—from law to social customs to religion—tended to be written from those perspectives, with the Alt/Noth school dominant in European scholarship and the Albright school dominant in North America.

Social Science Applications to the Hebrew Bible: Mendenhall, Gottwald, and Beyond

A brief, programmatic essay by George Mendenhall, "The Hebrew Conquest of Palestine" (1962, reprinted below, pp. 152–69), gave rise to the most recent wave of social science study of the Hebrew Bible. Mendenhall's contribution may be considered both in terms of the methodological issues it raises and the model he presents. Mendenhall critiques several commonly held but seldom discussed assumptions that underlie the then-dominant theories of the entry of Israel into Canaan suggested by Albright and Alt respectively. These assumptions were that the twelve tribes of Israel entered the land from another area, that the earliest Israelites were nomads who seized and then settled Palestine, and that the Israelite tribes were an ethnic entity, distinct from their Canaanite neighbors. To these, he might have added a fourth assumption: that there were twelve tribes constituting a historical Israel before the settlement in Palestine.

Mendenhall was particularly critical of an evolutionary trajectory implicit in Alt's model, which he claimed was based on idealized notions of nomadism. He argued that a pattern of "transhumant" nomadism, characterized by seasonal migration,[16] better fit ancient Israel's past. He also pointed out that the term *tribe* had been poorly defined by biblical scholars; a comprehensive definition should include not only ethnicity but should also account for social, religious, and kinship factors. He further questioned the widely held notion that pastoral and agrarian societies were in constant conflict and suggested instead that the basic conflict of the biblical world was between an urban elite and a village peasantry.

Mendenhall's own model places the emergence of Israel in the broader context of political and socioeconomic tensions in Late Bronze Age Palestine. He equates the Hab/piru of the Amarna correspondence with the "Hebrews" and suggests that Israel emerged as a result of a "peasant revolt." In this "revolt," disaffected peasants rebelled and/or withdrew from a highly stratified Canaanite culture and subsequently settled in the marginal and largely uninhabited central hill country. They then merged with the group of Israelite slaves who had escaped from Egyptian oppression and had committed themselves to Yahweh as their protective deity. What allowed the Canaanite peasants and these former slaves to unite was a similar past—rooted in oppression—their commitment to Yahweh and to each other as a sacred covenant community, and their mutual rejection of power.

All of Mendenhall's writings seek to look behind the biblical texts—as they are and as they are studied by scholars—and to identify the social world that produced them. In particlar, they examine the impact of Yah-

---

16. Lemche (1985: 3–4 n. 10) faults Mendenhall's use of the term *transhumant* because it refers to a particularly European type of nomadism that is not only seasonal but is associated with mountain regions. However, Lemche, while technically correct, seems unaware of the many other forms of *transhumant* pastoralism that do not fit his narrow definition. Gottwald has further applied the model of transhumant nomadism to ancient Israel in *Tribes* (1979: 435–63).

wism on Israelite society and culture. For Mendenhall, whether it is in Israel's laws, its emergence from oppression through peasant revolt, or its development toward petty statism, Israel's religion—its commitment to Yahweh as its covenantal deity—explains its social development.

If Mendenhall reintroduced the social science study of the Hebrew Bible, Norman Gottwald applied sociological and anthropological theory in a more systematic way, writing on methodology (1974, reprinted below, pp. 170–81; 1992, 1993b), the emergence and religion of earliest Israel (1979), economic structure in early Israel and during the monarchy (1985, 1993a), and social ethics (1989). Like Mendenhall, Gottwald addresses the basic assumptions underlying biblical studies, many of which are both unstated and untested (1974: 89). Gottwald identifies three such assumptions that undergird the regnant theories of Israel's emergence in Palestine, assumptions that view social change as external (primarily, population displacement) and "arbitrary" (resulting from "idiosyncratic or prominent cultural elements"). Instead of these views, he maintains that change often results from indigenous social conflicts and is complex and multifaceted (1974: 92–93). With these new assumptions in place, Gottwald suggests that the emergence of Israel in Palestine should be seen as an essentially internal development in which disaffected Canaanites withdrew from the stratified society in which they lived, "retribalized," that is, willingly adopted a village-based, egalitarian economy, organized around interrelated social groups, or "tribes." To this point, he has accepted the basic outlines of Mendenhall's model, though he has provided it with a more solid anthropological basis. However, he differs with Mendenhall over the role of Israel's commitment to Yahweh as the impetus for social cohesiveness and change. Mendenhall sees Yahwism as *the* dominant factor in Israel's establishment and views earliest Israel not only as anti-statist but also as opposed to any form of political power. Gottwald, on the other hand, views Yahwism as one of many factors contributing to Israel's formation and early development and sees its commitment to Yahweh as an assertion of political power, one fundamentally different from the Canaanite structures that had controlled them prior to their "retribalism." For Mendenhall, Israel's spirituality explains its social order, whereas for Gottwald, Israel's spirituality can only be explained by its materiality (1979: xxv).

What Gottwald suggested in seed form in his article on domain assumptions, he developed fully in his monumental *Tribes of Yahweh* (1979) and his *Hebrew Bible: A Socioliterary Introduction* (1985). Both volumes are marked by a conscious attempt to account for the complexities and nuances of biblical traditions and Israelite social structures and approach biblical society both from a structural-functional and cultural materialist perspective. The result is that his sociology of early Israel, far from being "the worst of armchair sociology" (Rainey 1987), presents an impressive array of ethnographic, archaeological, and social science data and theory on pastoral nomadism (1979: 435–67), tribal structure and segmentary societies (1979: 293–337), cultural materialism (1979: 650–63), and structural-functional theory (608–21) interacting frequently with the theory of Marx, Weber, Durkheim, Fried (1967), and Service (1962, 1975). Brueggeman's positive evaulation of Gottwald is therefore justified (1980: 443); he contends that *The Tribes of Yahweh* parallels Wellhausen's *Prolegomena* and Albright's *Stone Age to Christianity* in "significance, potential and authority."

It would be a mistake to see Mendenhall and Gottwald as the only, or even the primary, advocates of a social science approach to the Hebrew Bible. Their work may be more visible, owing to the introduction and nuancing of a new model for Israel's emergence in Palestine. However, during the past thirty years, substantial contributions to the study of Israelite culture have been made from all six of the basic models outlined above. The Society of Biblical Literature has sponsored sections on the sociology of the monarchy, sociology of the Second Temple, and the social science study of the Hebrew Bible; the Constructs of the Social and Cultural Worlds of Antiquity Group, jointly sponsored by SBL, AAR, and ASOR, analyzes the models or constructs used in reconstructing the ancient world and its literatures. Since the renaissance of social science criticism, two major areas have received the bulk of the attention: (1) the emergence of Israel in Palestine, early Israelite society, and the forces leading to state formation; and (2) institutions of ancient Israel, including prophecy, Israelite religion, and gender and sexuality in Israelite society.

Israel's Emergence and Early Political Development

The account of both Mendenhall and Gottwald of an internal revolt leading to the establishment of earliest Israel demonstrated that a theory that takes several factors into account is necessary to explain something as complex as Israelite society. Accordingly, Marvin Chaney (1983) and Gerhard Lenski (1980) would modify Gottwald's and Mendenhall's model of Israel's "peasant revolt." Lenski suggests that Gottwald's theory of an internal revolt is incomplete, since it does not explain why this revolt succeeded or why Israel reverted to a monarchy after its alleged "retribalization." He proposes instead that earliest Israel was a frontier society, an adaptation of agrarian society found in marginal economic areas beyond the effective control of their culture of origin. Such societies typically "revert" to their former patterns of political organization when they themselves grow in size and complexity. Chaney builds on Lenski's suggestion of a combined frontier and peasant revolt model, examining the nature of peasant unrest from a sociological standpoint and identifying evidence of such unrest within the traditions from Joshua and Judges.

Coote and Whitelam (1986, reprinted below, pp. 335–76) and Frick (1985) identify a combination of factors and pressures to account for Israelite political development. Coote and Whitelam place earliest Israel in the context of the breakdown of Late Bronze Age social structures and see elements such as population pressure, agricultural intensification, and gradual stratification as leading to the formation of the state. Frick likewise sees these multiple causes at work, so that a subsistence-level economy was transformed to a surplus-bearing economy. Once surplus was generated, the forces were in place for Israel's segmentary society to shift to a chiefdom, a society in which one family becomes dominant and extracts surplus in exchange for providing services to the larger society. Saul's kingship is therefore best understood as a chiefdom (see also Flanagan 1981, reprinted below, pp. 311–34; and Finkelstein 1989, reprinted below, pp. 377–403). Accounting for the same period and social forces, Malamat analyzes the period of the judges from the perspective of Weber's ideal types and the nature of charismatic leadership (1973, reprinted below, pp. 293–310). Flanagan (1988) applies the metaphor of a hologram to the monarchy under David. Just as a hologram combines parts of an image to make a composite picture, so multiple perspectives are necessary for a holistic understanding of the forces leading to the monarchy. Flanagan then combines literary and archaeological data with social theory to complete his multifaceted image of the early Israelite state.

Israelite Society and Institutions

Much of the study of Israelite institutions has centered around the prophetic movement. Robert Wilson (1979, reprinted below, pp. 404–22) and Thomas Overholt (1974; 1982, reprinted below, pp. 423–47) apply crosscultural parallels to Israelite prophecy. Wilson's study centers around the nature and function of intermediaries, the social forces necessary for successful intermediation, and the role or place of the intermediary within society. Central intermediaries are part of the established social structure, while peripheral intermediaries typically function outside the ruling structure, are critical of it, and often work as agents of social change. These "ideal types" do not exist in isolation, so prophets can function in either or both categories during their lifetimes. Thus, Elijah's prophecy should be seen in the light of peripheral intermediation, whereas Elisha's fluctuated between central and peripheral. Wilson then applies this basic model first to Ephraimite tradition (primarily prophets from the Northern Kingdom, including the deuteronomic tradition and Jeremiah) and then to Judean prophecy (those writing from a Southern perspective, both in the pre- and postexilic periods).

Thomas Overholt's studies address the social psychology of the prophets against the background of Native American culture. He develops a model of prophecy that emphasizes the interrelationship between the prophet, the deity, and the community to which the prophet speaks. Like Long (1977), he places the prophets' authority not only in their supernatural call but also in the community's belief in their office and its acceptance of their message as authentic. Feedback, or response from the community to the prophet, often influences and even shapes the prophet's future message and directly affects his/her authority.

The seeds of apocalypse are often found within the prophetic movement and its interaction with a new social dynamic. Paul Hanson's approach to the emergence of the apocalyptic tradition may be placed broadly within the conflict tradition (1975). Hanson suggests that the postexilic community was marked by conflict between the priestly or hierocratic party (represented by Zerubbabel and Joshua) and the visionary party reflected in the prophecies of Third Isaiah. Thus, the visionary party represents a *Gemeinschaft* (Mayes 1989: 14–15), a community whose identity rested in its resistance to the ruling Temple establishment, which it viewed as compromised, and who sought a radical inbreaking of God to validate its utopian vision.

Paralleling and contributing to the social science study of scripture has been the rise of feminist criticism. Although much of feminist criticism is literary in nature,[17] several scholars have produced anthropological, archaeological, and/or sociological studies that examine the role and place of women in the largely patriarchal society of ancient Israel. Carol Meyers concentrates on women from the ancestor traditions through the early monarchy and suggests that while women had limited authority in the public domain, they had considerable influence in the domestic sphere (1988; forthcoming). Further, she views several of the biblical narratives as reflecting the concerns of the community she believes produced them (taking a traditional date for the Yahwist). Thus, population pressure and subsistence struggles underlie the statement of God to the woman in Genesis 3—a statement referring not to pain in childbirth as traditionally understood, but to the many labor-intensive aspects of the domestic,

17. The bibliography of this growing field is extensive and impossible to summarize adequately here. It generally follows groundbreaking works by Rosemary Radford Reuther (1974) and Phyllis Trible (1978, 1984). For a helpful source for feminist studies of the Hebrew Bible, see Mayer I. Gruber, *Women in the Biblical World* (1995).

village-based economy of Early Iron Age Palestine (1983a; see also 1983b, reprinted below, pp. 489–514). More recently she has examined gender role in Canticles (1987) and women's roles in Israelite worship, and has used ethnoarchaeological data to shed light on sacrifice (1995).

Phyllis Bird (1987, reprinted below, pp. 515–36; 1989) examines the role and place of women in the Israelite cultus. She maintains that women had a larger role within Israelite worship than has been traditionally maintained, that their 'exclusion' has been as much a product of androcentric exegesis as of historical fact. In order to present a more balanced view, she provides a more holistic understanding of cultus (including public and private, sanctioned and suppressed) and examines the religious sphere in its relationship with wider Israelite institutions.

Critiques and Methodology

As social science criticism has taken its place alongside the more traditional methods of criticism, a constructive dialogue has arisen concerning its use and abuse. This discussion typically involves at least three major concerns and suggests that social science criticism (1) undermines the notion of ancient Israel's cultural and religious distinctiveness; (2a) is unevenly used and is therefore eclectic rather than systematic, and (2b) biblical scholars apply a particular theory or method after social scientists have abandoned it; and (3) social science criticism applies models external to the biblical world that are both reductionistic and deterministic so that it actually misrepresents the biblical world. Permit me to deal with these concerns point by point.

Social science criticism undermines the long-held assumption that Israel was distinct from its neighbors, particularly in its religious tradition. One of the presuppositions of the social sciences is that all cultures have inherent value, with no cultural or religious tradition given pride of place. Because of this, some consider social science method to be inimical to the theological study of scripture. The notion that religion was one of many cultural factors influencing or expressing Israelite identity rather than the prime mover in its history, and the use of terms like ideology rather than theology to describe Israelite beliefs, seem to undermine the once-prominent idea of "biblical theology."

Anderson (1987, excerpts reprinted below, pp. 182–200) and Oden (1987) both contend that theological explanations for Israelite ritual or beliefs—or even its purported distinctiveness from its neighbors—have been overdrawn. Israelite religion was much less different from other Near Eastern religious traditions than has generally been thought. The Israelites, like their neighbors, were concerned with fertility, thought that their sacrifices provisioned their God, Yhwh, and practiced forms of kinship-based religions. Furthermore, Anderson believes that one can arrive at an accurate understanding of sacrifice in Israelite tradition only when its social and socioeconomic settings are adequately examined.

Does this deemphasis of theology mean that a social science approach is diametrically opposed to the theological study of scripture? For some, the answer would be yes; social science criticism is yet another step in removing the academic study of Israel and its traditions from a theological stranglehold, a step that is deemed necessary for any "objective" study of religion (Oden 1987; Coote and Whitelam 1986; Davies 1992). Alternatively, a social science perspective may be viewed as one of many forms of scholarly analysis that provide a more complete understanding of the context of any religious tradition and in particular those of Israel. Thus it is not surprising to find in Gottwald's work an emphasis on modern social ethics that is informed by his understanding of Israel's communitarian ideals (1989, 1992). Israel's empowering Yahwistic ideology, in turn, is thought to provide hope or encouragement for any oppressed or voiceless minority (for a similar use of exilic and postexilic ideologies, see D. L. Smith 1989).

Social science criticism has been inconsistently applied to the study of ancient Israel and often lags behind recent sociological/anthropological developments.
For scholars not trained in either sociology or anthropology, gaining even a cursory understanding of the historical context of these disciplines (that is, reading the classic works of Weber, Durkheim, and Marx) and of current theory is time-consuming and challenging. Further complicating matters are the various methodologies advocated within each particular field: scholars must choose among and between such diverse approaches as conflict, structural-functional, cultural idealist, and cultural materialist models. The effect has been that many studies purporting to use social science methods are somewhat "eclectic" (Rogerson 1985; Lemche 1990) and have achieved rather uneven results. Equally problematic has been the failure of biblical scholars to remain current in their application of sociological or anthropological ideas to the biblical world. Anderson notes that long after J. Frazer's evolutionary approach to folklore had been abandoned, many biblical scholars still accepted his ideas and used them in the influential myth-and-ritual school. Thus, some biblical scholars continue to suggest that Canaanite religion was a "fertility cult" characterized by a deterministic understanding of magic while the Israelite cult was more ethically oriented, even though textual data show fertility and ethical concerns in both Canaanite and Israelite traditions (1987: 4–14). Many other views popular in the second phase of anthropology, marked by an evolutionary view of culture, have continued to be used by scholars

of the Hebrew Bible, even though they were rejected by anthropologists in anthropology's third, field-work phase (Rogerson 1978).

These criticisms are both well taken. However, the eclectic application of theory and uneven results are to be expected in early stages of a new form of a critical method. In that Mendenhall's and Gottwald's early work represents the initial forays into social science criticism, and since Mendenhall's initial study was intended to be programmatic rather than comprehensive, they should be judged in that light.[18] But as the method matures, it should become more sophisticated and comprehensive. The work of Weber can serve as a model in this regard. Although he was trained not as a biblical scholar but as a sociologist, his immersion in the best critical scholarship of his day perhaps accounts for his continuing influence in the field. Accordingly, it is only as biblical scholars become as well read in anthropological or sociological theory as they are in their own primary discipline that truly refined studies of Israelite society and its institutions emerge. The works of Wilson (1977, 1980), Frick (1985), and Meyers (1988) all achieve this level of sophistication.

The fact that biblical scholars have tended to use anthropological theories or data that are no longer espoused among anthropologists and that many of these ideas have a long "half-life" suggests that biblical studies should adopt social science methods as a necessary rather than an optional corollary to interpretation, just as one practices historical, literary, and form criticism. Only as scholars throughout the wider discipline are informed of significant developments in the social sciences will outdated theories cease to be applied to the biblical world.

Social science criticism applies models external to the biblical world that are deterministic and reductionistic so that it actually distorts our understanding of the biblical world. The use of models in the study of ancient Israel and its society has led to numerous concerns about the nature of these models and the ways they are applied. Some suggest that empirical models are inherently positivistic, that they are espoused as the only true scientific models (Hcrion 1986, reprinted below, pp. 230–57; Lemche 1990). This scientific orientation in turn leads to a false sense of objectivity. Essentially, the argument is that any attempt to construct a falsifiable model will fail, since controlled tests—the staple of the scientific method—cannot exist in human society. This is true in part because of the variables that exist in the physical environment that impinges on human societies and in part because humans are inherently unpredictable.

18. Lemche (1985, 1990) for example, is highly critical of Mendenhall's use of social theory. For a more positive assessment of Mendenhall's work, see Rogerson (1978: 98–101).

Models are also thought to be reductionistic in that they explain complex social processes in terms of narrowly defined hypotheses (Lemche 1990: 82), so that the models and the system they intend to explain are confused (Herion 1986). Further complicating the application of models to the biblical record is the danger of reading modern assumptions back onto ancient societies (Herion 1986; Sasson 1981). Sasson observes that biblical scholars often "base their visions upon analogs and models which have been used successfully to reconstruct pasts more immediate and more familiar to them" (Sasson 1981: 7).

Finally, the social science models that scholars apply to the Hebrew Bible are often critiqued as being overly deterministic. Some models may present belief systems as culturally bound or rooted in material realities (Herion 1986). Others may suggest that all cultures of a given type in a similar environment will pass through the same stages; thus, certain trajectories of cultural evolution may be considered "unavoidable," something "which no society living under the same general conditions can *possibly escape*" (Lemche 1990: 81, emphasis mine). This, however, distorts the nature of modeling. It is one thing to suggest that social development *tends to follow certain patterns*, as evidenced in a variety of cultures, adequately studied and compared; it is quite another to claim that all societies *must by definition pass through the same stages*, with no variation and no room for human innovation.

If these dangers exist, how then should biblical scholars proceed? What methods or cautions can they use to avoid the pitfalls outlined above? How can social science approaches contribute even more directly to our understanding of ancient Israel and its social setting? I would like to conclude with a few concrete suggestions.

Interdisciplinary cooperation. With the burgeoning of knowledge across all fields of inquiry and the improvement of information technology comes a recognition that research models must change. If scholars a generation ago could remain current in the major developments within their field and could contribute as individual researchers, the pressures of the development of new subdisciplines and new means of processing information point toward greater levels of collaboration. Not only should studies of Israelite society and its institutions approach their subject from a variety of perspectives but increasingly, scholars from different disciplines will need to work together on common projects. Dever (1993) and Gottwald (1993b) have suggested this type of cross-fertilization between biblical scholars and Syro-Palestinian archaeologists, and among the humanities, social sciences, and physical sciences respectively. The Constructs of the Social and Cultural Worlds of Antiquity group of SBL/AAR/ASOR has modeled this approach by bringing together biblical scholars and scholars from other disciplines in its recent discussions.

A neutral view of so-called "primitive" societies and a wider use of ethnographic data. The increase of ethnographic fieldwork in the twentieth century has had two welcome effects. On the one hand, it has improved the quality of information available on nonindustrial societies. Furthermore, an increased appreciation of these cultures as complex social systems has replaced the demeaning attitudes toward non-Western cultures that many social scientists held in the late nineteenth and early twentieth centuries. Characteristic of this change has been an attempt not only to evaluate these cultures from the perspective of the observer (the so-called etic perspective) but also from the perspective of the members of the culture itself (the emic approach; on the emic/etic distinction, see Harris 1980: 32–45). Yet Herion warns that a cultural bias has often crept into even the best of social science studies of the Hebrew Bible, so that the urban perspective of most scholars prevents them from adequately understanding the folk or village world of the ancient Israelites (1986: 23–24).

To the extent that this critique is true, one of the best correctives would be the increased use of ethnographic information from premodern cultures in studies of Israelite society (see also Herion 1986). With adequate controls (Carter 1991: 31–42, 319–44; 1997), many of these data have the potential to inform our understanding of simple and complex agrarian societies in general and the social setting and institutions of Israel in particular. Such data have been applied with considerable success to the questions of gender (Meyers 1983a, 1983b, 1988, forthcoming), the village economy and subsistence strategies (Finkelstein 1988), and religion (Frick 1979, reprinted below, pp. 448–70; Bird 1987).

An increased sensitivity to the complexity of social processes. Gottwald (1993b) urges biblical scholars to beome more aware of the complex *process* of social development by applying a series of overlaying "social data grids" to their analyses of Israelite culture. The *physical grid* deals with natural environment and the necessary technologies, population, skills, and social organization necessary to survive that physical setting. The *cultural grid* includes the basic symbols, language, expectations, behavior, and self-understanding of people within a given culture. The *social organizational/political grid* identifies the various structures within a society that govern the interaction among its various segments. It would include issues of land tenure, production, and legal traditions and is interested in "how social power, both by persuasion and coercion, is used to meet the needs and interests of some or all of the people" (Gottwald 1993b: 80*). The *religious grid* examines the rituals and the expressed and implied beliefs of a society. Each of the grids should be studied with respect to its development in the various phases of Israel's history. Further, the various types of data, from texts, artifacts, and the social sciences, must be considered together not as an aggregate but through a form of "triangulation." In

this way, scholars "work compositely toward a measure of certitude that
no one mode of inquiry alone can provide" (Gottwald 1993b: 81*).

*The most effective way to avoid overly reductionistic or deterministic analyses
of Israelite society and culture is to adopt a methodology that is rigorous and self-
critical.* One of the contributions that both Mendenhall and Gottwald
made was to identify and critique the implicit assumptions that underlay
much of biblical scholarship. In addressing these assumptions, they were
then able to propose alternative models that account for Israelite origins
and social, political, and religious development. In effect, both were calling for a greater level of methodological sophistication. The question
remains, however: what constitutes adequate rigor? Certainly a methodology that is interdisciplinary and aware of social complexity is essential,
but I believe that even more intentionality is necessary. Herion has suggested that scholars who would apply the social sciences to the Hebrew
Bible should present and analyze the critical theory relevant to their
study (1986: 22–25). In addition, I would suggest that scholars identify
their working assumptions and, where relevant, develop falsifiable hypotheses for the models they apply or construct. The benefit of constructing models that can be tested is twofold: (1) what is often unstated and
ambiguous is forced to be clearly defined; (2) when hypotheses are
falsified, alternative models can be constructed and tested. This in turn
leads to the improving of our models and of our understanding of the
social forces operative in a given culture. It is just this type of rigor that
will lead not just to the proliferation of social science studies of ancient
Israelite society but to the ultimate maturation of the approach.[19] The
ultimate goal, then, is to produce studies that are acceptable to both biblical scholars and social scientists (Malina 1982: 241).

Conclusion

The use of social science models in the study of the Hebrew Bible has developed well beyond its origins as an ancillary and sometimes suspect tool
within the interpretive process. The conclusions of many of its early practitioners may have been surpassed, but the questions that they raised and
the ways in which they raised them have had an enormous impact on
biblical studies. The social science approach promises to broaden our
understanding not only of aspects of Israelite life long examined by social
sciences, such as its origins, early political development, and the pro-

---

19. In this statement, I have adapted the comments of G. Lenski (1988: 165) concerning rigor in sociology to the social science study of the Hebrew Bible.

phetic movement, but in ways not otherwise possible, it also promises to illuminate other areas of the biblical past, such as the social settings of wisdom, Israelite law, the exilic and postexilic periods, and the social and religious dynamics of emergent Judaism.

Bibliography

Alt, Albrecht
  1929 *Der Gott der Vater: Ein Beitrag zur Vorgeschichte der israelitischen Religion.* Beiträge zur Wissenschaft zur Alten und Neuen Testament. Stuttgart: Kohlhammer.
  1930 *Die Staatenbildung der Israeliten in Palästina: Verfassungsgeschichtliche Studien.* Reformationsprogramm der Universität. Leipzig: Edelmann.
Albright, William F.
  1946 *Archaeology and the Religion of Israel.* 2d ed. Baltimore: Johns Hopkins University Press.
  1957 *From the Stone Age to Christianity: Monotheism and the Historical Process.* 2d ed. Garden City, New York: Doubleday.
  1974 *The Archaeology of Palestine and the Bible.* Cambridge, Massachusetts: American Schools of Oriental Research. [Memorial edition]
Anderson, Gary
  1987 *Sacrifices and Offerings in Ancient Israel: Studies in Their Social and Political Importance.* Atlanta: Scholars Press.
Beidelman, Thomas
  1974 *W. Robertson Smith and the Sociological Study of Religion.* Chicago: University of Chicago Press.
Bird, Phyllis
  1987 The Place of Women in the Israelite Cultus. Pp. 397–419 in *Ancient Israelite Religion: Essays in Honor of Frank Moore Cross, Jr.,* ed. Paul D. Hanson, S. Dean McBride, and Patrick D. Miller. Philadelphia: Fortress. [Reprinted in this volume, pp. 515–36]
  1989 Women's Religion in Ancient Israel. Pp. 283–98 in *Women's Earliest Records from Ancient Egypt to Western Asia,* ed. Barbara F. Lesko. Atlanta: Scholars Press.
Bright, John
  1981 *A History of Israel.* 3d ed. Philadelphia: Westminster.
Brueggemann, Walter
  1980 *The Tribes of Yahweh:* An Essay Review. *Journal of the American Academy of Religion* 48: 441–51.
Carter, Charles
  1991 *A Social and Demographic Study of Post-Exilic Judah.* Ph.D. Dissertation, Duke University.
  1997 Ethnoarchaeology. Pp. 280–84 in vol. 2 of *The Oxford Encyclopedia of Archaeology in the Near East,* ed. Eric M. Meyers. New York: Oxford University Press. [Forthcoming]

Causse, Antonin
    1922   Les "pauvres" d'Israël: Prophetes, psalmistes, messianistes. Strasbourg: Librairie Istra.
    1929   Les dispersés d'Israël: Les origines de la diaspora et son rôle dans la formation du Judaïsme. Paris: Alcan.
    1934   Du groupe ethnique à la communauté religieuse. Le problème sociologique du judaïsme. *Revue d'histoire et de philosophie religieuses* 14: 285–335. [Translated, revised, and reprinted in this volume, as From an Ethnic Group to a Religious Community: The Sociological Problem of Judaism, pp. 95–118]
    1937   Du groupe ethnique à la communauté religieuse: Le problème sociologique de la religion d'Israël. Études d'histoire et de philosophie religieuses 33. Paris: Alcan.
Chaney, Marvin
    1983   Ancient Palestinian Peasant Movements and the Formation of Premonarchic Israel. Pp. 39–90 in *Palestine in Transition: The Emergence of Ancient Israel*, ed. David Noel Freedman and David F. Graf. Sheffield: Almond.
Coote, Robert, and Whitelam, Keith
    1986   The Emergence of Israel: Social Transformation and State Formation following the Decline in Late Bronze Age Trade. Pp. 109–47 in *Semeia 37: Social Scientific Criticism of the Hebrew Bible and Its Social World: The Israelite Monarchy*. [Reprinted in this volume, pp. 335–76]
Cross, Frank Moore
    1973   Canaanite Myth and Hebrew Epic: Essays in the History of the Religion of Israel. Cambridge: Harvard University Press.
Dalman, Gustav
    1928–39 Arbeit und Sitte in Palästina. Gütersloh: Bertelsmann.
Davies, Philip R.
    1992   In Search of "Ancient Israel." Sheffield: Sheffield Academic Press.
    1994   The Society of Biblical Israel. Pp. 22–33 in *Second Temple Studies 2: Temple and Community in the Persian Period*, ed. Tamara C. Eskenazi and Kent H. Richards. Sheffield: Sheffield Academic Press.
    1995   Method and Madness: Some Remarks on Doing History with the Bible. *Journal of Biblical Literature* 114: 699–705.
Dever, William G.
    1988   The Impact of the "New Archaeology." Pp. 337–57 in *Benchmarks in Time and Culture: An Introduction to Biblical Archaeology*, ed. Joel F. Drinkard, Gerald L. Mattingly, and J. Maxwell Miller. Atlanta: Scholars Press.
    1993   Biblical Archaeology: Death and Rebirth. Pp. 706–22 in *Biblical Archaeology Today, 1990: Proceedings of the Second International Congress on Biblical Archaeology, Jerusalem (June–July 1990)*, ed. Avraham Biran and Joseph Aviram. Jerusalem: Israel Exploration Society and Israel Academy of Sciences and Humanities.

Douglas, Mary
   1966   *Purity and Danger: An Analysis of the Concepts of Pollution and Taboo.* London: Routledge and Kegan Paul. [The essay in her book entitled The Abominations of Leviticus is reprinted in this volume, pp. 119–34]
Evans-Pritchard, E. E.
   1951   *Social Anthropology.* London: Cohen & West.
Finkelstein, Israel
   1988   *The Archaeology of the Israelite Settlement.* Jerusalem: Israel Exploration Society.
   1989   The Emergence of the Monarchy in Israel: The Environmental and Socio-Economic Aspects. *Journal for the Study of the Old Testament* 44: 43–74. [Reprinted in this volume, pp. 377–403]
Flanagan, James W.
   1981   Chiefs in Israel. *Journal for the Study of the Old Testament* 20: 47–73. [Reprinted in this volume, pp. 311–34]
   1988   *David's Social Drama: A Hologram of Israel's Early Iron Age.* Social World of Biblical Antiquity Series, 7. Sheffield: Almond.
Freedman, David Noel, and Graf, David F., eds.
   1983   *Palestine in Transition: The Emergence of Ancient Israel.* Social World of Biblical Antiquity Series 2. Sheffield: Almond.
Frick, Frank S.
   1979   Religion and Socio-Political Structure in Early Israel: An Ethno-Archaeological Approach. Pp. 233–53 in *Society of Biblical Literature, 1979: Seminar Papers,* vol. 2, ed. Paul J. Achtemeier. Society of Biblical Literature Seminar Papers 17. Missoula, Montana: Scholars Press. [Reprinted in this volume, pp. 448–70]
   1985   *The Formation of the State in Ancient Israel: A Survey of Models and Theories.* The Social World of Biblical Antiquity Series 4. Decatur, Georgia: Almond.
Fried, Morton H.
   1967   *The Evolution of Political Society.* New York: Random.
Gaster, Theodor H.
   1950   *Thespis: Ritual, Myth and Drama in the Ancient Near East.* New York: Schuman.
Gerth, Hans H., and Mills, C. Wright
   1947   Introduction: The Man and His Work. Pp. 1–74 in *From Max Weber: Essays in Sociology.* London: Kegan Paul, Trench, Trübner.
Gottwald, Norman K.
   1974   Domain Assumptions and Societal Models in the Study of Pre-Monarchic Israel. Pp. 89–100 in *Congress Volume: Edinburgh, 1974.* Supplements to Vetus Testamentum 28. Leiden: Brill. [Reprinted in this volume, pp. 170–81]
   1979   *The Tribes of Yahweh: A Sociology of the Religion of Liberated Israel, 1250–1050 B.C.E.* Maryknoll, New York: Orbis.
   1985   *The Hebrew Bible: A Socio-Literary Introduction.* Philadelphia: Fortress.

1989   The Exodus as Event and Process: A Test Case in the Biblical
           Grounding of Liberation Theology. Pp. 250–60 in *The Future of Liber-
           ation Theology: Essays in Honor of Gustavo Gutiérrez*, ed. M. H. Ellis and
           O. Maduro. Maryknoll, New York: Orbis.
1992   Sociology of Ancient Israel. Pp. 79–89 in vol. 6 of *Anchor Bible Dictio-
           nary*, ed. David Noel Freedman, David F. Graf, and Gary A. Herion.
           Garden City, New York: Doubleday.
1993a   A Hypothesis about Social Class in Monarchic Israel in the Light of
           Contemporary Studies of Social Class and Social Stratification. Paper
           presented to the Sociology of the Monarchy Group, ASOR-SBL an-
           nual meeting, November, 1985. Pp. 139–64 in *The Hebrew Bible in Its
           Social World and in Ours*. Society of Biblical Literature Semeia Studies
           25. Atlanta: Scholars Press.
1993b   Reconstructing the Social History of Early Israel. Pp. 77*–82* in
           Eretz-Israel 24: Malamat Volume.

Gruber, Mayer I.
1995   *Women in the Biblical World—A Study Guide: Women in the World of He-
           brew Scripture*. American Theological Library Association Bibliogra-
           phy Series 38. Lanham, Maryland: American Theological Library
           Association / London: Scarecrow.

Gunkel, Hermann
1920   *Das Märchen im Alten Testament*. Tübingen: Mohr.

Halpern, Baruch
1988   *The First Historians: The Hebrew Bible and History*. New York: Harper & Row.

Hanson, Paul D.
1975   *The Dawn of Apocalyptic*. Rev. ed. Philadelphia: Fortress.

Harris, Marvin
1968   *The Rise of Anthropological Theory: A History of Theories of Culture*. New
           York: Columbia University Press.
1974   *Cows, Pigs, Wars and Witches: The Riddles of Culture*. New York: Random.
1980   *Cultural Materialism: The Struggle for a Science of Culture*. New York:
           Vintage.
1987   *The Sacred Cow and the Abominable Pig: Riddles of Food and Culture*. New
           York: Simon & Schuster. [The essay in his book entitled The Abomi-
           nable Pig is reprinted in this volume, pp. 135–51]

Herion, Gary A.
1982   *The Social Organization of Tradition in Monarchic Judah*. Ph.D. Disserta-
           tion, University of Michigan.
1986   The Impact of Modern and Social Science Assumptions on the Re-
           construction of Israelite History. *Journal for the Study of the Old Testa-
           ment* 34: 3–33. [Reprinted in this volume, pp. 230–57]

Hopkins, David
1985   *The Highlands of Canaan: Agricultural Life in the Early Iron Age*. Decatur,
           Georgia: Almond.
1987   Life on the Land: The Subsistence Struggles of Early Israel. *Biblical
           Archaeologist* 50: 178–91. [Reprinted in this volume, pp. 471–88]

Kimbrough, S. T.
1972   A Non-Weberian Sociological Approach to Israelite Religion. *Journal of Near Eastern Studies* 31: 197–202.
1978   *Israelite Religion in Sociological Perspective: The Work of Antonin Causse.* Studies in Oriental Religions 4. Wiesbaden: Harrassowitz.

King, Philip J.
1983   *American Archeology in the Mideast: A History of the American Schools of Oriental Research.* Philadelphia: American Schools of Oriental Research.

Lang, Bernhard
1983   *Monotheism and the Prophetic Minority: An Essay in Biblical History and Sociology.* Social World of Biblical Antiquity Series 1. Sheffield: Almond.

Lemche, Niels Peter
1985   *Early Israel: Anthropological and Historical Studies on the Israelite Society before the Monarchy.* Leiden: Brill.
1990   On the use of "System Theory," "Macro Theories," and "Evolutionistic Thinking" in Modern Old Testament Research and Biblical Archaeology. *Scandinavian Journal of the Old Testament* 2: 73–88. [Reprinted in this volume, pp. 273–86]

Lenski, Gerhard
1980   Review of Norman K. Gottwald's *The Tribes of Yahweh. Religious Studies Review* 6/4: 275–78.
1988   Rethinking Macrosociological Theory. *American Sociological Review* 53: 163–71.

Lenski, Gerhard, and Lenski, Jean
1987   *Human Societies: An Introduction to Macrosociology.* 5th ed. New York: McGraw-Hill.

Long, Burke O.
1977   Prophetic Authority as Social Reality. Pp. 3–20 in *Canon and Authority,* ed. George W. Coats and Burke O. Long. Philadelphia: Fortress.

Malamat, Abraham
1973   Charismatic Leadership in the Book of Judges. Pp. 152–68 in *Magnalia Dei—The Mighty Acts of God: Essays on the Bible and Archaeology in Memory of G. Ernest Wright,* ed. Frank M. Cross, Werner E. Lemke, and Patrick D. Miller Jr. Garden City, New York: Doubleday. [Reprinted in this volume, pp. 293–310]

Malina, Bruce
1982   The Social Sciences and Biblical Interpretation. *Interpretation* 37: 229–42.

Marx, Karl
1936   *Capital: A Critique of Political Economy,* trans. Samuel Moore and Edward Bibbins. New York: Modern Library. [Original German pub., 1887]

Mayes, Andrew D. H.
1988   Idealism and Materialism in Weber and Gottwald. *Proceedings of the Irish Biblical Association* 11: 44–58. [Reprinted in this volume, pp. 258–72]
1989   *The Old Testament in Sociological Perspective.* London: Pickering.

Mendenhall, George
    1962   The Hebrew Conquest of Palestine. *Biblical Archaeologist* 25: 66–87.
                [Reprinted in this volume, pp. 152–69]
    1973   *The Tenth Generation: The Origins of Biblical Tradition.* Baltimore: Johns
                Hopkins University Press.
Meyers, Carol L.
    1983a   Gender Roles and Genesis 3:16 Revisited. Pp. 337-54 in *The Word of
                the Lord Shall Go Forth: Essays in Honor of David Noel Freedman in Cele-
                bration of His Sixtieth Birthday,* ed. Carol L. Meyers and M O'Connor.
                Winona Lake, Indiana: Eisenbrauns.
    1983b   Procreation, Production, and Protection: Male-Female Balance in
                Early Israel. *Journal of the American Academy of Religion* 51: 569–73.
                [Reprinted in this volume, pp. 489–514]
    1987   Gender Imagery in the Song of Songs. *Hebrew Annual Review* 10: 209–23.
    1988   *Discovering Eve: Ancient Israelite Women in Context.* New York: Oxford
                University Press
    1995   An Ethnoarchaeological Analysis of Hannah's Sacrifice. Pp. 77–91 in
                *Pomegranates and Golden Bells: Studies in Biblical, Jewish, and Near Eastern
                Ritual, Law, and Literature in Honor of Jacob Milgrom,* ed. David P.
                Wright, David Noel Freedman, and Avi Hurvitz. Winona Lake, Indi-
                ana: Eisenbrauns.
    forth-   The Family in Early Israel. In *The Family in Ancient Israel and Early Ju-
    coming   daism,* ed. Leo G. Purdue. Religion, Culture, and Family Series. Louis-
                ville, Kentucky: Westminster/John Knox.
Meyers, Carol L., and Meyers, Eric M.
    1989   Expanding the Frontiers of Biblical Archaeology. Pp. 140*–147* in
                Eretz-Israel 20: Yadin Volume.
Miller, J. Maxwell
    1985   Israelite History. Pp. 1–30 in *The Hebrew Bible and Its Modern Interpreters,*
                ed. Douglas A. Knight and Gene M. Tucker. Chico, California: Schol-
                ars Press.
Mowinckel, Sigmund
    1921–24   *Psalmenstudien: 1–3, 5–6.* Kristiania: Dybwad. Translated as *The Psalms
                in Israel's Worship.* New York: Abingdon, 1962.
Noth, Martin
    1930   *Das System der zwölf Stäme Israels.* Beiträge zur Wissenschaft vom Alten
                und Neuen Testament 4/1. Stuttgart: Kohlhammer.
    1960   *The History of Israel.* 2d ed. London: Black.
Oden, Robert
    1987   *The Bible without Theology: The Theological Tradition and Alternatives to
                It.* San Francisco: Harper & Row. [Excerpts reprinted in this volume,
                pp. 201–29]
Overholt, Thomas W.
    1974   The Ghost Dance of 1890 and the Nature of the Prophetic Process.
                Ethnohistory 21: 37–63.

1982   Prophecy: The Problem of Cross-Cultural Comparison. Pp. 55–78 in
            Semeia 21: *Anthropological Perspectives on Old Testament Prophecy.* [Re-
            printed in this volume, pp. 423–47]
Pedersen, Johannes
1920   *Israel: Its Life and Culture, I–IV.* London: Oxford University Press.
Provan, Iain W.
1995   Ideologies, Literary and Critical: Reflections on Recent Writing on
            the History of Israel. *Journal of Biblical Literature* 114: 585–606.
Rainey, Anson
1987   Review of *The Tribes of Yahweh: Sociology of the Religion of Liberated Is-
            rael. Journal of the American Oriental Society* 107: 541–43.
Rogerson, John
1978   *Anthropology and the Old Testament.* Oxford: Blackwell.
1985   The Use of Sociology in Old Testament Studies. Pp. 245–56 in *Congress
            Volume: Salamanca, 1983.* Vetus Testament Supplements 36. Leiden:
            Brill.
Reuther, Rosemary Radford
1974   *Religion and Sexism: Images of Women in the Jewish and Christian Tradi-
            tions.* New York: Simon & Schuster.
Sasson, Jack
1981   On Choosing Models for Recreating Israelite Pre-Monarchic History.
            Journal for the Study of the Old Testament 21: 3–24.
Service, Elman R.
1962   *Primitive Social Organization.* 2d ed. New York: Random.
1975   *Origins of the State and Civilization.* New York: Norton.
Smith, Daniel L.
1989   *The Religion of the Landless: The Social Context of the Babylonian Exile.*
            Bloomington, Indiana: Meyer-Stone.
Smith, W. Robertson
1885   *Kinship and Marriage in Early Arabia.* Cambridge: Cambridge Univer-
            sity Press.
1889   *Lectures on the Religion of the Semites: First Series, The Fundamental Insti-
            tutions.* 2d ed. London: Black, 1894. 3d ed. New York: Macmillan,
            1927. [The essay in his book entitled Sacrifice: Preliminary Survey is
            reprinted from the 1927 edition, in this volume, pp. 43–64]
1995   *Lectures on the Religion of the Semites: Second and Third Series,* ed. John
            Day. Sheffield: Sheffield Academic Press.
Stager, Lawrence E.
1985   The Archaeology of the Family. *Bulletin of the American Schools of Ori-
            ental Research* 260: 1–35.
Talmon, Shemaryahu
1987   The Emergence of Jewish Sectarianism in the Early Second Temple
            Period. Pp. 587–616 in *Ancient Israelite Religion: Essays in Honor of Frank
            Moore Cross, Jr.,* ed. Paul D. Hanson, S. Dean McBride, and Patrick D.
            Miller. Philadelphia: Fortress. Reprinted from Jüdische Sektenbildung

in der Frühzeit der Periode des Zweiten Tempels. Pp. 233–80 in *Max Webers Sicht des antiken Christentums*. Frankfurt a/M: Suhrkamp, 1985. Also under the English title, pp. 165–20 in *King, Cult and Calendar in Ancient Israel*. Jerusalem: Magnes, 1986.

Thompson, Thomas L.
1995   A Neo-Albrightean School in History and Biblical Scholarship? *Journal of Biblical Literature* 114: 683–98.

Tönnies, Ferdinand
1963   *Community and Society*, trans. C. P. Loomis. New York: Harper & Row. [Translation of *Gemeinschaft und Gesellschaft*, 1887]

Trible, Phyllis
1978   *God and the Rhetoric of Sexuality*. Philadelphia: Fortress.
1984   *Texts of Terror: Literary Feminist Readings of Biblical Narratives*. Philadelphia: Fortress.

Vaux, Roland de
1965   *Ancient Israel, Volume 1: Social Institutions. Volume 2: Religious Institutions*. New York: McGraw-Hill.

Wallis, Louis
1907   Sociological Significance of the Bible. *American Journal of Sociology* 12: 532–52.
1912   *Sociological Study of the Bible*. Chicago: University of Chicago Press.
1935   *God and the Social Process: A Study in Hebrew History*. Chicago: University of Chicago Press.
1942   *The Bible Is Human: A Study in Secular History*. New York: Columbia University Press.

Weber, Max
1952   *Ancient Judaism*. Trans. H. Gerth and D. Martindale. Glencoe, Illinois: Free Press. [Numerous excerpts from his book are reprinted in this volume, pp. 65–94]
1988   *The Agrarian Sociology of Ancient Civilization*. Trans. R. I. Frank. London: Verso.

Wilson, Robert R.
1977   *Genealogy and History in the Biblical World*. New Haven: Yale University Press.
1979   Prophecy and Ecstasy: A Reexamination. *Journal of Biblical Literature* 98: 321–37. [Reprinted in this volume, pp. 404–22]
1980   *Prophecy and Society in Ancient Israel*. Philadelphia: Fortress.
1984   *Sociological Approaches to the Old Testament*. Philadelphia: Fortress.

Part 1

Anthropologists, Sociologists, and the Biblical World

Introduction

Part 1 of this volume is designed to demonstrate the different types of contributions the social sciences can make to the study of the Hebrew Bible and the cultures that produced it. Section i contains seminal studies by social scientists and biblical scholars that have led to the rise of social science criticism. Section ii includes essays that critique particular social science reconstructions of ancient Israel and raise methodological issues.

W. Robertson Smith, the founder of social anthropology, was the first scholar to apply anthropological approaches to the Hebrew Bible in a systematic way. Lecture VI of his monumental *Lectures on the Religion of the Semites* lays the foundation for his analysis of the Israelite sacrificial system that followed in lectures VII through XI. In this excerpt, entitled "Sacrifices: Preliminary Survey" (pp. 43–64 below), one sees many of the assumptions that undergird his larger work. Based on his evolutionary perspective, he suggests that all Semitic culture was originally nomadic and maintains that sacrifice was transformed from an "act of social fellowship" to its later tributary and pecuniary significance. He envisions an early phase of human socioreligious development that was totemic: the sacrificial animal represented the deity to whom it was offered. One can also see the notion of survivals (or relics, as he calls them) in his treatment of the origin of the blood libation and in his consistent use of nomadic Arab culture as a backdrop for his discussion of Israelite religion. His familiarity with traditions ranging from Old South Arabic to Classical Greek, Canaanite, Carthaginian, Egyptian, and even rabbinic and medieval Jewish sources facilitated his use of the comparative method, a method that has characterized anthropology since the late nineteenth century.

Max Weber and Antonin Causse present complementary, yet different, pictures of ancient Israel. Weber begins his *Ancient Judaism* with the question "Why did the Jews become a pariah people?" (p. 68 below) and from that basis analyzes Israelite culture as it developed from the period of the ancestors to nascent Judaism in the Second Temple Period. In the excerpt reprinted here (pp. 65–94 below), we see some of the issues that influenced biblical scholars from Albrecht Alt to Robert Wilson: the social

39

setting of Israelite culture; the significance of the covenant and the tribal league; the role of the judges as "charismatic" leaders; the conception of Yahweh as a "war god"; and the social location of the prophets.

Causse's contribution is taken from a study that he subsequently expanded and included in his *Du groupe ethnique à la communauté religieuse.* In this study (translated here as "From an Ethnic Group to a Religious Community: The Sociological Problem of Judaism," pp. 95–118 below), he traces the salient features that characterized Israelite and subsequent Jewish tradition after the crisis of the exile. Specifically, he demonstrates a shift from the concept of corporate responsibility envisioned in the deuteronomic history to that of individual accountability displayed in Ezekiel and other prophets of the exile. He also examines the development and social significance of the apocalyptic traditions and contrasts them with the priestly perspective and its concern for ritual purity. Causse sees the subsequent emergence of various sects as one of the distinctive elements of Jewish tradition in the fifth and fourth centuries B.C.E. In general, his work seeks to trace religion in Israel from its earliest pre-logical and communal forms to its more fully developed individual forms.

The essays by Mary Douglas ("The Abominations of Leviticus," pp. 119–34) and Marvin Harris ("The Abominable Pig," pp. 135–51) represent the attempts of two prominent anthropologists to solve the riddle of the Israelite dietary laws. Douglas's contribution is part of a book that examines the entire concept of Israelite ritual purity and its opposite concept, pollution; Harris's contribution is from a work that seeks to provide answers for a variety of cultural conundrums. Douglas's approach to purity laws and ritual taboos represents the perspective of cultural idealism; Harris's represents that of cultural materialism. Douglas sees the taboo concerning pigs as part of the larger system of establishing social and ritual boundaries, whereas Harris suggests that the pork taboo results from the interface between physical environment and competition over resources.

After a lengthy decline in the use of the social sciences in studying the Hebrew Bible, George Mendenhall and Norman Gottwald once again bring sociological questions to the fore. Mendenhall does much more than propose a new model for the emergence of Israel in Palestine at the end of the Late Bronze Age in his programmatic article "The Hebrew Conquest of Palestine" (pp. 152–69 below). He also critiques assumptions that had dominated biblical scholarship since the work of W. Robertson Smith and Julius Wellhausen. These include the notions that Israel was initially a nomadic society and that nineteenth-century C.E. Arab Bedouin culture could serve as an adequate model for that society. He points out that the basic conflict in Syria–Palestine in the thirteenth century B.C.E. was not between settled and sown but between urban elites and oppressed peasants. This conflict, he claims, provides a more accurate context from which to view Israel's emergence: it was neither a rapid conquest nor a peaceful infiltration of land-hungry nomads that gave birth to Israel but rather a peasant revolt.

Gottwald's "Domain Assumptions and Societal Models in the Study of Pre-Monarchic Israel" (pp. 170–81 below) accepts the main lines of Mendenhall's critique and seeks to refine the peasant revolt model. He too questions assumptions that were dominant in biblical scholarship but does so in a more systematic way. In this article he critiques what he considers the three basic or "domain" assumptions concerning Israelite social development and proposes three alternatives that he believes make better sense of the available data. He advocates an approach to the study of the Hebrew Bible that goes beyond the traditional "humanities" approach, with its textual, linguistic, and historical orientation, and suggests that scholars supplement their study of ancient Israel with a social science orientation.[1]

Section ii on critical perspectives begins with two contributions that examine the relationship between scholarly presuppositions and reconstructions of ancient Israelite culture. Gary Anderson's "Sacrifices and Offerings in Ancient Israel: An Introduction" addresses a question raised by W. Robertson Smith: What is the role and function of sacrifice in Israelite society? His larger work provides an answer from a socioeconomic rather than a uniquely religious perspective. In this excerpt (pp. 182–200 below), Anderson illustrates the questionable anthropological assumptions, by means of which biblical scholars demonstrate Israel's distinctiveness from its neighbors. For example, by using Sir James Frazer's caricature of "primitive religion" as magic, they typically differentiated Israelite religion from Canaanite "magical" tradition because of its supposedly more ethical orientation. However, as Anderson points out, this distinction misunderstands the nature of Canaanite and Israelite religion and, more basically, the nature of religion itself. He then critiques the contrast of nomadic and settled cultures that W. Robertson Smith used to explain the evolution of Israelite sacrificial system. In *The Bible without Theology*, Robert Oden traces the impact the theological perspective that has dominated biblical scholarship has had on our understanding of the biblical world(s). In his view, the theological agenda has often led

1. Professor Gottwald recommended that we use his essay "Reconstructing the Social History of Early Israel" (*ErIsr* 24 [Malamat Volume; 1993] 77*–82*) instead of "Domain Assumptions." While his more recent essay reflects, in his words, a more mature understanding of the issues involved in social science studies of biblical Israel, we included "Domain Assumptions" due to its impact on the wider discipline.

scholars to inappropriate interpretations. In "Historical Understanding and Understanding the Religion of Israel" (pp. 201–29 below), he places developments in critical scholarship within the larger context of the German idealism of the late nineteenth century. He demonstrates the effect of the German historiographic tradition on biblical scholars and on their reconstructions of Israelite religion.

The essays by Gary Herion, Andrew D. H. Mayes, and Niels Peter Lemche address methodological issues inherent within social science criticism. Gary Herion (pp. 230–57 below) examines two prominent social science interpretations of ancient Israel and finds within them four specific dangers to avoid: positivism, relativism, reductionism, and determinism. Positivism involves an overly confident view of empirical or scientific models; relativism denies the possibility of any absolute moral value in a given text or situation in the biblical world; reductionism explains the complex in overly simple terms; and determinism presents social developments as the necessary effect of particular environmental or cultural factors.

Mayes (pp. 258–72 below) refers to the studies by Max Weber and Norman Gottwald on ancient Israel to argue that the assumed dichotomy between idealist and materialist perspectives is often presented in an overly simplistic manner. Weber, whose work is typically thought to demonstrate the idealist viewpoint, often showed a sensitivity to the influences of material realities on beliefs and other aspects of culture. And while Gottwald's *Tribes of Yahweh* is written from the tradition of cultural materialism, Mayes shows that the prominence Gottwald gives to Yahwism in the Israelite sources is idealist in nature.

Lemche (pp. 273–86 below) critiques the use of macrosociology, systems theory, and heuristic models by biblical scholars. He suggests that these models are typically reductionistic and deterministic in nature. He further contends that biblical scholars use social science theory in an eclectic manner and often in ways that social scientists would find troubling. In his view, models are particularly problematic when the same data are accounted for by two different models but both are "verified," because "only one model can be true." He also believes that many models are flawed in that they do not account adequately for the variables of human behavior. Of the three essays, Lemche's is the most negative in its assessment of the value of social science approaches. Mayes and Herion both close their articles with concrete proposals for more sophisticated methodology. Taken together, the five articles represent the rich dialogue within the field of biblical studies concerning the usefulness and limits of the social sciences.   (C. E. C.)

Sacrifice:
Preliminary Survey

WILLIAM ROBERTSON SMITH

[[213]] We have seen in the course of the last lecture that the practices of ancient religion required a fixed meeting-place between the worshippers and their god. The choice of such a place is determined in the first instance by the consideration that certain spots are the natural haunts of a deity, and therefore holy ground. But for most rituals it is not sufficient that the worshipper should present his service on holy ground: it is necessary that he should come into contact with the god himself, and this he believes himself to do when he directs his homage to a natural object, like a tree or a sacred fountain, which is believed to be the actual seat of the god and embodiment of a divine life, or when he draws near to an artificial mark of the immediate presence of the deity. In the oldest forms of Semitic religion this mark is a sacred stone, which is at once idol and altar; in later times the idol and the altar stand side by side, and the original functions of the sacred stone are divided between them; the idol represents the presence of the god, and the altar serves to receive the gifts of the worshipper. Both are necessary to constitute a complete sanctuary, because a complete act of worship implies not merely that the worshipper comes into the presence of his god with gestures of homage and words of prayer, but also that he lays before the deity some material oblation. In antiquity an act of [[214]] worship was a formal operation in which certain prescribed rites and ceremonies must be duly observed.

Reprinted from *Lectures on the Religion of the Semites—First Series: The Fundamental Institutions* (2d ed.; London: Black, 1894) 213–43.

And among these the oblation at the altar had so central a place that among the Greeks and Romans the words ἱερουργία and *sacrificium,* which in their primary application denote any action within the sphere of things sacred to the gods, and so cover the whole field of ritual, were habitually used, like our English word sacrifice, of those oblations at the altar round which all other parts of ritual turned. In English idiom there is a further tendency to narrow the word sacrifice to such oblations as involve the slaughter of a victim. In the Authorised Version of the Bible 'sacrifice and offering' is the usual translation of the Hebrew *zébah uminha,* that is, "bloody and bloodless oblations." For the purposes of the present discussion, however, it seems best to include both kinds of oblation under the term "sacrifice"; for a comprehensive term is necessary, and the word "offering," which naturally suggests itself as an alternative, is somewhat too wide, as it may properly include not only sacrifices but votive offerings, of treasure images and the like, which form a distinct class from offerings at the altar.

Why sacrifice is the typical form of all complete acts of worship in the antique religions, and what the sacrificial act means, is an involved and difficult problem. The problem does not belong to any one religion, for sacrifice is equally important among all early peoples in all parts of the world where religious ritual has reached any considerable development. Here, therefore, we have to deal with an institution that must have been shaped by the action of general causes, operating very widely and under conditions that were common in primitive times to all races of mankind. To construct a theory of sacrifice exclusively on the Semitic evidence would be unscientific [[215]] and misleading, but for the present purpose it is right to put the facts attested for the Semitic peoples in the foreground, and to call in the sacrifices of other nations to confirm or modify the conclusions to which we are led. For some of the main aspects of the subject the Semitic evidence is very full and clear, for others it is fragmentary and unintelligible without help from what is known about other rituals.

Unfortunately the only system of Semitic sacrifice of which we possess a full account is that of the second temple at Jerusalem;[1] and though the ritual of Jerusalem as described in the Book of Leviticus is undoubtedly

---

1. The detailed ritual laws of the Pentateuch belong to the post-exilic document commonly called the Priestly Code, which was adopted as the law of Israel's religion at Ezra's reformation (444 B.C.). To the Priestly Code belong the Book of Leviticus, together with the cognate parts of the adjacent Books, Exodus 25–31, 35–40, and Numbers 1–10, 15–19, 25–36 (with some inconsiderable exceptions). With the Code is associated an account of the sacred history from Adam to Joshua, and some ritual matter is found in the historical sections of the work, especially in Exodus 12, where the law of the Passover is mainly priestly,

based on very ancient tradition, going back to a time when there was no substantial difference, in point of form, between Hebrew sacrifices and those of the surrounding nations, the system as we have it dates from a time when sacrifice was no longer the sum and substance of worship. In the long years of Babylonian exile the Israelites who remained true to the faith of Jehovah had learned to draw nigh to their God without the aid of sacrifice and offering, and, when they returned to Canaan, they did not return to the old [[216]] type of religion. They built an altar, indeed, and restored its ritual on the lines of old tradition, so far as these could be reconciled with the teaching of the prophets and the Deuteronomic law—especially with the principle that there was but one sanctuary at which sacrifice could be acceptably offered. But this principle itself was entirely destructive of the old importance of sacrifice, as the stated means of converse between God and man. In the old time every town had its altar, and a visit to the local sanctuary was the easy and obvious way of consecrating every important act of life. No such interweaving of sacrificial service with everyday religion was possible under the new law, nor was anything of the kind attempted. The worship of the second temple was an antiquarian resuscitation of forms which had lost their intimate connection with the national life, and therefore had lost the greater part of their original significance. The Book of Leviticus, with all its fulness of ritual detail, does not furnish any clear idea of the place which each kind of altar service held in the old religion, when all worship took the form of sacrifice. And in some particulars there is reason to believe that the desire to avoid all heathenism, the necessity for giving expression to new religious ideas, and the growing tendency to keep the people as far as possible from the altar and make sacrifice the business of a priestly caste, had introduced into the ritual features unknown to more ancient practice.

The three main types of sacrifice recognised by the Levitical law are the whole burnt-offering (ʿōla), the sacrifice followed by a meal of which the flesh of the victim formed the staple (shélem, zébaḥ), and the sin-offering (ḥaṭṭāth), with an obscure variety of the last named called asham (A.V. 'trespass-offering'). Of these ʿōla and zébaḥ are frequently

---

and represents post-exilic usage. The law of Deuteronomy (seventh cent. B.C.) and the older codes of Exodus 20–23, 34, have little to say about the rules of ritual, which in old times were matters of priestly tradition and not incorporated in a law-book. A just view of the sequence and dates of the several parts of the Pentateuch is essential to the historical study of Hebrew religion. Readers to whom this subject is new may refer to J. Wellhausen's *Prolegomena* [[to the History of Ancient Israel]] (Eng. trans., Edinburgh, 1883), to the article "Pentateuch," *Encycl. Brit.*, 9th ed., to my *Old Test. in the Jewish Church* (2nd ed. [[New York: Appleton, 1892), or to Professor Driver's *An Introduction* [[to the Literature of the Old Testament* (9th ed.; New York: Scribner's, 1899)]].

mentioned in the older literature, and they [[217]] are often spoken of
together, as if all animal sacrifices fell under one or the other head. The
use of sacrifice as an atonement for sin is also recognised in the old
literature, especially in the case of the burnt-offering, but there is little or
no trace of a special kind of offering appropriated for this purpose before
the time of Ezekiel.[2] The formal distinctions with regard to Hebrew
sacrifices that can be clearly made out from the pre-exilic literature are—

1. The distinction between animal and vegetable oblations (*zebah*
   and *minha*).
2. The distinction between offerings that were consumed by fire
   and such as were merely set forth on the sacred table (the shewbread).
3. The distinction between sacrifices in which the consecrated gift
   is wholly made over to the god, to be consumed on the altar or
   otherwise disposed of in his service, and those at which the god
   and his worshippers partake together in the consecrated thing.
   To the latter class belong the *zebahim*, or ordinary animal sacrifices, in which a victim is slain, its blood poured out at the altar,
   and the fat of the intestines with certain other pieces burned,
   while the greater part of the flesh is left to the offerer to form
   the material of a sacrificial banquet.

These three distinctions, which are undoubtedly ancient, and applicable to the sacrifices of other Semitic nations, suggest three heads under
which a preliminary survey of the subject may be conveniently arranged.
But not till we reach the third head shall we find ourselves brought face
to face with the deeper aspects of the problem of the origin and significance of sacrificial worship. [[218]]

(1) *The material of sacrifice.* The division of sacrifices into animal and
vegetable offerings involves the principle that sacrifices—as distinct from
votive offerings of garments, weapons, treasure and the like—are drawn
from edible substances, and indeed from such substances as form the
ordinary staple of human food. The last statement is strictly true of the
Levitical ritual; but, so far as the flesh of animals is concerned, it was
subject, even in the later heathen rituals, to certain rare but important exceptions, unclean or sacred animals, whose flesh was ordinarily forbidden
to men, being offered and eaten sacramentally on very solemn occasions.

2. See Wellhausen, *Prolegomena*, chap. ii. The Hebrew designations of the species of
sacrifices are to be compared with those on the Carthaginian tables of fees paid to priests
for the various kinds of offerings, *CIS.* Nos. 165, 166ff., but the information given in these
is so fragmentary that it is difficult to make much of it. See below, p. 60 n. 61.

We shall see by and by that in the earliest times these extraordinary sacrifices had a very great importance in ritual, and that on them depends the theory of the oldest sacrificial meals; but, as regards later times, the Hebrew sacrifices are sufficiently typical of the ordinary usage of the Semites generally. The four-footed animals from which the Levitical law allows victims to be selected are the ox, the sheep, and the goat, that is, the "clean" domestic quadrupeds which men were allowed to eat. The same quadrupeds are named upon the Carthaginian inscriptions that give the tariff of sacrificial fees to be paid at the temple,[3] and in Lucian's account of the Syrian ritual at Hierapolis.[4] The Israelites neither ate nor sacrificed camels, but among the Arabs the camel was common food and a common offering. The swine, on the other hand, which was commonly sacrificed and eaten in Greece, was forbidden food to all the Semites,[5] and occurs as a sacrifice only in certain exceptional rites of the kind already alluded to. Deer, gazelles and other kinds of game were eaten by the Hebrews, but not sacrificed, and from Deut 12:16 we may conclude that this was an [[219]] ancient rule. Among the Arabs, in like manner, a gazelle was regarded as an imperfect oblation, a shabby substitute for a sheep.[6] As regards birds, the Levitical law admits pigeons and turtledoves, but only as holocausts and in certain purificatory ceremonies.[7] Birds seem also to be mentioned in the Carthaginian sacrificial lists; what is said of them is very obscure, but it would appear that they might be used either for ordinary sacrifices (*shélem kalīl*) or for special purposes piacular

---

3. *CIS.* Nos. 165, 167.

4. Lucian, *ut sup.* (Syrians); Sozomen, vi. 38 (all Saracens).

5. *Dea Syria,* liv.

6. Wellhausen p. 115; Ḥārith, *Moʿall.* 69; especially *Lisān,* vi. 211. The reason of this rule, and certain exceptions, will appear in the sequel.

7. Lev 1:14; 12:6, 8; 14:22; 15:14, 29; Num 6:10. Two birds, of which one is slain and its blood used for lustration, appear also in the ritual for cleansing a leper, or a house that has been affected with leprosy (Lev 14:4f., 49f.). Further, the turtle-dove and nestling (pigeon) appear in an ancient covenant ceremony (Gen 15:9ff.). The fact that the dove was not used by the Hebrews for any ordinary sacrifice, involving a sacrificial meal, can hardly be, in its origin, independent of the sacrosanct character ascribed to this bird in the religion of the heathen Semites. The Syrians would not eat doves, and their very touch made a man unclean for a day (*Dea Syria,* liv). In Palestine also the dove was sacred with the Phœnicians and Philistines, and on this superstition is based the common Jewish accusation against the Samaritans, that they were worshippers of the dove (see for all this S. Bochart, *Hierozoicon,* [[*sive, bipertitum opus De animalibus Sacrae Scripturae* [London: Roycroft, 1663]]] II. i. 1). Nay, sacred doves that may not be harmed are found even at Mecca. In legal times the dove was of course a "clean" bird to the Hebrews, but it is somewhat remarkable that we never read of it in the Old Testament as an article of diet—not even in 1 Kgs 5:2ff.[4:22ff.]—though it is now one of the commonest table-birds all over the East.

and oracular. That the quail was sacrificed to the Tyrian Baal appears from Athenæus, ix. 47, p. 392*d.* See p. 469 ⟦not reprinted in this volume⟧.

Fish were eaten by the Israelites, but not sacrificed; among their heathen neighbours, on the contrary, fish—or certain kinds of fish—were forbidden food, and were sacrificed only in exceptional cases.[8]

Among the Hebrew offerings from the vegetable kingdom, meal, wine and oil take the chief place,[9] and these were also the chief vegetable constituents of man's daily food.[10] ⟦220⟧ In the lands of the olive, oil takes the place that butter and other animal fats hold among northern nations, and accordingly among the Hebrews, and seemingly also among the Phœnicians,[11] it was customary to mingle oil with the cereal oblation before it was placed upon the altar, in conformity with the usage at ordinary meals. In like manner no cereal offering was complete without salt,[12] which, for physiological reasons, is a necessary of life to all who use a cereal diet, though among nations that live exclusively on flesh and milk it is not indispensable and is often dispensed with. Wine, which as Jotham's parable has it, "cheereth gods and men,"[13] was added to whole burnt-offerings and to the oblation of victims of whose flesh the worshippers partook.[14] The sacrificial use of wine, without which no feast was complete, seems to have been well-nigh universal wherever the grape was known[15] and even penetrated to Arabia, where wine was a scarce and costly luxury imported from abroad. Milk, on the other hand, though one of the commonest articles of food among the Israelites, has no place in Hebrew sacrifice, but libations of milk were offered by the Arabs, and also at Carthage.[16] Their absence among the Hebrews may perhaps be explained by the rule of Exod 23:18, Lev 2:11, which excludes all ferments from presentation at the altar; for in hot climates milk ferments rapidly and is generally eaten sour.[17] The same principle covers the

---

8. See below, pp. 292ff. ⟦not included here⟧.

9. Cf. Mic 6:7 with Lev 2:1ff.

10. Ps 104:14f.

11. In *CIS.* No. 165, line 14, the בלל is to be interpreted by the aid of Lev 7:10, and understood of bread or meal moistened with oil.

12. Lev 2:13.

13. Judg 9:13.

14. Num 15:5.

15. For some exceptions see Aesch., *Eum.* 107; Soph., *Oed. Col.* 100, with Schol.; Paus. ii. 11. 4; v. 15. 10 (Greek libations to the Eumenides and to the Nymphs); and Athen. xv. 48 (libations to the sun at Emesa).

16. Wellhausen p. 114f.; *CIS.* No. 165, line 14; No. 167, line 10.

17. The rule against offering fermented things on the altar was not observed in northern Israel in all forms of sacrifice (Amos 4:5), and traces of greater freedom in this respect appear also in Lev 7:13, 23:17. It seems strange that wine should be admitted in sacrifice and

⟦221⟧ prohibition of "honey,"[18] which term, like the modern Arabic *dibs*, appears to include fruit juice inspissated by boiling—a very important article of food in modern and presumably in ancient Palestine. Fruit in its natural state, however, was offered at Carthage,[19] and was probably admitted by the Hebrews in ancient times.[20] Among the ⟦222⟧ Hebrews vegetable or cereal oblations were sometimes presented by themselves, especially in the form of first-fruits, but the commonest use of them was as an accompaniment to an animal sacrifice. When the Hebrew ate flesh, he ate bread with it and drank wine, and when he offered flesh on the table of his God, it was natural that he should add to it the same concomitants which were necessary to make up a comfortable and generous meal.

---

leaven excluded, for leaven is a product of vinous fermentation, and leavened bread equally with wine is to the nomad a foreign luxury (*al-khamr wal-khamir* ⟦'both wine and that which is leavened'⟧, *Agh.* xix. 25), so that both alike must have been wanting in the oldest type of Hebrew sacrifices. Thus the continued prohibition of leaven in sacrifice, after wine was admitted, can hardly be regarded as a mere piece of religious conservatism, but must have some further significance. It is possible that in its oldest form the legal prohibition of leaven applied only to the Passover, to which Exod 23:18, 34:25, specially refer. In this connection the prohibition of leaven is closely associated with the rule that the fat and flesh must not remain over till the morning. For we shall find by and by that a similar rule applied to certain Saracen sacrifices nearly akin to the Passover, which were even eaten raw, and had to be entirely consumed before the sun rose. In this case the idea was that the efficacy of the sacrifice lay in the living flesh and blood of the victim. Everything of the nature of putrefaction was therefore to be avoided, and the connection between leaven and putrefaction is obvious.

The only positive law against the sacrificial use of milk is that in Exod 23:19, 34:26: "Thou shalt not seethe a kid in its mother's milk." Mother's milk is simply goat's milk, which was that generally used (Prov 27:27), and flesh seethed in milk is still a common Arabian dish; sour milk is specified as the kind employed in *PEF. Qu. St.* 1888, p. 188. The context of the passages in Exodus shows that some ancient form of sacrifice is referred to; cf. Judg 6:19, where we have a holocaust of sodden flesh. A sacrificial gift sodden in sour milk would evidently be of the nature of fermented food; but I do not feel sure that this goes to the root of the matter. Many primitive peoples regard milk as a kind of equivalent for blood, and thus to eat a kid seethed in its mother's milk might be taken as equivalent to eating "with the blood," and be forbidden to the Hebrews along with the bloody sacraments of the heathen, of which more hereafter.

18. Lev 2:11.

19. *CIS.* No. 166.

20. The term *hillūlīm*, applied in Lev 19:24 to the consecrated fruit borne by a new tree in its fourth year, is applied in Judg 9:27 to the Canaanite vintage feast at the sanctuary. The Carthaginian fruit-offering consisted of a branch bearing fruit, like the "ethrog" of the modern Jewish feast of Tabernacles. The use of "goodly fruits" at this festival is ordained in Lev 23:40, but their destination is not specified. In Carthage, though the inscription that speaks of the rite is fragmentary, it seems to be clear that the fruit was offered at the altar, for incense is mentioned with it; and this, no doubt, is the original sense of the Hebrew rite also. Cf. the raisin-cakes (A.V. "flagons of wine"), Hos 3:1, which from the context appear to be connected with the worship of the Baalim.

Of these various oblations animal sacrifices are by far the most important in all the Semitic countries. They are in fact the typical sacrifice, so that among the Phœnicians the word *zébaḥ*, which properly means a slaughtered victim, is applied even to offerings of bread and oil.[21] That cereal offerings have but a secondary place in ritual is not unintelligible in connection with the history of the Semitic race. For all the Semites were originally nomadic, and the ritual of the nomad Arabs and the settled Canaanites has so many points in common that there can be no question that the main lines of sacrificial worship were fixed before any part of the Semitic stock had learned agriculture and adopted cereal food as its ordinary diet. It must be observed, however, that animal food—or at least the flesh of domestic animals, which are the only class of victims admitted among the Semites as ordinary and regular sacrifices—was not a common article of diet even among the nomad Arabs. The everyday food of the nomad consisted of milk, of game, when he could get it, and to a limited extent of dates and meal—the latter for the most part being attainable only by purchase or robbery. Flesh [[223]] of domestic animals was eaten only as a luxury or in times of famine.[22] If therefore the sole principle that governed the choice of the material of sacrifices had been that they must consist of human food, milk and not flesh would have had the leading place in nomad ritual, whereas its real place is exceedingly subordinate. To remove this difficulty it may be urged that, as sacrifice is food offered to the gods, it ought naturally to be of the best and most luxurious kind that can be attained; but on this principle it is not easy to see why game should be excluded, for a gazelle is not worse food than an old camel.[23] The true solution of the matter lies in another direction. Among the Hebrews

---

21. *CIS.* No. 165, line 12; 167, line 9. In the context צד can hardly mean game, but must be taken, as in Josh 9:11ff., of cereal food, the ordinary "provision" of agricultural peoples.

22. See the old narratives, *passim,* and compare C. M. Doughty, *Travels in Arabia Deserta* (Cambridge: Cambridge University Press, 1888) i. 325f. The statement of Fränkel, *Fremd-wörter,* p. 31, that the Arabs lived mainly on flesh, overlooks the importance of milk as an article of diet among all the pastoral tribes, and must also be taken with the qualification that the flesh used as ordinary food was that of wild beasts taken in hunting. On this point the evidence is clear; Pliny, *H. N.* vi. 161, "nomadas lacte et ferina carne useci" [['the nomads are accustomed to use milk and the flesh of game']]; Agatharchides, *ap.* Diod. Sic. iii. 44. 2; Ammianus, xiv. 4, 6, "uictus uniuersis caro ferina est lactisque abundans copia qua sustentantur" [['the universal sustenance is wild flesh and an abounding supply of milk, by means of which they are sustained']]; Nilus [[*Nili opera quaedam nondum edita* (Paris, 1639) 27]]. By these express statements we must interpret the vaguer utterances of Diodorus (xix. 94. 9) and Agatharchides (*ap.* Diod. iii. 43. 5) about the ancient diet of the Nabatæans: the "nourishment supplied by their herds" was mainly milk. Certain Arab tribes, like the modern Sleyb, had no herds and lived wholly by hunting, and these perhaps are referred to in what Agatharchides says of the Banizomenes, and in the Syriac life of Simeon Stylites (Assemani, *Mart.* ii. 345), where, at any rate, *besrd d'haiwāthā* means game.

23. Cf. Gen 27:7.

no sacrificial meal was provided for the worshippers unless a victim was sacrificed; if the oblation was purely cereal it was wholly consumed either on the altar or by the priests, in the holy place, i.e., by the representatives of the deity.[24] In like manner the only Arabian meal-offering about which we have particulars, that of the god Ocaiṣir,[25] was laid before the idol in handfuls. The poor, however, were allowed to partake of it, being viewed no doubt as the guests of the deity. [224] The cereal offering therefore has strictly the character of a tribute paid by the worshipper to his god, as indeed is expressed by the name *minḥa*, whereas when an animal is sacrificed, the sacrificer and the deity feast together, part of the victim going to each. The predominance assigned in ancient ritual to animal sacrifice corresponds to the predominance of the type of sacrifice which is not a mere payment of tribute but an act of social fellowship between the deity and his worshippers. Why this social meal always includes the flesh of a victim will be considered in a subsequent lecture.

All sacrifices laid upon the altar were taken by the ancients as being literally the food of the gods. The Homeric deities "feast on hecatombs,"[26] nay, particular Greek gods have special epithets designating them as the goat-eater, the ram-eater, the bull-eater, even "the cannibal," with allusion to human sacrifices.[27] Among the Hebrews the conception that Jehovah eats the flesh of bulls and drinks the blood of goats, against which the author of Psalm 50 protests so strongly, was never eliminated from the ancient technical language of the priestly ritual, in which the sacrifices are called לחם אלהים 'the food of the deity'. In its origin this phrase must belong to the same circle of ideas as Jotham's "wine which cheereth gods and men." But in the higher forms of heathenism the crass materialism of this conception was modified, in the case of fire-offerings, by the doctrine that man's food must be etherealised or sublimated into fragrant smoke before the gods partake of it. This observation brings us to the second of the points which we have noted in connection with Hebrew sacrifice, viz., the distinction between sacrifices that are merely set forth on the sacred table before the deity, and such as are consumed by fire upon the altar. [225]

(2) The table of shewbread has its closest parallel in the *lectisternia* of ancient heathenism, when a table laden with meats was spread beside the idol. Such tables were set in the great temple of Bel at Babylon,[28] and, if any weight is to be given to the apocryphal story of Bel and the Dragon

---

24. Lev 2:3, 5:11, 6:16[23].
25. Yācūt, *s.v.*; Wellhausen, p. 62ff.
26. *Iliad*, ix. 531.
27. αἰγοφάγος, χριοφάγος, ταυροφάγος, Διόνυσος ὠμηστής.
28. Herod. i. 181, 183; Diod. Sic. ii. 9. 7.

in the Greek Book of Daniel, it was popularly believed that the god actually consumed the meal provided for him,[29] a superstition that might easily hold its ground by priestly connivance where the table was spread inside a temple. A more primitive form of the same kind of offering appears in Arabia, where the meal-offering to Ocaiṣir is cast by handfuls at the foot of the idol mingled with the hair of the worshipper,[30] and milk is poured over the sacred stones. A narrative of somewhat apocryphal colour, given without reference to his authority by A. Sprenger,[31] has it that in the worship of ⁽Amm-anas in Southern Arabia, whole hecatombs were slaughtered and left to be devoured by wild beasts. Apart from the exaggeration, there may be something in this; for the idea that sacred animals are the guests or clients of the god is not alien to Arabian thought,[32] and to feed them is an act of religion [[226]] in many heathen systems, especially where, as in Egypt,[33] the gods themselves are totem-dieties, i.e., personifications or individual representations of the sacred character and attributes which, in the purely totem stage of religion, were ascribed without distinction to all animals of the holy kind. Thus at Cynopolis in Egypt, where dogs were honoured and fed with sacred food, the local deity was the divine dog Anubis, and similarly in Greece, at the sanctuary of the Wolf Apollo (Apollo Lycius) of Sicyon, an old tradition preserved—though in a distorted form—the memory of a time when flesh used to be set forth for the wolves.[34] It is by no means impossible that something of the same sort took place at certain Arabian shrines, for we have already

29. The story, so far as it has a basis in actual superstition, is probably drawn from Egyptian beliefs; but in such matters Egypt and Babylon were much alike; Herod. i. 182.

30. The same thing probably applies to other Arabian meal-offerings, e.g., the wheat and barley offered to Al-Kholaṣa (Azrāci, p. 78). As the dove was the sacred bird at Mecca, the epithet *Moṭ⁽im al-ṭair* 'he who feeds the birds', applied to the idol that stood upon Marwa (ibid.), seems to point to similar meal-offerings rather than to animal victims left lying before the god. The 'idol' made of *ḥais*, i.e., a mass of dates kneaded up with butter and sour milk, which the B. Ḥanîfa ate up in time of famine (see the *Lexx. s.v.* تباعة; Ibn Coteiba, ed. Wüst. p. 299; Birūnī, *Chron.*, p. 210), probably belonged to the widespread class of cereal offerings, shaped as rude idols and eaten sacramentally (F. Liebrecht, *Zur Volkskunde: Alte und neue Aufsätze* [Heilbronn: Henninger, 1879] 436; *ZDMG* 30, p. 539).

31. [[*Das Leben und die Lehre des Mohammed* (Berlin: Nicolai, 1861–65)]] iii. 457.

32. See above, p. 142ff. [[not reprinted in this volume]], and the god-name Moṭ⁽im al-ṭair in the last note but one; also Hamdāni's account of the offerings at Sāwid, *supra*, p. 177 [[not reprinted in this volume]].

33. Strabo, xvii. lines 39f. (p. 812).

34. Pausanias, ii. 9. 7. The later rationalism which changed the Wolf-god into a Wolf-slayer gave the story a corresponding twist by relating that the flesh was poisoned, under the god's directions, with the leaves of a tree whose trunk was preserved in the temple, like the sacred erica at Byblus.

learned how closely the gods were related to the *jinn* [['genie']] and the *jinn* to wild animals, and the list of Arabian deities includes a Lion-god (Yaghūth) and a Vulture-god (Nasr),[35] to whose worship rites like those described by Sprenger would be altogether appropriate.

But while it cannot be thought impossible that sacrificial victims were presented on holy ground and left to be devoured by wild beasts as the guests or congeners of the gods, I confess that there seems to me to be no sufficient evidence that such a practice had any considerable place in Arabian ritual. The leading idea in the animal sacrifices of the Semites, as we shall see by and by, was not that of a gift made over to the god, but of an act of communion, [[227]] in which the god and his worshippers unite by partaking together of the flesh and blood of a sacred victim. It is true that in the case of certain very solemn sacrifices, especially of *piacula* [['propitiatory sacrifices']] to which class the sacrifices cited by Sprenger appear to belong, the victim sometimes came to be regarded as so sacred that the worshippers did not venture to eat of it at all, but that the flesh was burned or buried or otherwise disposed of in a way that secured it from profanation; and among the Arabs, who did not use burning except in the case of human sacrifices, we can quite well understand that one way of disposing of holy flesh might be to leave it to be eaten by the sacred animals of the god. Or again, when a sacrifice is expressly offered as a ransom, as in the case of the hundred camels with which ʿAbd-al-Moṭṭalib redeemed his vow to sacrifice his son, it is intelligible that the offerer reserves no part of the flesh, but leaves it to anyone who chooses to help himself; or even (according to another reading) leaves it free to man and beast.[36] On the whole, however, all the well-authenticated accounts of Arabian sacrifice seem to indicate that the original principle, that the worshippers must actually eat of the sacred flesh, was very rigorously held to.[37] Wellhausen indeed is disposed to think that the practice of slaughtering animals and leaving them beside the altar to be devoured by wild beasts was not confined to certain exceptional cults, but prevailed generally in the case of the *ʿatāir* (sing. *ʿatīra*) or annual sacrifices presented by the Arabs in the month Rajab, which originally corresponded

---

35. See W. R. Smith, *Kinship* [[*and Marriage in Early Arabia*]] (Cambridge: Cambridge University Press, 1885)]] 223, 242; T. Nöldeke, *ZDMG* (1886) 186. See also, for the Himyarite Vulture-god, *ZDMG* 29, p. 600, and compare the eagle standard of Morra, Nābigha, iv. 7, Ahlw. = xxi. 7, Der.

36. Ibn Hish. p. 100, line 7; Ṭabarī, i. 1078, line 4 (Wellhausen, p. 116).

37. The evidence of Nilus is very important in this connection; for the interval between his time and that of the oldest native traditions is scarcely sufficient to allow for the development of an extensive system of sacrifice without a sacrificial meal; *infra*, p. 338 [[not reprinted here]].

to the Hebrew Passover-month (Abib, Nisan).[38] [[228]] "It is remarkable," says Wellhausen, "how often we hear of the *ʿatāïr* lying round the altar-idol, and sometimes in poetical comparisons the slain are said to be left lying on the battlefield like *ʿatāïr.*"[39] But on the Arabian method of sacrifice the carcases of the victims naturally lie on the ground, beside the sacred stone, till the blood, which is the god's portion, has drained into the *ghabghab*, or pit, at its foot, and till all the other ritual prescriptions have been fulfilled. Thus at a great feast when many victims were offered together, the scene would resemble a battlefield; indeed, it is impossible to imagine a more disgusting scene of carnage than is still presented every year at Minā on the great day of sacrifice, when the ground is literally covered with innumerable carcasses. It is not therefore necessary to suppose that the *ʿatāïr* at Rajab were left to the hyæna and the vulture; and, as the name *ʿatīra* seems to be also used in a more general sense of any victim whose blood is applied to the sacred stones at the sanctuary, it is hardly to be thought that there was anything very exceptional in the form of the Rajab ceremony.

In the higher forms of Semitic heathenism offerings of the shewbread type are not very conspicuous; in truth the idea that the gods actually consume the solid food deposited [[229]] at their shrines is too crude to subsist without modification beyond the savage state of society; the ritual may survive, but the sacrificial gifts, which the god is evidently unable to dispose of himself, will come to be the perquisite of the priests, as in the case of the shewbread, or of the poor, as in the meal sacrifice to Ocaiṣir. In such cases the actual eating is done by the guests of the deity, but the god himself may still be supposed to partake of food in a subtle and supersensuous way. It is interesting to note the gradations of ritual that correspond to this modification of the original idea.

In the more primitive forms of Semitic religion the difficulty of conceiving that the gods actually partake of food is partly got over by a predominant use of liquid oblations; for fluid substances, which sink in and

---

38. Cf. Wellhausen, pp. 94f. [[1st ed.]], 98f. [[2d ed.]]. To complete the parallelism of the Passover with the Rajab offerings, Wellhausen desiderates evidence connecting the *ʿatāïr* of Rajab with the sacrifice of firstlings. The traditionists, e.g., Bokhārī, vi. 207 (at the close of the *Kit. al-ʿacīca*), distinguish between firstlings (*faraʿ*) and *ʿatīra*, but the line of distinction is not sharp. The lexicons apply the name *faraʿ*, not only to firstlings sacrificed while their flesh was still like glue (*Lisān*, x. 120), but also to the sacrifice of one beast in a hundred, which is what the scholiast on Ḥārith's *Moʿall.* 69 understands by the *ʿatīra*. Conversely the *Lisān*, vi. 210, defines the *ʿatīra* as a firstling (*awwal mā yuntaj* [['first that is brought']]) which was sacrificed to the gods. If we could accept this statement without reserve, in the general confusion of the later Arabs on the subject, it would supply what Wellhausen desiderates.

39. Wellhausen, p. 115 [[1st ed.]], cf. 121 [[2d ed.]]; cf. the verses cited ibid. pp. 18, 61; and, for the poetical comparisons, Ibn Hishām, 534. 4; Alcama, vi. 3, Soc.

disappear, are more easily believed to be consumed by the deity than obstinate masses of solid matter.

The libation, which holds quite a secondary place in the more advanced Semitic rituals, and is generally a mere accessory to a fire-offering, has great prominence among the Arabs, to whom sacrifices by fire were practically unknown except, as we shall see by and by, in the case of human sacrifice. Its typical form is the libation of blood, the subtle vehicle of the life of the sacrifice; but milk, which was used in ritual both by the Arabs and by the Phœnicians, is also no doubt a very ancient Semitic libation. In ordinary Arabian sacrifices the blood which was poured over the sacred stone was all that fell to the god's part, the whole flesh being consumed by the worshippers and their guests; and the early prevalence of this kind of oblation appears from the fact that the word נסך 'to pour', which in Hebrew means to pour out a drink-offering, is in Arabic the general term for an act of worship.

In the North Semitic ritual the most notable feature in ⟦230⟧ the libation, which ordinarily consisted of wine, is that it was not consumed by fire, even when it went with a fire-offering. The Greeks and Romans poured the sacrificial wine over the flesh, but the Hebrews treated it like the blood, pouring it out at the base of the altar.[40] In Ecclesiasticus the wine so treated is even called "the blood of the grape,"[41] from which one is tempted to conclude that here also blood is the typical form of libation, and that wine is a surrogate for it, as fruit-juice seems to have been in certain Arabian rites.[42] It is true that the blood of the sacrifice is not called a libation in Hebrew ritual, and in Ps 16:4 "drink-offerings of blood" are spoken of as something heathenish. But this proves that such libations were known; and that the Hebrew altar ritual of the blood is essentially a drink-offering appears from Ps 50:13, where Jehovah asks, "Will I eat the flesh of bulls or drink the blood of goats?" and also from 2 Sam 23:17, where David pours out as a drink-offering the water from the well of Bethlehem, refusing to drink "the blood of the men that fetched it in jeopardy of their lives." Putting all this together, and noting also that libations were retained as a chief part of ritual in the domestic heathenism of the Hebrew women in the time of Jeremiah,[43] and that private service is often more conservative than ⟦231⟧ public worship, we are led

40. Sir 50:15; Jos. *Ant.* iii. 9. 4. Num 15:7 is sometimes cited as proving that in older times the wine was poured over the sacrificial flesh, but see against this interpretation Num 28:7.

41. The term αἷμα βοτρύων occurs in the Tyrian legend of the invention of wine, Ach. Tatius, ii. 2, and may possibly be in the translation of an old Phœnician phrase.

42. *Kinship*, p. 59 n.; Wellhausen, p. 125.

43. Jer 19:13, 32:29, 44:17, 18. With this worship on the house-tops, cf. what Strabo, 16:4, 26, tells of the daily offerings of libations and incense presented to the sun by the

to conclude (1) that the libation of blood is a common Semitic practice, older than fire-sacrifices, and (2) that the libation of wine is in some sense an imitation of, and a surrogate for, the primitive blood-offering.

Whether libations of water can properly be reckoned among the drink-offerings of the Semites is very doubtful. David's libation is plainly exceptional, and in the Levitical ritual offerings of water have no place. In the actual practice of later Judaism, however, water drawn from the fountain of Siloam, and carried into the Temple amidst the blare of trumpets, was solemnly poured out upon the altar on seven days of the Feast of Tabernacles.[44] According to the Rabbins, the object of this ceremony was to secure fertilising rains in the following year. The explanation is doubtless correct, for it is a common belief all over the world that pouring out water is a potent rain-charm.[45] This being so, we can well understand that the rite derives no countenance from the law; in truth it does not belong to the sphere of religion at all, but falls under the category of sympathetic magic in which natural phenomena are thought to be produced by imitating them on a small scale. In some forms of this charm thunder is imitated as well as rain;[46] and perhaps the trumpet-blowing at the Temple is to be explained in this way.

The closest parallel to the water-pouring of the Feast [[232]] of Tabernacles is found in the rite of Hierapolis, described by Lucian.[47] Twice a year a great concourse of worshippers assembled at the Temple bearing water from "the sea" (i.e., the Euphrates[48]), which was poured out in the Temple and flowed away into a cleft which, according to tradition, absorbed the waters of Deucalion's flood, and so gave occasion to the erection of a sanctuary, with commemorative services on the spot.[49]

Nabatæans at an altar erected on the house-tops. The sacrificial act must be done in the presence of the deity (cf. Nilus, pp. 30, 117), and if the sun or the queen of heaven is worshipped, a place open to the sky must be chosen. See Wellhausen, p. 41.

44. See *Succa,* iv. 9; J. B. Lightfoot on John 7:37; A. Reland, *Antiquitates sacrae veterum Hebraeorum,* pp. 448f., with the refs. there given. The water was poured into a special channel in the altar.

45. Numerous examples are given by J. G. Frazer, *Golden Bough,* 1.248ff., to which I may add the annual "water-pouring" at Ispahan (M. Bîrûnî [[*The Chronology of Ancient Nations* (London: Allen, 1879)]] 228ff.; Cazwînî, i. 84).

46. Frazer, i. 303; a very curious Arabian rain-charm, where cattle (or perhaps antelopes) are driven into the mountains with firebrands attached to their tails, seems to be an imitation of lightning. See Wellhausen, p. 167; *Lisân,* v. 140; Râghib, i. 94.

47. *Dea Syria,* §13, cf. §48. The same rite is alluded to by Melito in W. Cureton [[*Spicilegium Syriacum* (London: Rivingtons, 1855)]] 25.

48. To the dwellers in Mesopotamia the Euphrates was "the sea"; Philostratus, *Vita Apollonii,* i. 20.

49. The ritual of pouring water into the cleft has its parallel in the modern practice at the fountain of water before the gates of Tyre, when in September the water becomes red

In Hebrew ritual oil is not a libation, but when used in sacrifice serves to moisten and enrich a cereal offering. The ancient custom of pouring oil on sacred stones[50] was presumably maintained at Bethel according to the precedent set by Jacob; and even in the fourth Christian century the Bordeaux pilgrim speaks of the "lapis pertusus" [['perforated stone']] at Jerusalem "ad quem ueniunt Iudæi singulis annis et ungunt eum" [['toward which Jews came yearly and anointed it']]; but, as oil by itself was not an article of food, the natural analogy to this act of ritual is to be sought in the application of unguents to the hair and skin. The use of unguents was a luxury proper to feasts and gala days, when men wore their best clothes and made merry; and from Ps 45:8[7] compared with Isa 61:3, we may conclude [[233]] that the anointing of kings at their coronation is part of the ceremony of investing them in the festal dress and ornaments appropriate to their dignity on that joyous day (cf. Cant 3:11). To anoint the head of a guest was a hospitable act and a sign of honour; it was the completion of the toilet appropriate to a feast. Thus the sacred stone or rude idol described by Pausanias (x. 24. 6) had oil poured on it daily, and was crowned with wool at every feast. We have seen that the Semites on festal occasions dressed up their sacred poles, and they did the same with their idols.[51] With all this the ritual of anointing goes quite naturally; thus at Medina in the last days of heathenism we find a man washing his domestic idol, which had been defiled by Moslems, and then anointing it.[52] But apart from this, the very act of applying ointment to the sacred symbol had a religious significance. The Hebrew word meaning to anoint (*mashaḥ*) means properly to wipe or stroke with the hand, which was used to spread the unguent over the skin. Thus the anointing of the sacred symbol is associated with the simpler form of homage common in Arabia, in which the hand was passed over the idol (*tamassoḥ*). In the oath described by Ibn Hishām, p. 85, the parties dip their hands in unguent and then wipe them on the Caaba. The ultimate source of the use of unguents in religion will be discussed by and by in connection with animal sacrifice.

---

and troubled, and the natives gather for a great feast and restore its limpidity by pouring a pitcher of sea-water into the source (C. F. Volney, *État pol. de la Syrie*, chap. viii.; Mariti, ii. 269). Here the ceremony takes place at the end of the dry season when the water is low, and may therefore be compared with the legend that Mohammed made the empty well of Ḥodaibiya to overflow by causing it to be stirred with one of his arrows after a pitcher of water had been poured into it [[J. Wellhausen, *Mohammed in Medina* (Berlin, 1882) 247]]. As a rule the pouring out of water in early superstition is, as we have already seen, a rain-charm, and possibly the rite of Hierapolis was really designed to procure rain, but only in due measure.

50. Gen 28:18, 35:14.
51. Ezek 16:18.
52. A. Ibn Hishām, p. 303.

The sacrificial use of blood, as we shall see hereafter, is connected with a series of very important ritual ideas, turning on the conception that the blood is a special seat of the life. But primarily, when the blood is offered at the altar, it is conceived to be drunk by the deity. Apart from Ps 50:13 the direct evidence for this is somewhat scanty, so far as the Semites are concerned; the authority usually [[234]] appealed to is Maimonides, who states that the Ṣabians looked on blood as the nourishment of the gods. So late a witness would have little value if he stood alone, but the expression in the Psalm cannot be mere rhetoric, and the same belief appears among early nations in all parts of the globe.[53] Nor does this oblation form an exception to the rule that the offerings of the gods consist of human food, for many savages drink fresh blood by way of nourishment, and esteem it a special delicacy.[54]

Among the Arabs, down to the age of Mohammed, blood drawn from the veins of a living camel was eaten—in a kind of blood pudding—in seasons of hunger, and perhaps also at other times.[55] We shall find, however, as we proceed, that sacrificial blood, which contained the life, gradually came to be considered as something too sacred to be eaten, and that in most sacrifices it was entirely made over to the god at the altar. As all slaughter of domestic animals for food was originally sacrificial among the Arabs as well as among the Hebrews, this carried with it the disuse of blood as an article of ordinary food; and [[235]] even when slaughter ceased to involve a formal sacrifice, it was still thought necessary to slay

53. See E. B. Tylor, *Primitive Culture: Researches into the Development of Mythology, Philosophy, Religion, Language, Art and Custom* (4th ed.; London: Murray, 1903) ii. 381f. The story told by Yācūt, ii. 882, of the demon at the temple of Riām to whom bowls of sacrificial blood were presented, of which he partook, seems to have a Jewish origin. According to one version this demon had the form of a black dog (cf. Ibn Hishām, p. 18, line 3).

54. See, for America, H. H. Bancroft, *Native Races* (San Francisco: The History Company, 1886) i. 55, 492, ii. 344. In Africa fresh blood is held as a dainty by all the negroes of the White Nile (E. Marno, *Reise [[in der ägyptischen Aequatorial-Provinz und in Kordofan in den Jahren 1874–1876* [Vienna: Holder, 1878]]] 79); it is largely drunk by Masai warriors (J. Thomson, p. 430); and also by the Gallas, as various travellers attest. Among the Hottentots the pure blood of beasts is forbidden to women but not to men; Kolben, *State of the Cape*, i. 205, cf. 203. In the last case we see that the blood is sacred food. For blood-drinking among the Tartars, see Yule's *Marco Polo* [[H. Yule, *The Book of Marco Polo, the Venetian, concerning the Kingdoms and Marvels of the East* (London)]] i. 254, and the editor's note. Where mineral salt is not used for food, the drinking of blood supplies, as Thomson remarks, an important constituent to the system.

55. Maidānī, ii. 119; *Hamāsa*, p. 645, last verse. From *Agh.* xvi. 107. 20, one is led to doubt whether the practice was confined to seasons of famine, or whether this kind of food was used more regularly, as was done on the other side of the Red Sea, by the Troglodytes (Agatharchides in *Fragmenta Geographus Graeca* i. 153). See further the *Lexx. s. vv. faṣada, ʿilhiz, bajja, musawwad.*

the victim in the name of a god and pour the blood on the ground.[56] Among the Hebrews this practice soon gave rise to an absolute prohibition of blood-eating; among the Arabs the rule was made absolute only by Mohammed's legislation.[57]

The idea that the gods partake only of the liquid parts of the sacrifice appears, as has been already said, to indicate a modification of the most crassly materialistic conception of the divine nature. The direction which this modification took may, I think, be judged of by comparing the sacrifices of the gods with the oblations offered to the dead. In the famous νέκυια [['séance']] of the *Odyssey*[58] the ghosts drink greedily of the sacrificial blood, and libations of gore form a special feature in Greek offerings to heroes. Among the Arabs, too, the dead are thirsty rather than hungry; water and wine are poured upon their graves.[59] Thirst is a subtler appetite than hunger, and therefore more appropriate to the disembodied shades, just as it is from thirst rather than from hunger that the Hebrews and many other nations borrow metaphors for spiritual longings and intellectual desires. Thus the idea that the gods drink, but do not eat, seems to mark the feeling that they must be thought of as having a less solid material nature than men.

[[236]] A further step in the same direction is associated with the introduction of fire sacrifices; for, though there are valid reasons for thinking that the practice of burning the flesh or fat of victims originated in a different line of thought (as we shall by and by see), the fire ritual readily lent itself to the idea that the burnt flesh is simply a food-offering etherealised into fragrant smoke, and that the gods regale themselves on the odour instead of the substance of the sacrifice. Here again the analogy of gifts to the dead helps us to comprehend the point of view; among the Greeks of the seventh century B.C. it was, as we learn from the story of Periander and Melissa, a new idea that the dead could make no use of the gifts buried with them, unless they were etherealised by fire.[60] A

---

56. Wellhausen, 1st ed., pp. 113–14; 2d ed., p. 117. In an Arab encampment slaves sleep beside "the blood and the dung" (*Agh.* viii. 74. 29); cf. 1 Sam 2:8.

57. Whether the blood of game was prohibited to the Hebrews before the law of Lev 17:13 is not quite clear; Deut 12:16 is ambiguous. In Islām as in Judaism the prohibition of blood-eating and the rule that carrion must not be eaten go together (Lev 17:15; Ibn Hishām, p. 206, line 7).

58. Bk. xi.; cf. Pindar, *Olympian Odes* i. 90, where the word αἱμακουρίαι [['offerings of blood made to the dead']] is explained by Hesychius as τὰ ἐναγίσματα τῶν κατοιχομένων [['the offerings of the ones who have departed (died)']]; Pausanias v. 13, §2; Plutarch, *Aristides*, 21 [[*The Life of Aristides* 21.5]].

59. Wellhausen, p. 182.

60. Herodotus, v. 92; cf. Joannes Lydus; [[*Lypsiae* (Liepzig: Teubner, 1827)]] iii. 27, where the object of burning the dead is said to be to etherealise the body along with the soul.

similar notion seems to have attached itself to the custom of sacrifice by fire, combined probably at an early date with the idea that the gods, as ethereal beings, lived in the upper air, towards which the sacrificial smoke ascended in savoury clouds. Thus the prevalence among the settled Semites of fire sacrifices, which were interpreted as offerings of fragrant smoke, marks the firm establishment of a conception of the divine nature which, though not purely spiritual, is at least stripped of the crassest aspects of materialism.

(3) The distinction between sacrifices which are wholly made over to the god and sacrifices of which the god and the worshipper partake together requires careful handling. In the later form of Hebrew ritual laid down in the Levitical law, the distinction is clearly marked. To the former class belong all cereal oblations (Heb. *minḥa*; A.V. 'offering' or 'meat-offering'), which so far as they are not burned on the altar are assigned to the priests, and among [[237]] animal sacrifices the sin-offering and the burnt-offering or holocaust. Most sin-offerings were not holocausts, but the part of the flesh that was not burned fell to the priests. To the latter class, again, belong the *zebaḥīm* [['animal sacrifices']] or *shelamīm* [['peace offerings']] (sing. *zébaḥ, shélem*, Amos 5:22), that is, all the ordinary festal sacrifices, vows and freewill offerings, of which the share of the deity was the blood and the fat of the intestines, the rest of the carcass (subject to the payment of certain dues to the officiating priest) being left to the worshipper to form a social feast.[61] In judging of the original scope and meaning of these two classes of sacrifice, it will be convenient, in the first instance, to confine our attention to the simplest and most common forms of offering. In the last days of the kingdom of Judah, and still more after

61. In the English Bible *zebaḥim* is rendered 'sacrifices', and *shelamīm* 'peace-offerings'. The latter rendering is not plausible, and the term *shelamīm* can hardly be separated from the verb *shillem*, to pay or discharge, e.g., a vow. *Zébaḥ* is the more general word, including (like the Arabic *dhibḥ*) all animals slain for food, agreeably with the fact that in old times all slaughter was sacrificial. In later times, when slaughter and sacrifice were no longer identical, *zébaḥ* was not precise enough to be used as a technical term of ritual, and so the term *shelamīm* came to be more largely used than in the earlier literature.

On the sacrificial lists of the Carthaginians the terms corresponding to עלה [['burnt offering']] and זבח [['animal sacrifice']] seem to be כלל [['expiation sacrifice']] and צועת [['communion sacrifice']]. The former is the old Hebrew כליל [['complete burnt offering']] (Deut 33:10; 1 Sam 7:9), the latter is etymologically quite obscure. In the Carthaginian burnt-sacrifice a certain weight of the flesh was apparently not consumed on the altar, but given to the priests (*CIS.* 165), as in the case of the Hebrew sin-offering, which was probably a modification of the holocaust. The שלם כלל [['whole peace offering(?)']], which appears along with כלל and צועת in *CIS.* 165 (but not in *CIS.* 167), is hardly a third co-ordinate species of sacrifice. The editors of the *Corpus* regard it as a variety of the holocaust (*hol. eucharisticum*), which is not easily reconciled with their own restitution of line 11 or with the Hebrew sense of שלם. Perhaps it is an ordinary sacrifice accompanying a holocaust.

the Exile, piacular sacrifices and holocausts acquired a prominence which they did not possess in ancient times. The old history knows nothing of the Levitical sin-offering; the atoning function of sacrifice is not confined to a particular class of oblation, but belongs to [[238]] all sacrifices.[62] The holocaust, again, although ancient, is not in ancient times a common form of sacrifice, and unless on very exceptional occasions occurs only in great public feasts and in association with *zzebaḥîm* [['animal sacrifices']]. The distressful times that preceded the end of Hebrew independence drove men to seek exceptional religious means to conciliate the favour of a deity who seemed to have turned his back on his people. Piacular rites and costly holocausts became, therefore, more usual, and after the abolition of the local high places this new importance was still further accentuated by contrast with the decline of the more common forms of sacrifice. When each local community had its own high place, it was the rule that every animal slain for food should be presented at the altar, and every meal at which flesh was served had the character of a sacrificial feast.[63] As men ordinarily lived on bread, fruit, and milk, and ate flesh only on feast days and holidays, this rule was easily observed as long as the local sanctuaries stood. But when there was no altar left except at Jerusalem, the identity of slaughter and sacrifice could no longer be maintained, and accordingly the law of Deuteronomy allows men to slay and eat domestic animals everywhere, provided only that the blood—the ancient share of the god—is poured out upon the ground.[64] When this new rule came into force men ceased to feel that the eating of flesh was essentially a sacred act, and though strictly religious meals were still maintained at Jerusalem on the great feast days, the sacrificial meal necessarily lost much of its old significance, [[239]] and the holocaust seemed to have a more purely sacred character than the *zébah*, in which men ate and drank just as they might do at home.

But in ancient times the preponderance was all the other way, and the *zébah* was not only much more frequent than the holocaust, but much more intimately bound up with the prevailing religious ideas and feelings of the Hebrews. On this point the evidence of the older literature is decisive; *zébah* and *minha*, sacrifices slain to provide a religious feast, and vegetable oblations presented at the altar, make up the sum of the ordinary religious practices of the older Hebrews, and we must try to understand these ordinary rites before we attack the harder problem of exceptional forms of sacrifice.

62. To *zébah* and *minha*, 1 Sam 3:14, 26:19, and still more to the holocaust, Mic 6:6–7.
63. Hos 9:4.
64. Deut 12:15–16; cf. Lev 17:10f. The fat of the intestines was also from ancient times reserved for the deity (1 Sam 2:16), and therefore it also was forbidden food (Lev 3:17). The prohibition did not extend to the fat distributed through other parts of the body.

Now, if we put aside the *piacula* [['propitiatory sacrifices']] and whole
burnt-offerings, it appears that, according to the Levitical ritual, the distinction between oblations in which the worshipper shared, and oblations
which were wholly given over to the deity to be consumed on the altar or
by the priests, corresponds to the distinction between animal and vegetable offerings. The animal victim was presented at the altar and devoted by
the imposition of hands, but the greater part of the flesh was returned to
the worshipper, to be eaten by him under special rules. It could be eaten
only by persons ceremonially clean, i.e., fit to approach the deity; and if
the food was not consumed on the same day, or in certain cases within two
days, the remainder had to be burned.[65] The plain meaning of these rules
is that the flesh is not common but holy,[66] and that the act of eating it is
a part of the service, which is to be completed before men break up from
the sanctuary.[67] The *zébaḥ*, therefore, is [[240]] not a mere attenuated
offering, in which man grudges to give up the whole victim to his God.
On the contrary, the central significance of the rite lies in the act of
communion between God and man, when the worshipper is admitted to
eat of the same holy flesh of which a part is laid upon the altar as "the food
of the deity." But with the *minḥa* nothing of this kind occurs; the whole
consecrated offering is retained by the deity, and the worshipper's part in
the service is completed as soon as he has made over his gift. In short,
while the *zébaḥ* turns on an act of communion between the deity and his
worshippers, the *minḥa* (as its name denotes) is simply a tribute.

I will not undertake to say that the distinction so clearly laid down in
the Levitical law was observed before the Exile in all cases of cereal
sacrifices. Probably it was not, for in most ancient religions we find that
cereal offerings come to be accepted in certain cases as substitutes for
animal sacrifices, and that in this way the difference between the two
kinds of offering gradually gets to be obliterated.[68] But in such matters
great weight is to be attached to priestly tradition, such as underlies the
Levitical ritual. The priests were not likely to invent a distinction of the
kind which has been described, and in point of fact there is good evidence that they did not invent it. For there is no doubt that in ancient
times the ordinary source of the *minḥa* was the offering of first-fruits—
that is, of a small but choice portion of the annual produce of the

---

65. Lev 7:15ff., 19:6, 22:30.

66. Hag 2:12; cf. Jer 11:15, LXX.

67. The old sacrificial feasts occupy but a single day (1 Samuel 9), or at most two days
(1 Sam 20:27).

68. So at Rome models in wax or dough often took the place of animals. The same
thing took place at Athens: Hesychius, *s.vv.* βοῦς and ἕβδομος βοῦς; cf. Thucyd. i. 126 and *schol.*
At Carthage we have found the name *zébaḥ* applied to vegetable offerings [[p. 50 n. 21]].

ground, which in fact is the only cereal oblation prescribed in the oldest laws.[69] So far as can be seen, the first-fruits were always a tribute wholly made [[241]] over to the deity at the sanctuary. They were brought by the peasant in a basket and deposited at the altar,[70] and so far as they were not actually burned on the altar, they were assigned to the priests[71] not to the ministrant as a reward for his service, but to the priests as a body, as the household of the sanctuary.[72]

Among the Hebrews, as among many other agricultural peoples, the offering of first-fruits was connected with the idea that it is not lawful or safe to eat of the new fruit until the god has received his due.[73] The offering makes the whole crop lawful food, but it does not make it holy food; nothing is consecrated except the small portion offered at the altar, and of the remaining store clean persons and unclean eat alike throughout the year. This, therefore, is quite a different thing from the consecration of animal sacrifices, for in the latter case the whole flesh is holy, and only those who are clean can eat of it.[74]

In old Israel all slaughter was sacrifice,[75] and a man could never eat beef or mutton except as a religious act, but cereal food had no such sacred associations; as soon as God had received His due of first-fruits, the whole domestic store was common. The difference between cereal and animal food was therefore deeply marked, and though bread was of course brought to the sanctuary to be [[242]] eaten with the *zebaḥīm* [['animal sacrifices']], it had not and could not have the same religious meaning as the holy flesh. It appears from Amos 4:4 that it was the custom in northern Israel to lay a portion of the worshipper's provision of ordinary leavened bread on the altar with the sacrificial flesh, and this custom was natural enough: for why should not the deity's share of the sacrificial meal have the same cereal accompaniments as man's share? But there is no indication that this oblation consecrated the part of the

---

69. Exod 22:29, 23:19, 34:26.

70. Deut 26:1ff.

71. Lev 23:17; Deut 18:4. For the purpose of this argument it is not necessary to advert to the distinction recognised by post-Biblical tradition between *rēshīth* [['firstling']] and *bikkūrīm* [['firstfruits']] on which we see Wellhausen, *Prolegomena*, 3rd ed., pp. 161f. (Eng. trans., p. 157f.).

72. This follows from 2 Kgs 23:9. The tribute was sometimes paid to a man of God (2 Kgs 4:42), which is another way of making it over to the deity. In the Levitical law also the *minḥa* belongs to the priests as a whole (Lev 7:10). This is an important point. What the ministrant receives as a fee comes from the worshipper, what the priests as a whole receive is given them by the deity.

73. Lev 23:14; cf. Pliny, *H. N.* xviii. 8.

74. Hos 9:4 refers only to animal food.

75. The same thing is true of Old Arabia; Wellhausen, p. 117.

bread retained by the worshipper and made it holy bread. The only holy bread of which we read is such as belonged to the priests, not to the offerer.[76] In Lev 7:14, Num 6:15, the cake of common bread is given to the priest instead of being laid on the altar, but it is carefully distinguished from the *minḥa* [['grain offering']]. In old times the priests had no altar dues of this kind. They had only the first-fruits and a claim to a piece of the sacrificial flesh,[77] from which it may be presumed that the custom of offering bread with the *zébah* was not primitive. Indeed Amos seems to mention it with some surprise as a thing not familiar to Judæan practice. At all events no sacrificial meal could consist of bread alone. All through the old history it is taken for granted that a religious feast necessarily implies a victim slain.[78]

[[243]] The distinction which we are thus led to draw between the cereal oblation, in which the dominant idea is that of a tribute paid to the god, and animal sacrifices, which are essentially acts of communion between the god and his worshippers, deserves to be followed out in more detail. But this task must be reserved for another lecture.

---

76. 1 Sam 21:4.

77. Deut 18:3, 4; 1 Sam 2:13ff.

78. What has been said above of the contrast between cereal sacrificial gifts and the sacrificial feast seems to me to hold good also for Greece and Rome, with some modification in the case of domestic meals, which among the Semites had no religious character, but at Rome were consecrated by a portion being offered to the household gods. This, however, has nothing to do with public religion, in which the law holds good that there is no sacred feast without a victim, and that consecrated *aparchæ* [['firstlings']] are wholly given over to the sanctuary. The same thing holds good for many other peoples, and seems, so far as my reading goes, to be the general rule. But there are exceptions. My friend Mr. J. G. Frazer, to whose wide reading I never appeal without profit, refers me to G. A. Wilken's *Alfoeren van het eiland Beroe*, p. 26, where a true sacrificial feast is made of the first-fruits of rice. This is called "eating the soul of the rice," so that the rice is viewed as a living creature. In such a case it is not unreasonable to say that the rice may be regarded as really an animate victim. Agricultural religions seem often to have borrowed ideas from the older cults of pastoral times.

Ancient Judaism

MAX WEBER

Prefatory Note: The Sociological Problem
of Judaic Religious History

[[3]] The problem of ancient Jewry, although unique in the socio-historical study of religion, can best be understood in comparison with the
problem of the Indian caste order. Sociologically speaking the Jews were
a pariah people, which means, as we know from India, that they were a
guest people who were ritually separated, formally or de facto, from their
social surroundings. All the essential traits of Jewry's attitude toward the
environment can be deduced from this pariah existence—especially its
voluntary ghetto, long anteceding compulsory internment, and the dual-
istic nature of its in-group and out-group morality.

Numerous excerpts reprinted with permission from *Ancient Judaism* (trans. and ed. Hans H.
Gerth and Don Martindale; Glencoe, Ill.: Free Press, 1952) 3–5, 13–19, 75–86, 130–38,
278–86, and 425–55.

Editor's note: Max Weber's *Ancient Judaism* has profoundly influenced the social science
study of the Hebrew Bible. In order to give the reader a sense of the breadth of Weber's
contribution, I have chosen several shorter segments rather than one lengthy section of the
book. In the interests of space, I have edited both text and footnotes; in doing so, I trust
that the brilliance of Weber's work will be demonstrated rather than diminished (CEC).

Author's note: It would require more than a lifetime to acquire a true mastery of the literature concerning the religion of Israel and Jewry, especially since this literature is of exceptionally high quality. For ancient Israelite religion, modern Protestant, especially
German, scholarship is acknowledged to be authoritative to this day. For talmudic Judaism,
on the whole, the considerable superiority of Jewish scholarship is unquestionable.

From the outset, in our attempt to present developmental aspects of Judaic religious history relevant to our problem, we entertain but modest hopes of contributing anything essentially new to the discussion, apart from the fact that, here and there, some source data
may be grouped in a manner to emphasize some things differently than usual. Our questions may, of course, vary in some points from those which Old Testament scholars legitimately raise.

The differences between Jewish and Indian pariah tribes consist in the following three significant circumstances:

1. Jewry was, or rather became, a pariah people in a surrounding free of castes.

2. The religious promises to which the ritual segregation of Jewry was moored differed essentially from those of the Indian castes. Ritually correct conduct, i.e., conduct conforming to caste standards, carried for the Indian pariah castes the premium of ascent by way of rebirth in a caste-structured world thought to be eternal and unchangeable.

The maintenance of the caste status quo involved not only the continued position of the individual within the caste, but also the position of the caste in relation to other castes. This conservatism ⟦4⟧ was pre-requisite to salvation, for the world was unchangeable and had no "history."

For the Jew the religious promise was the very opposite. The social order of the world was conceived to have been turned into the opposite of that promised for the future, but in the future it was to be over-turned so that Jewry would be once again dominant. The world was conceived as neither eternal nor unchangeable, but rather as having been created. Its present structures were a product of man's activities, above all those of the Jews, and of God's reaction to them. Hence the world was an historical product designed to give way again to the truly God-ordained order. The whole attitude toward life of ancient Jewry was determined by this conception of a future God-guided political and social revolution.

3. This revolution was to take a special direction. Ritual correctitude and the segregation from the social environment imposed by it was but one aspect of the commands upon Jewry. There existed in addition a highly rational religious ethic of social conduct; it was free of magic and all forms of irrational quest for salvation; it was inwardly worlds apart from the paths of salvation offered by Asiatic religions. To a large extent this ethic still underlies contemporary Mid Eastern and European ethic. World-historical interest in Jewry rests upon this fact.

Actual harm has been done to purely historical inquiry into Judaic religious history, as elsewhere, only where value judgments have been allowed to interfere with detached analysis. No strictly empirical, historical, or sociological discipline can ever answer questions such as whether the Mosaic conception of God or the Mosaic ethic, assuming them to be reliably ascertainable, are superior to those of the surrounding world. Such questions can only be raised on the basis of given religious premises. Religious premises have strongly influenced the methodology of some relevant part of purely empirical research into Israelite religious history. . . . The literature (including literature of highest quality) is so extensive, that, in general, we quote only when a special substantive reason warrants it. For once there seemed little danger to me that an omission might give the appearance as if I were claiming to present "new" facts and views. That is out of the question. Somewhat new are some of the sociological viewpoints and questions which we address to the data.

The world-historical importance of Jewish religious development rests above all in the creation of the Old Testament, for one of the most significant intellectual achievements of the Pauline mission was that it preserved and transferred this sacred book of the Jews to Christianity as one of its own sacred books. Yet in so doing it eliminated all those aspects of the ethic enjoined by the Old Testament which ritually characterize the special position of Jewry as a pariah people. These aspects were not binding upon Christianity because they had been suspended by the Christian redeemer.

In order to assess the significance of this act one need merely conceive what would have happened without it. Without the adoption of the Old Testament as a sacred book by Christianity, gnostic sects and mysteries of the cult of Kyrios Christos would have existed on the soil of Hellenism, but providing no basis for a Christian church or a Christian ethic of workaday life. Without [[5]] emancipation from the ritual prescriptions of the Torah, founding the caste-like segregation of the Jews, the Christian congregation would have remained a small sect of the Jewish pariah people comparable to the Essenes and the Therapeutics.

With the salvation doctrine of Christianity as its core, the Pauline mission in achieving emancipation from the self-created ghetto, found a linkage to a Jewish—even though half buried—doctrine derived from the religious experience of the exiled people. We refer to the unique promises of the great unknown author of exilic times who wrote the prophetic theodicy of sufferance (Isaiah 40–55)—especially the doctrine of the Servant of Yahweh who teaches and who without guilt voluntarily suffers and dies as a redeeming sacrifice. Without this the development of the Christian doctrine of the sacrificial death of the divine redeemer, in spite of the later esoteric doctrine of the son of man, would have been hardly conceivable in the face of other and externally similar doctrines of mysteries.

Jewry has, moreover, been the instigator and partly the model for Mohammed's prophecy. Thus, in considering the conditions of Jewry's evolution, we stand at a turning point of the whole cultural development of the West and the Middle East. Quite apart from the significance of the Jewish pariah people in the economy of the European Middle Ages and the modern period, Jewish religion has world-historical consequences. Only the following phenomena can equal those of Jewry in historical significance: the development of Hellenic intellectual culture; for western Europe, the development of Roman law and of the Roman Catholic church resting on the Roman concept of office; the medieval order of estates; and finally, in the field of religion, Protestantism. Its influence shatters this order but develops its institutions.

Hence we ask, how did Jewry develop into a pariah people with highly specific peculiarities?

. . . .

The Cities and the Gibborim

[[14]] Economically and politically, the cities of the [[biblical]] tradition represent very different phenomena. The city could be but a small fortified agricultural community with a market. In this case it differed only in degree from a village. If fully developed, however, the city throughout the ancient Orient was not only a market place, but above all a fortress and, as such, seat of the army, the local deity, his priests, and the respective monarchical or oligarchical authorities of the body politic. This clearly suggests the Mediterranean polis.

The political constitution of the Syrian–Palestine city actually represents a developmental stage of urbanism which resembles that of the old-Hellenic "polis of the gentes." Even in pre-Israelite times the sea-cities of the Phoenicians and the Philistines were organized into full cities. For the time of Tuthmose III, Egyptian sources reveal the existence of many city-states in Palestine, among them even the kind that continue to be found during Canaanite times of Israel (according to Lakisch).[1]

In the Tell-el-Amarna correspondence there appears under Amenophis IV (Akhenaten) in the larger cities, most distinctly in Tyre and Byblos, an urban stratum beside the vassal kings and regents of the Pharaoh with their garrisons, magazines and arsenals. This urban group controlled the city hall (*bitu*) and pursued an independent policy which often was inimical to Egyptian rule.[2]

Whatever other traits may have characterized this group, it was obviously in the nature of an armed patriciate.[3] Its relations to the vassal princes and regents of the Pharaoh were apparently already similar to

1. Cf. W. Max Müller in *JQRNS*, vol. 4 (1913/14) 65.

2. The *bitu* of Tyre is distinguished (Knudtzon No. 89) [[J. A. Knudtzon et al., *Die El-Amarna Tafeln* (Leipzig: Hinrichs, 1915)]] from that of the regent, the appointee of the Pharaoh. The correspondent draws the attention of the Pharaoh to the fact that, not the regent, to whom he always addresses himself, but the circles in control of the city hall determine the politics of Tyre. The regent later was slain.

3. If (in Knudtzon No. 129) "the Great" of a city are mentioned it remains questionable whether officials or patrician sib elders are meant; in any case, the urban populace has political influence. The people of Dunip (cf. No. 50) request from the king a certain man for regent. The city dwellers of Byblos, in common with the regent's renegade brother, close the city gates on the regent, a Canaanite. Elsewhere, city people made common cause with the advancing foreign invaders: death threatens the regents. The city is lost when the Egyptian garrison withdraws or rebels because provisions fail to arrive or because people refuse corvées on the official fiefs of the regents and the military. This seems to me the in

those we find later between the urban Israelite sibs and such military princes as Abimelech, Gideon's son. . . .

[[15]] Obviously, this state of affairs existed throughout known history wherever the urban defense organization attained to full political and economic development. The dependent places are, then, in the situation of *periocoi* places, i.e., without political rights. The master sibs are, or are held to be, city dwellers. In Jeremiah's home town, Anathoth, there are "only small people" who lack understanding of his prophecy (Jer 5:4), so he goes into the city of Jerusalem where the "great men" are, in hope of better success. All political influence lies in the hands of these "great men" of the capital city. When under Zedekiah, at Nebuchadnezzar's command, at times, others than the "great men" are in power and, particularly, control the office, it is held to be an anomaly. It is a possibility that Isaiah holds out as just punishment for continual profligacy of the mighty ones, at the same time, however, as a terrible evil for the community. However, the people of Anathoth are considered to be neither metics nor a special status group, but Israelites who simply do not belong to the "great men."[4]

Here the type of the prevailing polis of the gentes is developed in the very manner of early antiquity: with *periocoi* places devoid of political rights, but considered to be settlements of freemen.

The organized sib, also, remains basic in the city. However, while it has exclusive significance for the social organization of the Bedouin tribes, in the cities, the distribution of landownership has made its appearance as the foundation of rights and has finally outweighed the former. In Israelite antiquity, social organization is usually articulated in terms of father

---

escapable interpretation of conditions touched upon in Nos. 117:37; 138; 77:36; 81:33; 74; 125 and more often. . . . But the μάχιμοι [['troops']] of the Pharaoh were in the main invested with very small fiefs (enfeoffed foot soldiers), and thus the *hubšu* [[traditionally, 'peasant']] mentioned in the documents are probably liturgically enfeoffed military prebendaries as are typically found in the Middle East and in Egypt. In No. 74 the field, that is the fief of the regent, has remained untilled because people have refused to render the corvée; therefore he is in need. The garrison fares similarly and that is why it is disloyal. Obviously, the garrisons are numerically very small: occasionally the regents put through new requests for 50 or less men. Petty conditions prevail generally: a tribute to the prince of Meggido amounts to 30 head of cattle.

4. It seems to me, the only shortcoming in Eduard Meyer's excellent presentation cf. *Die Israeliten und ihre Nachbarstämme* [[with *addenda* by Luther; Halle, 1906]] and *Enstehung des Judentums* [[Halle: Niemeyer, 1896]] is that this distinction running throughout early antiquity to the time of establishment of "democracy" is not emphasized. Not all free landowners in ancient states, especially the city-states, are full citizens or political peers, but only those economically qualified for war service; that is, in Israel, the *gibbor chail* [['mighty warrior']]. There are, in the fully developed Israelite city-states, certainly, also free Israelite landowners, who do not belong to these and who therefore like the Hellenic *periocoi* [[free citizens without political rights in Sparta]] and the Roman plebs stand outside the full citizenry.

houses (*beth ʾaboth*). These household communities are considered to be subdivisions of the sib (*mishpacha* ⟦'family'⟧), which, in turn, is a subdivision of the tribe (*shebet*).

⟦16⟧ We saw, however, that the tradition of the Book of Joshua already has the tribe subdivided into cities and villages rather than into sibs and families. Whether every Israelite belonged to a "sib," might, by analogies, be questioned. The sources assume it, inasmuch as every Israelite freeman qualifies for war service. However, an increasing differentiation among the armed freemen was occurring. Occasionally tradition (in Gibeon, Josh 10:2), expressly identifies all citizens (ʾanashim, elsewhere, e.g., Josh 9:3, *yoshebim*) of a city with the *gibborim*, the warriors (knights). But this is not the rule. Rather, the term *gibborim* refers regularly to the *bne chail*, the 'sons of property', i.e., the possessors of inherited land called *gibbore chail* in contrast[5] to ordinary men (ʿam), the militarily trained section of whom are later (Josh 8:11, 10:7; 2 Kgs 25:4) called the warriors (ʿam hamilchamah). . . .

Also where, as so often in early antiquity, a hereditary charismatic city prince (*nasi*) stood at the head of the city, he had to share power as *primus inter pares* ⟦'first among equals'⟧, with the elders (*zekenim*) of the sibs, and with the family heads (*roshi beth ʾaboth*) of his own sib. The power of these latter could become so great and at the same time the predominance of the princely sib over all ⟦17⟧ other sibs of the city and their elders could become so extensive that the city appeared as an oligarchy of the family heads of the princely sib, as we find quite regularly in Israelite history. But conditions may well have differed. In the Genesis account, Shechem is ruled by a rich sib, the *bne chamor* ⟦'sons of Ḥamor'⟧, the head of which holds the title *nasi* (prince) and is called "Father of Shechem" (Judg 9:28). For important transactions, for example, for the reception of strangers into the association of citizens and landowners, this

---

5. The indiscriminate use of ʿam ⟦'people'⟧ and *gibborim* ⟦'mighty men'⟧ beside one another is to be found in a somewhat corrupted passage in the Song of Deborah (Judg 5:13). If one accepts Kittel's reading and at the end reads *kaggiborim* ⟦'like the mighty men'⟧ as Gressmann proposes, the meaning is clear. This presupposes, however, that ʿam and *gibborim* were two different groups, the latter the Israelite knights, the former the Israelite peasants who fought 'like knights' but simply were not knights (cf. vv. 11 and 14). Against this, the city of Meroz (according to v. 23) seems to have had the duty to come to the aid of the confederacy with knights (*gibborim*). The victory song characteristically curses this city, hence deems it deserving to be outlawed and destroyed in holy war, but not the peasant tribes who likewise had broken the covenant.

As a rule the *gibbor* is the knightly hero as in Genesis 6 or in the lists of David's paladines. Colorless is the term used especially in the Book of Joshua, but also in the Book of Kings, ʿam hamilchamah meaning 'warrior people'. In Josh 10:7 it is used beside *gibbore chail*, *gibbor* and ʿam hamilchamah appearing beside one another in Isa 6:22, and the fighters per se are by no means all *gibborim*, cf. Jer 5:16, where the foreign nation, approaching to punish Judah, is said to be all *gibborim*, which, in this case, means trained warriors.

city head required the assent of the "armed" men (*?anashim*) of Shechem. Alongside this old master sib there appeared after the war against the Midianites Gibeon's sib as an overpowering competitor, which, in its turn, was displaced by Hamor's sib in the revolt against Abimelech.

The sibs, as in early Hellenic times, often settled interlocally; at times, a sib was predominant in several, particularly in small, towns. Thus, Jair's sib in Gilead held sway over an entire group of tent villages, which were later, also, occasionally called "cities." As a rule, actual power was in the hands of the elders (*zekenim*). These appear in all those parts of the tradition for which city constitutions are basic. Hence, they appear, above all, in Deuteronomic law as the *zikne ha-?ir* [['city elders']], permanent public authorities who sit "in the gate," that is to say, administer and hold court in the market place at the gates of the city. The Book of Joshua presupposes their existence for Canaanite as well as Israelite cities. For the city Jezreel, besides the elders, 'nobles' (*chorim*) are mentioned. Elsewhere, heads of the father's house (*roshi beth ?aboth*) appear beside the elders; the family heads, also, in later times (Ezra) appear as representatives of the city beside the *zekenim* and the magistrates, differently named at the time, who are obviously identical with the latter. In the first case a permanent charismatic preference seems to have been accorded to one or several sibs constituting the magistracy, in the latter, the family heads of all arms-bearing sibs of the city are concerned. Such distinctions are also found in the older traditions. Whether and to what extent actual organizational variations corresponded to these terminological differences, however, is neither transmitted nor evident. The charismatic position of a sib of notables depends, of course, above all, on its military strength, and connected with this, its wealth. . . .

[[18]] A comparison of Israelite with pre-Israelite, and with Mesopotamian conditions, shows that in Israel, never a single elder, but always several elders are mentioned in place of the single city king of the Amarna times and still later epoch of the Rameses and the one local elder of Babylonian documents.[6] This is a reliable indication of sib rule as is the plurality of *suffits* [['magistrates']] and consuls.

Conditions differed when a charismatic war lord succeeded as lord of the city in making himself independent of the aristocracy of elders by winning a personal following, or by hiring paid, frequently foreign-born, mercenaries, who constituted a bodyguard only to him. He might recruit

---

6. The contrast is not absolute. In the Babylonian myth of the flood, the fold and "elders" of a city are presupposed (translated by H. Gunkel, *Schöpfung und Chaos* [[Göttingen: Vandenhoeck & Ruprecht, 1895]] 424, line 33). And, on the other hand, *Hamor* means the "father" of Shechem, of course, only as a kinship-eponym. A single elder already occurs in the old texts from Ur; H. de Genouillac, "Textes juridiques de l'époque d'Ur," *Revue d'Assyriologie*, vol. 8 (1911) 2.

personally devoted officials (*sarim*) from his following or from among slaves, from freedmen or the politically disqualified lower classes. If he based his rule completely on these power sources, that form of princely rule emerged which, in later inimical perspective, was associated with "kingship." The legitimate, hereditarily-charismatic "prince" of old was viewed as a kind of man who rode an ass. Therefore, the messianic prince of the future should come once again on this riding animal of pre-Solomon times.

A "king," on the other hand, is viewed as a man who has war horses and chariots in the manner of the Pharaoh. From his castles, he holds sway over the city and the dependent region by means of his treasure, his magazines, his eunuchs, and, above all, his bodyguard, which he provisions. The king installs regents over the city, probably giving his followers, officers and officials, fiefs, especially castle fiefs—such as "the men of the castle" (*millo*) in Shechem presumably had (Judg 9:6, 20). The king imposes forced labor, and increases, therewith, the proceeds of his own land holdings. . . .

⟦19⟧ The transition between princehood and city kingship was actually quite fluid. For, throughout Israelite antiquity, even for the mightiest kings, the great landowning sibs and their elders as a rule remained an element not to be permanently ignored. As it was a rare exception in early times to report of a harlot's son, hence, an upstart (Jephthah) as a charismatic leader, so in the time of Kings, upstart royal officials are the exception rather than the rule. To be sure, in the Northern Kingdom there were to be found several kings without father's names, hence, without descent from fully qualified sibs; Omri did not even bear an Israelite name. The priestly kings' law in Deuteronomy, therefore, deems it necessary to stress pure Israelite blood as a prerequisite to kingship. But the king everywhere has to reckon with the *gibbore chayil*, the militarily full-qualified landowners and the representatives of the notables, the *zekenim* of the great sibs, who, also, by the editors of the genuine political tradition in Deuteronomy (chaps. 21, 22, 25 in contrast to the theologically influenced places 16:18 and 17:8, 9), are considered to be the sole legitimate representatives of the people.

· ·

The Berith

⟦75⟧ A peculiarity of the Israelite social order finds expression in the very name of the oldest law book; *sefer haberith* 'Book of the Covenant'. What interests us is the important concept of *berith*.[7]

7. The work of R. Kraetzschmar, *Die Bundesvorstellung im Alten Testament* (Marburg: Elwert, 1896), differs in many ways from what follows and was not available to me during

A *coniuratio* or oathbound league of opponents of Egyptian rule was already mentioned in the Amarna letters.[8] Also the name *Ḥabiri* for the enemies of the Egyptian governors appears in the Amarna tablets, which is sometimes identified with *ʿIbri* (Hebrews). In view of certain linguistic difficulties, recently the term has been related occasionally to the Jewish term *chaber*, i.e., 'comrade'. In post-exilic times this term signifies the 'ritually correct full Jews' as well as *cheber* 'confederation'. On the coins of the Maccabees[9] it designated the full Jewish community and in the older tradition too (for example, Judg 20:11), it was occasionally utilized to designate the confederation army (loc. cit., in a holy war because of religious crime).[10] To be sure, the derivation of *Ḥabiri* from this word remains improbable.[11]

The fact that various oathbound confederations under divine protection existed throughout Israelite history per se is not peculiar. In Antiquity every political alliance, in fact almost every private contract was normally confirmed by an oath, i.e., the curse of self. Rather, the peculiarity consists in the first place in the extensive employment of the religious *berith* as the actual (or construed) basis of the most varied legal and moral relations. Above all, Israel itself as a political community was conceived as an oathbound confederation.

An Israelite, including a member of another tribe, who stood only in the relation of a *ger* [['sojourner']] to one spoken to, nevertheless addressed him as 'brother' (*ʾachim*) even as the Swiss speaker on official occasions must address his Swiss compatriots as *Eidgenossen* [['Swiss

---

the conclusion of this work. Stade, who maintains that the idea of the confederacy appears only late, in the last analysis wishes to say only that the *berith* of Moses did not have the form of a legal enactment, which is certainly correct. However, the paramount significance of the *berith* idea will be witnessed ever anew.

8. Knudtzon No. 67.

9. The coinage inscription of the Maccabean priest-princes reads *kohen ha gedol w cheber hayyehudim* 'high priest and confederation of the Jews'.

10. In the war against Benjamin because of the offense of Gibeah. Otherwise the word occurs with Isaiah (47:9, 12) for the confederation of magicians and robbers; in Hosea (6:9) for the confederation of priests; Prov 21:9 and 25:24 for the house community; in the Psalms (119) for the brothers in belief. The word was, at the time, utilized somewhat as an equivalent to the expression of the oldest tradition for 'friend, neighbor' *reaʿ*, which characteristically is derived from *raʿah* 'to graze', Piel: *reʿah* 'to choose a companion', hence it is probably derived from the camp-community of the Bedouins or the cattle-breeding sibs.

11. See the discussion of F. M. T. Böhl, "Kanaanäer und Hebräer," *BWAT*, vol. 9, 1911, p. 85. The identification with *ʿIbrim* appears possible and probable. In any case the concept of the "brother in belief" was not absent in pre-Israelite times as a later-to-be mentioned letter of a Canaanite from the 15th century indicates. When addressing a fellow Israelite, however, the expression *chaber* was not used but apparently always *ʾach* (brother).

subjects']]. [[76]] And as David, according to the official tradition, through *berith*, became the legitimate king, this tradition also makes the elders of the northern tribes negotiate his recognition with David's grandson Rehoboam in the manner of an imperial capitulation. However, it is also true that incorporation of cattle-breeding sibs in a Canaanite city, or, in reverse, the affiliation of, for instance, the Gibeonites as a tributary community with Israel was always consummated through a *berith* named sworn brotherhood. All *gerim* [['sojourners']], including the patriarchs, are in their legal situation through *berith*.[12]

According to tradition, the sworn fraternizations were ritualistically consummated by the establishment of common meals among the participants (compare Gen 26:30 with Josh 9:14). The collection of laws which Moses announced at the behest of God was (Exod 24:7) named the 'Book of the Covenant' (*sefer haberith*)[13] and so, too, were called the religious

12. Abraham through *berith* [['covenant']] became a *ger* [['sojourner']] in Beer-Sheba (Gen 21:31, 34). Isaac formed a sworn bond with Abimelech of Gerar (Gen 26:28). Abimelech appears, despite verse 31 which emphasized the reciprocity of the obligation, just as lonely as the one who makes the *berith* (26:8), as later Yahweh over and against Israel, because in both cases the side of the weaker is less privileged (Israel as Yahweh's *ger!*). Similarly, Israel over and against Gibeon (Josh 9:6ff.). In the Deborah tradition the husband of Jael fixed his tents by virtue of *berith* as a *ger* on Canaanite royal territory. King Asa sent, by power of *berith*, tribute to Ben-hadad (1 Kgs 15:19). Ahab and his prisoner Ben-hadad concluded a *berith* (1 Kgs 20:34) as Jonathan did with David (1 Sam 18:3; 20:8); David with Abner (2 Sam 3:12). Jabesh asked Nahash for one (1 Sam 11:1). In all these cases, as between Yahweh and Israel, it is a matter of a *feodus iniquum* [['treaty of unequals']] among unequals; in contrast the *berith* between Jacob and Laban is a *feodus aequum* [['treaty of equals']] (Gen 31:44). The international law, which supported Tyre, was called (Amos 1:9) 'brotherhood' (*berith ʾachim*). Already from these examples it follows in any case that *berith* is rightly rendered through 'confederation', and E. Kautzsch (*Biblische Theologie des Alten Testaments* [Tübingen: Mohr, 1911] 60) is quite wrong in denying this meaning which is the absolutely central point for the whole of ancient Israelite religion. David (2 Sam 5:3) became king of Israel in the same sense through *berith* with the elders as previously Yahweh became its God. . . . "P" never refers to the Sinai law as *berith*, whereas for the Yahwist ("Y") the Horeb confederation and the *berith* on the fields of Moab are typical bilateral *feodera* [['treaties']]. According to Isa 24:5 Israel has broken the 'eternal covenant' (*berith ʿolam*). The expression *karat berith* corresponds, as often noted, quite to the *feodus icere*, ὅρκιατέμνειν [['make a covenant']] of the Romans and Hellenes. With Nehemiah this linguistic usage has faded and *ʾamanah* [['pledge']] is used instead of *berith* (10:1).

13. With regard to the Book of the Covenant, as well as to these words of the covenant, it remains, of course, questionable to which parts the terms of the earliest tradition referred. The previously discussed legal collection which at the indicated place is now called Book of the Covenant, is never so designated in its own text, where the word 'covenant', indeed, does not appear, while the ritual prescriptions Exodus 34 are expressly introduced as *berith*, and through the bilateral nature of the pledges, agree better with the character of a covenant than do the other collections which essentially contain unilateral prescriptions (*mishpatim*). The 'words of the covenant', Exod 34:28, are identified by the presumably later addition of

prescriptions which on God's request, he wrote on two tablets (Exod 34:28) 'Words of the Covenant' (*dibre haberith*). Likewise the Deuteronomic *sefer hattorah* the 'Book of Teaching', which as such first appeared in 2 Kings 22 is called the 'Book of the Covenant', its contents 'Words of the Covenant' in the following account of its acceptance as law under Josiah (2 Kgs 23:2).

In the Book of Joshua a tradition is preserved in which Joshua, after the complete conquest of the land, allegedly made a covenant (*berith*) with the people and wrote down its content in the 'Book of the Torah of God'. It cannot be established which of the different legal collections is referred to. Against this (Judg 9:4) it is transmitted that in Shechem at Abimelech's time there is a 'house' of a 'covenant-baal' (*Baal berith*), the temple treasure of which served at the same time as the city treasure. And the tradition of Deuteronomy (chiefly, Deut 27:14–15)[14] recognizes a solemn ceremony, which was allegedly first held with the conquest of the land. According to later versions it was held by the representatives of six tribes on the Mountain of Gerizim [[and]] by six others on the Mountain of Ebal (between which lies Shechem). The four or five variations of the account give the following picture. The priests on Mount Gerizim pronounce a solemn blessing on those who observe the holy commandments [[77]] and on Mount Ebal they pronounce a solemn curse against those who violate them. . . .

The Yahweh Confederacy and Its Organs

In historical times the inner political history of Israel developed through ever repeated ritualistic confederate resolutions toward the establishment in Jerusalem under Joash of the pure Yahweh cult. It led, later, under Josiah to the reception of the law of Deuteronomy which, according to tradition, occurred [[78]] through *berith*.[15] Likewise, it led to the

---

'the ten words' with the Decalogue. But originally the expression referred obviously to the just mentioned directly preceding ritualistic prescriptions. (See on the whole question B. Baentsch, loc. cit. [[*Exodus-Leviticus-Numbers* [HKAT 1/2; Göttingen: Vandenhoeck & Ruprecht, 1903]]].)

14. The respective chapter (27) of Deuteronomy is held to be a recent compilation and insertion. But its original material could hardly be of recent origin. The great contradictions of the account and the representation of the twelve tribes by one man each may well be credited to the editor, likewise the unclear change of place references (on the Ebal or below in the valley of Shechem). Probably the fragment is held rightly as of Elohistic origin.

15. In these cases the *berith* was concluded 'before' Yahweh, not 'with' Yahweh. This is readily explained from the fiction that this *berith* represented only a renewed vow of one party to the contract, namely the people, to fulfill the obligations of the old covenant with the God. Allegedly they had failed to honor it.

resolution under Zedekiah to obey the law and release debt slaves (Jer 34:8–9) and then again the solemn acceptance of the congregational constitution under Nehemiah. As in the cursing ceremony, numbers of particularly important statutes were seized upon and solemnly signed and sealed by the synactic sib heads in agreement with the meanwhile usual practice of officializing documents (Nehemiah 10). Decisive for the context under consideration were precisely the ancient, pre-exilic and, in these cases, law-producing *berith* of the people of Israel as a whole.

In clear contrast to the *berith*-contracts among individuals or contracts with metics, they were not contracts and fraternizations among partners placed under the protection of God as a witness and avenger of perjury. But for the old conception, advanced primarily by the so-called "Yahwist," the pre-exilic *b'rithot* [['covenants']] were confederate covenants with God Himself. Hence, in avenging the violation of the covenant He insisted on His own violated treaty rights and not only on the claims of the contract observing party placed under His protection.[16] This important conception profoundly influenced the development of Israelite religiosity. The god of the prophets based his frightful threats of disaster on the violation of the contractual good faith sworn personally to him as a contractual partner. He in turn is reminded of the pledges which he has given by oath to the forefathers (thus, first Mic 7:20). From the very beginning the entire relation even of the legendary forefathers of Israel to god, in the conception later established by the Exile priests, was consummated through ever renewed covenants; through the covenant with Noah, that with Abraham, Isaac, Jacob, and, finally, the covenant of Sinai. Meanwhile, with the change of the idea of god the anthropomorphic conception of a bilateral pact had weakened into the concept of a divine ordainment, which was merely guaranteed by a special pledge. Inherently Jeremiah's hope for the future, too, is for Yahweh to conclude another covenant with his people only under more lenient conditions than given the fathers.

Whence stems this peculiarity of the Israelite conception? Some general political conditions and a special event in religious history conjoined in its origin.

[[79]] The "covenant" concept was important for Israel because the ancient social structure of Israel in part rested essentially upon a contractually regulated, permanent relationship of landed warrior sibs with guest tribes as legally protected metics: itinerant herdsmen and guest ar-

---

16. The one-sided loyalty oath of the people under Nehemiah was not called *berith* [['covenant']] but *ʾamanah* [['pledge']] (Neh 10:1 [[9:38]]).

tissans, merchants and priests. An entire maze of such fraternal arrangements, we saw, dominated the social and economic structure. That the
covenant with the god, Yahweh himself, became a fundamental conception for Israel's own judgment of its place among nations was bound up
with the following circumstances.

As observed earlier, all political organizations among Bedouins and
stock-breeders were quite unstable due to their life conditions. All these
tribal organizations tended now to split into sibs, again to coalesce. The
fate of the tribes Reuben, Simeon, Levi, Machir on the one hand, Judah
on the other, offers examples. With this instability contrasts strikingly
the extraordinary stability of a definite type of organization to be found
precisely among these unsettled strata: namely, the religious order or
"cult" organization of similar pattern. Apparently only such a religious
organization provided solid basis for permanent political and military
structures. Such an organization was that of the Rechabites: for centuries,
from Jehu's time to Jeremiah we see their continued existence and reli-
gious-political activities. In the Nehemiah chronicle a Rechabite is mentioned. In the Middle Ages still, Benjamin of Tudela claims to have
encountered them under a *nasi* (leader) in the Babylonian desert. And
other travelers thought even to find traces of them in the nineteenth
century near Mecca. Also, the strictly Yahwistic Kenite tribe, to which the
Rechabites belonged, seems to have based its cohesion on religion. For
Stade has made it at least very probable that the "sign of Cain," that is to
say the tribal tattoo of the Kenites[17] was no mere tribal badge, but rather
a primary sign of the cult community.[18]

The Indian badges of sect would represent the analogous phenomena. The grand example of a religious quasi-order of fundamentally
the same kind on the same soil was, of course, Islamism and its warrior
orders, which established the numerous and, indeed, lasting Islamic
states.

Now, the point at issue is not that the life conditions of the [[80]]
Bedouins and semi-nomads had "produced" an order whose establishment could be considered as something like the "ideological exponent"
of its economic conditions. This form of historical materialistic construction is here, as elsewhere, inadequate. The point is, rather, that once
such an order was established the life conditions of these strata gave it by
far the greater opportunity to survive in the selective struggle for existence against the other, less stable political organizations. The question,

17. How old the Yahweh piety of the Kenites was remains an open question. König
(*ZDMG* 69, 1915) draws attention to the fact that the first well ascertained name is that of
Jonadab ben Rechab.

18. "Das Kainzeichen," *ZAW*, vol. 14, 1894, p. 250–51.

however, why such an order emerged at all, was determined by quite concrete religious-historical and often highly personal circumstances and vicissitudes. Once the religious fraternization had proven its efficiency as a political and economic instrument of power and was recognized as such it contributed, of course, tremendously to the diffusion of the pattern. Mohammed's as well as Jonadab ben Rechab's religious promises are not to be "explained" as products of population phenomena or economic conditions, though their content was co-determined thereby. They were, rather, the expression of personal experiences and intentions. However, the intellectual and social means which they utilized and further the great success of creations of this very type are indeed to be understood in terms of such life conditions. The same goes for ancient Israel. . . .

[[81]] The Israelite confederacy itself, according to unambiguous tradition, represented a war confederation under and with Yahweh as the war god of the union, guaranteeing its social order and creator of the material prosperity of the confederates, especially of the requisite rain. This is brought to expression by the name "Israel" which was meant to designate directly "the people of the fighting god" or originally to be pronounced *Yesorel,* and hence to signify the god 'in whom one trusts'. This last is improbable. In any case, "Israel" was no tribal name but the name of an association, at that, of a cult league.[19]

The name Israel has been made the designation of an eponym only by the theological revision of the legend of the hero Jacob, hence the shadowy character of this personification.

We must examine the structure of the league somewhat more closely.

[[82]] The scope of the league varied. Israel must have existed in Palestine even in the time of King Merneptah, the alleged Pharaoh of the Exodus, for it was mentioned in a well known inscription[20] of the time that the attacks of the royal army had decimated Israel's manpower and possessions. The manner in which it is mentioned shows that Israel, in contrast to the small and large city states, was considered to be a non-urban association. As we saw in the Deborah war, the peasants on foot and their princes taking to the field on white asses, formed the core of the army fighting against the chariot-drawn knights of the city kings. The Song of Deborah recognized as confederate members the co-belligerent mountain tribes of Ephraim and its two derivative groups, Machir and Benjamin. Furthermore, Zebulon, Napthtali, Issachar, and the tribes of Asher and Dan settled near the sea were included. Moreover, it recog-

---

19. In the myth Jacob received the name Israel after his *berith* with God (Gen 35:10).

20. W. Spiegelberg in *Berichte der Berliner Akademie der Wissenschaften* 1896. G. Steindorf in *ZAW* vol. 16.

nized the stock-breeding tribes of Reuben and Gilead from east of the Jordan, which failed, however, to come to the aid of the confederacy. The Song mentioned the city of Meros separately as violating the covenant. The two collections of Blessings recognized the usual twelve-fold number of tribes: Machir was replaced by Manasseh, Gilead by Gad, Judah and Simeon were added and according to whether Levi was included or, as in Moses' Blessing, was counted separately as a priestly tribe, Ephraim and Manasseh were counted as two tribes or jointly as the "house of Joseph."

In the time of the Song of Deborah, doubtlessly, neither Judah nor Simeon nor Levi was considered a member tribe. At that time and later Ephraim or Joseph were undoubtedly held to be the core tribes of the confederation. This is proven by its precedence in the Song, its descent from the favorite wife of Jacob, and its characterization as her favorite son (grandson respectively). . . . Hence, Ephraim was doubtlessly important in the events which led to the reception of Yahweh as the war god of Israel. The first army leader of the confederacy [[83]] to bear a Yahwistic name in the tradition, Joshua, was an Ephraimite and was buried in Ephraimite territory. It was Yahweh who from Seir in Edom drew near in the storm and destroyed the Canaanites and was praised in the Song of Deborah as war god of the confederacy standing under Ephraim's hegemony. Among the Yahweh shrines belonging to Ephraim's territory was, above all, Shechem with the confederation stone. Yet it appears that the cult place proper lay outside the city which the tradition long held to be Canaanite. . . .

As far as can be determined this unstable Israelite confederation till the time of kings had no permanent political organs at all. The tribes engaged in occasional feuds with one another. The religious international law, which, for example, prohibited the cutting down of fruit trees, applied—if at all extending back to ancient times—presumably to such feuds as occurred within the organization. The league members in the Song of Deborah partly withheld their support. Occasionally this led to their being cursed and to holy war against the oath-breaking member. There existed no common citizenship. Such was present, apparently, only in the tribe. To be sure, grave violation of metic rights, which every Israelite enjoyed in every other tribe, under certain circumstances was revenged by the confederacy. But there existed, obviously, no unitary court or unified administrative organ of any sort in times of peace. Confederate unity found expression in that a Yahweh-certified war hero or war prophet regularly claimed authority also beyond the boundaries of his tribe. People came to him from afar to have him settle their [[84]] legal disputes or to seek instruction in ritual or moral duties.

Such is told of Deborah (Judg 4:5), and the present-day version of the tradition transformed all charismatic war heroes of ancient confederate times into *shofetim*, i.e., into 'judges' of Israel who allegedly followed one another in an uninterrupted series and had legal authority throughout Israel. Their last representative, Samuel, during his office allegedly yearly visited Beth-el, Gilgal and Mizpeh (1 Sam 7:15, 16) in order to 'speak justice'. Then, after the election of the king and his own discharge, he is said to have solemnly retired from office like a Roman or Hellenic polis-official, leaving public account and the summons to raise possible complaints against him (1 Samuel 12). The Samuel tradition is without question an anti-royalist construction of Deuteronomy which presents the behavior of a Yahweh-pleasing prince as a paradigm in contrast to the kings of the present.

What fundamentally was the place of the *shofetim*? Stade maintains[21] that the later tradition simply elevated the ancient war heroes of Yahweh to the status of peaceful "judges," while Klostermann, in a spirited manner, compared the "judges" of Israel to the 'law speakers' (*lögsögumadr*) of the Nordic, particularly Icelandic practice, the bearers of the oral legal tradition and the forerunners of the fixation of law in writing.[22] In this way he sought particularly to explain the origin and literary peculiarities of the pre-exilic law books, which allegedly originated in the public instructions in the law by 'law speakers'. The hypothesis which Puukko especially criticized in detail, according to numerous socio-legal analogies has some validity.

Law has always developed first through legal oracles, precedents, responses of charismatically qualified bearers of legal wisdom. But such charismatic law speakers have not always had the specific place of the Nordic law speakers, whose office—for office it was—was closely bound up with the organization of the Germanic judicial community. The "judges" so-called in the present revision of the tradition, had clearly quite different imprint. They were, in general, far from actual bearers of legal wisdom. Tradition placed the normal legal counsel in the hands of the *zekenim* (elders). The ordeal, on the other hand, and the regular trial-oracle were the business of the priests. And, as will ⟦85⟧ be noted later, the oracle in early times was obtained purely by mechanical means (lot). For the rest, the tradition mentions very different types of digni-

21. B. Stade, *Biblische Theologie des Alten Testament* (Tübingen: Mohr, 1905) 285–86.

22. A. Klostermann, *Der Pentateuch* (Leipzig: Bohme, 1907) has been criticized in detail by A. F. Puukko, *Das Deuteronomium* ⟦BWAT; Leipzig: Hinrichs, 1910⟧ 176–202. K. sought through his hypothesis to render understandable the peculiar literary character of Deuteronomy. He maintains that it was an eschatology lecture on religious laws. The comparison of the story of the "find" with the "law" of Numa can hardly be called fruitful.

taries who enjoyed traditional authority within the single tribe. Hence, there could be room for a charismatic juridical procedure only alongside all these sources of legal finding.

The figures of the *shofetim* whom the present day version of the so-called Book of Judges presents vary greatly in nature. If one disregards those merely reported existing (Jair, Ebzon, Elon, Abdon), we note that Samson was held to be a purely individual hero fighting out his feuds. Ehud, too, was an individual hero, only with the difference that he killed the oppressor of Israel. Othniel, Shamgar, Barak, Gideon, Jephthah and probably also Tola were considered to be successful army leaders of Israel, in truth, apparently, of their own and neighboring tribes. Only a part of them were "judges" in Israel in time of peace. And this "fact" is only quite generally noted. The whole emphasis lies rather on their accomplishment as "redeemers," that is to say, saviors in grave war emergencies.

Beside this, in a police action of the confederacy represented as a holy war (Judg 20:28), a priest from Elide lineage (Phinehas) appeared as oracle giver of the army. Eli is a pure priest. His sons were presented as priests, but at the same time as chosen leaders of the summons against the Philistines. This last named tradition concerning the Elides is highly dubious and late, the tradition concerning Samuel, however, is completely useless. He is at one time treated as a *Nabi* [['prophet']], at another as a seer, at still others as a preacher (1 Sam 4:1), also as a Nazirite, as priest, and, finally, as a military leader. The time in which these representations were revised clearly no longer had any certain knowledge of the actual conditions of the times of the confederacy. The most reliable source, the Song of Deborah, shows the prophetess beside the leading Naphtalite war hero, Barak, who as army leader had quite a few allied dignitaries of other tribes at his side.

The tradition expressly knows and reports of Deborah and Samuel only that they "spoke law" regularly, that is to say, gave trial oracles upon request. The same is reported in the present-day revision of the Hexateuch of Moses. The establishment of [[86]] "objective," permanently valid, legal norms and their fixation in writing is reported only of Moses and of Joshua, besides Samuel, in a certain legendary case of the determination of the king's prerogative after Saul's decision. In any case there was no room with the *shofetim* for a continuously functioning "law speaking" according to the analogy of the Germanic Nordics. Political oracles, not trial oracles, were given by "prophets" like Deborah. And politico-military decisions, not legal decisions or wisdom, were the specific function of charismatic *shofetim*.

With all this it is quite probable that both proven prophets as well as war heroes, were, in times of peace, requested to settle conflicts and that the secular war heroes, as usual, took these matters in hand as their prerogatives once they had succeeded in stabilizing the rule to the extent, for instance, of Abimelech. But even the first kings were not yet considered primarily to be bearers or even creators of law, but war leaders. With David, the tradition (2 Sam 14:2ff.) supposes that the king, in a given case, intervenes in a blood feud. Solomon, however, was the first apparently, systematically to take the administration of justice into his hands (1 Kgs 3:16–17). There is the account of the construction of a hall of justice under Solomon (1 Kgs 7:7). Presumably because of this innovation he was held by posterity as a source of judicial wisdom. But at first there is no mention of an official concern for the unity of law even with the kings.

. . . .

Social Reception of the War God

⟦130⟧ What mattered practically was that Yahweh, despite this nature, became and continued to be a god of social organization, at least for old Israel. This must be properly understood. We must assume that, since Moses, he was the god of the covenant of the Israelite confederacy, and, corresponding to the purpose of the confederacy, he was primarily its war god. He played this role in a very special manner. He became war god by virtue of a treaty of confederation. This contract had to be concluded, not only among confederates, but also with him, for he was no god residing in the midst of the people, a familiar god, but rather a god hitherto strange. He continued to be a "god from afar." This was the decisive element in the relationship. Yahweh was an elective god. The confederate people had chosen him through *berith* ⟦'covenant'⟧ with him, just as, later, it established its king by *berith*.

Yahweh, in turn, had chosen this people before all others by free resolve. This is what he constantly brings home to the people through the priestly Torah and the prophetic oracles. By free grace he has chosen this and no other people. He has given them promises as to no other people and in compensation accepted their pledges. Hence, whenever the confederate people per se entered a *berith*, he, the god, was an ideational party to it. All violations of the holy enactments were not merely violations of orders guaranteed by him as other gods guarantee their orders, but violations of the most solemn contractual obligations toward him personally. He who failed to accept the army summons, failed not merely to serve the confederacy, but to serve ⟦131⟧ him personally and "came not to the help of the Lord" (Judg 5:23). The members of the confederate army were called 'men of God' (*ᶜam haᵓelohim* Judg 20:1–2).

In this manner Yahweh became not only the war god of the confederacy but also the contractual partner of its law established by *berith*,
above all of the socio-legal orders. Since the confederacy was at first a
stateless association of tribes, new statutes, whether cultic or legal in nature, could in principle originate only by way of agreement (*berith*) based
on oracle like the original covenant. Therewith, all statutes were based
on the same ground as the old contract relation which existed between
the god and the people. Considered in terms of public law, the *berith*, before the advent of kingship, was no mere theoretical construction. The
same holds for the religious conception. With Jeremiah (2:5) Yahweh
asks "what iniquity have your fathers found in me?" And for his part,
Jeremiah admonishes him not to break his covenant with Israel.

Being considered a contractual partner, this god of the covenant
could be viewed in Israel neither as a mere functional deity of some process of nature or of social institutions, nor as a local deity in the manner
everywhere characteristic of Oriental cities. He was no mere god of the
"land." Rather, the human community of the Israelite confederate army
had to be considered as his people, joined to him through common covenant. This was, in fact, the classical view of the tradition. The transfer of
holiness to the political territorial holding, making it a "holy land," is but
a later conception, probably suggested by heterogeneous conceptions of
deity in part derived from Baal worship, in part from the localization of
Yahweh as the god of the king's residence. This conception of the "holy
land" is first documented for David in the time of kings in a tradition of
uncertain age, then in the Northern kingdom at the occasion of Elisha's
conversion of Naaman.

As guardian of confederate orders, Yahweh protects the customs and
mores. That which is "unheard of" in Israel is an abomination to him.
In agreement with his original nature, however, and unlike Varuna and
similar deities, he was not the guardian of the confederate law and mores
in the sense of sanctifying an already existing immutable order of law or
a [[132]] "righteousness" measurable in terms of fixed norms. On the contrary, this positive law for Israel was created through *berith* [['covenant']]
with him. It had not always been in existence and it was possible that by
new revelation and new *berith* with God it could be changed again. . . .

The law was no eternal Tao or Dharma but a positive divine enactment. Its observance was jealously watched by Yahweh. On the later occasions, God's law was called "eternal" by the ethical rationalism of the
Deuteronomic school (Deut 4:2) and the original moral perfection of
God's just orders was praised as peculiar to no other people (4:8). These
occasional exhortatory arguments, however, do not embody the typical
stand unavoidably following from the *berith* character of the law. God's

ordainments come from his hand and are as *such* changeable. He may bind himself to his enactments by *berith*, but that is the result of His free resolve. Only the priestly revision knows of eternal orders. Almost all of these are cultic norms or they pertain to rights of the Aaronites who gained ascendancy only in Exile times becoming monopolists of cult leadership. Just because these norms were innovations they were designated with this emotionally charged expression (*ḥūqqath ᶜolam* [['everlasting statute']]). (Exod 27:21; Lev 3:17; 16:31; 23:14, 41; Deut 12:1 pertain to cultic orders. Lev 7:37; Num 18:23 pertain to priestly law of Exile times. Gen 9:14 *berith ᶜolam* [['everlasting covenant']] pertains to the theological constructions of Noah's covenant.) . . .

[[133]] From the beginning, in Yahwism there were features transcending Israel and in this sense a certain universalism was inherent in the conception of Yahweh. Rather, such elements of a potential universalism were inherent in the peculiar relationship in which, for purely historical reasons, the Israelite confederacy stood to this god. There has been recent controversy as to whether monolatry (the exclusive worship of one of several deities), henotheism (consideration of the implored god as alone mighty) or monotheism (singularity in principle) have governed the ancient conception of Yahweh. This may be a misleading formulation of the question. The conception of Yahweh has not only undergone changes, but at any given time it varied according to different social groups. The warrior knew clearly that the god whom he implored was his god and consequently that the god of the enemy was different. The gods Yahweh and Chemosh are thus treated in the Book of Judges (11:24) in the story of Jephthah and in the Book of Kings in the account of the Moabite war (2 Kgs 3:1–2). (Apparently Chemosh was also a god common to several tribes.) With regard to the king and the urban strata, especially those of the temple priests and patricians, but also of the urban masses, a different conception of Yahweh obtained. The god was considered to be localized in the temple of the city and there were other gods elsewhere. One's own god stood and fell with the existence of the city. Anyone who had to leave the city (or its jurisdictional area) could not serve its god but had to serve strange deities, as did David (1 Sam 26:19). The newcomer from a foreign land, however, had better serve the native god, because he might otherwise revenge himself as did Yahweh on the Assyrian colonists in Samaria (2 Kgs 17:25–26). This is the product of urban culture. For the Israelite of a temple city, especially Jerusalem, Yahweh resided in the Temple. The Ark of Yahweh always facilitated such localization. The transmitted ritual shows that warriors in the field conceived of Yahweh as present on this camp shrine.

⟦134⟧ Naturally, the attitude of semi nomadic stock-breeding tribes was quite different. The tradition influenced by them takes it for granted that god is with the Israelites wherever they are (Gen 28:20). They know full well that non-Israelite tribes also worship Yahweh, hence their legends presuppose the same not only for Laban (Gen 24:50; 31:49), after all a relative, but also for Abimelech of Gerar (Gen 20:11; 21:23). In the Joseph legend (Gen 41:39–40) one can trace views typical of overseas trading peoples such as the Hellenes and the later Romans, namely, the naive identification of certain foreign deities with their own. In post-exilic Judaism this is to be found in the identification of Yahweh with the god of Nebuchadnezzar (with Daniel) and that of the Persian king. On the whole, however, this tendency was alien to early Israel because Yahweh by *berith* ⟦'covenant'⟧ had become its god. In the original view, this precluded the possibility that Yahweh, as for example, Marduk and Ahuramazda, could be the tutelatory god of foreign kings in the same manner as of Israel. The professional Yahweh prophets of olden times, the Nebiᵖim and seers, were evidently neither convinced of Yahweh's uniqueness, nor of the fact that their god had been domiciled only in Israel. In part these prophets had an international clientele. The Elijah tradition presupposes, at least in one place (1 Kgs 17:9), that also the widow of Sidon receives Yahweh's commandments. For the rest, their god was, if not the only one, naturally the strongest of them all and other gods were "nobodies." This was true also for the old Yahwistic warrior tradition (Josh 2:9). What mattered to it most was the special position of Israel by *berith*. This tradition held that while others may worship Yahweh, Israel stands under his special protection. Yahweh was not considered to be the enemy of other nations. Only the nationalistic fanaticism of the kingly prophets of good fortune and the confessional fanaticism of the priests after the Exile occasionally approached this view. What mattered to Yahweh was Israel alone, as was, after all, expected at all times of every local god, or local saint, and every localized madonna. However, in the case of Yahweh, views leading to similar results did not derive originally from the localization but, indeed, from a (relative) universalism and the particularized *berith* with Israel.

The different conceptions of Yahweh stood side by side and ⟦135⟧ their logical contradiction was usually not perceived. In any case, one should beware of viewing the more "particularistic" conception of god as necessarily older. To some extent, the opposite holds and this was unavoidably the case with Yahweh. In the rhythmic, ancient, divine speech (Exod 19:5) Yahweh, before announcing the substance of the covenant to be concluded which will make Israel his treasure, refers to himself as "lord of the earth." This view, alongside others, is to be found even in pre-prophetic times. The gods of other nations, after all, also make their appearance "universalistically" in this sense. This is true particularly of the gods of the great kings of the capitals of the world empires. Amon, in Egypt under the priestly rule of the later Rameses, claimed universal power of ministering grace.[23] The councillors and court prophets of the Israelite kings will have pronounced similar things of Yahweh in memory of David's kingdom.[24]

Historically the special (relative) universalism of Yahweh did not rest on this foundation, but rather on the fact of his reception. Yahweh had simply existed already and had proven his power in a manner different from other deities before Israel offered him sacrifices. This had consequences for worship. Even if he enjoyed sacrifices and these, accordingly, were considered adequate means to win his favor, nevertheless, the idea frequent elsewhere that god's existence depended upon the offering of sacrifices[25] could hardly emerge. Yahweh had his throne afar on his mountain height and had no need for sacrifices, even though he enjoyed them. Besides, note this, in the pre-kingly times during periods of peace, there existed no political or hierocratic authority whatsoever which could have offered sacrifices in the name of the confederacy. We have no knowledge of such, and its existence seems impossible. Hence, the sacrifice in ancient times simply could not gain the significance in relation to Yahweh which it obtained elsewhere. Thus, the prophets later were perfectly justified in emphasizing that not only for the time of the desert but for the Israelite confederation generally, people did not worship god by offering sacrifice. As the *berith* [['covenant']] was the specific form through which the confederate people constantly renewed contact with Yahweh, the idea suggested itself to deem the fulfillment of his *berith*-sanctified commandments [[136]] at least of equal or actually greater importance than occasional sacrifices offered by individuals and later by

23. Wen Amon (according to J. H. Breasted, [[*Ancient Records of Egypt* [Chicago: University of Chicago Press, 1906–7]]] vol. 4, p. 80) presents to the king of Byblos that the Pharaohs (whose shipments of silver the king of Byblos misses) were unable to accomplish what god Amon could accomplish (who for this very reason sends no material gifts) namely give him long life and good health (this, to be sure, does not agree with the courtly style of the Old Kingdom). Also the king of Byblos is said to "belong" to Amon, whom to obey allegedly brings good fortune to every man.

24. The differences in the deities of the surrounding world especially of Mesopotamia, are excellently presented by J. Hehn in his *Die biblische und die babylonische Gottesidee* (Leipzig [[Hinrichs]], 1913).

25. In contrast, the gods in Egypt require nourishment through man's sacrificial offerings just as do dead souls (see [[F. W. Bissing, *Prähistorische Topfe aus Indien und aus Aegypten* [SBAWG; Munich: Königlich Bayerischen Akademie der Wissenschaften, 1911]]]).

kings and temple priests. This is asserted ever anew by part of the pure Yahweh worshippers.[26]

During the later time of kings there was always a party in Israel—and, indeed, it included the most powerful scriptural prophets such as Amos and Jeremiah—who kept the memory of this condition alive and presented any and all sacrifices as ultimately quite indifferent to Yahweh. It is understandable that people least firmly settled at fixed places of worship, hence, strata of small-stock-breeders, most closely adhered to this view. Obviously, what the mighty heavenly warlord actually demanded was the precise observation of his specific rites, and, for the rest, obedience to his revelations. This view, replete with consequences—again for political reasons—from the beginning remained alive among the very guardians of the old tradition. However primitive and barbaric the ethical commandments may have been (which today can no longer be ascertained) which he imposed on the warrior confederacy, Yahweh was simply and unavoidably and far more than any other deity a "jealous" god, quite specifically securing the observance of certain ritualistic and social-ethical workaday norms.

He was not a god—note this—who esteemed an eternally valid ethic or who could himself be ethically judged. This last notion emerged only gradually as a product of intellectual rationalism. Nay, he behaved as a king, given to wrath and passion if the obligations due him through *berith* remained unfulfilled. Duties such as the chosen lord demands of his subject were at issue; they were quite positive obligations. From the first people did not and had nothing to ponder as to their absolute ethical value. What was owed was substantially the avoidance of things "unheard of in Israel" and positive obligations fixed by *berith*. According to an early and widely diffused opinion, these were more insisted upon by god than sacrificial offerings. Even quite early, the tradition presents him in a great state of rage not only because of ritualistic, but ethical abominations. And it is presupposed that the holy war of the confederacy could be declared to confederate members because of grave offenses, because of deeds such as had not been "done nor seen from the [[137]] day that the children of Israel came up out of the land of Egypt" (Judg 19:30). What led the confederacy to intervene in such matters and hence led to a specifically strong ethical orientation of old Israelite confederate law, was the joint religious liability of confederate members for the offenses of each individual. This presupposition of collective liability for each

26. For this entire context see, especially, Budde's cycle of lectures on ancient Israelite religion [[K. Budde, *Die altisraelitische Religion* (3d ed.; Giessen: Alfred Töpelmann, 1912)]]. He may well have most clearly seen and emphasized the determination of the ethical nature of the religion of Israel by the character of the godhead as elective.

offender, knowingly or unwittingly held, was of great consequence. Like the right to employ repressive measures in all international relations to this day, it was taken as a matter of course in the religious belief of people who, like Israel, stood opposite their god as an association of freemen.

Whereas in Babylonian hymns the liability of the individual for the sins of his ancestors and close relatives is to be found, joint liability of the people as a whole for each and every individual—the precondition for all prophetic prediction of doom—naturally, was ideologically undeveloped in a purely bureaucratic state. Hence, also in this the political structure played a decisive role. As the members of the collectivity are liable for one another, so the descendants are liable for the offenses of their ancestors down to remote generations. The same held for blood revenge, hence was nothing startling. With the weakening of blood revenge, changes came about. The Deuteronomic speculation considered both kinds of liability, for compatriots and ancestors, a hardship without being able actually to abolish the view. For Israel it resulted from *berith* with god himself.

A further important peculiarity results from the quality of the god as guardian of the confederate law and as war god accepted through a special contract: the god was and continued to be, in spite of all anthropomorphism, unmarried and, hence, childless. . . . With Yahweh, however, this circumstance from the beginning contributed substantially to his appearance, as something unique and more removed from this world, in contrast to other divine figures. This, above all, blocked the formation of true myths which is always [[138]] "theogony." Hence also this important peculiarity was probably determined through the peculiar political origin of his worship.

As we have seen, such traits of preeminence of the god of the confederacy by no means necessarily constituted a claim to exclusive recognition. The external relationship to the deities of other peoples has already been discussed. Jephthah takes for granted the reality and might of the Ammonite and later, also, Moabite god Chemosh. The view is still the same under Ahab. The Moabite king by the sacrifice of his own son was able to much to strengthen Chemosh that his anger against Israel and its god gained the upper hand. But what matters here is that de facto the exclusiveness of the god also did not exist within the group. It is highly probable that for the semi-Bedouins of the steppe, from the outset the great war god of the covenant was the only important deity. This monolatry is explained quite simply from the fact that they had no differentiated culture productive of functional deities and that the po-

litical community only served militarily to protect and/or conquer grazing grounds. Hence, these semi-nomadic tribes, especially in the South,
were presumably from the outset the representatives of a conception of
the "singularity" of Yahweh in the sense of monolatry.

This view was taken up by the professional group which was, from the
beginning, peculiar to Yahweh worship: the war prophets. The oldest
document which mentions with disapproval the worship of "new gods"
in Israel is the Song of Deborah (Judg 5:8). All wars against the urban
patricians, Canaanite as well as Philistine, were fought in the name of
Yahweh. Understandably, on such occasions, the view always emerged
that exclusive worship of Yahweh who had promised military aid was a
covenant duty. All non-secular, but prophetic, male or female leaders in
the wars of liberation were hostile to all other deities or became so in war.
For the rest, nothing is better ascertained for the settled Israelites than
the fact that they possessed "other gods" besides Yahweh. Originally this
was perfectly legitimate. The possession of other gods meant merely that
other cults not dedicated to Yahweh existed and that their importance
quite apart from imported foreign *numina* was such that the priestly
revision was unable to efface.[27]

. . . .

Social Context of the Prophetic Message

[[278]] One important principle united the prophets as a status group:
the gratuitous character of their oracles. This separated them from the
prophets of the king, whom they cursed as destroyers of the land. And it
distinguished the prophets from all groups that made an industry of
prophecy in the manner of the old seers or dream-interpreters whom
they despised and rejected. The complete inner [[279]] independence of
the prophets was not so much a result as a most important cause of their
practice. In the main they prophesied disaster and no one could be sure
whether on request, like King Zedekiah, he might not receive a prediction of doom and therewith an evil omen. One does not pay for evil
omens nor expose oneself to them. Primarily unbidden and spontaneously impelled, rarely on request, the prophets hurled their frequently
frightful oracles against their audience.

27. Against the very pronounced view of B. D. Eerdmans in the *Altestamentliche Studien*
[[Giessen: Alfred Töpelmann, 1908–12]] to the effect that some parts of the Old Testament
do not at all know Yahweh, that they were in fact specifically polytheistic, see C. Steuernagel
in the *Theologische Rundschau*, 1908, pp. 323–33.

However, as a status principle this gratuitous practice is, indeed, characteristic of a stratum of genteel intellectuals. The borrowing of this principle, later, by the plebeian intellectual strata of the rabbis and, from them, by the Christian apostles form exceptions of great importance for the sociology of religion. Moreover, the prophets did not by any means find their "community," so far as that term applies (of which more later) either solely or primarily in the demos. On the contrary, if they had any personal support at all, it was from distinguished, individual, pious houses in Jerusalem. Sometimes for several generations such served as their patrons. Jeremiah was supported by the same sib which also took part in the "finding" of Deuteronomy. Most sympathetic supporters were found among the *zekenim* [['elders']], as the guardians of the pious tradition and, particularly, the traditional respect for prophecy. Such was the case for Jeremiah in his capital trial; it was also true of Ezekiel, whom the elders consulted in Exile.

The prophets never obtained support from the peasants. Indeed, all prophets preached against debt slavery, the pawning of clothes, against all violation of the charity commandments, which benefited the little man. In Jeremiah's last prophecy, peasants and shepherds were the champions of piety. However, this form of prophecy was true only for Jeremiah. The peasants belonged as little to his following as the rural squirearchy; in fact, the ʿ*am ha-*ʾ*aretz* [['people of the land']] were among the more important opponents of the prophets, especially of Jeremiah who was opposed by his own sib. Because they were strict Yahwists, the prophets declaimed against the rural orgiasticism of the fertility cults and the most tainted rural places of worship. Above all the prophets declaimed against the shrines of Baal, which meant much to the rural population for economic as well as ideal reasons.

The prophets never received support from the king. For the [[280]] prophets were champions of the Yahwistic tradition opposing kingship which was compromised by politically necessary concessions to foreign cults, intemperant drinking, and by the innovations of the Solomonic corvée state. Solomon was not of the slightest importance for any of the prophets. When a king is mentioned at all, it is David who is the pious ruler. Hosea viewed the kings of the Northern realm as illegitimate, because they had usurped the throne without the will of Yahweh. Amos mentioned the Nazirites and Nebiʾim [['prophets']] among the institutions of Yahweh, but not the kings. Indeed, none of the prophets denied the legitimacy of the Davidians. However, respect even for this dynasty, such as it was, was only conditional. Isaiah's Immanuel-prophecy, after all, may well be considered as the prediction of a God-sent usurper. Yet it was for Isaiah that David's age represented the climax of national history. Relentless attacks against the conduct of the respective contemporary kings grew in intensity. Such raging outbursts of wrath and scorn as those of Jeremiah against Jehoiakim are rarely to be found. Jehoiakim shall go to earth like an ass (22:19) and the queen mother who apparently participated in the Astarte-cult, shall have her skirt pulled over her head that all might see her shame (13:18ff.). But even Isaiah called his woe down on the land the king of which "is a child and is led by women" and he stood up boldly to the grown-up king in a personal encounter.

With obvious intent the prophetic tradition preserved the account of Elijah's conflicts with Ahab. The kings returned these antipathies in kind. They tolerated the prophets only in uncertain times, but, whenever they felt sure of themselves, they had recourse, like Manasseh, to bloody persecution. Beside the politically conditioned worship of foreign deities or incorrect cults, the wrath of the prophets against the kings was, above all, directed at world politics per se, the means and presuppositions of which were unholy. This applied particularly to the alliance with Egypt. Although fugitive Yahweh prophets, such as Uria, sought refuge in Egypt, and although Egyptian rule was lenient and certainly religiously non-propagandistic, the prophets rebelled with especial bitterness against this alliance. The reason is made obvious in Isaiah (28:18).

Dealings with Egypt are an "agreement with Sheol," that is to [[281]] say with the chthonian gods of the realm of the dead which they loathed.[28] Obviously in this the prophets rest their political attitudes solidly on the priestly tradition; their political stand is throughout religiously conditioned. As against the king, so the prophets declaimed against the mighty, particularly the *sarim* [['princes']] and *gibborim* [['mighty men']]. Along with the injustice of their courts, the prophets cursed, above all, their impious way of life and debauchery. But obviously the opposition of the prophets was independent of such single vices. The king and political-military circles could make no use whatever of the purely utopian exhortations and counsels of the prophets.

The Hellenic states of the sixth and fifth centuries regularly consulted oracles but in the end and precisely in the days of decision, as, for example, during the Persian war, they failed to honor the advice of their oracles even though they were politically oriented. As a rule, it was politically impossible for the kings of Judah to heed the advice of the prophets. And the knightly sense of dignity which here as elsewhere is aloof

28. For the conception of sin and its development in Babylonian religion see A. Scholl-meyer, "Sumerisch-babylonische Hymnen und Gebete an Samas," *Studien zur Geschichte und Kritik des Altertums*, Supplement (Paderborn: Schoningh, 1912), and J. Morgenstern, "The Doctrine of Sin in the Babylonian Religion," *Mitteilungen des Vereins für Alte Geschichte* (Berlin, 1905) vol. 3.

from prophetic belief, necessarily made them reject as beneath them Jeremiah's advice with respect to Babylon. They disdained these screaming ecstatics of the streets.

On the other side, the popular opposition against the distinguished knights and patricians of the time of the kings which the intellectual strata had nourished played its part in the attitude of the prophets. Avarice is the preeminent vice, that is to say, usurious oppression of the poor. The prophets are not interested in the royal army. Their future kingdom is a kingdom of peace. In this they did not by any means represent something like "Little Judah" pacifists. Amos promised to Judah dominion over Edom and over those people which are called by Yahweh's name (9:12). The old popular hope of world domination recurred repeatedly. Increasingly, however, the idea gained currency that the political aspirations of Israel would only be realized through a miracle of God, as once at the Red Sea, but not through autonomous military power, and, least of all, through political alliances. Ever anew the wrath of the prophets turned against such alliances. The basis of the opposition was again religious. It was not simply because of the danger of strange cults that such antipathy was felt. Rather, Israel stood in the *berith* [['covenant']] with Yahweh. Nothing must enter competition [[282]] with the *berith*, especially not trust in human help, which would bespeak of godless disbelief and evoke Yahweh's wrath. As Jeremiah saw the matter, if Yahweh had ordained the conquest of the people by Nebuchadnezzar, one must accept the fact.

Defensive alliances against the great kings were offenses against God so long as the great kings were executors of his will. If they were not and if He wished to help Israel, He would do so alone, Isaiah taught. Probably he was the first for this reason to preach indefatigably against all and every attempt to work out an alliance. Clearly, the whole attitude toward internal as well as foreign affairs was purely religious in motivation, nothing bespeaks of political expediencies. The relationship to the priests also was religiously conditioned.

No prophet before Ezekiel spoke favorably of the priests. Amos recognized, as noted, only the Nazirites and *Nebi²im* [['prophets']] as Yahweh's tools, but he failed to mention the priests. The very existence of their type of free prophecy was, from the time of its appearance, a clear symptom of the weakness of priestly power. Had the place of the priest been like that in Egypt, or even in Babylon, or in Jerusalem after the Exile, free prophecy would doubtlessly have been suppressed as dangerous competition. Since originally, in the confederate time, there was no central shrine and no official sacrifice, this was impossible. Meanwhile the prestige of the old royal prophets and seers and then of Elijah and the Elisha-school was firmly established. Powerful sibs of pious laity backed the prophets. Therefore, the priests had to tolerate them despite frequent and sharp antagonisms. But, they were by no means always antagonistic to the priests. Isaiah had close relations with the priests of Jerusalem and Ezekiel was throughout priestly in outlook. On the other hand, we find the sharpest conceivable personal conflicts with the cult priests, first with Amos in Beth-el and last with Jeremiah in Jerusalem. . . .

Jeremiah was charged with a capital crime because he had prophesied for the Temple the fate of the shrine in Shiloh which the Philistines once had destroyed. He was dragged before the court of officials and elders, and the priests and prophets of salvation [[283]] acted as his accusers. However the difference of the times is evident in the result. Jeremiah was acquitted on advice of the elders, in spite of the complaint of the priests, on the ground that there existed the precedent of Micah's case. Micah, they said, had prophesied under Hezekiah similar events.[29] The occurrence indicates that prophecies against the Temple itself were rare. Above all such oracles in the last analysis implied no doubt in the Temple's legitimacy. Later, to be sure, Jeremiah readily comforted himself and others for the loss of the Ark of the Covenant under Nebuchadnezzar. His prophecy, nevertheless, deals with the destruction of the Temple as a grievous misfortune which was only conditionally held out as a punishment for sins in case of failing conversion (26:13).

In fact, no prophet attacked the Temple proper. Amos called the sacrifice in Beth-el and Gilgal transgressions (4:4, 5:5) presumably meaning by this only the cult practices of the peasants. Such cult practices were deeply hated by all representatives of shepherd piety. The people should not frequent these places, but "seek Yahweh" (ibid.). Amos knew Zion as the seat of Yahweh in the same manner as Hosea acknowledged Judah as the one undefiled seat of Yahweh. Isaiah's trust in the invincibility of Jerusalem in his late oracles doubtlessly rested on the presence there of the Temple. It was in a temple vision during his youth that he had seen the heavenly court. For Micah, despite his oracle of doom, Mount Zion remained the future place of the pure Torah and prophecy of Yahweh. The prophets preached only against the impurities of the cult practiced there, particularly against defilement by sacred courtesans. In the case of Hosea almost the whole strength of the prophet was absorbed by the fight against the worship of Baal, a fight which runs through pre-exilic prophecy. But they never preached for the correct priestly cult. . . .

[[284]] In characteristic fashion, the bearer of personal charisma refused to recognize office charisma as a qualification to teach if the

---

29. See, for instance, the prohibition against depriving a poor man of his position during his corvée service for the king (nineteenth Dynasty). Breasted, *Records*, vol. 3, p. 51.

priestly teacher is personally unworthy. For, the prophet who did not participate in the cult naturally considered the teaching of God's word (*dabar*) as he received it as religiously all-important. Hence also in priestcraft, the teaching (*torah*), not the cult [[was important]] (Jer 8:6, 18:18). This held also for Jerusalem (Mic 4:2). Likewise the prophet naturally considered as important for the people only obedience to the *debarim* [['words']] and the *torah* and not the sacrifice or ritualistic pre-scriptions like observance of the Sabbath and circumcision which later in the Exile obtained such decisive significance. Even with Amos, a shep-herd, Yahweh is impatient with the Sabbath of the disobedient people,[30] and Jeremiah opposes to external circumcision the "circumcision of the foreskin of the heart" (9:24ff.) as the only truly important fact. . . .

[[285]] The total attitude of the prophets has often been described as "culture hostility." This should not be understood to mean their per-sonal lack of culture. The prophets are conceivable only on the great sounding board of the world-political stage of their times. Similarly, they are conceivable only in connection with extensive cultural sophistication and a strong cultured stratum, though, for the reasons previously dis-cussed, only in the frame of a small state somewhat similar to Zwingli in a single canton. They were all literate and on the whole obviously well informed as to the peculiarities of Egyptian and Mesopotamian culture, especially, also, in astronomy. The manner in which the prophets used sacred numbers, for example Jeremiah's use of the number "70" may well permit us to infer that they had more than a hazy knowledge of Babylonian astronomy. In any case, tradition records no trait that would permit the inference of any attempts at flight from the world or the de-nial of culture in the Indian sense.

In addition to the *torah*, the prophets knew also the *chokma* [['wis-dom']] or *ᶜeṣah* [['counsel']] (Jer 18:18) of the teachers of prudent living (*chakamin*). However, the educational level of the prophets may well have been more comparable to that of the Orphics and folk prophets of Hellas than to that of the genteel sages as represented by Thales. Not only all aesthetic and all values of genteel living in general, but, also, all worldly wisdom was viewed by them with quite alien eyes. These attitudes were sustained by the anti-chrematistic tradition of the puritanically pious in their environment who were [[286]] suspicious of the court, the officials, the *gibborim* [['mighty men']] and the priests. In its inner structure, how-ever, these attitudes of the prophets were purely religiously conditioned by the manner in which they elaborated their experiences.

---

30. Breasted, *Records*, vol. 1, pp. 239, 240, 281, 328–29, 459, 523. All these inscriptions stem from the time of the Old Kingdom and begin with the first Dynasty.

From an Ethnic Group to a Religious Community:

The Sociological Problem of Judaism

ANTONIN CAUSSE

[[285]] In order to formulate a proper view of Jewish origins, it is necessary to forsake common notions, such as the "Jerusalem-centeredness" typical of the majority of Old Testament scholars from Wellhausen through Kittel and on to Sellin. One generally studies the formation of Judaism as an institution that appeared first in Babylon among the remnant of Benjamin and Judah that Nebuchadnezzar had led captive, and then a half-century later, in Jerusalem among the exiles who returned to rebuild the Temple and reestablish the theocracy.[1]

Translated, revised, and reprinted with permission from "Du groupe ethnique à la communauté religieuse: Le problème sociologique du judaïsme," *Revue d'histoire et de philosophie religieuses* 14 (1934) 285–335. Translated by David W. Baker.

    Editor's note: In order to shorten the article for inclusion here, I have altered Causse's original in three ways. Lengthy quotations from the Hebrew Bible have generally been replaced by a simple citation; references following these have been included in parentheses within the text instead of in footnotes; and the body and notes have been edited where it was deemed possible to shorten without altering the flow or substance of Causse's arguments. (CEC)

    1. See J. Wellhausen, *Israelitische und jüdische Geschichte* (Berlin: Reimer); R. Kittel, *Geschichte des Volkes Israel* (4th ed., Gotha: Perthes, 1923–29; 7th ed., Stuttgart: Kolhammer, 1925–32) 3.29; E. Sellin, *Geschichte des israelitisch-jüdischen Volkes* (Leipzig: Quelle & Meyer, 1924–32), vol. 2; and . . . W. O. E. Oesterley, *A History of Israel* (Oxford: Clarendon, 1933) vol. 2. . . . The point over which the critics differ is the greater or lesser importance of the role of the Jewish element remaining in Palestine during the Exile. . . . These historians remain unanimous in their "Jerusalem-centric" concept of Judaism's formation. The

⟦286⟧ This conception is only following the traditional presuppositions of the Chronicler in the first chapters of Ezra. However, a more attentive and expanded study of the biblical texts, confirmed by the discovery of such documents as the Aramaic contracts from Nippur and the Elephantine papyri, leads us to a very different view. The formation of Judaism is not primarily a question of a Jerusalemite restoration, a return of the "captivity of Babylon"; it is, rather, a question of the evolution of a Judaism that would henceforth be a diaspora and its transition from an ethnic group to a religious community.

The Diaspora and the Crisis of the Ethnic Group

The facts are as follows: from 586, Judah, which, since the destruction of Samaria and the Assyrian deportations had preserved the tradition of Israel, disappears itself as a political organization. Jerusalem is in ruins, the palace and Temple torched; the elite of the population, the princes, the priests, and the men at arms have been taken away into Chaldea.

From the moment of deportation, Israel no longer appears as a group tied to a fixed geographical location. It is already a people without a country. Of course, there are still some more-or-less important remnants in the Judean hills: "the people of the land" whom the Chaldeans have left as laborers and vinedressers and who have established themselves as well as possible under the circumstances in the most fertile and least devastated regions.[2]

Babylonian Exile is presented as a temporary accident, and the existence of an active diaspora outside of a Babylonian contingent is not sufficiently taken into consideration. Meanwhile, Max Haller (in his introduction to the volume *Das Judentum*, which is vol. 3 in *Die Schriften des Alten Testaments in Auswahl* [ed. H. Gressmann; Göttingen: Vandenhoeck & Ruprecht, 1925] 13–24) and Gustav Hölscher (in his *Geschichte der Israelitischen und Jüdischen Religion* [Giessen: Alfred Töpelmann, 1922] 116–24) have already elaborated on more complex aspects of the problem and have taken note of the larger role of the Egyptian and Mesopotamian colonies in the history of Judaism in the Persian Period.

2. The notice of the Chronicler in 2 Chr 36:20–21, according to which Nebuchadnezzar had led captive "all those who had escaped the sword in order to enslave them," leaving Palestine absolutely devastated . . . during ten sabbaths of years, is doubtlessly nothing more than a haggadic interpretation. . . . But it certainly appears that the towns and chief villages of the province suffered less than the capital and that . . . those of Judah who escaped the deportation maintained themselves in the land by cultivating the vines and olives that the enemy had not destroyed and planting grain in the most fertile soil. However, it does not seem that Jerusalem was immediately restored from its ruin, and it is asking too much to claim with Hölscher that "the cult would have been regularly celebrated on the *bāmâ* ⟦'high place'⟧ of Zion and that the sacral tradition was continued there without interruption" (Hölscher, *Geschichte der israelitischen Religion*, 117–18; idem, "Les origines de la communauté juive," *RHPR* 6 [1926] 110–11). . . .

¶287¶ However, they were still too few in number and too disorganized to occupy all of the land, and groups coming from neighboring countries, Ammonites, Edomites, and Moabites, had infiltrated certain parts of Judah in order to fill the vacuum there. As for central Palestine, the ancient realm of Ephraim, it was inhabited by an extremely mixed population of Assyrian settlers who associated themselves with the ancient Israelites. . . . But the center of gravity and the vital forces of Judaism during the Neo-Babylonian and Persian Periods were elsewhere—they were among the colonies of the diaspora, established among the nations.

[288] Far from the ancestral land, far from their country, there where the fortunes of deportation or emigration had dispersed them, there were groups of Jews. Some were set up as fellahs who labor in the fields and plant orchards along the rivers, like those referred to in the letter of Jeremiah to the exiles (Jer 29:6) and the Jews in Tel-abib and Tel-harsa (Ezra 2:59, Neh 7:61, Ezek 3:15). Others were tradesmen in the area of the cities, at the populated crossroads, in Damascus (1 Kgs 20:34) and Phoenicia;[3] in the villages of Lower Egypt (Hos 9:3, 6; 8:13; Isa 19:18–25; Jer 24:8; 26:22, 23; 42:14; 44:1); in Babylon and Nippur, such as the people we know from the Murašû documents;[4] still others were soldiers in the service of princes, such as the Jewish army of Elephantine and Syene at the edge of Upper Egypt.[5]

The formation of this diaspora is, in the majority of cases, of a relatively early date, prior to what is commonly called the Babylonian captivity. In an earlier book, I thought it necessary to insist on the fact that there was an Israelite and Judean diaspora throughout the Orient during the ninth and eighth centuries, and I tried to show that only the existence of such a diaspora would explain the conservation and development of

3. The numerous allusions to islands and coastlands (*ʾiyyîm*) in Deutero-Isaiah and to the cedars of Lebanon seem to indicate that the Deuteronomist was addressing himself to colonies established on the Phoenician coast.

4. Concerning the Murašû documents, see H. V. Hilprecht and A. T. Clay, *Business Documents of the Murashû Sons of Nippur Dated in the Reign of Artaxerxes I (464–424 B.C.)* (The Babylonian Expedition of the University of Pennsylvania, series A, vols. 9–10; Philadelphia: University of Pennsylvania, 1898–1906); and idem, *Business Documents of the Murashû Sons of Nippur Dated in the Reign of Darius II (424–404 B.C.)* (The Babylonian Expedition of the University of Pennsylvania, series A, vol. 10; Philadelphia: University of Pennsylvania, 1906); S. Daiches, *The Jews in Babylonia in the Time of Ezra and Nehemiah according to the Babylonian Inscriptions in London* (Jews College Publication 2; 1910); A. Causse, *Les dispersés d'Israël: Les origines de la diaspora et son rôle dans le formation du Judaïsme* (Paris: Alcan, 1929) 67–68.

5. On the Elephantine papyri, see A. H. Sayce and A. E. Cowley, *Aramaic Papyri Discovered at Assuan* (London, 1906); E. Sachau (ed.), *Aramäische Papyrus und Ostraka aus einer jüdischen Militarkolonie zu Elephantine* (Leipzig: Hinrichs, 1911); E. Meyer (ed.), *Der Papyrusfund von Elephantine* (1912); van Hoonacker, *Une communauté judéo-araméenne à Éléphantine* (1915); Causse, *Dispersés d'Israel,* 77–95.

Judaism after the Exile.[6] But whatever [[289]] the numerical importance and predominant role of any of these groups had been previously, . . . the fact is that Israel appears as an outcast people who live in the towns of others; it no longer is a political entity. The organization of the different Jewish groups is varied, like the conditions of their social life and habitat. In the majority of cases, they are headed by elders. We know specifically, for instance, that the exiles of the time of Jeremiah and Ezekiel had elders.[7] Elders were at this time a permanent institution in the Orient. They were charged with directing the group, with representing it before the pagan authorities, and with judging between its members in case of conflict. Their role was all the more extensive due to the lack of a national organization and the fact that the great states only intervened with their lives from afar, and this solely for taxes and recruitment of forced labor or military service.

In the new conditions in which Israel found itself, the activity of the elders was not especially original, and it [[290]] would not have been a problem to maintain the traditional institution of the *mišpāḥâ* [['family']]. The authority of the collective conscience and the feeling of social unity must have been gravely weakened by the fact that the exiles lacked a territorial base and had been tossed about and scattered by political crises. It was only in Palestine that the clan groupings were still able to maintain themselves to a certain degree. In the description of the rebuilding of the walls of Jerusalem under Nehemiah, the Judeans appear to be organized both by *mišpāḥôt* [['families']] and by districts. That is to say, the patriarchal groupings were maintained at the same time as the geographical and political groupings.[8] In the same chapter, occupational groups are discussed alongside clans and districts. Thus, the *netînîm* (Temple ser-

6. Causse, "Origines préexiliques de la diaspora," *Dispersés d'Israël*, 9–24. In this chapter, I tried to demonstrate the importance that the exiles of the twelve tribes, after the Assyrian deportations and the Egyptian diaspora of the eighth and ninth centuries, would have had for the subsequent destiny of Judaism. The theory accepted by Wellhausen and most critics, according to which the exiles of the Northern Kingdom would have disappeared from history, and the Israelite and Judean émigrés established in the Delta villages would have mixed with the pagan mass, is more radical than realistic. . . .

7. See Jer 29:1, where the elders are named before the priests and prophets; Ezek 8:1 and 14:1, where the elders of Israel (and of Judah) gather together in the house of the prophet and seat themselves before him. In Ezra 8:1, we see the scribe gathering the family chiefs [[*rōʾšîm*]] to go up with him to Jerusalem.

8. Neh 3:1–32; cf. 11:3–36. The towns and villages were governed by elders and judges (Ezra 10:14). Even in Jerusalem, where the authority of the High Priest was strong, elders (*zěqēnîm*) and nobles (*śārîm* and *ḥôrîm*) were set up to exercise justice and guide the people (Ezra 4:3; 10:8, 14; Neh 5:7). There were also representatives of the Persian government, with, in certain cases, a special chief like Nehemiah, but usually a delegated manager accountable to the Samarian governor (Neh 12:24).

vants), goldsmiths, perfumers, and merchants are mentioned with the sons of Senah, the Tekoites, the men of Gibeon, and the inhabitants of Zanoah as people who built the gates or a part of the walls.[9] The occupational groups, in different forms, must have experienced a great development in the towns of the diaspora. The documents speak to us only of the *ḥûṣôt* [['streets']] of Damascus and the *degel* [['flag']] companies of the Jewish army of Elephantine.[10] But it is also probable that the tradesmen and the Jewish artisans of the towns [[291]] of the Delta and of Mesopotamia–Chaldea[11] had their guilds. People join together according to common interests and labor opportunities as much as for the preservation of tradition. Circumstances frequently required groups to establish relations with pagans and at times also to become personally associated with them.

On the whole, one can say that of all the pre-diaspora social forms, the only stable one remaining is the family. However, the Jewish family is no longer the relatively extended social group that can be observed in the early period. The family has transformed itself. To the extent that its mobility has increased, it has lost its primitive character and some of its political, economic, and cultic distinctiveness. In addition, the traditional older mores have weakened. The power of the father is less absolute, and the woman tends to assert more influence.[12] Thus, constituted as [[292]] a restrained and rigorously monogamous paternal family, the Jewish family

9. Neh 3:3–31. Professional groupings already existed in ancient Israel and among the Canaanites; see Causse, *RHPR* 10 (1930) 34–35. But it is during the postexilic period that they are mentioned most often; see 1 Chr 4:14, 21, 23; Neh 3:8, 31.

10. The *ḥûṣôt* 'streets' doubtless designate the area in which the merchants have their bazaars. See my *Dispersés d'Israel*, 9–12; concerning the societies at Elephantine, see ibid., 78–79; and A. van Hoonacker, *Une communauté judéo-araméene à Éléphantine, en Égypte aux VIᵉ et Vᵉ siècle av. J.-C.* (London: British Academy, 1915) 6–8.

11. On the commercial activity of the Jews of Babylonia, see the Murašû documents, Hilprecht and Clay, *Business Documents of the Murashû Sons of Nippur*; Causse, *Dispersés d'Is-raël*, 65–68.

12. See *RHPR* 13 (1933) 290–91. For the study of the rights and influence of women in the Jewish period, we have the case of Zelophahad's daughters in the Priestly Code (Num 27:1–10, 30:1–12). . . . In the epilogue of the book of Job, we see Job's daughters receiving a part of the inheritance along with their brothers (Job 42). In Prov 31:10–31, the mistress of the house appears as a morally and socially independent person. . . . This conception of the virtues and social dignity of women is much closer to the concepts current in Babylonia, where in certain cases a woman had the right to dispose of her fortune and to make contracts. . . . See E. Révillout, *Cours de droit égyptien* (1884) 194–226. From this perspective it is interesting to consider the relatively independent situation of women in the Elephantine papyri, which contain both Egyptian and Babylonian law. Mibtakyah, son of Mahseya, upon marrying Ashkor, reserved the same right as her husband to request a divorce before the assembly (*Papyrus Sayce-Cowley* F). There, the woman had the right to possess not only the *môhar* [['dowry']] that she had received upon marrying but also the inheritance that she

in the diaspora became the foundation for an effective preservation, not only for maintaining the race but also for moral education. This new form would tend to strengthen the family rather than weaken it.[13] . . .

Meanwhile, it became more difficult to maintain the cohesion and purity of the clans [[293]] among the populations where they were now established. In an age when the reign of Torah had not yet begun, there were bound to be many inroads and assimilations in Judaism. In the lists of Ezra 2 and Nehemiah 7, for instance, it is explicitly stated that certain groups sought their genealogical titles in vain: they "could not make known their paternal house or their ancestry in order to prove that they were of Israel" (Ezra 2:59–63, Neh 7:61–65). The protests of the reformers of the fifth century are proof of the frequency of mixed marriages in Jerusalem and in Palestine (Mal 2:10–12; Ezra 9–10; Neh 13:23–27). Among the Jews established in Chaldea, Mesopotamia, and Egypt, or following deportations and emigrations, the population's equilibrium is even more broken, and . . . the Israelites are led to ally themselves with pagan families.[14] The Murašû documents and the Elephantine papyri are conclusive in this regard. There at times the fathers have foreign theophoric names, and the sons, Hebrew names, or vice versa.[15] None of this supports a [[294]] very rigorous group dynamic but, rather, a relatively unstable environment, vulnerable to pagan influence and syncretism from the outside.[16]

A disturbing problem that must have been considered by the exiles from the outset was their cultic situation. The old tie that united God, people, and land had been severed. The exiles now lived far from the ancestral land and far from the ancient sanctuaries where Yahweh had

---

had received from her father. See van Hoonacker, *Une communauté judéo-araméenne à Éléphantine*, 25–30; J. Türck, "Die Stellung der Frau in Elephantine als Ergebnis persische-babylonischen Rechtseinflusses," *ZAW* 40 (1928) 166–69.

13. Concerning the fact that the evolution of the family from the maternal family to the patriarchal family to the monogamous paternal family and then to the conjugal family leads toward a foundation that is clearly more ethical and more effective religiously and morally (see E. Durkheim, *Revue philosophique* [1921/1]; and idem, *L'Année sociologique* 1 [1896–97]).

14. The deportations of the Assyro-Chaldean Period had established in the region of Mesopotamia–Chaldea many remnants of people groups, that were brought in to compensate for the depletion of the original population that the conquest had created. In addition, the fact that Babylon was a capital city and that the cities of the Egyptian Delta were very active from an international business standpoint must have greatly enhanced international contact and the mixing of the races.

15. See S. Daiches, "Einige nach babylonischen Mustern gebildete hebräische Namen," *Orientalische Literaturzeitung* (1908) 276–77; van Hoonacker, *Une communauté judéo-araméenne à Éléphantine*, 24–26.

16. See Causse, *Dispersés d'Israël*, 65–71.

established his name. Further, after the destruction of Samaria and the ruin of Jerusalem, Israel's God appeared to be a vanquished God, chased from his sanctuary and without earthly habitation. . . . According to the popular Semitic concept, vanquished gods who succeeded in escaping from their town continued to live in heaven, since they were of a celestial nature. This is how Yahweh now resided on the mountain of God, the Mountain of the North.[17] Even if Yahweh did still sojourn in heaven, however, his cult seemed possible only on the earth, in the ancient social framework, manifested by the magic of ritual sacrifice and by covenant ties. When a person had left the soil of his ancestors, as well as the family and clan to which he belonged, he felt separated from his God; he was without religion, just as he was without citizenship rights (1 Sam 26:19).

Practically speaking, the problem was more or less resolved by the exiles. They had finished by admitting that Yahweh could follow his people in a strange land as he had previously followed the patriarchs among the nations and had led the Israelites, wandering from one wilderness to the next. In addition, sanctuaries were raised in various parts of the diaspora where the people offered Yahweh sacrifices, offerings, and fragrances.[18] However, for the people deported to Babylon, who had [[295]] accomplished the deuteronomic reform, the question of cult still remained unanswered. Deuteronomy had centralized the cult in Jerusalem; apart from the holy mountain there was no licit divine rite, and one could not offer a sacrifice or sing the hymn of Yahweh on unclean ground (Ps 137:3–4).

This was more than enough to shatter the spirit of that elite and to destroy forever its strength and its hope. But if the sanctuary was in ruins, the sacred word remained; not only the word of the prophets but also the word of the book, the commandments, the statutes and the ordinances of the Torah.[19] This was the source of Israel's preservational energy during this decisive crisis. At the very moment when the foundations of the life of the people and its religion seemed to collapse, Judaism would still maintain itself . . . in the face of the *gôyîm* [['nations']],

17. On the Mountain of the North, where Yahweh resides in the midst of the *ʾelohîm* [[gods]], see H. Gressmann, *Der Ursprung der israelitisch-jüdischen Eschatologie* (Göttingen: Vandenhoeck & Ruprecht, 1905) 113ff. and 221ff.

18. On the sanctuary at Elephantine, see *Papyrus Sachau* I and II.

19. We have seen that, with Deuteronomy, Judaism had already begun to assert itself as a religion of the book. See *RHPR* 13 (1933) 22–24. The importance of sacred scripture must necessarily have increased in the diaspora, either to establish tradition or to legitimize propaganda. Prophecy itself, instead of being an ecstatic oracle from the mouth of the inspired one, tended to become literature. . . .

as both a race and a religious tradition . . . more the latter than the former.[20]

Thanks to the prophets of the Exile (Ezekiel and the school that formed around his name, the disciples of Jeremiah, Deutero-Isaiah and his followers), the groups in the diaspora were made conscious of the community to which they aspired, while the Babylonian scribes preserved the best of the heritage of the past, the words of the men of God [[296]] of old. They drafted anew the ancient books, history and prophecy, and zealously prepared the utopian legislation and cultic institution of the future.[21] This would be the great awakening of Israel in the diaspora, a movement that showed itself first and with the most intensity in the eastern colonies, particularly in the Babylonian *gôlâ* [['exile']]. This awakening would result, during the Persian Period, in a coalescence of Judaism with Jerusalem as its spiritual capital and the Torah as its norm and ideal.

Thus, it was not in any way a question of restoring a political past, with its social organization and national life, which had deteriorated from the time of the judges and first kings to the eventual fall of the two kingdoms. It was, rather, a question of a new sociological formation that would be neither a federation of clans nor a nation but a religious community whose destiny would not necessarily be tied to the conditions of an ethnic group or to a state.

A Split from the Past and Group Solidarity

Events had made the split with the past . . . catastrophic and brutal. The prophets had boldly played their part in it. We have already seen the attitude of Jeremiah, who announced the triumph of Yahweh and the advent of the new covenant in a day when the realm and the city were going to ruin. The same concept of history and of divine justice[22] was affirmed by Ezekiel at the time of the last deportation. With audacious clarity, the prophet whom Yahweh had called to announce his word throughout the world of the Exile proclaims that the ancient things are abolished; it is necessary for the last vestiges of the royal civilization, with [[297]] impure mores and paganized cult, to disappear.[23] . . . It will be for Jerusalem as it was for Samaria and Sodom. . . . The sword of

---

20. See E. Renan, *Le judaïsme comme race et comme religion: Conférence faite au cercle Saint-Simon, le 27 janvier 1883* (Paris: Calmann-Levy, 1883) 351–65. Haller, *Das Judentum*, 13–14.

21. Concerning the preservation and development of Jewish literature in Babylon and in the diaspora, see my *Dispersés d'Israël*, 26–50, 103–16.

22. See *RHPR* 12 (1932) 135–39; and *RHPR* 13 (1933) 320–23.

23. This is the theme of the central and most incontestably original part of the book of Ezekiel (3:22–24:27) and the leitmotiv of the prophet's message.

Yahweh will accomplish his work (Ezekiel 21): the last remnants of the Judean monarchy will collapse, and the princes who violated the covenant will be torn from their country and led captive in the streets (Ezek 17:9, 10, 19–21). And when the prophet learns the news of the supreme catastrophe and the profanation of the sanctuary, he refuses to cry and lament, since he knows that the justice of Yahweh has been served (Ezekiel 24).

Is this not the argument that the deuteronomic redactor is trying to develop in his exposé of the deeds and exploits of the Israelite and Judean kings? What is striking from the first, when one considers this historiography, is the parenetic tendency driving the author, as well as his lack of political sense or interest in social life and military heroism. In that past of glory and misery, . . . the reformer/historian seeks only material for moral lessons for the present. . . . His goal [[298]] is to exhort and to illustrate.[24]

. . . .

Thus, the deuteronomistic historian continues the theme of collective sanctions[25] in order to exhort the exiles to repentance and a new life. On this decisive point he remains faithful to the popular conception and to the tradition of ancient prophetism. However, in this area, he differs profoundly [[300]] with Ezekiel, for insofar as Ezekiel breaks with the past, he abandons the old idea of group solidarity. At the same time that Ezekiel is breaking with the past, he is abandoning the old concept of group solidarity and no longer admits that the individual must pay for the crimes of the people. The individualistic theory of sanctions that occasionally appears in Jeremiah and the seventh-century reformers[26] now finds its full expression. On various occasions Ezekiel insists on the personal character of retribution, and he derives all of his conclusions from that claim. . . .[27]

24. For the deuteronomic concept of history, see *RHPR* 13 (1933) 17–22. See also Karl Budde, *Geschichte der althebräischen Literatur* (Leipzig: Amelang) 115–35; and J. Hempel, *Die althebräische Literatur* (Wildpark / Potsdam: Akademische Verlagsgesellschaft Athenaion, 1930) 149–51.

25. In spite of the text of 2 Kgs 12:5–6, concerning Amaziah's sparing of the sons of the murderers of Jehoash his father, the deuteronomistic historian considers it completely normal that the individual suffer for the group and especially that the group be struck for the crimes of its leaders (2 Kgs 21:10–15, 22:15–17, 23:25–27). It is the impiety of the kings that provokes the misfortunes of Israel and Judah and their dispersion. At most, the historian/prophet recognized that in certain cases Yahweh had temporarily delayed the execution of his sanctions. . . .

26. Concerning the individualism of Jeremiah and the seventh-century reformers, see *RHPR* 12 (1932) 137–38; and 13 (1933) 319–23.

27. See Ezek 18:2–3, 20–21, 24. In fact, the doctrine of national retribution was not abandoned, and it is to Jerusalem and Judah as collective entities that the prophet addressed

Thus the rigid law that sacrificed the individual to the fate of the social group is abolished. Now there is hope for the righteous sufferer. The sinner who repents of his faults can be offered pardon by Yahweh. It is not for the nation that Yahweh pardons sin; it is for the person as a person. The sin of the people is unforgivable. Even Noah, Daniel, and Job would not have been able to turn aside [[301]] its effects (Ezek 14:12, 23),[28] but if a sinner turns aside from his evil path, his transgressions will be forgotten. It is this call to personal repentance and salvation that the prophet insists on with almost evangelistic tones: "That which I desire is not that the wicked die, oracle of Yahweh. Is it not rather that he turn aside from his wicked way and live?" (Ezek 18:23, 30–32; 33:11).[29] The prophet considers himself a sentinel standing guard over the house of Israel, looking over the dispersed members of Yahweh's people, and calling them to salvation (Ezek 3:17–19; cf. 33:7–9). . . .

[[302]] This reformulation of the ethical and religious problem, which placed individual behavior over that of the group, be it political, social, or cultural, would be Judaism's great innovation. Hereafter, the religion of the Torah as well as the piety of the psalms and the ethics of wisdom literature would assume an individualistic stance regarding the relationship between humanity and God.

The Myth of the Reestablishment of Israel and of the New Jerusalem

The former vision of Israel as a whole, such as was expressed in Deuteronomy (*kōl-Iśrā'ēl* [['all Israel']]) did not disappear. It remained on the horizon as a hope and as a program. The exilic prophets announced their message in order to recall the people to life, to console the dispersed, and to restore the holy nation. It is necessary that a new Israel arise and become exalted in the midst of its ordeal. But this vision unfolds in a distant utopian future and becomes refined outside of the realities of history.

First, Yahweh will revive the desiccated bones of his people, and he will place the breath of life in them (Ezek 37:1–14). He will reassemble

---

his threats. The old concept coexisted with the new. However it was the new that prevailed (18:29–30). The entire chapter is a long discussion trying to prove that it was not because of the sins of the ancestors but because of their own sins that the present generation was struck by Yahweh.

28. The prayer of the just for the guilty is useless; they can only save themselves (see Ezek 14:17–18).

29. See Lucien Gautier, *Le mission du prophète Ézéchiel* (1891) 265–73.

the exiles who are among the nations and will bring them back to their land. He will purify them of their defilement and give them a new spirit, and they will be his people and he will be their God (Ezek 36:13–23). . . . ⟦303⟧ The mountains of Palestine will be cultivated and verdant as a garden of Eden (Ezek 34:23–30; 36:6, 11, 33–38). The old things, the times of error and curse, will be forgotten. Israel and Judah, the brothers at enmity, long separated by political rivalries and diverse sanctuaries, will form a single family, a single people (Ezek 37:15–28). . . .

⟦304⟧ The stereotypical themes of exilic eschatology now begin to take shape. The majority of these motifs go back to an already ancient mythology that can be found in fragmentary form in the blessings and curses of the prophets of the eighth and seventh centuries. . . . However, in the predictions of the former prophets, this traditional eschatological material was still relatively moderate and stayed in the background. Its main point was not the mythical drama of the end of time but rather the ethical and historical drama of the present Israel: the infidelity of the nation, chastisement of Israel, conversion of a "remnant," salvation in the context of catastrophe, and establishing a just society in which the will of Yahweh would be realized. When they appealed to the future, that future did not appear precisely outside of history, miraculously separated from the present world. That future was above all the result of their actions, and it appeared in a very near future, holding on with strong roots to immediate reality. . . . ⟦305⟧ ⟦But⟧ to the extent that the political circumstances became increasingly unfavorable, Jewish hope tended to detach itself from its present reality and its historical framework in order to be exalted in a utopian and transcendent future.[30]

* * *

What was already tangible in the eschatology of Ezekiel and his immediate disciples became even more concrete with the visionaries of the second exilic generation. This is true in particular in the description of the new Jerusalem that concludes the book of Ezekiel (chaps. 40–48)[31] and also in the poems of the great prophet of the diaspora, Deutero-Isaiah.

30. See A. von Gall, "Enstehen und Entwiklung der jüdischen Reich-Gottes," and "Hoffnung im persischen Zeitalter," Βασιλεία τοῦ θεοῦ (Heidelberg: Carl Winter, 1926) 175–261. The influence of Iranian concepts on the formation and development of Jewish apocalyptic myth in these chapters is clearly overestimated. The problem deserves to be considered in a more critical fashion and in all of its complexity, whether regarding the development of Avestic religion or by taking into consideration the syncretic assimilations of the Babylonian East.

31. The attribution of this vision to Ezekiel, or to the first redactors of his text, can only be maintained with difficulty, even though the manner and style of the visionary at

⟦306⟧ In the vision of the new Jerusalem, we have the plan of an ideal Palestine and a utopian city, described with details that were simultaneously very precise and perfectly fantastic. In the first place, in the middle of a vast plain, a high mountain arises, from which one can see all of the land (Ezek 40:2, 18:12). It is the Temple city. It no longer has anything in common with the historical Jerusalem. It bears a new name, *Yahweh šāmmâ* ('Yahweh is here'; Ezek 48:35). Its twelve doors are oriented toward the four points of the compass and toward the twelve tribes of Israel (Ezek 48:30–34). It causes one to think of the heavenly vault with the constellations of the zodiac. The Temple is in the center, built according to a plan conceived in large scale in order to be a town for priests.[32] A river, large and deep, leaves the sanctuary and flows from the eastern side toward "the sea of the plain," which it purifies. It is the River of Paradise, whose banks are planted with fruit trees in great number and with luxuriant vegetation (Ezek 48:1–12).

The rest of the land is divided from east to west into twelve equal, rectangular strips of land, according to the number of the Israelite tribes. The visionary enumerates these twelve tribes, along with the territory assigned to them, without concern that the number twelve does not correspond precisely to any ⟦307⟧ historical reality and that a number of these tribes had disappeared long before (Ezekiel 47). . . . There is now hardly any question of social and political organization. There is no longer any question of the Davidic son of messianic hope. The prince who is established over the country and who is to practice righteousness and justice appears only as a figure of sacred pomp, chiefly occupied with ensuring the observation of the liturgical forms and providing sacrifices.[33]

* * *

times bears the mark of the exilic prophet. However, the preoccupation with the cult and with priestly organization is that of the school of scribes from the Babylonian *gôlâ* ⟦'exile'⟧, especially of the author of the Holiness Code. One can place the composition of that part of the book at the end of the sixth century. . . .

32. Ezekiel 40–43. This Temple plan, in spite of the magnitude of the dimensions, is not unrealistic from an architectural point of view. In certain ways it recalls the older Solomonic sanctuary, which it would greatly surpass in splendor.

33. Nevertheless, one cannot say that the *nāśîʾ* ⟦'prince'⟧ is without political attributes. Repeatedly the visionary speaks of him as of a true chief. . . . He exhorts the princes to content themselves in the future with the territory that was assigned to them by tribes, "so that they no longer oppress the people of Yahweh" (45:9, 46:14). Even more than the deuteronomic legislator, he seeks to reduce the power of the state to a minimum . . . so that the exercise of justice will remain in the hands of the priests alone (44:23). The *nāśîʾ* is nothing more than a survivor of the past who has lost his original, mystical prestige, and whom the visionary legislator inserts in the framework of his priestly city after having carefully regulated and delimited his place in the Temple and his actions and functions in sacred ceremonies (Ezek 45:7–17).

In the chapters of Deutero-Isaiah, we find the same eschatological idealism, expressed in all of its [[308]] magnificence, with only organizational and legalistic tendencies appearing to alter the splendor. First and foremost is the myth of the epiphany of Yahweh, who comes to manifest himself on behalf of his own in all of his power, in order to justify his people in front of all of the *gôyîm* [['nations']] (Isa 40:3–7, 42:10–16). Yahweh comes, and the nations see his glory as far as the ends of the earth (Isa 45:21).[34]

Second is the myth of the gathering of the exiles: Israel had to pass through a time of testing. It appears as a crumbling nation, dispersed to the four corners of the earth, from the land of Sinîm [['Syene']] to the distant islands and from Lebanon to the towns of Chaldea. Israel has no unity, no point of support, no sanctuary, but now the time of servitude is finished. Yahweh will "bring back the tribes of Jacob and restore the rest of Israel" (Isa 43:5–6, 49:12).

[[309]] Yahweh himself will lead his captives in triumphal procession. A route will be opened for them through the wilderness like the processional track around the sanctuary in the sacred ceremonies. . . .

Jerusalem/Zion will no longer be in distress like a neglected wife, like a captive on the roads, like a city in ruins battered by storms. Yahweh wants to lift the city up from the dust and give it abundance and joy (Isa 49:14–23; 52:7–10; 54:1–15). The returnees will rebuild the ruined walls. The deserted towns will be restored. They will overflow with inhabitants. . . . A numerous and prosperous crowd will sing hymns commemorating God's gracious acts. This will be a people of righteousness, disciples instructed by Yahweh (Isa 54:11–13).

Commentators generally see in these prophecies hyperbolic descriptions of the historical events of Cyrus's giving the deportees permission to return to their country and rebuild the Temple of Jerusalem after his victorious campaign against Babylon. However, the vision of Deutero-Isaiah goes far beyond the scope of these historical events, and what we have here are variations on [[310]] what will hereafter become classical apocalyptic motifs. All of this apocalyptic language is significant only if it is understood as signs that are precursors of the future and of the great deliverance by Yahweh.[35] However, the prophet does not seem to give much consideration to the circumstances and conditions by which this

---

34. Concerning the epiphany of Yahweh, see H. Gressmann, *Der Ursprung des israelitisch-jüdischen Eschatologie* (Göttingen: Vandenhoeck & Ruprecht, 1905); and S. Mowinckel, *Psalmenstudien*, vol. 2: *Der Thronbesteigungsfest Yahwäs und der Ursprung der Eschatologie* (Kristiania: Dybwad, 1922). . . .

35. The description of the destruction of Babylon (chaps. 47–48) and the allusion to Cyrus, conqueror of the people, who is viewed as the liberator of the tribes of Israel and restorer of the city and the Temple (45:13), can be applied to a very near future, which the

deliverance will be accomplished, and his presentation of actual history, in spite of the acclamation of the conquering Achaemenid hailed as Yahweh's envoy, is imprecise and poorly defined.[36] The geographical horizon remains uncertain, in spite of the splendor of the descriptions; there are only allusions to mountains, valleys, and ruins that revive.[37] Although pagan masters are still part of the picture, the messianic David has dropped out of the picture.[38] Yahweh suffices as [[311]] king of his people. Although the restoration of the holy Temple is mentioned (Isa 44:28), a description of the building like that of Ezekiel 40–48 is not given, nor is there any reference to priests or cultic rites.

In addition to themes of people and race, the prophet expands his writing to embrace the entire world, both the universe and humanity (Isa 41:5; 42:10–11; 45:22–23; 49:1, 6; 55:4–5). Not only are all of the nations called, but Israel's hope tends to blossom into a dream of nature transformed, in the vision of a new heaven and a new earth. This eschatology finds its climax in the description of the new Jerusalem found in the prophecy of Trito-Isaiah, the city of light toward which the multitudes stream . . . (see Isa 60:1–3, 19–20).

[[312]] Then in Isa 65:17–25, we find the announcement of the re-creation of the world, where the redemptive action of Yahweh on behalf of his people climaxes in a transformation of nature, a second creation.[39]

[[313]] In these visions, where the traditional great dichotomy of oriental thought between light and darkness, cursing and blessing, and life

---

prophet announces with a mysterious imprecision. On the other hand, they could also be a recalling of the great events of the past, precursive signs of the eschatological manifestation of Yahweh.

36. Concerning Palestine, the prophet appears to know only of Jerusalem/Zion, the holy mountain, with devastated and abandoned country all around it (49:18; 54:3). This is a traditional, schematic concept, such as we find in Jer 44:2, 6 and in the account of 2 Chr 36:20–21. . . .

37. Effectively, Cyrus is saluted as the messiah of Yahweh (45:1). But, as Isadore Loeb previously maintained (*La littérature des pauvres dans la Bible* [1892] 223), it is not necessary to see in these oracles impressions left by the victorious march of the great Achaemenid on a prophet contemporary with the events. We can simply consider them an apocalyptic vision on a theme that belongs to the past as well as the present. Thus, the Cyrus of Deutero-Isaiah is an ideal figure, a sort of pagan messiah.

38. When, according to the formula of H. Gressmann (*Der Messias* [Göttingen: Vandenhoeck & Ruprecht, 1929]), we consider the ʿEbed-Yahweh [['Servant of Yahweh']] to be "the Messiah of Deutero-Isaiah," we give the term *messiah* the very broad sense, which it only took on in the Jewish and Christian literature of the first centuries [[C.E.]]. One would search in vain for a tie between the righteous servant, even when represented as an eschatological figure, and the king as divine hero of traditional messianic hope. Those are notions from different origins and fundamentally of a different order. As regards the mention of David (55:4), one must view it as with the mention of Jacob and of the Abrahamic race as a designation of Israel considered as a unity; there is no messianic allusion.

39. Isa 65:17–23. The concept of a utopian life in the peace of a new Eden is not a new idea. But in Isaiah 65, the theme is being expanded to a new level, where the liberating

and death has expressed itself in both an ethical and cosmic sense,[40] the prophetic ideal is increasingly evolving beyond the conditions of what is possible in the distant future, to a world of the supernatural and of miracles. This evolution, increasingly characterized by apocalypticism, will have sociological significance: from now on Israel will live for its myths and by its myths . . . and in the re-creation of Judaism, the sociological impact of myth will be greater than the impact of organizations and institutions. How mediocre and obscure is literary realism next to the dreams of visionaries! The arrival of Sheshbazzar and Zerubbabel with the first caravans of returnees and the reconstruction of the Temple and [[314]] of the walls of Jerusalem during the early days of Darius are conventionally called the restoration of Judaism. All of this movement consisted in the establishment of Jerusalemite community, a colony of the *běnê haggôlâ* [['children of the exile']], sustained by the eastern diaspora and by its successive contributions. All of this was with the consent and protection of the Persian authorities, interested in encouraging the restoration of local traditions and ancient religions in their empire.

Moreover, these historical events had meaning only in their relation to the great hopes that the prophets of the Exile had evoked. To realize this, one need only read the writings of Haggai and Zechariah, where one can sense in the lackluster style the decline of prophecy. However, Israel's faith remains and is now forward-looking: "Rebuild the house of Yahweh, offer him suitable worship, and you will receive peace and blessing. The ground will bring forth its fruit, and the treasures of the nations will flow into the sanctuary" (Hag 2:3–9, 15–19). *Yahweh Ṣěbāôt* [['the Lord of armies']] will be in your midst, Judah will be his heritage, and Jerusalem his chosen city (Zech 2:8–13, 8:2–19). The power of the inspired word is markedly weakened, but the myth is still alive,[41] and the deceptiveness of reality does not matter.

---

action of Yahweh on behalf of his people shows itself by a restoration of heaven and earth, a creation more perfect and harmonious than the first. Perhaps we have in these concepts traces of the influence of Iranian eschatology, where the *frashôkéréti* is represented as a revolution of nature or a renewing of the world (see N. Söderblom, *La vie future d'après le mazdéisme à la lumière des croyances parallèles dans les autres religions: École d'eschatologie comparée* (Paris: Leroux, 1901).

40. "Darkness covers the earth; deep darkness the people" (Isa 60:2). The Gentile world lives in darkness because it does not know God. However, the beneficiaries of Yahweh will be the children of light. This concept, which will find its full expression in the Jewish apocalypses of the first centuries after Christ (see *Enoch* 58, *Testament of Levi* 19), had its origins in the astrological syncretism of Babylonia and Syria (see F. Cumont, *Les religions orientales dans le paganisme romain* [Paris: Leroux, 1906] 151–55).

41. This life manifests itself in new apocalyptic variations. The great diversity of mythological motifs that we find in Zechariah 1–9—the four horsemen (1:7–13), the four horns and four craftsmen (1:18–21), the four chariots that come out from between two bronze mountains (6:1–8), the seven lamps of the candelabra that are "the seven eyes of Yahweh,

It is evident that this myth could not have had its origin in the political context of Jerusalem and Judah at the end of the Chaldean Empire and at the beginning of the Achaemenid era as the product of an exalted national sentiment and the idealization [[315]] of a previously-existing state of affairs. It is commonly assumed that the last half of the sixth century, particularly the years immediately preceding and following the restoration of the Temple was the time of a great revival of messianism in Palestine. But in fact, political messianism along with the proclamation of a reestablishment of the Davidic dynasty, which historians of the Wellhausen school saw as essentially postexilic,[42] appears to have played only a relatively secondary role in the formation of Judaism. It seems more than probable that there had been a movement around Zerubbabel, especially during the times of crisis that heralded the end of the reign of the imposter Smerdis and the beginning of the reign of Darius, and that there is an allusion to this movement in Hag 2:20–23 and in Zech 6:11–13. But it remains uncertain, according to the reading of the text, whether this culminated in a marked national upheaval, having as its goal the reestablishment of the Davidic monarchy. The ingenious critics who assure us that the rise of Zerubbabel would have caused offense to the Persian authorities and therefore would have caused the mysterious disappearance or assassination of the governor of Judah leave too much to conjecture.[43] In any case, it can only refer to a [[316]] localized agitation, restricted to certain circles in Jerusalem, and not to a fundamental shift in Judaism.[44] Furthermore, this movement appears to

---

which range throughout the earth" (4:2, 10)—attest, as in Ezekiel, an increasingly marked predilection for astral theology. Typical of this development is the vision of the new Jerusalem that no longer appears as the result of crises of Oriental history but interposes itself into the cosmic drama as the realization of a divine plan in the supraterrestrial world.

42. See, for example, in the *Introduction to the Book of Isaiah* (London: Black, 1895) of T. K. Cheyne, and, in the commentaries of Duhm and Marti, the interpretation and dating of the eschatological fragments and poems of the Second David (Isa 2:2–5, 4:2–6, 9:1–6, 11:1–10, 33:13–24). It would appear that, for these critics, eschatological messianism in a prophetic portion was of necessity a sign of inauthenticity, of being postexilic. . . .

43. A lively, colorful picture of the messianic movement at the end of the sixth century has been produced by E. Renan in his *Histoire du peuple d'Israël* (Paris: Colmann-Levy, 1893), vol. 4. Since then, the question of the alleged revolt of Zerubbabel has been, because of its own mystery, fertile material for audacious and ingenious hypotheses. . . . E. Sellin . . . (in *Serubabel* [1899] and his *Geschichte des israelitisch-jüdischen Volkes*, 2.96–113) . . . suggested that Zerubbabel would have followed the enthusiasts and accepted the responsibility of carrying out the oracles of Haggai and Zechariah by rebelling against the Persian authority (see Haller, *Das Judentum*, 78–80; and Kittel, *Geschichte des Volkes Israel*, 3.441–83). See also the restatement of Gressmann in *Der Messias*, 256–63 and the prudent and measured conclusions of A. Bentzen, in *RHPR* 10 (1930).

44. The Davidic dynasty, which had played a role in the restoration of Jerusalemite Judaism (Sheshbazzar and Zerubbabel were of royal lineage), must have remained significant,

have been essentially [[317]] religious and peaceful and, as such, remains in line with prophecy. The rebuilding of Jerusalem and the Temple, like the return of the first caravans of exiles to the holy mountain, was not the outcome of a Zionist movement, the effort of a people who wanted to repossess the land of their fathers. It was the aspiration of religious communities who were seeking a common point to rally around. For the exiles, Jerusalem was less the city of the house of David than it was the city of the Temple, the city of pilgrimages, the holy place around which the faithful tended to gather.[45]

The Program of Theocracy:
The Temple Cult and the Law

[[318]] Jewish literature from this period is full of contrasts. Nothing re sembles less the lyric verve and fervent anticipation of the Deutero-Isaianic prophets than the scribal curriculum of the Babylonian school and the system of traditions and laws organized by the author of the Priestly Code. On the other hand, the visionary of the city of the Temple in Ezekiel 40–48, in his legislative literature, has given us a foretaste of it. After all, prophets and reforming scribes were energized by the same faith, tended toward the realization of the same myth, and had common sociological concepts. The author of the Priestly Code also has a utopian agenda, but instead of casting it as a vision of the future, as the seer of Ezekiel 40–48 does, he finds his motifs in the patriarchal and Mosaic past. He frames his legislation in a large-scale philosophy of history, a description of the origins of Israel and of humanity. . . .[46]

[[320]] [[U]]nderlying all of the systematic and dogmatic tendencies that dominate the historian/scribe is the theme of the development of

---

at least for a time, to the elders and heads of households who led the people. The care with which the Chronicler has preserved the genealogy of Jekoniah for us up to the end of the fifth century (1 Chr 3:17–24) is witness to this. However, with the development of the Temple cult and the growth in power of the priestly aristocracy, the secular aristocracy must have lost prestige, and in the times that follow, from the fourth century on, we find no further trace of the lineage of the ancient kings.

45. This objection should be directed at men like B. Stade, R. Emend, E. Meyer, and finally, R. Kittel (*Geschichte des Volkes Israel*, 3.326–28), who speak of the return from captivity as a national restoration carried out according to a previously prepared plan, where each clan, each family among the exiles was to provide representatives. This concept, based on the tradition of the Chronicler (Ezra 1:5–11), and a far too literal interpretation of Ezra 2 and Nehemiah 7, presupposes an organization and social stability among the Babylonian diaspora that is hardly creditable, considering the circumstances of the Exile (see my *Dispersés d'Israël*, 51–58). . . .

46. There already was, as we have seen, a philosophy of history in the deuteronomistic redaction of the J and E documents and of the books of Judges, Samuel, and Kings. But, with

races and peoples since prehistory, following a well-determined plan leading to the foundation of the Jewish community by Moses and Aaron and the peregrinations of the tribes through the desert, following the cultic objects and the ark of acacia wood.

It is here that one finds the decisive moment and the goal of the new legislation, no longer to organize a just society as in Deuteronomy, but rather to form a religious community with its ritual. This is what is called *theocracy*.[47] There is no secular society but only a priestly hierarchy and worshipers. It is true that on several occasions mention is made of the assembly of the children of Israel, *ᶜēdâ*,[48] but the role of this assembly is more circumscribed and passive than that of the *kōl-Iśrāᵓēl* [['all Israel']] of Deuteronomy. . . .

[[321]] The legislator applies himself to describing at great length the rights and functions of the priests and the organization of the hierarchy. Already the author of the ritual law of the book of Ezekiel had set out to distinguish between the priestly descendants of Zadok and the Levites. The priests are given special dignity and have the sole right to perform the sacrifices and to approach the very holy places. The priestly author sharpens the distinction. The holy descendants of Aaron[49] are the only ones charged with the sacrificial cult. . . . [[322]] All Israelites not de-

---

the Priestly Code, we begin a new stage, no longer the prophetic stage . . . , but the theological stage. . . . A construction of erudite theology comes to replace the living, brightly colored legends of the ancient story tellers who were themselves still very close to the stories' popular origins.

47. *Theocracy* is the traditional term used to designate the Jewish community and the ideal society of the Holiness Code. Nevertheless, the word does not adequately define the concept. In reality, ancient national Yahwism was already based on a theocratic concept, Yahweh being considered master and lord of his people, and the king being the viceroy of God. . . . What is new about the Priestly Code is the essentially clerical character of the ideal society, theocracy tending toward its realization in hierarchy. The Torah is ritualistic. It not only is taught and guaranteed by the priests, but it reduces civil activity to a minimum and tends to gather all human activity into the network of cultic prescriptions and sacred practices.

48. The word *ᶜēdâ* is used in place of *qāhāl*. This change of name is already significant. The term *qāhāl* designated the popular assembly reunited to participate in the functions of national life, deliberations, festivals, military parades. The *ᶜēdâ*, on the other hand, is the cultic assembly. Furthermore, the sacred tent, where Moses and Aaron consult Yahweh and around which the children of Israel gather, is itself called the tent of meeting, *ᵓōhel môᶜēd*.

49. It is the priestly historian who created the myth of Aaron as founder of the priestly dynasty and as prototype of the *kōhēn haggādôl* [['high priest']]. He no longer comments on the human frailties and faults of this brother of Moses who, according to ancient tradition, had favored Israelite idolatry by fashioning the golden calf (Exod 31:1–6, 21–24, 35) and . . . had murmured against Moses . . . with his sister Miriam . . . (Num 12:1–15). . . . From the first, Aaron appeared as an indispensable collaborator with Moses, the one God

scended from Aaron are excluded from the priesthood under penalty of death (Num 3:10, 16:1–40). As for the Levites, they are only the servants of the house of God, the slaves who were taken from among Israelite children as redemption for all the firstborn (Num 3:11–13, 8:14–18). They are charged with the heavy labor of the sanctuary, from guarding the gates to caring for the tabernacle, the candlestick, and the sacred objects, which they could not touch except with special precautions (Num 4:8). At the head of the priestly hierarchy is the high priest, the *kōhēn haggādôl*, who appears here in the fullness of his role, master of the sanctuary, chief sacrificer. The priestly writer does not stop at telling us that the high priest was elevated over his brothers; he describes for us the consecration ceremony, the costume, and the sacred ornaments . . . (Exod 39:27–31). [T]he vestments mark the social dignity and importance of the function.[50] It is the *kōhēn haggādôl* who replaces the king-priest. ‖323‖ It is he who has mystical powers and who serves as intermediary between God and his worshipers.[51]

The Priestly Code also describes the sacrifices and festivals. It gives us a carefully organized sacrificial system, distinguishing with authority between the types of sacrifice at the level of form, offering, and motive. There are various groups of sacrifices, distributed and combined according to the days, the circumstances, and the needs of the worshipers: the offerings, the vegetable offering *minḥâ*, the libation *nesek*, the perfume offering *qĕṭōret*, and the blood offerings, the peace offering *zebaḥ šĕlāmîm*,

---

had appointed to make up for the insufficiencies of Moses and to speak in his place (Exod 4:10–17). He was with him before Pharaoh. He had magical powers, and he was the one who carried the rod, who performed miracles and unleashed the plagues on Egypt (Exodus 7–8 and passim). After the revelation at Sinai, when Moses had built the tabernacle, the Ark, the altar, and the holy objects, Aaron and his four sons were chosen to be consecrated to Yahweh and to exercise the priesthood forever (Exodus 28–29, Lev 8:1–10:7).

50. The attention given by the Priestly writer to the details of decoration and the description of the priestly vestments is not primitive, but it does show the same tendency toward the organization of the sacred. This tendency was found not only in Judaism but also in Egypt, Syria, Asia Minor, and Babylon. The political institutions of kingdom and city were in decline; however, the clerics of the ancient sanctuaries or syncretistic religions gained in prestige before the devoted throngs.

51. The theory of the Priestly Code only serves to sanctify the historical evolution. Before the Exile, the king possessed, among other attributes, supreme priesthood. . . . However, now that there is no longer a Judean king but only a delegate of the Persian king and the Zion sanctuary has a more widespread appeal as the central sanctuary of the diaspora, the importance of the head of the priestly hierarchy becomes more evident. However, it would be incorrect to consider the *kōhēn haggādôl* the supreme leader of the Jewish community, even at the height of his power. The Priestly writer, while exalting his dignity, restricts his activities to the cultic [realm]. . . . (see A. F. Loisy, *La religion d'Israël* [3d ed.; Paris] 240).

with the different types—*tôdâ* [['thank-offering']], *neder* [['vow']], *nĕdābâ* [['free-will offering']]—and the greatest of them, the burnt offering *ʿōlâ*, the complete sacrifice, where the entire victim is consumed by fire.[52] This classification, which the oldest documents of the Pentateuch and preexilic historiography do not seem to have [[324]] known, did not appear simply as a result of "a synthesis of ancient sacrifices to the Canaanite Baals and to the God of Israel, old practices of cultic purification and also of magic."[53] One can also perceive traces of later syncretism within Judaism, due to contact with the Syrian and Babylonian East.[54]

A number of the sacrifices concern the community and the regular worship of God during festivals, Sabbaths, and the daily cult, while others are occasional private sacrifices intended to procure particular favors for the one offering them. As is typical of complex sacramental organizations, the essential goal is less that of maintaining and renewing the covenant between the people and their God than it is of assuring the purity of the community and its members. The sacred was rigorously distinguished from the profane, daily life being profane. It is essential first of all to put a worshiper into a normal relationship with the divine. Furthermore, the concept of sin developed in proportion to the individualization of religion. . . . The Priestly Code shows a particularly varied and detailed ritual of purification and sin sacrifices. The sin sacrifice (*ʾāšām*) and the reparation sacrifice (*ḥaṭṭāʾt*) are minutely described in chaps. 4–5 of Leviticus. [[325]] Voluntary sins are distinguished from involuntary sins, and for each of the various cases the legislator indicates the victim and the way in which it is to be sacrificed, the offerings and fines that are to accompany the sacrifice. After each case comes this formula, repeated in almost the same words: "thus shall the sacrificer make atonement for that man, for the sin which he committed, and he will be pardoned for it." In other cases, the expiation of the sin of a priest is

---

52. Concerning the sacrificial system of the Priestly Code, see the accounts of I. Benzinger, *Hebräische Archäologie* (3d ed.; Leipzig: Pfeiffer, 1927) 364–78; and Loisy, *La religion d'Israël*, 233–38 and 246–49. Cf. A. F. Loisy, *Essai historique sur le sacrifice* (Paris: Nourry, 1920), chaps. 11–12, §4, and passim.

53. Ibid., 351–62 and 513–14.

54. These influences did not stem solely from Canaanite syncretism from the period of the divided monarchy or from Assyrian syncretism under Ahaz and Manasseh (see 2 Kgs 16:10–20, 21:2–9, 22:4–15); there also could have been influences on the scribal schools in Babylon and on the diaspora in general. In any case, the Priestly Code should not be considered a simple, tentative organization of ancient cultic tradition. It is possible to perceive in it traces of new rites and, especially, new tendencies and a new spirit, particularly in the sacrifices of penitence and the exorcism of sickness. One must approach R. Dussaud's *Origines cananéennes du sacrifice israélite* (Paris: Leroux, 1921) with reservation for these reasons, though his work is in other regards a solid and singularly penetrating exposition.

addressed, and a bull is immolated; and in another case the sins of a leader, and a he-goat without defect is burnt; in yet another case, the sins of the assembly are addressed, and the substitutionary sacrifice is a bull upon whose head the Israelite elders have previously laid their hands and whose remains are consumed outside the camp (Lev 4:26). However, the most distinctive rite is the expulsion of the scapegoat combined with the sacrifice of the expiatory bull for the great Day of Atonement. . . .[55] All of this is fairly distant from the moralism of the prophets, and in all of this expiatory system, the ethical aspect of the notion of sanctity and the call to individual and social repentance is absent. In its place is a purely magical concept of purity and impurity, with primitive notions of [[326]] participation, sin being considered a kind of contagion that pollutes the individual, the group, or the race by contact. It also pollutes material objects and even pollutes the earth. The expulsion of evil is accomplished by elimination and substitution, thanks to the efficacy of the sacrificial rite. . . .[56]

[[327]] This system . . . presupposes the cult of a people rooted to the land, celebrating seasonal sacrifices. However, the Priestly compiler, while maintaining the ancient rituals, for example the rite of the first sheaf of the crop waved before Yahweh and the offerings of bread made with the new wheat flour for the Feast of Weeks,[57] has forgotten the primitive significance of this agrarian magic (Exod 12:1–15). It signifies to him homage to Yahweh, master of the land, who gives riches and prosperity to

55. Leviticus 16. This use of the especially crude, primitive superstitions that characterize the penitential rituals of the levitical code seems to have been typical of the Oriental piety of that period. Compare this with the development of penitential magic in the second Babylonian Empire (C. Fossey, *La magie assyrienne: Étude suivie de textes magiques* (Paris: Leroux, 1902); E. Dhorme, *La religion assyro-babylonienne: Conférences données à l'Institut Catholique de Paris* [Paris: Victor Lecoffre, 1910]). Concerning the rites for exorcism and expiation among primitives in the mystery religions, see the rich accumulation of facts presented by J. Frazer in *The Golden Bough: A Study in Magic and Religion* (London: Macmillan, 1907–15); see the volume on *Le bouc émissaire*, French translation; and see also Loisy, *Essai sur le sacrifice*, 307–62.

56. Under Wellhausen's influence we have certainly overestimated the value and role of this cultic systematization of the Priestly Code, when we see there above all the end of a purifying work destined to make of the Temple cult "the solid framework of spiritual monotheism" (see . . . Loisy, . . . *La religion d'Israël*, 246). It remains, nevertheless, that the general tendency of the Priestly legislator is, from a religio-ethical point of view, clearly a regression from that of Deuteronomy, who boldly interpreted the institutions and rites, trying to adapt them to his gracious concepts and his human ideal (see *RHPR* 13 [1933] 289–323).

57. Lev 23:9–17. For the interpretation of these rituals of agrarian magic and for the numerous parallels in primitive religions and in modern folk practices, see Frazer, *The Golden Bough*, French edition, in the chapters on the agrarian and sylvan cults. See also Loisy, *Le sacrifice*, 202–57.

his people. As for the sacrifice of the paschal lamb, it was instituted for the redemption of the firstborn because Yahweh struck the firstborn of the Egyptians and spared the Hebrews. The tents of foliage of the Feast of Tabernacles do not celebrate the enchantment of vegetation and the joy of the harvest but recall the forty years when Israel wandered in the wilderness to atone for its sins, living in tents (Lev 23:41–43). However, the most distinctive holy day of the Priestly Code, the spirit of which is more or less reflected in the other festivals, is the Day of Atonement. Here none of the traditional rejoicing and happiness remains: of farmers celebrating life in the midst of nature, made fertile through their labors. Rather, it entails the purification of the community of its sins, humility before Yahweh, and expiation through the blood of the sacrifice and through propitiatory rites. . . .

[328] This organization of priesthood and cult in an idealized sanctuary was still a system, an a priori construction, as it were, as in Ezekiel. . . . Moreover, it was not just scribal fantasy. In some ways the Priestly legislators codified the ancient cultic practices, the rites and institutions of the old Israelite sanctuaries, which were to be restored and reorganized in Second Temple practice. But this practice and all of its organization, which the priests and the reforming scribes imposed upon the Jerusalem community after the Exile, was not a precise realization of the plans of the theocratic legislator. . . .

[329] As for the situation in Jerusalem after these reforms—from the little that we know either from (1) the writings of the end of the fifth or fourth centuries (Joel, Deutero-Zechariah, and the Chronicler's compilations) or (2) from the letters of the Jews from Elephantine to [330] Governor Bagoas and to the sons of Sanballat, or (3) from the few traditions collected by Josephus in his *Antiquities* concerning the government of Bagoas, or (4) from the history of Palestine in the last part of the Achaemenid Period and the first part of the Greek Period—this evidence does not appear to support such a pure cult and such a strongly established organization. In fact, Jerusalem was only now beginning to emerge as the preeminent cultic center, as pilgrims streamed toward it from various points of the diaspora. As a result, a certain unification of Judaism must have occurred in practice as well as in literature and religious thought.[58] At the same time the priesthood of the Temple was establishing itself as a power. It enriched itself through the numerous offerings brought to the sanctuary. The high priest appeared before foreign governors, as much a national leader as a religious one. However,

---

58. Concerning the role of Jerusalem during the second half of the Persian Period, see my *Dispersés d'Israël*, 54–58 and 161–64.

this temporal supremacy, which was to assert itself definitively with the priest-kings of the Hasmonaean dynasty, was not precisely in line with the Priestly Code: the legislator had conceived of his *kōhēn haggādôl* ⟦'high priest'⟧ as the great Temple dignitary and the leader of those performing the sacrifices, political order being so foreign to his way of thinking, that he did not conceive of a high priest as a leader similar to the princes who governed the other nations. . . .

⟦331⟧ Furthermore, we have witnesses to the fact that despite the pretensions of the Jerusalemite clergy, other sanctuaries outside of Jerusalem had maintained their importance during the Persian Period and on into the Greek Period. . . . ⟦T⟧he text of Isa 19:19 concerning the altar and the *maṣēbâ* ⟦'sacred pillar'⟧ that would be erected in Egypt, the polemic of Isa 66:1–4 against those who would build a sanctuary for Yahweh, and above all the text of Mal 1:10–11 concerning the offerings and sacrifices that are being offered in the name of Yahweh among the nations are rather explicit in this regard. And what we know elsewhere through the Elephantine documents about the cult of the Temple of Yeb reinforces these data.[59]

The Priestly legislator, who probably belonged to the schools of the Babylonian *gôlâ* ⟦'exile'⟧, could not ignore this situation in Judaism, and one would be wrong to think that his reform plan exclusively concerned Jerusalem and ⟦332⟧ the Palestinian community. Next to the laws concerning the cult and the priestly organization in the ideal sanctuary, there are other laws that apply to all of Israel, elemental and permanent precepts that the faithful person must observe wherever he lives, laws concerning the Sabbath, circumcision, impurity, and fasting. . . .

⟦333⟧ The Torah thus has a dual purpose: in the first place, it accomplishes in a permanent way what the simple sacrificial cult accomplished only at certain times of life, the union of God and the worshiper. . . . Piety from now on consists of "keeping the commandments, the statutes, ⟦334⟧ and the ordinances," and in "putting them into practice." Thus, in this religion of law, the continual presence of Yahweh affirms itself in the life of his worshipers. It is no longer simply a question of entering into a relationship with the God of the community through the community's intermediary; it is a question of a sanctified and perfect life. . . .

---

59. See van Hoonacker, *Une communauté judéo-araméenne à Éléphantine*; and my *Dispersés d'Israël*, 77–95. In the letter of Jedoniah and the priests of Yeb to Bagohi, the importance of Jerusalem as the center of Judaism is explicitly recognized. However, the importance of Samaria is also recognized. Neither of these things kept the Jews of Elephantine from offering *oblation, incense, and burnt offering* on the altar of the sanctuary of Yeb as soon as that sanctuary could be built.

At the same time, the law is the bonding element of the religious community. The religious assemblies of the diaspora tended to group themselves around communal practice. In the midst of the *gôyîm* 〚'nations'〛, Israel affirms its distinctive traits. Israel is a people living as strangers among the nations. However, they zealously and proudly observe the laws and rituals that they received from their fathers, which are the mark of the holy race. The Israelites must practice the prescribed commandments and must abstain from the foul customs of the pagans, so that the name of Yahweh will not be profaned among his people.

> Be holy, because I am holy, I, Yahweh your God. Keep, therefore, all
> of my laws and my statutes and put them into practice. . . . Do not
> follow the laws of the nations whom I drive out before you. . . . I am
> Yahweh your God, who has separated you from the other peoples. You
> shall be holy for me, because I am holy, I, Yahweh (Lev 19:2, 20:22–
> 26, 22:31–32).

〚335〛 Thus it is said in the Holiness Code. The entire spirit of philosophy and history and priestly legislation is there. It is a question of not letting oneself be influenced by the pagan masses and of maintaining one's religious tradition intact. This is the price to be paid for retaining the identity of small dispersed groups.[60] A minority only survives by fanatical conviction and rigorous practice.

However, under this guise, and in spite of the traditionally maintained framework, the religion of the Torah resulted not in theocracy, a holy nation, or a great organized religious community, but in a sect. As we have seen, Judaism became focused on the future, a far-off and imprecise one at that. Sectarianism was the creative and conserving element of Judaism during the period of its formation (the sixth and fifth centuries) that assured its survival in the midst of crises in the diaspora. . . .

---

60. Max Weber has shed light on this role of the law in the preservation of Judaism and the setting apart the "pariah people" (*Aufsätze zur Religionsoziologie*, vol. 3: *Das Antike Judentum*, 365–70). Cf. Kittel, *Geschichte des Volkes Israel*, 3.655–56. See also my *Dispersés d'Israël*, 48–50, 121–26.

The Abominations of Leviticus

MARY DOUGLAS

[[41]] Defilement is never an isolated event. It cannot occur except in view of a systematic ordering of ideas. Hence any piecemeal interpretation of the pollution rules of another culture is bound to fail. For the only way in which pollution ideas make sense is in reference to a total structure of thought whose key-stone, boundaries, margins and internal lines are held in relation by rituals of separation.

To illustrate this I take a hoary old puzzle from biblical scholarship, the abominations of Leviticus, and particularly the dietary rules. Why should the camel, the hare and the rock badger be unclean? Why should some locusts, but not all, be unclean? Why should the frog be clean and the mouse and the hippopotamus unclean? What have chameleons, moles and crocodiles got in common that they should be listed together (Lev 11:27)?

To help follow the argument I first quote the relevant versions of Leviticus and Deuteronomy using the text of the new Revised Standard Translation.

Deuteronomy 14

3. You shall not eat any abominable things. 4. These are the animals you may eat: the ox, the sheep, the goat, 5. the hart, the gazelle, the roe-buck, the wild goat, the ibex, the antelope and the mountain-sheep. 6. Every animal that parts the hoof and has the hoof cloven in two, and chews the cud, among the animals you may eat. 7. Yet of those that chew the cud or have the hoof cloven you shall not eat these: The camel, the hare and

Reprinted with permission from *Purity and Danger: An Analysis of the Concepts of Pollution and Taboo* (London: Routledge and Kegan Paul, 1966) 41–57.

the rock badger, because they chew the cud but do not part the hoof, are unclean for you. 8. And the swine, because it parts the hoof ⟦42⟧ but does not chew the cud, is unclean for you. Their flesh you shall not eat, and their carcasses you shall not touch. 9. Of all that are in the waters you may eat these: whatever has fins and scales you may eat. 10. And whatever does not have fins and scales you shall not eat; it is unclean for you. 11. You may eat all clean birds. 12. But these are the ones which you shall not eat: the eagle, the vulture, the osprey, 13. the buzzard, the kite, after their kinds; 14. every raven after its kind; 15. the ostrich, the night hawk, the sea gull, the hawk, after their kinds; 16. the little owl and the great owl, the water hen 17. and the pelican, the carrion vulture and the cormorant, 18. the stork, the heron, after their kinds; the hoopoe and the bat. 19. And all winged insects are unclean for you; they shall not be eaten. 20. All clean winged things you may eat.

Leviticus 11

2. These are the living things which you may eat among all the beasts that are on the earth. 3. Whatever parts the hoof and is cloven-footed and chews the cud, among the animals you may eat. 4. Nevertheless among those that chew the cud or part the hoof, you shall not eat these: The camel, because it chews the cud but does not part the hoof, is unclean to you. 5. And the rock badger, because it chews the cud but does not part the hoof, is unclean to you. 6. And the hare, because it chews the cud but does not part the hoof, is unclean to you. 7. And the swine, because it parts the hoof and is cloven-footed but does not chew the cud, is unclean to you. 8. Of their flesh you shall not eat, and their carcasses you shall not touch; they are unclean to you. 9. These you may eat of all that are in the waters. Everything in the waters that has fins and scales, whether in the seas or in the rivers, you may eat. 10. But anything in the seas or the rivers that has not fins and scales, of the swarming creatures in the waters and of the living creatures that are in the waters, is an abomination to you. 11. They shall remain an abomination to you; of their flesh you shall not eat, and their carcasses you shall have in abomination. 12. Everything in the waters that has not fins and scales is an abomination to you. 13. And these you shall have in abomination among the birds, they shall not be eaten, they are an abomination: the eagle, the ossifrage, the osprey, 14. the kite, the falcon according to its kind, 15. every raven according to its kind, 16. the ⟦43⟧ ostrich and the night hawk, the sea gull, the hawk according to its kind, 17. the owl, the cormorant, the ibis, 18. the water hen, the pelican, the vulture, 19. the stork, the heron according to its kind, the hoopoe and the bat. 20. All winged insects that go upon all fours are an abomination to you. 21. Yet among the winged insects that go on all fours you may eat those which have legs above their feet, with which

to leap upon the earth. 22. Of them you may eat: the locust according to its kind, the bald locust according to its kind, the cricket according to its kind, and the grasshopper according to its kind. 23. But all other winged insects which have four feet are an abomination to you. 24. And by these you shall become unclean; whoever touches their carcass shall be unclean until the evening, 25. and whoever carries any part of their carcass shall wash his clothes and be unclean until the evening. 26. Every animal which parts the hoof but is not cloven-footed or does not chew the cud is unclean to you: everyone who touches them shall be unclean. 27. And all that go on their paws, among the animals that go on all fours, are unclean to you; whoever touches their carcass shall be unclean until the evening, 28. and he who carries their carcass shall wash his clothes and be unclean until the evening; they are unclean to you. 29. And these are unclean to you among the swarming things that swarm upon the earth; the weasel, the mouse, the great lizard according to its kind, 30. the gecko, the land crocodile, the lizard, the sand lizard and the chameleon. 31. These are unclean to you among all that swarm; whoever touches them when they are dead shall be unclean until the evening. 32. And anything upon which any of them falls when they are dead shall be unclean. 41. Every swarming thing that swarms upon the earth is an abomination; it shall not be eaten. 42. Whatever goes on its belly, and whatever goes on all fours, or whatever has many feet, all the swarming things that swarm upon the earth, you shall not eat; for they are an abomination.

All the interpretations given so far fall into one of two groups: either the rules are meaningless, arbitrary because their intent is disciplinary and not doctrinal, or they are allegories of virtues and vices. Adopting the view that religious prescriptions are largely devoid of symbolism, Maimonides said:

[44] The Law that sacrifices should be brought is evidently of great use . . . but we cannot say why one offering should be a lamb whilst another is a ram, and why a fixed number of these should be brought. Those who trouble themselves to find a cause for any of these detailed rules are in my eyes devoid of sense. . . . [Friedländer, trans. 1885]

As a mediaeval doctor of medicine, Maimonides was also disposed to believe that the dietary rules had a sound physiological basis, but we have already dismissed in the second chapter [not reprinted here] the medical approach to symbolism. For a modern version of the view that the dietary rules are not symbolic, but ethical, disciplinary, see Epstein's English notes to the Babylonian Talmud and also his popular history of Judaism (1959: 24):

Both sets of laws have one common aim . . . Holiness. While the positive precepts have been ordained for the cultivation of virtue, and for the promotion of those finer qualities which distinguish the truly religious and ethical being, the negative precepts are defined to combat vice and suppress other evil tendencies and instincts which stand athwart man's striving towards holiness. . . . The negative religious laws are likewise assigned educational aims and purposes. Foremost among these is the prohibition of eating the flesh of certain animals classed as "unclean." This law has nothing totemic about it. It is expressly associated in Scripture with the ideal of holiness. Its real object is to train the Israelite in self-control as the indispensable first step for the attainment of holiness.

According to Professor Stein's "The Dietary Laws in Rabbinic and Patristic Literature" [[1957]], the ethical interpretation goes back to the time of Alexander the Great and the Hellenic influence on Jewish culture. The first century A.D. Letter of Aristeas teaches that not only are the Mosaic rules a valuable discipline which "prevent[s] the Jews from thoughtless action and injustice," but they also coincide with what natural reason would dictate for achieving the good life. So the Hellenic influence allows the medical and ethical interpretations to run together. Philo held that Moses' principle of selection was precisely to choose the most delicious meats:

> The lawgiver sternly forbade all animals of land, sea or air whose flesh is the finest and fattest, like that of pigs and scaleless fish, knowing that they set a trap for the most slavish of senses, the taste, and that they produced gluttony [[*Special Laws* 4.100]],

[[45]] (and here we are led straight into the medical interpretation):

> an evil dangerous to both soul and body, for gluttony begets indigestion, which is the source of all illnesses and infirmities.

In another stream of interpretation, following the tradition of Robertson Smith and Frazer, the Anglo-Saxon Old Testament scholars have tended to say simply that the rules are arbitrary because they are irrational. For example, Nathaniel Micklem [[1953]] says:

> Commentators used to give much space to a discussion of the question why such and such creatures, or such and such states and symptoms were unclean. Have we, for instance, primitive rules of hygiene? Or were certain creatures and states unclean because they represented or typified certain sins? It may be taken as certain that neither hygiene, nor any kind of typology, is the basis of uncleanness. These regulations

are not by any means to be rationalised. Their origins may be diverse, and go back beyond history. . . .

Compare also S. R. Driver (1895):

The principle, however, determining the line of demarcation between clean animals and unclean, is not stated; and what it is has been much debated. No single principle, embracing all the cases, seems yet to have been found, and not improbably more principles than one cooperated. Some animals may have been prohibited on account of their repulsive appearance or uncleanly habits, others upon sanitary grounds; in other cases, again, the motive of the prohibition may very probably have been a religious one, particularly animals may have been supposed, like the serpent in Arabia, to be animated by superhuman or demoniac beings, or they may have had a sacramental significance in the heathen rites of other nations; and the prohibition may have been intended as a protest against these beliefs. . . .

P. P. Saydon takes the same line in the *Catholic Commentary on Holy Scripture* (1953), acknowledging his debt to Driver and to Robertson Smith. It would seem that when Robertson Smith applied the ideas of primitive, irrational and unexplainable to some parts of Hebrew religion they remained thus labelled and unexamined to this day.

Needless to say such interpretations are not interpretations at all, since they deny any significance to the rules. They express [[46]] bafflement in a learned way. Micklem says it more frankly when he says of Leviticus:

Chapters XI to XV are perhaps the least attractive in the whole Bible. To the modern reader there is much in them that is meaningless or repulsive. They are concerned with ritual "uncleanness" in respect of animals (11), of childbirth (12), skin diseases and stained garments (13), of the rites for the purgation of skin diseases (14), of leprosy and of various issues or secretions of the human body (15). Of what interest can such subjects be except to the anthropologist? What can all this have to do with religion?

Pfeiffer's general position is to be critical of the priestly and legal elements in the life of Israel. So he too lends his authority to the view that the rules in the Priestly Code are largely arbitrary:

Only priests who were lawyers could have conceived of religion as a theocracy regulated by a divine law fixing exactly, and therefore arbitrarily, the sacred obligations of the people to their God. They thus sanctified the external, obliterated from religion both the ethical ideals of Amos and the tender emotions of Hosea, and reduced the Universal Creator to the stature of an inflexible despot. . . . From immemorial custom P derived the two fundamental notions which characterise its legislation: physical holiness and arbitrary enactment—archaic conceptions which the reforming prophets had discarded in favour of spiritual holiness and moral law [[Pfeiffer 1957: 91]].

It may be true that lawyers tend to think in precise and codified forms. But is it plausible to argue that they tend to codify sheer nonsense—arbitrary enactments? Pfeiffer tries to have it both ways, insisting on the legalistic rigidity of the priestly authors and pointing to the lack of order in the setting out of the chapter to justify his view that the rules are arbitrary. Arbitrariness is a decidedly unexpected quality to find in Leviticus, as the Rev. Prof. H. J. Richards has pointed out to me. For source criticism attributes Leviticus to the Priestly source, the dominant concern of whose authors was for order. So the weight of source criticism supports us in looking for another interpretation.

As for the idea that the rules are allegories of virtues and vices, Professor Stein [[1957]] derives this vigorous tradition from the [[47]] same early Alexandrian influence on Jewish thought (pp. 145–46). Quoting the letter of Aristeas, he says that the High Priest, Eleazar:

> admits that most people find the biblical food restrictions not understandable. If God is the Creator of everything, why should His law be so severe as to exclude some animals even from touch (128f.)? His first answer still links the dietary restrictions with the danger of idolatry. . . . The second answer attempts to refute specific charges by means of allegorical exegesis. Each law about forbidden foods has its deep reason. Moses did not enumerate the mouse or the weasel out of a special consideration for them (143f.). On the contrary, mice are particularly obnoxious because of their destructiveness, and weasels, the very symbol of malicious tale-bearing, conceive through the ear and give birth through the mouth (164f.). Rather have these holy laws been given for the sake of justice to awaken in us devout thoughts and to form our character (161–168). The birds, for instance, the Jews are allowed to eat are all tame and clean, as they live by corn only. Not so the wild and carnivorous birds who fall upon lambs and goats, and even human beings. Moses, by calling the latter unclean, admonished the faithful not to do violence to the weak and not to trust their own power (145–148). Cloven-hoofed animals which part their hooves symbolise that all our actions must betray proper ethical distinction and be directed towards righteousness. . . . Chewing the cud, on the other hand stands for memory.

Professor Stein goes on to quote Philo's use of allegory to interpret the dietary rules:

Fish with fins and scales, admitted by the law, symbolise endurance and self-control, whilst the forbidden ones are swept away by the current, unable to resist the force of the stream. Reptiles, wriggling along by trailing their belly, signify persons who devote themselves to their ever greedy desires and passions. Creeping things, however, which have legs above their feet, so that they can leap, are clean because they symbolise the success of moral efforts.

Christian teaching has readily followed the allegorising tradition. The first century epistle of Barnabas, written to convince the Jews that their law had found its fulfilment, took the clean and unclean animals to refer to various types of men, leprosy to mean sin, etc. A more recent example of this tradition is in [[48]] Bishop Challoner's notes on the Westminster Bible in the beginning of this century:

> Hoof divided and cheweth the cud. The dividing of the hoof and chewing of the cud signify discretion between good and evil, and meditating on the law of God; and where either of these is wanting, man is unclean. In like manner fishes were reputed unclean that had not fins and scales: that is souls that did not raise themselves up by prayer and cover themselves with the scales of virtue. (Footnote verse 3)

These are not so much interpretations as pious commentaries. They fail as interpretations because they are neither consistent nor comprehensive. A different explanation has to be developed for each animal and there is no end to the number of possible explanations.

Another traditional approach, also dating back to the Letter of Aristeas (139–142), is the view that what is forbidden to the Israelites is forbidden solely to protect them from foreign influence. For instance, Maimonides held that they were forbidden to seethe the kid in the milk of its dam because this was a cultic act in the religion of the Canaanites. This argument cannot be comprehensive, for it is not held that the Israelites consistently rejected all the elements of foreign religions and invented something entirely original for themselves. Maimonides accepted the view that some of the more mysterious commands of the law had as their object to make a sharp break with heathen practices. Thus the Israelites were forbidden to wear garments woven of linen and wool, to plant different trees together, to have sexual intercourse with animals, to cook meat with milk, simply because these acts figured in the rites of their heathen neighbours. So far, so good: the laws were enacted as barriers to the spread of heathen styles of ritual. But in that case why were some heathen practices allowed? And not only allowed—if sacrifice be taken as a practice common to heathens and Israelites—but given an absolutely central place in the religion. Maimonides' answer, at any rate in

The Guide to the Perplexed, was to justify sacrifice as a transitional stage, regrettably heathen, but necessarily allowed because it would be impractical to wean the Israelites abruptly from their heathen past. This is an extraordinary statement to come from the pen of a rabbinical scholar, and indeed in his serious rabbinical writings Maimonides did not [[49]] attempt to maintain the argument: on the contrary, he there counted sacrifice as the most important act of the Jewish religion.

At least Maimonides saw the inconsistency and was led by it into contradiction. But later scholars seem content to use the foreign influence argument one way or the other, according to the mood of the moment. Professor Hooke and his colleagues have clearly established that the Israelites took over some Canaanite styles of worship, and the Canaanites obviously had much in common with Mesopotamian culture (1933). But it is no explanation to represent Israel as a sponge at one moment and as a repellent the next, without explaining why it soaked up this foreign element but repelled that one. What is the value of saying that seething kids in milk and copulating with cows are forbidden in Leviticus because they are the fertility rites of foreign neighbours (1935), since Israelites took over other foreign rites? We are still perplexed to know when the sponge is the right or the wrong metaphor. The same argument is equally puzzling in Eichrodt [[1961: 230–31]]. Of course no culture is created out of nothing. The Israelites absorbed freely from their neighbours, but not quite freely. Some elements of foreign culture were incompatible with the principles of patterning on which they were constructing their universe; others were compatible. For instance, Zaehner suggests that the Jewish abomination of creeping things may have been taken over from Zoroastrianism (1961: 162). Whatever the historical evidence for this adoption of a foreign element into Judaism, we shall see that there was in the patterning of their culture a pre-formed compatibility between this particular abomination and the general principles on which their universe was constructed.

Any interpretations will fail which take the Do-nots of the Old Testament in piecemeal fashion. The only sound approach is to forget hygiene, aesthetics, morals and instinctive revulsion, even to forget the Canaanites and the Zoroastrian Magi, and start with the texts. Since each of the injunctions is prefaced by the command to be holy, so they must be explained by that command. There must be contrariness between holiness and abomination which will make over-all sense of all the particular restrictions.

Holiness is the attribute of Godhead. Its root means 'set apart'. What else does it mean? We should start any cosmological enquiry by seeking the principles of power and danger. In the Old [[50]] Testament we find blessing as the source of all good things, and the withdrawal of blessing as the source of all dangers. The blessing of God makes the land possible for men to live in.

God's work through the blessing is essentially to create order, through which men's affairs prosper. Fertility of women, livestock and fields is promised as a result of the blessing and this is to be obtained by keeping covenant with God and observing all His precepts and ceremonies (Deut 28:1–14). Where the blessing is withdrawn and the power of the curse unleashed, there is barrenness, pestilence, confusion. For Moses said:

> But if you will not obey the voice of the Lord your God or be careful to do all his commandments and his statutes which I command you this day, then all these curses shall come upon you and overtake you. Cursed shall you be in the city, and cursed shall you in the field. Cursed shall be your basket and your kneading trough. Cursed shall be the fruit of your body, and the fruit of your ground, the increase of your cattle, and the young of your flock. Cursed shall you be when you come in and cursed shall you be when you go out. The Lord will send upon you curses, confusion, and frustration in all that you undertake to do, until you are destroyed and perish quickly on account of the evil of your doings, because you have forsaken me. . . . The Lord will smite you with consumption, and with fever, inflammation, and fiery heat, and with drought, and with blasting and with mildew; they shall pursue you till you perish. And the heavens over your head shall be brass and the earth under you shall be iron. The Lord will make the rain of your land powder and dust; from heaven it shall come down upon you until you are destroyed. (Deut 28:15–24)

From this it is clear that the positive and negative precepts are held to be efficacious and not merely expressive: observing them draws down prosperity, infringing them brings danger. We are thus entitled to treat them in the same way as we treat primitive ritual avoidances whose breach unleashes danger to men. The precepts and ceremonies alike are focussed on the idea of the holiness of God which men must create in their own lives. So this is a universe in which men prosper by conforming to holiness and perish when they deviate from it. If there were no other clues we should be able to find out the Hebrew idea of the holy by examining the precepts by which men conform to ⟦51⟧ it. It is evidently not goodness in the sense of an all-embracing humane kindness. Justice and moral goodness may well illustrate holiness and form part of it, but holiness embraces other ideas as well.

Granted that its root means separateness, the next idea that emerges is of the Holy as wholeness and completeness. Much of Leviticus is taken up with stating the physical perfection that is required of things presented in the temple and of persons approaching it. The animals offered in sacrifice must be without blemish, women must be purified after childbirth, lepers should be separated and ritually cleansed before being allowed to approach it once they are cured. All bodily discharges are defiling and disqualify from approach to the temple. Priests may only come into contact with death when their own close kin die. But the high priest must never have contact with death.

Leviticus 21

17. Say to Aaron, None of your descendants throughout their generations who has a blemish may approach to offer the bread of his God. 18. For no one who has a blemish shall draw near, a man blind or lame, or one who has a mutilated face or a limb too long, 19. or a man who has an injured foot or an injured hand, 20. or a hunch-back, or a dwarf, or a man with a defect in his sight or an itching disease or scabs, or crushed testicles; 21. no man of the descendants of Aaron the priest who has a blemish shall come near to offer the Lord's offerings by fire; . . .

In other words, he must be perfect as a man, if he is to be a priest.

This much reiterated idea of physical completeness is also worked out in the social sphere and particularly in the warriors' camp. The culture of the Israelites was brought to the pitch of greatest intensity when they prayed and when they fought. The army could not win without the blessing and to keep the blessing in the camp they had to be specially holy. So the camp was to be preserved from defilement like the Temple. Here again all bodily discharges disqualified a man from entering the camp as they would disqualify a worshipper from approaching the altar. A warrior who had had an issue of the body in the night should keep outside the camp all day and only return after sunset, having washed. Natural functions producing bodily waste were to be performed outside the camp (Deut 23:10–15). In short the idea of holiness was given an external, [[52]] physical expression in the wholeness of the body seen as a perfect container.

Wholeness is also extended to signify completeness in a social context. An important enterprise, once begun, must not be left incomplete. This way of lacking wholeness also disqualifies a man from fighting. Before a battle the captains shall proclaim:

Deuteronomy 20

5. What man is there that has built a new house and has not dedicated it? Let him go back to his house, lest he die in the battle and another man dedicate it. 6. What man is there that has planted a vineyard and has not enjoyed its fruit? Let him go back to his house, lest he die in the battle and another man enjoy its fruit. 7. And what man is there that has betrothed a wife and has not taken her? Let him go back to his house, lest he die in the battle and another man take her.

Admittedly there is no suggestion that this rule implies defilement. It is not said that a man with a half-finished project on his hands is defiled in the same way that a leper is defiled. The next verse in fact goes on to say that fearful and faint-hearted men should go home lest they spread their fears. But there is a strong suggestion in other passages that a man should not put his hand to the plough and then turn back. Pedersen goes so far as to say that:

> in all these cases a man has started a new important undertaking without having finished it yet . . . a new totality has come into existence. To make a breach in this prematurely, i.e. before it has attained maturity or has been finished, involves a serious risk of sin (Vol. 3, p. 9).

If we follow Pedersen, then blessing and success in war required a man to be whole in body, whole-hearted and trailing no uncompleted schemes. There is an echo of this actual passage in the New Testament parable of the man who gave a great feast and whose invited guests incurred his anger by making excuses (Luke 14:16–24; Matthew 22. See Black and Rowley 1962: 836). One of the guests had bought a new farm, one had bought ten oxen and had not yet tried them, and one had married a wife. If according to the old Law each could have validly justified his refusal by reference to Deuteronomy 20, the parable supports Pedersen's view that interruption of new projects was held to be bad in civil as well as military contexts.

[[53]] Other precepts develop the idea of wholeness in another direction. The metaphors of the physical body and of the new undertaking relate to the perfection and completeness of the individual and his work. Other precepts extend holiness to species and categories. Hybrids and other confusions are abominated.

Leviticus 18

> 23. And you shall not lie with any beast and defile yourself with it, neither shall any woman give herself to a beast to lie with it: it is perversion.

The word 'perversion' is a significant mistranslation of the rare Hebrew work *tebel*, which has as its meaning mixing or confusion. The same theme is taken up in Lev 19:19.

> You shall keep my statutes. You shall not let your cattle breed with a different kind; you shall not sow your field with two kinds of seed; nor shall there come upon you a garment of cloth made of two kinds of stuff.

All these injunctions are prefaced by the general command:

> Be holy, for I am holy.

We can conclude that holiness is exemplified by completeness. Holiness requires that individuals shall conform to the class to which they belong. And holiness requires that different classes of things shall not be confused.

Another set of precepts refines on this last point. Holiness means keeping distinct the categories of creation. It therefore involves correct definition, discrimination and order. Under this head all the rules of sexual morality exemplify the holy. Incest and adultery (Lev 18:6–20) are against holiness, in the simple sense of right order. Morality does not conflict with holiness, but holiness is more a matter of separating that which should be separated than of protecting the rights of husbands and brothers.

Then follows in chapter 19 another list of actions which are contrary to holiness. Developing the idea of holiness as order, not confusion, this list upholds rectitude and straight-dealing as holy, and contradiction and double-dealing as against holiness. Theft, lying, false witness, cheating in weights and measures, all kinds of dissembling such as speaking ill of the deaf (and presumably smiling to their face), hating your brother in your heart (while presumably speaking kindly to him), these are ⟦54⟧ clearly contradictions between what seems and what is. This chapter also says much about generosity and love, but these are positive commands, while I am concerned with negative rules.

We have now laid a good basis for approaching the laws about clean and unclean meats. To be holy is to be whole, to be one; holiness is unity, integrity, perfection of the individual and of the kind. The dietary rules merely develop the metaphor of holiness on the same lines.

First we should start with livestock, the herds of cattle, camels, sheep and goats which were the livelihood of the Israelites. These animals were clean inasmuch as contact with them did not require purification before approaching the Temple. Livestock, like the inhabited land, received the blessing of God. Both land and livestock were fertile by the blessing, both were drawn into the divine order. The farmer's duty was to preserve the blessing. For one thing, he had to preserve the order of creation. So no hybrids, as we have seen, either in the fields or in the herds or in the clothes made from wool or flax. To some extent men covenanted with their land and cattle in the same way as God covenanted with them. Men respected the first born of their cattle, obliged them to keep the Sabbath. Cattle were literally domesticated as slaves. They had to be brought into the social order in order to enjoy the blessing. The difference between cattle and the wild beasts is that the wild beasts have no covenant to protect them. It is possible that the Israelites were like other pastoralists who do not relish wild game. The Nuer of the South Sudan, for instance, apply a sanction of disapproval of a man who lives by hunting. To be driven to eating wild meat is the sign of a poor herdsman. So it would be probably wrong to think of the Israelites as longing for forbidden meats and finding the restrictions irksome. Driver is surely right in taking the rules as an *a posteriori* generalisation of their habits. Cloven-hoofed, cud-chewing ungulates are the model of the proper kind of food for a pastoralist. If they must eat wild game, they can eat wild game that shares these distinctive characters and is therefore of the same general species. This is a kind of casuistry which permits scope for hunting antelope and wild goats and wild sheep. Everything would be quite straightforward were it not that the legal mind has seen fit to give ruling on some borderline cases. Some animals seem to be ruminant, such as the hare and the hyrax (or rock badger), whose constant grinding of their [55] teeth was held to be cud-chewing. But they are definitely not cloven-hoofed and so are excluded by name. Similarly for animals which are cloven-hoofed but are not ruminant, the pig and the camel. Note that this failure to conform to the two necessary criteria for defining cattle is the only reason given in the Old Testament for avoiding the pig; nothing whatever is said about its dirty scavenging habits. As the pig does not yield milk, hide nor wool, there is no other reason for keeping it except for its flesh. And if the Israelites did not keep pig they would not be familiar with its habits. I suggest that originally the sole reason for its being counted as unclean is its failure as a wild boar to get into the antelope class, and that in this it is on the same footing as the camel and the hyrax, exactly as it is stated in the book.

After these borderline cases have been dismissed, the law goes on to deal with creatures according to how they live in the three elements, the water, the air and the earth. The principles here applied are rather different from those covering the camel, the pig, the hare and the hyrax. For the latter are excepted from clean food in having one but not both of the defining characters of livestock. Birds I can say nothing about, because, as I have said, they are named and not described and the translation of the name is open to doubt. But in general the underlying principle of cleanness in animals is that they shall conform fully to their class. Those species are unclean which are imperfect members of their class, or whose class itself confounds the general scheme of the world.

To grasp this scheme we need to go back to Genesis and the creation. Here a three-fold classification unfolds, divided between the earth, the waters and the firmament. Leviticus takes up this scheme and allots to each element its proper kind of animal life. In the firmament two-legged fowls fly with wings. In the water scaly fish swim with fins. On the earth four-legged animals hop, jump or walk. Any class of creatures which is not equipped for the right kind of locomotion in its element is contrary to holiness. Contact with it disqualifies a person from approaching the

Temple. Thus anything in the water which has not fins and scales is unclean (11:10–12). Nothing is said about predatory habits or of scavenging.
The only sure test for cleanness in a fish is its scales and its propulsion by
means of fins.

Four-footed creatures which fly (11:20–26) are unclean. Any ⟦56⟧
creature which has two legs and two hands and which goes on all fours like
a quadruped is unclean (11:27). Then follows (v. 29) a much disputed list.
On some translations, it would appear to consist precisely of creatures endowed with hands instead of front feet, which perversely use their hands
for walking: the weasel, the mouse, the crocodile, the shrew, various kinds
of lizards, the chameleon and mole (Danby, 1933), whose forefeet are
uncannily hand-like. This feature of this list is lost in the new Revised
Standard Translation which used the word 'paws' instead of hands.

The last kind of unclean animal is that which creeps, crawls or
swarms upon the earth. This form of movement is explicitly contrary to
holiness (Lev 11:41–44). Driver and White use 'swarming' to translate
the Hebrew *shéreṣ*, which is applied to both those which teem in the waters and those which swarm on the ground. Whether we call it teeming,
trailing, creeping, crawling or swarming, it is an indeterminate form of
movement. Since the main animal categories are defined by their typical
movement, 'swarming' which is not a mode of propulsion proper to any
particular element, cuts across the basic classification. Swarming things
are neither fish, flesh nor fowl. Eels and worms inhabit water, though
not as fish; reptiles go on dry land, though not as quadrupeds; some
insects fly, though not as birds. There is no order in them. Recall what
the Prophecy of Habakkuk says about this form of life:

> For thou makest men like the fish of the sea,
>   like crawling things that have no ruler. (1:14)

The prototype and model of the swarming things is the worm. As fish
belong in the sea so worms belong in the realm of the grave, with death
and chaos.

The case of the locusts is interesting and consistent. The test of
whether it is a clean and therefore edible kind is how it moves on the
earth. If it crawls it is unclean. If it hops it is clean (11:21). In the Mishnah it is noted that a frog is not listed with creeping things and conveys
no uncleanness (Danby, p. 722). I suggest that the frog's hop accounts
for it not being listed. If penguins lived in the Near East I would expect
them to be ruled unclean as wingless birds. If the list of unclean birds
could be retranslated from this point of view, it might well turn out that
they are anomalous because they swim and dive as ⟦57⟧ well as they fly,
or in some other way they are not fully bird-like.

Surely now it would be difficult to maintain that "Be ye Holy" means no more than "Be ye separate." Moses wanted the children of Israel to keep the commands of God constantly before their minds:

Deuteronomy 11

18. You shall therefore lay up these words of mine in your heart and in your soul; and you shall bind them as a sign upon your hand, and they shall be as frontlets between your eyes. 19. And you shall teach them to your children, talking of them when you are sitting in your house, and when you are walking by the way, and when you lie down and when you rise. 20. And you shall write them upon the doorposts of your house and upon your gates.

If the proposed interpretation of the forbidden animals is correct, the dietary laws would have been like signs which at every turn inspired meditation on the oneness, purity and completeness of God. By rules of avoidance holiness was given a physical expression in every encounter with the animal kingdom and at every meal. Observance of the dietary rules would thus have been a meaningful part of the great liturgical act of recognition and worship which culminated in the sacrifice in the Temple.

Bibliography

Black, M., and Rowley, H. H. (editors)
   1962   *Peake's Commentary on the Bible.* London: Thomas Nelson.
Danby, Herbert
   1933   *The Mishnah.* Oxford: Clarendon.
Driver, S. R.
   1895   *International Critical Commentary on Holy Scriptures of the Old and New Testaments: Deuteronomy.* International Critical Commentary. Edinburgh: T. & T. Clark.
Eichrodt, W.
   1961   *Theology of the Old Testament,* Trans. John A. Baker. London: SCM / Philadelphia: Westminster. ⟦Translated from German⟧
Epstein, I.
   1959   *Judaism.* London: Penguin.
Friedländer, M. (translator)
   1885   Moses Maimonides. *Guide for the Perplexed,* 1st ed. London: Trübner.
Hooke, Samuel Henry, editor
   1933   *Myth and Ritual: Essays on the Myth and Ritual of the Hebrews in Relation to the Cultural Pattern of the Ancient East.* London: Oxford University Press.

1935   *The Labyrinth: Further Studies in the Relation between Myth and Ritual in the Ancient World.* London: SPCK.

Micklem, Nathaniel
1953   Leviticus. *The Interpreter's Bible*, volume 2. Nashville: Abingdon.

Pedersen, Johannes
1926   *Israel: Its Life and Culture*, volume 3. London: Oxford University Press.

Pfeiffer, R. H.
1957   *Books of the Old Testament.* New York: Harper.

Saydon, P. P.
1953   Leviticus. *Catholic Commentary on the Holy Scripture*, ed. B. Orchard. New York: Nelson.

Smith, W. Robertson
1889   *The Religion of the Semites.* Edinburgh: Black.

Stein, S.
1957   The Dietary Laws in Rabbinic and Patristic Literature. *Studia Patristica* 64: 141ff.

Zaehner, R. C.
1961   *The Dawn and Twilight of Zoroastrianism.* London: Weidenfeld & Nicolson.

The Abominable Pig

MARVIN HARRIS

‖67‖ An aversion to pork seems at the outset even more irrational than an aversion to beef. Of all domesticated mammals, pigs possess the greatest potential for swiftly and efficiently changing plants into flesh. Over its lifetime a pig can convert 35 percent of the energy in its feed to meat compared with 13 percent for sheep and a mere 6.5 percent for cattle. A piglet can gain a pound for every three to five pounds it eats while a calf needs to eat ten pounds to gain one. A cow needs nine months to drop a single calf, and under modern conditions the calf needs another four months to reach four hundred pounds. But less than four months after insemination, a single sow can give birth to eight or more piglets, each of which after another six months can weigh over four hundred pounds. Clearly, the whole essence of pig is the production of meat for human nourishment and delectation. Why then did the Lord of the ancient Israelites forbid his people to savor pork or even to touch a pig alive or dead?

> Of their flesh you shall not eat, and their carcasses you shall not touch; they are unclean to you [Lev 11:1] . . . everyone who touches them shall be unclean [Lev 11:24].

Unlike the Old Testament, which is a treasure trove of forbidden flesh, the Koran is virtually free of meat taboos. Why is it the pig alone who suffers Allah's disapproval?

> ⟦68⟧ These things only has He forbidden you: carrion, blood, and the flesh of swine [Holy Koran 2, 168].

Reprinted with permission from *The Sacred Cow and The Abominable Pig: Riddles of Food and Culture* (New York: Simon & Schuster, 1987) 67–87.

For many observant Jews, the Old Testament's characterization of swine as "unclean" renders the explanation of the taboo self-evident: "Anyone who has seen the filthy habits of the swine will not ask why it is prohibited," says a modern rabbinical authority. The grounding of the fear and loathing of pigs in self-evident piggishness goes back at least to the time of Rabbi Moses Maimonides, court physician to the Islamic emperor Saladin during the twelfth century in Egypt. Maimonides shared with his Islamic hosts a lively disgust for pigs and pig eaters, especially Christian pigs and pig eaters: "The principal reason why the law forbids swine-flesh is to be found in the circumstance that its habits and food are very filthy and loathsome." If the law allowed Egyptians and Jews to raise pigs, Cairo's streets and houses would become as filthy as those of Europe, for "the mouth of a swine is as dirty as dung itself." Maimonides could only tell one side of the story. He had never seen a clean pig. The pig's penchant for excrement is not a defect of its nature but of the husbandry of its human masters. Pigs prefer and thrive best on roots, nuts, and grains; they eat excrement only when nothing better presents itself. In fact, let them get hungry enough, and they'll even eat each other, a trait which they share with other omnivores, but most notably with their own masters. Nor is wallowing in filth a natural characteristic of swine. Pigs wallow to keep themselves cool; and they much prefer a fresh, clean mud-hole to one that has been soiled by urine and feces.

In condemning the pig as the dirtiest of animals, Jews and Moslems left unexplained their more tolerant attitude toward other dung-eating domesticated species. Chickens and goats, for example, given motivation and opportunity, also readily dine on dung. The dog is another domesticated creature which easily develops an appetite for human feces. And this was especially true in the Middle East, where dung-eating dogs filled the scavenging niche left vacant by the ban on pigs. Jahweh prohibited their ⟦69⟧ flesh, yet dogs were not abominated, bad to touch, or even bad to look at, as were pigs.

Maimonides could not be entirely consistent in his efforts to attribute the abstention from pork to the pig's penchant for feces. The Book of Leviticus prohibits the flesh of many other creatures, such as cats and camels, which are not notably inclined to eat excrement. And with the exception of the pig, had not Allah said all the others were good to eat? The fact that Maimonides's Moslem emperor could eat every kind of meat except pork would have made it impolitic if not dangerous to identify the biblical sense of cleanliness exclusively with freedom from the taint of feces. So instead of adopting a cleaner-than-thou attitude, Maimonides offered a proper court physician's theory of the entire set of biblical aversions: the prohibited items were not good to eat because not only was one of them—the pig—filthy from eating excrement but all of them were not good for you. "I maintain," he said, "that food forbidden by the Law is unwholesome." But in what ways were the forbidden foods unwholesome? The great rabbi was quite specific in the case of pork: it "contained more moisture than necessary and too much superfluous matter." As for the other forbidden foods, their "injurious character" was too self-evident to merit further discussion.

Maimonides's public health theory of pork avoidance had to wait seven hundred years before it acquired what seemed to be a scientific justification. In 1859 the first clinical association between trichinosis and undercooked pork was established, and from then on it became the most popular explanation of the Jewish and Islamic pork taboo. Just as Maimonides said, pork was unwholesome. Eager to reconcile the Bible with the findings of medical science, theologians began to embroider a whole series of additional public health explanations for the other biblical food taboos: wild animals and beasts of burden were prohibited because the flesh gets too tough to be digested properly; shellfish were to be avoided because they serve as vectors of typhoid fever; blood is not good to eat because the bloodstream is a perfect medium for microbes. In the case of pork this line of rationalization [70] had a paradoxical outcome. Reformist Jews began to argue that since they now understood the scientific and medical basis of the taboos, pork avoidance was no longer necessary; all they had to do was to see to it that the meat was thoroughly cooked. Predictably, this provoked a reaction among Orthodox Jews, who were appalled at the idea that the book of God's law was being relegated to the "class of a minor medical text." They insisted that God's purpose in Leviticus could never be fully comprehended; nonetheless the dietary laws had to be obeyed as a sign of submission to divine will.

Eventually the trichinosis theory of pork avoidance fell out of favor largely on the grounds that a medical discovery made in the nineteenth century could not have been known thousands of years ago. But that is not the part of the theory that bothers me. People do not have to possess a scientific understanding of the ill effects of certain foods in order to put such foods on their bad-to-eat list. If the consequences of eating pork had been exceptionally bad for their health, it would not have been necessary for the Israelites to know about trichinosis in order to ban its consumption. Does one have to understand the molecular chemistry of toxins in order to know that some mushrooms are dangerous? It is essential for my own explanation of the pig taboo that the trichinosis theory be laid to rest on entirely different grounds. My contention is that there is absolutely nothing exceptional about pork as a source of human disease. All domestic animals are potentially hazardous to human health. Undercooked beef, for example, is a prolific source of tapeworms, which can grow to a length of sixteen to twenty feet inside the human gut, induce a severe case of anemia, and lower the body's resistance to other diseases. Cattle, goat, and sheep transmit the bacterial disease known as brucellosis, whose symptoms include fever, aches, pains, and lassitude. The most dangerous disease transmitted by cattle, sheep, and goats is anthrax, a fairly common disease of both animals and humans in Europe and Asia until the introduction of Louis Pasteur's anthrax vaccine in 1881. Unlike trichinosis, which does not produce symptoms in the majority of [[71]] infected individuals and rarely has a fatal outcome, anthrax runs a swift course that begins with an outbreak of boils and ends in death.

If the taboo on pork was a divinely inspired health ordinance, it is the oldest recorded case of medical malpractice. The way to safeguard against trichinosis was not to taboo pork but to taboo undercooked pork. A simple advisory against undercooking pork would have sufficed: "Flesh of swine thou shalt not eat until the pink has been cooked from it." And come to think of it, the same advisory should have been issued for cattle, sheep, and goats. But the charge of medical malpractice against Jahweh will not stick.

The Old Testament contains a rather precise formula for distinguishing good-to-eat flesh from forbidden flesh. This formula says nothing about dirty habits or unhealthy meat. Instead it directs attention to certain anatomical and physiological features of animals that are good to eat. Here is what Lev 11:1 says:

> Whatever parts the hoof and is cloven footed and chews the cud
> among animals, you may eat.

Any serious attempt to explain why the pig was not good to eat must begin with this formula and not with excrement or wholesomeness, about which not a word is said. Leviticus goes on to state explicitly of the pig that it only satisfies one part of the formula. "It divideth the hoof." But the pig does not satisfy the other part of the formula: "It cheweth not the cud."

To their credit, champions of the good-to-eat school have stressed the importance of the cud-chewing, split-hoof formula as the key to understanding Jahweh's abomination of the pig. But they do not view the formula as an outcome of the way the Israelites used domestic animals. Instead they view the way the Israelites used domestic animals as an outcome of the formula. According to anthropologist Mary Douglas, for example, the cud-chewing, split-hoof formula makes the split-hoof but non−cud-chewing pig a thing that's "out of place." Things that are "out of place" are dirty, she argues, for the essence of dirt is "matter out of place." The [[72]] pig, however, is more than out of place; it is neither here nor there. Such things are both dirty and dangerous. Therefore the pig is abominated as well as not good to eat. But doesn't the force of this argument lie entirely in its circularity? To observe that the pig is out of place taxonomically is merely to observe that Leviticus classifies good-to-eat animals in such a way as to make the pig bad to eat. This avoids the question of why the taxonomy is what it is.

Let me attend first to the reason why Jahweh wanted edible animals to be cud-chewers. Among animals raised by the ancient Israelites, there were three cud-chewers: cattle, sheep, and goats. These three animals were the most important food-producing species in the ancient Middle East not because the ancients happened capriciously to think that cud-chewing animals were good to eat (and good to milk) but because cattle, sheep, and goats are ruminants, the kind of herbivores which thrive best on diets consisting of plants that have a high cellulose content. Of all domesticated animals, those which are ruminants possess the most efficient system for digesting tough fibrous materials such as grasses and straw. Their stomachs have four compartments which are like big fermentation "vats" in which bacteria break down and soften these materials. While cropping their food, ruminants do little chewing. The food passes directly to the rumen, the first of the compartments, where it soon begins to ferment. From time to time the contents of the rumen are regurgitated into the mouth as a softened bolus—the "cud"—which is then chewed thoroughly and sent on to the other "vats" to undergo further fermentation.

The ruminant's extraordinary ability to digest cellulose was crucial to the relationship between humans and domesticated animals in the Middle East. By raising animals that could "chew the cud," the Israelites and their neighbors were able to obtain meat and milk without having to share with their livestock the crops destined for human consumption. Cattle, sheep, and goats thrive on items like grass, straw, hay, stubble, bushes, and leaves—feeds whose high cellulose content renders them unfit for human [[73]] consumption even after vigorous boiling. Rather than compete with humans for food, the ruminants further enhanced agricultural productivity by providing dung for fertilizer and traction for pulling plows. And they were also a source of fiber and felt for clothing, and of leather for shoes and harnesses.

I began this puzzle by saying that pigs are the most efficient mammalian converters of plant foods into animal flesh, but I neglected to say what kinds of plant foods. Feed them on wheat, maize, potatoes, soybeans, or anything low in cellulose, and pigs will perform veritable miracles of transubstantiation; feed them on grass, stubble, leaves, or anything high in cellulose, and they will lose weight.

Pigs are omnivores, but they are not ruminants. In fact, in digestive apparatus and nutrient requirements pigs resemble humans in more ways than any mammal except monkeys and apes, which is why pigs are much in demand for medical research concerned with atherosclerosis, calorie-protein malnutrition, nutrient absorption, and metabolism. But there was more to the ban on pork than the pig's inability to thrive on grass and other high-cellulose plants. Pigs carry the additional onus of not being well adapted to the climate and ecology of the Middle East. Unlike the ancestors of cattle, sheep, or goats, which lived in hot, semiarid, sunny grasslands, the pig's ancestors were denizens of well-watered, shady forest glens and riverbanks. Everything about the pig's body heat-regulating system is ill suited for life in the hot, sun-parched habitats which were the homelands of the children of Abraham. Tropical breeds of cattle, sheep, and goats can go for long periods without water, and can either rid their bodies of excess heat through perspiration or are protected from the sun's rays by light-colored, short fleecy coats, (heat-trapping heavy wool is a characteristic of cold-climate breeds). Although a perspiring human is said to "sweat like a pig," the expression lacks an anatomical basis. Pigs can't sweat—they have no functional sweat glands. (Humans are actually the sweatiest of all animals.) And the pig's sparse coat offers little protection against the sun's rays. Just how does the pig keep cool? It does [[74]] a lot of panting, but mostly it depends on wetting itself down with moisture derived from external sources. Here, then, is the explanation for the pig's love of wallowing in mud. By wallowing, it dissipates heat both by evaporation from its skin and by conduction through the cool ground. Experiments show that the cooling effect of mud is superior to that of water. Pigs whose flanks are thoroughly smeared with mud continue to show peak heat-dissipating evaporation for more than twice as long as pigs whose flanks are merely soaked with water, and here also is the explanation for some of the pig's dirty habits. As temperatures rise above thirty degrees celsius (eighty-six degrees Farenheit), a pig deprived of clean mudholes will become desperate and begin to wallow in its own feces and urine in order to avoid heat stroke. Incidentally, the larger a pig gets, the more intolerant it becomes of high ambient temperatures.

Raising pigs in the Middle East therefore was and still is a lot costlier than raising ruminants, because pigs must be provided with artificial shade, extra water for wallowing, and their diet must be supplemented with grains and other plant foods that humans themselves can eat.

To offset all these liabilities pigs have less to offer by way of benefits than ruminants. They can't pull plows, their hair is unsuited for fiber and cloth, and they are not suited for milking (I'll explain why in a later chapter [[not reprinted here]]). Uniquely among large domesticated animals, meat is their most important produce (guinea pigs and rabbits are smaller equivalents; but fowl produce eggs as well as meat).

For a pastoral nomadic people like the Israelites during their years of wandering in search of lands suitable for agriculture, swineherding was out of the question. No arid-land pastoralists herd pigs for the simple reason that it is hard to protect them from exposure to heat, sun, and lack of water while moving from camp to camp over long distances. During their formative years as a nation, therefore, the ancient Israelites could not have consumed significant quantities of pork even had they desired it. This historical experience undoubtedly contributed to the development [[75]] of a traditional aversion to pig meat as an unknown and alien food. But why was this tradition preserved and strengthened by being written down as God's law long after the Israelites had become settled farmers? The answer as I see it is not that the tradition born of pastoralism continued to prevail by mere inertia and ingrown habit, but that it was preserved because pig raising remained too costly.

Critics have opposed the theory that the ancient Israelite pork taboo was essentially a cost/benefit choice by pointing to evidence of pigs being raised quite successfully in many parts of the Middle East including the Israelites' promised land. The facts are not in dispute. Pigs have indeed been raised for ten thousand years in various parts of the Middle East— as long as sheep and goats, and even longer than cattle. Some of the oldest Neolithic villages excavated by archaeologists—Jericho in Jordan, Jarmo in Iraq and Argissa-Magulla in Greece—contain pig bones with features indicative of the transition from wild to domesticated varieties. Several Middle Eastern pre–Bronze Age villages (4000 B.C. to 2000 B.C.) contain concentrated masses of pig remains in association with what archaeologists interpret as altars and cultic centers, suggestive of ritual pig slaughter and pig feasting. We know that some pigs were still being raised in the lands of the Bible at the beginning of the Christian era. The New Testament (Luke) tells us that in the country of the Gadarenes near Lake Galilee Jesus cast out devils from a man named Legion into a herd of swine feeding on the mountain. The swine rushed down into the lake and drowned themselves, and Legion was cured. Even modern-day Israelis continue to raise thousands of swine in parts of northern Galilee. But from the very beginning, fewer pigs were raised than cattle, sheep, or goats. And more importantly, as time went on, pig husbandry declined throughout the region.

Carlton Coon, an anthropologist with many years of experience in North America and the Levant, was the first scholar to offer a cogent explanation of why this general decline in pig husbandry had occurred. Coon attributed the fall of the Middle Eastern pig to deforestation and human population increase. At the beginning 〖76〗 of the Neolithic period, pigs were able to root in oak and beech forests which provided ample shade and wallows as well as acorns, beechnuts, truffles, and other forest floor products. With an increase in human population destiny, farm acreage increased and the oak and beech forests were destroyed to make room for planted crops, especially for olive trees, thereby eliminating the pig's ecological niche.

To update Coon's ecological scenario, I would add that as forests were being destroyed, so were marginal farmlands and grazing lands, the general succession being from forest to cropland to grazing land to desert, with each step along the way yielding a greater premium for raising ruminants and a greater penalty for raising swine. Robert Orr Whyte, former director general of the United Nations Food and Agriculture Organization, estimated that in Anatolia the forests shrank from 70 percent to 13 percent of the total land area between 5000 B.C. and the recent past. Only a fourth of the Caspian shorefront forest survived the process of population increase and agricultural intensification; half of the Caspian mountainous humid forest; a fifth to a sixth of the oak and juniper forests of the Zagros Mountains; and only a twentieth of the juniper forests of the Elburz and Khorassan ranges.

If I am right about the subversion of the practical basis of pig production through ecological succession, one does not need to invoke Mary Douglas's "taxonomic anomaly" to understand the peculiarly low status of the pig in the Middle East. The danger it posed to husbandry was very tangible and accounts quite well for its low status. The pig had been domesticated for one purpose only, namely to supply meat. As ecological conditions became unfavorable for pig raising, there was no alternative function which could redeem its existence. The creature became not only useless, but worse than useless—harmful, a curse to touch or merely to see—a pariah animal. This transformation contrasts understandably with that of cattle in India. Subject to a similar series of ecological depletions—deforestation, erosion, and desertification—cattle also became bad to eat. But in other respects, especially for traction power and milk, they became more useful 〖77〗 than ever—a blessing to look at or to touch—animal godheads.

In this perspective, the fact that pig raising remained possible for the Israelites at low cost in certain remnant hillside forests or swampy habitats, or at extra expense where shade and water were scarce, does not contradict the ecological basis of the taboo. If there had not been some minimum possibility of raising pigs, there would have been no reason to taboo the practice. As the history of Hindu cow protection shows, religions gain strength when they help people make decisions which are in accord with preexisting useful practices, but which are not so completely self-evident as to preclude doubts and temptations. To judge from the Eight-fold Way or the Ten Commandments, God does not usually waste time prohibiting the impossible or condemning the unthinkable.

Leviticus consistently bans all vertebrate land animals that do not chew the cud. It bans, for example, in addition to swine, equines, felines, canines, rodents, and reptiles, none of which are cud-chewers. But Leviticus contains a maddening complication. It prohibits the consumption of three land-dwelling vertebrates which it specifically identifies as cud-chewers: the camel, the hare, and a third creature whose name in Hebrew is *shāphān*. The reason given for why these three alleged cud-chewers are not good to eat is that they do not "part the hoof":

> Nevertheless, these shall ye not eat of them that chew the cud . . . the camel because he . . . divideth not the hoof. And the *shāfān* because he . . . divideth not the hoof. . . . And the hare, because he . . . divideth not the hoof. [Lev 11:4–6]

Although strictly speaking camels are not ruminants, because their cellulose-digesting chambers are anatomically distinct from those of the ruminants, they do ferment, regurgitate, and chew the cud much like cattle, sheep, and goats. But the classification of the hare as a cud-chewer immediately casts a pall over the zoological expertise of the Levite priests. Hares can digest grass but only by eating their own feces—which is a very uncudlike [[78]] solution to the problem of how to send undigested cellulose through the gut for repeated processing (the technical term for this practice is coprophagy). Now as to the identity of the *shāphān*. As the following stack of Bibles shows, *shāphān* is either the 'rock badger', 'cherogrillus', or 'cony':

BIBLES TRANSLATING SHĀPHĀN AS 'ROCK BADGER'
   The Holy Bible. Berkeley: University of California Press.
   The Bible. Chicago: University of Chicago Press, 1931.
   The New Scofield Reference Library Holy Bible. (Authorized King James Version). New York: Oxford University Press, 1967.
   The Holy Bible. London: Catholic Truth Society, 1966.
   The Holy Bible. (Revised Standard Version). New York: Thomas Nelson and Sons, 1952.
   The American Standard Bible. (Reference Edition). La Habra, CA: Collins World, 1973.
   The New World Translation of the Holy Scriptures. Brooklyn, NY: Watchtower Bible and Tract Society of Pennsylvania, 1961.

BIBLES TRANSLATING SHĀPHĀN AS 'CONY'

The Pentateuch: The Five Books of Moses. Edited by William Tyndale. Carbondale: Southern Illinois University Press, 1967.

The Interpreter's Bible: The Holy Scriptures. 12 vols. New York: Abingdon Press, 1953.

The Holy Bible: King James Version (Revised Standard Version). Nashville: Thomas Nelson and Sons, 1971.

Holy Bible: Authorized version. New York: Harpers.

Holy Bible: Revised. New York: American Bible Society, 1873.

Modern Readers Bible. Edited by Richard Moulton. New York: Macmillan, 1935.

BIBLES TRANSLATING SHĀPHĀN AS 'CHEROGRILLUS'

Holy Bible. (Douay, translated from Vulgate). Boston: John Murphy and Co., 1914.

The Holy Bible (translated from the Vulgate by John Wycliffe and his followers). Edited by Rev. Josiah Forshall and Sir Frederick Madden. Oxford: Oxford University Press, 1850.

〚79〛 All three terms refer to a similar kind of small, furtive, hoofed herbivore about the size of a squirrel that lives in colonies on rocky cliffs or among boulders on hilltops. It has two other popular aliases: "dassie" and "damon." It could have been any of these closely related species: *Hyrax capensia, Hyrax syriacus,* or *Procavia capensis.* Whichever it was, it had no rumen and it did not chew the cud.

This leaves the camel as the only bona fide cud-chewer that the Israelites couldn't eat. Every vertebrate land animal that is not a ruminant was forbidden flesh. And only one vertebrate land animal that is a ruminant, the camel, was forbidden. Let me see if I can explain this exception as well as the peculiar mixup about hares and *shāphān.*

My point of departure is that the food laws in Leviticus were mostly codifications of preexisting traditional food prejudices and avoidances. (The Book of Leviticus was not written until 450 B.C.—very late in Israelite history.) I envision the Levite authorities as undertaking the task of finding some simple feature which good-to-eat vertebrate land species shared in common. Had the Levites possessed a better knowledge of zoology, they could have used the criterion of cud-chewing alone and simply added the proviso, "except for the camel." For, as I have just said, with the exception of the camel, all land animals implicitly or explicitly forbidden in Leviticus—all the equines, felines, canines, rodents, rabbits, reptiles, and so forth—are nonruminants. But given their shaky knowledge of zoology, the codifiers could not be sure that the camel was the only undesirable species which was a cud-chewer. So they added the criterion of split hooves—a feature which camels lacked but which the other familiar cud-chewers possessed (the camel has two large flexible toes on each foot instead of hooves).

But why was the camel not a desirable species? Why spurn camel meat? I think the separation of the camel from the other cud-chewers reflects its highly specialized adaptation to desert habitats. With their remarkable capacity to store water, withstand heat, and carry heavy burdens over great distances, and with their long eyelashes and nostrils that shut tight for protection [[80]] against sandstorms, camels were the most important possession of the Middle Eastern desert nomads. (The camel's hump concentrates fat—not water. It acts as an energy reserve. By concentrating the fat in the hump, the rest of the skin needs only a thin layer of fat, and this facilitates removal of body heat.) But as village farmers, the Israelites had little use for camels. Except under desert conditions, sheep and goats and cattle are more efficient converters of cellulose into meat and milk. In addition, camels reproduce very slowly. The females are not ready to bear offspring and the males are not ready to copulate until six years of age. To slow things down further, the males have a once-a-year rutting season (during which they emit an offensive odor), and gestation takes twelve months. Neither camel meat nor camel milk could ever have constituted a significant portion of the ancient Israelites' food supply. Those few Israelites such as Abraham and Joseph who owned camels would have used them strictly as a means of transport for crossing the desert.

This interpretation gains strength from the Moslem acceptance of camel meat. In the Koran, pork is specifically prohibited while camel flesh is specifically allowed. The whole way of life of Mohammed's desert-dwelling, pastoral Bedouin followers was based on the camel. The camel was their main source of transport and their main source of animal food, primarily in the form of camel milk. While camel meat was not daily fare, the Bedouin were often forced to slaughter pack animals during their desert journeys as emergency rations when their regular supplies of food were depleted. An Islam that banned camel flesh would never have become a great world religion. It would have been unable to conquer the Arabian heartlands, to launch its attack against the Byzantine and Persian empires, and to cross the Sahara to the Sahel and West Africa.

If the Levite priests were trying to rationalize and codify dietary laws, most of which had a basis in preexisting popular belief and practice, they needed a taxonomic principle which connected the existing patterns of preference and avoidance into a comprehensive cognitive and theological system. The preexisting ban on [[81]] camel meat made it impossible to use cud-chewing as the sole taxonomic principle for identifying land vertebrates that were good to eat. They needed another criterion to exclude camels. And this was how "split hooves" got into the picture. Camels have conspicuously different feet from cattle, sheep, or goats. They have split toes instead of split hooves. So the priests of Leviticus added "parts the hoof" to "chews the cud" to make camels bad to eat. The misclassification of the hare and *shāphān* suggests that these animals were not well known to the codifiers. The authors of Leviticus were right about the feet—hares have paws and *Hyrax* (and *Procavia*) have tiny hooves, three on the front leg and five on the rear leg. But they were wrong about the cud-chewing—perhaps because hares and *shāphān* have their mouths in constant motion.

Once the principle of using feet to distinguish between edible and inedible flesh was established, the pig could not be banned simply by pointing to its nonruminant nature. Both its cud-chewing status and the anatomy of its feet had to be considered, even though the pig's failure to chew the cud was its decisive defect.

This, then, is my theory of why the formula for forbidden vertebrate land animals was elaborated beyond the mere absence of cud-chewing. It is a difficult theory to prove because no one knows who the authors of Leviticus were or what was really going on inside their heads. But regardless of whether or not the good-to-eat formula originated in the way I have described, the fact remains that the application of the expanded formula to hare and *shāphān* (as well as to pig and camel) did not result in any dietary restrictions that adversely affected the balance of nutritional or ecological costs and benefits. Hare and *shāphān* are wild species; it would have been a waste of time to hunt them instead of concentrating on raising far more productive ruminants.

To recall momentarily the case of the Brahman protectors of the cow, I do not doubt the ability of a literate priesthood to codify, build onto, and reshape popular foodways. But I doubt whether such "top-down" codifications generally result in adverse nutritional or ecological consequences or are made with blithe [[82]] disregard of such consequences. More important than all the zoological errors and flights of taxonomic fancy is that Leviticus correctly identifies the classic domesticated ruminants as the most efficient source of milk and meats for the ancient Israelites. To the extent that abstract theological principles result in flamboyant lists of interdicted species, the results are trivial if not beneficial from a nutritional and ecological viewpoint. Among birds, for example, Leviticus bans the flesh of the eagle, ossifrage, osprey, ostrich, kite, falcon, raven, nighthawk, sea gull, hawk, cormorant, ibis, waterhen, pelican, vulture, stork, hoopoe, and bat (not a bird of course). I suspect but again cannot prove that this list was primarily the result of a priestly attempt to enlarge on a smaller set of prohibited flying creatures. Many of these "birds," especially the sea birds like pelicans and cormorants, would rarely be seen inland. Also, the list seems to be based on a taxonomic principle that has been somewhat overextended: most of the creatures on it are carnivores and "birds of prey." Perhaps the list was generated from this principle applied first to common local "birds" and then extended to the exotic sea birds as a validation of the codifiers' claim to special knowledge of the natural and supernatural worlds. But in any event, the list renders no disservice. Unless they were close to starvation and nothing else was available, the Israelites were well advised not to waste their time trying to catch eagles, ospreys, sea gulls, and the like, supposing they were inclined to dine on creatures that consist of little more than skin, feathers, and well-nigh indestructible gizzards in the first place. Similar remarks are appropriate vis-à-vis the prohibition of such unlikely sources of food for the inland-dwelling Israelites as clams and oysters. And if Jonah is an example of what happened when they took to the sea, the Israelites were well advised not to try to satisfy their meat hunger by hunting whales.

But let me return to the pig. If the Israelites had been alone in their interdictions of pork, I would find it more difficult to choose among alternative explanations of the pig taboo. The recurrence of pig aversions in several different Middle Eastern cultures strongly supports the view that the Israelite ban was a [[83]] response to recurrent practical conditions rather than to a set of beliefs peculiar to one religion's notions about clean and unclean animals. At least three other important Middle Eastern civilizations—the Phoenicians, Egyptians, and Babylonians—were as disturbed by pigs as were the Israelites. Incidentally, this disposes of the notion that the Israelites banned the pig to "set themselves off from their neighbors," especially their unfriendly neighbors. (Of course, after the Jews dispersed throughout pork-eating Christendom, their abomination of the pig became an ethnic "marker." There was no compelling reason for them to give up their ancient contempt for pork. Prevented from owning land, the basis for their livelihood in Europe had to be crafts and commerce rather than agriculture. Hence there were no ecological or economic penalties associated with their rejection of pork while there were plenty of other sources of animal foods.)

In each of the additional cases, pork had been freely consumed during an earlier epoch. In Egypt, for example, tomb paintings and inscriptions indicate that pigs were the object of increasingly severe opprobrium and religious interdiction during the New Kingdom (1567–1085 B.C.). Toward the end of late dynastic times (1088–332 B.C.) Herodotus visited

Egypt and reported that "the pig is regarded among them as an unclean animal so much so that if a man in passing accidentally touches a pig, he instantly hurries to the river and plunges in with all his clothes on." As in Roman Palestine when Jesus drove the Gadarene swine into Lake Galilee, some Egyptians continued to raise pigs. Herodotus described these swineherds as an in-marrying pariah caste who were forbidden to set foot in any of the temples.

One interpretation of the Egyptian pig taboo is that it reflects the conquest of the northern pork-eating followers of the god Seth by the southern pork-abstaining followers of the god Osiris and the imposition of southern Egyptian food preferences on the northerners. The trouble with this explanation is that if such a conquest occurred at all, it took place at the very beginning of the dynastic era and therefore does not account for the evidence that the pig taboo got stronger in late dynastic times.

My own interpretation of the Egyptian pig taboo is that it ⟦84⟧ reflected a basic conflict between the dense human population crowded into the treeless Nile Valley and the demands made by the pig for the plant foods that humans could consume. A text from the Old Kingdom clearly shows how during hard times humans and swine competed for subsistence: ". . . food is robbed from the mouth of the swine, without it being said, as before 'this is better for thee than for me,' for men are so hungry." What kinds of foods were robbed from the swine's mouth? Another text from the Second Intermediate period, boasting of a king's power over the lands, suggests it was grains fit for human consumption: "The finest of their fields are ploughed for us, our oxen are in the Delta, wheat is sent for our swine." And the Roman historian, Pliny, mentions the use of dates as a food used to fatten Egyptian pigs. The kind of preferential treatment needed to raise pigs in Egypt must have engendered strong feelings of antagonism between poor peasants who could not afford pork and the swineherds who catered to the tastes of rich and powerful nobles.

In Mesopotamia, as in Egypt, the pig fell from grace after a long period of popularity. Archaeologists have found clay models of domesticated pigs in the earliest settlements along the lower Tigris and Euphrates rivers. About 30 percent of the animal bones excavated from Tell Asmar (2800–2700 B.C.) came from pigs. Pork was eaten at Ur in predynastic times, and in the earliest Sumerian dynasties there were swineherds and butchers who specialized in pig slaughter. The pig seems to have fallen from favor when the Sumerians' irrigated fields became contaminated with salt, and barley, a salt-tolerant but relatively low-yielding plant, had to be substituted for wheat. These agricultural problems are

implicated in the collapse of the Sumerian Empire and the shift after
2000 B.C. of the center of power upstream to Babylon. While pigs continued to be raised during Hammurabi's reign (about 1900 B.C.), they virtually disappear from Mesopotamia's archaeological and historical
record thereafter.

The most important recurrence of the pig taboo is that of Islam. To
repeat, pork is Allah's only explicitly forbidden flesh. Mohammed's Bedouin followers shared an aversion to pig found [[85]] everywhere among
arid-land nomadic pastoralists. As Islam spread westward from the Arabian Peninsula to the Atlantic, it found its greatest strength among North
African peoples for whom pig raising was also a minor or entirely absent
component of agriculture and for whom the Koranic ban on pork did
not represent a significant dietary or economic deprivation. To the east,
Islam again found its greatest strength in the belt of the semiarid lands
that stretch from the Mediterranean Sea through Iran, Afghanistan, and
Pakistan to India. I don't mean to say that none of the people who
adopted Islam had previously relished pork. But for the great mass of
early converts, becoming a Moslem did not involve any great upending of
dietary or subsistence practices because from Morocco to India people
had come to depend primarily on cattle, sheep, and goats for their animal products long before the Koran was written. Where local ecological
conditions here and there strongly favored pig raising within the Islamic
heartland, pork continued to be produced. Carlton Coon described one
such pork-tolerant enclave—a village of Berbers in the oak forests of the
Atlas Mountains in Morocco. Although nominally Moslems, the villagers
kept pigs which they let loose in the forest during the day and brought
home at night. The villagers denied that they raised pigs, never took
them to market, and hid them from visitors. These and other examples
of pig-tolerant Moslems suggest that one should not overestimate the
ability of Islam to stamp out pig eating by religious precept alone if conditions are favorable for pig husbandry.

Wherever Islam has penetrated to regions in which pig raising was a
mainstay of the traditional farming systems, it has failed to win over substantial portions of the population. Regions such as Malaysia, Indonesia,
the Philippines, and Africa south of the Sahara, parts of which are ecologically well suited for pig raising, constitute the outer limits of the active spread of Islam. All along this frontier the resistance of pig-eating
"pagans," pig-eating Moslem heretics, and pig-eating Christians has prevented Islam from becoming the dominant religion. In China, one of the
world centers of pig production, Islam has made small inroads and is
[[86]] confined largely to the arid and semiarid western provinces. Islam,
in other words, to this very day has a geographical limit which coincides

with the ecological zones of transition between forested regions well suited for pig husbandry and regions where too much sun and dry heat make pig husbandry a risky and expensive practice.

While I contend that ecological factors underlie religious definitions of clean and unclean foods, I also hold that the effects do not all flow in a single direction. Religiously sanctioned foodways that have become established as the mark of conversion and, as a measure of piety, can also exert a force of their own back upon the ecological and economic conditions which gave rise to them. In the case of the Islamic pork taboos, the feedback between religious belief and the practical exigencies of animal husbandry has led to a kind of undeclared ecological war between Christians and Moslems in several parts of the Mediterranean shores of southern Europe. In rejecting the pig, Moslem farmers automatically downgrade the importance of preserving woodlands suitable for pig production. Their secret weapon is the goat, a great devourer of forests, which readily climbs trees to get at a meal of leaves and twigs. By giving the goat free reign, Islam to some degree spread the conditions of its own success. It enlarged the ecological zones ill suited to pig husbandry and removed one of the chief obstacles to the acceptance of the words of the Prophet. Deforestation is particularly noticeable in the Islamic regions of the Mediterranean. Albania, for example, is divided between distinct Christian pig-keeping and Moslem pig-abominating zones, and as one passes from the Moslem to the Christian sectors, the amount of woodland immediately increases.

It would be wrong to conclude that the Islamic taboo on the pig caused the deforestation wrought by the goat. After all, a preference for cattle, sheep, and goats and the rejection of pigs in the Middle East long antedated the birth of Islam. This preference was based on the cost/benefit advantages of ruminants over other domestic animals as sources of milk, meat, traction, and other services and products in hot, arid climates. It represents ⟦87⟧ an unassailably "correct" ecological and economic decision embodying thousands of years of collective wisdom and practical experience. But as I have already pointed out in relation to the sacred cow ⟦in a chapter not reprinted here⟧, no system is perfect. Just as the combination of population growth and political exploitation led to a deterioration of agriculture in India, so too population growth and political exploitation took their toll in Islamic lands. If the response to demographic and political pressures had been to raise more pigs rather than more goats, the adverse effects on living standards would have been even more severe and would have occurred at a much lower level of population density.

All of this is not to say that a proseletyzing religion such as Islam is incapable of getting people to change their foodways purely out of obedience to divine commandments. Priests, monks, and saints do often refuse delectable and nutritious foods out of piety rather than practical necessity. But I have yet to encounter a flourishing religion whose food taboos make it more difficult for ordinary people to be well nourished. On the contrary, in solving the riddle of the sacred cow and abominable pig, I have already shown that the most important food aversions and preferences of four major religions—Hinduism, Buddhism, Judaism, and Islam—are on balance favorable to the nutritional and ecological welfare of their followers.

The Hebrew Conquest of Palestine

GEORGE E. MENDENHALL

Introduction

⟦66⟧ There is no problem of biblical history which is more difficult than that of reconstructing the historical process by which the Twelve Tribes of ancient Israel became established in Palestine and northern Transjordan. The historical traditions in the Bible emphasize the religious significance of narrated events to the virtual exclusion of the kinds of information which the modern historian looks for and utilizes in his reconstruction of the past. This biblical emphasis upon the "acts of God" seems to modern man the very antithesis of history, for it is within the framework of economic, sociological and political organization that we of today seek understanding of ourselves and consequently of ancient man. When the scholar lacks sufficient data, he must resort to hypothesis either deliberately or unconsciously. He constructs an "ideal model" of what ought to have been the case, and his "ideal model" is inevitably based upon that which is known to have been true of other times and other places. The biblical scholar has utilized as an "ideal model" the process of sedentarization of nomadic tribes, or the irruption of barbaric hordes into civilized society. In the nineteenth century, when little was known of ancient Near Eastern history, the Islamic conquest or the Gothic sack of Rome perhaps seemed the most accessible analogies to the Israelite conquest of Palestine, but both of these events now appear in a light quite different from the views held of them in the nineteenth century. This paper represents a conscious attempt to substitute a quite different "ideal model" for that which has so long been held; the purpose of hypothesis ⟦67⟧ is not to give dogmatic

Reprinted with permission from *Biblical Archaeologist* 25 (1962) 66–87.

Editors' note: In the original article, several photos appeared that are not reproduced in this reprint.

answers to historical problems, but rather to suggest further fruitful lines of inquiry, and to suggest relationships between seemingly unrelated bits of information.

Present Views of the Conquest

There have been only two important views of the conquest of Palestine by ancient Israel. The traditional view presented in the biblical narratives has the Twelve Tribes invading en masse, conducting a systematic and progressive military campaign beginning in Transjordan and ending with the conquest of northern Palestine. Everyone will agree that the narrative is oversimplified, but many scholars hold that it is essentially correct. The correlation of the biblical narratives with archaeological investigation of cities mentioned is then used to support the validity of the narratives. Many of the Canaanite cities were destroyed about the middle of the thirteenth century B.C.E.[1]

The other scholarly hypothesis completely disconnects the Hebrew "conquest" from archaeological evidence of destruction, holding instead that the Hebrew Tribes merely infiltrated peacefully into the settled land and gradually became sedentary.[2] The destruction of cities had nothing to do with Israel. These radically different views of Israelite origins are the best indication of unfinished scholarly business; the impossibility of harmonizing the accounts of modern scholars which are based upon the same evidence makes it necessary to re-examine fundamental assumptions which underlie both reconstructions of early biblical history.

The tacit or expressed assumptions on which both reconstructions rest are the following:

a. That the Twelve Tribes entered Palestine from some other area just prior to or simultaneously with the "conquest."
b. That the Israelite tribes were nomads, or in more recent literature, "semi-nomads," who seized land and settled upon it during and after the conquest.
c. That the solidarity of the Twelve Tribes was an "ethnic" one, and that kinship was the basis of the contrast between Israelite and Canaanite.

There can be little doubt that the first and third assumptions are insisted upon by the biblical narratives with considerable emphasis, and

---

1. See G. E. Wright, *Biblical Archaeology* (Philadelphia [[Westminster]], 1957) 69–84.
2. Martin Noth, *The History of Israel* [[London: Black, 1960]] 146.

that insistence must be accounted for by any alternative theory. The assumption that the early Israelites were nomads, however, is entirely in the face of both biblical and extra-biblical evidence, and it is here that the reconstruction of an alternative must begin.

Nomadism in the Ancient World

[[68]] The Bedouin has been the object of considerable romancing for some time. The pattern of Bedouin life described in detail by Doughty[3] and Musil[4] has been utilized in an entirely uncritical fashion by biblical scholars[5] simply because it has been assumed that the Israelites *must* have been nomads before they became sedentary. The sharp contrast between nomad and sedentary villager then supposedly "explained" the peculiar religious and cultural traits of early Israel. That sharp contrast is hardly a justifiable conclusion in modern Saudi Arabia, as Matthews has recently pointed out.[6] There is hardly a Bedouin tribe which does not include some sedentary persons. The wanderings of the Bedouin are essentially "transhumance"; that is, migration from one particular area to another under the influence of seasonal changes in weather. Since the camel was not effectively domesticated until the Late Bronze Age or later, it is very precarious method to conclude from modern [[69]] Bedouin culture to early Israelite. Since even the modern Bedouin often have tribal ties with villages, no conclusions based upon an assumption of a radical contrast between nomad and villager are at all justifiable. That people wandered in the fringe areas of the desert in antiquity is certain; the evidence from both the Bible and the Mari documents very strongly suggests, however, that the pastoralist was a villager who specialized in animal husbandry, primarily because there was not enough tillable land to support the entire population of the village.[7] The Cain and Abel story presupposes as a matter of course that the shepherd and the farmer were brothers, just as most references to shepherds in ancient

3. C. M. Doughty, *Travels in Arabia Deserta* [[New York: Random, 1936]].

4. A. Musil, *Manners and Customs of the Rwala Bedouins* [[New York: American Geographical Society, 1928]].

5. Notably, in the writer's opinion, by J. Pedersen, *Israel* [[*Its Life and Culture* (London: Oxford University Press, 1926–40]], and S. Nyström, *Yahwismus und Bedouinentum* [[CWK Gleerup, 1946]]. At best, Bedouin may have preserved archaic culture traits which once were more widespread.

6. C. D. Matthews, "Bedouin Life in Contemporary Arabia," *Rivista degli Studi Orientali* 35 (1960) 31–61.

7. J. R. Kupper, *Les nomades en Mesopotamie* [[*au temps des rois de Mari* (Paris: Belles Lettres, 1957]], has greatly overestimated the amount of true nomadism in the Mari period. Much of the material refers simply to the seasonal transhumance of sheepherding villagers.

sources presuppose that the shepherd is a member of a city or village community subject to its law and entitled to its protection. The patriarchal narratives of the Bible present just this picture of the pastoralist. Jacob's sons travel with their flocks as far north as Dothan, but Jacob remains at home—he has a residence. Jacob himself is a shepherd in the service of Laban, but Laban and his family are resident in a city or village. There can be no doubt that sheepherding on a large scale existed already in the Bronze Age; the Mari documents refer incidentally to very large flocks of sheep and also to far-flung travels in search of pasture. But there is no justification for the conclusion as to a radical contrast between the shepherd culture and that of the village. There may have been true nomads during the Bronze Age; i.e., groups with no permanent habitations, such as the Sutu in the Mari letters, but they can, like the modern Bedouin, be safely regarded as statistically and historically negligible.[8] That such groups may have become sedentary in the course of time can be assumed; the present hypothesis concerning the conquest of Palestine merely maintains that this process had nothing to do with early Israel.

Tribes in the Ancient World

It is perhaps the fact that early Israel is divided into twelve "tribes" which accounts for the obsession of scholars that they must have been nomads originally. The city of Athens was divided into "tribes," as was Byblos at the time of the Execration Texts; but most of the people of modern Baghdad regard themselves as members of some "tribe."[9] In modern north Syria, villages are regarded as "non-tribal," or "tribal," or "mixed."[10] Furthermore, most non-urban cultures of the whole world have some kind of "tribal" organization.[11] [[70]] There is no justification whatever for the idea that a tribal organization must be an indication of an originally nomadic background. Finally, the Jericho and Jarmo excavations give full evidence of sedentary, agricultural communities at very remote periods of time; it is not necessary to assume a neat, unilinear evolutionary pattern of development from nomad to village to city which must be imposed upon every emergent culture, even though the development did take place from the Magdalenian cave-paintings to Jarmo to Nippur, and

8. Matthews, op. cit.

9. So I am informed by Mr. Sami Ahmed.

10. Louise Sweet, *Tell Toqaan: A Syrian Village* (Ann Arbor [[Museum of Anthropology, University of Michigan]], 1960) 18.

11. See the discussion, for example, of G. P. Murdock, *Social Organization* [[Washington, 1949]].

urbanization has been a characteristic of almost every culture termed civilization by the modern urbanized scholar.

What a "tribe" actually was in the Bronze Age is very difficult to determine. The tribe of Benjaminites of the Mari letters is certainly a large social complex with considerable geographical range and with at least four subsections. It is hardly likely that genealogical descent actually produced this, or any other tribe in antiquity. What constituted membership in a tribe was essentially a subjective feeling of belonging and loyalty, no doubt conditioned by the entire childhood and adult experience in the group and the orientation and indoctrination process which is an inevitable concomitant of a close-knit group in constant competition and conflict with outside groups. Added to this subjective attitude toward the group is the objective fact that the group would act in a concerted fashion to defend any member against the outside. Whatever else it may have been, tribal religion must inevitably have been an identification of deity with the social, economic, and political concerns of the "tribe," for the deity is constantly referred to in proper names as a kinsman of individuals. A tribe must be considered, then, as a larger unit of society which transcended the immediate environment of an individual, usually a village, upon which the village could rely for aid against attack too strong for it to cope with unaided. Because of this larger group loyalty, a village headman could treat even the royal officer with ill-disguised contempt,[12] and the policies of the tribe could impose limits upon the royal monopoly of force.[13] Urbanization eventually neutralizes tribal identity, for the urbanized society has rewards to offer which the tribe cannot approach, in wealth, power, and prestige plus the more intangible rewards of excitement, freedom from boredom, and magnificent spectacles which make the simple village celebrations seem naive and quaint if not laughable. The greater elaboration of urban culture, its wealth, pride and prestige, creates a deep schism between city and village. The problems which face urbanized man in competition with his fellow man are radically different from those of the villager [[71]] who must compete with the grasshopper, drought and weeds, in addition to the constant attempt to salvage as much as possible of his crop from the tax collector. It is between the city and the village that the primary contrast of ancient

12. See the classic retort of the *suqaqu* of Dumteti, a Benjaminite village, when called upon evidently to furnish persons for the corvée: "Let the enemy come and take us away from our village." [[J. R. Kupper,]] *Correspondance de Kibri-Dagan* [[ARM 3; Paris: Imprimerie Nationale, 1950]] 38, lines 15–22.

13. See the warning of Shamshi-Adad to Iasmakh-Adad not to carry out a *tebibtum* (military registration) of the Benjaminites. [[G. Dossin,]] *Correspondance de Samsi-Addu* [[ARM 4; Paris: Imprimerie Nationale, 1951]] 6, lines 6–13.

times lies, not between the village farmer and the shepherd who may be typically blood-brothers.

Hebrews in the Ancient World

This picture is, of course, highly theoretical and in part is a transference from observations of the modern world. It is of value, however, since it offers an alternative to the classical, indefensible, concept of the origins of the twelve tribes of Israel. One may begin by discussing the concept of "withdrawal." There can be no doubt that the conditions of urban society in antiquity as also today, resulted in the disvaluation of that society on the part of groups and individuals. The Code of Hammurabi already must make provision for the situation in which a person states, whether overtly or in effect, "I hate my king and my city." By this hatred, he has renounced any obligation to the society in which he formerly had some standing (if not status), and has in turn deprived himself of its protection. This is all that is meant by the term 'Hebrew' *Ḫab/piru*, *ʿApiru*, which recurs in many sources from 2000 B.C. to its last occurrences in the Hebrew Bible about the time of David, who was himself a Hebrew in this sense when he was fleeing from King Saul—not through choice, but through necessity of self-preservation. The very fact, then, that Israelite and Hebrew are practically synonymous terms in the Hebrew Bible itself should speak volumes to any sensitive historical imagination. For if the early Israelites were called 'Hebrews', they could be termed so only from the point of view of some existing, legitimate political society from which they had withdrawn. In other words, no one could be born a 'Hebrew'; he became so only by his own action, whether of necessity or by the inability any longer to tolerate the irrationalities of the society in which he was born.[14] The person who thus became a Hebrew would of necessity, whether in the ancient or the modern world, find some kind of acceptance in some other society, and the gamut of possibilities are well presented in the various treatments of the *Ḫab/piru* problem already published.[15] The Hebrew entered the service of a citizen in some other political community as a slave, or he banded together with other persons in a similar predicament to form a gang of freebooters like King David, or the group individually or as a unit entered the service of a foreign king, also like David in the service of Achish, king of Gath.

14. It might be comforting to realize that "gangs" and gang warfare have been an almost constant problem of highly developed states since before 2000 B.C.

15. See especially, Moshe Greenberg, *The Ḫab/piru* (New Haven [American Oriental Society], 1955), for a most useful collection of the materials.

⟦72⟧ The very valuable study of the Amarna *Ḫabiru* of Professor Campbell shows, however, that another alternative was known by those of Palestine and Syria who wished to withdraw from a political orientation.[16] Here we come face to face with a situation which has overtones of delicious irony. The similarity of the Amarna *Ḫabiru* to the Israelite Hebrews has been known for a long time, and even been utilized in the attempt to reconstruct early biblical history, but in an entirely misguided fashion. The biblical tradition ⟦73⟧ with its insistence upon invasion of Palestine by alleged nomads was unconsciously assumed to be the inevitable pattern, which was then imposed upon the Amarna letters, even though there is not the slightest hint of any outside invading forces being involved in the *Ḫabiru* activities of the Amarna period. The fact is, and the present writer would regard it as a fact though not every detail can be "proven," that both the Amarna materials and the biblical events represent politically the same process: namely, the withdrawal, not physically and geographically, but politically and subjectively, of large population groups from any obligation to the existing political regimes, and therefore, the renunciation of any protection from those sources. In other words, there was no statistically important invasion of Palestine at the beginning of the twelve tribe system of Israel. There was no radical displacement population, there was no genocide, there was no large scale driving out of population, only of royal administrators (of necessity!). In summary, there was no real conquest of Palestine at all; what happened instead may be termed, from the point of view of the secular historian interested only in socio-political processes, a peasant's revolt against the network of interlocking Canaanite city states.

What is a Hebrew Tribe?

Individuals who withdraw from an urbanized society rarely can cause a situation in which the society is threatened with extinction, but organized resistance within a political society is infinitely more dangerous than the plaintive voice of dissent of an individual, who can always be dismissed as a lunatic, or at least be decently put out of his misery by respectable, legal processes. There can be no doubt, however, that whole groups of persons possessed a solidarity of action in the ancient world which could be a great danger to constituted political organizations. This is the "tribe." The Hebrew conquest of Palestine took place because a religious movement and motivation created a solidarity among a large

16. *BA* 23 (1960) 1–22.

group of pre-existent social units, which was able to challenge and defeat the dysfunctional complex of cities which dominated the whole of Palestine and Syria at the end of the Bronze Age.

As is true of most such movements, the Israelite movement had most unlikely beginnings. A group of slave-labor captives succeeded in escaping an intolerable situation in Egypt. Without any other community upon which they could rely for protection and support, they established a relationship with a deity, Yahweh, who had no antecedents except in human traditions about ways in which God manifested Himself to human beings. A new God cannot create immediately a new language and a new culture. Contrary to older scholarly theories, the relationship to that deity was conditioned by an absolute obedience to certain norms in inter-personal relationships as well as [74] an absolute loyalty to the deity. From its very beginnings, the Yahwistic faith transcended tribal religion, for it was intended and actually functioned in a way to create a community above the tribal level. It is only a subsequent period of the religious history which made out of the faith a tribal religion, in which the function of the deity was regarded by a blind nationalism as merely the protection of tribal-national political and economic interests.

It was the common loyalty to a single Overlord, and obligation to a common and simple group of norms which created the community, a solidarity of loyalty which was attractive to all persons suffering under the burden of subjection to a monopoly of power which they had no part in creating, and from which they received virtually nothing but tax-collectors. Consequently, entire groups having a clan or "tribal" organization joined the newly-formed community, identified themselves with the oppressed in Egypt, received deliverance from bondage, and the original historic events with which all groups identified themselves took precedence over and eventually excluded the detailed historical traditions of particular groups who had joined later. It is for this reason that the covenant tradition is so overwhelmingly important in biblical tradition, for this was the formal symbol by which the solidarity was expressed and made functional. The symbolization of historical events was possible because each group which entered the covenant community could and did see the analogy between bondage and Exodus and their own experience.[17] Only when the tie between religious symbol and the primary historical experience of individuals and groups had become lost, did the cultic celebration become mere "re-enactment" and consequently mere ritual without the moral and ethical dynamic which was essential to the

17. Cf. Judg 6:9.

formative period of the faith. It is the prophetic tradition which preserved this essential tie between religious symbols and qualitative obligation, over against their society which since Saul had attempted to make
cultus a substitute for obedience (1 Sam 15:22–23), or simply a guarantee of security (Jer 7:1–15).

It was this religious affirmation of the value of historical events which
is still felt to be the unique feature of Israelite faith, and quite correctly,
but any cultic separation of religious values from the brute facts of historical reality must inevitably result in a radical transformation of the nature of religious obligation. It is for this reason that theology and history
must be inseparable in the biblical faith; biblical theology divorced from
historical reality ends in a kind of ritual docetism, and history apart from
religious value is a valueless secularized hobby of antiquarians.

⟦75⟧ The *value* of events which actually happened to the groups in
Transjordan and Palestine is thus the mainstream of biblical religion;
but it was the events which constituted the conquest, which became an
historical necessity once entire groups had joined the religious community. Not even the "city invincible" could coerce an entire countryside
into obedience. The subjection of individuals and groups to a non-human
Overlord by covenant, the solidarity of the newly formed community
meant that they could and did reject the religious, economic, and political obligations to the existing network of political organizations. By this
process, they became "Hebrews." The religious community of early Israel
created a contrast between the religious and the political aspects of
human culture which had been inseparable in the idea of the "divine
state" or the "divine kingship," for a complete identification of religious
with political authority and obedience, so characteristic of ancient and
modern paganism, became impossible. The early community created a
concept of obedience to norms which took precedence over the demands of any monopoly of force, and which was regarded as binding
upon the state when it was finally established with Saul and David. But the
state could not create the biblical norms of personal relationships by
power alone, and when the preservation of the state became the primary
concern of official political and religious leaders, the exercise of power,
unrestrained except by opposing power, became dominant, and the
prophets had to predict its ⟦76⟧ destruction. If politics be the science, or
more properly the art, of manipulating the monopoly of force which
every political state must be, the biblical faith was originally a most cou-
rageous, and one must add irrational, affirmation of the position that
above the monopoly of force stood a Power which judged and destroyed
power-monopolies. The ancient monopolies of force are now a subject of
investigation by eccentric academicians and cartoonists; the affirmation

of the biblical religious community still stands as a potential but recently dormant factor in human history, primarily because of an obsession with the concern for obtaining influence in modern power-monopolies, an obsession which is a tacit capitulation to the position of ancient paganism, that it is power which determines legitimacy, and therefore, right. Early Israel thus cannot be understood within the framework of traditional academic ideas about a primitive society gradually becoming urbanized, and therefore civilized. Its very beginnings involved a radical rejection of Canaanite religious and political ideology, especially the divine authority underlying the political institutions, and the Canaanite concept of religion as essentially a phenological cultic celebration of the economic concerns of the group—the fertility cult. Only under the assumption that the groups involved had actually experienced at first hand over a period of time the malfunctioning of Canaanite kingship, can one understand the concept of God in early Israelite religion, for the usual functions, authority, and prestige of the king and his court are the exclusive prerogative of deity. So, land tenure, military leadership, "glory," the right to command, power, are all denied to human beings and attributed to God alone. In this way, even the theological aspects of OT religion represent a transference from the political to the religious. Not until David is the old Canaanite legitimacy of kingship re-introduced, but considerably modified at first by the entrenched Israelite system of religious values. The best illustration of the continuity of Canaanite and indeed international patterns of thought is to be found in the covenant itself, the foundation of the religious unity of early Israel.[18]

Palestinian Politics and Society in the Late Bronze Age

Early Israelite tradition everywhere presupposes Canaanite culture as a contrast, or as the origin of certain features. The very insistence of early Israelite law upon a single norm or procedure to be binding upon every person, the amazingly tender concern for the slave which in effect made slavery a voluntary status, and for the non-citizen, presupposes a violent rejection of the highly stratified society of Late Bronze Canaan. Though many more illustrations of this conscious contrast could and should be offered, this is not the place. It can be summed up in the observation that Canaan is consistently ⟦77⟧ presented as the polar opposite to that which early Yahwism represented. This is best understood under the assumption that the earliest Israelites actually had been under the domination of the Canaanite cities, and had successfully withdrawn. Having become

18. See "Covenant Forms in Israelite Tradition," *BA* 17 (1954) 49–76.

independent, they were determined not immediately to reconstruct the same sort of power-centered, status-centered society as that which they had escaped, even though it was a constant temptation (Abimelech) to which they finally succumbed (Solomon).

Another impressive concern of early Israelite religion which is a striking contrast to Late Bronze Age Canaan is the preservation of the peace over a large territory. The Amarna letters illustrate beautifully the internecine warfare of city-state against city-state, in which the peasant must inevitably have suffered. The deliberate attempt of ambitious politicians to alienate the peasantry by making it impossible for them to till their fields is specifically mentioned in the Rib-Addi correspondence.[19] This cold-blooded policy was based upon the assumption that the masses would follow anyone who could exhibit [[78]] power, and therefore guarantee their security. To lay bare the powerlessness of Rib-Addi and the Egyptian empire meant to win the peasantry over, and the calculation evidently succeeded, for Rib-Addi had to confess that only half of even his own city, Byblos, "loved" the king of Egypt.[20] Here lies the basis of the biblical concept of the power of God, not in metaphysical speculation or ontology. It is a normative concept inseparable from ethical value, not a mere theological or cultic cliche. By making the struggle for power an illicit assumption of the prerogatives of God alone, the early Israelite religion laid the foundations for an internal peace which Canaanite society evidently could not do.

The activities of *Habiru* groups in the Amarna period break down into a rather well-formed pattern. In the first place, there is a conscious attempt to win support for the *Habiru* leader especially from the less privileged group (the *Khubšu*) in society. The exhibition of the powerlessness of the existing regime is only one such technique. Secondly, there is a constant threat to the existing king of assassination, to be followed by the replacement of a ruler who would be sympathetic to the *Habiru* leader—for the ruler would owe his royal throne to the *Habiru*.[21] Third, there would be an attempt to organize the whole of the disaffected on a broad territorial basis under the leadership of the *Habiru* chieftain, so that massive retaliation on the part of the Egyptian Empire could be warded off.[22] Though the conclusion is precarious, it is certainly worth recalling here the references to the "Gods of the *Habiru*" in Hittite suzerainty treaties—by making them witnesses to the treaty, attempt was

19. J. A. Knudtzon et al., *Die El-Amarna Tafeln* [[VAB 2; Leipzig: Hinrichs, 1915]] 81, lines 34–41.

20. Ibid., 138, lines 71–73.

21. Ibid., 73, lines 26–33.

22. Ibid., 74, lines 31–41.

made to make impossible any other *Ḫabīru* covenant community which would endanger the state.

Finally, a few remarks about land tenure are in order. Though very little evidence is available, there can be little doubt that land was often held, and perhaps always, as a grant, one might almost say fief, from the king. The wholesale buying and selling of villages attested in the Alalakh documents is a good indication of the complexity of real estate holdings in the North, in which the peasant farmer seems to have had little freedom, whatever his legal status may have been. When early Israel in effect declared that every farmer received his fief directly from Yahweh, each family enjoyed on a smaller scale the status of feudal lord, exactly as the covenant relationship to Yahweh conferred upon each person the status of vassal king, subject only to the will of God stipulated in the covenant itself. In this framework of religious conviction must be sought the origins of the idea of a "promised" or [[79]] a "holy" land. Territorial boundaries are a function of political administrators, and are probably an anachronism in the traditions of the twelve tribes, projected into the past from the administrative organization of the kingship. The land that belonged peculiarly to Yahweh was that which He had granted to anyone who stood in covenant relationship to Him. Tribal territory was similarly a function of the identification of persons who held land with a tribe; wherever a member of Yahweh's community tilled his own soil under the protection of deity and the religious community, there was "holy" (belonging to Yahweh) land.

The Process of Conquest

As mentioned above, the religious community had its beginnings in the escape from Egypt and the religious bond of the covenant which formalized and determined the responsibility and freedom of each member of the group. The mixed multitude and persons with tribal identification (Num 11:4) was thus formed into a community named Israel. All scholars seem to agree that this can have been only a small group; possibly the biblical tradition of 70 families is not too far from historical reality. The community survived in the desert by a succession of miracles, which is sufficient indication that the traditions at least did not regard them as nomads entirely adapted to desert environment. Miracle was necessary also to defend them against other tribal groups in the area, which emphasizes the lack of real military power in the group. Yet within the lifetime of Moses, Israel succeeded in destroying the two kingdoms which controlled the most fertile and wealthy areas of Transjordan, those of Sihon and Og, and are already settled in the whole land of Transjordan from the River Arnon to the land of Bashan. In another generation,

Israel is settled in Palestine proper from Beersheba to northern Galilee,
[[80]] and by the middle of the next century numbers some quarter of
a million people. It is no wonder that biblical scholars have questioned
the historical validity of the biblical narratives; but that doubt was based
entirely upon an entirely mistaken concept of the process, an assumption that the Israelites must originally have been nomads, and that they
are a distinct ethnic group [[81]] from the very beginning. The biblical
traditions give no hint of migration during this period from any other
source than Egypt, and the only demonstrable source of accessions is
from the population who were already settled on the land. In other
words, the appearance of the small religious community of Israel po-
larized the existing population all over the land: some joined, others,
primarily the kings and their supporters, fought. Since the kings were
defeated and forced out, this became the source of the tradition that all
the Canaanites and Amorites were either driven out or slain en masse,
for the only ones left were the predominant majority in each area—now
Israelites. It is for this reason that the king of Moab resorts to a curse,
not to attack, to neutralize Israel, for it is the alienation of persons in his
own kingdom which he wishes to prevent, not the defense of his kingship which was otherwise in no danger. There is no hint of any attempt
to follow up the victory over Sihon by taking over his previous domination of Moab. The curses which the Moabite king expected from Balaam
are the reverse side of the Baal-Peor incident (Num 25:1–9). If there
was to be no church unity, neither side would tolerate church merger!

This Transjordanian phase of the conquest has not received adequate attention, at least until quite recently. In the first place, the preservation of the taunt-song over the defeat of Moab by Sihon in Numbers
21 is of significance. Since the victory of Sihon must have taken place
some time before the appearance of Israel on the scene, the most likely
explanation for the inclusion of the poem in Israelite tradition is the
assumption that the event celebrated involved the interests of the group
who preserved it. Biblical tradition assigns the territory involved (South
of the Wadi Abu Gharaba) to the tribe of Reuben, according to tradition
the firstborn of Jacob/Israel. Since the entire area had very little if any
sedentary occupation before about 1300 B.C., the events may be reconstructed as follows.

With the increasing social and political instability in Palestine proper,
and the northern regions as well, groups migrated to the fringe areas
from the more populous regions to the West and North. The close connections of the Reubenites with Palestine proper have been noted by
Martin Noth.[23] Immediately the Moabite and Edomite kingdoms erected

---

23. *The History of Israel*, 63ff.

border fortresses, found by Nelson Glueck, to preserve their territorial integrity; these peoples cannot have been far removed culturally and linguistically from the group called Reuben. Migrations from the North brought organized military gangs (like that of Jephthah later), who established a military domination over the area which was populated by similar migrations from the central and northern parts of Palestine as well as by migrations from the north and northeast. These ⟦82⟧ military kingdoms of Sihon and Og were destroyed in battle, according to the biblical tradition, but those of Moab and Edom were not even attacked. Though the latter two refused transit to the Israelites, there was no actual attack. Sihon did attack, for in the meantime the population of his kingdom had been attracted by and perhaps already had joined the religious community of Israel; his army would consist of the professional soldiers who owed personal allegiance to him, but the population under his rule did not identify themselves with his regime, as did presumably the Edomites and Moabites. Therefore, the defeat was possible because of the support of a very large part of the villagers and shepherds of the region. Though the Midianites were ⟦83⟧ vassals (what does *nasik* mean in Josh 13:21? the verbal root would indicate a meaning nearly identical to messiah—one installed with authority by anointing) of Sihon, the defeat of Sihon did not result in their joining Israel; instead, we next hear of them as part of the kingdom of Moab (Balaam stories). A similar process involved northern Transjordanian peoples. Most interesting is the fact that the biblical traditions indicate close relationships between all these Transjordanian tribes and those of Palestine proper. Reuben's connections with Cisjordan have been mentioned above. Gilead is in early tradition taunted with being escapees from from Ephraim (Judg 12:4), and north Transjordan is from the very beginning populated by a "half-tribe" of Manasseh. In other words, existing social relationships antedated the beginnings of the "Conquest," and greatly facilitated, indeed made inevitable the crossing of the Jordan. For the destruction of undesired political domination over part of a larger social group would have been a success which attracted the rest with a hope for similar independence. A very considerable military potential was thus created practically overnight, and similar local actions of related groups in Palestine proper followed with rapidity. The oft-repeated observation that there is no account of the Conquest of the central hill country is negated by the list of kings in Joshua 13, which mentions kings of Tappuah, Hepher, Aphek, and Tirzah. Two of these names appear in Numbers 26 as subclans of Manasseh, actually village units as military recruiting districts.[24] Since the removal of these kings was done by local, indigenous groups, probably with

---

24. "The Census Lists of Numbers 1 and 26," *Journal of Biblical Literature* 77 (1958) 52–66.

no important military action involved, no narrative was preserved, but the significance of the event would not have been lost upon the other more powerful kings of the region. Since the independence movement already involved a solidarity of many groups over a large territory the immediate reaction would necessarily be that of age-old response to formidable opponents. Coalitions of city kings were hastily formed to meet the threat or to punish the rebels; no Canaanite king could have been without allies in that time and place. Battle became inevitable, for the kings were understandably unwilling to see their tax-basis reduced to nothing by the withdrawal of the food producers. However the details of crossing the Jordan, Jericho and Ai may eventually be resolved, there can be little doubt that the major threat to early Israel came from coalitions of kings; as this threat was successfully neutralized, victories were followed up by the destruction of cities some of which were resettled, some of which, like Lachish, could not be successfully held. It is not inconceivable that the campaign of Merneptah may have resulted in a considerable set-back to the progress of the destruction of the [[84]] royal powers, and dampened the enthusiastic optimism of the rapidly growing movement of Israel. In a period of considerable instability it is not at all inconceivable that certain territories or city regions might have changed hands twice or even more frequently.

The very strong tendency for down-dating the narratives attributed to the early period has been thus based upon a complete misconception as to what actually happened during the so-called Conquest. The rapid "settlement" of the Transjordanian lands is no problem at all, for the process had already taken place during the first half of the thirteenth century. Furthermore, the case of the taunt-song over Moab may be taken as illustrative of the process by which the pre-Mosaic traditions were preserved. Local populations which became Israelite by "conversion" continued to value their own traditions, poetry, historical narratives, and customs. These are only incidentally *ortsgebundene Traditionen* (traditions bound to geographical locations); they are traditions which were preserved because there is a continuity of population, and a continuity also of every feature of culture which was not a flagrant violation of the religious obligation to Yahweh.

Who Were the "Twelve Tribes" of Israel?

The narrative of Joshua 24 may be taken to be essentially historical, even though particular details may be indefensible. There can be no doubt any longer that important migrations from NE Syria had taken place perhaps as early as the Early Bronze IV period (2300–2000 B.C.). There can be no doubt that the religion of peoples from NE Syria, Amorites, was strongly tribe-centered, with the deity regarded as a member, so to speak, of the tribe. Joshua 24 cannot have any context in the entire history of Israel other than the very beginning, for it was only at the formative period of the community that existing social units were, or could have been, called upon to forsake their inherited tribal religion for the worship of Yahweh. Only here, and in the Song of Deborah (though the text is difficult) is there any hint of the idea of a deliberate choice of gods in the whole biblical literature. Early Israelite religion was thus emphatically not a "tribal" religion; tribal religion was one of the possible dangers which had to be outgrown for the sake of creating a larger unity among a most diverse and far-flung population. Early Yahwism continually had to cope with the dangers of a local particularism over against a larger unity necessary to meet the dangers from better organized and better armed political organizations. The sharp break with tribal religion emphasized in Joshua 24 contrasts as sharply as possible to the narrative in Exodus 3 and 6, in which Yahweh is deliberately identified with the god of the fathers. Yet both narratives in their historical context may well be correct, though the necessity of a break with the past at the beginning of the new [[85]] community is much more likely than the more compromising position of identifying Yahweh with the god of pre-Yahwistic times. In view of the strong appeal to the patriarchal period during the united monarchy, it seems much more likely that the idea of continuity, minimizing the discontinuity of religious tradition which was introduced with Yahwism, may have become much more useful at that time.

It would be naive in the extreme, however, to assume that all the twelve tribes were lineal descendants of immigrants from NE Syria. In the first place the *shibboleth* incident (Judg 12:6) demonstrates that the different segments of Israel did not even speak the same dialect of the NW Semitic language. Furthermore, the near identity of Hebrew to Canaanite proves that there could hardly have been any considerable contrast linguistically or ethnically between the Israelite tribes and the population of the Canaanite cities. Finally, the old tradition of Deuteronomy 26 which calls Jacob a "fugitive Aramean" cannot be lightly dismissed, particularly when there is good reason to think that the Transjordanian *shibboleth* dialect is proto-Aramaic, and the Song of Deborah contains a number of Aramaisims in spite of its early date. There can be nothing upon which the biblical traditions insist more strongly than the fact that "Israel" is specifically a *religious* community; the tradition that all the tribes were lineal descendants from a single ancestor is an attempt to give expression to a unity which was created by the religious factor, and is paralleled exactly by the attempt to express cultural relationships in [[86]] ancient civilizations generally by the identical procedure. So, the non-Semitic Elamites

become descendants of Shem; Philistines and Cretans are descendants of
Egypt, and so on. These express correctly important cultural connections,
the direction of cultural diffusion, but cannot be used as any indication
of any biological connection. The old thesis of Causse, *Du groupe ethnique
à la communauté religieuse* [an excerpt, "From Ethnic Group to Religious
Community," is reprinted in this volume, pp. 95–118], is exactly the
reverse of the historical truth. Israel began as a specifically religious community; only in the course of time and historical calamity did the religious community eventually rely largely upon biological continuity based
upon endogamy and considerable resistance to the access of ethnic outsiders. The Deuteronomic law presupposes that captive women from non-
Israelite cities taken in war will be married by the captor, and nowhere
is there any indication that marriage to a non-Israelite is a violation of
religious obligation. Early Israel was an ecumenical faith, a catholic religion in the best sense of the term the very purpose of which was to create
a unity among a divided and warring humanity. This it succeeded in mi-
raculous fashion in doing, until the blows of historical calamity, the
conflict with non-Yahwist neighbors, and the gradual dilution of the religious fervor reduced religion to the status of mere marker, mere support
for a political system, and finally a system of ritual and a cultural tradition
which served as a marker in a hostile world. From a source of unity, it became, like Islam and Christianity, a source of division and hostility.

From formation to fixed tradition takes only about three centuries, a
dozen generations. But the prophets, and ultimately Christianity kept
the older tradition alive. That is another story. There cannot longer be
much doubt that there was no basis for the unity of the twelve tribes before Moses; that unity was the function of the religion, and it is for this
reason that the religious obligation of relationship to a single deity was
so strongly emphasized during this period. Whether it should be called
monotheism is entirely a question of the modern definition of the term.
The religion itself was, however, almost the opposite to that which has
survived in manifold expressions of the biblical religion in the modern
world. Certainly each tribe had its particular traditions, its favorite ritual
and festival customs, its peculiar solidarity which threatened to take precedence over the religious obligations to the whole group. The uniqueness of early Israelite faith lies in the fact that these particularisms were
neither commanded nor prohibited except where they were clearly incompatible with the covenant obligations to Yahweh. Every man (and
every cult community!) was free to do what was right in its own eyes.
There is here a maturity of vision, a recognition of a concept of obligation which far transcends the narrow parochialism to which religion has
so tragically and frequently fallen, a parochialism which effectively bears

[[87]] witness to a substitution for a concern to realize in human life some quality which would be worthy of God, the universally human, divisive, and at worst vicious concern only for self-preservation of a particular group at the expense of humanity—and of God. It is not an instinct for self-preservation which kept the religious tradition alive, for it is this which induces groups and individuals to violate the tradition of religious obligation with a clear conscience, once the deity has become merely a symbol (a myth) for the existing cultural or cultic tradition of the cult-organization. The function of religion in human society varies greatly through time, but the formation of new religious communities cannot be explained simply as the result of the revelation of more effective ways of "worship." Religion in its formative period was simultaneously a bond between persons in an intolerable situation, and a way of life. In a period of traditionalism it becomes merely a way of worship, and a part of the total situation which makes life intolerable.

Israelite religion was then originally a view of man and of history which regarded sociological factors and economic or political power as secondary concerns of human beings; as such they were not the basis for understanding history, and for this reason the traditions tell little about them. All emphasis was upon the major symbolic expressions of divine aid, the Exodus and Sinai covenant; with these symbols the tribes identified their own predicament and delivery, and the mainstream of tradition emphasized what all had in common instead of particular acts or experiences of a single group. It may well have been also that the official version of Israelite history during the Monarchy was understandably loathe to describe the process by which villagers rejected the sovereignty of the kings who ruled them. One suspects that the northern ten tribes were acting with good religious precedent behind them when they cried, "What stake have we in David? To your tents, O Israel" (1 Kgs 12:16).

Domain Assumptions and Societal Models in the Study of Pre-Monarchic Israel

NORMAN K. GOTTWALD

[[89]] The American sociologist Alvin Gouldner speaks of "domain assumptions," by which he means the key or master conceptual frames of reference which affect the kinds of models and hypotheses that are imaginable—and therefore possible—in an epoch or circle of scholarship. The commanding domain assumptions are characteristically unexpressed or half-expressed and unargued. Shifts in models and hypotheses occur when new domain assumptions arise under the pressure of accumulating evidence and, more especially, under the impact of new extrascholarly intellectual and cultural climates.[1]

Precisely such a shift in domain assumptions is under way in the study of Israelite beginnings. In a volume shortly to be published, I attempt to articulate the old and the new domain assumptions and to offer a societal model for pre-monarchic Israel consonant with the new domain assumptions. I shall here summarize the main outlines of my argument, with particular attention to the links between the domain assumptions in ancient Near Eastern and biblical studies, on the one hand, and the models

Reprinted with permission from *Congress Volume: Edinburgh, 1974* (Vetus Testamentum Supplements 28; Leiden: Brill, 1975) 89–100.

Author's note: The theses advanced in this lecture will appear in greatly expanded and documented form in the lecturer's forthcoming study, *A Sociology of the Religion of Liberated Israel, 1250–1000 B.C.* [[published as *The Tribes of Yahweh: A Sociology of the Religion of Liberated Israel 1250–1050 B.C.E.* (Maryknoll, New York: Orbis, 1979 / London: SCM, 1980)]].

1. A. W. Gouldner, *The Coming Crisis of Western Sociology* [[New York: Basic Books]], 1970.

of Israelite society, on the other. By way of more detailed application, I shall have a few comments about the historical peculiarity of Israelite tribalism or "retribalization."

The history of the study of Israelite beginnings is a history of very slowly emerging self-consciousness about domain assumptions and societal models, chiefly I think because anthropology and sociology never have had the impact on biblical studies that the humanities have had. The traditional conquest/invasion model of Israelite origins scarcely raised a single sociological question because it [[90]] contained an implicit unexamined, albeit rudimentary, sociology of Israel. It assumed a twelve-tribe system composed of clans and families as sub-sets of tribes operating as an unquestioned counterpart to the miraculously formed religious community of Israel. The immigration model, especially in the form it assumed under Noth's amphictyonic analogue,[2] pushed sociological considerations a bit farther into the foreground, but not so far after all—and perhaps for three main reasons:

1. Noth's welcome systemic approach to Israel was really mainly focused on one societal segment, the cultic institutions, rather than on the entire social system.
2. Noth's approach took for granted the semi-nomadic origins of Israel without argument.
3. Noth failed to compare the structural locus of the amphictyony in Greece with the structural locus of the "amphictyony" in Israel. Had he done so, it would have been clear that the amphictyony in Greece was a secondary or tertiary formation within the wider society, whereas the presumed "amphictyony" in Israel was the encompassing framework of the entire society.

Within the last decade the revolt model of Israelite origins has exposed the social structural and developmental questions about early Israel in an emphatic and insistent manner. The fact that Mendenhall prefaced and framed his model of "peasant revolt" or "withdrawal" with a discussion of pastoral nomadism and tribalism in relation to urban and rural modes of ancient Near Eastern life thrusts the problem of the modes of Israel's occupation of the land into a larger context, namely, the problem of the social organizational modes of the Israelite occupiers.[3]

2. M. Noth, *Das System der zwölf Stämme Israels*, 1930 [[Stuttgart; repr., Darmstadt: Wissenschaftliche Buchgesellschaft, 1966]], and, in brief compass, *The History of Israel*, 2nd ed., 1960 [Eng. trans. [[New York: Harper]] 1960] 85–138.

3. G. E. Mendenhall, "The Hebrew Conquest of Palestine," *The Biblical Archaeologist Reader* 3 (1970) 100–120 = *The Biblical Archaeologist* 25 (1962) 66–87; *The Tenth Generation. The Origins of the Biblical Tradition* [[Baltimore: Johns Hopkins University Press]], 1973.

Until very recent years the inquiry into Israel's early history was massively under the sway of at least three master ideas which I shall characterize as:

1. The Domain Assumption of Social Change by Population Displacement.
2. The Domain Assumption of the Creativity of the Desert in Initiating Social Change in Sedentary Regions. ⟦91⟧
3. The Domain Assumption of Arbitrary Social Change Produced by Idiosyncratic or Prominent Cultural Elements.

These domain assumptions may be briefly stated as follows:

1. It is assumed that a major socio-political shift or hiatus is most likely to have been the result of one demographic or ethnic group displacing another, either wholesale or as a ruling elite, whether by immigration or by military conquest.
2. It is assumed that the breeding ground and source of many such population displacements in the ancient Near East was the desert and that these displacements entailed an influx of military and cultural élan typical of the desert group, followed by an eventual transition of the immigrants or invaders from nomadic to sedentary life with resulting socio-political acculturation.
3. It is assumed that the most idiosyncratic, prominent or distinctive element of a new socio-political phase, especially as viewed in retrospect, must have been the nuclear factor which initiated other sorts of changes and constellated them into a new social system or culture. Since the religio-symbolic and cultic dimensions of Israelite society appear to be the most idiosyncratic elements, particularly as viewed from the perspective of later Judaism and Christianity, Yahwism is to be regarded as the isolate source and agent of change in the emergence of Israel.

The pressures and forces which have eroded these long-standing domain assumptions are numerous and I shall cite only a few of them in catalogue form: evidence from pre-history and ethnography that pastoral nomadism is a secondary outgrowth of plant and animal domestication in the sown land; indications from the study of zones of social organization and from cultural anthropology that seemingly sudden cultural and social change is as often the consequence of slow growth and sharpening social conflict within a population continuum as it is the result of fresh incursions of peoples, that conflict occurs as regularly within societies under single political regimes as between opposing states, and that technology and social

organization shape ideas more profoundly by far than humanities-oriented
scholars have understood; demonstrations from sociology of religion that
the social functions of religion are intrinsic to the form religion takes even
in its most distinctive higher features; signs from historical data on the
ancient Near East and early Israel of the subsidiary role [[92]] of pastoral
nomadism within the village-based economy, of the desert as a zone of
political resistance and asylum rather than the locus of alien political and
military initiatives, and of Israel's fundamental cultural continuity with
Canaan over a very wide repertory, including language and religious formations, simultaneously combined with Israel's sharp divergence from
Canaan in the development both of tribalism in opposition to the state and
of a distinctively elaborated religious system. Probably not the least as a
general encompassing factor in the deterioration of the old domain assumption is the direct experience of social upheaval in the modern world
which more often follows from technological change and from tension and
conflict within populations over control of resources and their distribution
than from actual population displacements.

New domain assumptions are implicit in sociological work on Israelite
beginnings now going on in the United States, so far most fully published
by George Mendenhall, soon to be enlarged by this lecturer's publication,
and shared in by a growing number of younger scholars. Among others,
students of Mendenhall at the University of Michigan and of Frank Cross
and Ernest Wright at Harvard University have contributed measurably to
this development, generally in the form of unpublished dissertations and
brief articles. Similar trends toward the application of social scientific
methods to ancient Israel are beginning to surface in Israel, in western
Europe and in the third world. A parallel phenomenon is visible among
students of the ancient Near East.

The emerging master concepts, in each case challenging and replacing its outmoded predecessor, may be characterized as:

1. The Domain Assumption of the Normalcy of Social Change by
   Inner Societal Pressure and Conflict.
2. The Domain Assumption of the Subordinate Role of the Desert
   in Precipitating Social Change.
3. The Domain Assumption of Lawful Social Change Produced by
   the Interaction of Cultural Elements at Many Levels.

The substance of these new domain assumptions may be briefly stated as
follows:

1. It is assumed that major socio-political shifts or hiatuses are to
   be expected within societies as the result of new technological

forces, social conflicts and contending ideas in volatile interaction [[93]] and that social change due to population displacement or political conquest is to be posited only when specific evidence warrants.

2. It is assumed that semi-nomadism in the ancient Near East was economically and politically subordinate to and broadly integrated within the dominant agricultural zone and was never the source of massive population displacement or political conquest as commonly attributed to it.[4]

3. It is assumed that the initially or ultimately prominent or distinctive features of a society or culture must be viewed in the total matrix of generative elements and not over-weighted in advance as the all-powerful sources of inspiration or as the selective survival factors in the societal development. Thus, a critical generative role may well have been played by cultural elements which have been lost to view and must be recovered by careful research. In particular, ideational factors must be looked at not as disembodied prime movers but as the ideas of human beings in determinate technological and social settings in which the total mix of culture will tend to exhibit lawful or patterned configurations.[5]

Congruent with these domain assumptions, I propose a societal model for early Israel along the following lines: Early Israel was a slowly converging and constellating cluster of rebellious and dissenting Canaanite peoples distinguished by an anti-statist form of social organization with de-centralized leadership. This Israelite "devolution" or "winding down" from the city-state form of social organization took the shape of a "re-tribalization" movement among agriculturalists and pastoralists organized in economically self-sufficient extended families with egalitarian access to basic resources. Israel's religion, which had intellectual and cultic foundations in ancient Near Eastern-Canaanite religion, was idiosyncratic or mutational in a manner that its society was idiosyncratic and mutational, i.e., one integrated divine being existed for one integrating

4. For the evidence, see N. K. Gottwald, "Were the Early Israelites Pastoral Nomads?" *Proceedings of the Sixth World Congress of Jewish Studies* held in Jerusalem, 13–19 August, 1973 [[(Jerusalem: Magnes, 1977) 1.165–89 = *Rhetorical Criticism: Essays in Honor of James Muilenberg* (ed. J. J. Jackson and M. Kessler; Pittsburgh Theological Monograph Series 1; Pittsburgh: Pickwick, 1974) 223–55]].

5. For a cogent, methodical, richly illustrated presentation of theories of lawful cultural change, see M. Harris, *The Rise of Anthropological Theory. A History of Theories of Culture* [[New York: Crowell]], 1968.

and egalitarianly structured people. Israel became that segment of Canaan which wrested sovereignty from another segment of Canaan in the ⟦94⟧ interests of village-based tribally-oriented "low politics" over against city-state hierarchic "high politics."

So far it can be seen that I am in broad agreement with Mendenhall's basic design of Israelite origins. One of the points where we diverge, however, is the point at which he denies the sphere of politics to early Israel. Mendenhall reads Israel's rejection of state power as tantamount to the rejection of socio-political power per se: "The starting point of politics is the concern for power, but the whole theme of early biblical history . . . is the rejection of power."[6] It is obvious, however, that without a central concern for marshalling and employing power Israel could never have come into existence. Prompted by his fascination with the suzerain-vassal treaty as the supposed model for Israel's early covenant, Mendenhall has bracketed out the divine monopoly of power from socio-political analysis. Clearly, we face two interlocking sociological phenomena to be accounted for in their peculiar combination: (1) Israel challenged one form of power by means of another form of power, and (2) Israel consciously exercised power even as it consciously attributed the source of all power to its deity. In failing to deal with the Israelite power formation sociologically, it appears to me that Mendenhall has not adequately assimilated the new domain assumption concerning lawful social change.

At this juncture I propose to follow up and extend somewhat the tribal model of early Israel, first in synchronic terms and then in diachronic terms.

A considerable body of social organizational work on the tribe suggests the following broad formal features or traits of tribal organization:[7]

1. The tribe represents a sharp increase in demographic size over the hunting and gathering or primitive agricultural band, normally a leap from fewer than one hundred people to several hundreds or thousands.
2. The population increase is closely connected with a more secure control over an enlarged food surplus.
3. The enlarged food surplus is secured not only by technological improvements but by more intricate social bonding by means of

6. G. E. Mendenhall, *The Tenth Generation*, 195.
7. See, for example, M. Sahlins, *Tribesmen* ⟦Englewood Cliffs, N.J.: Prentice-Hall⟧, 1968, and J. Helm (ed.), *Essays on the Problem of Tribe* (Proceedings of the 1967 Annual Spring Meeting of the American Ethnological Society ⟦Seattle: University of Washington Press⟧, 1968).

⟦95⟧ many cross-cutting associations or sodalities which inter-
connect the residential units, notable among these associations being the exogamous clan.
4. The sub-divisions of the tribe are typically segmented, i.e., they
   are structurally and functionally equivalent and politically equal,
   so that in principle any one of them could be destroyed and the
   tribe would survive.
5. The tribe carries out its political functions by diffused or temporary role assignments in such a way that there is no political
   leadership network distinguishable from the network of social
   leadership, although the rudiments of specialized political leadership appear with the tribal chiefdom.

Viewed in the broad design of social forms, pre-monarchic Israel was
clearly tribal in character. Israel's economy was a form of intensive rain
agriculture with animal husbandry, an economy which capitalized on the
recent introduction into the highlands of Canaan of iron implements
for clearing and working the land, of slaked lime plaster for constructing
water-tight cisterns to hold reserve water through the annual dry season,
and of the art of rock terracing to retain and control the erratic rainfall. The members of Israelite society were arranged not only in large
extended residence groups which were relatively self-contained socioeconomic units and political equals but also in cross-cutting sodalities or
sodality equivalents. Among these cross-cutting groupings were the protective associations of extended families (the *mishpāḥoth*, which were *not*
exogamous clans in my view), the citizen army, the ritual congregation,
the Levites (landless and distributed among the tribes), and probably
also the Rechabites (understood as itinerant specialists in metal).[8]

On the other hand, Israel was not yet a state, which it became only
fully under David. Tendencies toward the chiefdom and monarchy are
clearly evidenced in Saul and even earlier in some of the diverse functionaries called obscurely "judges," notably Gideon and Abimelech, and
perhaps also some of the so-called "minor judges" such as Ibzan. At its
founding Israel had no specialized political offices rooted in a superordi-
nate sovereignty and it resisted such institutions and offices strenuously
even after reluctantly resorting to them in the in face of the mounting
Philistine military threat, which was itself a powerful and effective re-
grouping of socio-political ⟦96⟧ formations from the preceding era of
Egyptian imperialism and Canaanite quasi-feudalism.

The defining feature of politics in old Israel was that political functions were diffused throughout the social structure or focused in tempo-

8. F. S. Frick, "The Rechabites Reconsidered," *JBL* 90 (1971) 279–87.

rary ad hoc role assignments. While the details of Israel's social structure (and especially of its "offices") are as yet unrecoverable in many respects, so that we do not possess the fully rounded cross-section we desire, all available information supports consistently the view that early Israel was tribal with fiercely resisted tendencies toward the chiefdom. And we are also able to establish beyond any shadow of doubt that this political feature of Israelite tribalism was not derived from pastoral nomadism but was securely rooted in a form of agricultural tribalism for which there are ample parallels in ethnography.

Of course the gross typological-evolutionary scale of band, tribe and state does not provide a finely calibrated historical understanding of specific societies. The historical locus of early Israel is thus of decisive importance for understanding the precise mix of factors and tendencies at work in its social organizational development.

The insights of Morton Fried concerning tribal formations as "secondary phenomena" are pertinent for understanding Israel's peculiar tribalism, granting that Fried's position is adjudged extreme by most anthropologists when applied to all tribal societies.[9] Fried points out that many tribes are known to us in colonial situations where the external pressure of more highly organized and dominant civilizations leads to administrative synthesis and consolidation of the threatened society internally, so that it comes to present the form of a tribe to those who dominate the society. He cites the Makah of Washington State, the Tonga of northern Rhodesia and the Chiga of Uganda.

> Most tribes seem to be secondary phenomena in a very specific sense: They may well be the product of processes stimulated by the appearance of relatively highly organized societies amidst other societies which are organized much more simply. If this can be demonstrated, tribalism can be viewed as a reaction to the formation of complex political structure rather than a necessary preliminary stage in its evolutions.[10]

[[97]] Fried notes that this is hardly a development peculiar to European colonialism since "the Roman, the Chinese, and other expanding state societies had grasped the essentials of divide and rule."[11]

---

9. M. H. Fried, *The Evolution of Political Society. An Essay in Political Anthropology* [[New York: Random]], 1967, pp. 154–74, and with some expansion in "On the Concepts of 'Tribe' and 'Tribal Society,'" *Essays on the Problem of Tribe* (ed., J. Helm), 1968, pp. 3–20, accompanied by caveats and alternative views in several essays in the same volume, particularly those by G. E. Dole, by H. S. Lewis, and by R. Cohen and A. Schlegel.

10. M. H. Fried, *The Evolution of Political Society*, 170.

11. Ibid., 173.

If we modify his "most tribes" to "some tribes" or "many tribes," Fried's insight may be taken seriously as an indication of the way a centralized state may intrude on simpler societies and harden them into certain social formations. But surely Fried does not mean to imply that these simpler societies were entirely indisposed to the tribal direction in which the more organized societies pushed them. It would be stretching his argument ridiculously far to claim that segmentation and the exogamous clan were imposed by colonial powers. These integral elements of tribalism must be closely connected with economic production. Fried himself admits the pertinence of Elman Service's contention that the tribal organization extends the peace group and enhances military effectiveness in a world of competing bands and tribes, quite apart from and prior to the entrance of state societies on the tribal scene.[12]

Under the circumstances, Fried's model must be altered considerably to apply to Israel. This can be done fruitfully if we allow not only that colonial centralized states can shape tribalism within a subject people, solidifying and skewing elements already present, but if we also posit that elements of the population within or adjacent to a centralized state may withdraw from it or rebel against it and develop less centralized social forms both as defensive mechanisms against the state and as constructive alternatives to the state. What these two versions of the social organizational effect of opposed centralized and uncentralized societies have in common is the abrasive or openly conflicting juxtaposition of societies at different organizational levels and the critical selective organizational impact of the "stronger" and more complex party upon the "weaker" and less complex party.

In my assessment we should view Israelite tribalism as a form chosen by people who consciously rejected Canaanite centralization of power and deliberately aimed to defend their own uncentralized system against the effort of Canaanite society to crush their movement. Israel's tribalism was an autonomous project which tried to roll back the zone of political centralization in Canaan, to claim territories and peoples for an egalitarian mode of agricultural and pastoral life. Unquestionably there were significant antecedent forms of struggle [[98]] and modes of organization which fed into Israelite tribalism,[13] but in terms of demographic size, organizational novelty and political effectiveness there was a far greater qualitative leap from pre-Israelite to Israelite tribalism than

12. Ibid., 164–65.
13. For an explication of the immediate antecedents of Israelite tribalism, see N. K. Gottwald, *A Sociology of the Religion of Liberated Israel, 1250–1000 B.C.*, to be published in 1975, chaps. 8 and 9 [[part VI of *The Tribes of Yahweh*, 1979]].

there was from pre-colonial to post-colonial tribalism among the Makahs, Tongas or Chigas. The sum of these qualitative differences suggests that we should speak of Israel's adaptive tribalism as a "re-tribalization" movement.

All the evidence for early Israel points to its tribalism as a self-constructed instrument of resistance and of decentralized self-rule rather than tribalism as an administrative structure imposed by Canaanite rulers in order to govern their proto-Israelite or Israelite subjects. Seen from the perspective of Canaanite society, Israel was not a resistant colonial underling to be subdued but a foreign growth in its own body to be cut out. Seen from Israel's perspective, its tribalism was not a continuous ancient development to be preserved but a freshly constructed instrument for "cracking open" the centralized and stratified appropriation of natural and human resources of which the people forming Israel were an essential part prior to their act of revolt. Israel's tribalism was politically conscious social revolution and, more loosely, a civil war in that it divided and counterposed peoples who had previously been organized within Canaanite city-states.

At this point, however, I would introduce another factor into the socio-political dynamics of Israelite origins, for it is the omission of this factor from Mendenhall's model which contributes to the air of unreality which many critics have detected in his hypothesis. I refer to the fact that in virtually all such revolutions and civil wars the polarization of the populace is far from complete. There is evidence that a sizable part of the Canaanite populace was "caught in the middle," staying neutral as long as possible and only reluctantly moving toward one side or the other, thus constituting a socio-political segment whose loyalty or passive cooperation was actively sought by the contending parties.[14]

The implications of this concrete historical understanding of Israel's leap to tribalism are enormous. It means that our image of Israel's formation cannot be that of a continuous line of cultural evolution upwards from the band society to tribal forms of segmentation [[99]] and sodality formation, nor can our image be that of a spill-over or eruption of pastoral nomadism from the desert into the settled land. Our image of Israel's formation must be that of a profound discontinuity in the hierarchic feudal social fabric of Canaan, a rupture from within centralized society. This rupture was accomplished by an alliance of peoples who withdrew directly from the Canaanite system with other peoples who, beyond the centralized system's immediate reach in the hinterland of

14. Cf. ibid., chap. 9 [[parts VIII and IX in *The Tribes of Yahweh*]], for a treatment of Canaanite enemies, converts, neutrals and allies vis-à-vis Israel.

Canaan, refused the customary path of being drawn into that system and accommodating themselves to it.

In terms of Fried's typology, Canaan did not make an "appearance" in a long-developed or latent tribal society called Israel. To the contrary, Israel, with a mutant sophisticated tribal mode of organization, made an "appearance" within the social system and territorial domain of Canaan. The people who came to be Israelites countered what they experienced as the systematic aggression of centralized society by a concrete, coordinated, symbolically unified social revolutionary action of aggressive self-defense against that society. Appropriating the land and economic modes of production, this body of people organized its production, distribution and consumption along essentially egalitarian lines. The specific historic rise of old Israel was thus a conscious improvisational reversion to egalitarian social organization which displaced hierarchic social organization over a large area which had been either directly or indirectly dominated by Canaanite centralization and stratification for centuries.

The above model of Israelite re-tribalization as an inner Canaanite phenomenon raises whole chains of additional questions for further research and theoretical reflection. Is anything to be learned about the re-tribalizing confederacy of Israel from the history and typology of other inter-tribal confederacies such as the Iroquois Five Nations? Is there an analogy between post-Minoan and post-Mycenean Greek society and early Israel, as Mendenhall has briefly suggested? Is anything further to be learned about the earliest Greek amphictyony of pre-Delphic times which centered at Pylae and which might after all be more cogently analogous with early Israel than the relatively late, perhaps already much decomposed, form of the amphictyony which Noth treated? With what relevant social systems are we to compare early Israel? Certainly the Canaanite city-state and the Egyptian empire are prime units for comparison. But what of the ʿapiru which appear in part as a special deviant form of passive ⟦100⟧ resistance to Canaanite society and in part as a forerunner and contributory component of early Israel? How can our view of the previously over-inflated and misconstrued pastoral nomadic society be phrased so as to include it as a special ecological nuancing either of the city-state system or of the village-based agricultural system in conflict with the city-state? What allowance must be made for Mendenhall's recent contention that there was a considerable movement of Luwians, Hittites, Hurrians and other northerly peoples into Palestine attendant on the incursion of the Sea Peoples?[15] Were these people carriers of a major new social system or, more likely, did they join the ranks of

---

15. Mendenhall, *The Tenth Generation*, chap. 6.

both sides of the inner-Canaanite struggle between low and high politics, or opt for uneasy neutrality? What are we to make of the Ammonites, Moabites and Edomites of whose beginnings we still know so appallingly little? Will the present slight improvement in our archaeological data on these trans-Jordanian peoples allow us to form any clearer picture of their social structure? This glaring blank in our knowledge of Israel's neighbors becomes all the more tantalizing in the light of the model advanced above for early Israel's social origins. Why were those Ammonites, Moabites and Edomites, whose origins are presumed to have been rather similar to Israel's origins, *not* a part of Israel? Why did the social revolutionary movement of early Israel extend only so far in the trans-Jordanian highlands and no farther? Were social elements among the Ammonites, Moabites and Edomites part of the general social uprising which failed to develop to a breakthrough point as it did with Israel? Finally, can a re-oriented Palestinian archaeology be of increasing assistance in checking social and cultural hypotheses, comparable for example with the function of "the new archaeology" in checking out hypotheses in new world ethnography?[16]

These are but a few of the proliferating questions which sharply pose the need for new research strategies and new forms of collaboration among specialists in order to seek additional evidence and to reassess old evidence within the framework of rapidly maturing sociological analyses of old Israel.

16. A. E. Glock, director of excavations at Taanach, has proposed an ethnographic model for Palestinian archaeology in a paper on "Archaeological Systematics" which he presented to a seminar of resident fellows at the Albright Institute of Archaeological Research in Jerusalem on 3 May 1974. It is anticipated that a revised and enlarged form of this paper will be shortly published.

Sacrifices and Offerings in Ancient Israel: An Introduction

GARY A. ANDERSON

The Distinctive Nature of the Israelite Cult

⟦1⟧ The most important social and political institution in tribal Israel was the cult of the league's patron deity.[1] The cultic gatherings of the Israelites were the primary fashioners of social and religious unity. The league shrine functioned as the meeting place for the muster of the militia and it was to this shrine that the victorious warriors returned with the spoils of

Reprinted with permission from *Sacrifices and Offerings in Ancient Israel: Studies in Their Social and Political Importance* (Harvard Semitic Monographs 41; Atlanta: Scholars Press, 1988) 1–14, 19–23.

Editors' note: We have deleted section C, "Sacrifice as Food for the Gods?" from our excerpt. In it, Anderson questions the commonly held distinction between Israel and its neighbors concerning the function of sacrifice. He shows that there are numerous examples in the Hebrew Bible of Israelites perceiving sacrifice as food for Yahweh, contra R. de Vaux (*Studies in Old Testament Sacrifice* [Cardiff: University of Wales Press, 1964]), who held that this notion was either a vestige of earlier, primitive Canaanite ideas or a result of Mesopotamian influence on the Priestly school during the exilic period. Anderson further shows, by a comparative analysis of the Old Babylonian and Standard Babylonian texts of the Atrahasis Epic, that Mesopotamian scribes had adopted a more cosmic view of sacrifice over time.

1. This study is concerned exclusively with the pan-tribal YHWHistic cult. Although Israel's religion will be spoken of only in terms of this public manifestation the writer acknowledges the varied types of religious expression which were to be found in the private cults of individual families or extended clan groups. The public cult of YHWH was not the only form of religious expression in ancient Israel, but it is one of the few to which modern scholarship has access.

battle.[2] Unlike the city-state which had enforceable, centralized programs of military conscription and taxation, the tribal league's constitution was much more tenuous. The league had to depend on tribal participation in the cult of the league shrines for both its muster and its collection of offerings.[3] Indeed it is difficult to speak of an entity "Israel" in the tribal period outside of the gathered body of clan members around the shrines of their patron, YHWH.[4]

It is most likely for this reason that the religion of a tribal confederation is typologically distinct from that of the city-state. As Cross has noted: "In Phoenician and Aramean city states there are city gods, triads of city gods, and patron gods of the king who often differ from the chief city gods, but in both documentary evidence and in the onomastica, we find multiple state deities [[2]] and personal deities."[5] It is different in the tribe. There the tribal members bind themselves to one particular god, the patron of that tribe.

. . . .

The concept of a tribal clan bound to a single patron deity presumes some type of covenant.[6] For tribal groups, the language of kinship was

2. On the role of the cult in early Israelite wars see von Rad, *Der heilege Kreig im alten Israel* (Zürich: Zwingli Verlag, 1951). One should also note the reaction of M. Weippert, "'Heiliger Kreig' in Israel und Assyrien: Kritische Anmerkungen zu Gerhard von Rads Konzept des 'Heiligen Kreiges im alten Israel,'" *ZAW* 84 (1972) 460–93.

3. Note the strong injunctions of the Covenant Code (Exod 23:14–17): all the men of Israel were required to participate in the pilgrim festivals and not to come empty-handed! Both of these injunctions were lost in the later priestly recensions of this list (Leviticus 23 and Numbers 28–29).

4. This position was classically stated by M. Noth in his *Das System der zwölf Stämme Israels* (Stuttgart: Kohlhammer, 1930). See also G. von Rad, *Theology of the Old Testament*, vol. 1 (New York: Harper and Row, 1962) 17ff. for a concurring view. Noth's perspective is, of course, firmly grounded in his theory of an early Israelite amphictyony. This theory has been subject to a number of criticisms in recent years. Especially problematic is his thesis that there was a central shrine for all of Israel. Yet Gottwald, one of Noth's strongest critics, agrees with Noth's basic premise—the cult is the center of early Israelite life (*The Tribes of Yahweh* [Maryknoll: Orbis, 1979] 63–125 and 252–59).

5. F. Cross, "The Epic Traditions of Early Israel," 36, in R. Friedman, ed., *The Poet and the Historian* (HSS 26, Chico: Scholars Press, 1983).

6. This idea is somewhat controversial, and, it should be noted, is not crucial to our thesis. There are still a number of scholars who feel that the covenantal theology of Israel is a late development. See for example, L. Perlitt, *Bundestheologie im alten Testament* (WMANT 36, Neukirchen-Vluyn: Neukirchener Verlag, 1969). Their arguments have some basis. The Hittite formulary does not neatly fit any of the early pre-deuteronomistic narratives. Joshua 24 is probably the first biblical text to clearly outline Israelite belief on a covenantal model. Though this text is pre-deuteronomic, it cannot be conclusively put in the early period. On the other hand though, one must reckon with the fact that the Sinai narratives are the most

the favored means of expressing the mutually assumed covenantal obligations. Ideally, each clan stood on equal footing with the others; the political [[3]] constitution, like the genealogy, was segmented.[7] The tenuous link between these loosely articulated clans was the cult of the patron deity. It is no surprise that the very first commandment found in the Sinai material (Exod 20:3) is: 'You shall have no other gods before me' (*lōʾ yihyeh lĕkā ʾĕlōhîm ʾăḥērîm ʿal-pānāy*). To abstain from participation in the league cult was to absolve the covenantal bonds of the tribal group. In the later language of the Deuteronomist this commandment was couched in even more explicit covenantal idiom. The rubric 'to go after other gods' (*laleket ʾĕlōhîm ʾăḥērîm*), found everywhere in Deuteronomy, was borrowed directly from covenantal charters.[8]

But what of the actual cult of YHWH? There can be little doubt that it was very different from that of Canaan. The Deuteronomistic redaction of Israel's early history clearly sets Israelite religion apart from its Canaanite environment. But the distinction does not begin at this late period. Already, in earliest Israel, one of YHWH's cultic epithets shows the self-conscious distinction Israel herself made. YHWH is called *ʾēl qannāʾ* 'a jealous God'. But of what did this jealousy consist? Was Israel's actual cultic service distinct?

The most basic answer to this question—which presumes no value judgment concerning the ethical or religious value of the two cultic systems—is that the Israelite cult consisted of those sacrificial gifts and offerings which were donated to YHWH (*lĕ-YHWH*). *The distinctiveness of the Israelite cult is nothing other than the limitation of cultic activity to one particular patron deity.* This view makes no claim to the superiority of the Is-

---

heavily redacted narratives in the Bible. A neat survival of an original covenant formulary in this corpus is impossible to expect. Even with these reservations, though, one must come up with some type of legal or religious formula which enabled a diverse group of independent tribal clans to participate regularly in the militia and pilgrim feasts of a tribal confederacy and share a distinctive onomastic pattern. *These were not natural developments!* To disallow the existence of a covenantal agreement in the early period would pose more problems than it would solve. For a similar position see J. Barr, "Some Semantic Notes on the Covenant," in *Beiträge zur Alttestamentlichen Theologie: Festschrift für Walther Zimmerli*, ed. H. Donner et al. (Göttingen: Vandenhoeck und Ruprecht, 1977) 37: "Yet with all the will in the world it is a little hard to believe that the covenant of Yahweh with Israel became significant only so late.

　　7. On the political importance of segmented genealogies see R. Wilson, *Genealogy and History in the Biblical World* (New Haven: Yale University Press, 1977).

　　8. See W. Moran, "The Ancient Near Eastern Background of the Love of God in Deuteronomy," *CBQ* 25 (1963) 82 n. 35.

raelite cult We could just as easily have said the distinctiveness of the Moabite cult is the limitation of public cult to its patron god, Chemosh. This provisional statement will guide the beginning of this study.

This definition might appear so general as to be without value. But such a statement is of primary importance for the beginning of any discussion of the Israelite cult. For one, this statement presupposes that the Israelite rites were not significantly different from Canaanite rites. As de Vaux has observed, the Bible itself makes this observation.[9] In the sacrificial rites mentioned in Elijah's confrontation with the prophets of Baal, the holocaust offering is [[4]] prepared in exactly the same way between the two parties.[10] The story presumes that the outward form of the rite itself was undifferentiated. Also the story of Naaman's allegiance to YHWH presumes that it is not how the rite is executed, but to whom the sacrifice is offered which is significant.[11] Finally we would mention the evidence of the Punic cultic tariff texts whose sacrificial terminology parallels so closely that found in the Bible.[12] This terminological similarity is an indication of the basic continuity of cultic rites between Israel and Canaan.

Canaanite Magic and Israelite Ethic?

Many scholars have not been satisfied with this sparse and unnuanced definition. More analytical and value-oriented differentiations have been proposed. By far the most common means of distinguishing the two cult spheres has been that of contrasting the Israelite ethical and covenantal religion with the magical rites of the Canaanite fertility cult. This view distinguishes the historical quality of YHWH's self-revelation from the pagan

---

9. R. de Vaux, *Studies in Old Testament Sacrifice* (Cardiff: University of Wales Press, 1964) 44. Also see I. Engnell, *A Rigid Scrutiny* (Nashville: Vanderbilt University Press, 1969) 35–39.

10. 1 Kgs 18:23–24. One should note that the priestly behavior of the Canaanites is portrayed differently by the biblical writer though the actual preparation of the animal is the same.

11. 2 Kgs 5:17.

12. This evidence was first used by R. Dussaud (*Les origines cananéenes du sacrifice israélite* [Paris: Leroux, 1921]) to argue against Wellhausen's assertion that Israelite sacrificial practice as described in the P code was exilic or later. When the Ugaritic material was first published, many of these same terms were found and, so given second millennium attestations. In light of this evidence, Dussaud revised his argument (2nd edition, 1941) and said Israel's earliest sacrifices paralleled that of Canaan. Some scholars (R. J. Thompson, *Penitence and Sacrifice in Early Israel outside the Levitical Law* [Leiden: Brill, 1963] 30–33 and J. Gray, *The Legacy of Canaan* [[*The Ras Shamra Texts and Their Reference to the Old Testament*]] [SVT 5, Leiden: Brill, 1965] 182–83, 195–204) deny the validity of such a claim on the basis of Israel's nomadic origins. The specious quality of such a counter-claim will be discussed below.

interests in natural religion and agrarian rites.[13] The agricultural festivals of Israel are suspect in this view. Their agrarian appearance is evidence of their pagan (Canaanite) background. These pagan agrarian rites become legitimate only when they are subordinated to the covenantal religion of Israel.[14] When the Israelite presents his produce to [[5]] the priest in a religious festival, the magical fertility elements are expunged in the act of reciting the Credo.[15] History has usurped Nature.[16]

Mary Douglas has recently addressed the contrast biblical scholars draw between magical activity and ethical religion in her work *Purity and Danger* [[see a reprinted extract from this work on pp. 119–34 in this volume]].[17] We mention her work because she perceives very clearly the intellectual foundations of such a view, which stem from anthropological methods that have long been dismissed. Biblical scholars borrowed these ideas when they were *au courant,* but many have not followed their development in the discipline from which they were taken.[18] The importance of this theory stems more from the vast quantity of publications which as-

13. The classic statement was made by J. Wellhausen in his *Prolegomena to the History of Ancient Israel* (Gloucester: Peter Smith, 1973) 92–112.

14. H. J. Kraus' remarks are typical here (*Worship in Israel* [Richmond: John Knox Press, 1965] 122): "The great achievement of the Old Testament is the inclusion of the whole sacrificial system within the saving events and the fact of the *berit* [['covenant']].

15. G. von Rad, in his *Old Testament Theology,* vol. 1 (New York: Harper and Row, 1962), speaks of the Canaanite agrarian rites (pp. 19–35) and the role of the divine word and saving event (p. 262). The summary of the divine activity (Credo) transformed the material observances of the cult to the true worship of YHWH.

16. This interpretive framework is often described as Hegelian because it assumes a logical progression from the realm of nature to history. This philosophical system was assumed by Wellhausen (and followed by Kraus, von Rad and others) in the writing of his classic *Prolegomena to the History of Ancient Israel.* The dependence of Wellhausen on Hegelian ideas has long been assumed by many biblical scholars, though there are dissenting voices. See H. J. Kraus, *Worship in Israel,* 6 and F. M. Cross, *CMHE* [[*Canaanite Myth and Hebrew Epic* (Cambridge: Harvard University Press, 1973)]] 82 for an analysis of Wellhausen's Hegelian presuppositions.

17. (New York: Praeger, 1966) 7–28, 58–72.

18. This is not an uncommon phenomenon in biblical studies. One could compare the development of Form Criticism. These methods were borrowed from Folklore and Classical studies of the late nineteenth century. They presumed, among other things, that the shorter the poetic unit the more archaic. Since then, modern studies of oral poetry have shown how unreliable a guide this is. Yet, many continue to operate under old assumptions. One could say the same about the recent use of anthropological methods in biblical studies. All scholars assume some sort of social model when writing about clans, tribes and city-states. Those who use these ancillary disciplines are said to be imposing models on the texts, but previous scholarship did the same thing. The only reason they are not perceived as such an imposition now is because of the vast amount of published material which presumes them.

sume its veracity than from the sophistication of its methodological underpinnings. It was Frazer who advanced most eloquently the theory that primitive religion was based on magic.[19] Although Frazer claimed to be an admirer of Robertson Smith, their views on primitive religion could not have differed more. For Smith, primitive religion began with ritual activity out of which ethical values were formed.[20] Mythology or belief structures were secondary to ritual. Magic was a peripheral concern for Smith. He saw it as an aberration in the evolution of humanity, something which occurred only in times of social duress. Frazer took the opposite view. He began with the [[6]] myth of the dying and rising god. From this myth, primitive society developed rituals as a magical aid in furthering the reproductive process.

Douglas characterizes Frazer as an evolutionist in the Hegelian sense. This is true, in part.[21] Like Hegel, Frazer believed that the ethical religion found in the biblical prophets—the highest form of religious thinking— was preceded by a magical understanding of the world.[22] But Frazer's particular characterization of this intellectual evolution was not altogether comparable to Hegel. For Frazer the dominant intellectual issue was how humankind perceived causality in the natural world. Specifically, how did people account for change in the natural environment, and how could the natural environment be manipulated by human agents? The first attempts to manipulate the natural environment were magical. Frazer believed magical activity had two forms, homeopathic or imitative magic and contagious magic.[23] Through these activities primitive people thought they could alter certain physical properties of the natural world. When primitive peoples discovered that magical activity did not always yield the predictable results a new theory of causality had to arise. Thus, the beginnings of religion. Now the somewhat fickle and often arbitrary

---

19. J. G. Frazer, *The Golden Bough: A Study in Magic and Religion*, vols. 1–13 (London: Macmillan, 1980). This edition is a reprint. It was originally published in London in 1890 with the subtitle, "A Study in Comparative Religion." The subtitle was changed in the 3rd edition. The change illustrates the development of Frazer's thought and the manner in which he has been appropriated by scholarship.

20. W. Robertson Smith, *Lectures on the Religion of the Semites* (New York: KTAV, 1969 [[excerpts from this work are reprinted in this volume, pp. 43–64]]). The original work was published in London in 1889, and was the subject of numerous editions and translations during the course of Robertson Smith's life.

21. See Frazer's appendix on the Hegel in the first volume of the third edition of *The Golden Bough.* He was not conscious of the Hegelian roots of his theory until they were pointed out to him after the publication of his work.

22. Frazer, *The Golden Bough*, vol. 1, pp. 50–51.

23. Frazer, *The Golden Bough*, vol. 1, pp. 11–47.

whims and desires of the gods could account for irregularity in the natural world. With the development of religious thinking, the control of nature was put in the hands of the gods instead of the artifice of the magician. Science is the apogee of this evolutionary sequence. With scientific thinking, humankind regained its desire to explain and control the natural environment through immutable laws. The arbitrary whims and desires of the gods no longer played a role in explaining causal relations in the natural world. Instead, empirical principles were developed which could explain and control the natural environment. As Frazer observes, there is greater similarity between science and magic than between religion and science. For both science and magic assert "that the succession of events is assumed to be perfectly regular and certain, being determined by immutable laws, the operation of which can be foreseen and calculated precisely; the elements of caprice, of chance and of accident are banished from the course of nature."[24] Religion, then, was not highly [[7]] esteemed in Frazer's system except when it expounded the values that he felt were found in the prophetic materials.

It is difficult, if not impossible, to find any modern anthropologist who respects Frazer's theoretical model.[25] He is extolled as an excellent composer of English prose and for the sheer massiveness of his folklore collection, but his theoretical and synthetic observations are dismissed if not scorned. He has been called an armchair anthropologist, one who spoke of primitive culture without ever leaving the world of the university. Douglas describes his contribution as a baneful one.[26] Burkert has even criticized his insights from a classicist's perspective.[27] He claims that Frazer's allegorizing of all myth into stories about natural process had precedents already in late antiquity!

Yet, as Burkert cynically observed, even when Frazer's position is destroyed it will rise again. In several areas of scholarly study, Frazer's presuppositions have had a lasting impact. In almost every biblical handbook one can read about the magical fertility rites of the Canaanites as

24. Frazer, *The Golden Bough*, vol. 1, p. 49.
25. Douglas, *Purity and Danger*, 13–28; E. Evans-Pritchard, *A History of Anthropological Thought* (New York: Basic Books, 1981) 132–52; M. Harris, *The Rise of Anthropological Theory* (New York: Harper and Row, 1968) 204–8; E. Leach, "On the Founding Fathers," *Current Anthropology* 7 (1966) 560–67; E. J. Sharpe, *Comparative Religion* (New York: Scribners, 1975) 87–94, and J. Z. Smith, "When the Bough Breaks," *History of Religions* 12 (1973) 342–71.
26. Douglas, *Purity and Danger*, 28.
27. W. Burkert, *The Structure and History of Greek Mythology and Ritual* (Berkeley: University of California Press, 1979) 35–36 and 99–122.

opposed to the ethical values of Israel's cult.[20] In spite of the fact that we have little knowledge of the Canaanite cult, it has become an assumed scholarly position that it was inherently magical. The imposition of this rubric has affected not only biblical studies, but also studies of other ancient civilizations. Douglas noted that the well-respected classicist M. Finley used an ethical test to distinguish earlier elements of belief from later in his work *The World of Odysseus*.[29] Cassirer uses magical, non-ethical superstition as his criterion for historical primitiveness in his study of Zoroastrianism.[30]

Let us turn to a Ugaritic text many scholars have used as evidence of Canaan's fertility religion. The text has been read: 'cook a kid in milk, a lamb in [[8]] curd'.[31] This harmless cultic directive becomes a symbol of fertility religion when it is contrasted with the biblical injunction not to cook a kid in its mother's milk (Exod 23:19). No reason is given in the Bible for such a prohibition, but some biblical scholars—under the influence of a Frazerian model—have been ready to supply one. The Canaanite rite has been called a "milk-charm . . . performed . . . in order to promote a flow of milk from the goats and cattle which was already failing in the summer drought."[32] The *only source* for such an idea is the assumption that Canaanite ritual is by definition magic, and Israelite resistance to it is derivable from her ethical sensitivities.

This is not to deny the existence of magical elements in Canaanite religion. Rather, the concern is to point out how Frazer's typology of development, from magic to religion, has been imposed on the ancient world. But magic, in the eyes of modern social scientists, has become a very difficult term not only to analyze but to define.[33]

28. On the priority of a primitive stage of magical thinking in Near Eastern lore see von Rad, *Theology of the Old Testament*, vol. 1, pp. 22–35. His summary statement is a classic expression of the ideas of late 19th century anthropology and folklore.

29. (New York: Penguin, 1979) 136–41.

30. E. Cassirer, *An Essay on Man* (Oxford: Oxford University Press, 1944) 100.

31. *CTA* 23.14. The irony of this reading is that it is erroneous. The word for 'kid', *gd*, is better translated 'coriander'. In Ugaritic we would expect the spelling *gdy* for 'kid'. The corrected translation renders unusable the supposed biblical parallel.

32. J. Gray, *The Legacy of Canaan*, 97. Maimonides (*Moreh Nebukhim* 3.48) first suggested that the rite must have been Canaanite. T. Gaster (*Thespis* [New York: Schuman, 1950] 244) also concludes that the rite concerned fertility.

33. Three volumes have appeared in the last fifteen years which address the issue of the rationality of magical behavior. These are: B. Wilson, ed., *Rationality* (Oxford: Basil Blackwell, 1970); R. Horton and Ruth Finnegan, eds., *Modes of Thought* (London: Faber and

Many discussions of magic in the anthropological literature trace their scholarly lineage to Evans-Pritchard's work on Azande witchcraft and Nuer religion.[34] Evans-Pritchard used the context of his ethnographic work among these peoples as a means of disposing with some of Lévy-Bruhl's concepts about primitive thought. Lévy-Bruhl, not unlike Frazer believed that primitive people inhabited a prelogical and mystical mental world unlike that of modern people. Evans-Pritchard argued against this assessment. By means of a careful ethnographic analysis he showed that primitive people lived in the same "world" that modern people do for the most part. Like modern people most of their lives were concerned with the "practical economic pursuits: gardening, hunting, fishing, care of cattle, and the manufacture of weapons, utensils and ornaments, and in their social contacts: the life of household, family and kin, relations with friends and neighbours, with superiors and inferiors, dances and feasts, legal [[9]] disputes, feuds and warfare."[35] Mystical thinking was restricted to certain situations in social life. Evans-Pritchard's comments are illuminating:

> I have often noticed Azande lean their spears up against, or hang baskets on, the shrines they build for the spirits of their ancestors in the centre of their homesteads, and as far as it is possible to judge from their behaviour they have no other interest in the shrine than as a convenient post or peg. At religious ceremonies their attitude is very different. Among the Ingassana of the Tabi Hills God is the sun and on occasions they pray to it but, as far as I could judge, in ordinary situations they looked upon the sun very much as I did as a convenient means of telling the time, as the cause of intense heat at midday, and so on. If one were not present at some religious ceremony on a special occasion, one would remain ignorant that the sun is God. Mystical thought is a function of particular situations.[36]

Evans-Pritchard suggests several reasons for why anthropologists believed primitive peoples think mystically. One would be the idiosyncratic fash-

---

Faber, 1973), and M. Hollis and S. Lukes, eds., *Rationality and Relativism* (Oxford: Basil Blackwell, 1982).

34. *Witchcraft, Oracles and Magic among the Azande* (Oxford: Clarendon Press, 1937) and *Nuer Religion* (Oxford: Clarendon Press, 1956).

35. E. Evans-Pritchard, "Lévy-Bruhl's theory of Primitive Mentality." *Bulletin of the Faculty of the Arts* (Egyptian University, Cairo) 2, 1 (1934) 9. A more recent opinion of Evans-Pritchard on Lévy-Bruhl can be found in his *Theories of Primitive Religion* (Oxford: Oxford University Press, 1965) 78–99.

36. "Lévy-Bruhl's Theory," 27.

ion by which ethnographic records take shape. European ethnographers were more likely to record the extraordinary experiences than the mundane.[37] It is also a fact that anthropologists were likely to devote most of their attention to those particular aspects of social life where mystical thinking is likely to appear, that is, in myth and ritual. Once these particular and highly selective segments of primitive life become the staples of the ethnographic record the tendency arises to compare these selective segments with our everyday vocabulary.[38] If the everyday events of primitive life are properly noted, their thought appears no different from ours. Finally one must be careful to understand "mystical" statements of primitive peoples in the context of their symbolic system. For example, a favorite 19th century example of primitive irrationality was the statement by the Bororo of Central Brazil, "We are red macaws." This apparently mystical and irrational statement was examined by Crocker. On a careful reinvestigation he found out that "(1) only men say 'We are red macaws'; (2) red macaws are owned as pets by Bororo women; (3) because of matrilineal descent and uxorilocal residence, men are in important ways dependent on women; (4) both men and macaws are thought to reach beyond the women's sphere through ⟦10⟧ their contacts with spirits."[39] Thus the statement, "We are red macaws," is hardly irrational or mystical, rather it is a symbol or metaphor of the masculine condition in Bororo culture. As Sperber notes, probably many such puzzling "irrational" statements in the ethnographic literature could be explained by such careful research.

But what of those special situations in the ritual life of a community which appear magical? How is the modern ethnographer to interpret these beliefs and rituals which seem, *prima facie*, irrational? Two schools of thought have arisen. On the one hand scholars like Horton argue that magical acts which attempt to bring rain, ward off disease and so forth are best understood as a primitive type of science.[40] They reflect attempts by pre-scientific peoples to construct a meaningful theory about causality in the world. Other anthropologists dislike this comparison of Horton's

---

37. "Lévy-Bruhl's Theory," 8.

38. On this misplaced comparison see M. Bloch, "The Past and the Present in the Present," *Man* 12 (1977) 278–92.

39. D. Sperber, "Apparently Irrational Beliefs," in *Rationality and Relativism*, 152–53. For this analysis, Sperber is recounting the article by J. C. Crocker, "My Brother the Parrot," in J. D. Sapir and J. C. Crocker, eds., *The Social Use of Metaphor: Essays on the Anthropology of Rhetoric* (Philadelphia: University of Pennsylvania, 1977) 164–92.

40. R. Horton, "African Traditional Thought and Western Science," *Africa* 37 (1967) 50–71 and 155–87.

because it necessarily makes primitive thought inferior to modern think-ing by compelling one to compare primitive religious thinking with mod-ern scientific theory.[41] Some argue that this is Frazer's error rising again. As an alternative to Horton, these anthropologists argue that primitive magical rites must be understood on a symbolic level. To see these rites simply as instrumental activity arising from misplaced ideas about natural causality is to misread them. The "symbolist school" argues the instrumen-tal aspect of primitive ritual is of negligible importance in understanding the rite. What is of real importance is the symbolism involved in the rite. Those who hold this symbolic perspective view primitive myths and rituals as a form of artistic or theological expression rather than a form of scientific speculation. Thus a sensitive aesthetic judgment is required for interpretation.

A good example of this symbolic mode of interpretation can be found in Lienhardt's analysis of Dinka rain rituals.[42] As Lienhardt observes, the Dinka know when the rainy season is approaching and this point is im-portant for the correct appreciation of their ceremony. These rain rituals are not simply an ⟦11⟧ attempt to control the environment. Rather, in these rituals, "their human symbolic action moves with the rhythm of the natural world around them, recreating that rhythm in moral terms and not merely attempting to *coerce* it to conformity with human desires."[43] The religious impulse in the rite *does not* stem from an attempt to assist this natural order. Rather, the moral life of the community itself is or-dered around the fixed cycle of the seasonal rains.[44]

We are left at an apparent impasse. How are we to interpret a ritual whose expressed purpose is to secure rain for a people? Is the rite to be understood as an instrumental act practiced only for the expectation of material consequences, or is the rite primarily a symbolic activity con-cerned with moral and aesthetic values? This impasse is not insoluble. In

41. For example see J. Beattie, *Other Cultures* (London: Cohen and West, 1964) 202–40 and "On Understanding Ritual," in B. Wilson ed., *Rationality*, 240–68; M. Douglas, *Purity and Danger*; E. Leach, *Political Systems of Highland Burma* (London: London School of Economics and Political Science, 1954); G. Lienhardt, *Divinity and Experience* ⟦ *The Religion of the Dinka*⟧ (Oxford: Clarendon Press, 1961).

42. For Lienhardt's views on symbolic action see his work, *Divinity and Experience*, 252–97.

43. Lienhardt, *Divinity and Experience*, 280.

44. Horton's review of Lienhardt's work is quite critical (in *Africa* 32 [1962] 78). He be-lieves Lienhardt does not "call a spade a spade." He observes, "though it seems clear from the material offered that the Dinka think certain actions symbolizing desired ends really do help in themselves to achieve those ends, the author seems at times to want to rationalize this magical element away."

commenting on this very problem several anthropologists have noted that the desire to distinguish between instrumental and symbolic meanings may be a peculiarity of the modern scholar. As Taylor observes: "It is a feature of our civilization that we have developed a practice of scientific research and its technological application from which the symbolic and expressive dimensions have been to a great extent purged."[45] In premodern cultures the distinction between controlling the world and understanding it symbolically is not made.[46] Thus when a primitive person both performs a rain ritual and waters his crop, chases birds away and provides natural fertilizers, he views this as all one technique. Modern persons, on the other hand, would separate this activity into two types.

. . . .

⟦12⟧ A sophisticated understanding of primitive ritual is not easy to arrive at. We must put aside our modern sensibilities which seek to distinguish empirical from symbolic understandings of the environment. But we also must have a certain theological sensitivity for the role of symbolic activity within a particular world-view or belief system. As Evans-Pritchard observed, many ethnographers would be greatly aided by acquainting themselves with the subtleties of classical theological dogma and ritual so that the distinctions between sacrament and magic, belief and superstition can be appreciated.[47] Many of the same sorts of subtle dialectics which exist in Western theological traditions can be found elsewhere.

The student of ancient civilizations can learn a number of things from this discussion. Firstly, one should recall Evans-Pritchard's comment about the selectivity of many ethnographic reports. A comparable phenomenon exists in the studies of ancient Near Eastern documents. The propensity of modern scholars to describe the thought of ancient civilization through its mythological and ritual texts is a highly selective procedure. Yet, it is to these very texts that scholars turn in hope of discerning the ancients' views on the relationship between fertility and agriculture. These mythological texts obviously emphasize supernatural and sometimes "irrational" concerns. Yet mythic texts comprise only a small percentage of the information which is available for the study of ancient civilizations. The mythic

45. C. Taylor, "Rationality" in *Rationality and Relativism*, 94.

46. See I. C. Jarvie and J. Agassi, "The Problem of the Rationality of Magic," in *Rationality*, 172–93.

47. *Theories of Primitive Religion*, 16–17. Evans-Pritchard observes that many anthropologists in the past viewed religion from a very unsympathetic vantage point and often imported their prejudices into their ethnographies and analyses.

view is hardly the perspective of everyday affairs. The greatest percentage
of texts available in the ancient Near East are concerned with the practical side of agricultural life, when to plant, what to plant, who is to receive
the harvest and so forth. These texts show us that ancient Near Eastern
peoples had a very rational understanding, in the main, of agricultural
affairs. Secondly one should be cognizant of the context of a ritual or
symbolic statement. What often appears *prima facie* irrational often fits
quite well into a larger symbolic frame. Finally one must be cognizant of
the fact that modern culture devalues religious ritual and that this devaluation has affected the way scholars approach the study of ritual. As
Douglas observes, this attitude is so pervasive that it is even common in
Catholic circles.[48] Again we are reminded of Evans-Pritchard's [[13]]
comments in regard to the study of primitive religion. One's appreciation
and insight into the way myth and ritual operate in contemporary religions often parallels one's appreciation of their operation in primitive or
archaic religions.

With these provisions in mind let us turn to another text which is often quoted as representative of magical Canaanite fertility rites. It is
found in the Baal cycle, after Mot has swallowed the Divine Hero, Baal.
As we join the text, Anat is effecting her revenge on Mot:

ta°ḥud bina °ili-mi môta	She seized El's son Mot
bi-ḥarbi tabaqqicunannu	with a sword she split him
bi-ḥaθri tadriyunannu	with a sieve she winnowed him
bi-°išti tašrupunannu	with fire she burnt him
bi-riḥêma tiṭhanannu	with two millstones she ground him
bi-šadī tidracunannu	in the field she scattered him
(*CTA* 6.2.30–35)	

Does this text require us to believe that Canaanite fertility rites were primarily an instrumental activity oriented toward altering the physical
environment? It is true that this text is related to the agricultural procedures of Canaan.[49] The narrative context is important too; the narrative
is about to foretell the rising of Baal again and the consequent return of

---

48. *Natural Symbols* (New York: Pantheon Books, 1970) 1–53. The result is that she, as
an anthropologist, produces a work which is more sensitive toward religious ritual than
many modern clerics and scholars of religion.

49. See Josephus (*Antiquities*, 3.250) regarding the preparation of grain for the new
year and J. Gray, *Legacy of Canaan*, 68–69 (esp. p. 68, note 3) for a good discussion of this.
S. Loewenstamm ("The Ugaritic Fertility Myth—The Result of a Mistranslation" *IEJ* 12
(1962) 87–88. U. Cassuto ("Baal and Mot in the Ugaritic Texts," *IEJ* 12 [1962] 79) and others have said it is not a fertility rite.

ıaın to the land. But can we extrapolate from this that the Canaanite peasant thought that he or she was somehow assisting this process through the sowing of grain? Is this action to be understood only in an instrumental fashion? What about the practical steps which were also taken to insure a productive crop yield; and what about the symbolic dimensions of such a rite? The legacy of Frazer would impel us to see this rite as irrational primitive magic which was one step below a higher form of intellectual life, ethical religion. Some modern biblical scholars have found this an attractive position because it allows them to set Israel's belief structure over and against that of her immediate environment for an apologetic goal. But the intellectual [[14]] foundations of such an apologetic—though appropriate several generations back—are no longer adequate.[50]

· ·

Tribal and Urban Cults

[[19]] Another method used to distinguish earliest Israel's cult employs the typological contrast of nomadic and sedentary culture. This view has been championed in the work of Robertson Smith and Julius Wellhausen. It was Robertson Smith who had the greatest effect in this area.[51] He attempted to divide early Israel's cultic life on the basis of nomadic and sedentary

50. See J. Roberts, "Myth *versus* History: Relaying the Comparative Foundations," *CBQ* 38 (1976) 1–13. We should note that the Scandinavian school does not do this. The remarks of Engnell (*A Rigid Scrutiny*, 39–40) are quite contrary to the standard German view: "The argument that Israel took over the Canaanite cult and all its external furnishings, but not the ideas associated with this cult, cannot be successfully defended. This argument implies an abstraction which cannot be assumed in an era when cult and religion were to a great extent synonymous ideas. In opposition to this, it should be pointed out that the usual picture of Canaanite cultic religion needs to be radically revised. We are not to think of a sensuous and amoral cult which is supplanted by the elevated and pure faith of the Mosaic period. Behind its partly highly orgiastic cult, as is often the case in strongly emotional forms of religion, the Canaanite religion had room for profound and valuable ideas." Unfortunately, Engnell lapses into the Hegelian framework later in the same essay, "the general tendency is toward emancipation from the substratum of nature religion. . . . Out of this gradually changing cultic form, a new cult emerges which will prove revolutionary for all future time, even for the Christian age." He even adheres to the traditional Christian view of post-exilic biblical faith when he says that Ezra-Nehemiah "represent the beginning of Pharisaism . . . Here, legalism is triumphant" (p. 47).

51. W. Robertson Smith, *Lectures on the Religion of the Semites*. [[Excerpts reprinted in this volume, pp. 43–64]]

existence. The former represented the purest form of Israelite religion, while the latter was the source of syncretistic agricultural rites.

Based on his own ethnographic research among contemporary Arab tribesmen, Robertson Smith formulated a number of hypotheses about the primitive characteristics of Semitic religion. Because he felt that the nomad and the sedentary citizen were such contrasting social types, he concluded that their religious rituals must be different as well. This impulse to understand religious [[20]] practice as fundamentally related to social structure remains as one of the lasting contributions of his work. Its influence, especially among French sociologists such as Durkheim, has long been noted.[52]

For Robertson Smith, the contrast between nomad and village dweller was well displayed in their different types of sacrificial ritual. He argued that the *zĕbaḥ* or 'slain offering' typified the religion of the nomad whereas the *minḥâ* or 'tribute offering' characterized the religion of sedentary culture.[53] Behind this contrast was the assumption that nomadic culture preceded settled life. Thus the "logical" conclusion: the *zĕbaḥ* sacrifice was the most primitive sacrificial type.

It was from his observations of animal sacrifice in various cultures that Robertson Smith formulated his theories regarding their meaning. The most basic characteristic of these rites was the feeling of *communitas* enjoyed by its partakers. These feelings were of such a profound character that the kinspeople felt that their patron deity was sharing in the meal with them. This joyous sharing of a common slain animal communally among one's kin had an ethical quality as well. Because this sacrificial meal was a communal experience, the tribesmen and women learned the value of pursuing the common good as opposed to their own individual desires.[54] The intensity of the experience fostered a commitment to the kin-group and an obligation to uphold its ideals.

It was only much later when nomads settled down, that the slain offering was replaced in importance by the *minḥâ* or tribute offering. Behind the idea of this tribute offering stood the image of Baal, the feudal lord of the land. Baal was inextricably tied to the growth of agriculture and the accumulation of tillable land by the ruling elite. Here, Robertson Smith rightly observed that the basic Semitic meaning of the noun *baʿl*

52. Smith's influence on Durkheim has been well summarized by T. Beidelman, *W. Robertson Smith and the Sociological Study of Religion* (Chicago: University of Chicago Press, 1974) 55–68.

53. Smith, 244.

54. Smith, 263–68.

was 'owner' or 'lord' of. The religious image of a vegetable offering due to this feudal lord, Baal, reflected the social setting of the Canaanite city-state.[55]

For Robertson Smith, the worship of Baal, with its urban, non-kin based setting was far removed from the earlier commensal feast. The very concept of a vegetable offering (*minḥâ*) due a feudal lord assumed a rigorously stratified [[21]] society. It reflected the luxurious public religion of the nobles which replaced the more spontaneous kin-based religion of earlier nomads.

The value of Robertson Smith's work is still apparent to those who choose to read him. Although his work is thoroughly ingrained with a romanticism about Semitic nomadism, he is very cognizant of the social ramifications of religious ceremony. For this reason his work continues to have a profound effect on modern anthropology.[56] Religious ritual was not a secluded sector of ancient civilization; it was at the very heart of its existence.

At the center of his concerns was the social structure of the community. His relatively sophisticated anthropological sensitivities allowed him to see how kin obligations were lessened in urban life. In the urban situation, the more egalitarian distribution systems of the extended family broke down. As a result, access to resources became unequal and asymmetrical so that craft-specialists and military and religious specialists could evolve.

For Robertson Smith, this inequitable arrangement was well demonstrated in the Temples of Syria–Palestine. He asserted that the Temple of Melcarth at Tyre was hardly different from the state treasury, and sacred offerings sent to Tyre by the Phoenicians in Carthage were the functional equivalent of the tribute won from conquered colonies. City-states claimed that their collections for public feasts and rituals were sacred donations, but Smith realized their affinity to other taxes. In a highly stratified urban setting, there were unequal levels of distribution. The vegetable offerings due Baal, the divine "feudal lord," were simply a theological legitimation for a system of exploitation in the city-state. Some gave more than they received, while others received more than they gave.

---

55. Smith, pp. 244–47.

56. Anthropologists representing widely variant methodologies appreciate the anthropological instincts of Robertson Smith even if a number of his assertions are questioned. Among these anthropologists we would note: M. Harris, *The Rise of Anthropological Theory*, 204–5, 207–8; E. Evans-Pritchard, *A History of Anthropological Thought*, 69–81; and M. Douglas, *Purity and Danger*, 13–28.

This urban "Baal religion" was in vast contrast to the kin-group celebrations of nomadic culture with its egalitarian social structure. Among
nomads, only the joyous celebrations of the clan were needed to impress
group obligations. In the city-state, only a monopoly of force could uphold its system of unequal distribution of resources. The prophetic critique of sacrifice, to Robertson Smith, stemmed from the realization that
the earlier egalitarian kin- or clan-based festivals had turned into ban-
quets for the urban elite. Contributions to these [[22]] affairs depended
no longer on the voluntary generosity of the individual family unit, but
on forced imposts of the king.

Our major criticism of Robertson Smith concerns his sharp distinction between nomadic and sedentary culture. Modern study of nomadism
in the second millennium B.C.E. has overturned most of his assumptions.[57] One can no longer assume that nomadic culture is prior to settled
life on an evolutionary scale. Just the opposite pattern is documented.
Nomadism develops as a specialization within village life. Nomads in the
second millennium B.C.E. are dependent on the produce of the village
and are bound inseparably to it. Rowton labels this type of nomadism "enclosed nomadism" because of its close ties to settled life. Because of these
close ties, it is best to speak of nomads within their larger tribal framework. This tribal framework in the second millennium B.C.E. was vastly
different from that of 19th and 20th century Arab bedouin. These tribes
were a mixture of settled and pastoral folk. Of this mixture, only a small
minority practiced pastoralism with regularity. By far the largest part of

---

57. The most comprehensive study is that undertaken by M. B. Rowton. He prefers
to list his work in a logical as opposed to chronological sequence: "Autonomy and Nomadism in Western Asia," *Or* 42 (1973) 247–58: "Urban Autonomy in a Nomadic Environment,"
JNES 32 (1973) 201–15; "Enclosed Nomadism," *JESHO* 17 (1974) 1–30; "Dimorphic Structure and the Tribal Elite," *Studia Instituti Anthropos* 30 (1976) 219–58; "The *Abu Amurrim*,"
Iraq 31 (1969) 68–73; "Dimorphic Structure and Topology," *OA* 15 (1976) 17–31; "The Physical Environment and the Problem of the Nomads," *RAI* 15 (1967) 109–21; "The Woodlands of Ancient Western Asia," *JNES* (1967) 261–67; "The Role of Watercourses in the
Growth of Mesopotamian Civilization," *Alter Orient und Altes Testament* 1 (1969) 301–16;
"Watercourses and Water Rights in the Official Correspondence from Larsa and Isin," *JCS* 21
(1967) 267–74; "The Topological Factor in the ᶜapirû Problem," *AS* 16 (1965) 375–87; "Dimorphic Structure and the Problem of the ᶜApirû-ᶜIbrim," *JNES* 35 (1976) 13–20; "Dimorphic Structure and the Parasocial Element," *JNES* 36 (1977) 181–98. Biblical scholars have
also attempted to update the description of tribalism in the late second millennium. Two
of the more important treatments are: G. Mendenhall, *The Tenth Generation* (Baltimore:
The Johns Hopkins University Press, 1973) 174–97 and N. Gottwald, "Were the Early Israelites Pastoral Nomads?" in J. J. Jackson and M. Kessler eds., *Rhetorical Criticism: Essay in Honor
of James Muilenburg* (Pittsburgh Theological Monographs Series 1, Pittsburgh: Pickwick,
1974) 223–55.

the tribe was sedentary. The tribe, then, was primarily a village-centered community, with a portion of its population practicing pastoralism.[58]

Most recent research supports the idea that early Israelite tribalism was agrarian and village-centered.[59] Roughly around 1200 B.C.E. we witness a [[23]] sizable increase in the number and density of permanent settlements in the hill country of Judea and Ephraim. The material cause for this rapid growth was the development of terraced farming. Terracing allowed the previously unusable land of the hill country to become productive agriculturally. These terraces had their origins in Canaanite civilization, but served a special purpose in the Israelite settlements. As Stager has shown, the terraces were best suited for growth of grapes and olives. Yet in earliest Israel, the probable use for these terraces was the production of grain. Thus terraced farming in the hill country allowed Israel to set up a grain economy independent of the Canaanite grain economies of the surrounding coastal plain.[60] Israel's very existence as an autonomous political unit depended on the grain produced on these terraced fields.

The picture of earliest Israel as an aggregation of small rural villages in the hill country organized into a tribal league does not render obsolete the typological contrast Smith made between the religion of the tribe and the state. Rather, it forces us to rethink the specific methods Smith proposed for discussing this contrast. No longer can we neatly separate a tribal *zĕbaḥ* [['slain']] sacrifice from an urban *minḥâ* [['tribute']] type. In earliest Israel, both existed side by side. In this respect we return to the point we made at the beginning of this chapter. Israel's sacrificial rites were, by and large, very similar to Canaanite rites. But this is not to say that the cults were identical. Our initial proposition was that the early Israelite cult was distinctive due to its limitation of cultic activity to a patron tribal deity YHWH. Now we are prepared to say a little more.

---

58. The discovery that tribalism in the second millennium B.C.E. is a mixture of settled and pastoral people is very damaging for the theory of a peaceful nomadic settlement (*Landnahme*) advocated by the Alt school. As Rowton's studies show, the pastoral element within a tribe is small and does not naturally seek sedentary life. Nomadism was, in fact, a specialization away from that very way of existence. When pastoral folk do settle down, it is most often only the poorest or the wealthiest who do. The notion of land-hungry tribes is a fiction of some modern historians. Outside of the imposed programs of some modern states (such as the Ottoman empire, Saudi Arabia) the ethnographic literature knows no examples of whole tribes settling down in the fashion that is sometimes proposed for the Israelite settlement.

59. See L. Stager, "The Archaeology of the Family in Ancient Israel," *BASOR* 260 (1985) 1–36; N. Gottwald, *The Tribes of Yahweh*, 237–337.

60. See L. Stager, "Agriculture," in the *IDBS*, 11–13.

Along with Robertson Smith we believe the manner by which sacred offerings were collected and distributed was vastly different in tribal and state polities. In other words the contrast is no longer to be made on sacrificial types—*měnāḥōt* versus *zěbāḥîm*—but rather on the manner by which the *měnāḥōt* and *zěbāḥîm* are collected and used by the community. This is exactly the manner in which contemporary anthropologists describe the contrast between tribe and state economies.[61]

61. See for example: R. Firth, *Primitive Polynesian Economics* (London: Routledge and Kegan Paul, 1965); C. D. Forde and M. Douglas, "Primitive Economics," in H. Shapiro, ed., *Man, Culture and Society* (New York: Oxford University Press, 1960) 330–44; M. Fried, *The Evolution of Political Society* (New York: Harper and Row, 1967); B. Malinowski, *Argonauts of the Western Pacific* (London: Routledge and Kegan Paul, 1965); and M. Sahlins, "Political Power and the Economy in Primitive Society," in G. Dole and R. Carneiro, eds., *Essays in the Science of Culture in Honor of Leslie White* (New York: T. Y. Crowell, 1960) 390–415, and *idem*, "Economic Anthropology and Anthropological Economics," in M. Fried, ed., *Explorations in Anthropology* (New York: T. Y. Crowell, 1973) 274–88.

Historical Understanding and Understanding the Religion of Israel

ROBERT ODEN

Understanding "Traditions" of Scholarship

[[1]] When the intellectual history of the twentieth century comes to be written, the following will loom large among the noteworthy discoveries of the latter half of this century: the discovery of the surprisingly revealing and broadly applicable conclusions that can result from the study of individual traditions of learning. Like most discoveries, this is in fact a rediscovery. The enterprise of closely following the development of a single area of investigation is not really a new one. But this enterprise's most recent applications have reached conclusion that have generated both excitement and controversy in the past quarter of a century.

In important ways, the heightened interest in following the histories of particular areas of learning began with the publication of Thomas Kuhn's *The Structure of Scientific Revolutions.*[1] As is widely known, his central argument was that the standard and accepted view of how learning progresses in science was incorrect. Scientific progress was seen as gradual and linear. Such progress was "development-by-accumulation" in a steady "process of accretion."[2] Kuhn's investigations of a number of advances within the natural sciences persuaded him that these advances

Reprinted with permission from *The Bible without Theology* (San Francisco: Harper & Row, 1987) 1–9, 15–39, 167–75.

1. Thomas S. Kuhn, *The Structure of Scientific Revolutions*, 2d ed. (Chicago: University of Chicago, 1970).

2. Kuhn, *Scientific Revolutions*, 2–3.

came about through nothing like such gradual, linear progress. Rather, science develops much more dramatically, through revolutions signalled by what Kuhn came to call paradigm shifts. Kuhn defined these paradigms as "universally recognized scientific achievements that for a time provide model problems and solutions to a community of practitioners."[3] [[2]] When such paradigms no longer seem able to make sense of new data, or of old data seen in a new way, there is a shift of paradigm that is soon apparent throughout an entire community of scholars. So dramatic is this shift that Kuhn is not afraid to speak of the "conversion" of scientists to a new paradigm, a new model of comprehension.[4] Another name for a shift like this is a scientific revolution. A scientific revolution thus is "a transformation of the world within which scientific work was done," and the history of science properly understood is the history of these "noncumulative developmental episodes in which an older paradigm is replaced in whole or in part by an incompatible new one."[5]

To say that the central argument of Kuhn's volume has sparked a controversy and that not all historians, philosophers of science, and social theorists agree with the volume's central thesis in all its details is a significant understatement.[6] However, even Kuhn's sharpest critics agree that a great deal is to be learned in pursuing the issue of central traditions of learning and of how these traditions quite unconsciously shape the working methods and the conclusions of those utilizing any model of understanding. Moreover, there is no question but that this issue is one of importance in areas of investigation well beyond that of the natural sciences. When asked whether his central thesis seemed applicable to other areas—to history, literature, and a host of additional academic disciplines—Kuhn answered that of course it was. Indeed, he went on to say, it was precisely the work already done in other disciplines that prompted him to apply his revolutionary model to the natural sciences.[7]

Whatever be the ultimate fate of the several specific arguments advanced in Kuhn's *The Structure of Scientific Revolutions*, he is surely right in claiming both that great dividends can accrue to those who look carefully at a particular tradition of learning and that doing just this has

---

3. Kuhn, *Scientific Revolutions*, viii.

4. Kuhn, *Scientific Revolutions*, 19 or 144, for example.

5. Kuhn, *Scientific Revolutions*, 6, 92.

6. For an introduction to the many issues raised by Kuhn and his critics, see the essays by Karl Popper, Paul Feyerabend, Imre Lakatos, and others in Imre Lakatos and Alan Musgrave, eds., *Criticism and the Growth of Knowledge*, Proceedings of the International Colloquium in the Philosophy of Science, London, 1965, vol. 4 (Cambridge: Cambridge University, 1970).

7. Kuhn, *Scientific Revolution*, 208.

already paid dividends in areas outside the natural sciences. Within the area of concern in the present volume, T. K. Cheyne began his classic and still valuable inquiry into the history of Old Testament scholarship with the modest claim that "it is not unimportant to notice how the intellectual phases and material [[3]] surroundings of a writer have affected his criticism."[8] Within a field long allied to that of biblical studies, that of classics and ancient history, the task of the scholar has long been understood to include not just the investigation of the ancient past but also the examination of influential students of antiquity. And some of the most brilliant advances of the past quarter century have come from the two classicists, Arnaldo Momigliano and M. I. Finley, who resolutely include within their central vision sustained inquiry into various intellectual traditions that have held the field for a time.[9]

Still, if scholars from widely disparate disciplines have observed that a neglected and vital subject for further research is that of the traditions in which the most influential thinkers of any discipline have stood, it remains true that there are a number of ways of conducting this further research. Some of these ways seem of more lasting value than others. Perhaps the least well controlled of these is to speak of the "influence" of a specific figure, usually from the field of literature or philosophy, upon the thought of others. . . . Such studies have also appeared in the domain of biblical scholarship. Of these, perhaps the best known are those that argue that the scholarship of F. C. Baur, the Tübingen historian of early Christianity, and of Julius Wellhausen, of whom I will speak at length, is heavily influenced by Hegel, or that the demythologizing program of Rudolf Bultmann is purely the result of the influence of various existentialist philosophers.[10] . . .

---

8. T. K. Cheyne, *Founders of Old Testament Criticism: Biographical, Descriptive, and Critical Studies* (London: Methuen, 1893). This volume was composed before Cheyne, who was for a time the Oriel Professor of the Interpretation of Scripture at Oxford, began to advocate some of the less sustainable hypotheses for which he was eventually to become notorious.

9. The works of both scholars are of sufficient number and depth that no attempt is made here to list, much less survey, them all. For studies of direct relevance to biblical scholarship, see especially Arnaldo Momigliano, *Quarto Contributo alla storia degli studi classici e del mondo antico* (Rome: Edizioni di storia e letteratura, 1969); *Quinto Contributo alla storia degli studi classici e del mondo antico*, 2 vols. (Rome: Edizioni di storia e letteratura, 1975); and M. I. Finley, *The Use and Abuse of History* (New York: Viking, 1975).

10. For an introduction to the work of F. C. Baur and an assessment of the value of viewing this work against the thought of Hegel, see Peter C. Hodgson, *The Formation of Historical Theology: A Study of Ferdinand Christian Baur* (New York: Harper & Row, 1966), especially 54–70. The issue of Wellhausen's alleged "Hegelianism" will be treated briefly in this chapter; it is the chief focus of Lothar Perlitt's *Vatke und Wellhausen*, BZAW 94 (Berlin: Alfred Töpelmann, 1965). Bultmann's work is treated briefly in Chapter 2 [[not reprinted here]].

[[4]] Better controlled and more broadly useful ways of approaching the issue of an intellectual tradition's strengths and weaknesses are available. One of these, which is best seen as an instance of the sociology of knowledge, is the investigation of the complete set of institutional, economic, political, and personal affiliations of a particular community of scholars.[11] Though the present study will take a rather different direction, the potential significance of this kind of sociological study for the history of biblical scholarship is great. For example, the institutional setting for the majority of biblical scholarship has long been that of the Christian seminary or of universities committed to training Christian ministers. This setting is quite different from that which exists today for the study of the Bible, especially in the United States, and from what has long existed for other disciplines. So, too, the field of biblical study has witnessed a far higher degree of "self-recruitment" than is true for other fields. To take the example of the nineteenth-century German university (the setting for almost all the material investigated in the present chapter), even if it is true that scholars in many disciplines were disproportionately the offspring of other scholars, this kind of self-recruitment has been demonstrated to have reached its peak in the particular discipline of theology.[12] . . .

[[5]] As with the inquiry into the influence that a specific thinker may have had upon a single scholar or upon an entire discipline, this kind of sociological study both poses special problems in the area of the logic of explanation and carries with it some clear dangers. That a biblical scholar was both the descendant of a Christian minister and was himself (and the scholars in question here are all males, which is also not without potential significance) employed by a Christian seminary need not alone account for all or any of his views. Certainly, sociologists of knowledge know this and attempt to put careful controls on their conclusions to guard against any facile generalizations. There seems little doubt that

---

11. A superb and evenhanded introduction to the contributions of the sociology of knowledge to issues often treated only within intellectual history is Barry Barnes, *Scientific Knowledge and Sociological Theory* (London/Boston: Routledge & Kegan Paul, 1974). Barnes's chief conclusion with regard to scientific research is coincident with the conclusions of the present study with regard to research into the religion of Israel: "Those general beliefs which we are most convinced deserve the status of objective knowledge—scientific beliefs— are readily shown to be overwhelmingly theoretical in character" (p. 10); in the natural sciences, as elsewhere, there is in fact no "clear fact-theory boundary" (p. 21).

12. See Fritz K. Ringer, *Education and Society in Modern Europe* (Bloomington/London: University of Indiana, 1979) 87, 100. Together with other work of Ringer cited in this chapter, this volume is of great and unexpected value for those interested in the course of biblical research.

controlled research of this kind will eventually produce important results for the area of biblical scholarship.

A third way of engaging the history of an intellectual discipline is to be distinguished both from the discussion of specific influences and from the practice of the sociology of knowledge. This is the construction of intellectual history in its broadest sense. It is this method that will occupy our attention for the remainder of the present chapter. Rather than risking the trivialization of the work of committed, often brilliant scholars by tracing their central assumptions to a single mentor, and rather than speaking of the political, institutional, and personal loyalties of these same scholars, I wish instead to speak of an entire tradition of understanding in which biblical scholarship has long taken its stand. It is against this broad tradition of understanding, I believe, that the conclusions of the great nineteenth-century biblical scholars can be both best understood and most fairly evaluated. Nor is this purely a historical exercise. In important ways the tradition of understanding here surveyed has continued to shape the questions and answers of much Hebrew Bible study in the present century.

The intellectual paradigm in question here is a particular and definable way of understanding human history. This tradition for the practice of understanding history arose in Germany and exercised a powerful appeal to German biblical scholars. Because of this, and in company with others, I will generally refer to this paradigm as "the German tradition of historiography," or the like. [[6]] It is not, however, limited to Germany. As this historical paradigm shaped biblical study generally, as the conclusions of German biblical study made their way to other locations on the Continent and to England and the United States, and as the German university became the model for graduate education in the United States especially, many of the essentials of this tradition became a part of biblical study everywhere, however unconsciously.

This particular tradition of comprehending human phenomena made great claims for the discipline of history. History, its adherents never ceased to repeat, is a unique, indeed an autonomous, discipline. Because there is nothing in the world truly comparable to human beings and to their achievements, there is in turn no academic discipline fairly comparable to history.

The German historiographic tradition that made these claims and many others began to take clear shape at the end of the eighteenth century and during the first decades of the nineteenth century. It reached an initial peak in the years just before 1850. Then, after a period of doubts and of competition from other models of understanding, it was revived with a new combativeness in the decades around 1900. Debate about its

possible merits and weaknesses has continued for much of the present
century—and continues still.

The study of this historiographic tradition and its relationship to biblical study that will occupy our attention for the remainder of the present
chapter offers three related arguments. (1) The first is, simply but most
significantly, that biblical scholarship throughout the nineteenth century
and beyond always saw itself as a part, often as the key part, of the broader
tradition against which it arose. This is not, then, a question of "influence." Rather, the broader historiographic tradition and biblical study
shared the same methods, the same goals, the same prejudices, and the
same world of understanding. (2) Secondly, placing the study of the religion of Israel in this, its proper intellectual context, suggests some new
ways to view what appear otherwise as puzzling debates and developments within biblical scholarship. (3) Finally, and most critically significant for the wider thesis of the present 〚7〛 volume, an inquiry into
the German historiographic tradition and its particular manifestations
among biblical scholars reveals that the internal tensions, perhaps even
the self-contradictions, of this tradition were and remain the internal
tensions of biblical study. . . .

The German Tradition of Historical Understanding

> Because it is now deeply entrenched in our thought, it is easy to forget
> that the tendency to view all matters in terms of their histories may
> itself have had a history.[13]

Among the many studies of the German tradition of historical understanding,[14] none fails to note the power of this tradition, a power so
apparent that it gave to the entire nineteenth century the title "The Historical Century." Nor is there any doubt that it is a single concept of

13. Maurice Mandelbaum, *History, Man, and Reason: A Study in Nineteenth-Century
Thought* (Baltimore/London: Johns Hopkins University, 1971) 51.

14. Given the rightful emphasis that students of historiography have placed upon this
particular tradition, these studies abound. See, for a start, G. P. Gooch, *History and Historians
in the Nineteenth Century*, 2d ed. (London: Longmans, Green, and Co., 1952); Friedrich
Meinecke, *Die Entstehund des Historismus*, ed. Carl Hinrichs (Munich: R. Oldenbourg, 1959);
Perlitt, *Vatke und Wellhausen*, 57–85; George Iggers, *The German Conception of History: The National Tradition of Historical Thought from Herder to the Present* (Middletown, Conn.: Wesleyan
University, 1968); Fritz K. Ringer, *The Decline of the German Mandarins: The German Academic
Community, 1890–1933* (Cambridge, Mass.: Harvard University, 1969) 90–102; and Mandel-
baum, *History, Man, and Reason*, 39–138. That the present study is especially indebted to the
ground-breaking work of Iggers will be apparent.

understanding with which we are here dealing. Despite the number and variety of names linked to this tradition, in Germany there was, as perhaps nowhere else, "one main tradition" [[8]] behind which stood an interlocking set of "theoretical convictions in regard to the nature of history."[15] This single tradition, bolstered as it was by these firmly defended convictions, yielded what Georg Iggers, perhaps the most astute chronicler of the tradition, fairly calls "a comprehensive philosophy of life," one which subsumed all value judgments and all categories of logic, to the greater power of history's incomparable and unrepeatable progression.[16]

Though there are risks in periodizing human history, since all such periodization gains clarity at the risk of some accuracy,[17] the German historiographic tradition can usefully be seen both as originating in the eighteenth-century Enlightenment (*Aufklärung*) and as a protest against some Enlightenment views. For a long time, the latter alone was emphasized, and this tradition's polemical stance against rationality and against natural law was pointed to as fundamentally in conflict with the Enlightenment. Recently, however, this exaggerated view has received corrections. Intellectual historians have discovered that the essential premise of the German historiographic tradition—the premise that all inquiry into things human must begin with historical inquiry—is itself a result of Enlightenment thought.[18] Though this correction has been useful, it ought not to obscure the differences that those who shaped the German understanding of history intended between their views and Enlightenment views. Especially in such areas as the concentration upon individuals, upon artistic and intuitive comprehension as a replacement for what was seen as an Enlightenment stress upon "the cold light of reason," the tradition that was soon to proclaim itself with self-conscious pride is a distinct departure from the eighteenth-century Enlightenment.[19]

If some risks accompany the schematizing of history into separate periods, the risks are greater in pointing to a single figure as the one who inaugurates a new historical epoch. Still, the arguments are powerful for discovering the theoretical basis for the German historiographic tradition

---

15. Iggers, *German Conception of History*, 4.

16. Iggers, *German Conception of History*, 30.

17. Among contemporary philosophers of history, Mandelbaum has been especially wise in pointing out the inaccuracies and dangers in any wanton periodization of history; see Maurice Mandelbaum, *The Anatomy of Historical Knowledge* (Baltimore/London: Johns Hopkins University, 1977) 22–23, 134–36.

18. This is the central thesis of Peter H. Reill's *The German Enlightenment and the Rise of Historicism* (Berkeley/Los Angeles/London: University of California, 1975).

19. Mandelbaum, *History, Man, and Reason*, 57.

in the thought of Johann Gottfried Herder (1744–1803).[20] Indeed, Herder's 1774 volume *Also a Philosophy of History for the "Development" of Humanity* has been labeled [[9]] the "first formal statement" of the German stream of historical understanding.[21] Among the key theses of this book and of Herder's thought generally is that all nations and cultures are properly viewed as individual organisms, each with its own distinctive characteristics and defining "spirit." Every people (*Volk*) should be viewed not as are the inert phenomena of nature but rather as "a genetic individual."[22] Nations, and every person in them, thus live under a divine mandate fully to develop their "unique individuality."[23] As vital for the further development of the German tradition of historical understanding as is Herder's insistence that every people is an individual organism, equally so is his strident claim that the history of any people can only be comprehended through acts of intuition and imagination. The historian, Herder said, must loathe metaphysical abstractions and purely rational constructs. The proper historian must rather work as does an artist or a poet.[24] Terms like *immediate, natural,* and *naive* are terms of high praise from Herder, as he sought to combat rationalism with "a kind of aesthetic submissiveness to each ancient depiction."[25]

Those German historians who came to maturity as the Enlightenment gave way to the Romantic era, and then their successors in the decades that followed, found in Herder's proclamations the keys for their ambitious program to compose the first authentic histories of humanity. Selecting representative scholars from the burgeoning German tradition of historical understanding is made difficult by the number of these, undoubtedly of the first rank, who were active during the nineteenth century. Still, the names of three historians do stand out: Wilhelm von Humboldt, Leopold von Ranke, and Johann Gustav Droysen. Emphasiz-

20. Studies that accent Herder's role in the shaping of the following century's historical (including biblical) research include Perlitt, *Vatke und Wellhausen*, 15–24; J. W. Rogerson, *Myth in Old Testament Interpretation*, BZAW 134 (Berlin/New York: Walter de Gruyter, 1974) 9–15; and Hans W. Frei, *The Eclipse of Biblical Narrative: A Study in Eighteenth- and Nineteenth-Century Hermeneutics* (New Haven/London: Yale University, 1974) 183–201.

21. Hayden V. White, "On History and Historicisms," translator's introduction to Carlo Antoni, *From History to Sociology: The Transition in German Historical Thinking* (Detroit, Mich.: Wayne State University, 1959 [originally published in 1940]) xviii. The German title of Herder's ground-breaking work is *Auch eine Philosophie der Geschichte zur Bildung der Menschheit.*

22. Perlitt, *Vatke und Wellhausen*, 18–19 (citing Herder). On Herder's plea that we view peoples as individuals, see also Iggers, *German Conception of History*, 35.

23. Iggers, *German Conception of History*, 46 (citing Herder). The German term for this most important concept is *Eigentümlichkeit.*

24. For the demonstration that Herder's hermeneutic comes from a poetic, rather than a scientific, spirit [*Geist*], see Perlitt, *Vatke und Wellhausen*, 31–32.

25. Frei, *Eclipse of Biblical Narrative*, 184–93.

ing these three, as we will here, does mean omitting all but the most fleeting reference to further representatives of this tradition. Among the most important of these are Barthold Georg Niebuhr, Freidrich Carl von Savigny, and Theodor Mommsen, along with many others.[26]

. . . .

Common Themes in the German Historiographic Tradition

[[15]] In spite of some differences of focus and of the choice of disparate nations and eras to be treated, it is overwhelmingly clear that all three of these historians stand firmly within a single tradition of understanding. What is impressive is the number of themes shared by Humboldt, Ranke, and Droysen. First, there is the conviction that nations and epochs are best viewed as individuals. This means initially that the historian's subject matter is to be treated as a living organism, like an individual human being. The historian searches for an appreciation of the unique individuality of every nation, and hence must not import foreign concepts into his construction of the life of that nation. The emphasis on individualism also means that for these historians the best society is that which allows every human being to develop his own individual characteristics most fully. Clearly, these views carried with them political implications.

Secondly, the various representatives of the German tradition of historical thought here summarized all view the writing of history as the tracing of human development. Humboldt, Ranke, Droysen, and others all "affirmed that the nature of any particular phenomenon was entirely comprehended in its development."[27] Further, the assessment of human change and growth accorded to history by each of these historians was a positive one. Some idea—a world spirit or the hand of God or the ethical world—was progressing through history, to a higher end.

---

26. [[In the rest of this section, Oden examines the thought of these three major German historians. Wilhelm von Humboldt (1767–1835) is perhaps best known for his essay "On the Task of the Historian" (1822) and his assertion that while the historian is to represent "that which happened," he must present this history with creativity, as a "poet," using "intuition." Leopold von Ranke (1795–1886) is often misunderstood as approaching history only empirically (due, according to Oden, to his often-quoted remark that the goal of the historian is "to portray what actually happened"). Yet, he too suggested that the historian meld empirical "objectivity" with a spiritual sensitivity that could discern what Oden calls "the hand of God" behind history. Johann Gustav Droysen (1808–84) concentrated on the rise and rule of Alexander the Great and the Hellenistic period and spoke often of the role of both spirit and idea in history. Oden concludes that his work "represents an uneasy alliance of 'critical historical science' with 'idealistic historical philosophy' " (p. 14) [[not reprinted here]].

27. Michael Ermarth, *Wilhelm Dilthey: The Critique of Historical Reason* (Chicago/London: University of Chicago, 1978) 56.

Thirdly, there is throughout this tradition a loathing of all abstracting, theorizing, or law making. Indeed, Iggers's superb account of this tradition centers upon its "anti-conceptual" character. The tradition repeatedly rejected all abstract and purely conceptual thought, which was thought to risk emptying history of its vital reality.[28] It is this particular element within the nineteenth-century German view of history that accounts for the firm ⟦16⟧ division advocated between natural science (*Naturwissenschaft*) on the one hand and the human science of history (*Geisteswissenschaft*) on the other. The same element accounts for the constant insistence that the historian work as does a poet or an artist, utilizing imagination, intuition, and divination rather than purely rational analysis.

Fourthly, every figure within this overall tradition elevates history to a special rank as an autonomous discipline. History is alone at the top of all learning because solely from historical investigation comes a glimpse of the guiding hand behind all human development. From historical investigation alone comes revelation. History, said Ranke, is "a holy work," which is best approached as one might approach prayer or worship.[29] The logic of this position is well summarized by a recent philosopher: "If all of reality is One, and the Divine is present in all the manifestations of this One, then what occurs within the process of history is itself a Revelation."[30]

Finally, and perhaps most obviously, this whole tradition is a representation of German idealism. This stance "holds that within natural human experience one can find the clue to an understanding of the ultimate nature of reality, and this clue is revealed through those traits which distinguish man as a spiritual being."[31] Whether any or all of the historians whose views were just summarized were specifically "Hegelians" is a question of lesser importance than is their fundamental standing in the broader idealistic stream. Droysen, as we have noted, denied he was a Hegelian. And yet his use of "the supra-empirical level of spirit" and his conviction that history's "movement from natural determinism to the freedom of ethical choice consists of a necessary logic" are both very much in keeping with Hegel's philosophy of history.[32] And the same might be said with fairness of others within this same tradition.

28. Iggers, *German Conception of History*, 10.

29. Gooch, *History and Historians*, 73; and Theodore Von Laue, *Leopold Ranke: The Formative Years*, Princeton Studies in History, no. 4 (Princeton, N.J.: Princeton University, 1950) 44.

30. Mandelbaum, *History, Man, and Reason*, 58.

31. This is Mandelbaum's definition of "metaphysical idealism" (*History, Man, and Reason*, 6).

32. Michael J. Maclean, "Johann Gustav Droysen and the Development of Historical Hermeneutics," *HT* 21 (1982) 363–64. Cf. also Iggers, *German Conception of History*, 95.

Empirical Research versus Intuitive Contemplation

Before turning to a look at biblical historians, an issue directly related to the idealist foundations of the German tradition of [[17]] historical understanding needs some further comment. This is the issue of the tension between this tradition's emphasis upon empirical, objective investigation on the one hand, and the equally firm emphasis upon intuiting history's larger process on the other. Perhaps we can enter into this discussion again by asking what the content of history's grander process was for these historians. If there is development within history, and if the historian must apprehend this development for his results to be worthy of the name of history, just what is it that develops? What develops is some sort of idea or spirit, something quite abstract—and this despite this entire tradition's otherwise steadfast refusal to grant any explanatory power to abstract concepts. However this apparent inconsistency be explained, it is undeniable that the ultimate keys to historical thought turn out to be some quite "elusive abstractions," concepts like a "spiritual principle" or "the hand of God."[33] Though the terms various nineteenth-century historians use in description of the larger processes of history differ in detail, they are without exception disconcertingly abstract, beyond discovery by any ordinary means of investigation. And, as Mandelbaum cogently argues, "all such conceptions are faced by fundamental empirical difficulties which they cannot overcome and cannot avoid."[34]

There thus appears to be a basic inconsistency, if not an essential contradiction, at the heart of this particular concept of historical understanding. So important is the realization of this potential contradiction, especially when we turn to biblical scholarship, that it is worth the risk of some redundancy in citing several recent scholars' formulations of this problem. Iggers, whose portrait of the German understanding of history has proved basic for all subsequent research in this area, has observed that despite the steadfastness with which those within this tradition claimed themselves free of any philosophical or political bias, in fact "German historicism, as a theory of history, possessed many of the characteristics of an ideology."[35] Indeed, in a perhaps curious way, it is precisely *the denial of philosophical presuppositions*, in the face of much evidence of the force of these presuppositions, that suggests [[18]] most strongly that this tradition might be characterized as an ideology. Hans Frei's formulation of the central difficulty here is similarly forceful:

33. Von Laue, *Leopold Ranke*, 93.
34. Mandelbaum, *History, Man, and Reason*, 130.
35. Iggers, *German Conception of History*, 17.

On the one hand, historicism was an apprehension of the specificity and irreducibly historical particularity of cultural change. But on the other hand, as a movement in German thought it led to the very opposite of this apprehension, to a vast universalization in defining the content of historical change.[36]

Finally, the conclusion to a recent study of Droysen's thought is also relevant: By his emphasis upon the progress of "ethical powers" working toward individual freedom, Droysen's "interpretive categories remain ideologically fixed" and his claims for the autonomy of historical understanding are, in the end, mired "in the *Tendenzgeschichte* [partisanship] he wished so much too avoid."[37]

The results of this internal tension, between (1) scrupulous, objective investigation and (2) the imaginative search for the spiritual forces connecting phenomena, are everywhere apparent. At the very moment when the nineteenth-century German historians who shaped this tradition were advocating a careful relativism so that the historian sought to understand each nation on its own terms, as an individual, they were bringing into their own historical thought the most obvious kinds of value judgments. These judgments include a Protestant loathing for the Middle Ages, and especially for the Roman Catholic church, a distaste for the French and the results of the French Revolution, or a pronounced prejudice toward things German—judgments, one critic correctly notes, "so patently narrow that it is difficult to see any tendency toward relativism at all."[38] In short, following the dictates of this tradition led, inevitably, to anything but an objective portrait of matters "as they really were."

The History of Israel in the Nineteenth-Century Context

The present context plainly prohibits anything like a fair portrait of the chief biblical scholars of the past several centuries or of their many and monumental contributions.[39] Still, before we move on to the mid–

---

36. Frei, *Eclipse of Biblical Narrative*, 213.

37. Maclean, "Johann Gustav Droysen and the Development of Historical Hermeneutics," 362.

38. Reill, *German Enlightenment and the Rise of Historicism*, 190–91.

39. For an introduction to the history of Old Testament scholarship, see the following volumes: Cheyne, *Founders of Old Testament Criticism*; Emil G. Kraeling, *The Old Testament since the Reformation* (New York: Harper & Brothers, 1955); Hans-Joachim Kraus, *Geschichte der historisch-kritischen Erforschung des Alten Testaments*, 2d ed. (Neukirchen-Vluyn: Neukirchener, 1969); Herbert F. Hahn, *The Old Testament in Modern Research* (Philadelphia, Pa.: Fortress, 1970); and, for the most recent period alone, Ronald E. Clements, *A Century of Old Testament*

nineteenth century, it is worthy of note that [[19]] critical biblical scholarship began, as did the broader movement of historical understanding, with the eighteenth-century Enlightenment.[40]

. . . .

Julius Wellhausen

Since Julius Wellhausen (1844–1918) is remembered above all for his massive and systematic presentation of the argument that [[20]] the prophets predate the law, it is plain that the separate pieces of this argument had been constructed before him. To say as much is to take nothing away from the achievement of Wellhausen, who is beyond all doubt one of the handful of scholars of genius ever to have devoted themselves to the study of Israelite religion.[11] . . . After an early brilliant career at Göttingen, where he studied under Ewald and others, Wellhausen was for a decade a professor at Greifswald. It was at Greifswald that he wrote the work of chief concern here, a volume now generally known as the *Prolegomena to the History of Ancient Israel.*[12] . . .

Wellhausen's *Prolegomena*, as we have just noted, is best remembered for the comprehensive treatment of the sources of the Pentateuch and of other blocks of material in the Hebrew Bible for which Wellhausen similarly attempted to fix a chronology. The central thesis, that the prophets preceded the law, Wellhausen attributes to Graf, Reuss, and

---

Study (Guilford/London: Lutterworth, 1976). For the New Testament, see Werner Georg Kümmel, *The New Testament: The History of the Investigation of Its Problems,* trans. S. M. Gilmour and H. C. Kee (Nashville, Tenn./New York: Abingdon, 1972). A truly comprehensive, multi-volume history of biblical scholarship, such as exists for classical scholarship, for example, is one of the clear needs in this discipline.

40. [[In the section omitted, Oden provides a brief summary of the developments in critical scholarship from Richard Simon and Jean Astruc through W. M. L. de Wette, Heinrich Ewald, Wilhelm Vatke, and Karl Graf.]]

41. The literature on Wellhausen is, fully appropriately, immense. For a beginning, see the following works and the bibliographies therein: Perlitt, *Vatke und Wellhausen;* Kraus, *Geschichte der historisch-kritischen Erforschung,* 255–74; and all of the essays in Douglas A. Knight, ed., *Julius Wellhausen and His Prolegomena to the History of Israel,* Semeia 25 (Chico, Calif.: Scholars, 1983). The last work contains a piece of great interest by Rudolf Smend, for whose complete biography of Wellhausen the scholarly world awaits with much expectation; for now, see also Smend's "Wellhausen in Greifswald," *ZTK* 78 (1981) 141–76.

42. Originally published as *Geschichte Israels. In zwei Bänder: Erster Band* (Berlin: G. Reimer, 1878), the 2d edition was entitled *Prolegomena zur Geschichte Israels, Zweite Ausgabe der Geschichte Israels, Band I* (Berlin: G. Reimer, 1883). Citations here are from this edition of 1883 and from the English translation, *Prolegomena to the History of Ancient Israel,* which was first published in 1885, with a reprint of "Israel" from the *Encyclopaedia Britannica* and a preface by W. Robertson Smith (Gloucester, Mass.: Peter Smith, 1973).

Vatke and less directly to the pioneering historical work of de Wette.[43] Wellhausen presents and defends this thesis not just with wide-ranging evidence from throughout the Hebrew Bible but also with a superb literary style. . . . [21] So powerfully is the whole presented that Robertson Smith could write a few years later that, thanks to the work of Wellhausen above all, "nothing of vital importance for the historical study of the Old Testament religion remains uncertain."[44]

Our chief concern here, however, is not so much the status of the central thesis of the *Prolegomena*. We are concerned rather with the extraordinary extent to which the foundations of Wellhausen's arguments can be shown to correspond to the theoretical bases of the German tradition of historical understanding. This appears perhaps most clearly in the undisguised evaluative statements that run through the work. As Patrick Miller has recently observed, "one of the things that is always startling in reading Wellhausen is that along with the wealth of data he marshalled to argue his case there is a significant amount of value judgment running throughout the *Prolegomena*."[45] The first, and probably least startling, of these that is fully within the broader nineteenth-century historiographic tradition is Wellhausen's praise for anything that expresses or allows for human individualism. For example, Wellhausen leaves no doubt but that authentic religion entails "the spontaneous sacrifice of the individual" rather than "the prescribed sacrifice of the community."[46] That Wellhausen prefers the spontaneous to the prescribed has long been observed, but of even greater significance for his overall conception of religious development is his emphasis on individual freedom. Nor is this judgment limited to comments on sacrifice. The tribal period Wellhausen praises as the era that witnessed "the divineness of heroical self-sacrifice of the individual for the good of the nation."[47] So too Wellhausen's high regard for Israelite prophets is most truly a result of his vision of history progressing toward individual self-expression. For Wellhausen, the prophets are responsible for "the great metamorphosis" of Israelite religion.[48] The reason for the prophets' ability to effect such a change is what is of greatest interest. The importance of the prophets, writes Wellhausen, [22] "rests on the individuals. . . . [The prophets are] always single, rest-

43. Wellhausen, *Prolegomena*, 4 (English trans., 3–4).

44. William Robertson Smith, *The Religion of the Semites: The Fundamental Institutions* (New York: Schocken, 1972 [originally published in 1889]) vii.

45. Patrick D. Miller, Jr., "Wellhausen and the History of Israel's Religion," in Knight, *Julius Wellhausen*, 63.

46. Wellhausen, *Prolegomena*, 107 (English trans., 103).

47. Wellhausen, "Israel," in the English edition of the *Prolegomena*, 448.

48. Wellhausen, *Prolegomena*, 390 (English trans., 368).

ing on nothing outside themselves. . . . [The prophets represent] the inspiration of awakened individuals. . . . They do not preach on set texts;
they speak out of the spirit."[49] Individual freedom climaxes, of course,
only in the New Testament, where Wellhausen finds expressed "the freedom of the children of God."[50]

Both this high praise for individual expression and the underlying
belief that the world has progressed under providential design to allow
for more and more such individual expression are, as we have seen,
themes Wellhausen shares with the broader tradition of historical understanding. Wellhausen's reliance upon the basic historicist premise, that
history represents an unceasing course of development, is clear throughout, even if this course is not always progressive for him. Thus, that prophetic individualism previously noted and responsible in Wellhausen's
eyes for "ethical monotheism" is itself a result of "a progressive step
which had been called forth simply by the course of events. The provi-
dence of God brought it about."[51] Such citations could be multiplied
but are perhaps unnecessary in view of a most important sentence Wellhausen writes in the introduction to the *Prolegomena*, which explicitly presents his central assumption of method: "It is necessary to trace the
succession of the three elements [the Jehovist, the Deuteronomic, and
the Priestly] in detail, and at once to test and to fix each by reference
to an independent standard, namely, the inner development of the history of Israel."[52] That "the inner development" of an individual nation's
life should offer one "an independent standard" was self-evident *only* to
those who stood squarely within a particular tradition of historical understanding—the tradition of Humboldt, Ranke, and Droysen. Moreover,
just as that which develops in a nation's progress for these historians
was morality or ethics, Wellhausen too finds in the moral the most significant arena of religious worth. The prophets, for Wellhausen, are moved
"by ethical motives, which manifest themselves in them for the first time
in history."[53] Again, in the most authentic representatives of Israelite
religion, "sin or offence to the Deity is [[23]] a thing of purely moral
character. . . . Morality is that for the sake of which all other things exist;
it is the alone essential thing in the world."[54]

---

49. Wellhausen, *Prolegomena*, 422–23 (English trans., 398–99).
50. Cited by Perlitt, *Vatke und Wellhausen*, 234 ("die Freiheit der Kinder Gottes").
51. Wellhausen, "Israel," 474.
52. Wellhausen, *Prolegomena*, 13 (English trans., 12) ("mittelst eines unabhängigen
Masses . . . nämlich mittelst des inneren Ganges der israelitischen Geschichte").
53. Wellhausen, *Prolegomena*, 49–50 (English trans., 47). It will be remembered that
Droysen spoke explicitly of the same movement of "ethical forces."
54. Wellhausen, "Israel," 472.

Another vital area of agreement between Wellhausen and the broad stream of nineteenth-century historiography is a pronounced bias against all abstraction, theory, and nomothetic thought—even though both Wellhausen and this broad stream were themselves deeply indebted to their own abstract concepts. It is this above all that accounts for Wellhausen's extraordinarily harsh condemnations of the Priestly Codex and for the work of the Chronicler. While the Jehovist (Wellhausen uses this to refer to a combination of the Yahwist and the Elohist) expresses "genuine antiquity," "sacred mystery," and "living poetic detail," the Priestly Codex represents "theological abstraction," "mere fact," and the "pedantry" of theory.[55] Again, further documentation is perhaps unnecessary. Throughout the *Prolegomena* we find the Priestly Code and the work of the Chronicler everywhere stigmatized as "an abstraction," "mechanical," "a theory," "a pattern," "a system," something static and beyond the reality of growth and development. As with the German historiographic tradition generally, what is here remarkable is Wellhausen's condemnation of the theoretical and the abstract on the one hand, and yet his fundamental reliance upon highly theoretical—and theological—abstractions on the other hand.

It seems clear, then, that the basic precepts of the German tradition of historical understanding are also the basic precepts out of which Wellhausen composes the history of Israelite religion and literature. That Wellhausen stands squarely within this tradition is a far more significant conclusion than is the issue of the extent to which he was or was not a Hegelian, an issue that has loomed large in the assessment of Wellhausen for many decades.[56] It has so partly because Wellhausen admitted his great debt to Vatke, who was openly Hegelian. For example, Wellhausen wrote in a letter to Vatke's son, "I have learned from none more, from few as much, as I have learned from your father. . . . Hegelian or not, that is immaterial to me."[57] But more basic and more important [[24]] here, as in the case of Droysen for example, is the essential idealistic philosophy of history shared by so many in the nineteenth century.

Smend has recently written that "Wellhausen stood at as great a remove from Hegelian speculation as a German historian of the nineteenth

---

55. Wellhausen, *Prolegomena*, 320–23, 357 (English trans., 304–7, 337).

56. The chief aim of Perlitt, in *Vatke und Wellhausen*, is to refute the charge that Wellhausen was a Hegelian. For an expression of a contrary argument, see Kraus, *Geschichte der historisch-kritischen Erforschung*, 260–68.

57. The letter is cited in Perlitt, *Vatke und Wellhausen*, 152 ("Ich habe von keinem Menschen mehr, von kaum Einem so viel gelernt, als von Ihrem Herrn Vater. . . . Hegelianer oder nicht: das ist mir einerlei").

century could without falling right out of context."[58] Smend's statement is well and carefully put. But the context of which he speaks, the context of both Wellhausen and the historians summarized earlier in this chapter, is the key to following the course of nineteenth-century biblical criticism. That this is the case, that Wellhausen is hardly alone in his situation within a broader stream of learning, can be made clear by a briefer glance at Robertson Smith.

William Robertson Smith

The course of the career of William Robertson Smith (1846–94) is in many ways not unlike that of Wellhausen. In May 1881, almost precisely a year before Wellhausen resigned his chair at Greifswald, Robertson Smith was removed from his chair at the Free Church of Scotland College in Aberdeen. He too moved to an allied field and in 1883 became the professor of Arabic at Cambridge. And Robertson Smith's work was in many ways as creative and influential as was that of Wellhausen. This is most especially true in the area of religion's social background and social impact. It is not going too far to claim that Robertson Smith "discovered" the social function of religions generally. And from a single sentence in his *The Religion of the Semites* [for an excerpt from Robertson Smith's book, see "Sacrifice: Preliminary Survey," pp. 43–64 in this volume] arose an entire tradition of twentieth-century studies in religion, the sentence that reads: "Religion did not exist for the saving of souls but for the preservation and welfare of society."[59] What is of chief concern here, however, are not those areas in which Robertson Smith anticipated and shaped future studies, by those like Émile Durkheim, but rather the extent to which his portrait of the religion of Israel grows out of the historiographical tradition in which Wellhausen so clearly stands.

In his comparative study of Israelite religion, Robertson Smith [25] offers continued praise for religious developments that result in the heightening of individual expression. For example, he labels both Judaism and Christianity "*positive* religions," by which he understands them to be religions "which did not grow up like the systems of ancient heathenism, under the action of unconscious forces operating silently from age to age, but trace their origin to the teaching of great religious innovators."[60] For Israel, the chief such innovators are the prophets, who acted under providential guidance to produce the uniquely individual and ethical

58. Rudolf Smend, "Julius Wellhausen and His *Prolegomena to the History of Israel*," in Knight, *Julius Wellhausen*, 14.

59. Robertson Smith, *Religion of the Semites*, 29.

60. Robertson Smith, *Religion of the Semites*, 1.

religion of the Old Testament. While the preprophetic religious world thought "much of the community and little of the individual life," the prophets, acting according to "a series of special providences," ensured that Israel's religion would concern itself with "the welfare of every individual."[61] That this is the case, Robertson Smith argues, ought to be plain to anyone "who has faith enough to see the hand of God as clearly in a long providential development as in a sudden miracle."[62] Further, for Robertson Smith as for Wellhausen and the tradition behind both, what develops providentially in Israel's religion is not just an increase in individual freedom but also a heightened sense of the ethical. While other religions remained tied to a reward and punishment system of a purely "mechanical character," in "the religion of the Old Testament" the historian witnesses a "development of the higher sense of sin and responsibility."[63]

It was observed earlier that Wellhausen utters a surprising number of evaluative judgments in the course of his reconstruction of Israelite literary development. The same is true of Robertson Smith. Here, such judgments are if anything even more curious, given the high regard Robertson Smith has for the exercise of comparative religion. He opens *The Religion of the Semites* with the proclamations that "comparative religion . . . is indispensable to the future progress of Biblical research" and that the materials in the Old Testament "cannot be thoroughly comprehended until they are put into comparison with the religions of the nations akin to the Israelites."[64] Yet the remainder of the volume proves that Robertson Smith does not have in mind anything like the modern [[26]] enterprise of comparative religion. It is not *comparison*, as objectively and fairly as is possible, that he exercises but rather a series of *contrasts* between the ethical, individual, fully developed religion of Israel on the one hand, and the restricted and communal religions of Israel's neighbors on the other. Thus, these other religions remained satisfied with a "crassly materialistic conception of the divine nature," while Israel alone "had learned to draw nigh to their God without the aid of sacrifice and offering."[65]

The End of the Nineteenth Century and the "Crisis" in Historical Understanding

The internal tension between empirical investigation and a reliance upon highly abstract, theoretical and theological, presuppositions that

61. Robertson Smith, *Religion of the Semites*, 258–59.
62. Robertson Smith, "Preface" to the English trans. of Wellhausen's *Prolegomena*, ix.
63. Robertson Smith, *Religion of the Semites*, 415.
64. Robertson Smith, *Religion of the Semites*, v–vi.
65. Robertson Smith, *Religion of the Semites*, 215 [[reprinted in this volume, p. 43–64]].

existed in the German historiographic tradition was noted with increasing frequency in the period from 1850 onward. The observation of this tension, and the implication that its presence might mean this tradition could not achieve anything like the full historical portraits it was after, was one of the sources for what came to be seen as a "crisis" in historical understanding as the nineteenth century came to a close. This crisis was met by a wide attempt on many fronts to reassert, with a new combativeness, the fundamental postulates of the German tradition of historical understanding. The "enemy" against which these combative blows were directed was largely positivism. Positivism was, of course, associated in its origin above all with the name of August Comte (1798–1857), who had argued that the best model for the explanation of any phenomenon was the model provided by the natural sciences. Many in Europe professed to see in the years following 1850 "a wave of anti-Hegelian positivist reaction," a reaction that "swept German intellectual (including theological) circles."[66] The historiographic tradition begun by Herder, Humboldt, and others responded to this perceived threat from positivism by attempting "to restore the Romantic sense of the historical and the ideal world."[67] As the nineteenth century came to a close, the battle lines were thus firmly drawn. On one side stood positivism; on the [[27]] other stood a neo-idealist, neo-Romantic, anti-rationalist front that sought to restore the authentic spirit of historical understanding.

The sense that a formerly clear tradition of understanding was under attack and was no longer adopted uncritically by a new generation of thinkers was akin to a wider sense, which stretched far beyond the boundaries of the university, that the world had changed—and changed for the worse. There was continual talk of the evils of commercialism and materialism, of the destruction of the old culture and its ideal of the full development of human potential (*Bildung*). What had replaced the former sense of history and poetry was now the ills of "mechanization, specialization, fragmentation."[68] In the 1870s, toward the ends of their lives, both Ranke and Theodor Mommsen expressed their dismay at what they claimed to see as "the dehumanizing tendencies of the time."[69] In roughly the same period, the letters of Droysen are filled with fulminations against "Positivism," "Materialism," and "the polytechnic

66. Frei, *Eclipse of Biblical Narrative*, 225.

67. [[H. Stuart]] Hughes, *Consciousness and Society* [[*The Reorientation of European Social Thought 1890–1930* (rev. ed.; New York: Vintage, 1977)]] 189.

68. Ringer, *Decline of the German Mandarins*, 220–23, 265.

69. Gooch, *History and Historians*, 469.

Method."[70] The wider context of this "crisis" means, of course, that the term *positivism* was really a kind of catchall negative, utilized in much the same way that the term *Fascism* has been used in the present century. That is, positivism was not so much a particular model of understanding based upon the natural sciences as it was a symbol for all things against which the neo-Romanticism of the end of the nineteenth century wished to do battle.

Probably this era's most vital spokesman on behalf of a historical understanding that could retrieve the best of the former tradition and yet still be a proper science was Wilhelm Dilthey (1833–1911).[71] Dilthey can with justice be called the founder of historical hermeneutics, at least in the modern period. Hughes, for example, finds in his work "the first thoroughgoing and sophisticated confrontation of history with positivism and natural science."[72] It was Dilthey who first "truly perceived the epistemological inconsistency of the claim of the German 'historical school' to 'objectivity' as an uncritical mixture of the idealist and realist perspectives."[73]

[[28]] In a sense, then, the problem Dilthey confronted is the problem at the base of the present study—and perhaps too the issue at the center of much of nineteenth-century thought. Where does historical understanding fit in the relationship between positivism and idealism, or between the natural sciences (*Naturwissenschaften*) and the human sciences (*Geisteswissenschaft*).[74] And can historical understanding make claims to objectivity? Dilthey saw his task as that of guiding "a recalcitrant and rebellious historiography into the frame of science, after its autonomy *vis-à-vis* the natural sciences had been established."[75] His answer was to develop a notion of 'understanding' (*Verstehen*) that he saw as both objective and yet still distinct from what existed in the natural sciences. . . .

Biblical Scholarship at the End of the Nineteenth Century

Just as Wellhausen, Robertson Smith, and many others demonstrate repeatedly that the theoretical foundation of their scholarship [[29]] is

70. Joachim Wach, *Das Verstehen: Grundzüge einer Geschichte der hermeneutischen Theorie im 19 Jahrhundert*, 3 vols. (Tübingen: J. C. B. Mohr, 1926–33) 3:154, citing Droysen's correspondence.

71. On Dilthey, see Richard E. Palmer, *Hermeneutics: Interpretation Theory in Schleiermacher, Dilthey, Heidegger, and Gadamer* (Evanston, Ill.: Northwestern University, 1969) 98–123; Iggers, *German Conception of History*, 133–44; Ringer, *Decline of the German Mandarins*, 316–23; Hughes, *Consciousness and Society*, 192–200; and especially Ermarth, *Wilhelm Dilthey*.

72. Hughes, *Consciousness and Society*, 194.

73. Palmer, *Hermeneutics*, 99.

74. White ("On History and Historicisms," xv) views this as the central problem of all of nineteenth-century German intellectual history.

75. Antoni, *From History to Sociology*, 7.

identical with that of the tradition of Herder, Humboldt, Ranke, and Droysen, so too there is a group of biblical scholars who worked in the years immediately following, the years at the end of the nineteenth century, whose works show them as full participants in the attempt to revitalize this same tradition of historical understanding. This group includes Albert Eichhorn, Hermann Gunkel, W. Wrede, Wilhelm Bousset, Ernst Troeltsch, and W. Heitmüller, all of whom were born within the first two decades following 1850, and a second group born only shortly thereafter: Hugo Gressmann, Hans Schmidt, Walter Baumgartner, Emil Balla, and Otto Pfleiderer. At one time or another, all of these scholars were associated with something commonly called the "History of Religions School."[76] As one of its members, Hugo Gressmann, frequently said, the title is not quite accurate if it suggests all these scholars worked together at a single location. Gressmann preferred the title "circle" or "movement."[77] Whatever be the most appropriate title, what is important here is that all these scholars shared an interest in defending the basic, German historiographic tradition and in defining their own work as an authentic representation of this tradition.

The History of Religions School's birthplace was the Göttingen of the 1880s, and its father was Albert Eichhorn. Even though Eichhorn wrote far less than did Gunkel or Gressmann, for example, the members of this school were unanimous in looking to him as their "undisputed spokesman."[78] Much that would become central to this school and much that demonstrates the school's participation in the end-of-the-century defense of historical understanding is implicit already in a set of twenty-four theses that Eichhorn defended publicly in 1886. The set includes the theses that "every explanation of a myth is false which does not bear in mind the origin and development of the myth" and that "the composition of history is an art"[79] —both of which might have been uttered by Herder. Gressmann attributes the great influence of Eichhorn over the

76. On this School ("die religionsgeschichtliche Schule"), see Hugo Gressmann, *Albert Eichhorn und die religionsgeschichtliche Schule* (Göttingen: Vandenhoeck und Ruprecht, 1914); Werner Klatt, *Hermann Gunkel, zu seiner Theologie der Religionsgeschichte und zur Entstehung der formgeschichtlichen Methode*, FRLANT 100 (Göttingen: Vandenhoeck und Ruprecht, 1969); Kraus, *Geschichte der historisch-kritischen Erforschung*, 327–40; and Kümmel, *New Testament*, 206–324.

77. Gressmann, *Albert Eichhorn*, 25 ("Kreise" or "Bewegung").

78. Klatt, *Hermann Gunkel*, 20–21 ("unbestrittener Wortführer").

79. All twenty-four theses may be found in Gressmann, *Albert Eichhorn*, 8. ("Jede Deutung eines Mythus ist falsch, welche nicht die Entstehung und Ausbildung des Mythus berücksichtigt"; "Die Geschichtschreibung ist eine Kunst"). On the significance for the future of the History-of-Religions School of this event, see also Kraus, *Geschichte der historisch-kritischen Erforschung*, 328.

others in the school to Eichhorn's passionate search for "the progress of human spiritual life," to his great "love for history and for historical development," and to his equally pronounced distaste for philosophy and natural science.[80] As [[30]] Gunkel was to later write in a letter to Gressmann, Eichhorn showed all of those in this school that the truth was to be found in "realities, not theories," and thus "in history and not in philosophy."[81]

If Eichhorn was of early significance in shaping the essential concerns of the History of Religions School, it is the work of Johannes Heinrich Hermann Gunkel (1862–1932) that has had the greatest impact on twentieth-century biblical scholarship.[82] Gunkel's many contributions, all of which (including the form-critical method) are best seen against the background of the end-of-the-century reaffirmation of the German tradition of historical understanding, have justly been called "epoch making." Gunkel himself has been labeled "doubtless the most important Old Testament scholar since Wellhausen," one whose methods and goals "have been appropriated, in one fashion or another, by all who move in the mainstream of contemporary biblical studies."[83] Gunkel was the first (in 1889) to use the adjective *religionsgeschichtliche* ('History of Religions') to describe what this movement wanted to achieve. He was also the first openly to proclaim that he and the others in this school "stand at the beginning of a new epoch in the interpretation of Old Testament religious and literary history."[84] And his 1895 volume *Creation and Chaos*, which followed the life of a single mythic structure from Genesis in the Hebrew Bible through the Book of Revelation in the New Testament, marked the formal inauguration of the History of Religions School.

So voluminously did Gunkel write, and so plainly do his theoretical assumptions match those of the wider attempt to defend and reassert the basic postulates of the German tradition of historical understanding, that one can find evidence in his work for every one of these postulates. Just as Eichhorn had done in one of his public theses, Gunkel tirelessly

80. Gressmann, *Albert Eichhorn*, 8–14 ("die Entfaltung des menschlichen Geistesleben"; "seine Vorliebe für Geschichte und geschichtliche Entwicklung").

81. Gunkel's letter of June, 1913, is cited by Kraus, *Geschichte der historisch-kritischen Erforschung*, 330 (not "Theorien, sondern Wirklichkeiten": "Geschichte, aber nicht Philosophie").

82. For the life and thought of Gunkel, see Klatt, *Hermann Gunkel*; and Kraus, *Geschichte der historisch-kritischen Erforschung*, 341–67.

83. These three judgments come, respectively, from Kraus (*Geschichte der historisch-kritischen Erforschung*, 341), from Kraeling (*Old Testament since the Reformation*, 298), and from James Muilenburg ("Introduction" to Hermann Gunkel, *The Psalms: A Form-Critical Introduction* [Philadelphia, Pa.: Fortress, 1967] iii).

84. Klatt, *Hermann Gunkel*, 25 n. 39, and p. 74 ("wir am Anfang einer neuen Epoche in der Auffassung der alttestamentlichen Religions- und Literaturgeschichte stehen").

repeated that to understand is to follow a phenomenon's providential growth. "We had come to see," Gunkel wrote in description of the origins of the History of Religions School, that the religion of Israel "can be understood only when it is understood in its history, in its growth and becoming."[85] [[31]] What is it that progresses and develops in this religion? The same concept that progresses and develops for Wellhausen and the tradition in which he stood: the idea of human individualism. For Gunkel, the Old Testament yielded "the highest that was achieved anywhere throughout the East—human personality living its own life."[86] To the religion of Israel Gunkel attributes the very "origin of individualism."[87] If the Israelite prophets initiated this process, as they did in Gunkel's vision, the process is only complete in the New Testament. There, we see, Gunkel argues, that "in the teachings of Jesus everything centers about an ethical imperative born of supreme religious individualism."[88] The Old Testament, then, "is on a lower level, for in its pages religion deals in the first instance with national life, although it was out of this national religion that the higher religion of the individual gradually arose."[89]

How does one apprehend the central developmental message of the Old Testament? Here Gunkel speaks in a way that reveals most clearly his participation in the neo-Romantic, antipositivist revolt that characterized the final decade of the nineteenth century. One understands, Gunkel says again and again, not rationally, but poetically, not as a scientist but as an artist. Arguing that too much dry rationality has characterized biblical scholarship (in fact, there is very little that is anything like dry rationality), Gunkel pleads for "a certain flair or artistic sense."[90] Since exegesis is after the secret inner life, the spiritual fullness, of biblical literature, "exegesis in the highest sense is more an art than a science."[91] Gunkel says he began his scholarship to combat "the modernizings of

85. Hermann Gunkel, "The 'Historical Movement' in the Study of Religion," *Expository Times* 38 (1926–27) 533.

86. Hermann Gunkel, "What Is Left of the Old Testament," in *What Remains of the Old Testament and Other Essays* (London: Allen & Unwin, 1928) 52–53.

87. Hermann Gunkel, "Die israelitischen Literatur," in *Die Kultur der Gegenwart: Die orientalischen Literaturen*, ed. Paul Hinneberg (Berlin/Leipzig: Teubner, 1906) 78 ("die Entstehung des Individualismus").

88. Hermann Gunkel, "The Religio-Historical Interpretation of the New Testament," *The Monist* 13 (1902–3): 449. This lengthy essay was also published as *Zum religionsgeschichtlichen Verständnis des Neuen Testaments* (Göttingen: Vandenhoeck und Ruprecht, 1903).

89. Gunkel, "What Is Left of the Old Testament," 42.

90. Hermann Gunkel, "Jakob," in *What Remains of the Old Testament*, 157.

91. Hermann Gunkel, "Ziele und Methoden der Erklärung des Alten Testaments," in Hermann Gunkel, *Reden und Aufsätze* (Göttingen: Vandenhoeck und Ruprecht, 1913) 14 ("Exegese im höchsten Sinne ist mehr eine Kunst als eine Wissenschaft").

exegetes who, without historical reflection and influenced by rationalism, know nothing of the 'effects' of the *pneuma* [spirit] and render 'Spirit' a pure abstraction."[92]

Further, such statements about biblical scholarship's task are buttressed by more general laments over the mechanical and impersonal course of recent events—laments we have seen to have been echoed everywhere in this era. Gunkel often railed against "materialism" and looked for a new religious awakening to return Germans to their spiritual roots.[93] In a sentence of extraordinary [[32]] significance, a sentence that might serve as a kind of epigram for the real goals of Gunkel and the History of Religions School, Gunkel pauses in the midst of an essay on the Old Testament and offers the following reflection: "The conditions of modern life, especially in large cities, have become so unnatural, so complicated and chaotic, that the modern child . . . finds it extremely difficult to gain clear and simple conceptions."[94] This sentence is of vital significance partly because this nostalgic vision included also a specific nostalgia for the methods and aims of the German tradition of historical understanding—methods and aims that Gunkel, in company with others, knew to be under attack and in need of dramatic rearticulation.

The History of Religions School is often praised and perhaps chiefly remembered for its work in the area of comparative religion. According to the standard view, discoveries like that of the Amarna Tablets in 1887–88 led Gunkel and others to a new appreciation of the contribution that might come from such comparative work. Certainly, there is some truth to this conventional view. Gunkel did say, for example, that "the religion of the New Testament, in important, and even in some vital, points can be interpreted only in the light of the influence of extraneous religions."[95] However, whenever Gunkel, Gressmann, or others within this school were questioned about their comparative work, they replied with vigor that this was most emphatically *not* the central emphasis of this school. Gunkel, for example, repeatedly said that it was the history of *a religion* (i.e., biblical religion), not the history of *various religions*, that was his concern. The History of Religions School's title, Gunkel wrote, never meant "a dragging down of what is Biblical to the level of the non-Biblical." Rather, "the thoughts that then [in the period when this school was founded] filled our minds had arisen within the-

92. Hermann Gunkel, *The Influence of the Holy Spirit: The Popular View of the Apostolic Age and the Teaching of the Apostle Paul,* trans. R. A. Harrisville and P. A. Quanbeck II (Philadelphia, Pa.: Fortress, 1979 [originally published in 1888]) 12.

93. See Klatt, *Herman Gunkel,* 86.

94. Gunkel, "What Is Left of the Old Testament," 31.

95. Gunkel, "Religio-Historical Interpretation," 398.

ology itself . . . Before our eyes, uplifting us and bearing us onward, stood a wondrous picture—the Religion of the Bible in all its glory and dignity."[96] Gressmann too wrote that the real "kernel of the movement" was never comparative work; it was rather the attempt to reconstruct "the history of a single religion."[97] Hence, this school did engage [[33]] in a sort of comparative work. But it was comparative work very much like that of Robertson Smith or of Humboldt and Ranke. It was an enterprise that made claims to objectivity and yet whose central aim was plainly apologetic. The more comparative material was assembled, the more brightly shone the superiority of Israel's religion.

That the entire History of Religions movement was deeply immersed in the turn-of-the-century afterlife of the German idealist historiographic tradition is not solely a conclusion from data such as that just presented. The members of this school themselves readily granted this. Gressmann, for example, wrote that this school flourished despite some initial opposition precisely because its goals corresponded to "the general current of the era," a current defined as "an awakening sharpness of historical sensibility." Hence for Gressmann, "the appearance of the History of Religions School upon the theological scene is nothing but one manifestation of a larger, total movement which is now noticeable within scholarship everywhere."[98] The "larger, total movement" to which Gressmann refers is plainly an attempt to recapture the idealist and Romantic spirit of the historical tradition begun in Herder, to whom several of these scholars, and Gunkel especially, pay continued tribute. For Gunkel, the History of Religions School properly viewed is "nothing but a new wave of the mighty historical current set in motion by our great idealist thinkers and poets, which has affected our entire mental life, and has now long influenced our theological outlook also."[99] It comes as no surprise, then, that Gunkel finds in the Israelite prophets the expression of "the imperishable power of the Moral Idea," or that he believed always in "the revelatory power of history."[100]

When Gunkel and the others are thus placed within the particular context of turn-of-the-century polemics, the History of Religion School's

96. Gunkel, "Historical Movement," 533.

97. Gressmann, *Albert Eichhorn*, 30 ("Kern der Bewegung": "die Geschichte der eigenen Religion").

98. Gressmann, *Albert Eichhorn*, 27–28 ("die allgemeine Zeitströmung . . . die wachsende Verfeinerung des historischen Sinnes"; "Das Aufkommen der religionsgeschichtlichen Schule auf theologischen Gebiet ist demnach nur die Teilerscheinung einer grösseren Gesamtbewegung, die sich überall in der Wissenschaft bemarkbar macht").

99. Gunkel, "Historical Movement," 533.

100. Gunkel, "What Is Left of the Old Testament," 21; and Klatt, *Hermann Gunkel*, 269 ("die Offenbarungsmächtigkeit der Geschichte").

so-called battle with Wellhausen becomes far more intelligible. Certainly, the members of this school were careful to voice their debts to Wellhausen. Gunkel, typically, claimed that he "was a true Wellhausian" and that he and the others belonged in a sense to the larger school of Wellhausen.[101] But this movement's [[34]] representatives also convicted Wellhausen for not being historical enough. For Gunkel, "Wellhausen falls into conflict with fundamental principles which are everywhere recognized in historical science" because "the cardinal principle of historical study is this: That we are unable to comprehend a person, a period, or a thought dissociated from its antecedents. . . . [Only such inquiry yields a] true and living understanding of the subject."[102]

This is the central accusation by this school against Wellhausen: not that he insufficiently utilized comparative materials, as is often claimed, but that his failure to go backward far enough behind the historical sources meant that Wellhausen was, in the end, *not* a true historian. But such a claim in isolation makes no sense at all. Surely Julius Wellhausen deserves the title of "historian" as much as anyone in the entire nineteenth century. But in the context of the decades of the 1890s and beyond, this claim makes a good deal of sense. Wellhausen is condemned, when he is, largely as a representative of the period between 1850 and 1890, a period that for Gunkel and for many others stood under the suspicion of making concessions to "positivism" and thus of not upholding the idealist historical tradition with sufficient vigor. In fact, there is very little even faintly positivist about Wellhausen's work. And he can compete admirably with Gunkel in his nostalgia for a rural, simpler world of greater poetry and less rationality or in his passion for pursuing the larger processes of history. So, too, can Wellhausen's nearest contemporaries. To the great Dutch scholar Abraham Kuenen, for example, a historian's task is completed only when he can offer a portrait "above all of spiritual life and activity," while for Bernhard Duhm the prophets are vital for their revolutionary break with demonism into "the spiritual sphere of ethics."[103] But Wellhausen and the others stood under indictment because the decades in which they worked stood under indictment. The battle with Wellhausen, then, is more a result of the History of Religions School's participation in the larger war against those positivistic powers seen to have emerged shortly after mid-century than it is a result of anything Wellhausen did or failed to do. . . .

101. Klatt, *Hermann Gunkel*, 179 ("ich ein echter Wellhausianer gewesen bin"); and Gunkel, "Historical Movement," 533.

102. Gunkel, "Religio-Historical Interpretation," 404.

103. Kraus, *Geschichte der historisch-kritischen Erforschung*, 251 (citing Keunen) ("vor allem geistiges Leben und Tätigkeit") and 282 ("die geistige Sphäre des Ethos").

Conclusion: Objectivity and the
Nineteenth-Century Heritage

[[35]] That the present century's biblical scholarship is massively indebted to the conclusions and the methods of Wellhausen, Gunkel, and the contemporaries of each need not be demonstrated here. The author of a recent account of the historical-critical method says with unquestionable correctness that "it is difficult to overestimate the significance the nineteenth century has for biblical interpretation. It made historical criticism *the* approved method of interpretation."[104] Where that debt is most notable, beyond the [[36]] basic commitment to historical study, is precisely in that area of the internal tension implicit within nineteenth-century historical understanding to which we have repeatedly pointed. The nineteenth-century historical tradition made high claims for objectivity, for a portrait of matters as they really were, and for avoiding any philosophical commitments in favor of the data themselves. And yet both this tradition and its inheritors among biblical scholars everywhere are revealed to be founded upon obviously extraempirical, theoretical, and theological commitments.

To choose but a single example in demonstration of this point, both nineteenth-century scholars and their successors in the present century repeat in almost liturgical fashion their methodological rooting in "the text itself." Gressmann argues at length that the student of the Bible guard above all against importing any alien ideas into and upon the text itself.[105] So too, that same recent introduction to the historical-critical method just cited proclaims that the biblical historian's "first task" is "simply to hear the texts with which he is working. . . . to hear the text apart from the mass of biblical interpretation that has been laid over it in the history of its use."[106] Such advice is well meant. But just about the *only* tradition within learning ever to argue that such a naked confrontation with the text itself might be possible is the very historiographic tradition that is everywhere clothed in commitments to highly philosophical and theological principles—principles that come from somewhere beyond the text itself.

Let it be clear that the argument here presented is *not* that this tradition of learning is rooted in theory while other traditions are blissfully free from theory. The argument is rather that the claim of this particular historiographic tradition to be theory-free and hence to offer

104. Edgar Krentz, *The Historical-Critical Method*, Guides to Biblical Scholarship, ed. Gene M. Tucker (Philadelphia, Pa.: Fortress, 1975) 30.
105. See Kraus, *Geschichte der historisch-kritischen Erforschung*, 397, and the article of Gressmann cited there.
106. Krentz, *Historical-Critical Method*, 39.

supremely objective conclusions is simply not sustainable. That this is the claim of this tradition is everywhere apparent. It appears in Perlitt's argument, as a part of his attempt to acquit Wellhausen of the charge of Hegelianism, that for Wellhausen "any general, comprehensive philosophical or theological systematic held no appeal."[107] And it appears in that polemic against the nomothetic model of the natural sciences to which [37] every historian surveyed in this chapter gives voice. . . .

The particular assumptions and judgments of both the broad historical tradition of understanding and the reflexes of this in biblical scholarship are not just those of the idealist tradition. They are also those of specific commitments to equally specific traditions of faith. As early as the eighteenth century, J. G. Eichhorn defended historical criticism on the ground that such criticism will in the end "establish the credibility and truth of the gospel story on unshakable foundations."[108] Eichhorn is hardly alone in articulating such a view. F. C. Baur, too, said both that the "sole purpose" of his research was "to comprehend the historically given in its pure objectivity" and also that the results achieved would then "contend for the positivity of Christianity on scientific grounds."[109] Similarly, Gunkel can allege both that "Old Testament Science justly claims to be a fully qualified member of the circle of historical Sciences," and yet also that "the historical movement, by shedding new light on ancient Scriptures, is truly serving genuine religion."[110] Or, after offering a nearly identical defense of biblical history as objective in its methods and results, Gressmann too concludes that "the last goal of all our endeavors is to illuminate the essence and truth of the Christian religion."[111] If a historian begins any investigation with such a clear view in advance of what the results of that investigation will be, then it is obviously folly to lay claim to anything like objectivity.

Whether any research in the human sciences can aspire to, much less attain, something like purely objective results is, needless to say, no simple matter.[112] Once again, however, that is not the [38] point at issue in the preceding argument. This point is rather that the recent origins of biblical scholarship are beyond doubt a monument to sustained

107. Perlitt, *Vatke und Wellhausen*, 182; cf. 213–15.

108. Cited by Kümmel, *New Testament*, 79.

109. See Hodgson, *Formation of Historical Theology*, 161 and 186.

110. Gunkel, "What Is Left of the Old Testament," 19; and "Historical Movement," 536.

111. Gressmann, *Albert Eichhorn*, 51 ("Das letzte Ziel aller unserer Bemühungen ist, das Wesen und die Wahrheit der christlichen Religion zu erhellen").

112. The most sophisticated recent discussion of objectivity in historical learning of which I am aware is Mandelbaum's *The Anatomy of Historical Knowledge*. Mandelbaum, it might be noted, concludes that objectivity here is in the end a worthy and attainable goal (pp. 150–51).

Industry, creativity, and piety. But the biblical scholarship of the past several centuries and for the most part still today, which is thoroughly and unapologetically theological scholarship, is no monument to disengaged objectivity. If it is true, as Iggers argues at length and with elaborate documentation, that the theoretical foundations of the German tradition of historical understanding have continued to live a life of their own in other disciplines "long after these theories had been abandoned or at least seriously questioned by philosophers and cultural scientists,"[113] of no discipline is this more true than it is of biblical scholarship.

There is, then, an important and unfortunate division between biblical study and a variety of other academic fields of inquiry. The latter joined in formulating a sustained critique of a model of historical understanding, a model that could not deliver on its promises to achieve objective historical reconstruction because its theoretical foundations prohibited precisely this. Biblical study, even into the present century, long seemed either unaware of the consequences of this critique or unwilling to allow these consequences to alter its portrait of Israelite religion. Though the motives responsible for such apparent ignorance or unwillingness are probably complex and beyond full recovery, among them surely was the congenialness of the idealist historiographic tradition for theology. This tradition allowed biblical scholars to absolutize and particularize the religion of Israel beyond any meaningful comparison, on the ground that every culture was an organic individual, incomparable with any other individual. The tradition also granted legitimacy to vague and unverifiable claims about the subtlety and yet the certainty of divine guidance to Israel's history, on the ground that authentic historical reconstruction would always discover the workings of God's hand. Finally, the same historiographic tradition supported the regular affirmations by theologians engaged in biblical research that their work was at [[39]] once empirical and objective and yet capable of proving the unique superiority of biblical religion.

113. Iggers, *German Conception of History*, 25.

The Impact of Modern and Social Science Assumptions on the Reconstruction of Israelite History

GARY A. HERION

[[3]] The past few years have witnessed an increasing interest in using the social sciences to elucidate the history of ancient Israel. This interest is typically expressed in the biblical scholar who re-examines the historical data in terms of particular models or theories borrowed from this or that social science discipline. The results of this cross-disciplinary activity generally have been positive, if for no other reason than because they sensitize biblical historians to the nomothetic aspects (as opposed to the idiographic features) of ancient Israel,[1] and because they force them to confront the social dimension of Israelite religion (see the important statement of Gottwald 1979: 8–17).

However, there are also some problems inherent in this cross-disciplinary activity, problems related to what is commonly labelled "the

Reprinted with permission from *Journal for the Study of the Old Testament* 34 (1986) 3–33.

Author's note: The author wishes to thank the James A. Gray Endowment, whose post-doctoral fellowship at the University of North Carolina at Chapel Hill provided him with both the opportunity and the resources to prepare this paper. He also wishes particularly to thank University of North Carolina professors Gerhard Lenski (Sociology) and Jack Sasson (Religious Studies) for their very helpful comments and criticisms of earlier drafts of this manuscript. The author assumes full responsibility for all the inadequacies that remain, as well as for all opinions expressed in this paper.

1. Wilhelm Windelband formulated the classic distinction between the idiographic aims of the historian and the nomothetic objectives of the sciences; the former being a concern for specific or unique traits while the latter is an interest in observed regularities and explanatory generalizations. Cf. Mandelbaum 1977: 4–14.

sociology of knowledge." Most biblical scholars have become increasingly aware of the subtle ways in which scholars' backgrounds and training, heritage, social-class position and even gender influence their views about ancient Israel. Yet there is at least one other factor that plays a crucial role in shaping the sociology of their knowledge: modernism. This paper will focus on the ways in which scholars' distinctively modern social contexts and experiences of society help to shape the "pre-understandings" they have about what is generally "true" of human social life, and about what is particularly "true" of ancient Israelite society.[2]

This has an important bearing on biblical studies' interest in social science, since in many respects the assumptions of the social sciences and those of the modern social context are similar.

[4] They came into existence together and are indissolubly inter-linked. A critique of social science cannot but be a critique of modern society, and vice versa (Bellah 1981: 8).

These modern assumptions or perspectives that helped to bring the social sciences into existence may be listed as positivism, reductionism, relativism and determinism. By viewing the "social scientizing" of biblical studies in terms of these four assumptions, this paper will exhibit a superficial dependency upon Robert Bellah's somewhat polemical and over-simplified article "Biblical Religion and Social Science in the Modern World" (1981). However, it must be pointed out that Bellah's description there of the nature of the social sciences is hardly an accurate portrayal of the current state of social science inquiry since each of these four assumptions has fallen under critical review and has been rejected by large portions of the social science community. Nevertheless, he has identified certain tendencies that come to play powerful roles when students of biblical religion begin utilizing the social sciences (cf. the very useful introduction in Wilson 1984: 1–29).

Modern Assumptions and the Scholarly Perspective

An important part of scholars' modernism is the extent to which they live in a complex society and are thereby thoroughly accustomed to the vital and seemingly natural social roles played by formal institutions. A

2. Cf. Sasson 1981, who provides a succinct statement about the relationship between modernism and the scholar's pre-understandings: "Thus whenever a scholar compares kingship, democracy, absolutism, etc., in the Ancient Near East and in the OT, his comparison is understood by his audience—and by him, for that matter—not so much because he has recreated the political realities in Israel and in the Ancient Near East, but because he is using currently understood models as frames of reference" (p. 8).

consequence of this is that sometimes the modern person tends to assume that social organization should typically proceed through such formally organized, collective bodies or institutions (Wirth 1938: 23), taking for granted what economist Kenneth Boulding has called "the organizational revolution."[3] Sometimes, however, this can lead even some scholars to assume that formal, organizational or institutional structure is a universal prerequisite in all other societies as well, including ancient Near Eastern and village-based societies. Thus, the experiences of society built into the modern context can sometimes operate to limit the number of understandable options available to historians when they reconstruct the past.[4]

The past eighty years of inquiry into the Hebrew prophets may well be called an illustration. The old nineteenth-century view of the prophet as "inspired individual" has given over to the twentieth-century view of the prophet as "organizational spokesman," a view [[5]] that reached an extreme forty years ago with the thesis that every prophet held an "office" or was a member of some "guild" or "cult association." The current interest in the prophets' "support groups" or "followings" is yet a more recent illustration of how modern, scholarly understandings of "social organization" can sometimes be confused with distinctively different concepts such as "political organization" or "professional organization," all of which are more familiar to the scholar living in the modern world.

As one example of such a modernist view of social organization one may cite Odil Steck's article on "Theological Streams of Tradition" (1977), noting especially his assumption that the prophetic stream (like the wisdom stream of the royal court and the cultic stream of the temple) must have had some kind of institutional "centers" associated with formally organized, collective bodies:

3. "The past fifty or a hundred years have seen a remarkable growth in the number, size and power of organizations of many kinds, ranging through all areas of life. . . . Yet this revolution has received little study, and it is not something of which we are particularly conscious. It has crept upon us silently. It is something we accept as 'natural' almost without thinking" (Boulding 1953: 3–4).

4. While kinship is the organizational basis of most simple societies, it is rare these days to find it discussed as a significant aspect of Israelite social organization. In part this is the consequence of kinship's close tie a century ago to now-discredited hypotheses about Israel's nomadic origins; in part its neglect may also stem from a belief that its impact on Israelite society was negligible compared to the impact of formally organized institutions (military, priesthood, bureaucracy, etc.), on the assumption that Israel was a relatively complex society like our own. No one can deny that certain segments of Israelite society indeed resemble modern society (cf. Rosenbloom 1972), but other segments undoubtedly were simpler, and functioned as such. The point is: Can we understand these simpler functions? For example, to what extent can we fully appreciate the social function of kinship systems as long as we experience kinship in a modern setting that has translated many of its traditional functions into formal institutional structures (e.g., daycare centers for children, formal schooling for youths, government assistance for impoverished relatives, nursing homes for the elderly)?

Distinctive, long-lasting intellectual movements of this kind are not borne by individuals but only by groups in which the tradition streams are kept in flux through transmission, learned discussion, and development of new witnesses to the tradition. For carrying out their activities and training their successors these groups need fixed meeting places and durable, more or less established institutions (pp. 197–98).

Although Steck admits that "we do not have a concrete historical picture of these centers of prophetic tradition" (pp. 201–2), this notable lack of evidence does not prompt him to re-evaluate his assumptions or to consider alternative hypotheses. In fact, his assumptions appear specifically to rule out other possibilities—e.g., that "prophetic" traditions may have been nurtured and transmitted outside such institutional settings and without official maintenance, perhaps being part of the more loosely structured "cultural repertoire" of peasant villages. Steck's assumption might be attributed in part to a modern context that naturally associates religious (and political) expression with formally organized, institutional settings, groups and activities. Thus, a modern tendency to assume society's prerequisite need for formal institutions may interfere when reconstructing the tradition-process behind the Hebrew prophets by limiting scholars' pre-understanding (and therefore limiting the number of intelligible options available to them).[5]

Social Science Assumptions and the Scholarly Perspective

[[6]] In order to demonstrate more precisely the variety of ways in which distinctively modern social contexts and experiences can shape one's pre-understandings of what was "true" (or at least possible) in ancient Israel, one must examine in more detail the four assumptions that sometimes

5. We also tend to retroject modern notions of "authority" into the past where they do not belong (cf. Arendt 1958). While we have a tendency to institutionalize authority and associate it with the political monopoly of force, this is not at all how authority operates in the more folk-like setting of simple societies. Authority there has nothing to do with coercive force, persuasive argumentation or institutional organization. Because it is so prevalent, so absolute and yet so diffuse as to defy anthropological attempts to "locate" it, authority in these settings is unlike anything with which we "politicized" moderns are familiar. Perhaps the closest we in biblical studies have come to recognizing this general type of authority in ancient Israel was in our rather imprecise references to the authority of the judges as being "charismatic." Initially there was never any doubt that the word "charismatic" cautioned against any association of authority with institutional organization; similarly it was understood to refer to something quite different than a judge's ability to coerce or persuade others rationally. Subsequently, however, some scholars have begun to coin qualifying terms such as "institutional charisma" or "office charisma," which have not necessarily provided a more accurate picture of the judges, only one that is more easily comprehended in modern terms.

play powerful roles when social science is used—positivism, reductionism, relativism and determinism. It is important to keep in mind that these
four basic assumptions are usually interwoven with one another, often
making it difficult to isolate clearly the unadulterated influence of any
one of them. Nevertheless, it is possible to view these four in terms of two
pairs of influences: (1) the way in which positivism and reductionism
combine to influence cross-disciplinary methodology; and (2) the way in
which relativism and determinism combine to shape a more "scientific"
view of Israelite religion.

Positivism, Reductionism and the Cross-Disciplinary Method

Positivism may be defined broadly as the desire to emulate the empirical
methods of natural science in the quest for knowledge. At best, positivism encourages methodological and intellectual rigor while stressing the
central role that reason must play in scholarship. However, positivism
can sometimes degenerate into a form of "scientism" in which science is
no longer understood as one form of knowledge but where the nomothetic character of science comes to be viewed as the only valid terms in
which any "knowledge" can be achieved (Habermas 1972: 4). In such an
intellectual climate, many scholars trained in the more "subjective" approaches of the humanities (history, theology and philosophy) may come
to believe that the "more objective" social sciences per se can render a
more accurate picture of what was "real" in ancient Israel. Consequently
there may arise certain inhibitions about criticizing the more "presti-
gious" social sciences.[6]

Ideally, responsible interdisciplinary activity is a "two-way street,"
meaning that the historical and the social scientific approaches to knowledge inevitably affect and alter one another when they are brought together. Most social scientists concede this, viewing the tasks of the social
sciences and history (as well as the humanities in general) as being complementary. However, it seems that sometimes in the appeal to the social
sciences positivist inclinations may operate in such a way that the interdisciplinary "two-way street" carries [[7]] mainly "one-way traffic" from the
social sciences into historical studies, but not vice versa. As a result, biblical studies sometimes witnesses the uncritical (not necessarily inaccurate
always, but unquestioning) use of social science models and theories.

It is impossible to appreciate fully this impact of positivism without simultaneously appreciating the impact of reductionism. *Reductionism* generally is the tendency to explain as much of the complex as possible in

---

6. As Robert Bellah has noted, what often guarantees the authority and even the power
of professional social scientists is "the theoretical and methodological prestige of social
science as science" (1982: 36).

terms of the simple. This means that if one is to handle complex phenomena, one has little choice but to "chunk" or abstract similarities, thereby reducing the number of items being considered (Malina 1982: 231–32). Such abstractions of similarities are called "models" or "typologies" in the social sciences. While no model has yet been devised that can explain 100% of the variance, the study of any real social phenomena would be difficult if not altogether impossible without the aid of models. Yet models or typologies must be used with a conscientious regard for their limitations; the reduction of complexity always entails a certain methodological risk since the line separating the enlightening epitome from the vulgarized distortion can sometimes be very fine.

Since the construction and use of models have been integral parts of the "social scientizing" of biblical studies, a few remarks about the nature of models seem in order. All societies are alike in some respects, and each differs from others in other respects. Yet some social phenomena have certain features in common enabling us to designate them as a "type" of phenomenon. This "type" or "model" is constructed by assembling and listing only those common features, temporarily ignoring the existing differences, divergences, inconsistencies and irregularities. For this reason it must never be forgotten that a "type" is not "real":

> The type is an imagined entity, created only because through it we may hope to understand reality. Its function is to suggest aspects of real societies which deserve further study, and especially to suggest hypotheses as to what, under certain defined conditions, may be generally true about society (Redfield 1947: 295).

Three important points emerge: (1) models are hypothetical entities, not real descriptions; (2) they are to be used to analyze existing data, not to serve as substitutions in the absence of data; and (3) they do not conclude a study or provide definitive answers, but rather they (a) summarize current thought, or they (b) help to raise new questions [8] for study, suggest fresh lines of inquiry, and expose relevant topics for research when used as a basis of comparison with real phenomena. It is suggested here that positivist and reductionist tendencies sometimes combine in such a way that these three important points become lost, and that consequently the application of social science models and theories to biblical studies sometimes lack proper methodological rigor and balance.

Relativism, Determinism and the Scientific Study of Religion

In focusing on the remaining two assumptions, it should be noted that relativism and determinism have dovetailed to shape an empirical approach to the study of religion that is often associated with the social sciences, and that in this respect they can influence scholarly pre-understandings and reconstructions of ancient Israel. *Relativism* is here defined as the assumption that issues of morality and religion can never be considered truly right or wrong in any "absolute" sense, rather that they vary with (or are "relative" to) persons, societies and cultures. In conjunction with this, *determinism* may be defined as the general tendency to think that human values, choices and actions are caused (or "determined") by certain variables in the social and cultural environment.[7]

These assumptions can combine to produce a general view of human values that denies the individual any genuine claim to socially autonomous or "transcendent" beliefs. In this view, it is characteristically assumed that human values—including religious beliefs—are not held independently or actively but rather that they result from socialization. In other words, values are not seen as reflecting any deep-seated, personal belief in anything truly universal; instead, they become indications of one's acquiescence to a particular set of norms prevalent in the immediate social environment. If a person should claim to possess a deep-seated, autonomous belief in certain transcendent "things," this is typically dismissed as simply an example of the extent to which "superstructural" social concerns and interests have successfully been internalized by the individual.[8]

This general view of human values is in some respects similar to certain social science theories of religion. From its inception in the French enlightenment, sociology was committed to the positivist view that religion is institutionalized ignorance, a vestige of man's primitive past doomed to disappear in an era of scientific rationalism. This view was laid to rest when Emile Durkheim's celebrated study [[9]] of totemism (1912) demonstrated that religion often functions in a very sophisticated manner to help control, stabilize and legitimize social systems. Ever since, the social sciences have tended to consider "religion" primarily as a public, not a private phenomenon, and they have tended to find beneath it particular social control interests, but not more transcendent values or beliefs.

7. Both relativism and determinism have been subjects of debate within the social sciences, and most social scientists probably would no longer accept our admittedly reductionistic definitions of these two tendencies. However, there are noticeable traces of these tendencies still lingering in the social sciences, and some social scientists still feel compelled to criticize the ways in which these assumptions dominate some social science studies. Cf. Haes 1980 and McGhee 1982.

8. It is important for biblical scholars to appreciate that social science consensus on these matters has disappeared. There is now significant dissatisfaction within the social sciences over such a one-sided appeal to the passive conception of man as implied in Marxian historical materialism. Many—even many neo-Marxists—are trying to strike a more reasonable and accurate balance by supplementing it with the view of active, autonomous man implied in Kantian transcendental idealism (Habermas 1971, 1973, 1976; Dawe 1970; Haes 1980).

This view of passive man and ideological religion may be associated generally with the rise of modernism and urbanism, wherein "the juxtaposition of divergent personalities and modes of life tends to produce a relativistic perspective and a sense of toleration of differences which . . . lead toward the secularization of life" (Wirth 1938: 15). The modern, urban context requires religious groups and individuals to interact with others on the basis of some "relative moral minimum" rather than a "transcendent moral absolute," compromising internally held values and beliefs for the rational pursuit of shared social, economic and political interests (Lenski 1961: 9; Wirth 1938: 18).

This truism of modern, urban society has been summed up by the theologian Harvey Cox, who notes that "in the secular city, it is not religion but politics that brings unity and meaning to human life and thought" (1965: 254). There is a two-part corollary to this statement: (1) religion remains meaningful in such an environment only to the extent that it, too, is secularized and "politicized" (relativism); and (2) when religious views are expressed in this milieu, it is likely that certain (sometimes latent) social, economic or political interests underlie and prompt them (determinism—more specifically, social or economic determinism).

It is interesting to note what might result if this modern truism were read into the ancient past. One might assume *a priori* that ancient persons were not individuals actively motivated by or autonomously voicing their deep-seated private beliefs and values. Guided by these relativist and determinist assumptions, one might be more inclined to view the ancients as being influenced by and giving expression to the social, economic and political interests of the immediate social group of which they were a part. Consequently, the religious mindset of the ancient Near Easterner could be portrayed as being every bit as secular in its orientation as is the modern mindset.[9] It is important to note that when this happens one is not necessarily rendering a picture of the past that is more accurate (or more erroneous), only one that is more understandable, meaningful or "relevant" to a modern audience.

Example A: The Impact of These Assumptions on Reconstructions of the Hebrew Prophets

[[10]] Robert Wilson's *Prophecy and Society in Ancient Israel* (1980) provides a useful illustration of how these modern, social science assumptions can

---

9. Given the fact that most "religious" texts recovered from the ancient Near East originally were public and ideological in nature, this view would not be at all improper when applied to such texts. The question is: Is it proper to extend this view into a generalization about every "religious" expression originating in the ancient Near East?

sometimes play a decisive role in shaping reconstructions of the past. In this important work, Wilson examines the entire range of phenomena associated with Hebrew prophecy in terms of I. M. Lewis's anthropological model of central/peripheral intermediation. In many cases the model clarifies certain instances of prophecy recorded in the Hebrew Bible, and if biblical scholars possessed a complete record of all "prophetic" activity occurring in Palestine during the OT period (including especially the activities of the so-called "false prophets"), Wilson's study probably would describe very well the aggregate of such activities.[10]

Yet even a brief review of Wilson's study reveals the unmistakable impact that relativism and determinism have had upon his view of prophetic religion, and that positivism and reductionism have had upon his cross-disciplinary method. The issue at hand concerns the extent to which Wilson's reconstruction might have been unduly determined by these assumptions.

The Impact of Relativism and Determinism

At the heart of Wilson's study lies the suggestion that the anthropological model of intermediation provides a close parallel to biblical "prophecy." Wilson points out that

> Intermediaries do not operate in a vacuum. They are integral parts of their societies and cannot exist without social guidance and support (p. 51)

and that consequently

> On the basis of the comparative evidence, we may expect Israelite society to have been involved in every phase of prophetic activity, from the prophet's "call" to the delivery of his message (p. 86).

His description of how external group processes shape or determine the content of an intermediary's/prophet's message is quite detailed (pp. 51–62). He notes that the "candidate is frequently trained at the request of the society and is encouraged in his attempts to bring about the expected intermediation" (p. 53).[11] His study then proceeds to promote the view that every prophet in Israel (writing and non-writing, [11] "true" and

---

10. In noting that Wilson's thesis may very well describe what was typical of prophetic phenomena, we must remember that it might not apply at all to those prophets who were not typical. Were Amos, Hosea, Micah, Isaiah or Jeremiah "typical" pre-exilic prophets? If so, why were their words initially remembered, valued and preserved while those of countless others were not? See Heschel (1962: 2.252–53), who argues that these individuals represent a type *sui generis*.

11. Wilson's use of the word "expected" is quite revealing: the intermediary's/prophet's message can be predicted once we know which group he represents. Wilson's actual method

"false," cultic and non-cultic, court and non-court, Yahwist and non-Yahwist) should be approached less as an individual autonomously voicing his inner convictions and more as a group spokesman whose message has been shaped by some external social forces and interests.

By tying the prophet so closely to group processes, Wilson has appreciably limited the range within which one is now permitted to understand the historical nature of the prophet and his message. The religious "tone" of a prophet's message may now be explained, at best, as indicative of the extent to which he had internalized the interests of his support group or, at worst, as mere ideological "forms of speech" under which may be found a particular sociopolitical or socioeconomic agenda. In this view, the prophet's autonomy and individuality essentially have been stripped from him: his personal convictions, values and beliefs are either nonexistent (which makes him a hypocrite) or more simply they are reflective of his particular (central or peripheral) group's interests (which makes him a spokesman). The prophet's genuine sense of any "good" transcending his social group's interests has been effectively denied.

The point here is not to deny that Hebrew prophets could be group spokesmen, even though Wilson's blanket application of this conclusion to every single prophet is arguable (cf. Herion 1982: 245–53). Rather it is to note that Wilson's reconstruction of this ancient Israelite phenomenon amounts to a classic description of modern, urban relativism and social determinism.[12] The diminished capacity of the individual to believe autonomously in absolutes—which is characteristic of the secular, modern world—has been projected on to the world of the ancient Near East. The result is the view that in ancient Israel, as in the modern "secular city," it was not any socially transcendent religious values or convictions but relative (and partisan) sociopolitical goals or socioeconomic interests that brought unity and meaning to the life and thought of the Hebrew prophet.

The Impact of Positivism and Reductionism

It was noted above that at the heart of Wilson's study lies the assumption that there can be no socially isolated intermediaries. Wilson's reconstruction concludes that in ancient Israel there indeed were no socially

---

is the reverse of this: since we know the prophet's message from the biblical text, we can predict the group to which he belonged. The potential for circular reasoning here should be obvious.

12. "The individual counts for little, but the voice of the representative is heard with a deference roughly proportional to the numbers for whom he speaks." Interestingly, this statement was not made by Wilson with respect to the ancient Hebrew prophets (although it seems to apply quite well to his thesis); rather it was made by a sociologist with respect to modern, urban society (Wirth 1938: 14).

isolated prophets. There is a perfect correlation here between assumption and conclusion. The issue is whether there might be something in Wilson's cross-disciplinary methodology that accounts for such neat symmetry.

⟦12⟧ Perhaps a good place to begin is with the observation that there exists some evidence which could easily be interpreted in such a way as to challenge the validity of the assumption and the accuracy of the conclusion, and thereby to disturb the symmetry of the reconstruction (cf. Heschel 1962: 1.3–26, especially pp. 17–19). As one important example one may note Jeremiah's lament to Yahweh: "I sat alone because your hand was upon me" (15:17). While it would be possible simply to reinterpret this passage (e.g., as a mere figure of speech that should not be taken literally), Wilson ignores it altogether. This is significant because it provides a useful glimpse into how the cross-disciplinary method often operates: data are consistently manipulated to the distinct advantage of the model, although the reverse is never attempted. In order to fit the historical data into the central/peripheral scheme of the model that necessarily ties prophets to support groups, some evidence is omitted (e.g., Jer 15:17; 1 Kgs 19:10, 14) and a great deal is simply explained away—e.g., Micaiah had a "weak" support group in 1 Kgs 22 (p. 211), or Jer 20:10 refers to the prophet being rejected by "portions" of his support group (p. 246).

When Wilson does attempt to reinterpret the evidence, this often involves questionable and sweeping re-creations of entire prophetic biographies and careers. In short, the methodological stance toward the historical data seems highly critical (even revisionist at times), while the stance toward the social science model seems credulous. Wilson has permitted the model to interpret the data for him—in fact, he seems improperly to have permitted it to fill in gaps existing in the data—but he has not permitted the data reciprocally to address, much less to challenge the model. This is not an appropriate method for using models since basic to all models is their falsifiability (cf. the critique by Long 1982: 251).

It is here suggested that this methodological oversight may, in part, result from a positivist bias about the supremacy of more "scientific" approaches to knowledge, a bias that inhibits one from critically reviewing those approaches—e.g., passive acceptance of the more "scientific" definitions (of religion) or the more "scientific" models (of intermediation). Another part of the oversight might well be attributed to a reductionism that leads one to confuse a simple, abstract model with an actual description of complex reality. Despite these problems, however, it must be underscored that Wilson has provided biblical scholars with an important aid for the study of the Hebrew prophets. His model of intermediation is an extremely useful one, but not ⟦13⟧ because it necessarily fills in any gaps in data or serves as a possible description of what was "real" in ancient Israel. It is important because, when used properly and critically, it can point scholars to potentially fruitful areas for further study.

The model performs this service only to the extent that one permits it and the data to go their separate ways. Unfortunately, in the quest for precise and definitive (not to mention publishable) results, many biblical scholars utilizing social science seem reluctant to permit this, perhaps believing incorrectly that unless there is a direct and consistent correlation between model and data their theses were wrong and their research was a waste of time and effort. Thus scholars may be found overlooking data (probably subconsciously) that do not mesh with their models or else straining them in such a way that they do mesh. Yet the point where the social science model and the historical data diverge is precisely the area where further study should be directed. Without the model there could be no such divergence, and without the divergence it would be much more difficult to ascertain what are the truly exceptional (and therefore important) historical features of ancient Israel. Social science models, therefore, have great heuristic value. One must then seek not to gloss over or to downplay the divergences between data and model but rather to recognize them, to underscore them for colleagues, and to invite those colleagues to join in the task of trying to account for the divergences.

Thus, for example, Wilson's study now invites scholars to raise important questions about the nature of a prophet's "support group." What does it mean to say that these groups were *socially* organized, as opposed to being politically, professionally, religiously or culturally organized? What does it mean to say that they were socially *organized*, as opposed simply to "being present" in society? In what sense did "support groups" provide the impulse behind a prophet's outspokenness, and in what sense did they coalesce as a response to his message? More fundamentally, however, the divergence between the model of intermediation and the data about Hebrew prophecy suggests that Wilson may have initiated his study with too narrow a concept of "support group" in mind. In the future, it might be more appropriate (as well as less relativistic and deterministic) to begin more generally with references to a prophet's "support structure," noting that in some instances this may indeed have been a tangible (central or peripheral) social group, but that in other instances a [[14]] prophet's "support structure" may have been something more intangible and internalized such as a cultural heritage or a religious tradition. These things also exist in society, although they do not necessarily manifest themselves as an identifiable, socially organized "group."[13] To the extent that cultural

---

13. Jack Sasson has reminded me furthermore that one must be very cautious when undertaking "scientific" inquiries dependent on evidence found in literary pieces (e.g., the

and religious values (not just social solidarities) can give an individual
both vision and resolve, it seems fair to consider them important potential
elements in a prophet's "support structure."

Example B: The Impact of These Assumptions
on Reconstructions of Premonarchic Israel

Norman Gottwald's *Tribes of Yahweh* (1979) provides another useful illustration of how modern, social science assumptions can sometimes play a
decisive role in shaping reconstructions of the past. In this extensive re-
examination of the nature of premonarchic Israel, Gottwald introduces
a wealth of social science material presented against the backdrop of the
macro-sociological theories of Durkheim, Weber and Marx. The cumulative effect of this is to underscore in a most convincing manner the
importance of the social dimension in ancient Israel—more specifically,
the relationship between Israelite religion and society.

A brief review of Gottwald's study also reveals the impact that relativism and determinism have had upon his view of premonarchic religion,
and that positivism and reductionism have had upon his sociological
method. Once again, the issue at hand concerns the extent to which
Gottwald's reconstruction might have been unduly determined by these
assumptions.

The Impact of Relativism and Determinism

At the core of Gottwald's study lies the assumption that "only as the full
materiality of ancient Israel is more securely grasped will we be able to
make proper sense of its *spirituality*" (p. xxv). In light of this assumption,
it is not surprising that Gottwald tends to locate causality as low as possible
on the "conceptual pyramid of culture,"[14] with technological innovations

---

non-writing prophets who appear in Deuteronomistic literature). One would somehow feel
it inappropriate to apply anthropological models to gain scientific information about the
"seers" found in Homer or in the plays of Sophocles.

14. The anthropological "pyramidization" of culture conceives of a culture's economic
institutions as the base of a conceptual, three-tiered "pyramid" anchored to the ecosystem
by a technology that can exploit and capitalize upon existing resources, both natural and
human. Above this economic base is the middle tier representing the social structures that
exist to insure orderly (although not necessarily equitable) economic activity—chief among
these is the political monopoly of force (i.e., instruments of government). At the peak of the
"pyramid" are the ideological symbols, including religion and morality, which work to provide a sense of legitimacy and stability for everything underneath. Economic determinism
conceives of causation as being from the bottom up (materialism), and religion thus comes
to be viewed as the ultimate "effect." This has reinforced the relativist tendency to view religion as a public phenomenon related to social control interests, not as a private phenomenon related to personal experience.

(iron, waterproof plaster, agricultural terracing) providing a new basis for social relations among now-relative equals; and this, in turn, engendering an "egalitarian" ethic in early Israel that became ideologically enshrined in Yahwist religion (pp. 650–63). Thus, in premonarchic Israel religion (Yahwism) was ⟦15⟧ essentially a projection of the economic and political interests of the social organization (tribal confederacy).

This hypothesis draws heavily upon relativist and determinist notions about religion, and perhaps nowhere does this surface more clearly than in Gottwald's critique of John Bright and George Mendenhall (pp. 592–602), both of whom generally share his view of the social process while disagreeing with his views about the accompanying religious process.

Religion Related to Society. Contra John Bright.   According to Gottwald, Bright improperly severs religion from society by claiming that the religion of early Israel was unique and that its socio-political origins, while revolutionary, were not. The issue here seems to be the applicability of relativism—the assumption that religion must necessarily be tied to the social sphere.

Gottwald counters Bright first with a questionable testimony to the uniqueness of Israel's socio-political origins,[15] and secondly with an imaginative (and admittedly caricatured) reconstruction of how unexceptional Israel's rituals and beliefs in God must have seemed to Israel's neighbors (pp. 595–96). From this it logically follows that if Israel's religion was unique it was so only because it was tied to its unique socio-political existence.

However, this conclusion is sustained only by misconstruing or ignoring Bright's understanding and use of the word "religion." One does not have to read much that Bright has written to realize that he characteristically used the word "religion" as it is often used in the humanities, to refer to constitutive factors of human cognitive existence. For him, "religion" is largely synonymous with "world view" or "faith"; it is a process whereby people attempt to make sense out of their experiences of existence. It might be fair to say that Bright presumes a "religion-experience" nexus, with the understanding that many human experiences come from outside the "conceptual pyramid of culture"—i.e., beyond a given society's range of control. It seems that it is in this "area beyond" that Bright presumes the

15. "Gottwald claims that there is no parallel for this development in the Middle East, and I cannot suggest one. I am not persuaded, however, that the dynamics of the process by which Israel came into existence are quite as unique as Gottwald sometimes implies" (Lenski 1980: 275). One wonders if an enterprising Egyptologist could argue a "peasant revolt" hypothesis to describe the First (or Second) Intermediate period at least as plausibly as Gottwald had done for ancient Israel. Perhaps an enterprising Assyriologist could do the same for the end of the Ur III period.

existence of a Truly Other, and hence he feels one is justified in talking
about a God "acting" and "being revealed" in history (i.e., in human
experience).

Gottwald, however, characteristically uses the word "religion" as it is
often used in the social sciences, to refer to symbolic elements of human
social existence. He tends to presume a "religion-society" nexus wherein
it is proper to speak of religion narrowly in terms of [[16]] organized "belief
systems" (doctrines) and "cult practices" (rituals). By imposing this definition on Bright's use of the word "religion," Gottwald effectively side-steps
Bright's claim that the uniqueness of Israel's religion is to be found in its
peculiar way of discovering meaning and coherence in human existence
(cf. Bright 1972: 140–56), and thus he is able to rule out any possible connection between religion and factors outside the social domain. By sub-
stituting his narrow social science definition of religion ("set of beliefs and
cult practices," p. 595), he is able to view religion in such a way that it must
be linked to the social process. Thus, Gottwald's ability to demonstrate
that relativism was as pervasive in ancient Israel as it is in modern society
(and as it is in the theories of Durkheim, Weber and Marx) hinges on little
more than the way he has chosen to define the word "religion."

Religion Determined by Society: Contra George Mendenhall.   Having thereby
demonstrated the exclusive connection between religion and social processes, Gottwald moves on to address the ways in which one influences
the other. His concern here seems to be one of priority: Which came first,
the religion or the society? According to Gottwald, Mendenhall improperly
derives early Israelite society from its religion instead of vice versa. The issue here, of course, is the applicability of social determinism—the assumption that social processes influence or determine religious ideas and values.

One does not have to read Mendenhall too deeply to appreciate that
he characteristically makes two basic connections when he writes about the
relationship of religion to social processes. First, like Bright, he uses the
word "religion" in a much broader sense than doctrines and rituals. It may
be fair to say that Mendenhall presumes a "religion-ethical values" nexus
(with these values understood to originate in historical experiences). Thus
Mendenhall concludes that since human values influence human choices,
and since the sum of these choices patterns the character of social relations
and structure, then one correctly may assert that "religion" (i.e., ethical values) shapes society. Second, Mendenhall tends to contrast his "religion-
ethics" nexus with a "politics-power" nexus, thereby drawing a sharp distinction between ethical values ("religion") and social control interests
('politics'; cf. especially Mendenhall 1975; and 1973: 198ff.).[16]

16. Mendenhall seems to agree with the social sciences (and with Gottwald) that doctrines and rituals play important roles in social control (cf. 1973: 72–73); but for that reason

In his response to this, Gottwald again either misconstrues or ignores how Mendenhall uses the word "religion," and again substitutes ⟦17⟧ his narrower social science definition (doctrines and rituals). It is at this point that Gottwald introduces the concept of "politics" in order to demonstrate "religion's" dependence upon social processes. Moreover, he avoids a precise, analytical, social science definition of the word in order to embrace a more intuitive, Christian, theological view of politics as "ethics" (p. 601)—the substance of both in early Israel being "egalitariansim."[17] This semantic "twist" serves Gottwald's thesis well since it enables him to co-opt all of Mendenhall's categories by rearranging all the connections. Thus, Mendenhall's "religion-ethics" and "politics-power" connections (and all the issues Mendenhall raised through those connections) are replaced with Gottwald's connections of "religion" to "cult" and "ethics" to "politics."

By connecting "ethics" to "politics," Gottwald has appreciably limited our options in trying to identify the prime factors of causation. First, he can now agree with Mendenhall in principle that "ethical values" are the primary determinants, but in practice he can identify these with "political interests," not with "religion," and therefore he can locate them lower on the "conceptual pyramid of culture." Second, he can agree with Mendenhall that there are certain ways in which "religion" can be regarded

---

he tends to think of them in terms of political (power) functions, not religious (ethical) ones. To some extent the differences here between Mendenhall and Gottwald are primarily semantic and emphatic. However, there are very sharp confessional differences in their personal evaluations of political power. Mendenhall, apparently employing a Lutheran "two-kingdom" concept, seems to concede the necessity of social control interests while secularizing them. Gottwald, apparently employing a Marxist-style liberation theology, seems to regard upper-class power as illegitimate (even "evil"?) while lower-class power is justified (even "righteous"?).

17. One is reminded of theologian Paul Lehmann's definition of politics as "activity, and reflection on activity, which aims at and analyzes what it takes to make and keep human life human in the world" (1963: 85), or Harvey Cox's statement that politics is what makes human life and thought meaningful (1965: 254), or Miguez Bonino's contention that politics is the outward form of love (1983), or John Howard Yoder's *The Politics of Jesus* (1972), which is really about the ethics of Jesus. Certainly this confusion of "politics" with "ethics" is the consequence of commendable efforts to encourage Christians to act out their values rather than passively to pay them lip-service; the use of the word "politics" underscoring this call to act. But such naive definitions (conveniently?) avoid the ethically troublesome problem of power—i.e., "playing to win" instead of "playing with integrity." No social scientific study of political phenomena can hope to be taken seriously if it refuses to recognize that "politics" refers to the manipulation of coercive force in an orderly and prescribed manner. It necessarily assumes a highly utilitarian view of humans as manipulable objects. Thus, the paradox of "politics" in Gottwald's (and the others') ingenuous sense of the word is that at times it must be somewhat de-humanizing, unloving and unethical if it is to promote humanity, love and ethics. Cf. Mendenhall 1973: 196–97.

as a cause, but he identifies these with the ways in which the cult provides secondary, ideological legitimation and reinforcement of existing social, political and economic norms (Yahwism as a "societal 'feedback' servomechanism," pp. 642–49). Once again, Gottwald's ability to demonstrate that social determinism was as pervasive in ancient Israel as it is in modern society (or in Durkheim, Weber and Marx) hinges on little more than the way he has chosen to define such key words as "religion" and "politics." The result is an historical reconstruction unable to concede the Israelite peasants' ability to possess any genuine sense of "good" transcending their own sociopolitical goals and socioeconomic interests.

The point here is not to assert that early Israel was an exceptional time and place wherein self-interest largely disappeared (not even the Bible makes that statement!); nor is it to deny that premonarchic Yahwism may indeed have come to serve as an ideological projection of social, political and economic interests for a majority of Palestinian peasants (although one may debate Gottwald's assertion that this was the unique aspect of Yahwism from its inception). Rather it is to note that Gottwald's reconstruction amounts to a classic description of modern, urban relativism and social determinism. The result is the ⟦18⟧ view that in premonarchic Israel, as in the modern "secular city" (or in modern radical political movements, whether of the left or the right), it was not any socially transcendent ethical values or convictions but relative political interests and economic goals that brought unity and meaning to premonarchic Yahwism. Gottwald has not necessarily rendered a picture of ancient Israel that is more accurate (or erroneous), only one that is more intelligible, meaningful and "relevant" to a modern audience whose perspective is similarly imbued with relativist and determinist assumptions.

The Impact of Positivism and Reductionism

In summarizing his critique of Mendenhall, Gottwald offers a statement reflecting the relativism and determinism that inform his assumptions and that are confirmed by his conclusions. Despite this, the following statement will probably strike most modern scholars as self-evidently true:

> Yet to grant that the religion of the state serves the interests of the state, but to deny that the religion of the tribe or of the intertribal confederacy serves the interests of the tribe or intertribal community, is to desert sociological method at a decisive juncture (1979: 601).

As with Wilson, there is almost a perfect correlation between Gottwald's assumption that religion serves the interests of the social organization and his conclusion that in premonarchic times Yahwism served the political and economic interests of the Israelite tribal organization. Early Israel obeys all the rules laid out in the macro-sociological theories of Durkheim, Weber and Marx. The issue here is whether there might be something in Gottwald's sociological methodology that accounts for this neat symmetry.

As noted earlier, Gottwald depends heavily upon the macro-sociological theories of Durkheim, Weber and Marx. All "theories" are somewhat like "models" in that they often constitute summaries of current (or in these specific cases, nineteenth-century) thought and that they provide heuristic standards against which "reality" may be measured. Macro-sociological theories in particular exhibit a much higher level of theoretical abstraction than, say, do micro-sociological theories. Like models, theories are hypothetical entities that are falsifiable in the sense that one expects divergences to result when abstract hypotheses and concrete realities are brought together.

[[19]] Indeed, the past century has witnessed the application of these macro-sociological theories to countless, concrete social phenomena, and consequently professional social scientists (more so than non-social scientists) have become sensitized to the shortcomings and inadequacies of these theories. The nineteenth-century confidence in relativism and determinism that originally helped to fuel these theories (and which still helps to drive Gottwald's study) has noticeably drained away in most social science academies. In fact, almost all social scientists today would not consider themselves "materialists" but rather "idealists" in the sense that they see values and beliefs—including economic self-interest—as the chief driving forces in society. Thus, contra Gottwald, one could say that most social scientists themselves have "deserted sociological method" in that they no longer depend dogmatically upon relativist and determinist (much less materialist) explanations of social phenomena. As a result of a number of related developments within the social sciences, an increasing number of social scientists have become sensitized to the sometimes powerful influences arising outside the "conceptual pyramid of culture," and have challenged the truism that religion necessarily serves the interests of society.

In the first place, even classical nineteenth-century studies of the different bases of social solidarity (Durkheim 1893) suggest that religion functions quite differently in folk (or tribal) and urban (or state) types of societies. For example, the notion of religion serving the material interests of the social or political organization makes very little sense when applied to the ideal-typical folk society (Redfield 1947). This does not deny that religion functions to sustain society by promoting the solidarity of its members, but it points out that a wide range of possible relations between religion and society may be found beneath such simple truisms as "religion serves the interest of society," especially when those interests can be so radically different typologically. The truism only serves to obviate further study and to encourage modern and ethnocentric views about religion's "social utility" (cf. the comments in Malina 1982: 240–41).

Second, several prominent social science theorists from Tönnies (1887) to Parsons (1960) have hinted at the initial autonomy and independence of inner values by basing their respective social typologies (dependent variables) upon underlying typologies of personal values and volitional processes (independent variables). While few have considered such values and processes under the [20] rubric of "religion," the important works of Weber (1930) and Lenski (1961) have demonstrated that distinctively "religious" factors can inform these values and processes in profound ways, helping to shape the "moral ecology" upon which social relations, institutions and organizations are established.[18]

Third, recent sociological inquiry into the nature and origin of human values has demonstrated that values ultimately arise not from social structures / economic interests per se (as social and economic determinists maintain) but rather from human experiences (Rokeach 1979). This insight is significant because it no longer limits one to looking for causation exclusively within the "conceptual pyramid of culture." To the extent that social, economic and even technological factors are parts of those experiences, and to the extent that social organizations can control and meaningfully integrate both its constituents and their experiences, they can all determine human values. Causation can indeed exist within the pyramid of culture, and Gottwald has provided a necessary reinforcement of this important point. However, no social system exists that can completely control this process of integration, no matter how "totalitarian" it strives to be. Therefore, the potential for new values (or for the resurgence of older, dormant values) is forever present, constantly presenting a challenge or even threat to the social organization (cf. Heirich 1976). Thus, to the extent that experiences lie outside the "cultural domain" and beyond human personal or social control, the re-

---

18. The very important concept of "moral ecology" is analogous to the biological concept of "gene pool"; it refers to the *pre-existing* "raw material" out of which selections can be made so as to produce a unique and viable social (or biological) organism (cf. Sullivan 1982). The values constituting the "moral ecology" are not created by the social organization but rather are presupposed by it. To be sure, all social organizations inevitably turn around and actively promote an ideology to bolster those select values upon which its existence absolutely depends; but many values thus remain untouched or unincorporated by the social organization, and are still capable of inspiring individual and mass divergences from the social norm.

sultant values likewise originate outside the human consciousness. No person or society "plans" what its values will be. This is the significant element of truth underlying Bright's and Mendenhall's understanding of the potential "transcendence" of religion.[19]

The above three areas of development within the social sciences reflect if not an abandonment at least a critical revision of nineteenth-century macro-sociology's comfortable dependence upon neat relativist and determinist assumptions. Yet these very important advancements and revisions seem not to have been significantly incorporated into Gottwald's study. While a number of factors may account for this,[20] it seems also that positivism and reductionism may have played decisive roles in bringing about this methodological omission. Positivism may have had a hand to the extent that the more scholars are convinced of the validity of the "scientific" nature of the theories being used, the less they may be inclined to appreciate their falsifiability. Simultaneously, reductionism may have worked to blur 〚21〛 the distinction between abstract theories about general social tendencies and concrete descriptions of actual social realities.[21] Under the influence of these two factors, it is relatively easy to see why one might avoid dealing with those more-recent developments that would only serve to complicate matters further.

The solution to the methodological problems in *The Tribes of Yahweh* seems to be not so much a matter of recognizing the inevitable divergences between social science theories and historical data but rather the demanding task of incorporating the subsequent criticisms, modifications, qualifications and even the affirmations of the basic social science theories being used. Even though Gottwald seems not to have done this, it must be underscored that he has nevertheless introduced into the discussion a very important theoretical framework from which it is possible

19. This also helps to clarify something that historians take for granted but that social scientists often tend to be confounded by: change.

20. One factor undoubtedly is the inevitable "interdisciplinary lag" and "academic specialization" that make it impossible to keep abreast of developments in other fields. Another factor may be certain personal ideological or partisan political reasons that make these theoretical abstractions attractive and useful in their unrevised, nineteenth-century forms (see excursus).

21. The temptation to rely heavily upon theories (or upon intuition) is perhaps especially strong for historians of the ancient past who often have very little "concrete reality" (i.e., data) to begin with. It is perhaps in this light that we should try to understand Gottwald's appeal to "imagination" in lieu of evidence. Thus we must appreciate that some of his confident remarks about the state of our knowledge (e.g., "We know very well what these contemporaries noticed in Israel . . . ," 1979: 596) are really highly subjective intuitions. In fact, on a number of occasions Gottwald seems to recommend as proper methodology the reading of such modern intuitions into the ancient past (1979: xxv and 801 n. 644).

to explore a whole new range of issues related to early Israel. The theories of Durkheim, Weber and Marx are extremely important ones, but not because they provide a definitive statement about the "religion-society" nexus in ancient Israel (or anywhere else for that matter). They are important because they continue to raise issues for scholars subsequently to test, and for this reason these theories must be used with respect to the subsequent qualifications that have resulted from those tests.

When viewed in light of these more recent developments in sociology, Gottwald's study now urges biblical scholars to be much more cautious in making sweeping statements about the necessary "religion-society" nexus in early Israel. There is still much to understand about how religion may have been related to values, and more specifically about how values in ancient Israel were tied to human experiences. It might well be that experiences such as the collapse of Late Bronze Age civilization (1225–1175 B.C.) loom large in accounting for the expression of certain "religious" values or concepts in early Israel; perhaps they may even loom larger as "value determinants" (particularly for the first generation or so) than do particular social structures (such as an "egalitarian" confederation of tribes.[22] But even if they do not, the narrow view of religion serving the interests of the social structure can no longer be sustained as an unequivocal, "scientific" truism.

Finally, Gottwald's study also encourages biblical scholars to be more truly interdisciplinary when using the word "religion." He is correct in noting that one cannot continue to use the word exclusively in a humanities sense that overlooks the cult and how it comes to [[22]] function systemically to symbolize and legitimize the social order and its interests. Conversely, it must now also be recognized that one cannot use the word "religion" in such a restricted social science sense that values become linked narrowly to social interests instead of more properly (and more broadly) to human experiences. Religion is not entirely a subset or an extension of society; it is a subset and an extension of human experience (a part of which is the experience of society). This suggests that in order fully to ascertain the historical nature and impact of religion in early Israel (or among the Hebrew prophets), biblical scholars must utilize an interdisciplinary method wherein they can prevent positivist and reductionist assumptions from leading them to embrace the more "scientific"

---

22. We might also apply these insights to Wilson's *Prophecy and Society in Ancient Israel.* It might well be that experiences such as the westward march of the Assyrian army in the second half of the eighth century B.C. loom large in accounting for the outburst of prophetic activity in Israel at the time. Perhaps such experiences were more significant in stimulating their religious value than were specific central or peripheral support groups.

theories of religion without first criticizing them or without appreciating that they still remain just theories.

Conclusion

Hopefully, this focus on *Prophecy and Society in Ancient Israel* and *Tribes of Yahweh* has illustrated that even in the best studies utilizing the social sciences a special set of modern assumptions can come to play a pronounced role in shaping the sociology of knowledge in biblical studies and, therefore, in shaping conclusions about ancient Israel. This paper has not intended to suggest that positivism, reductionism, relativism and determinism are wholly "bad" influences on scholarship, for they certainly are not. Rather, it has been suggested that these modern assumptions often work to restrict historical reconstructions by imposing limits on the range of understandable options available to historians even prior to an examination of the evidence. Such "problems" related to the sociology of knowledge can never be eliminated, but at least they can be acknowledged, and at most one can hope that some ways may be found to compensate for their restrictive influences and to broaden the base of scholarly pre-understandings about society.

It is also hoped that this paper will help to stimulate efforts to discover those ways in which biblical scholars can acquire this greater range of options for reconstructing the historical nature of Israelite religion and society. The present writer feels that four such ways of improving cross-disciplinary research seem to follow naturally from everything that has been said above. They are offered here as tentative suggestions to help biblical scholarship more responsibly [[23]] refine its use of social science models and theories.

First, there seems to be a crucial need for a truly interdisciplinary understanding of what is meant by the words "religion" and "religious values" (see above). Distortions seem to result when either the definitions current in the humanities or those current in the social sciences begin to dominate historical reconstructions. This suggests that biblical scholars ought to exercise special care when using models and theories in a "social-anthropological" perspective. "Social anthropology" is that branch of the social sciences that seeks the social and political interpretation of essentially non-political, symbolic expressions and activities (cf. Cohen 1969). This discipline can tend to rely heavily upon relativist and determinist assumptions that religious expressions and activities have socio-political interpretations. Scholars must first have a reasonable level of certainty that religion indeed has a socio-political function in a given historical context before attempting to interpret the nature of that function. Admittedly, this is a somewhat circular approach to the material; nevertheless, this seems preferable to an uncritical positing of socio-political functions in areas where such might not exist.

For example, this suggests that for the moment scholars avoid the popular temptation of examining premonarchic Israel and the Hebrew prophets in social-anthropological terms. While these arguably are the most important, unique and interesting aspects of ancient Israel, the social and political realities associated with them are notoriously ill-defined. (In fact, we have seen that both Gottwald and Wilson for the most part had to "create" these realities). Perhaps biblical scholars' social-anthropological skills first ought to be sharpened against the wisdom texts of the monarchic period or the pre-exilic psalms (cf. Herion 1982: 110–92) since in both these cases scholars have better (even cross-cultural) control of the data, fairly straightforward symbolic and/or religious expressions, and a relatively well-defined socio-political context within which to place the data.

Second, the need for scholars to expand their pre-understandings beyond their own modern experiences of complex, urban society suggests that scholars need to acquire a more sympathetic awareness of the simple, "folk" or primitive types of societies that are typologically contrary to modern society. An informed appreciation of these types of societies should help to counterbalance or nullify the influences of modernism (a) by sensitizing biblical scholars to their own modern tempocentrism and urban ethnocentrism, and (b) by enabling them [[24]] to recognize a conceptual "continuum" of societal typologies against which specific features of ancient Israel may be viewed.

Third, because historians of ancient Israel cannot observe firsthand the object of their study as can most scientists, they are always searching for possible analogies to ancient Israelite phenomena. Thus, in addition to studying other texts recovered from the ancient Near Eastern (and Mediterranean) world, biblical scholars may look for possible analogies in that specific branch of the social sciences known as cultural anthropology—more specifically, ethnography. Ethnographic studies of Arab peasant village life may be particularly beneficial to those ancient Near Eastern and biblical scholars who have few occasions to travel the backroads of the Middle East. The conservative aspects of village life there may provide revealing glimpses into the ancient past, and it is curious that more biblical scholars have not sought for analogies in this corpus of material. In many pockets of the Middle East, modernism and industrialism have had little impact, and consequently these cultures can still be comparatively close to those of the ancient Near East both geographically and culturally—although due consideration must be given to the historical variables (notably Islam). Ethnographic studies of more recent non-Semitic societies (e.g., medieval European, Latin American, sub-Saharan African, Far Eastern) will probably yield less convincing analogies to ancient Israel since they are so widely separated historically, geographically and culturally.[23] The least convincing analogies of all will probably be those drawn between ancient Israel and the modern, industrial (and post-industrial) West. Thus, to the extent that the specific branch of the social sciences known as sociology derives its models and theories from the study and observation of this type of society, one may seriously question what it has to contribute to our understanding of ancient Israel.

Fourth, biblical scholars need to adopt a more rigorous method of using social science models and theories. Perhaps this means that every social science study of ancient Israel should begin not simply with a description of a particular model or theory but also with a critical evaluation of it, especially noting how subsequent social science study has qualified, modified or revised that model or theory. It follows from this that every social science study of ancient Israel should be committed to pointing out not only the parallels but more importantly the inevitable divergences that will result whenever social science models or theories are brought together with historical [[25]] data. This heuristic value of social science models and theories finally suggests that every social science study of ancient Israel should conclude with a directive for the continued investigation of the phenomenon in question. In short, those who engage in this cross-disciplinary study should be as committed to pointing out new and often more subtle question and lines of investigation as they are committed to answering and clarifying the old ones.

Excursus on "Genre-Confusion"

I hope that the preceding comments will not be construed either as a general assault on interdisciplinary study or as an attack centering on the works of Robert Wilson and Norman Gottwald. Whatever sharpness one may detect in my criticisms of these works is probably due to the uncertainty and frustration I felt when reading *Prophecy and Society* and *Tribes of Yahweh*: I was never sure what I was supposed to read those books "as."

---

23. In utilizing contemporary Third World ethnography, biblical scholars must appreciate that extensive and sometimes intensive colonialism, Protestant and Catholic evangelism, industrialism and more recently Marxism have all helped to modernize and westernize even the peasant villages there. Significantly, the Arab Third World has most successfully resisted these influences, although even that has begun to change in the past twenty years.

I have gradually begun to suspect that one of the casualties of inter-disciplinary study is clarity about "genre." For example, I had no doubt that I was supposed to read both these books generally "as" historio-graphy, but the difficulty I still experienced in trying to determine what the respective authors were intending to accomplish sensitized me to the wide range of sub-genres associated with history-writing. What "type" of historiography are these books?

For example, all biblical scholars are familiar with academic histori-ography. But even within this sub-genre, distinctions must be made be-tween a work that tests an hypothesis and one that more fundamentally proposes a reconstruction of the past. These distinctions easily become confused in an interdisciplinary study when the researcher fails to note the inevitable divergences between social science models and theories and the historical data. This was the confusion I had in reading *Prophecy and Society in Ancient Israel.* Had Wilson looked for and pointed out the divergences then it would have been more obvious that he was testing an hypothesis rather than proposing a (sweeping) reconstruction. I believe this would have made it easier to respond more fairly to his study since I would then have been more sensitive to what he was trying to accomplish.

Also, when an interdisciplinary study fails to include a critique of the social science theories being applied, the careful reader begins to ques-tion how "realistic" is the resulting picture of the past. In fact, the [[26]] reader may no longer be certain that the writer is primarily motivated by a "dispassionate," academic quest for the "reality" of the past in its own terms. This suggests another type of history-writing: ideological histori-ography. Here the past becomes an authoritative vehicle for expressing and legitimizing contemporary concerns (Plumb 1971; B. Lewis 1975). In fact, the use of social science can actually facilitate such history-writing, since social science can also be highly ideological in its own right.[24] When the authority of "the past" is combined with the authority of "sci-ence"—not to mention the additional sense of authority that in certain religious circles adheres to any statement made about the Bible or an-cient Israel—an interdisciplinary study combining history, social science and biblical studies becomes ripe for ideological exploitation. One is no longer certain whether the study is an objective accounting of the "real" past or a partisan advocacy of a desirable future. This was the con-fusion I had in reading *Tribes of Yahweh.* Had Gottwald criticized the

24. Over thirty years ago Reinhold Niebuhr commented that "While the ideological taint upon all social judgments is most apparent in the practical conflicts of politics, it is equally discernible, upon close scrutiny, in even the most scientific observations of social scientists" (1953: 75). Even in America today sociologists are often viewed as progenitors of social vision and political directions (cf. Bellah 1982: 35).

nineteenth-century macro-sociological theories he used, the resulting picture of premonarchic Israel would certainly have been more "realistic" and less "utopian"; it would then have been more obvious that Gottwald was indeed writing academically about ancient Israel instead of ideologically about (legitimate) contemporary political concerns, and it would have been easier for me to know how to respond to his study.

Hopefully a more rigorous methodological use of social science models and theories will help clear up much of the historiographic "genre-confusion" that has accompanied the social scientific study of ancient Israel.

Bibliography

Arendt, H.
   1958   What Was Authority? Pp. 81–112 in *Authority.* Nomos 1, ed. C. J. Friedrich. Cambridge, Mass.: Harvard University Press.
Bellah, R.
   1981   Biblical Religion and Social Science in the Modern World. *The National Institute for Campus Ministries Journal* 6/3: 8–22.
   1982   Social Science as Practical Reason. *The Hastings Center Report* 12/5: 32–39.
Bonino, J. M.
   1983   *Toward a Christian Political Ethics.* Philadelphia: Fortress.
Boulding, K.
   1953   *The Organizational Revolution.* New York: Harper.
Bright, J.
   1972   *A History of Israel.* 2d ed. Philadelphia: Westminster. In the third edition (1981) Bright responds to Gottwald (1979).
Cohen, A.
   1969   Political Anthropology: The Analysis of the Symbolism of Power Relations. *Man* 4: 217–35.
Cox, H.
   1965   *The Secular City: Secularization and Urbanization in Theological Perspective.* New York: Macmillan.
Dawe, A.
   1970   The Two Sociologies. *British Journal of Sociology* 21/2: 207-18.
Durkheim, E.
   1893   *De la division travail social.* Paris: Alcan; 5th ed., 1926. ET *The Division of Labor in Society.* New York: Macmillan, 1933; repr. Glencoe, Ill.: Free Press, 1949.
   1912   *Les formes élémentaires de la vie religieuse.* Paris: Alcan.
Gottwald, N.
   1979   *The Tribes of Yahweh.* Maryknoll, New York: Orbis.
Habermas, J.
   1971   *Towards a Rational Society.* London: Heinemann.

1972   *Knowledge and Human Interests.* London: Heinemann.
1973   *Theory and Practice.* Boston: Beacon.
1976   *Legitimation Crisis.* London: Heinemann.
Haes, J.
1980   The Problem of Cultural Relativism. *Sociological Review* 28/4: 717–43.
Heirich, M.
1976   Cultural Breakthroughs. *American Behavioral Scientist* 19/6: 685–702.
Herion, G.
1982   *The Social Organization of Tradition in Monarchic Judah.* Ph.D. disserta-
          tion, University of Michigan. Ann Arbor: University Microfilms.
Heschel, A.
1962   *The Prophets: An Introduction,* vols. 1–2. New York: Harper and Row.
Lehmann, P.
1963   *Ethics in a Christian Context.* New York: Harper and Row.
Lenski, G.
1961   *The Religious Factor.* Garden City, N.Y.: Doubleday
1980   Review of Gottwald's *Tribes of Yahweh. Religious Studies Review* 6/4:
          275–78.
Lewis, B.
1975   *History: Remembered, Recovered, Invented.* Princeton: Princeton Univer-
          sity Press.
Long, B.
1982   The Social World of Ancient Israel. *Interpretation* 37/3: 243–55.
Malina, B.
1982   The Social Sciences and Biblical Interpretation. *Interpretation* 37/3:
          229–42.
McGhee, C.
1982   Spiritual Values and Sociology: When We Have Debunked Every-
          thing, What Then? *The American Sociologist* 17: 40–46.
Mandelbaum, M.
1977   *The Anatomy of Historical Knowledge.* Baltimore: Johns Hopkins Uni-
          versity Press.
Mendenhall, G.
1973   *The Tenth Generation.* Baltimore: Johns Hopkins University Press.
1975   The Conflict between Value Systems and Social Control. Pp. 169–80
          in *Unity and Diversity,* ed. H. Goedicke and J. J. M. Roberts. Balti-
          more: Johns Hopkins University Press.
Niebuhr, R.
1953   *Christian Realism and Political Problems.* New York: Scribner.
Parsons, T.
1960   Pattern Variables Revisited. *American Sociological Review* 25: 467–83.
Plumb, J. H.
1971   *The Death of the Past.* Boston: Houghton Mifflin.
Redfield, R.
1947   The Folk Society. *American Journal of Sociology* 52: 293–308.

Rokeach, M,
   1979   *Understanding Human Values.* New York: Free Press.
Rosenbloom, J.
   1972   Social Science Concepts of Modernization and Biblical History. *JAAR*
            40: 437–44.
Sasson, J.
   1981   On Choosing Models for Recreating Israelite Pre-monarchic History.
            JSOT 21: 3–24.
Steck, O.
   1977   Theological Streams of Tradition. Pp. 183–214 in *Tradition and Theol-*
            ogy in the Old Testament, ed. D. Knight. Philadelphia: Fortress.
Sullivan, W.
   1982   *Reconstructing Public Philosophy.* Berkeley. University of California Press.
Tönnies, F.
   1887   *Gemeinschaft und Gesellschaft.* Leipzig: Reisland.
Weber, M.
   1930   *The Protestant Ethic and the Spirit of Capitalism,* trans. T. Parsons. Lon-
            don: Allen & Unwin.
Wilson, R.
   1980   *Prophecy and Society in Ancient Israel.* Philadelphia: Fortress.
   1984   *Sociological Approaches to the Old Testament.* Philadelphia: Fortress.
Wirth, L.
   1938   Urbanism as a Way of Life. *American Journal of Sociology* 44: 1–24.
Yoder, J.
   1972   *The Politics of Jesus.* Grand Rapids: Eerdmans.

Idealism and Materialism in Weber and Gottwald

ANDREW D. H. MAYES

I

[[44]] Weber's study of ancient Judaism[1] is widely acknowledged as a seminal contribution to the sociological study of ancient Israel. The work does not, on Weber's own admission,[2] present any new facts, but it does reflect a new approach to and a use of known data, the results of which were to be highly influential in subsequent Old Testament study, especially as represented in the work of Alt and Noth.

Gottwald's study, *The Tribes of Yahweh*,[3] has been described in these terms:

> Gottwald's book should not be taken simply as another critical analysis, but as a reorganization of the data around quite new categories. . . . In this book we have a programmatic hypothesis which holds the potential of being an important historical moment in the discipline . . . the book holds promise of being a point of reference parallel in significance, potential and authority to Wellhausen's *Prolegomena*, and Albright's *From the Stone Age to Christianity*. . . . Wellhausen established a new scholarly

Reprinted with permission from *Proceedings of the Irish Biblical Association* 11 (1988) 44–58.

1. M. Weber, *Ancient Judaism* (translated and edited by Hans H. Gerth and Don Martindale), Free Press, New York 1952. First published as a series of essays in *Archiv für Sozialwissenschaft und Sozialforschung* 1917–19, and subsequently as vol. 3 of M. Weber, *Gesammelte Aufsätze zur Religionssoziologie*, J. C. B. Mohr, Tübingen 1921.

2. Op. cit., 429.

3. N. K. Gottwald, *The Tribes of Yahweh. A Sociology of the Religion of Liberated Israel 1250–1050 B.C.E.* [[Orbis, Maryknoll, N.Y., 1979]] / SCM, London 1980.

basis for criticism, both literary and historical, with his massive and ingenious synthesis. . . . In turn Albright broke with the evolutionism of Wellhausen. In a parallel move Gottwald proposes a break with *idealism* toward a religious functionalism that reflects a dialectic which is profoundly materialistic, and a materialism which is profoundly dialectical.[4]

There is indeed much in favour of highlighting Wellhausen, Albright and Gottwald as decisive turning points in the history of the study of ancient Israel; with equal justification the work of Weber could be put in place of that of Albright, for here too there is a historical exposition which on the one hand fundamentally modifies the evolutionary interpretation of Wellhausen, and on the other hand reflects, at least in Gottwald's view, an idealism for which Gottwald aims to substitute a comprehensive historical materialism.

This essay falls into three major sections: the first is a rather bald sketch of arguments which Weber and Gottwald put forward [[45]] with considerable care and subtlety; the second compares and contrasts their approaches, with some reference to the methodological presuppositions on which they are based; and the third offers some very tentative pointers to further development of the sociological study of ancient Israelite religion and society.

II

Weber's studies were in large measure concerned with the nature and origin of capitalism. His early work on *The Protestant Ethic and the Spirit of Capitalism*[5] indicated Calvinistic Protestantism as one factor in the rise of capitalism; and a strong echo of this is to be found in his later work on Israel. If *The Protestant Ethic* was written in part to demonstrate the error of the materialist thesis that all ideas, including religious ideas, have a socio-economic materialist basis, and to show that the relationship between religion and society could be the reverse, then this was found to be confirmed in *Ancient Judaism*: Israel has a religious foundation; it is not her social existence which is basic to her religion.

The first few chapters of *Ancient Judaism* reflect Weber's particular method and approach. He begins with a discussion of the social structure

4. W. Brueggemann, "Review of N. K. Gottwald, *The Tribes of Yahweh*," *The Bible and Liberation. Political and Social Hermeneutics*, ed. N. K. Gottwald, Orbis Books, New York 1983, 174.

5. M. Weber, *The Protestant Ethic and the Spirit of Capitalism* (translated by Talcott Parsons, with an introduction by Anthony Giddens), Allen & Unwin, London 1930 and [[New York: Scribner's]] 1976. First published in *Archiv für Sozialwissenschaft und Sozialpolitik* 1904–5, and subsequently, in revised form, in M. Weber, *Gesammelte Aufsätze zur Religionssoziologie*, vol. 1, J. C. B. Mohr, 1920, 1–206. The translation is from the revised version.

of nomadic bedouin, then he turns to the same subject in relation to
cities in Palestine, then to the peasant farmer and then to the semi-
nomadic herdsman. Following on this he turns his attention to the laws
of the Book of the Covenant and Deuteronomy and finally to the question of the covenant. The relationship between these different topics is
not made explicit, and where and how "Israel" fits into the picture is at
first obscure. The various forms of life in Palestine are discussed as not
only independent but hostile social forms,[6] and we are kept guessing as
to where exactly, and on what basis, Weber sees Israel's existence to lie.

Weber approaches his subject here as elsewhere by means of constructing "ideal types." In this he does not consider that he is doing anything new, but rather that he is simply making explicit what is already
done in practice. In that the process involved, however, is usually carried
through automatically and unconsciously, the concepts, or "ideal types,"
tend to be ambiguous or imprecise. Weber's approach is consciously to
construct such ideal types before the specific historical questions are
considered. Giddens has defined the approach in these terms:

> An ideal type is constructed by the abstraction and combination of
> an indefinite number of elements which, although found in reality, are
> rarely or never discovered in this specific form. . . . Such an ideal type is
> neither a "description" of any definite aspect of reality, nor, according to
> ⟦46⟧ Weber, is it a hypothesis; but it can aid in both description and
> explanation. An ideal type is not, of course, ideal in a normative sense:
> it does not carry the connotation that its realisation is desirable. . . . An
> ideal type is a pure type in a logical and not an exemplary sense. . . . The
> creation of ideal types is in no sense an end itself . . . the only purpose of
> constructing it is to facilitate the analysis of empirical questions.[7]

It is this ideal type approach which Weber brings to bear on premonarchic social forms in Palestine. He does not isolate any one of
these types historically as a description of Israel. These are types of life
in Palestine, and within their general context Israel is to be historically
located. Once one begins to speak of Israel, however, one moves away
from the typological approach, which by nature is ahistorical, to the historical approach, which by nature presupposes movement and development. Israel was a historical entity and so cannot, without risk of great
distortion, be described simply within the framework of an exclusively

---

6. Cf. Weber, *Ancient Judaism*, 54.

7. A. Giddens, *Capitalism and Modern Social Theory. An Analysis of the Writings of Marx,
Durkheim and Max Weber*, Cambridge University Press 1971, 141f. For a critical assessment of
the effects of the ideal type approach, cf. R. Bendix, *Max Weber: an intellectual portrait*, Doubleday, New York 1960, and University of California Press 1977, 274ff.

typological analysis. It is within this context that Weber writes: "This complex, unstable social composition of the Israelites gradually moved in the direction of urban patrician rule over the countryside. The development is mirrored in a peculiar manner in the legal collections which have come down to us from pre-exilic times."[8] From within the various social types which concurrently existed in Palestine, the historical Israel can be discerned emerging as a developing historical reality, by reference to the Old Testament lawcodes.

The primary concern of the Book of the Covenant is with peasant property in cattle. Since these laws, however, regulate money loans and deposits with the interest payable, it is clear that the social group in view, the landed peasant, is not treated in isolation; rather, it is the peasant in his relations with other social groups, especially the developing urban patriciate which would have been the source of such loans, who is the focus of the laws. Likewise, the peasant has contacts with the *gerim* [['sojourners']], among whom were to be found semi-nomadic herdsmen, and his behaviour towards that group is regulated. The Book of the Covenant reflects the need for codification arising from social tensions and antagonisms *within* the developing society of Israel, a society not confined to any one social type.[9] Further social development in Israel is reflected in the revision of the Book of the Covenant in Deuteronomy: "With the growing accumulation of pecuniary funds through commerce, the tensions between the urban patrician and the usuriously exploited peasant developed into a typical class antagonism."[10]

So it is clear that for Weber Israel is not simply to be identified with a semi-nomadic society, or a peasant society, or an urban [[47]] society. Israel was to be found in the city, among the peasantry and among the semi-nomads, and it is for the regulating of relations between them that the lawcodes came into existence. Moreover, it is not a case of Israel being first semi-nomadic, then peasant, then urban; rather, all types existed at the same time within this people Israel, a people which in general terms was in the process of a gradual development towards urbanization.

But how was Israel as such constituted within such varying and antagonistic social forms? Within what framework and on what basis were its internal differences overcome so that one people could emerge? Weber sees the clue to the answer in the increasingly *theological* elaboration of the law. The laws of the Old Testament gradually develop to meet changing situations, but what is distinctive is that they develop in terms

8. *Ancient Judaism*, 61.
9. Op. cit., 65.
10. Op. cit., 68.

of being laws of Yahweh. They are not simply laws regulating social relations; they are laws of the covenant between Yahweh and Israel. It is on
this that Israel's original unity is founded, on a union of different groups
in covenant with Yahweh.

How did this happen? Here we find a characteristic Weberian conception:

> the point at issue is not that the life conditions . . . "produced" an order
> whose establishment could be considered as something like the "ideo-
> logical exponent" of its economic conditions. This form of historical
> materialist construction is here, as elsewhere, inadequate. . . . The ques-
> tion . . . why such an order emerged at all was determined by quite con-
> crete religious-historical and often highly personal circumstances and
> vicissitudes.[11]

What Weber here apparently refers to is the exodus from Egypt and the
role of Moses as charismatic prophet and leader in that event. Israel is a
society comprising diverse social groups, a society founded on the unity
of such groups in covenant with Yahweh, a unity in covenant established
by the charismatic prophet Moses.

Gottwald is concerned less with the history of Israel than with the
nature of Israel. Historical questions mainly arise in relation only to the
origins of Israel. This in itself is significant, especially in the context of
contrasting Weber and Gottwald; with the latter it is not a matter of the
history of Israel in the period of the judges, but rather of the history of
origins of this Israel which then simply existed in the period of the judges.
The focus is not on the history of Israel but on the nature of Israel, and
the history only comes in at the point of accounting for the origins of
Israel.

Gottwald is thus concerned primarily not with a diachronic view of
a people existing over time, but with a synchronic cross ⟦48⟧ section of
Israel which attempts to elucidate its structure of internal relationships
at one particular time. So he determines that the basic economic unit is
the family. This was a self-sufficient unit in that it produced the basic
means of subsistence for all its members.[12] A number of such families
was contained in an association loosely referred to as a clan. The tribe
is a secondary and developed social unit, based primarily on territorial
contiguity rather than on kinship. As far as the foundations of society
are concerned, they lie at the level of the family. This is the primary

---

11. Op. cit., 80.
12. Gottwald, *The Tribes of Yahweh*, 292.

social unit, though that does not mean that all power resided at this bottom level. In the course of time instruments of government were formed, such as the council of elders at the tribal level, so that there developed a complex process of interaction from the bottom up and from the top down. This ensured the uniform development of tribal society throughout Israel and at the same time preserved its fundamental egalitarian, non-authoritarian character.

A basic uniformity of social and economic structure thus formed the foundation of Israel. Yet Israel did comprise some social diversity. This existed not mainly in the common distinction which is drawn between farmers and semi-nomads, for in fact these two types belong to the one socio-economic way of life. Semi-nomadism is simply a specialized offshoot of agriculture and belongs with agriculture in different forms of very close interaction.[13] The main diversity existed, rather, in that Israel comprised diverse underclasses in society: *habiru*, pastoralists and depressed peasantry. The bulk of the population indeed shared a common way of life and social structure, but the binding into this group of the *habiru* especially, a group distinguished by its opposition to established authority rather than by any specific social structure, means that the existence of the tribal people Israel is not based solely on the fortuitous existence of a single economic and social form.

The identity of Israel as a single people has its primary basis and focus not, as with Weber, in a common religion, but in an anti-feudal egalitarian social commitment. The wider society of Canaan within which Israel emerged was a feudalized society in which city-states exercised, or attempted to exercise, control over the rural peasantry. The city-state system, and the urban ruling class which it incorporated, could prosper only to the extent that it succeeded in levying taxes on a subject population, and in this pre-industrial age the subject population inevitably comprised mainly peasant farmers and pastoralists. Thus, the division in society existed not between the semi-nomad and the settled, as commonly understood, but between the urban and the rural. It was in the context of the decline of the city-states and their increasing inability to control the subject peasantry ⟦49⟧ that an anti-urban rural tribal alliance gradually emerged. In this alliance,

> tribalism was an autonomous project which tried to roll back the zone of political centralization in Canaan, to claim territory and peoples for an egalitarian mode of agricultural and pastoral life. . . . All the evidence of early Israel points to its tribalism as a self-constructed instrument of resistance and of decentralized self-rule. . . . Israel's tribalism was politically

13. Ibid., 438ff.

conscious and deliberate social revolution and, more loosely, a civil war in that it divided and counterposed peoples who had previously been organized within Canaanite city-states.[14]

If Israel's unity as a single people is of this kind, then how is the role of the religion of Israel to be described? Gottwald marks off his own position in the first instance by a criticism of what he describes as religious idealism. The view that the religion of the Canaanites was a justification and a projection of a particular social form, while that of Israel was not, implies a desertion of sociological method at a crucial juncture. It is an indefensible philosophical idealism which sees Yahwism as "an unmoved mover of people and events."[15] In place of the vagaries of non-methodical idealism, which severs Israelite religion from Israelite society (Bright), or arbitrarily derives Israelite society from Israelite religion (Mendenhall), or establishes social structural influences that merely affect the surface form and not the deep substance of Israelite religion (Fohrer), the subject requires, firstly, a method that will plot the correlations between Israelite society and Israelite religion; secondly, a method that will clarify the causal relationships between them; thirdly, a method that will facilitate the comparative differentiation of the Israelite religion-society complex from other religion-society complexes, both historically and typically.[16]

It is the structural functionalist approach which fulfils most of these purposes. Religion belongs in the total field of social relations and is a particular symbolic code articulating the whole network. In the Israelite context, Yahwism is a function of society; that is to say, Yahwism is dependably related to Israelite society in the sense that any change in society would have corresponding effects in Yahwism. Israelite society was egalitarian; correspondingly, Israelite faith was non-dominating in the sense that it involved the worship of one God whose cult laid little claim on communal resources. All the symbols of Yahweh (patron deity, leader in war, judge, sovereign) refer to "socio-economic desiderata in the community."[17] Thus, Yahwism was a pervasive social force with a central position in the Israelite social structure. As such, this faith not only symbolized the community, but also acted back upon society in order to sustain the foundational egalitarian social [[50]] relations. It is thus in the first instance a symbolic objectification of society which then, secondly, works back upon society to strengthen its egalitarian structure and to inhibit any developments which might threaten it.[18]

14. Ibid., 325.
15. Ibid., 602.
16. Ibid., 608.
17. Ibid., 615.
18. Ibid., 618ff.

III

At first glance the contrast between Weber and Gottwald is clear: for the former religion is the foundation of society, for the latter the reverse. In the one case religion exercises a primary causative influence, in the other the causative role is secondary to the origins of religion as a reflection of society. This distinction is, however, something we must qualify. There are differences of a very significant nature between Weber and Gottwald, differences which may be appreciated when the work of each is put into its wider sociological context; but it is potentially distorting to summarize those differences in terms of the relationship between religion and society in the way that this has just been done.

For Weber, sociology meant the study of the understandable behavior and actions of individuals who actively create the structures and institutions within which they live; and, arising from this, his critique of historical materialism was a critique of that form of historical materialism which put the relationship between the individual and society the other way around, seeing the individual as a creation of the society into which he was born. In line with this, Weber criticized the historical materialist explanation of religion simply as a product of social and economic conditions as inadequate. His own view of the relationship between religion and society is not, however, as easy to determine as is sometimes supposed. In *The Protestant Ethic* he noted that it was not his intention to maintain "such a foolish and doctrinaire thesis as that the spirit of capitalism could only have arisen as the result of certain effects of the reformation. . . . On the contrary, we only wish to ascertain whether and to what extent religious forces have taken part in the qualitative formation and quantitative expansion of that spirit in the world";[19] and on the last page of that book he wrote that, having discerned the contribution of ascetic Protestantism to the formation of capitalism, "it would also further be necessary to investigate how Protestant asceticism was in turn influenced in its development and its character by the totality of social conditions, especially economic"; he then concluded by affirming that "it is not my aim to substitute for a one sided materialistic an equally one sided spiritualistic causal interpretation of culture and of history."[20]

If this is so, how then are we to understand Weber's [[51]] affirmations in *Ancient Judaism* where, having criticized historical materialism, he stated that the rise of the pre-monarchic community of Israel "was determined by quite concrete religious historical and often highly personal circumstances and vicissitudes," and, further, that "Muhammed's

19. Weber, *The Protestant Ethic*, 91.
20. Ibid., 183.

as well as Jonadab ben Rechab's religious promises are not to be 'explained' as products of population phenomena or economic conditions, though their content was co-determined thereby. They were, rather, the expression of personal experiences and intentions."[21] At first sight, this seems to presuppose what Gottwald[22] dismissively refers to as "the idealist 'escape hatch' of the great personalities as the mysterious sources of religions," that ultimately the religious idea came first and on its basis the social structures were developed, and yet that would be exactly the sort of one sided causal interpretation which Weber earlier emphatically rejected.

There are two terms which Weber used to express the relationship between the religious ideas of an individual or group and the social and economic circumstances of that individual or group. One, which appears in the quotation just given, is "co-determination": the religious ideas are not explicable as products of social and economic conditions, "though their content was co-determined thereby." The other, which is used synonymously, is 'elective affinity' (*Wahlverwandtschaft*). The latter does not appear frequently and it is nowhere given clear definition, and yet it seems to express what Weber believed as an alternative to the materialistic view of religion.[23] It is, in fact, a somewhat paradoxical term:[24] "elective" implies the existence of free choice, while "affinity" implies the determined, non-elective relationship between one thing and another. It is in origin a chemical concept which is used of the propensity of elements to combine with each other in certain proportions, to split apart and to re-combine in new compounds. The expression was transferred by Goethe, in his novel *Elective Affinities*,[25] to the human sphere, where he used it to describe the attraction of one individual to another, their breaking apart and being drawn into new relationships. According to an interpretation of this novel current in Weber's time, Goethe was concerned with themes such as chance and necessity, freedom and determinism, and by means of the concept of "elective affinity" he attempted to overcome the dualism which these alternatives imply.

Weber was very probably well acquainted with this novel and with that interpretation of it; and his use of the idea is likewise an attempt to

21. Weber, *Ancient Judaism*, 80.

22. *The Tribes of Yahweh*, 630.

23. Cf. *From Max Weber. Essays in Sociology* (translated and edited by H. H. Gerth and C. Wright Mills), London 1948, 62f., 284f. Other references are noted in J. J. R. Thomas, "Ideology and Elective Affinity," *Sociology* 19, 1985, 53 n. 10.

24. For what follows, cf. Thomas, op. cit., 39–54.

25. J. W. Goethe, *Elective Affinities* (translated by R. J. Hollingdale), Penguin Books, London 1971.

overcome a similar dualism of chance and necessity, freedom and determinism. In the context of the relationship between religion and society, it affirms the inextricable interlocking of the ⟦52⟧ socially determined and the individually free in the origin of religious ideas; neither determines the other in any absolute sense. In his biography of Weber, Bendix has quoted the German historian Otto Hintze as providing a formulation of the perspective that governed Weber:

> All human action arises from a common source, in political as well as in religious life. Everywhere the first impulse to social action is given as a rule by real interests, i.e., by political and economic interests. But ideal interests lend wings to these real interests, give them a spiritual meaning, and serve to justify them. Man does not live by bread alone. He wants to have a good conscience as he pursues his life-interests. And in pursuing them he develops his capacities to the highest extent only if he believes that in so doing he serves a higher rather than a purely egoistic purpose. Interests without such "spiritual wings" are lame; but on the other hand, ideas can win out in history only if and insofar as they are associated with real interests.[26]

In similar vein, Weber himself argued thus:[27] very frequently the world images that have been created by "ideas" have, like switchmen, determined the tracks along which action has been pushed by the dynamic of interest.

That understanding of Weber's alternative to materialism is the framework within which we must understand his view of the relationship between religion and society, and indeed, the relationship between them not only in the ongoing history of religion but also in its beginnings. The charismatic founder is not removed from society and material interests, and in that respect cannot be regarded as, to use Gottwald's terms, an "idealist 'escape hatch'" which sets the origins of religion in unknowable mystery.

The structural functionalist approach used by Gottwald reflects a sociological approach fundamentally different from that of Weber, and one which is to be traced back to the French sociologist Émile Durkheim.[28] For Durkheim, society is the prior reality and determinative influence on the individual; man is knowable only as a manifestation of community; normal personality is the reflection of normal integration within community;

26. Bendix, op. cit., 46f.

27. *From Max Weber. Essays in Sociology*, 280.

28. Cf., e.g., A. Swingewood, *A Short History of Sociological Thought*, Macmillan, 1984, 227ff.

society is that which determines the individual materially, mentally and spiritually. Structural functionalism is used by Gottwald, however, only up to a certain point, viz., to describe the interacting relationship of religion and society at a given moment. But this approach provides no ultimate causal explanation of this relationship; it leaves open the possibility that ultimately religion may be the primary causative element, and however far back in history that cause may lie it leaves its mark as an underived remnant which lies outside the social context of the relationship between religion and society. From a sociological point [[53]] of view, it is unacceptable that any part of the problem of religion and society should lie outside the scope of sociological enquiry.[29]

It is for this reason, and in order to provide a historical perspective, that Gottwald has supplemented the structural functionalist model with a historical materialism based on a fairly selective reading of Marx. Marx's view "that at the root of all social organization and mental ideation, including religion, is the way human beings within nature act upon nature to produce their means of subsistence and thereby fashion their own social nature,"[30] is accepted as being "the most coherent and promising understanding for developing research strategies in the social sciences. It provides a framework within which to include structural-functional models as stepping stones in the analytic task of determining how social evolution occurs."[31] In this view, according to Gottwald, "changes in the forms of production (including techniques and modes of cooperative labor) lead correlatively to changes in social and political forms and to changes in ideas, including religious ideas."[32] Modes of production do change with developing technology; these bring about increased population and new forms of social interaction; and these in turn lead to changes in ideas. Religious ideas in this context come to exercise the function of reflecting and providing a mystical validation of the social order as it undergoes evolutionary change.

A sociology of religion, based on an historical cultural materialist hypothesis of social evolution, "recognizes that it is not the mere givenness of society that projects a god image of the Yahweh type, but it is the tensions within the onward-moving social process, the breaks and leaps, the struggles and mutations in the 'distancing' process that occurs when a new social formation comes into being and people are 'stretched' to realize new possibilities of social interaction."[33] For Gottwald, those who

29. Cf. Gottwald, *Tribes of Yahweh*, 622ff.
30. Ibid., 631.
31. Ibid., 633.
32. Ibid., 634.
33. Ibid., 697f.

are "stretched to realize new possibilities" are not charismatic originators of new ideas, but rather the hapless victims of the "tensions within the onward-moving social process." Arising from changes in the economic base, tensions appear in the process of formation of new social structures, and then new ideas emerge as the deposit and reflection of these changes and developments. So Moses and the prophets, as indeed all religious innovators, must be seen as "propagandists for a religion already formed or forming in a given social field."[34]

This is the nub of the issue as it is defined by Gottwald: do we have in religious ideas, innovations and movements, the insights of individuals who are somehow free of the social and economic conditions in which they live; or do all such ideas, innovations and movements reflect social and economic innovations and movements which are taking place according to society's own internal laws?

IV

[[54]] What, then, can we derive from Weber and Gottwald by way of an understanding of the relationship between individual and society and the place of ideas and particularly religious ideas in this relationship? Pannenberg has written in a recent work:

> If theologians are not to succumb to self-deception regarding their proper activity, they must begin their reflection with a recognition of the fundamental importance of anthropology for all modern thought and for any present-day claim of universal validity for religious statements. Otherwise they will, even if unintentionally, play into the hands of their atheistic critics, who reduce religion and theology to anthropology, that is, to human assumptions and illusions. . . . Theologians will be able to defend the truth precisely of their talk about God only if they first respond to the atheistic critique of religion on the terrain of anthropology. Otherwise all their assertions, however impressive, about the primacy of the Goodness of God will remain purely subjective assurances without any serious claim to universal validity.[35]

In our present context this can be taken to imply: if we wish to respond to the view that the religion of Israel is but a mystical validation of its social structures, then we must begin with anthropology. Quite apart from its own intrinsic points of interest, the anthropological issue, and, by extension, the sociological issue, must be foundational also to the study of Israelite religion.

34. Ibid., 630.
35. W. Pannenberg, *Anthropology in Theological Perspective*, T. & T. Clark, 1985, 16.

But if anthropological study of ancient Israel is then to be the foundation for the study of Israelite religion, it is by no means implied that Gottwald's form of historical materialism is the best approach. Gottwald's theoretical understanding of the relationship between religion and society is a materialist one, and the programme of research which he outlines for the future is a materialist programme, and one which is currently being explored by Frick and others;[36] it involves the rejection, or at least the serious devaluing, of the biblical text in favour of archaeology and the study of patterns of agriculture and climate, on the basis of which the nature of society and its long-term developments can be objectively determined; so a reliable foundation for knowledge of ancient Israel can be created.

Undoubtedly this materialist programme has much to offer to the study of both the history and religion of Israel, in terms of the long-term processes of social change and the organization of institutions, within the framework of which lie Israel's life and history. Its assumption, however, that intentional and purposive human action is an irrelevance which obstructs the uncovering of reliable historical knowledge, seems to rest not on any reasoned sociological or anthropological [[55]] theory, but rather on generally unexamined dogmatic presuppositions of a neo-positivistic kind concerning both the relationship of man to society and also the so-called facts of history, and represents a reaction against the biographical understanding and writing of history which goes much too far to the opposite extreme. It is true that individuals act according to the conventions of their age and within limitations imposed by a physical environment, and to an extent, therefore, one may speak of human action as determined; the uncovering of these conventions and limitations is an essential sociological task. It is also true that our activities constantly have

36. There is certainly a fundamental theoretical inconsistency in Gottwald's study which should be noted. While his exposition of the relationship between religion and society and his proposed programme for future research are materialist, his own understanding of the way in which Israel actually came into existence cannot be so classified. As F. R. Brandfon, "Norman Gottwald on the Tribes of Yahweh," *JSOT* 21, 1981, 101–10, has noted, Gottwald has in fact an idealist approach to the origins of Israel: he presupposes that the people of Israel understood their economic plight and devised an ideal scheme as an alternative; Marxism is substituted for Yahwism as the driving force behind the social change. This is, however, by no means untrue to Marx, for the latter cannot be crudely classified as a materialist. For the dialectical materialism of Marx and the distortion of this towards a crude materialism in the work of M. Harris (on whom Gottwald heavily relies), cf. M. Bloch, *Marxism and Anthropology*, Oxford University Press, 1983, 124–40. For more recent materialist approaches to Israelite origins, cf. F. S. Frick, *The Formation of the State in Ancient Israel*, Almond Press, 1985; R. B. Coote and K. W. Whitelam, *The Emergence of Early Israel in Historical Perspective*, Almond Press, 1987 [[for a similar work by Coote and Whitelam, see pp. 335–76 in this volume]].

consequences that we do not intend or to which we are oblivious, and so "while as social agents we are necessarily the creators of social life, social life is at the same time not our own creation."[37] But these represent qualifications rather than negations of the freedom which is also part of the human condition. A useful analogy has been drawn[38] in this connection with Saussure's study of the structural qualities of language. Here structures consist of relations of absences and presences embedded in the instantiation of language in speech or in texts. So also in social theory "structure is both the medium and the outcome of the human activities which it recursively organizes."[39] Within this framework it is possible to understand the relationship of the individual to society as one in which society has a structure by virtue of the continuity of the actions of its component members, while at the same time these members of society carry out their day-to-day activities by virtue of their ability to instantiate that structure. The purposive action of individuals is thus far from irrelevant to the understanding of history and society.

If the relationship between individual and society is to be described in these terms, there seem to be certain implications with respect to our understanding of Israelite religion in its relationship with Israelite society. Religion, as a pattern of beliefs and rituals which gives meaning to human lives, is part of the process of culture creation by which the individual responds to his situation through the conventions available to his time. It must necessarily reflect and be expressed through those conventions, and so then be integral to the society which embodies them; it must necessarily also reflect that from which it derives, namely the human search for meaning expressed through those conventions. From this perspective, the distinction drawn by Miller between ideology and theology is potentially misleading. Miller[40] has defined ideology as a partial and interested view entertained by a particular group or society, in which its ideas are functions of the group's existence. In theology, on the other hand, the self-interest of the group is transcended; there is no immediate and exclusive relationship between the belief expressed [[56]] and the interests of the group. In fact, theology implies self-criticism, moral

---

37. Cf. A. Giddens, *Social Theory and Modern Sociology*, Polity Press, 1987, 10, 67f. Brandfon, op. cit., 108f., has also noted that Gottwald has neglected the (materialist) possibility that Israelite social egaliterianism may have been an unintended consequence of a variety of events in the Late Bronze Age.

38. Cf. Giddens, *Social Theory and Modern Sociology*, 61.

39. Ibid.

40. P. D. Miller, "Faith and Ideology in the Old Testament," *Magnalia Dei. The Mighty Acts of God* (*Essays on the Bible and Archaeology in Memory of G. Ernest Wright*), ed. F. M. Cross, W. E. Lemke, P. D. Miller, Doubleday, 1976, 464–79.

demand and universalism, the essential characteristic being the discontinuity between ideas and special interests. Miller then goes on to use an earlier study of the Yahwist by Wolff, to show that it contains both ideology and theology: ideology insofar as it speaks of the chosen people, the promise of land through the expulsion of its former inhabitants, and the great nation promised to Abraham; but theology in that the nation is to be characterized by justice and righteousness and also in that the descendants of Abraham are to be the channel of universal blessing.

Much of this is attractive, but it does seem to carry the implication that what is to be classified as theology must by definition be independent of social and human limitation, so that it in effect becomes open to the charge of being simply human assumption and illusion. The basic distorting element in it is the restriction of the notion of "interests" to *material* interests, the expression of which is ideology. If "interests" are understood, however, to include, as they surely must, both material and ideal interests, then one can say that theology also expresses the self-interests of the group or the individual. The study of Israelite religion, therefore, must necessarily recognize the social, conventional form which it takes. This does not mean, however, that it is then a simple projection of material conditions; rather, it is the expression, within the limitations of that time and place, of a human search for meaning, a search through which men sought to order material reality in terms of ultimate meaning.

On the Use of "System Theory," "Macro Theories," and "Evolutionistic Thinking" in Modern Old Testament Research and Biblical Archaeology

NIELS PETER LEMCHE

⟦73⟧ More often than not the title seems to be the most promising part of an article whereas the content may be rather indifferent. The theme of this article sounds very ambitious and I am, of course, afraid that it is impossible to repay the expectations in such a short communication. On the other hand, the title itself also indicates that it is not my intention to present a definitive settlement of the phenomenon, "system theory." I am only going to present some second thoughts on the application of the method in question, although I shall also question the basic epistemology behind the method.[1]

The application of "system theory" in humanistic scholarship introduces the concept of "heuristic models" to biblical studies. The system theoretical application of "heuristic models" is strictly deductive since the starting point for a system theoretical investigation is a basic model or idea of a certain phenomenon which we are going to study. By using a model the various single phenomena belonging to the object of study are analyzed not on behalf of their own content but on behalf of the content of the model as such.

Reprinted with permission from *Scandinavian Journal of the Old Testament* 4/2 (1990) 73–88.

This article represents a revision of the author's lecture at the SBL International Meeting, Sheffield, England, August the 3rd, 1988.

1. The following will expand and supplement the excursus on this theme in my *Early Israel* (*VTS* 37; Leiden, 1985) 216–19.

Originally this procedure belongs to the realm of science, especially theoretical mathematics and physics. A scientist may present a certain model which is thereafter either verified or falsified by the existing empirical facts. Well-known are such procedures also in the field of general economic studies.

The method also has many advocates in the social sciences. It is [74] very popular here to present general models for societies and to try to form societies according to such models—often to the detriment of the population in question. Such examples are by no means only modern. I believe the most famous example (apart, of course, from the modern marxist remoulding of Eastern European societies, the effects of which are all too obvious today) may be the endeavours by Plato in Syracuse, to mould the Syracusians according to his political thinking. However, the ancient Syracusians were perhaps more clever than most people have been in later times, since after having been the victim of the application of a "macro social theory" they expelled the philosopher who was at one moment nearly sold as a slave and at the next almost killed. Finally the Syracusians abolished the try forever in order to continue with their old habits.[2]

The classical procedures within the humanities have, however, mostly been inductive and positivistic. On the basis of a certain number of apparent "facts" or phenomena scholars work toward a general theory or model in order to present their views in the form of hypotheses which are considered wide enough to embrace all facts belonging to the subject in question in such a way that not a single fact contradicts the content of the hypothesis (the basic understanding being of course that facts cannot be contradictory—it is only our interpretation of the facts which may seem so). A question of another kind is whether such hypotheses will not later on develop into "heuristic models" or "macro theories" of a very particular kind. In the field of Old Testament studies I only have to refer to the perhaps most famous historical hypothesis of this century, Martin Noth's amphictyonic hypothesis which soon became a "macro theory" for the scholarly organization of the early Israelite society, properly speaking.[3]

---

2. The principal sources of these events are contained in Plato's letters (here disregarding the old discussion of whether or not some or all of these may be spurious), esp. letter no. 7 (to the relatives and friends of Dion of Syracuse). Certainly these sources express the view of the philosopher on these matters.

3. Cf. Noth's original "model" as presented in his *Das System der zwölf Stämme Israels* (*BWANT* 4/1; Stuttgart [Kohlhammer], 1930). I have described these effects of Noth's very effective construction of early Israelite society in several publications, notably my *Israel i Dommertiden* (Copenhagen [Gad], 1972), "'Israel in the Period of the Judges'—The Tribal League in Recent Research," *ST* 38 (1984) 1–28, and in *Early Israel*, 291–305.

That this procedure is problematic has become ever more evident. [[75]] Just as the new concept of "system theory" this procedure originates from outside the humanities since it is ultimately a procedure borrowed from more "complete" sciences (if I may say so) such as mathematics and physics in particular. The scientific epistemology of the modern age was so to speak implanted in a field of study of quite another kind. The fundamental issue must therefore be (and to a certain degree always has been) whether or not the concept of the modern science was applicable to humanistic studies, and whether or not the method in question is adequate to describe its humanistic subject.

It is therefore hardly surprising that it has been relatively easy to demonstrate the inadequacy of the classical scholarly procedures. We can easily say that the current crisis of the modern sciences but also of the modern concept of the world as such (which is expressed in current phenomena like "post-modernism") should be considered a result of the lack of confidence in the value of the traditional scientific epistemology.

I also believe that it is justifiable to argue that biblical scholarship presents a rather sad picture as to the applicability of this positivistic methodology. We should after all have reached reliable results a long time ago after having invested so much industry and ingenuity. Not least should we have reached a general scholarly consensus as to the basic historical facts which form the background of the biblical sources. But what do we actually meet today? We find biblical study in a critical situation where nothing is considered definitive, where every single topic seems to be in a state of dissolution and fluidity. I cannot at the moment of writing recollect a single scholarly position of yesterday which has not been called into question.

Is it hardly coincidental that in the field of OT studies it is nowadays nearly a slogan to ask for a return to Wellhausen who has been dead for more than seventy years.[4] And it is symptomatic for the ongoing crisis that during the last decade plenty of books have appeared which propagate at least three or four totally different explanations of how Israel came to Palestine, whether by conquest or [[76]] in the form of the settlement of semi-nomads or as the result of a general evolution (or revolution).[5] Even

---

4. Or to blame scholars for having retorted to arguments found in Wellhausen's work!

5. Although it should at the same time be stressed that the conquest theory in general is disregarded by most serious scholars today. This is also, indirectly, made clear by the desperate attempt by J. J. Bimson to redate the conquest on the basis of a number of more or less questionable archaeological arguments (*Redating Exodus and Conquest. JSOTSS* 5; Sheffield [[JSOT Press]], 1978). That the old theory of Alt and Noth as to the infiltration of semi-nomads is very popular even today is obvious when we are confronted by a number of modern German histories of Israel such as H. Donner's (easily the best of the lot) *Geschichte*

if we believe that we have a fairly coordinated picture of the later Israelite society, of its literature and religion, we are, nevertheless, unable to present a picture of the formation of this society which may be considered valid by all factions of OT scholarship. The problem is, actually, that too many conflicting proposals are often presented on the basis of the same source material.

One endeavour to solve this problem is "system theory." Another solution which is of course not my subject in this lecture, is to divert the attention from the source material as the object of study to the instrument used in analyzing the source material. In our case the instrument will always be the scholar who is studying the source material. This is to say that it has become clear to many who work in the field of humanistic studies that different positions of thought and theory are not necessarily the outcome of the diversity of the basic sources; it may just as well be explained as a result of different scholarly attitudes.

In the field of biblical studies it is, of course, easy to present a rather commonplace example of such differences. Certainly, the presuppositions found in a conservative, evangelical scholar and in an historical-critical scholar are so different in nature as to exclude any possibility of agreement between them.[6] The differences between [[77]] scholars belonging to the same general approach to biblical studies are, however, much more subtle, but even these differences may be explained as caused by factors, which in most cases might form the subject of psychological studies. This should be well-known to most people, and I feel certain that it is true to say that we know how to cope with such differences.[7]

---

des Volkes Israel und seiner Nachbarn in Grundzügen 1 (*Grundrisse zum Alten Testament* 4/1; Göttingen [[Vandenhoeck & Ruprecht]], 1984), or by a study on the early history of Israel like the one by K.-H. Hecke, *Juda und Israel. Untersuchungen zur Geschichte Israels in vor- und frühstaatlicher Zeit* (*Forschung zur Bibel* 52; Würzburg [[Echter]], 1985). According to Hecker the (last) "Wende in der Forschung" was Alt's study of the Israelite immigration dating back to 1925 [[A. Alt., *Die Landnahme der Israeliten in Palästina: Territorialgeschichtliche Studien* (Leipzig: Druckerei der Werkgemeinschaft, 1925)]].

6. I only need to refer to the excellent expositions of the attitudes not only of fundamentalism but also of a number of "conservative" directions of study in the works of James Barr. See especially his *Fundamentalism* (London [[SCM, 1977 / Philadelphia: Fortress, 1978]]) 120–59.

7. The fact that most students of Israelite history have emerged from theological institutions (irrespective of which denomination they belong to) and, only as a result of their training, escaped being "fundamentalists" is hardly an unfair evaluation of an important aspect of biblical scholarship. I simply do not believe that any serious scholar has not—at some point of his or her career—felt some kind of regret that so much of what appears to be the historical truth in the Old Testament has to be abandoned. I believe that most modern results have been "forced" upon the biblical scholar by his honesty.

I think it fair to say that "system theory" has been introduced in order to overcome some of these hermeneutical problems. By introducing their models the advocates of this procedure think they have invented tools which may be comparable to the instruments of the scientists, that is devices which may be used to analyse a certain object without the interference of the human mind (or to minimize the interference of it). Personally I think that they are deluding themselves and that the same fundamental hermeneutical problem is still very much alive.

At first I shall try shortly to describe a so-called "heuristic model" or "tool" of investigation. A "heuristic tool" is a "macro explanation" presenting a general, but constructed model which can be used to study a certain object. For practical reasons we have to deal with historical matters here but other topics may also be studied by applying heuristic models. The model as such has generally been constructed as simple as possible, and normally it includes a carefully selected and restricted number of variables, that is a limited range of phenomena which are the elements of the model and which together form its structure or framework.[8]

[[78]] A variable is a common phenomenon forming part of the human society which may vary according to time or place but where the variations are of decisive importance for the understanding of the society in question.

The application of the model is strictly deductive. The model is the instrument of the analysis, the device for the evaluation of the single facts which form part of a certain phenomenon. The aim of the analysis is to demonstrate the presence of as many of the constituent variables as possible in order to prove the general validity of the model. If enough variables are present the model is considered to be verified.

As regards the study of the history of Israel such heuristic models are first and foremost asked for when scholars deal with the oldest history of the nation before the monarchy. This is only natural since most models concern the development of human societies on a primitive stage. The

---

8. For example, when construing a basis on which to evaluate the status of a certain nomadic society, the discussion formerly concerned the general ratio of movement as compared to the ratio of settlement in a certain society. Thus, should more than fifty percent of the population be travelling around, then the society would be called nomadic, whereas a society in which the migratory movements did not comprise more than half the population would be called basically a settled society. This is basically the argument in a fairly recent study by E. E. Bacon, "Types of Pastoral Nomadism in Central and Southwest Asia," *Southwestern Journal of Anthropology* 10 (1954) 44–68. There is no reason to go into details at this place, but it should be remarked that such issues are now considered rather primitive by most specialists who prefer a much more complicated "model" of the kind which was proposed by P. C. Salzman, for example in his "Multi-Resource Nomadism in Iranian Baluchistan," in W. Irons & N. Dyson-Hudson (eds), *Perspectives on Nomadism* (Leiden [[Brill]], 1972) 60–68.

models mostly describe the evolution of human civilization from one societal level to another. According to the advocates of system theory it is possible to establish fixed and verified models for this evolution. According to the OT scholars of this school these very factors should also be verifiable in the case of the oldest Israelite society, and they should be discernible in the OT sources as well as in the archaeological material fiom Palestine. And when the variable factors are supposedly found the model in question is considered valid or true and providing a total explanation of the development of the Israelite society till monarchic times. It is, accordingly, right to maintain that it is the aim of the school not only to provide a verified model of the development of the early Israelite society, but to achieve a scientific description of the history of that society, or, simply, to write history about a pre-historic period.

This is completely in agreement with the spirit of the discipline where such systemic models first turned up in the humanities, that is pre-historic archaeology. The discipline in question may be better [[79]] known as "new archaeology." This archaeological school originates in the U.S.A. but has also found quite a number of European supporters. Evidently the psychological factor governing the mind of these archaeologists is the desperation caused by the fact they they exclusively deal with mute societies, that is societies from which no written sources have survived. And since the school is of American extraction it is clearly an outcome of the desire to write a history of America before Columbus. Thus they want to bridge the gap between what is —according to the classical definition—historical time and prehistorical time, and by creating their models these new archaeologists believe themselves able to write that history and to change prehistory into history.[9]

The systemic method is borrowed from sociology and social anthropology where macro theories have become the hallmark of that social anthropological school known as "cultural evolutionism."[10] That the method in question is borrowed is certainly not wrong in itself, and the fact is acknowledged by most of the advocates of "new archaeology," for instance by one of its leading members, the American archaeologist L. R. Binford,

9. An exposition of the methods and aims of the "school" is found in L. R. Binford, *An Archaeological Perspective* (New York [[Seminar Press]], 1972), and for a history of the Ancient Near East written from this perspective, C. L. Redman, *The Rise of Civilization. From Early Farmers to Urban Society in the Ancient Near East* (San Francisco [[Freeman]], 1978). The whole direction has been severely criticized by, among others, B. Trigger (belonging originally to the same archaeological tradition), *Time and Traditions. Essays in Archaeological Interpretations* (Edinburgh [[Edinburgh University Press / New York: Columbia University Press]], 1978).

10. Cf. on this direction of social anthropology the critical review in J. J. Honigman, *The Development of Anthropological Ideas* (Homewood [[Dorsey]], 1976) 273–373.

who expressly maintains that archaeology belongs to social sciences, not to humanities.

Therefore, when we try to evaluate some early endeavours to use macro models and system theory in the field of OT studies, as for instance Norman Gottwald's *The Tribes of Yahweh*,[11] it is too easy to dismiss the whole business as just outdated evolutionism (as is the case in George Mendenhall's notorious review of Gottwald's book).[12] [[80]] To believe that things develop and that it may be possible to discern the laws according to which things move on is in itself obviously legitimate. The question is alone whether we have obtained a sound methodology to describe how evolution takes place.

In my own volume, *Early Israel,* both Mendenhall and Gottwald are criticized because of their arbitrary use of macro theories. Both scholars are dependent on the same sociological school of cultural evolutionism and both have their specific sociological master—Mendenhall, the social anthropologist Elman Service; and Gottwald, Morton Fried. Both masters have presented their general models in well-known books, Service in his *Primitive Social Organization*,[13] and Morton Fried in his *The Evolution of Political Society*.[14]

The notorious problem in the works of Mendenhall and Gottwald is, however, not that they try to make use of these models, but that they use them in a way which can hardly be condoned by the sociologists themselves. Mendenhall makes use of the thoughts and theories of Service in an eclectic manner, in that he provides Service's model with some variables which would hardly be acknowledged as valid by Service himself, and Gottwald uses a kind of mixed model, composed by elements borrowed from both scholars, although Service and Fried themselves are well aware of the differences between their models.[15] But my criticism in this connection is not directed against macro models as such, only against the actual application of these models.

11. *The Tribes of Yahweh* ([[Maryknoll, N.Y.: Orbis]], 1979).

12. "Ancient Israel's Hyphenated History," in D. F. Graff and D. N. Freedman, *Palestine in Transition* (Sheffield [[Almond]], 1983) 95–103. I, however, believe that Gottwald is actually a far cry from being a true system theoretic and evolutionistic scholar. Irrespective of all its weaknesses, his *The Tribes of Yahweh* is far too unorganized and therefore indefinitely more inspiring than any example of a rigid application of system theory.

13. The edition used by Mendenhall is the 1st, from 1962, 2nd revised ed. New York [[Random]], 1971. See, however, also Service's more recent volume, *Origins of the State and Civilization: The Process of Cultural Evolution* (New York [[Norton]], 1975).

14. New York [[Random]], 1967.

15. I may in this connection refer to the discussion between the two in Ronald Cohen and Elman Service, *Origins of the State* (Philadelphia [[Institute for the Study of Human Issues]], 1978).

In my *Early Israel,* however, I have also presented a more general criticism of the whole idea of macro models and their general validity in humanistic research. Not least was I able to draw on the criticism already published by the British structuralist social anthropologist Edmund Leach several years ago. The crucial point is that system theoretics generally forget the presence of a kind of black box in their models, namely Mr. Man himself. Leach thinks that Man should be reckoned the most important single variable in any ⟦81⟧ heuristic model used to describe the evolution of human society.[16]

It will hardly be wrong to maintain that the advocates of cultural evolutionism lag behind in general anthropological knowledge, and this specifically applies to the members of the cultural evolutionistic sociological school. And by "anthropology" I certainly do not mean social anthropology, but the general knowledge of the nature of Man. In particular we should never forget the theological discussion of the importance of the free will of Man, that is the ability of man to choose for himself.

It is a fundamental part of system theory that human societies normally develop according to certain laws. The variables reckoned to be important when constructing a model must by force be limited in number, since, obviously, too many variations will make it difficult to control the model in question. It will indeed make the whole procedure null and void. It is the fundamental assumption of system theory that if specific variables are present, then the result must always be considered identical.[17] The development from band society to tribal society may for instance be described as a decision made by the members of the band society itself, a decision which is forced upon them by specific economic, environmental or politic conditions. System theory, however, invariably understands this decision to be predictable, to be something unavoidable which no society living under the same general conditions can possible escape. The problem is, nevertheless, whether Man is always forced to make identical decisions or whether there will always be one or more alternatives open to him. In short, is the evolution from, in this case, band society to tribal society always predictable?[18]

16. "Concluding Address," in C. Renfrew, ed., *The Explanation of Culture Change* (London ⟦Duckworth⟧, 1973) 761–71.

17. Therefore even climatic changes are not allowed to have taken place, at least not in a study of early Near Eastern history like the one mentioned above by C. L. Redman. Climatic factors or climatic changes will be considered illegitimate variables, since they cannot be controlled on a theoretical basis.

18. This is still not the same as to deny that an evolution has taken place. The general lines of evolution of the human world have, of course, been conspicuous and are certainly almost inevitable. However, this only applies to the macro evolution of the human world.

⟦82⟧ This is the first problematic issue. The second is the fact that a model can only contain a limited number of variables. Of course the possibility of verifying the model is reduced if the model contains a greater number of variables. If it were possible to verify a development from band society to tribal society on the basis of, say only five variables, then the chance of verification or falsification is naturally better than if the model contains fifty variables, and should we construct a model consisting of about five hundred variables, then such a model is hardly of any practical use. But the real problem is whether five variables is enough to describe any human society however primitive it may be (and I should like to stress that the number "five" is used here in an exclusively symbolic manner). I very much doubt it, and I have tried in my writings (especially in *Early Israel*) to argue that this is never the case.

The third problematic issue is the number of possible models. It would of course be vain to expect that social anthropologists or other peoples working with system theory should be able to come to a degree of concord seemingly denied to scholars of other schools of mind. I have already described how Mendenhall and Gottwald have made use of sociological macro theories borrowed from Service and Fried, although in an arbitrary fashion. Some younger scholars have gone further and later I shall mention some more recent examples.

But the fact that several competing models are in existence and moreover that too many of them can be verified on the basis of the same source material indicates the problematic character of "system theory" which can be compared to the general situation in our field of research. The fundamental hermeneutical problems have not been solved by introducing macro theories of any kind. Not least is the almost unpredictable character of the human variable unaccounted for.

This is not so say that it is illegitimate to construct and test, to verify or falsify heuristic tools or models. I believe that it is what we are always trying to do. So long as the sources themselves have the final word to say models are unharmful. But when the verification of different models always turns out positive, the procedure is of doubtful value. Only one model can be true.

Modern social anthropologists are very conscious of the problems involved, and a sure sign of this is the fact that the models become more and more complicated and refined as more and more variables are included in each heuristic model, or different models are worked ⟦83⟧ together in

---

Minor developments which, nevertheless, represent the differences between individual human societies, and which in the eyes of the more traditionally minded historian may be just as or even more interesting, are certainly not taken into proper consideration.

order to obtain a more comprehensive construction. One of the positive effects of this development is that the demand for refined methods have forced a change of the working processes of the archaeologist. In the archaeology of Palestine, this is most conspicuous because of the evident shift of interest. The obvious sign is the new interest in area studies and general surveys which in part replace the excavations of single major tells. To some degree the study of the remains of a seemingly unimportant village culture has become just as important as a big excavation at some renowned place.[19]

At the same time the refinement of the models is in itself a sign of crisis and testifies to the fact that the whole procedure is becoming increasingly impossible and meaningless. It is, or so I believe, by now evident that even the most primitive human society is indefinitely more complicated than any model trying to describe the subsistence of that particular society. The inclusion of more and more variables is a testimony of how desperately scholars in this field try to include everything of importance, since it has also been acknowledged that any society in the past may have contained far more variables—also important ones, perhaps even decisive—which may not always be present in the source material.[20]

I shall illustrate some of my points here by introducing a couple of more recent examples of macro theories in the study of early Israelite history. Both are found in books published in the Sheffield-Almond series *The Social World of Biblical Antiquity Series*.

[[84]] My first example is taken from Frank Frick's *The Formation of the State in Ancient Israel* from 1985.[21] I shall not discuss Frick's book as such, only his application of "catastrophe theory."

Briefly spoken the catastrophe theory is a macro theory which in mathematics is introduced to explain some hitherto unpredictable math-

---

19. How important the results of such archaeological approaches may be becomes apparent when one reads Israel Finkelstein's splendid volume, *The Archaeology of the Israelite Settlement* (Jerusalem [[Israel Exploration Society]], 1988). It should, however, be stressed that Finkelstein is not a representative of the "New Archaeology" direction of archaeological studies, and his conclusions would surely be considered far too vague and imprecise by the adherents of this direction, which makes them the more valuable.

20. An example of this in the field of OT studies may be the recent volume by James W. Flanagan, *David's Social Drama. A Hologram of Israel's Early Iron Age* (*JSOTSS* 73; Sheffield [[Almond]], 1988). In his book, Flanagan uses more than 150 pages to explain his procedure, or model if you like, and although it may, perhaps, not be fair to Flanagan to say so, I would nevertheless argue that, at the end of the book, we know more about holograms than about early Israel. This is not to demerit Flanagan's endeavours to reconstruct a comprehensive model of the past, only to exemplify the problems involved, if the scholar wants his model to be able to encompass a human society in its totality.

21. Frank S. Frick, *The Formation of the State in Ancient Israel* (*The Social World of Biblical Antiquity Series* 4; Sheffield [[Almond]], 1985).

ematical results whereas in the humanities it is intended to explain the disruption of a certain phenomenon (in reality the breakdown of a culture) as well as its resurrection. In its humanistic setting the theory includes very complicated variables to describe the count down before the catastrophe and the rebuilding after the catastrophe. Frick has borrowed his model from an article written by the well-known British archaeologist and exponent of "new Archaeology," Colin Renfrew, "Catastrophe and Anastrophe in Early State Societies."[22]

The subtitle "Mathematical Approaches" is, however, rather decisive, since it discloses that we are dealing with a general model borrowed from theoretical mathematics. The whole concept of catastrophe theory was invented by the French mathematician René Thom and was from the beginning intended to be a mathematical model and nothing more. Furthermore, its validity is still forming the subject of discussion in mathematical circles.[23] It is in this connection not without interest to understand that Thom expresses himself more reluctantly as to the applicability of his mathematical model in other fields of research.[24]

[[85]] The model does, however, contain a certain limited number of variables which according to Frick can be rediscovered in the archaeological sources from Palestine in the Late Bronze and Early Iron Ages. And by introducing this catastrophe theory it is Frick's aim not only to present a general survey of the societal development in Palestine until the end of the second millennium B.C., but actually to reconstruct the history of Israel in this period.

Many problematic issues are involved in this case: First of all we may question the application of a model borrowed from a field where the debate as to the validity of the total concept is by no means over. Should Thom's ideas be rejected by his fellow mathematicians (and I am in no position to say whether this will be the case)[25] then, of course, we should avoid the use of it.

22. The article was published in C. Renfrew and K. L. Cooke (eds), *Transformations: Mathematical Approaches to Cultural Change* (New York [[Academic]], 1979) 481–506.

23. Published in R. Thom, *Structural Stability and Morphogenesis* (Eng. transl. Reading, MA, 1975; the French original *Stabilité structurelle et morphogenèse* going back to 1972 [[Benjamin Press]]). The inventor of the name "catastrophe theory" was, however, not Thom himself, but the English mathematician C. Zeeman.

24. This author confesses not to have read the said volume by Thom. As to a discussion of Thom's theories, I can here only refer to an interview with Thom, published in a Danish journal devoted to the history of ideas, *Slagmark* ('Battlefield') 5 (1985) 31–41. The actual *sciences* where Thom himself considers his theory applicable are obviously biology, linguistics and semiotics.

25. But I can refer to the issue of *Slagmark* mentioned above, to an article by K. N. Olsen, "Udenfor paradigmerne—kort introduktion til René Thoms teorier," 28–30. Here the "extra-paradigmatical" status of Thom's catastrophe theory is clearly expressed.

Secondly: Is it at all advisable to introduce mathematical models in humanities? By doing this it is a presupposition that human societies are as predictable as mathematical issues are supposed to be.

And the final issue is the model itself. How far can we trace the content of the detailed mathematical model in our sources? Can we recover the details of it, thereby making the model a valuable heuristic tool, or are we only able to verify the model in a very superficial way, the result of which may seem rather common-place or even dull? In case the only thing we can say for sure is that at a certain point we are going to break the back of the camel then the model is really not worth very much and we hardly need mathematical formulas to tell us this.

I shall leave Frick here. I believe that the issues mentioned will suffice to illustrate some of the pitfalls of the procedure as such. A more detailed criticism of Frick's procedure must by necessity follow the guidelines presented in my *Early Israel*, that is to say, it must analyse the premises which form the basis of the model itself when used as a sociological tool of investigation.

My second example is borrowed from the recent book by Robert Coote and Keith Whitelam, *The Emergence of Early Israel*,[26] a book which in many respects must be considered a more serious study than ⟦86⟧ the previously mentioned book. Evidently the book by Coote and Whitelam is an important contribution to the study of early Israel, but its usefulness is, however, limited to the specialist in the field.

The model invoked by Coote and Whitelam is not the theme of this discussion. It can shortly be described as a combination of various earlier anthropological and economic macro theories, above all Robert Carneiro's "circumscription model" from the early seventies, which describes how a society is forced to change its degree of inner integration in order to cope with alterations of its living conditions.[27] Especially important is the combination of a growing population and limited natural resources. Coote and Whitelam combine this model, first of all with Thom's already mentioned catastrophe theory, and secondly with an economic theory about the impact of international trade relations. The model is used as an heuristic tool for the investigation of the societal development in Palestine in the second half of the second millennium B.C. and the emphasis is, of course, placed on the issue of the emergence of Israel.

26. R. B. Coote and K. W. Whitelam, *The Emergence of Early Israel in Historical Perspective* (*The Social World of Biblical Antiquity* Series 5; Sheffield ⟦Almond⟧, 1987).

27. R. L. Carneiro, "A Theory of the Origin of the State," *Science* 169 (1970) 733–38. See also by the same author "Political Expansion as an Expression of the Principle of Competitive Exclusion," in Cohen and Service, *Origin of the State*, 205–23.

I shall leave the model itself at this stage having already published a more detailed review elsewhere.[28] My issue in this paragraph is, however, the application of the written sources from Palestine in this connection.

If for a moment we return to Gottwald's *The Tribes of Yahweh* we find a pronounced evaluation of the written sources in the Old Testament. His treatment of the sources is amazingly conservative, although not in an evangelical manner. Most sources are analyzed according to the old concept of Martin Noth and the German school of OT research.

Coote and Whitelam are on their part more conscious about the present debate as to the historical value of the OT sources, and they summarily dismiss these sources as of no use at all when it comes to the early history of Israel.

Their dismissal of any other written source from Palestine is, however, rather distressing and bears evidence of a narrowness of mind which can be the outcome of a pronounced use of system [[87]] theory. By mentioning the other existent sources from second millennium Palestine I am not referring to the scattered inscriptions of Egyptian or Palestinian origin but to the corpus of the Amarna letters. So far as I can recollect, there is hardly a single reference to the Amarna letters in Coote's and Whitelam's volume.

Some may argue that the Amarna letters are immaterial in this connection since they only concern a very limited span of years in the first half of the thirteenth century B.C. and, moreover, they cover a political situation which was extraordinary in the history of Palestine in the Late Bronze Age. To this [[it must be said]] that it is becoming increasingly clear that as regards the situation in Palestine the Amarna Age was not an exceptional era. Therefore we had better speak of the letters as describing the usual picture of Palestinian policy during the whole period in question.

I have to cut the discussion short at this point. But I think that this last example is an indication of some of the shortcomings of the systemic approach. The Amarna letters tell us about the behaviour of human beings and that this behaviour is unpredictable is my major point in this lecture. Therefore the human factor can never form an important variable in systemic thought since it cannot be controlled.

My point is that as long as the members of the school leave this human factor out of consideration and as long as their work is not based on a proper anthropology in the theological (or humanistic or even psychological) sense of the word, their work is of limited use. The method in question considers Man a kind of robot or automaton. As such it would seem to be highly useful if we were to study the life of insects, ant hills or

28. In *Biblica* 69 (1988) 581–84.

beehives, but it is hardly adequate to analyze the whereabouts of beings as complicated as the human race.

It is not my intention to say that sociology is useless, nor that social anthropological knowledge is superfluous. To the contrary, sociological knowledge is mandatory to any scholar who wants to study the behaviour of man and it cannot be supplanted by so-called "common sense" evaluation of sociological phenomena which are all too common in works by biblical scholars. In contrast, I would prefer to draw attention to other schools of anthropological thought as represented for instance by the Norwegian social anthropologist Fredrik Barth (and the mentioning of Barth isn't arbitrary since he is a specialist in the study of the Near Eastern societies and a pioneer in the investigation of nomadism). It is always a problem when [[88]] theologians try to introduce the results from other disciplines, since very often they simply do not know what they are dealing with. The idea that you can just pick up a standard work of reference in social anthropology and make use of the ideas of that book is nonsense. Even the biblical scholar will have to acquire a broader and more diversified picture of the foreign discipline in question in order to form his own opinions.

Part 2

Case Studies—Israel and Its Institutions: Social Science Perspectives

Introduction

Part 2 of this volume includes a series of "case studies"—examples of social science applications to biblical studies. As a group, they represent two major foci of social science approaches: the emergence and early political development of Israel, and Israelite institutions and life.

Israel's Emergence and Early Political Development

Abraham Malamat's entry (pp. 293–310 below) applies Weber's notion of ideal types and the routinization of authority to the period of the judges, whom he identifies as "charismatic" leaders. In contrast to the family-based "traditional authority" that characterized earliest Israel and the "legal-rational" authority of the monarchy, "charismatic authority" arose in periods of crisis. Malamat identifies two aspects of crisis in this period: external enemies and an internal weakening of traditional authority. All of the judges gained authority in an ad hoc manner, without concern for their social class; all ruled for a limited time, so their leadership was non-hereditary. This phase of Israelite history set the stage for the monarchy to emerge, when internal factors (greater stability) and external threats (specifically the Philistines) combined to lead Israel toward an institutionalized form of authority.

James Flanagan's study (pp. 311–34 below) also uses anthropological theory to trace the development of ancient Israel from pre-state to state. Designating biblical Israel as a "secondary state"—one that is directly affected by developments in larger "pristine" or "primary" states, such as Egypt and Mesopotamia—he reconstructs Israel's sociopolitical trajectory from a tribal or segmentary society, to a chiefdom, and then to a monarchy. This evolutionary schema was proposed by Elman Service[1] and was used to analyze other Near Eastern societies but until Flanagan's study, had rarely been applied to Israel. Rather, scholars tended to follow

1. Flanagan refers readers to two major studies by Service: *Primitive Social Organization* (2d ed.; New York: Random, 1962); and *Origins of the State and Civilization* (New York: Norton, 1975).

the biblical tradition of a direct transition from a tribal to a monarchic structure. Flanagan systematically presents the social theory and then examines the biblical evidence, suggesting that under Saul and David the Israelite sociopolitical structure is best described as a chiefdom.

Coote and Whitelam (pp. 335–76 below) propose that a variety of factors together led to Israel's emergence in the central hill country of Palestine. They maintain that the most appropriate perspective from which to approach early Israelite history is the larger history of Syria–Palestine from 1250 to 920 B.C.E. Using the theory of Fernand Braudel (what he calls *la longue durée*, the long duration) and the macrosociological perspective of Gerhard Lenski and Jean Lenski,[2] Coote and Whitelam suggest that a combination of waning Egyptian power and stability, decline in trade, agricultural intensification, and increased stratification worked together to influence Israel's development. By analyzing these factors, they seek to understand the "history" of the thirteenth to tenth centuries B.C.E. and the reasons for social and political changes within early Israel.

Israel Finkelstein likewise considers multiple factors—environmental features, socioeconomic elements, and settlement patterns—in his study of the monarchy in ancient Israel (pp. 377–403 below). His contribution provides a useful summary of the prevailing social models concerning state formation and of the various social forces present in the highlands of Canaan in the Early Iron Age. He assesses them in light of the archaeological evidence now more readily available as a result of recent extensive surface surveys, which shows changing demographic patterns from the beginning of the Iron I through the middle of the Iron II periods (ca. 1200–722 B.C.E.). His article is important in that it brings together social science theory and archaeological data.

Israelite Life and Social Institutions

This section begins with two studies on Israelite prophecy, perhaps the most extensively analyzed aspect of Israelite culture. Robert Wilson (pp. 404–22 below) traces the contributions of form criticism to the study of the prophetic movement and identifies the problems that ecstatic prophecy posed for biblical scholars. Did the prophets deliver oracles during their ecstatic state or after the ecstatic trance ended? Or was ecstatic prophecy outside the realm of the writing prophet's experience?

2. Coote and Whitelam refer to three major studies by Braudel: *The Mediterranean and the Mediterranean World in the Age of Philip II*, vols. 1–2 (London: Collins, 1972); *On History* (London: Weidenfeld and Nicholson, 1980); and *Civilization and Capitalism, 15th–18th Century, Volume III: The Perspective of the World* (London: Collins, 1984). See also, G. Lenski and J. Lenski, *Human Societies: An Introduction to Macrosociology* (4th ed.; New York: McGraw-Hill, 1984).

Wilson addresses these questions and the nature of ecstatic prophecy from the perspective of anthropological observations of human-divine contact, typically referred to as trance states or spirit possession.

Thomas Overholt's study (pp. 423–47 below) considers the problems involved in making cross-cultural comparisons to understand biblical prophecy. He identifies three specific problems: the problem of various groups and their "cultural adjustment" or type; the content of prophetic messages in various cultures; and the danger of the observers misunderstanding the phenomenon they observe due to their own "ethnocentricity." He then compares two prophetic figures, Handsome Lake, a Seneca holy man of the eighteenth and nineteenth centuries C.E., and Jeremiah, the seventh- and sixth-century B.C.E. Judean prophet. He argues that although the content of their speech is distinctly different, other aspects of their prophetic activity are quite similar. Overholt uses this analysis to develop a refined model of prophetic authority.

Studies by Frank Frick (pp. 448–70 below) and David Hopkins (pp. 471–88 below) examine the archaeological record for evidence of Israel's religious and political setting on the one hand, and its subsistence strategy and social organization on the other. Frick approaches the religion and political development of ancient Israel from the perspective of processual and environmental archaeology, using ethnographic parallels to present a more nuanced understanding of Israelite society. He considers religion to be "the expression . . . of a particular cultural identity rather than its sole foundation" (p. 450 below). Accordingly, he views sociopolitical development as central to Israelite religion and, like both Finklestein and Flanagan, sees features of a "chiefdom" in Early Iron Age Israel. Archaeological data from Tel Masos in the eastern Negev provide important evidence for such a chiefdom.

David Hopkins's study focuses on the various ways the Israelites adapted to their physical environment. He examines soil types, rainfall patterns, and other climatic factors characteristic of the central hill country of Palestine. He then identifies the various technologies and subsistence strategies the Israelites employed first simply to survive and subsequently to flourish. He also views these technologies within the wider social context. The mixing of herding and agriculture and crop rotation were forms of risk-management; terrace agriculture required a greater level of social cooperation, since one family did not generally possess adequate labor resources to construct and maintain terraces. By tracing the interrelationship of environment, population, and technology in Iron Age Israel, Hopkins seeks to present a holistic picture of Israel's social setting in the highlands of Canaan.

Carol Meyers (pp. 489–514 below) and Phyllis Bird (pp. 515–36 below) have been pioneers in the use of social science models in feminist biblical scholarship. Meyers's study focuses on the male and female roles within Iron Age agrarian society. Identifying three basic spheres of activity—procreation, production, and protection—she examines the relative contribution of males and females in ancient Israel. With men necessarily active in the protective role in the beginning of the Iron Age, marked as it was by threats from other cultures, women were called upon to take on more responsibility for production. Meyers notes that generally, as women's activity in production increases, so does their relative status. This is borne out in her examination of the valuation of women in Leviticus 27, in the significance of biblical heroines such as Miriam and Deborah, and in the portrayal of female and male equality in the Genesis creation stories.

Phyllis Bird examines the role of women in Israelite religion, first placing the question in the context of biblical scholarship of the last century, then suggesting the necessary components for a truly balanced approach to the question. To find a balanced approach, one must look not only at the official Israelite traditions and forms of worship but also at women's roles in cultic activities that were heterodox or "foreign" in addition to those that were orthodox; those that were private in addition to those that were public. One must also view religious practices in relationship to other Israelite institutions (for example, the family) and in the wider socioeconomic and political context. In order to recover the essentially hidden role of women in the Israelite cultus, Bird draws from biblical traditions, archaeological records, ancient Near Eastern parallels, and ethnographic studies of preindustrial societies.

The final case study reflects one of the new directions of social science applications to the Hebrew Bible and is therefore a fitting conclusion to this volume. In proposing a "sociology" of the exilic and postexilic periods, Daniel Smith (pp. 537–56 below) first assesses the psychological impact of the defeat of Judah and the exile on the exilic community. He suggests that the exiles formed a "culture of resistance" in order to promote their survival and that they created social boundaries by establishing criteria to delineate people who were "inside" or "outside" of the group. He examines Ezra's mission, particularly his attempts to create a distinction between the "children of the Golah" or the "holy seed" and any number of "outsiders," in light of Mary Douglas's *Purity and Danger* (see part 1, pp. 119–34). Thus, he understands the purity laws of the postexilic period as an attempt to establish social boundaries and provide a sense of social solidarity and identity. In this fashion, he demonstrates the value of the social science method for looking behind a prevailing ideology and finding its social signficance, something that a strictly theological or historical approach could not do as well.   (C. E. C.)

Charismatic Leadership in the Book of Judges

ABRAHAM MALAMAT

[[152]] The history of Israel from the conquest of Canaan in the thirteenth century B.C. to the establishment of the monarchy at the close of the eleventh century was characterized by a unique political system. This regime of judges, which has no extant parallel among the peoples of the ancient Near East, was a response to a chronic state of war imposed upon the Israelites by their neighbors. It is not surprising, therefore, that its main manifestations are in the military sphere. In times of distress, charismatic leaders in the form of deliverer-judges arose sporadically among the Israelites and brought them out from under the hands of their oppressors. The Book of Judges, which is the principal source for observing this historical phenomenon (it is also intimated in the stories concerning Saul, in 1 Samuel), contains a collection of folk tales on the deliverer-judges, each of which portrays an encounter with an adversary of a particular type, as well as the specific challenge confronting the judge. The Book of Judges also attests to another kind of leader, known in biblical scholarship as the "minor judge" in contradistinction to the deliverers, the "major judges."

Reprinted with permission from *Magnalia Dei — The Mighty Acts of God: Essays on the Bible and Archaeology in Memory of G. Ernest Wright* (ed. F. M. Cross, W. E. Lemke, and P. D. Miller; New York: Doubleday, 1976) 152–68.

Author's note: This paper is based on a lecture given at a symposium on "Types of Leadership in the Biblical Period" held at the Israel Academy of Sciences and Humanities on 15 December 1971. Throughout this paper, references by chapter and verse alone are to the Book of Judges.

293

Since our discussion is devoted primarily to the historical category of charismatic leadership, we shall not delve into such specific problems of biblical criticism relating to the Book of Judges as the editorial strata, the technical terms *šopeṭ*—which we following convention shall render 'judge'—and *mošia^c* 'deliverer' or the relation between the "major" and the "minor judges."[1] Nor are we concerned with the "minor judge" per se, for he does not embody the characteristics of a deliverer, at any rate not according to the stereotyped chronicle sources drawn upon in the Book of Judges (10:1–5; 12:8–15). It should be noted, however, that at least some of the five "minor judges" may have engaged in military activities and relieved their people from oppression.[2] Further, the root *yš^c* 'to deliver, save' is employed in each of the narratives of the "major judges" with the exception of Deborah and Barak, either in an epithet, "deliverer" (applied to Othniel [[153]] and Ehud—3:9, 15), or in the verbal form *hošia^c* (besides in the account of Othniel, it is found relating to Gideon—6:14, etc.; 8:22; to Jephthah—12:2–3; to Samson—13:5; and to Tola, the first of the "minor judges"—10:1; but also to Shamgar the son of Anath—3:31, for which see below). On the other hand, the root *špṭ*, in the senses 'to rule', 'to champion', 'to judge', occurs in these stories in relation to Othniel, Deborah, Jephthah, and Samson (3:10; 4:4; 12:7; 15:20; 16:31) and regularly to all five "minor judges."[3]

I

The first of the deliverer-judges is Othniel, who defeated an invader who had penetrated deep into southern Palestine, the mysterious Cushan-

1. For a general survey, see A. Malamat, "The Period of the Judges," in *Judges, WHJP* 3, 129–63, 314–23. For the composition of the Book of Judges and its *Redaktionsgeschichte*, see the cited literature, ibid., 314, n. 1, and 350 (General Bibliography). Like its West Semitic cognates from the early second millennium B.C. on, the root *špṭ* in the Book of Judges signifies more than merely 'judging'; it covers the broad concept of rulership, including the aspects of judge and champion. Contrary to the generally accepted critical view, its presence in the deliverer narratives is no less primary than that of *yš^c*, *mošia^c*; see ibid., 130f.

2. The different representations of the "major" and the "minor" judges in the Bible may be merely a carry-over from the literary sources drawn upon by the compiler—colorful folk narratives on the one hand, and schematic family chronicles on the other hand. See ibid., 131. Y. Kaufmann, *The Book of Judges* [Hebrew] (Jerusalem, 1962) 47f., entirely assimilated the "minor" to the "major" judges, assuming that the stories of deliverance once associated with the former had been lost. But this is an extreme view.

3. For the literature on *špṭ, šopeṭ*, see *WHJP* 3, 314f., nn. 6–7; and see now also H. Reviv, "Types of Leadership in the Period of the Judges," in *Beer-Sheva. Annual, Studies in Bible . . .* [Hebrew] 1 (1973) 204–21 and T. Ishida, "The Leaders of the Tribal League 'Israel' in the Pre-Monarchic Period," *RB* 80 (1973) 514–30. On *yš^c*, see now J. F. A. Sawyer, *Semantics in Biblical Research—New Methods of Defining Hebrew Words for Salvation* (London [[SCM]], 1972) esp. 57f., 94f.

Rishathaim, king of Aram-Naharaim. Because of the vague, schematic formulation of this account, material details of the actual war are lacking. The episode of Deborah and Barak epitomizes the confrontation with the autochthonous Canaanite population in the northern part of the country. The chief military challenge in this case was the chariot-force of the Canaanites, confronting the Israelite foot soldiers who, moreover, were poorly equipped (5:8). By reading between the lines of the biblical account, we can reconstruct the Israelite plan of operation in overcoming the situation: exploiting climatic and topographical factors, they rendered the Canaanite chariotry inoperable. The story of Gideon illustrates the conflict with desert marauders headed by the Midianites, who were making incursions into the cultivated region from the eastern fringes of Transjordan. In this instance, the military problem was two-fold: the numerical superiority of the enemy and his skilled use of the camel in warfare, which necessitated the adoption of special tactics to which the Israelites were unaccustomed. Gideon found a solution by planning a night attack, enabling him to nullify both these factors. The narratives linked with the names of Ehud and Jephthah describe wars against Moab and Ammon, national states which arose in Transjordan in the thirteenth century B.C. and whose inhabitants, in contrast to the Israelites, were already organized under monarchical regimes at an early stage of their settlement. Finally, the Samson cycle represents the clash with the Philistines in the western part of the country, an enemy which by virtue of its superior technology and its military aristocracy (*sěrānim*) was destined to jeopardize the very existence of Israel.[4]

We are confronted by the conspicuous fact that in none of the episodes in the Book of Judges is there a recurrence of either the type of enemy fought or the arena of battle, or the ethnic-tribal origin of the "deliverer," who arises in each instance from a different tribe. Concerning the latter aspect, we long ago noted in an unpublished study a point generally overlooked—that the sequence of narratives in the Book of Judges may have been based essentially [[154]] on a geographical scheme which presents the judges in the order of their tribal-territorial affiliations, from the south of the country to the north: Othniel from Judah, Ehud from Benjamin, Deborah from the hill country of Ephraim (drawing along with her Barak of Naphtali), Gideon from Manasseh (so, too, Abimelech, on whom see the last part of this paper), and Jephthah the Gileadite, which brings us to the area of Gad in Transjordan. Likewise, the two

---

4. For an extensive historical survey of the above military encounters, see *WHJP* 3, 135–59. For the possible identification of King Cushan-Rishathaim, see our remarks in ibid., 25–27; on the Philistine threat see B. Mazar, "The Philistines and Their Wars with Israel," ibid., 164–79.

"minor judges" wedged in between the stories of Abimelech and Jephthah—Tola of the tribe of Issachar, and Jair of Gilead, who represents the
eastern half of the tribe of Manasseh—are in keeping generally with
the tribal-territorial scheme of the book. It is true that Samson, the last of
the "major judges," belonged to the tribe of Dan and was active in the
southern part of the country, but his cycle of tales constitutes a separate
literary pericope within the book. Moreover, from the viewpoint of the
later redactor, it was only proper to place the Danite hero at the end of
the sequence of judges, for his tribe had long since migrated to the
northern extremity of the land. Thus, too, it can hardly be accidental that
in Judges 1, where the Israelite tribes are listed also in a principally geographical order from south to north, Dan (in a southern context) appears at the very end of the list.[5] If we posit, however, the tribal-territorial
principle as a guideline in the present structure of the Book of Judges,
the chronological credibility of the actual sequence of historical events,
as presented in the book, is naturally impaired (and see below).

The absence of duplication in the type of enemy and the tribal
affinity of the judges raise the possibility that the compiler of the book en-
deavored to portray only models of oppressors, on the one hand, and of
deliverers, on the other hand, emphasizing the features specific to each
particular confrontation. In other words, in selecting the stories in the
Book of Judges, we deem that the compiler wittingly restricted his choice
so as to obtain a paradigmatic scheme of Israel's wars in the premonarchical period. These paradigms would serve a didactic purpose, seemingly
alluded to at the beginning of the body proper of the book (3:1–2): "Now
these are the nations which the Lord left, to test Israel by them . . . that he
might teach war to such at least as had not known it before."[6]

---

5. The biblical lists of tribes arranged on a geographical principle have been treated
most recently by Helga Weippert, "Das geographische System der Stämme Israels," *VT* 23
(1973) 76–89, where, *inter alia*, Dan's ultimate position in the list of Judges 1 is attributed
to a late redactor, ascribing the order there to the period of the united monarchy; for this
same dating, see Z. Kallai, *Proceedings of the Fifth World Congress of Jewish Studies* [Hebrew]
(Jerusalem, 1969) 133, n. 12. By analogy, we can perhaps ascribe the north-to-south sequence of the structure of the Book of Judges as a whole, as outlined above, to the same
period.

6. 'To test' (*lĕnassot*) in 3:1 is the subject of an exegetical controversy. One view (exemplified by Kaufmann [n. 2] 100) holds that a religious trial of Israel is intended, in the
face of heathen temptation. It is preferable, however, and in keeping with the context of
vv. 1–2 here, to regard the expression as referring to military experience; cf., for example,
C. F. Burney, *The Book of Judges*[2] (London [Rivingtons], 1920) 54; and esp. M. Greenberg,
JBL 79 (1960) 276 and n. 5 (where the term is translated as 'to give [Israel] experience').
See now also J. Licht, *Testing in the Hebrew Scriptures and in Post-Biblical Judaism* [Hebrew]
(Jerusalem [Magnes], 1973) 15ff.

An exception to this scheme, insofar as the identity of the enemy and the military action are concerned, is the heroic exploit of Shamgar the son of Anath: he "smote of the Philistines six hundred men with an ox-goad; and he also delivered Israel" (3:31), an event which recalls Samson's smiting a thousand Philistines with the jawbone of an ass (15:15–16). But it is generally conjectured that this event occurred in the north, and not in the area of Samson's exploit. It may well be that, precisely because of the paradigmatic intent of the Book of Judges, the redactor did not feel the need to give a full account of this event, contenting himself with a mere reference to Shamgar, apparently because his name occurs later, in the Song of Deborah (5:6). At all events, it is reasonable to suppose that not all the deliverers [[155]] active in the twelfth to eleventh centuries B.C. have found mention in the Book of Judges. This assumption is supported by Samuel's farewell address, in which he counts among Israel's deliverers, alongside Jerubbaal (i.e., Gideon) and Jephthah, the enigmatic Bedan (1 Sam 12:11), a deliverer who is otherwise unknown[7] and whose deed of deliverance is lost to us.

The Book of Judges "compensates" us for its material defects and limitations as a comprehensive, multi-faceted historical source by providing a conceptual schema regarding the unfoldment of the events of the period generally, and the appearance of the deliverer-judge in particular. This schema, unparalleled in the other biblical books for systematic consistency, is founded upon a pragmatic theological interpretation which forms both the general introduction to the events of the period (2:11–19) and the setting into which the narratives of the individual judges were integrated. In this manner, the episodes are concatenated into a single historical chain. It is true that the pragmatic, historiosophic framework is to be ascribed only to an editorial stage of the book—and, according to the prevalent view, to its last redactor, the so-called Deuteronomist. Nevertheless, the content of this framework is not necessarily the expression of a later ideological concept, as most scholars hold. It possibly, and even probably, contains authentic reflections and preserves elements of ancient historical reality.[8]

The following two doctrines are basic to the pragmatic exposition.

---

7. For the attempts to identify this personage, see *WHJP* 3, 315, n. 15.

8. This has been stressed in particular by Kaufmann [n. 2] 33, who, however, is too fundamentalistic in his regarding the framework as an early, primary "historical document," like the deliverer narratives themselves. On the literary complexity of the framework proper, including pre-Deuteronomic strands, cf. W. Beyerlin, "Gattung und Herkunft des Rahmens im Richterbuch," in *Festschrift A. Weiser* (Göttingen, 1963) 1–29; for the relationship between the framework and the Book of Judges as a whole, see esp. W. Richter, *Die Bearbeitungen des "Retterbuches" in der deuteronomischen Epoche* (Bonn [[Hanstein]], 1964).

(a) The concept of historical periodicity. According to this doctrine the events of the period of the judges formed a chain of recurring cycles, each comprising four successive stages: the people sinned by reverting to idolatry, which brought in its train subjugation by an adversary; thereupon the people invoked the Lord to deliver them and ultimately their redemption came about by the hand of a deliverer. The deliverer-judge secured for his people a protracted period of "rest"; to use biblical terminology—"The land was at rest for [twenty, forty, eighty] years." But "whenever the judge died, they turned back and behaved worse than their fathers, going after other gods, serving them and prostrating themselves to them" (2:19). This cyclic view imposes a picture of linear development in which the judges appear in succession, from Othniel to Samson, with gaps between, when there was no leader. In this manner a historical-chronological sequence was created, which cannot be accepted *prima facie* as reflecting actual reality, unless the order of events is corroborated by additional factors. Furthermore, this approach negates the possibility—which cannot be excluded *a priori*—of the contemporaneous existence of two or more judges, active in separate parts of the country.

On the other hand, it seems that the historiosophic framework expressed an immanent truth in regard to the conditions prevailing in the premonarchical period, when it emphasizes the frequent vicissitudes befalling the people politically and militarily, which to a great extent were the outcome of the national religious consciousness; its decline aggravated the nation's position, [[156]] while its reinforcement led to consolidation and prosperity. Moreover, it is a universal phenomenon that in time of danger and crises there is an upsurge of charismatic sensitivity among the people, which seizes upon a personality which is able to satisfy, as one sociologist phrases it, "the charismatic hunger"[9] of his contemporaries. This explains the recurring dependence of the Israelites upon deliverer-leaders in times of trouble.

(b) The concept of the pan-Israelite dimension. On the basis of this doctrine the tribal events of the period—including the scope of the judge's activity—were elevated to a broad, national level encompassing the entire people and country. Hyperbolic as this may be, the prevalent approach of biblical criticism is likewise unsatisfactory inasmuch as it holds that the judge's action was of only a restricted local and tribal background and confined his authority to a single tribe or even less. It would seem that this radical narrowing of horizon is equally a distortion of the

9. E. H. Erikson, quoted by D. A. Rustow, in *Philosophers and Kings: Studies in Leadership* (New York [[Braziller]], 1970) 15.

reality of the period.[10] In the actual situation, the individual tribal framework was of little significance to the Israelite judge (see below), and of even less to the external enemy who was not consciously attacking a specific tribe or its territory, but rather Israelites per se. Generally, several tribes were affected simultaneously, and the act of liberation from the foreign pressure, which exceeded the strength of any solitary Israelite tribe, necessitated the cooperation of a confederacy. Thus, any relatively local incident could readily reach a more national plane.

Indeed, the internal evidence within the narratives of the judges clearly reflects these conditions. Thus, for instance, Gideon assembles for his battle against the Midianites not only members of his own clan, Abiezer, and his fellow Manassite tribesmen, but also troops from Asher, Zebulon, and Naphtali (6:35) and, at a later stage, he even seeks the assistance of the Ephraimites (7:24f.). This is also true of other judges, although the scope of their activities was at times more limited. The high point in national solidarity in the period of the judges was achieved at the battle of Deborah and Barak. Here, according to the Song of Deborah, six tribes united in a concerted action—from Benjamin in the south to Naphtali in the north, who came "to the help of the Lord among the fighting men." Thus, the significant epithet "mother in Israel," bestowed upon Deborah (5:7), was quite appropriate.

To sum up, the authority of the deliverer-judge transcended the ambit of the individual tribe and was not confined to a restricted locale. It was only natural that his influence should embrace a tribal confederacy, whether broad or limited; and thus his mission and his charismatic attribute also assumed national dimension, instead of retaining a mere tribal flavor. The judge's action within the intertribal and supratribal framework, therefore, justifies historically the use in the Book of Judges of the designation "Israel" for the object of the judge's act of deliverance and rule; hence, this appellation should not be regarded as a later artificial amplification, under tendentious, pan-Israelite influence.[11] Although

---

10. Cf. Kaufmann [n. 2] 36ff.; *WHJP* 3, 129.

11. As widely held by Bible critics; contrasting this, see the references in the previous note, and now Ishida [n. 3] 165. Attention should be drawn to a similar phenomenon regarding leadership in today's developing nations: the expansion of dimensions in tribal leaders and their becoming "nationalized," tribe being "transcended, while the sacred earth [i.e., the optative domain] retains its sacredness, its charisma, although it is no longer circumscribed by the area within which one's particular tribe—one's kinship and ethnic group—dwells" (E. Shils, "The Concentration and Dispersion of Charisma, Their Bearing on Economic Policy in Underdeveloped Countries, *World Politics* 2 [1958–59] 1–19, quotation on p. 4).

this is still a far cry from pan-Israelite ⟦157⟧ rule, the judges were blazing the path to a new era of leadership—the Israelite monarchy.

II

The best starting point in examining the nature of the judges' regime and the specific characteristics of the deliverer-leader is the theory developed at the beginning of this century by Max Weber concerning the several types of leadership and domination, including charismatic rule. Weber was not the first to resort to the term *charisma* as indicating unique qualities—deviating from the common and routine. He expressly states that he borrowed the term from the church historian Rudolph Sohm (1841–1917). But he was the first to place the phenomenon of charismatic rule on a broad sociological and political plane, and to present it as a defined model of one of the types of authority or leadership wielded by extraordinary, singular persons within a society. Thereby he paved the way for the term to become common currency not only in the social and political sciences, but also in daily speech (frequently employed in doubtful usages). Weber himself used the word charisma primarily in the connotation of the New Testament,[12] namely, as a gift of divine grace. It is particularly his appraisement of the charismatic order as essentially a religious transcendental category—in contradistinction to the majority of his followers, who infused the concept with secular content—that makes Weber's analyses supremely relevant for the biblical phenomenon. Although biblical terminology does not contain the exact semantic equivalent for charisma, it approximates to the expression "spirit [*rûăḥ*] of the Lord," which is bestowed upon the leader and stirs him to action.

In his treatment of charismatic leadership, Weber unfortunately gave only marginal attention to the Israelite judge, for this personality could have served as an exemplar of his *Idealtypus* ⟦'exemplary type'⟧. In his empirical analyses he was less concerned with the military leaders than with another distinctly charismatic figure which appears in the Bible and in numerous societies, namely, the prophet and the various kinds of diviners. On the other hand, those Bible scholars who in dealing with the period of the judges have adopted Weber's concept of charisma—such as Alt, Buber, Eichrodt, and Albright, to mention only the most out-

---

12. Almost exclusively in the Pauline epistles (Romans and esp. Corinthians); see most recently H. Conzelmann, *Theologisches Wörterbuch zum Neuen Testament* 9, Lief. 7 (Stuttgart ⟦Kohlhammer⟧, 1971) 393–97, s.v. *charisma*.

standing pioneers—have relied mainly on his book *Das antike Judentum.*[13] In the latter, though indeed he did treat the Israelite judge per se, he did little to elucidate his views on charisma. And Bible scholars, on their part, have not generally consulted Weber's brilliant over-all analyses of the phenomenon, to be found in his monumental *Wirtschaft und Gesellschaft,* which presents his most comprehensive and systematic formulation of the types of domination.[14]

The concept of charisma has taken on further dimensions, especially in [[158]] the last decade or so, through the renewed interest in and re-appraisal of Weber's *oeuvre* [['work']],[15] as well as under the impetus of the emergence of the new states of Asia and Africa. The recent applications in the latter direction are of particular relevance to charismatic leadership in the Bible, despite the considerable differences in time and historical circumstances. The contemporary phenomenon—especially in Africa—has evolved out of tribal society still largely subject to

13. *Gesammelte Aufsätze zur Religionssoziologie* 3: *Das antike Judentum* (Tübingen [[Mohr]], 1923). English translation by H. H. Gerth and D. Martindale, *Ancient Judaism* (Glencoe, 1952 [[excerpts reprinted in this volume, pp. 65–94]]), index, s.v. *charisma, šopeṭim.* For the literature of the Bible scholars, see n. 28.

14. *Grundriss der Sozialökonomik: Wirtschaft und Gesellschaft* (Tübingen [[Mohr]], 1925); we use here the 4th edition (henceforth *WuG*), critically revised and with excerpts from Weber's other writings, by J. Winckelmann (Tübingen [[Mohr]], 1956) 1:122–76; 2:541–615. English edition by G. Roth and C. Wittich, *Economy and Society, an Outline of Interpretive Sociology* (New York, 1968) 1:212ff.; 3:1111ff. Earlier publications in English of sections on charisma appear in *Max Weber: The Theory of Social and Economic Organization,* ed. T. Parsons, trs. A. M. Henderson and T. Parsons (New York [[Free Press]], 1947) 358–92; and *Max Weber: On Charisma and Institution Building,* ed. S. N. Eisenstadt (Chicago-London [[University of Chicago Press]], 1968).

15. Of the abundant recent literature on Weber's conception of charisma, we may note the following: the numerous publications of T. Parsons (a most recent treatment in his *Politics and Social Structure* [New York-London [[Free Press]], 1969], chap. 5, pp. 98–110); the introductions by Parsons and Eisenstadt in the works edited by them [n. 14]; R. Bendix, *Max Weber—An Intellectual Portrait* (New York [[Doubleday]], 1962; repr. University Paperbacks, London, 1966), chap. 10; P. M. Blau, "Critical Remarks on Weber's Theory of Authority," *American Political Science Review* 57 (1963) 305–16; W. H. Friedland, "For a Sociological Concept of Charisma," *Social Forces* 43 (1964) 18–26; K. J. Ratman, "Charisma and Political Leadership," *Political Studies* 12 (1964) 341–54; K. Loewenstein, *Max Webers staatspolitische Auffassungen in der Sicht unserer Zeit* (Bonn, 1965) 74–88; W. J. Mommsen, "Universalgeschichtliches und politisches Denken bei Max Weber," *Historische Zeitschrift* 201 (1965) 557–612, esp. 586ff.; the articles by D. A. Rustow, "The Study of Leadership," 1–18, and R. C. Tucker, "The Theory of Charismatic Leadership," 69–94 in *Philosophers and Kings: Studies in Leadership,* ed. D. A. Rostow (New York [[Knopf]], 1970); A. Mitzman, *The Iron Cage—An Historical Interpretation of Max Weber* (New York [[Knopf]], 1970); J. Séguy, "Max Weber et la sociologie historique des religions," *Archives de Sociologie des Religions* 33 (1972) 71–103, esp. 94ff.; and see the works by E. Shils, cited below [n. 21] and by Ann R. Willner [n. 24].

religious-magical motivation and is in that respect closer to the biblical environment than Western civilization, from which most of the analogies hitherto adduced have been drawn.[16]

In order to comprehend the particular quality of the charismatic rule of the judges, we must juxtapose it to the two other basic forms of leadership or authority, included in Weber's classical tripartite typology of legitimate domination.[17] (1) The traditional authority; this was represented in Israel from earliest times by a patriarchal-tribal system, in which authority descended through family heads and resided in a gerontocracy. (2) The legal-rational authority; this approached realization among the Israelites upon the establishment of the monarchy and a budding bureaucratic apparatus (albeit patrimonial) which evolved around it.[18] By their very nature, these two types of rule are mutually antagonistic and are motivated by opposite aims. Traditional authority is inclined toward conservatism and endeavors to maintain the status quo in the life pattern, whereas legal authority is activated by dynamic and rational-utilitarian forces and seeks to adapt the pattern of life to ever-changing circumstances, despite sanctified tradition. But they have a common denominator in their desire for stability and permanence, inasmuch as the leadership is uninterrupted and conventional, and conforms with prevailing interests.

Diametrically opposed is charismatic authority, distinguished primarily by its exclusive, personal character, entirely independent of the hierarchic structure. It is sporadic, unstable, and transient by its very nature and is not subject to the accepted laws of government and the routine social system. In Weber's words, "[this authority] is expressly non-rational in the sense that it conforms to none of the rules." However, the emphatic statement "none of the rules" is undoubtedly exaggerated, as is the

16. Loewenstein [n. 15] 78ff., considers genuine charisma as particularly inherent in those political milieus characterized by "magical-ritualistic or mystical-religious elements," as in the pre-Cartesian West and in large parts of Asia and Africa still today.

17. Cf. *WuG* [n. 14] 122ff. Weber's concise formulation of his scheme, included only in the 4th edition of *WuG*, 551–58, did not belong originally to this work and was therefore removed from the subsequent editions (cf. *Studienausgabe* 1[Köln-Berlin, 1964] xv, and the English edition of 1968). The development of Weber's concept of charismatic rule is traced in A. Mitzman, index, s.v. *charisma.*

18. Strictly according to Weber, however, *true* legal rationality was achieved only in modern Western civilization (cf. Bendix, [n. 15], 385ff.). My colleague S. N. Eisenstadt has pointed out to me that the Israelite monarchical regime was essentially patrimonial (a traditional rather than legal-rational feature); and besides, all "old bureaucracies were essentially patrimonial in character" (J. Freund, *The Sociology of Max Weber* [New York ⟦Vintage Books⟧, 1968] 236).

apparent rigidity of a threefold typology of authority and leadership.[19] In reality, these types do not appear in their pure and pristine form, but in some measure mix and overlap. In other words, the other two legitimate forms do also contain charismatic traits, a phenomenon which Weber himself clearly acknowledged.[20] But both his followers and his critics have emphasized that the real problem lies in the degree of the charismatic quality—intense or attenuated—present in the several forms of domination.[21] These qualifications of the Weberian tripartite scheme fully apply to Israelite society in the biblical period.

According to Weber's definition, the charismatic leader was endowed from birth with physical and mental traits that differed from the ordinary [[159]] and commonplace qualities (his *Ausseralltäglichkeit* [['extraordinariness']]). Both the charismatic individual and his following regard these attributes as emanating from a higher force; in this sense, he possesses supernatural gifts and is a leader *Dei gratia* [['by the grace of God']]. The charismatic leader arises, in Weber's words, "in times of psychic, physical, economic, ethical, religious, or political distress." This maxim, now regarded as classic, together with the characteristics just mentioned, aptly suits the Israelite judge and the circumstances of his emergence, as revealed in the Book of Judges. The deliver-judge, distinguished by extraordinary qualities and gifts, appeared in his own estimation and in that of his devotees as a divine agent delivering his people from national crisis, an act which imbued him with supreme authority within his society.

This brings us to the other aspect of the charismatic phenomenon— the prerequisite of a society willing to recognize this type of authority. Without such recognition, charisma lacks all substantiality and remains meaningless. Hence, this phenomenon is to be regarded as a process of interaction between the personality of the leader, on the one hand, and his followers seeking to achieve desired objectives, on the other hand.[22]

19. See several of the authors mentioned above in n. 15, e.g., Eisenstadt (introduction, esp. pp. xxiff.); Blau; Ratman (esp. p. 344); Rustow (pp. 14ff.); and further, Shils' "Charisma, Order and Status" and his entry on "Charisma" in *International Encyclopedia of the Social Sciences* 2 [[New York: Macmillan, 1968–79]], esp. p. 390; both cited in n. 21, below.

20. Hence Weber's introduction of the concepts *Gentilcharisma* (lineage charisma) and *Amtscharisma* (charisma of office) for the "depersonalization" of the charismatic quality in traditional domination, on the one hand, and the rational-legal domination, on the other hand. See *WuG* [n. 14] 681ff., 700ff.; and cf. also Bendix [n. 15] 308ff.

21. See principally Shils' "The Concentration and Dispersion of Charisma" [n. 11]; "Charisma, Order and Status," *American Social Review* 30 (1965) 199–213; and "Charisma," in *International Encyclopedia of the Social Sciences* 2 (1968) 386–90.

22. Cf. W. E. Mühlmann, *Max Weber und die rationale Soziologie* (Tübingen, 1966) 18–21; Friedland [n. 15] 20f.; Rustow [n. 15] 15ff.

Viewed in this light the concept of charisma gains a socio-political dimension, which biblical scholarship, with its express theological interest, neglected.[23] Only in a given socio-historical context, the "situation" of the
sociologists, could the charismatic person prevail and his mission come to
fulfillment. The specific conditions or situational aspects conducive to the
charismatic emergence were not particularly treated by Weber in his
comparative analyses, though this facet has drawn great attention in post-
Weberian investigation, especially in connection with the nature of leadership in the developing countries.[24]

III

A climate favorable to the emergence of charismatic leadership in Israel's
history matured in the era of the judges. The "situation" entailed a dual
crisis: externally, enemies made for constant insecurity, with succeeding
disasters befalling the Israelites (as seen above); internally, traditional
authority was progressively undermined. Increasing sedentation in this
period, with its consequent adjustments to the conditions of permanent
settlement alongside partial adaptation to the Canaanite urban environment, led the Israelite tribes to a preference for territorial principles over
gentilic bonds and consanguinity. Thus, the tribal institutions—indeed
the entire inherited societal framework—were on the wane.

    Although the routine social system and day-to-day affairs continued
under the jurisdiction of the clan heads and the institution of the elders,
the traditional elite could no longer maintain its own prestige let alone
cope [[160]] with the task of maintaining Israelite autonomy. Ineluctably,
a crisis of trust was created, and with it a crisis of authority. The existing leadership which was held responsible for the people's straits was
forced aside, to make way for leaders of a new kind who were able to inspire confidence, to steer a course for the people, and to shoulder the task
of deliverance. The very weakening of traditional authority within clan
and tribe resulted in individuals breaking away from the tight bonds of
kinship, freeing them to exercise personal initiative which could even-

23. This interpretation may serve to mollify recent questioning of the application of
"charisma" to the Israelite judge, as notably in G. Fohrer, *Geschichte der israelitischen Religion*
(Berlin [[de Gruyter]], 1969) 87f., 138. For the stress on the theological aspect, see the literature cited below toward the end of n. 28.

24. See notably A. R. Willner and D. Willner, "The Rise and Role of Charismatic Lead-
ership," *Annals of the American Academy of Political and Social Science* 358 (1965) 77–88; A. R.
Willner, *Charismatic Political Leadership: A Theory* (Princeton [[Center of International Studies,
Princeton University]], 1968), chap. 3: "The Charismatic Phenomenon—Convergence and
Catalyst"; and, e.g., D. A. Rustow, *A World of Nations* (Washington [[Brookings Institution]],
1967) 148–69 (Charisma and the Founding of States).

tually lead to attaining a national commission.[25] This polar relationship within Israelite society—the decline of traditional authority and the rise of individuals outside the old order—finds ample expression in the Book of Judges:[26]

Deborah, as a woman, had no standing in the agnatic-patriarchal order; it was she, however, who roused the people to fight for their freedom, who stirred Barak to action and, in short, who was the driving force behind the battle. Gideon, "whose clan is the weakest in Manasseh" and who himself was "the least in his family" (6:15), initiated and stood at the head of the forces of liberation—he, not his father or senior brothers, or the representatives of more renowned families. But the most indicative example of the incompetency of the traditional leadership and the rise of a fringe personality is the episode of Jephthah, who stood outside the normal social framework. The elders of Gilead sought in their hour of peril a leader from their own midst, but in vain. Hard-pressed, they turned to Jephthah the outcast, "the son of a harlot"—who had been ousted by his brothers from his patrimony—for he possessed the requisite military qualifications, having gathered around him a band of fighters. The traditional rulers were forced to accede to Jephthah (11:6ff.) and appoint him not only as 'commander' ($q\bar{a}\d{s}\hat{i}n$), that is, as leader for the duration of the war, but also as 'head' ($r\hat{o}\check{s}$), that is, as supreme ruler in peace as well—all of which involved surrendering their authority and the powers vested in them.

In the social and political vacuum created by the crumbling of traditional authority, before the requisite instruments of the legal-rational establishment had been fashioned—such as a standing army and a bureaucratic apparatus—the "floruit" of the Israelite judge was born. The Israelites despaired of deliverance through the existing leadership and languished for a deliverer-leader. This protracted yearning under the harsh conditions of distress, which increased the emotional strain, generated a deep religious-national awakening among the people—intensifying the charismatic susceptibility. Yet the "situation" of collective crisis alone is insufficient to trigger a charismatic emergence, as is shown by the lengthy periods of oppression and subjugation preceding the deliverance. In any event, in no instance did a deliverer-judge arise immediately upon the inception of a crisis (see below). Clearly, therefore, a further prerequisite is the appearance of the potential leader, a personage able to

25. For a similar process in the developing states, see Shils [n. 11] 1, 16.

26. The relationship between the "establishment" and the charismatic leaders in the period of the judges was insufficiently elaborated upon in Weber's *Antike Judentum* [n. 13] 21ff., 92ff.; cf. now Reviv [n. 3], who, however, puts too much weight on the role of the elders *vis-à-vis* the judges.

alleviate the people's frustration and apathy, to define for them their national goals, and to serve as ⟦161⟧ a catalyst for their collective desires.[27] Only the integration of these conditions, in each and every case, could lead to charismatic leadership, personified in Israelite history by the deliverer-judge.

IV

We shall now outline the qualities and principle components inherent in the personality of the Israelite deliverer-judge and his charismatic rule, as can be deduced from Weberian and post-Weberian theories. Apart from and above these, emphasis must be placed, from the outset, on the focal element peculiar to the Israelite phenomenon, namely the politico-military facet of deliverer-leadership integrated with the religious aspect[28] and usually involving personal bravery. The schematic outline below[29] does not intend to minimize the variety and diversity indeed found in the personalities and deeds of the individual judges, just as the absence of one quality or another in a given judge cannot invalidate the basic model of his charismatic leadership. The lack of a particular constituent can be ascribed merely to the manner of presentation by the literary source.

(a) A prerequisite for the maturing of the charismatic attribute is a situation of major crisis, above all one induced by an infringement upon national and territorial integrity, in other words, subjugation by an enemy.[30] The appearance of each of the deliverer-judges occurred only

27. Cf. A. R. Willner, *Charismatic Political Leadership* [n. 24] 44ff.

28. There may well have been a gradual strengthening and emphasis on the religious aspect, due to later tendentious reflections upon the early historical events in the Bible; cf. the conclusions, though extreme, in L. Schmidt, *Menschlicher Erfolg und Jahwes Initiative* (Neukirchen-Vluyn, 1970); F. Stolz, *Jahwes und Israels Kriege* (Zürich ⟦Theologischer Verlag⟧, 1972) esp. 100ff., 172ff.; and the more cautious treatment in I. L. Seeligmann, "Menschliches Heldentum und göttliche Hilfe," *Theologische Zeitschrift* 19 (1963) 385–411, esp. 397ff. The primeval nature of "charisma" within Yahwistic faith, already existent in the period of the judges, has long been noted in literature: A. Alt, *Die Staatenbildung der Israeliten in Palästina* (Leipzig ⟦Edelmann⟧, 1930) 9; M. Buber, *Königtum Gottes* (Berlin ⟦Schocken⟧, 1932); W. Eichrodt, *Theologie des Alten Testaments* 1 (Leipzig ⟦Hinrich's⟧, 1933) 150ff., 237f. (in the seventh edition ⟦Stuttgart: Klotz⟧, 1962, 190ff., 298); and G. von Rad, *Theologie des Alten Testaments* 1 (Munich ⟦Kaiser⟧, 1957) 100ff.; and most recently, W. Zimmerli, *Grundriss der alttestamentlichen Theologie* (Stuttgart, 1972) 68–72.

29. I am indebted to Professor U. Tal for certain features in the outline, which he pointed out during a lecture before a seminar on the regime of the judges, conducted by the author at the Hebrew University in 1959. Of course, Professor Tal could not then utilize the recent abundance of literature on the application of charisma.

30. Cf. A. R. Willner, *Charismatic Political Leadership* [n. 24] 41, noting the ensuing effects of subjugation.

after oppression by an alien people, which lasted many years—for eight years prior to Othniel (3:8); eighteen before Ehud (3:14); twenty before Deborah (4:3); seven before Gideon (6:1); eighteen before Jephthah (10:8); and forty before and during Samson's time (13:1, and cf. 15:20).

(b) The charismatic trait involves direct contact with transcendental powers and identification with the symbols held most sacred by a people.[31] In Israel such experiences were realized in the intimate relationship of the charismatic personage with God, expressed in religious revelations and in the spirit (*rûăḥ*) of YHWH with which the hero has come to be associated, by himself and by the people. Running through the Book of Judges like a thread are the phrases: "And the spirit of the Lord came upon [Othniel]" (3:10); "But the spirit of the Lord took possession of Gideon" (6:34); "Then the spirit of the Lord came upon Jephthah" (11:29); "And the spirit of the Lord began to stir [Samson]" (13:25); and "And the spirit of the Lord came mightily upon [Samson]" (14:6, 19; 15:14).

(c) Sometimes the divine contact required public signs and acknowledgment prior to the act of deliverance, to affirm the authority of the charismatic person both in his own eyes and in the consciousness of the people. The outstanding example is the case of Gideon, who appeals to God, upon being consecrated for his mission, for "a sign that it is Thou who spokest with me" (6:17); and on the eve of his action he twice requests additional [[162]] signs (the episode of the fleece of wool). There are numerous signs mentioned in the stories of Samson, who was designated for his task even prior to his birth (13:3ff.). The signs in the "call narratives" of these two deliverers were associated with the apparition of an angel of the Lord announcing the mission of the deliverer, a motif intended to enhance the credibility of his mandate.[32]

(d) The authority bestowed upon the charismatic leader is characteristically spontaneous. The judges were appointed for their task *ad hoc*, and their nomination was specifically personal and consequently non-hereditary or non-transferable. (The sole exception, Abimelech's inheritance of Gideon's authority, is a case of usurpation; see below.)

(e) The authority of charismatic leadership, by nature, is not dependent on social class or status, nor on age-group or sex. This is attested to by such figures as Jephthah, who was of dubious descent, the "lad" Gideon, who was the youngest of his family, and Deborah, the judgess and prophetess. An indication that the deliverer-judges were not of

31. Cf. Shils' "Charisma, Order and Status" and "Charisma" [both in n. 21].

32. Contrasting critical analyses of the literary relationship between the themes of "sign," "call," and "theophanic angel," especially in the Gideon episode, are given by W. Richter, *Die sogenannten vorprophetischen Berufungsberichte* (Göttingen [[Vandenhoeck & Ruprecht]], 1970) and Schmidt [n. 28]; earlier literature is noted in both works.

noble lineage is the conspicuous fact that they or their forebears (except Othniel's and Ehud's fathers; see immediately below) do not find mention in the tribal genealogies of the Bible. On the other hand, an inferior social status is not, of course, an essential feature of the rise of a deliverer-judge. Besides Othniel the putative "son of Kenaz, Caleb's younger brother" (3:9), Ehud the son of Gera was a scion of a noble Benjaminite family (Gen 46:21; 1 Chr 8.3, 7), which was still renowned in David's time (2 Sam 16:5). Furthermore, it appears that even prior to his charismatic emergence Ehud held a prominent role within his tribe, for he stood at the head of a delegation bringing tribute to the king of Moab—precisely like a vassal chief would appear before his suzerain. This seems to be a rare instance of a leader who acquired the charismatic quality in the course of his official career, a phenomenon found at times also in other charismatic regimes.[33]

(f) The rise and activity of charismatic leaders are not necessarily linked to important religious or civil centers. In this respect it is noteworthy that not even one of the Israelite judges arose in a place of special status in Israel's history, and certainly not at any site of cultic significance such as Shechem, Bethel, or Shiloh. Deborah judges "between Ramah and Bethel in the hill country of Ephraim" (4:5); Gideon's residence, Ophrah, became an Israelite cultic seat only after the act of deliverance; Jephthah found refuge in the land of Tob, a fringe area, and only after his appointment did he move to Mizpah and make it his permanent abode (11:16, 34); while Samson's birthplace was at Zorah, and the beginning of his activity was "in the encampment of Dan, between Zorah and Eshtaol" (13:25).

(g) Finally, the specific relationship between the charismatic leader and the people, which is not based upon formal rules or administrative organization, and certainly not on coercion; rather, it rests upon emotion, the personal reverence toward the charismatic individual on the part of his devotees. [[163]] A following gathered around the Israelite judge of its own free will, placing its entire dependence upon him with unshaken faith in his mission (an exception here is Samson the Nazirite). The mustering of warriors took on the form of a voluntary militia—in contrast to a mercenary force—dedicated to the leader with no rational remuneration or predetermined material reward.

In the Book of Judges there is one exceptional figure of a leader who represents the complete antithesis of the above scheme—namely, Abimelech the son of Gideon. His detailed story (Judges 9) was probably included in the book because of its paradigmatic value—in this case, to

33. Cf. A. R. Willner, *Charismatic Political Leadership* [n. 24] 12.

furnish the model of what I would call an "anti-judge" or "anti-deliverer." Indeed, comparing Abimelech to the typical charismatic leader, following the above outline, we find diametrically opposed traits or no corresponding traits whatsoever:

(a) Abimelech's rise was not preceded by a period of foreign subjugation necessitating an act of deliverance, and consequently it did not result in an era of tranquillity.

(b–c) Abimelech did not act under divine inspiration, and received no religious revelations. His military engagements, daring as they may have been, hardly constitute acts of deliverance from a foe, but aimed at conquest, oppression, and destruction.

(d) Abimelech did not come upon the scene spontaneously, but paved his way to power to political maneuvering, including the slaughter of his brothers. He based his demands for authority on the inheritance of his father's position as ruler (9:2).

(c) In his climb to power, Abimelech was aided not only by his paternal pedigree, but also by familial ties on his maternal side since his mother was of the Canaanite nobility of Shechem.

(f) In contrast to the other judges, Abimelech became ruler in a key urban center, the city of Shechem, a site long-sanctified even in Israelite tradition.

(g) Abimelech's authority was cast in a conventional pattern, that of kingship; the local oligarchy, the 'lords of Shechem' (*baᶜălê šĕkem*), "made him king" (9:6). He instituted an administration in the city, as is indicated by his appointment of Zebul as 'official' (*pāqîd*) or 'governor of the city' (*śar haᶜîr*; 9:28, 30). Initially, Abimelech utilized a mercenary troop of "idle and reckless men," paid from the temple treasury of Baal-berit, the city's deity (9:4).

Abimelech's rule did not, therefore, emanate from any charismatic quality. His system of government, drawing in great measure upon the Canaanite concept of the city-state, was of a dimorphic structure, a combination of rule over a foreign urban center, on the one hand, and over the Israelite [[164]] rural, tribal elements, on the other hand.[34] In seizing the reigns of government he acted solely out of personal greed for power—a motive far removed from any legitimate form of domination,

34. For Abimelech's rule and its peculiar nature, see *WHJP* 3, 149ff. Its course of development can also be analyzed in the light of Weber's theorems on modes of domination (though *Antike Judentum* [n. 13] 16, n. 2, and p. 23, mistakenly we believe, refers to Abimelech as a charismatic leader): Abimelech initially sought support of the "lords of Shechem" and later clashed with them, exemplifying Weber's notion that early kings, originally rural war leaders, had to rely upon the support of cities but, once established, came into conflict with the urban oligarchy. Further, Abimelech attempted to neutralize the influence of the city aristocracy by appointing his own retainers as officials and by mobilizing

most especially charismatic. Indeed, in Israelite tradition, Abimelech's abortive regency was excoriated as a despotic usurpation of power. In summing up his rule, the biblical author avoids calling him king or judge, but employs the unique phrase: "he held sway [*wa-yāśar*] over Israel for three years" (9:22).

The natural desire to stabilize the sporadic leadership of the judges strengthened the tendency among the Israelites to give fixed and permanent form to the charismatic attribute that it might become a stable, organized, and hereditary function—a universal phenomenon known as the "routinization of charisma." Indeed, it is against this background that the kingship offered to Gideon by "the men of Israel" must be viewed: "Rule over us, you and your son and your grandson also; for you have delivered us out of the hand of Midian" (8:22). However, the time was not yet ripe for transmuting the Israelite order. Individual freedom and the egalitarian structure of Israelite society were still major obstructions to change, alongside the deeply rooted belief in the supremacy of the Heavenly Kingdom.[35]

It was only toward the end of the eleventh century B.C. that the requisite internal conditions in Israel matured for the establishment of a new regime, a process accelerated by weighty external factors—principally the Philistine threat. At this stage, charisma ceased to function in its pure, concentrated form and became institutionalized within the framework of the Israelite monarchy.[36]

---

troops from among the (loyal) Israelites; this conforms with the Weberian king counteracting his dependence upon the local oligarchy by installing personally devoted officials from the ranks of the populace and by recruiting mercenaries from outside. Cf. Bendix [n. 15] 211, basing on *WuG* [n. 14].

35. See esp. Buber's *Königtum Göttes* [n. 28], where he uses Gideon's rejection of the offer of kingship as a point of departure.

36. Such "routinization" into charismatic kingship is treated in general in Weber's *WuG* [n. 14] 678f., 684f.; for the phenomenon in Israel—beyond the scope of the present study—see in particular, recently, J. A. Soggin, *Das Königtum in Israel* (Berlin [A. Töpelmann], 1967), which gives the earlier literature, and now also F. M. Cross, *Canaanite Myth and Hebrew Epic* (Cambridge, Mass. [Harvard University Press], 1973) 219ff.

Chiefs in Israel

JAMES W. FLANAGAN

1

[[47]] In 1962 Elman Service delineated four stages through which societies evolve as their sociopolitical organization develops from simpler toward more complex forms. Although drawing comparisons among so cieties which are spatially and temporally separated as Service has done does not enable complete and flawless reconstruction of a single society's history, his conclusions have proved useful for analyzing a variety of primitive and archaic civilizations. Ancient Egypt and Mesopotamia have been tested, but neither he nor others have used the cultural evolutionary hypothesis for studying a secondary society such as Israel. The fact that Israel developed under the influence of foreign polities, however, need not prevent comparing her evolution to that of groups. To exclude Israel would isolate the nation from cross-cultural [[48]] comparisons, a practice which has proven to be counterproductive in the past.

In this essay, I propose to make the comparisons previously avoided. Israel's evolution from tribal organization toward full kingship will be reviewed in the light of cultural evolutionary theory, such as that of Service, and in comparison with the processes of succession to high office outlined and described by social anthropologists (Goody 1966). The comparisons will aid not only in outlining the stages of evolution, but also in identifying the principal prime movers that affected the nation's changing social organization (see Vogt 1968: 555) and in explaining the origins of hereditary inequality that eventually led to monarchy (see Flannery

Reprinted with permission from *Journal for the Study of the Old Testament* 20 (1981) 47–73.

Author's Note: I first presented evidence regarding chiefs in Israel in a paper delivered before the Pacific Northwest Region of the Society of Biblical Literature in April 1979. A second draft was delivered in the Israelite History Section of the SBL meeting in November of the same year. I am grateful to colleagues who offered encouragement and suggestions at those sessions.

1972). The patterns in Israel, however, cannot be constructed solely on the basis of comparison supported by isolated bits of information. Such a mosaic would be little more than conjectural history. Rather, the pattern of evolution must truly be in Israel, and the comparisons must be used as a heuristic device which helps us understand and describe the processes that were at work in the ancient society. In sum, we must be careful to discover the evolutionary pattern rather than anxious to create it.

Service's analysis of bands, tribes, chiefdoms, and states and his description of the factors which move a society along its evolutionary trajectory have been so compelling and the cross-cultural comparisons so strikingly consistent that scholars from many schools of thought within several disciplines have adopted his summary with little or no modification. Sahlins (1968), Sanders and Price (1968), Flannery (1972), and E. O. Wilson (1978) adopted the paradigm in their analyses of varied and scattered civilizations. Fried (1967), while agreeing with a four-part division in the evolutionary process, has differed with Service over the description of the stages and the role which stratification plays in bringing about a centralized monopoly of force (Fried 1978; Service 1978; see Redman 1978: 201–13). Like Fried, others have disagreed with portions of Service's description while accepting the general outline of his four stages (Renfrew 1974; Peebles and Kus 1977; see Cohen 1978a, 1978b; and Claessen and Skalník 1978a).

The impact of the 1962 study has overshadowed modifications Service introduced in 1975. By distinguishing primitive societies known through ethnographic studies from ancient societies that can be retrieved only by prehistoric archaeology, he reduced the discernible phases in the latter to three by combining bands [[49]] with tribes in a single stage (1975: 303–5). For ancient, prehistoric societies, Service now prefers a new classification with different nomenclature, namely, a tripartite division of segmental (i.e., egalitarian) society, chiefdom, and archaic civilization. Even in the new division, however, he has left his description of chiefdom intact and has continued to insist upon its universality in the evolutionary schema of both primitive and archaic societies (1975: 87). He now admits though that, while chiefdoms can be distinguished from segmented societies with relative ease, discriminating between them and the archaic civilizations is a more difficult task (Service 1975: 305; Sanders and Marino 1970: 9; Claessen and Skalník 1978b: 629).

Because of the universal claims that have accompanied the discussion of chiefdoms, it is well to note several limitations which cultural evolutionists place upon their assertions. First, a predictable evolutionary schema does not guarantee that every human society has evolved to full statehood. This is an obvious but easily forgotten limitation, especially when one is attempting to discern the boundaries between chiefdoms and kingdoms. Second, not all archaic civilizations and states reflect the same patterns of social organization (i.e., not all were monarchies). And finally, evolutionary schemata do not imply that every developing society changes at the same rate or exhibits all the characteristics which another society exhibits at its parallel stage of development. Human societies are not so easily typed, and thus the factors interrelating processual phenomena militate against facile generalizing (Vogt 1968: 554; Leach 1968: 344).

Secondary societies whose development is influenced by polities outside their borders call for additional caution beyond that needed when studying primary or pristine civilizations (Price 1978). In them, the developments already achieved in the alien influential group affect the formation of the subordinate or neighboring society, especially if the secondary group is caught in the throes of tumultuous and unstable conditions.

Caveats such as these explain why few scholars have considered the possibility of chiefs in ancient Israel. Anthropologists have chosen to ignore the Syro-Palestine region even when considering Egypt and Mesopotamia because they prefer to draw evidence from primary societies where the "natural" processes of development can be tested without concern for acculturation from the outside.[1] Biblical scholars, on the other hand, have accepted the dominant view of the biblical tradition, namely, that Israel moved immediately from tribal [[50]] confederation to monarchy. Only recently have they begun to analyze the sociopolitical forces that accompanied the change.[2]

II

Our investigation of Israel's steps toward monarchy may begin with the statement of Service's thesis on the origins of states:

> [The thesis] locates the origins of government in the institutionalization of centralized leadership. That leadership, in developing its administrative functions for the maintenance of the society, grew into a hereditary aristocracy. The nascent bureaucracy's economic and religious functions developed as the extent of its services, its autonomy,

1. Professor Roy A. Rappaport, Chairman of the Department of Anthropology at the University of Michigan, first suggested this reason to me.

2. Norman Gottwald made occasional references to Israel's tendency toward chiefdom in his study of Yahwistic tribes even though the subject fell outside the scope of his work (1979: 297–98, 322–23). Frank Frick (1979) has drawn attention to evidence, literary and archaeological, supporting a chiefdom hypothesis. I will present additional evidence in a fuller study which is in preparation.

and its size increased. Thus the earliest government worked to protect, not another class or stratum of society, but itself. It legitimized itself in its role of maintaining the whole society (1975: 8).

Here Service argued that the prominence and success of a leader contributes directly to his authority so that, in effect, the community creates its own leadership by becoming dependent upon an individual's charismatic talents. A reciprocal and spiraling relationship is established in which a leader's traits inspire the group's dependence. The dependency in turn enhances the role of the leader so that his success guarantees even greater dependence, and so on, until the role becomes institutionalized in an office.

The gradually ascending authority invested in leadership makes it difficult to draw definite boundary lines between the organizational stages. "Big man" leadership characteristic of segmental society embodies traits of an embryonic chieftaincy (Service 1975: 75), and a chief is himself an initiatory "king" whose office may develop into the centralized monopoly of force typically found in the subsequent stage of early state and archaic civilization (Service 1975: 86). So, while a chiefdom stands between segmental society and coercive state, it exemplifies traits of both.

Describing chiefdoms in this fashion introduces a problem which Service sought to avoid. Inherent in discussions of evolutionary processes is the implication that intermediate stages do not have a status of their own, i.e., that they are only [[51]] intermediate and cannot be examined in their own right. But to assume this about chiefdoms would be a fallacy and would jeopardize understanding the nature and role of chiefs in society (Renfrew 1974: 71; Earle 1978: 1).

Still, descriptions of chiefdoms in anthropological literature tend to be lists of similarities and differences comparing and contrasting them with preceding and succeeding phases. Unlike tribes, chiefdoms exhibit sumptuary rules and taboos surrounding the chief (Service 1962: 145). They have ranking systems which add a new structural principle to kinship ties whereby those nearest the chief assume the status of nobility (Service 1962: 141). An emphasis is placed upon the leader as redistributor or, in Harris' terminology, as warrior-intensifier-redistributor (1979: 94). Theocratic claims which are lacking in tribal societies are made on behalf of the chief, and a dichotomy between the chief's center and the dependent settlements develops (Sahlins 1968: 7).

In contrast with states, chiefdoms lack social stratification into classes based upon occupational specialization. They also lack the ability to impose coercive physical sanctions and have to rely upon non-legal enforcement (Flannery 1972: 403). The government of a state is more highly centralized, with a professional ruling class including priests and bureaucrats who function as substitutes for the king in his many expanded roles (Sahlins 1968: 9). In chiefdoms, such tasks are shared by the chief personally.

The character of chiefdoms has been conveniently summarized by Renfrew (1974: 73) who listed twenty traits which distinguish chiefdoms from egalitarian societies:

1. ranked society
2. the redistribution of produce organized by the chief
3. greater population density
4. increase in the total number in the society
5. increase in the size of individual residence groups
6. greater productivity
7. more clearly defined territorial boundaries or borders
8. a more integrated society with a greater number of socio-centric statuses
9. centers which coordinate social and religious as well as economic activity
10. frequent ceremonies and rituals serving wide social purposes
11. rise of priesthood [[52]]
12. relation to a total environment (and hence redistribution)—i.e., to some ecological diversity
13. specialization, not only regional or ecological, but also through the pooling of individual skills in large cooperative endeavors
14. organization and deployment of public labor, sometimes for agricultural work (e.g., irrigation) and/or for building temples, temple mounds, or pyramids
15. improvement of craft specialization
16. potential for territorial expansion—associated with the "rise" and "fall" of chiefdoms
17. reduction of internal strife
18. pervasive inequality of persons or groups in the society associated with permanent leadership, effective in fields other than the economic
19. distinctive dress or ornament for those of high status
20. no true government to back up decisions by legalized force

Chiefly authority, therefore, is rooted in skills of warfare, dancing, solidifying allegiances, and redistributing goods. These exhibit the chief's charisms and inspire confidence and a sense of solidarity in his followers

(Service 1975: 74). Eventually, the people begin to expect and hope that the chief's exceptional qualities will be passed on to his sons so that, over time, a system of succession gradually develops with devolution of office to the chief's offspring, usually to the eldest male. Successful and successive handing on of leadership within the chief's family (dynasty) eventually leads to primogeniture as a binding custom (Service 1962: 293).

Studies on succession have demonstrated that in spite of the stability which presumption of primogeniture brings to the transmission of office, no system of succession is completely automatic even where next-of-kin procedures are thought to be in force, (Goody 1966: 13). Succession to chieftaincy is often a highly competitive process with contenders vying for the paramount role both during and after the incumbent's reign (Robertson 1976). Struggles for power often leave a string of assassinations, frustrated pretenders, and exiled losers in their wake so that turbulence rather than tranquility governs the transferral of office in these cultures (Barth 1961: 84).

The competition and tension surrounding high office affects the relationship not only of incumbent to potential successors, but also of competing rivals to each other. The encroachment [[53]] and usurpation that competing chiefs and successors perpetrate upon one another is so extreme at times that in nomadic societies groups often migrate in order to find a strong chief who can bring a modicum of peace to their lives (Barth 1961: 85).

Goody (1966: 5–37) has identified four principal variables affecting the tranquility of successions: uniqueness of the office, time of succession, means of selecting a successor, and relationship between successive office holders. He has found that it is typical for societies to manipulate these in order to cope with disruptions that accompany the transferral of office.

The combined options available to a society are many. When a unique office is open to a number of potential successors, the tension among the eligibles can be reduced by restricting the pool of eligibles or by dividing the office or territory. Tension both between incumbent and successors and among successors can be regulated by adjusting the time of succession making it either premortem or postmortem in order to bring a strong leader to power at a convenient time. Interregnums, stand-ins, stake-holders, and co-regencies are typical forms of partial transfer of office which are employed in order to stabilize government and to insure continuity of mature leadership.

Even when the premortem traumas of dethronement, abdication, and usurpation are not factors, the means of selecting successors is often not left to chance. Procedures vary according to the needs of the office. Where special qualities are required, the selection is apt to be highly regulated so that even where primogeniture plays a major role, divination, appointment, and force—always the final arbiter (Goody 1966: 18)—are also used. The time of selection (not to be confused with the time of accession) can also be adjusted as a ploy for decreasing indeterminancy and diminishing competition among rival successors.

The relationship between successive office holders impinges upon other aspects of indeterminate succession. For example, the larger the pool of eligible successors, the greater the distance between the incumbent and his successor and, therefore, the less the tension within the organization itself (Goody 1966: 23). On the other hand, the greater the indeterminacy of succession, the greater the tension among eligibles and the more frequent the struggles for power.

Seen in the light of such variables, the customs and practices which societies including Israel have adopted assume new meaning. For instance, dynastic shedding can be recognized as a [[54]] common practice whereby a dynasty or group of eligibles is reduced. This can be accomplished in several ways. In some systems females are automatically excluded from office while distant males are not, or in others sons of a ruler's siblings are excluded so that the system limits succession to the lineal (vertical) line by transferring rights from father to son to grandson, and so on. In lateral systems, however, office is passed along within a single generation before being transferred to the next generation, making it highly unlikely that all males in each generation will survive long enough to assume office. In either system, rather than determining the priority of the sons themselves, elimination among a sibling group may be accomplished by designating a favored mother whose son will succeed. This practice, reminiscent of Bathsheba's choosing Solomon, arises where polygamous marriages make seniority by birth hard to determine or where office is restricted to sons born after the father assumed office (Goody 1966: 33; 1976: 86–98; Cuisenier 1980: 13–14).

A general movement in history from hereditary toward appointive office has accompanied the growing complexity of society and the consequent need for technical competence (Goody 1966: 44). But because appointment is seldom the sole means of selection for high office, in systems where hereditary practices are deeply rooted, appointive (or elective) procedures usually modify rather than replace them. In most cases, however, a candidate's economic and military resources affect his chances more than his access to royal ancestors (Goody 1970: 637).

Although the conditions described here apply to other high offices as well as to chiefdoms, they illustrate forces by which limited access to office can transform the kinship structures of a society in ways that affect succession (Service 1962: 155). Two principal effects which are important for understanding the affairs of Saul and David can be noted: the formation of conical clans and the emergence of ramage descent groups (Service 1975: 79). The former are unilineal kin groups in which, because of primogeniture, certain members are considered closer to the central line and have greater status and access to common property than do others (Alland and McCay 1973: 165). Since unequal access to property and office is a characteristic of ranked society, conical clans signal a move away from segmental social organization

A ramage descent group is one type of kinship structure [[55]] caused by limited access. Where first-born sons are expected to succeed their fathers, other sons splinter off to begin their own lineages with themselves as heads of the ramages or "branches" (Service 1962: 158). Although they retain rights in the central line, the sons' inheritance and office are passed on to their own sons rather than reverting to the father's line. However, if the first-born's line is truncated by the death of all heirs, a childless marriage, or other causes, the right of succession moves laterally to the second son's lineage, or as necessary, to the third and so on. An individual's relative position in this structure is ranked and regulated by genealogy (Earle 1978: 168). Shifts in genealogies therefore reflect shifts in the relative position of eligibles. Fluctuations in the priority list can be frequent and complex because of polygamous marriages and power struggles which can change the eligibility of individuals rapidly.

Optative affiliation can also affect kinship patterns by placing an exogamous male in line for succession, even in an unilineal descent group (Service 1962: 162; Earle 1978: 175). This is a strategy societies employ in order to insure heirs and successors where male descendants are lacking (Goody 1976: 93–96). The phenomenon, first identified by Firth, combines traits of the epiclerate (substitution of a daughter for a son) and adoption. It allows newly married couples to choose which parental group they will affiliate with, and usually includes a choice of residence as well (Service 1962: 153). The couple generally elects the family that will bestow the higher status upon them. If it is the wife's family, her husband may be taken into her kin group and eventually inherit the title and name of her father. Through this form of adoption, the children of the couple fall in line of succession with the maternal grandfather's line, so descent technically remains patrilineal. The practice will be recalled below when discussing David's marriage to Michal and the latter's barrenness.

III

This brief summary of the circumstances accompanying the development of chiefdoms and the transferral of high office in chiefly societies provides the background for examining premonarchic Israel. To compare the development of chiefdoms in other societies with the evolution of Israelite leadership, we need not delay to defend the existence of an egalitarian, segmental phase among the Yahwists. This stage has been amply [[56]] documented by the biblical writers and has been extensively analyzed in studies by Noth ([1930] 1966) and Gottwald (1979). The end of the Israelite tribal period coincided with a series of events that brought the Yahwists under Philistine domination and initiated the rise of a centralized leadership. For our purposes we may assume that the end of the segmental stage is symbolized in the Bible by the loss of the ark reported in 1 Samuel 4.

The literary record portrays the period following the loss of the ark in terms that can only be read as tumultuous and chaotic, an atmosphere which seems to have persisted until the completion of Solomon's succession and the slayings of Adonijah, Shimei, and Joab in 1 Kings 1–2. Beginning with Samuel's vacillation between legitimating the growing pressures toward centralized rule and refusing to sanction them, deeply felt tensions divided the communities of his, Saul's, and David's days (1 Samuel 5–8).

Saul's election and rule did little to stabilize the situation or to reassure the people. Even when we allow for intentional discrediting by later anti-Saul biblical writers, we are left with a picture of a tragic individual (Gunn 1980: 23–31). A tall, handsome agriculturalist who emerged as a leader because of his military prowess, Saul enjoyed some ability to evoke support of a militia (1 Sam 9:2; chap. 11), but he eventually failed and stood defenseless before his enemies and slayers, the Philistines (1 Samuel 31). He was a warrior and an intensifier who apparently performed rituals, a duty he shared with the priests (1 Sam 13:8–15), and who took part in ecstatic religious movements (1 Sam 10:9–14), although he eventually was chastised for cultic violations (1 Sam 14:31–35).

In retrospect his leadership can be recognized as having been handicapped from the start. Unlike the Philistines, Saul seems to have lacked the Iron Age technology needed to exploit the potential of the cattle and plough agriculture of his day or to wage effective war (1 Sam 13:19–22). He also suffered from periods of depression and jealousy so severe that a musician's service was required to calm him (1 Sam 15:23). Although history eventually confirmed that Saul's fear of those around him was justified, it prevented him from gaining a useful perspective upon his situation and crippled him when he was forced to compete. His personal weakness contributed directly to David's success, a situation which is typical of chiefs competing for the paramount power.

[[57]] By comparison, David was a much stronger person and an obvious potential successor. He was handsome, prudent, well-spoken, and one who made a good first impression (1 Sam 16:12–19). He was a musician and poet (1 Sam 16:16; 2 Samuel 1; chap. 22). He was a successful warrior as well as a popular leader of armies and of the oppressed (1 Sam 22:1–2; chap. 27; chap. 30). He created solidarity by his personal traits and by redistribution, and he enhanced his popularity on many occasions by sharing his booty with friends, allies, neighbors, and suzerains (1 Samuel 21; chap. 25; 27:9; chap. 30).

David's life was closely identified with Saul's house even though his personal relationship with Saul eventually deteriorated to the point of open hostility. He married Saul's daughter Michal after having been refused the hand of Merab and after paying the agreed bride price (1 Samuel 18); he struck a covenant with Jonathan, Saul's eldest son (1 Samuel 18). On separate occasions, both Michal and Jonathan helped David escape from their father's wrath (1 Samuel 19; chap. 20). Later, although David retained affection for Jonathan and his son (2 Samuel 9), he appears to have reduced Michal to a pawn who could be used in whatever manner he found advantageous (2 Sam 3:12–16; 6:20–23).

As would be expected of competing chiefs, the animosity between Saul and David spilled over into their houses and their entourages. After Saul died at the hands of an enemy David served, a long war was waged between their two houses (2 Sam 3:1). The conflict led to the treasonous negotiations between David and Abner, who bargained away the crown of Ishbosheth, Saul's son and successor (2 Samuel 3).

The rift between the factions deepened when David permitted the wholesale slaughter of Saul's family in a blood feud with the Gibeonites. The massacre cost the lives of all surviving male heirs in Saul's house except for Jonathan's son, the crippled Mephibosheth, and his son Micah (2 Sam 21:9). The consequences were widespread. Shimei, a supporter of Saul's house, cursed David for his complicity in the deaths, and the long-standing feud fed the imaginations of Absalom and Sheba who organized rebellions to topple David (2 Samuel 15; 16:5–8; 20).

Although the attempted premortem succession by rebellion failed for Absalom and Sheba, Adonijah, presumably the eldest survivor among David's sons, tried again when his father became incapacitated by old age (1 Kings 1). His efforts were [58] quashed, however, by the appointment of Solomon, the son of the favored wife Bathsheba. With Nathan, she arranged for her son to be named successor-designate.

This survey illustrates the competitiveness which characterized the emergence of centralized leadership in Israel and demonstrates how eligibles were pitted against incumbents and against each other: Saul feared David and warned Jonathan that his rights of inheritance were in danger; Ishbosheth's succession was challenged by the betrayal of his strong man and cousin, Abner; David's accession in Hebron after Ziklag was during a time of instability in the North and must have had the tacit approval of the Philistines. Absalom's revolt, Sheba's rebellion, and Adonijah's accession, linked with the murder of all the principal actors in the drama of succession except David, fit with other events to form a long chain of intrigues which reached from the early years of Saul down to the appointment of Solomon. When the murders of Joab (son of David's sister), Shimei, and Adonijah had been accomplished, a monopoly of force finally replaced chiefly rule in ancient Israel.

IV

This summary derived from the narrative potions of the books of Samuel can be tested against information retained in the genealogical sections of Ruth, Samuel, and Chronicles. There the counters in the chiefly games can be seen: kinship, politics, economics, and religion, the four rubrics anthropologists use to organize their discussions of primitive and archaic societies. Since narratives and genealogies are not subjected to the same reinterpretations at the hand of traditional scribes, parallels and agreements between the two types of literature make a particularly compelling case for the stages of development in an ancient society.

I have examined several of the genealogies elsewhere (Flanagan, n.d. [[1983]]) and have found that their function in Israel parallels genealogies in other cultures. A. Malamat (1973) and R. Wilson (1977) have demonstrated similar parallels for other sections of the Yahwistic tradition. Here, I rely heavily upon these earlier studies, including my own, for what I have to say about genealogical evidence.[3]

It is important to understand the function of genealogies in early pre-literate and literate societies and to be familiar with several of their most common traits. Genealogies typically [[59]] exhibit a characteristic called "fluidity," i.e., a moving of names within, onto, or off genealogical lists when the relationship of the named individuals or groups changes. Since genealogies record and regulate relationships in the domestic, politico-jural, and religious spheres of life, fluidity is demanded in order for a genealogy to remain functional. If genealogies were not adjusted as relationships changed, they would lose their meaning and would soon be lost (R. Wilson 1977: 27–54). As groups migrate, individuals die, or persons' statuses change, the effects of each are reflected in the genealogical record.

A comparison of 1 Sam 14:49–51, 1 Sam 31:2 (=1 Chr 10:2), 2 Sam 21:7–8, 1 Chr 8:33–40, and 1 Chr 9:39–43 illustrates how Israel's records were adjusted in order to keep them abreast of the rapidly

---

3. Documentation and references for the conclusions about genealogies stated here may be found in my earlier study.

changing alliances outlined above. Consequently, the genealogies serve as guides for reconstructing the history of the period and for tracing the fate of Saul's house. In diagram form, the genealogies appear in Table 1.

In the diagrams, we see that when Abner lost his life, and consequently neither he nor his lineage continued to figure prominently in the affairs of Israel, his name was dropped from the genealogy (compare 1 Samuel 14 with 1 Chronicles 8 and 9). Ner, on the other hand, was elevated to the vertical line above Kish and Saul, probably because his importance had already been deeply implanted in the consciousness of the community. Even though the reasons for his prominence are no longer evident to us, we might conjecture that as head of a ramage, Ner had been "ranked" because he stood high among the pool of eligibles if all male successors to Saul in the vertical line should have been eliminated. Unlikely as this may have seemed in the early days of Saul's reign, the eventual violent deaths of Saul's sons and grandsons made the possibility of lateral succession much less remote. Indeed, it appears as if Abner might have succeeded Ishbosheth if he (Abner) had been successful in the intrigues he initiated.

The order in the birth sequence of Saul's sons changed over time as their rank fluctuated (cf. 1 Samuel 14, 31; 1 Chronicles 8, 9). The elusive Ishvi/Eshbaal (elsewhere Ishbosheth/Ishbaal) moved between fourth- and second-born position, and Abinadab and Malchishua traded positions several times. It is important to observe, however, that Jonathan was consistently ranked as first-born, even after his death and the succession of Ishbosheth. His unwavering prominence demonstrates that the genealogists [[61]] remembered that Jonathan's line had continued through Meribaal/Mephibosheth, Micah, etc. (cf. 1 Chronicles 8 and 9). Because of his physical handicap, Mephibosheth did not succeed Saul, and as a result his name was not firmly set nor his generation clearly remembered (compare 2 Samuel 21 with 1 Chronicles 8 and 9). Nevertheless, after the Gibeonite massacre of Saul's house, his name was retained as an important link between Saul and later eligibles in Saul's lineage. The retention of the records of Jonathan's descendents explains why Mephibosheth expected the house of Israel to give him back the kingdom of his father when David was forced into exile by Absalom's coup (2 Sam 16:3). He assumed that David had been a stand-in who led in place of his wife Michal perhaps for one generation or until Micah achieved majority. Michal's barrenness was connected to Mephibosheth's fortunes because it contributed to the uncertainty of whether the office would pass on in her father's line or in David's through a son born of another wife. If Michal had had a son, the competitors might have chosen different sides.

David's marriage to Michal and his insistence that she be returned before negotiations with Abner could begin must be viewed in the light

Table 1

GENEALOGIES OF SAUL'S HOUSE

1 Sam 14:49–51

```
                              Abiel
                   ┌────────────┴────────────┐
   Ahimaaz               Kish                    Ner
      │                    │                       │
   Ahinoam    ===        Saul                    Abner
 ┌────┴────┐        ┌──────┼──────┐
Jonathan  Ishvi  Malchishua  Merab  Michal
```

1 Sam 31:2 (= 1 Chr 10:2)

```
                       Saul
         ┌──────────────┼──────────────────┐
     Jonathan       Abinadab            Malchishua
```

2 Sam 21:7–8

(A)   (B)   (C)

Saul   Aiah
  │   │
Jonathan   Merab = Adriel   Rizpah   (= Saul)
  │   ┌───┬──┼──┬───┐   ┌──────┴──────┐
Mephibosheth   (five sons)   Armoni   Mephibosheth

1 Chr 8:33–40 and 9:39–43

```
                        Ner
                         │
                        Kish
                         │
                        Saul
         ┌───────────────┼───────────┬───────────┐
     Jonathan      Malchishua    Abinadab      Eshbaal
        │
     Meribaal
        │
      Micah
        │
      (etc.)
```

of the intrigue and indeterminacy that was caused by the deaths and disabilities in Saul's house. The daughter's importance for David's rise within the North can hardly be overestimated. In ways similar to the case of Zelophehad's daughters in Numbers 27 and 36, the issue was inheritance and succession rights of brotherless daughters (cf. Jobling 1980:

203–4). In David's case, he cleverly employed optative affiliation as one ground upon which he could appeal to northern support.

Political factors also figured prominently in David's competition for the paramount chief's role. For instance, when Saul forced him to withdraw to a remote outlying area, he used the distance to build a personal power-base and to begin his own lineage while waiting for another chance at the chieftaincy. The circumstances were typical of a losing contender. David's rise in Ziklag was as vassal to the Philistines, the archenemy of Israel, and his accession in Hebron must have been with Philistine support or acquiescence. Because the biblical writers spent no time trying to connect these successes with David's affinity to the house of Saul, we must conclude that his rise in the South was predicated on different grounds than his succession in the North where optative affiliation played a part [[62]] that it did not in the affairs of Judah. This may explain why there is no genealogy in the Samuel material connecting the house of Jesse to the house of Saul even though there is narrative evidence of Jesse's sons serving Saul (1 Samuel 17–18). As a losing contender, David had begun his own ramage with its own rights. When the North was finally forced to turn to him for leadership, he accepted their charge from a position of strength and made no effort to subvert Judah to the primacy of Israel. Instead he maintained two bases of power (centered in a "neutral" Jerusalem) which he could juggle to his own advantage. In effect, he laid the foundation for the tortuous days that were to follow in the history of Israel and Judah.

The economic as well as the political maneuvers which took place in David's house are evident in the genealogical records of his family. These are found in lists preserved in Ruth 4:18–23, 1 Chr 2:9–17, 2 Sam 17:24, 2 Sam 3:2–5, 2 Sam 5:13–16, 1 Chr 3:1–9, 1 Chr 14:3–7, and 2 Samuel 11. (See Table 2, pp. 63–64 [[326-27]].)

Here again, we must point out several characteristics of genealogies, even though we must limit our remarks to those traits which show the chiefly nature of the early Davidic reign. Foremost is the difference between linear and segmental genealogies. Linear genealogies such as found in Ruth 4 serve to legitimate the last name by connecting it with the names of individuals, groups, or places (sometimes mixed together in the same list) which stand above it. Unlike segmental genealogies, the linear do not rank in priority a pool of eligibles who might all be competing for office simultaneously.

This difference has several causes, but here we may concentrate upon the different sociopolitical situation reflected in the two types. Segmented genealogies belong to segmented societies where kinship ties are stressed, while linear genealogies belong to societies where inheritance and succession are not determined completely by familistic concerns.

Since chiefdoms hang in the betwixt and the between, we must avoid making universal claims about this difference, but we can expect to find linear genealogies in ranked societies and segmental ones in egalitarian communities. A shift from one dominant form to the other, therefore, suggests a change in the sociopolitical organization of the time.

In David's case, we find both segmental and linear genealogies. For instance, in 1 Chr 2:9–17, which is similar to the linear genealogy in Ruth 4, segmented and linear genealogies [65] are combined to trace David's lineage from Hezron (from Perez in Ruth) and to record his position as youngest male among seven sons and two daughters of Jesse. In 2 Samuel 17, however, a segmented genealogy has been used to list his sister Zeruiah as mother of Joab, and Abigail as wife of Jether/Ithra, father of Amasa.

In other lists (2 Samuel 3 and 5; 1 Chronicles 3 and 14) the names of David's children have been recorded, but not without some discrepancies. The variations, however, are strikingly consistent. The sons born at Hebron were listed with their mothers' names, whereas those born in Jerusalem are listed without mothers. The dropping of mothers' names indicates that David was a chief at Hebron where the order within his ramage, ranked according to mothers because of polygamous marriages, had to be maintained for determining statuses and succession rights; but once the bureaucracy of a monarchy in Jerusalem made primogeniture less relevant for succession, the mothers' names were no longer remembered. Here Israel's genealogies functioned in the same manner as those in other societies. The only mother from Jerusalem who was named was Bathshua/Bathsheba, identified as mother of four sons, one of whom was Solomon (2 Samuel 11 and 1 Chronicles 3). In the Court History, even Solomon's name was confused with a variant, Jedidiah.

Dropping the mothers' names when the capital moved from Hebron to Jerusalem is typical of transitions from chiefdoms to archaic states. But the continuing competition for David's office after the relocation indicates that full statehood was not achieved at once. During the transitional period, succession remained indeterminate even though the growing complexity of the leader's tasks required candidates who were capable of administering the expanding bureaucracy of an empire. By the time Solomon had succeeded David, premortem, appointive measures complemented heredity as a means of stabilizing the situation. Solomon was chosen from among Bathsheba's sons, and almost as an echo from the past, her name was recorded because of his prominence.

V

Service and others stressed the role which redistributing, organizing, and military leadership play in a chief's rise. Although we have no record

Table 2

GENEALOGIES OF DAVID'S HOUSE

Ruth 4:18–23   *2 Sam 17:24*

```
        Perez                    Nahash
          |                    ┌─────┴─────┐
        Hezron             Zeruiah    Abigail – Ithra
          |                   |             |
         Ram                 Joab         Amasa
          |
      Amminadab
          |
       Nahshon
          |
        Salma
          |
         Boaz
          |
         Obed
          |
        Jesse
          |
        David
```

1 Chr 2:9–17

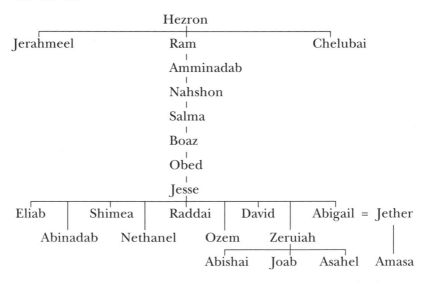

```
                        Hezron
        ┌──────────────────┼──────────────────┐
     Jerahmeel            Ram              Chelubai
                           |
                      Amminadab
                           |
                       Nahshon
                           |
                        Salma
                           |
                         Boaz
                           |
                         Obed
                           |
                         Jesse
   ┌────────┬─────────┬────┴────┬─────────┬──────────┐
  Eliab   Shimea    Raddai    David    Abigail = Jether
     Abinadab   Nethanel   Ozem   Zeruiah              |
                              ┌──────┼──────┐
                           Abishai Joab  Asahel    Amasa
```

Table 2, continued

GENEALOGIES OF DAVID'S HOUSE

---

2 Samuel 11

Eliam
|
David = Bathsheba
|
(unnamed)   Solomon (Jedidiah)

2 Sam 3:2–5		*1 Chr 3:1–9*		*1 Chr 14:3 7*
(Hebron)		(Hebron-Jerusalem)		(Jerusalem)
son	*mother*	*son*	*mother*	
Amnon	Ahinoam	Amnon	Ahinoam	
Chileab	Abigail	Daniel	Abigail	
Absalom	Maacah	Absalom	Maacah	
Adonijah	Haggith	Adonijah	Haggith	
Shephatiah	Abital	Shephatiah	Abital	
Ithream	Eglah	Ithream	Eglah	

2 Sam 5:13–16

(Jerusalem)			
Shammua		Shimea	Shammua
Shobab		Shobab	Shobab
Nathan		Nathan	Nathan
Solomon		Solomon (4 by Bathshua)	Solomon
Ibhar		Ibhar	Ibhar
Elishua		Elishama	Elishua
		Eliphelet	Elpelet
		Nogah	Nogah
Nepheg		Nepheg	Nepheg
Japhia		Japhia	Japhia
Elishama		Elishama	Elishama
Eliada		Eliada	Beelida
Eliphelet		Eliphelet	Eliphelet

---

of Saul's generosity, the narratives suggest that he was a solidifier who finally failed to knit firm [[66]] alliances between the village populations and his central administration (Mendenhall 1975: 162). This factor contributed to the decline in his popularity and to the growth of David's public favor. As a result, Saul was unable to establish a state of dependency through redistribution, which otherwise might have stabilized his leadership. The fact that Ishbosheth was forced to lead from afar, proba bly with only a fraction of Saul's following, also indicates the extent of Saul's failure. He was too weak to rout the Philistines, and they rather than he controlled many of the economic resources.

In contrast, David's rise was closely identified with his role as warrior-intensifier-redistributor. He distributed booty from his raids to his own followers, to the oppressed, to Achish of Gath, and to the elders of Judah—in effect, to those whom he depended upon for his rise. Yet in spite of this record, the difference between such earlier acts of generosity and the later parasitical dependency of his Jerusalem administration upon the resources of the people is striking. The lists of his Jerusalem court officers included commanders of armies and of the forced labor (2 Sam 20:23–26), and the census he ordered must have been intended as a basis for the taxation and conscription needed to staff and support these forces. The list and the census both reflect a dramatic shift in the values and organization of the Yahwistic community. David the chief had begun to act like a king.

As we would expect in chiefdoms, the religious functions mentioned in the biblical narratives also indicate that Saul's and David's reigns were theocracies. Both individuals were anointed by Samuel; performed cultic rites; both used priests and prophets. In short, religion was used by both to legitimate their authority and to help maintain social control.

This is especially obvious in David's case where the role of religion was displayed at every major step in his rise. He consulted Yahweh when considering the move to Hebron; he transferred the ark to Jerusalem; he took part in a ritual dance in order to legitimate his new center; and he relied upon a dynastic oracle to assure the continuation of his line. But do these religious functions suggest a chiefdom or a monarchy? Two episodes demonstrate that the people's religious feelings restrained a rapid, total transition to kingship during David's Jerusalem years. The first of these was the prohibition against building a temple (2 Samuel 24). The second was the punishment meted out to David for his taking the census. Each episode was [[67]] a limitation upon David's power, the likes of which were not evident later when Solomon completed the evolution to full monopoly of force. They suggest that David stood on the boundary line between chiefdom and kingdom.

VI

A review of the royal terminology associated with Saul's and David's reigns reveals a pattern of usage that parallels the stages of cultural evolution outlined here. Although the term is still under study and open to debate, we may suggest that *nāgîd* stands for the chiefly role of Saul and David.

A great deal of ambiguity has accompanied recent studies of the term. Since Albrecht Alt's classic study of the formation of the Israelite state, most scholars have followed him in assuming that *nāgîd* described the religious calling to leadership while *melek* designated the office conferred by the peoples' acclaim (Alt [1930] 1968: 274–80). The distinction according to Alt was between religious and political functions which were present simultaneously in a leader's reign.

Studies made since Alt have helped to clarify the meaning of the term, but they have not completely resolved the confusion between *nāgîd* and *melek*. Evidence from the Sefire treaties (Fitzmyer 1958: 459; 1967: 112–13) and the Nora stele (Peckham 1972: 457–68) have influenced Cross' translation of *nāgîd* as "commander" (Cross 1973: 220–21). For Cross, the term emphasized both the continuity with leadership in the time of the judges and the covenantal character of appointment to leadership roles. He distinguished its use from that of the later term, *melek*, which he believed was used to describe the "routinized" or dynastic kingship of David and Solomon.

Richter (1965) distinguished three phases in the development of the term. *Nāgîd* in the pre-Davidic period meant a type of military leader specially chosen and installed. During the Davidic monarchy, the title was applied to the king and was equated with *melek*. In the post-Davidic age, it became a title for religious functionaries and administrative officials.

A more recent examination of the term in 1 Samuel by McCarter takes up Mettinger's suggestion that a reigning king could designate a crown-prince, a *nāgîd*, to be his successor (Mettinger 1976: 151–84). McCarter's preference is for "king-designate" because "In every case the *nāgîd* is an individual singled out from among others as leader" and because the term [[68]] is usually applied to a king *before* he begins to reign (McCarter 1980: 178–79).

As a group these studies have shown that *nāgîd* underwent its own evolution corresponding to stages in the over-all development of Israel's sociopolitical organization. They have agreed upon the need for a distinction between *nāgîd* and *melek*, but they have also claimed that the terms cannot be completely separated. For these scholars, the words apply either to different aspects of a leader's authority or to different times in the office-holder's reign. This confusion can be explained by the gradual evolution in the role of the *nāgîd* as chiefdom gave way to monarchy.

The case for chiefs in Israel does not stand or fall with the meaning of *nāgîd*, but its use in the books of Samuel fits the developmental scheme we have outlined for chiefdom in the North. One of the earliest narrative traditions in the Samuel material is that of Samuel the seer in 1 Sam 9:1–10:16 which systematically avoided the use of *melek* in favor of *nāgîd* whenever referring to Saul. McKenzie (1962) suggested that the usage reflected the pro-Davidic prejudice of the biblical scribes who reserved *melek* for David who was for them the first true king. The explanation ignores Saul's historical role as chief and overlooks the fact that the term was used when Yahweh rejected Saul (1 Sam 13:14) and when the tribes of Israel selected David to be their *nāgîd* (2 Sam 5:2) as Abigail, wife of Nabal, had predicted (1 Sam 25:30). Each is an early use describing the historical role of Saul and David as chiefs.

David's role as *nāgîd* was also recalled when he chastised Michal (2 Sam 6:21) and in the Davidic oracle (2 Sam 7:8). Both references were made in connection with David's relationship to the house of Saul or with his humble pastoral origins. The passages recall David's early role before going on to celebrate and to symbolize his movement toward kingship. The ritualistic quality of these passages makes them especially important for analyzing the social structure of the period, but it also makes them exceptionally complex. Although they require more investigation than can be given here, we may emphasize that at the point of transition between Hebron and Jerusalem, between chief and king, between house of Saul and house of David, the ritualistic transfer of the ark and the utterance of the dynastic oracle were recalled. As in other societies, ritual was used to mediate the transitions and developments which were played out on the stage of history.

VII

[[69]] We may summarize and conclude. The literary record of the reigns of Saul and David reports a period of trauma and uncertainty when individuals competed forcefully for the paramount role. Murders, broken and restored alliances, marriages and separations, sharing of booty, unifying and leading militia, kinship ties, redistribution, and appeals to religious legitimacy all figured as strands in the warp and woof of the social, political, economic, and religious fabric of the day. Studies of the cultural evolutionary and succession patterns of other societies have described similar transitional circumstances and have concluded that such times were periods when the society was led by chiefs. The descriptions drawn from those non-Yahwistic and primary societies fit the evidence found in the literature of Yahwistic, secondary Israel. In fact, most of the elements on Renfrew's list of twenty characteristics of chiefdoms cited above can be documented in Israel. These indicate both the presence of chiefs and the absence of a strong centralized monopoly of force equipped with laws during the time of Saul and the early years of David. Since the parallels between Renfrew's list and the biblical evidence are not random, and because the evolutionary process outlined by Service is clearly evident in Israel, the cross-cultural comparisons are valid and productive. They have helped us understand the processes at work in ancient Israel and have aided in dismissing conjectures about the immediate transition from tribal league to full-blown monarchy.

In retrospect, we can see that Michal's childlessness left the future of Saul's house unclear, and it raised a question which optative affiliation usually did not raise: Should David's successor be from his house or Michal's? As would be expected, two views prevailed, one perhaps northern and pro-Saulide, the other southern and pro-Davidic. The appointment of Solomon temporarily resolved the question in favor of David by shifting the line of succession away from its northern Yahwistic roots. The outcome has left us to wonder what difference a male child born to David and Michal would have made for the history of Israel. But perhaps we do not have to conjecture. Solomon solidified kingship and a schism was avoided, but only for a generation.

References

Alland, Alexander, and McCay, Bonnie
    1973   The Concept of Adaption in Biological and Cultural Evolution. Pp. 143–78 in *Handbook of Social and Cultural Anthropology*, ed. John J. Honigmann. Chicago: Rand McNally.

Alt, Albrecht
    1968   The Formation of the Israelite State in Palestine. Pp. 223–310 in *Essays*
    [1930]   *on Old Testament Religion*, trans. R. W. Wilson. Garden City: Doubleday.

Barth, Fredrik
    1961   *Nomads of Southern Persia.* Boston: Little Brown.

Claessen, Henri J. M., and Skalník, Peter
    1978a   The Early State: Theories and Hypotheses. Pp. 3–29 in *The Early State*, ed. Henri Claessen and Peter Skalník. The Hague: Mouton.

    1978b   Limits: Beginning and End of the Early State. Pp. 619–35 in *The Early State*, ed. Henri Claessen and Peter Skalník. The Hague: Mouton.

Cohen, Ronald
  1978a   Introduction. Pp. 1–20 in *Origins of the State*, ed. Ronald Cohen and
           Elman Service. Philadelphia: Institute for the Study of Human
           Issues.
  1978b   State Origins: A Reappraisal. Pp. 31–75 in *The Early State*, ed. Henri
           Claessen and Peter Skalník. The Hague: Mouton.
Cross, Frank M.
  1973   *Canaanite Myth and Hebrew Epic.* Cambridge: Harvard University Press.
Cuisenier, Jean
  1980   Structural Anthropology and Historical Anthropology. Unpublished
           paper.
Earle, Timothy
  1978   *Economic and Social Organization of a Complex Chiefdom.* Ann Arbor:
           Museum of Anthropology, University of Michigan.
Fitzmyer, Joseph
  1958   The Aramaic Suzerainty Treaty from Sefire in the Museum of Beirut.
           Catholic Biblical Quarterly 20: 444–76.
  1967   *The Aramaic Inscriptions of Sefire.* Rome: Pontifical Biblical Institute.
Flanagan, James W.
  n.d.   Genealogy and Dynasty in the Early Monarchy of Israel. *Soundings.*
  〚1983〛   In press. 〚Appearing as "Succession and Genealogy in the Davidic
           Dynasty." Pp. 35–55 in *The Quest for the Kingdom of God: Studies in
           Honor of George E. Mendenhall*, ed. H. B. Huffmon, F. A. Spina, and
           A. R. W. Green. Winona Lake, Indiana: Eisenbrauns.〛
Flannery, Kent V.
  1972   The Cultural Evolution of Civilizations. *Annual Review of Ecology and
           Systematics* 3: 399–426.
Frick, Frank S.
  1979   Religion and Sociopolitical Structure in Early Israel: An Ethno-
           Archaeological Approach. Pp. 233–53 in *SBL 1979: Seminar Papers*,
           ed. Paul J. Achtemeier. SBLSP 18. Missoula, MT: Scholars Press 〚Re-
           printed in this volume, pp. 448–70〛.
Fried, Morton H.
  1967   *The Evolution of Political Society.* New York: Random House.
  1968   The State, the Chicken, and the Egg; or What Came First? Pp. 35–47
           in *Origins of the State*, ed. Ronald Cohen and Elman Service. Philadel-
           phia: Institute for the Study of Human Issues.
Goody, Jack R. (ed.)
  1966   *Succession to High Office.* Cambridge: Cambridge University Press.
Goody, Jack R.
  1970   Sideways or Downwards? *Man* 5:627–38.
  1976   *Production and Reproduction.* Cambridge: Cambridge University Press.
Gottwald, Norman K.
  1979   *The Tribes of Yahweh.* Maryknoll, NY: Orbis.
Gunn, David
  1980   *The Fate of King Saul.* Sheffield: JSOT Press.

Harris, Marvin
   1979   *Cultural Materialism.* New York: Random House.
Jobling, David
   1980   The Jordan: A Boundary. Pp. 183–207 in *SBL 1980: Seminar Papers,*
             ed. Paul J. Achtemeier. SBLSP 19. Chico, CA: Scholars Press.
Leach, Edmund
   1968   The Comparative Method in Anthropology. Pp. 339–45 in *Interna-
             tional Encyclopedia of the Social Sciences* 1. New York: Macmillan.
McCarter, P. Kyle, Jr.
   1980   *I Samuel.* Anchor Bible 8. Garden City: Doubleday.
McKenzie, John L.
   1962   The Four Samuels. *Biblical Research* 7: 3–18.
Malamat, Abraham
   1973   Tribal Societies: Biblical Genealogies and African Lineage Systems.
             Archives européenes de sociologie 14: 126–36.
Mendenhall, George E.
   1975   The Monarchy. *Interpretation* 29: 155–70.
   1978   Between Theology and Archaeology. *Journal for the Study of the Old
             Testament* 7: 28–34.
Mettinger, Tryggve N. D.
   1976   *King and Messiah.* Lund: GWK Gleerup.
Noth, Martin
   1966   *Das System der zwölf Stämme Israels.* Darmstadt: Wissenschaftliche Buch-
   [1930]   gesellschaft.
Peckham, Brian
   1972   The Nora Inscription. *Orientalia* 41: 457–68.
Peebles, Christopher, and Kus, Susan
   1977   Some Archaeological Correlates of Ranked Societies. *American An-
             tiquity* 42: 421–48.
Price, Barbara J.
   1978   Secondary State Formation: An Explanatory Model. Pp. 161–86 in
             Origins of the State, ed. Ronald Cohen and Elman Service. Philadel-
             phia: Institute for the Study of Human Issues.
Redman, Charles L.
   1978   *The Rise of Civilization.* San Francisco: Freeman.
Renfrew, Colin
   1974   Beyond a Subsistence Economy: The Evolution of Social Organiza-
             tion in Prehistoric Europe. Pp. 69–88 in *Reconstructing Complex Socie-
             ties,* ed. Charlotte B. Moore. Cambridge, MA: American Schools of
             Oriental Research.
Richter, Wolfgang
   1965   Die *nāgîd*-Formel. *Biblische Zeitschrift* 9: 71–84.
Robertson, A. F.
   1976   Ousting the Chief: Deposition Charges in Ashanti. *Man* 11: 410–27.
Sahlins, Marshall D.
   1968   *Tribesmen.* Englewood Cliffs, NJ: Prentice-Hall.

Sanders, William T., and Marino, Joseph
  1970   *New World Prehistory.* Englewood Cliffs, NJ: Prentice-Hall.
Sanders, William T., and Price, Barbara
  1968   *Mesoamerica.* Englewood Cliffs, NJ: Prentice-Hall.
Service, Elman R.
  1962   *Primitive Social Organization.* 2d ed. New York: Random House.
  1975   *Origins of the State and Civilization.* New York: Norton.
  1978   Classical and Modern Theories of the Origins of Government. Pp. 21–
          34 in *Origins of the State,* ed. Ronald Cohen and Elman R. Service.
          Philadelphia: Institute for the Study of Human Issues.
Vogt, Evon Z.
  1968   Cultural Change. Pp. 554–58 in *International Encyclopedia of the So-
          cial Sciences* 3. New York: Macmillan.
Wilson, Edward O.
  1978   *On Human Nature.* Cambridge: Harvard University Press.
Wilson, Robert R.
  1977   *Genealogy and History in the Biblical World.* New Haven: Yale University
          Press.

The Emergence of Israel:

Social Transformation and State Formation following the Decline in Late Bronze Age Trade

ROBERT B. COOTE AND KEITH W. WHITELAM

〚108〛 It may seem strange to many that a paper presented to the Sociology of the Monarchy Seminar should attempt to deal with the emergence of Israel. The justification for this lies in the thesis developed in this paper that the emergence of Israel and the development of the monarchy need to be studied as a continuum. The standard perception of the dichotomy between pre-monarchic Israel and the Israelite monarchy overlooks important aspects of the historical process. This paper will outline a number of methodological issues which inform our thinking before going on to offer an interpretation of the emergence of Israel and the implications for understanding the transition to statehood.

Some Methodological Considerations

The Debate

The debate on the emergence of Israel in Palestine is so well known that there is no need to rehearse the positions of the main protagonists

Reprinted with permission from *Semeia* 37 (*Social Scientific Criticism of the Hebrew Bible and Its Social World: The Israelite Monarchy*; ed. N. K. Gottwald; 1986) 107–47.

(Chaney 1983; Ramsey 1982). However, despite the deep disagreements, it is possible to identify an important underlying assumption shared by all in the debate. The problem of the origin of Israel as it has previously been formulated has been heavily influenced by the issue of literary interpretation. The beginning and end have been the biblical text. The chief question has been, how are the biblical texts pertaining to the origin of Israel to be understood? How are they to be illuminated by the archaeological evidence, as well as sociological and anthropological studies? The debate on the nature of the text has become particularly acute in the historiography of early Israel, enough so as to merit our considerable attention.

The most influential source of prevailing ideas of what Israel was and is is the Bible. Yet the Bible itself is largely a product of such ideas (and their historical basis) in effect during the lengthy period of composition, formation, and selection of the biblical documents, and among the limited sociopolitical groupings primarily responsible for its development. This observation applies with equal force to all periods of the Bible's formation and of its ostensible referents. Hence we assume as a starting point that the critique of biblical history is a function of the critique of Palestinian history rather than the other way around, as is so often the case.

The traditions of the Hebrew Bible with their theological stances and ⟦109⟧ complex and largely hidden history of development, transmission, adaptation and reformulation spanning a millennium or more, provide an immense obstacle for the historian. As often pointed out, the Hebrew Bible was not written to record the type of social scientific or historical data we as historians might wish to have. It cannot be stressed too strongly that what we are dealing with in the Bible are the religious traditions of early Israel. It is ultimately a document of faith that preserves the life, shape and identity of the communities of faith. By the same token, the traditions have developed along with the communities and been shaped accordingly. Kierkegaard's dictum has been aptly applied to these traditions: "It is no use remembering a past that cannot become a present." It is the adaptability of these traditions that gives the biblical literature its dynamism and life affirming qualities for the communities of faith.

The significance of this observation for historical reconstruction can be illustrated from the long narrative complex that begins the Hebrew Bible. The final shape of the canon as it addresses the identity and problems of the communities that preserved Israelite traditions in the sixth century B.C.E. has become an object of intense study in recent years (through the work of Sanders 1972, Childs 1979, and Blenkinsopp 1977).

Thc significance ot the narratives in their final form is that they address the problems and identity of the later community outside their homeland following the traumatic events of 587 B.C.E. They establish Israel's right to the land and contain an underlying promise for the future. Israel's final conquest will be the result of faithfulness to the law of Moses as set out in Deuteronomy (Mayes 1983: 56).

Nor is it simply a matter of using specialized tools to identify particular layers. Even if it is possible to show that particular narratives or units are contemporary with a particular period under study, it is important to be aware of the dangers in contemporary descriptions. What we are presented with is a particular perception of certain events and relationships (cf. Whitelam 1984). Braudel (1972: 21) expresses this most elegantly: "We must learn to distrust this history with its still burning passions, as it was felt, described, and lived by contemporaries whose lives are short and as shortsighted as ours. It has the dimensions of their anger, dreams or illusions . . . a world of strong passions certainly, blind like any other living world, our own included, and unconscious of the deeper realities of history. . . ."

It is these features over which the historian must stumble. The adaptation and reformulation of the various traditions mean that it is extremely difficult if not impossible to get behind or beneath to anything like an underlying historical "core." It is because they have faced this task squarely that many have simply abandoned the historical task. In the context of the present state of the discipline of biblical studies, with its [[110]] concern with literature, structure, canon, and philological minutiae, it is necessary to address this problem if the attempt to reconstruct the history of Israel is not to be looked upon with passing antiquarian interest or dismissed as the pursuit of the impossible.

The power of the past, in the form of our traditions, our perceptions of the past, exerts tremendous influence on the present which makes such a venture of utmost importance. Various political and religious communities view themselves as heirs to the biblical traditions, and their perceptions of the emergence of Israel in the distant past have tremendous repercussions in the modern world. This study is an attempt to provide a new synthesis of the history of early Israel by bringing together insights drawn from many disciplines as well as recent biblical studies.

The Power of the Past

If as many believe the study of history is really a dialogue about the present, then this task poses an awesome responsibility upon those who presume to undertake it. George Orwell dramatized the power of the social function of history writing—or rather its abuse—in his novel *1984*.

Winston Smith's work in Oceania is, in official parlance, to "rectify" previous newspaper reports now out of line with official reality. Thus the Party has the power to reach into the past and decree whether or not a particular event ever happened. The Party slogan decrees that "who controls the past controls the future; who controls the present controls the past" (cf. Plumb 1969; Herion 1981: 32–33). Orwell's nightmare is really an extention and perversion of the important historiographic principle that historians discuss the past using categories and paradigms drawn from the present. J. Sasson (1981) has illustrated how the models of previous scholarship, mainly those associated with American and German historiography, have been fractured by the altered historiographic perceptions of post-war Germany and post–Viet Nam America.

This raises further important questions about the nature of history writing in biblical studies. The most immediate question for biblical scholars is what type of history is possible or appropriate given the changed perspective of recent years, particularly with the influence of liberation theology as well. It is a task which, far from being worthless or peripheral, needs to be carried out with the greatest vigilance if the all-important dialogue between present and past is to continue rather than be abandoned to the kind of monologue conducted in Oceania and dictated solely by the present.

Rewriting the History of Israel

It has become apparent in recent years that the growing body of archaeological evidence from Palestinian sites cannot be fitted into any of the present dominant models of the emergence of Israel in Palestine [[111]] (Fritz 1981; Weippert 1979, 1982). The continued attempts to reconstruct the history of Israel from the starting point of minute literary study of the traditions of the Bible show little sign of real progress. Such studies run the risk of perpetuating the theological inclinations of their sources, whether from the Pentateuch, the Deuteronomistic History, or even the prophetic books. The more archaeological evidence that becomes available, the more questions it raises about the nature of our sources. The time seems ripe to attempt a fresh synthesis of the history of Israel from a different perspective.

The histories of Noth and Bright have dominated the field, shaping the perceptions of a generation of students and teachers. Despite the considerable differences between their presentations of the so-called patriarchal and conquest periods, these works concentrate on the nature of the literature. The picture of much of early Israel's history they share is remarkably one-dimensional. They are concerned to describe what happened but rarely ask why it happened. They present an odd world, drawn from the biblical traditions, populated by a few leading individuals (cf. Bloch 1954: 59) with a minimal and shadowy supporting cast. These reconstructions, dominated as they are by the events and individuals of the artful narratives of the Bible, are the epitome of Voltaire's complaint about French history: "It seems that, for fourteen hundred years, there have been none but kings, ministers, and generals in Gaul" (cited by Bloch 1954: 178). As such these standard presentations fail to account for or even investigate the underlying causes of social change (cf. Frick 1985).

A major debate has grown up in recent years concerning the historiographic intent of the biblical narratives themselves. J. Barr's seminal essay (1980) categorizing the narrative complex of the Hebrew Bible as story rather than history, along with the ever-increasing new literary studies, raises fundamental questions for the historian. The implications of this redefinition of the narratives as story rather than history, following Barr, has had its greatest effect upon biblical theology (see Collins 1982). The full implications of this shift have yet to be worked out for the historian and historical reconstruction. It might be thought that this debate strips the historian of the ability to write any kind of history of early Israel by removing the greatest body of information about its emergence and development that we have at hand (see Miller 1982: 215; cf. Thompson 1978a: 20). The result has been for many a retreat into historiographic nihilism.

It is by no means the case that the historian cannot or should not investigate periods devoid of usable written sources or should not seek to reveal those aspects of society which are not the subject of literary remains (cf. Febvre 1973: 34). The study of geography in combination with long-term settlement patterns is the foundation of such a history which transcends the short-term perspective of traditional political histories. [[112]] And settlement pattern is precisely the best historical evidence we are in possession of with respect to the emergence of Israel. The recent developments of Palestinian archaeology devoted to surface surveys and focusing upon anthropological, sociological and ecological concerns is obviously central to such a venture (cf. Thompson 1978b; Rainey 1983; Gonen 1984). This enables the historian to build up a network of mutually supporting relationships which make up for the absence of written documents. This is not simply an archaeological inventory but rather the attempt to analyze and interpret the data provided by the archaeologist's spade to throw light on settlement history, demography, economic and political relationships, that is, the internal shifts and strains which are vital for understanding social change. The correlation of evidence independently culled from the biblical traditions is secondary to this task (cf. Thompson 1980).

In order to illuminate a historical, social or political process, the historian often appeals to analogy from some other society or period of history. But it is not always clear how valuable particular analogies are, especially if they are drawn from societies that are considerably removed in time and space from the one under consideration (Hodder 1982: 11–27). The sea-change in the reception accorded Noth's hypothesis of a premonarchic amphictyony in Israel, which has changed in the last decade from general acceptance to general rejection, demonstrates the inherent risks of analogy. These are compounded by the lack of objective controls that provide a check upon free-ranging eclecticism. The importance of a consciously formulated research strategy or interpretative framework is that it provides some controls over analogical reasoning, although a greater knowledge of archaeology, anthropology, sociology, or other disciplines will not automatically produce a better result (Price 1980: 173). Data need to be categorized, organized, and structured, especially when they are as sparse as they are concerning early Israel. Admittedly, as many point out (Thompson 1978b: 11; Frick and Gottwald 1975: 172), structure is no substitute for data since the conclusions need to be drawn from data. Nonetheless "facts" are meaningless until placed within an interpretative framework. Explanation has to be imposed upon otherwise mute data. As C. Renfrew maintains, the past is not recovered but recreated (1973: 5). One of the essential elements of this recreation is inference based upon comparative material; but such inference can only be carried out in the context of a well-defined research strategy. It is then possible to make logical deductions or informed guesses on the basis of the comparative data.

One of the strongest objections to the use of social scientific categories in the study of ancient Israel is that it is impossible to use the field worker's notebook and observe Israelite society directly. Yoffee's rejoinder to the same objection made with respect to Mesopotamian studies [113] applies equally to the study of Israel: "If certain elements of Mesopotamian social systems will never be directly observable, it obviously does not follow that those unattested elements did not exist in the living culture, nor does it mean we cannot infer their presence in an orderly, rigorous way" (1982: 348). Inference is a dynamic process which allows the formulation of new questions, the investigation of previously unexplored areas and the refinement or reformulation of hypotheses to take account of new discoveries, fresh ideas or greater understanding of available data. It is precisely because of the lack of data, the inability to observe directly, and despite continued advances and refinements in archaeological techniques, that it will remain impossible to offer a definitive reconstruction of the emergence of Israel. But historical nihilism is not the only choice in the face of this residue of uncertainty. Certainty is not a prerequisite to understanding. It is the will to understand rather than simply the will to know for certain that is the motivation for the inquiry to be undertaken here (cf. Loyn 1980: 132).

The distractions of our own specialization within biblical studies need to be balanced by investigating how Israel fits into or differs from the regular and recurrent patterns of Palestinian history which can take centuries to work out. Thus it is necessary to extend the chronological perspective of biblical history, which spans the period from the thirteenth century B.C.E. to the second century C.E., to include the whole of Palestinian history from at least the inception of the Middle Bronze Age to the present day.

The myriad of social and political permutations throughout the kaleidoscopic history of Palestine proves a formidable obstacle to any attempt to provide a broad overview of Palestinian history. Only after this task has been faced, is it possible to achieve an important perspective from which to view the emergence of Israel and its transition to statehood as part of complex processes spanning many centuries. These processes are related to the geographical constants which provide the foundations on which the surface events are played out and in turn affect the range of possibilities open to any community. The domination of this area by outside political powers is one of the most important constants of Palestinian history which has had a profound effect upon settlement patterns. The rare periods of serious decline or absence of outside political influence, of which the period under study is an example, thus take on much greater significance but still need to be viewed in relation to the overall pattern rather than in isolation.

The works of authors like Braudel, Harris, and the Lenskis have had a particular influence on our thinking in this area. Braudel (1972; 1980) is perhaps the main source of our critical sense of periodization with his important distinction between different levels of historical time. The Lenskis are useful to us mainly for their description of the type of ⟦114⟧ "agrarian society," based on the use of metals for agriculture and warfare, although their distinction between advanced and simple agrarian societies based on the difference between iron and bronze use does not seem significant for the emergence of Israel, even though it occurs on the cusp of the Bronze and Iron ages. In addition, although the category agrarian society is based primarily on the history of technology, we do not subscribe to recent attempts to emphasize the significance of technological change in Palestine for the emergence of Israel. Further still, the Lenskis' exclusion of "nomadic" societies from their category of agrarian society means that the latter must be modified and adapted to the Palestinian setting, with its prevalent and politically significant pastoral nomadic component. And yet theirs is possibly the most astute justification of the sociohistorical category that allows us to make comparisons between ancient and modern Palestine, at least up to about the middle of the nineteenth century. They and others have worked out the basis for ascribing a degree of commonality among all periods of Palestinian history and culture from the early Bronze Age to the beginnings of industrialization. Harris's view of infrastructural causation requires considerable modification for certain aspects of Palestinian culture.

Such broad-gauge enterprises are not fashionable within biblical studies (cf. Mendenhall 1961: 38; 1976: 152) and certainly run the risk of attack from specialists in many disciplines. Yet there is pressing need to attempt a new synthesis of the history of Israel from this extended chronological perspective. It is an attempt to loose biblical studies from the merely descriptive or chronological histories which concentrate upon what happened, particularly in the political area, in order to ask the fundamental question of why it happened. The search for broad patterns and generalizations helps to throw valuable light on periods of social change. It is necessary to view the emergence of Israel within the context of millennia-long agrarian relations and processes from the Middle Bronze Age to the present.

Viewed from this perspective, the kaleidoscopic history of Palestine reveals a number of regular and recurrent patterns, of which the most significant is the domination of this area by major outside powers and their political economies. Biblical studies in the past have sought to illuminate only a small section of the rich and troubled history of Palestine. There is much to be gained by trying to see how biblical history fits into the tapestry of Palestinian history, a tapestry still being woven with many of the same threads. This is an awesome task. But Palestinian history is so rich that it draws the researcher on, wanting to know more, ever conscious of the vast array of material that beckons. The dangers of such an approach are partly offset by the rewards of fresh understanding.

This approach offers a fresh perspective on the emergence of Israel in Palestine while providing a corrective to a number of damaging assumptions 〚115〛 which underlie much of biblical scholarship. It is the regular and recurrent that shapes the possibilities open to a particular society but that so often escapes the awareness of the social actors themselves. Febvre (1973: vii) notes that with regard to the environment "there are no necessities but everywhere possibilities." This extended chronological perspective helps to overcome the problem of periodization, that is, the belief that social, economic, political and religious change can be neatly compartmentalized with overly precise chronology without distortion. The emergence of Israel datable to about 1250–920 B.C.E. is, to use concepts popularized by Braudel, a surface event that is understandable only in terms of the wider, slower movement of much longer duration, what Braudel styles *la longue durée*. Human beings in history are constrained by climate, vegetation, animal population, agricultural potentialities, and the like. Surface events, primarily those events which are most often the focal point of traditional political histories, are played out around more permanent elements such as urban sites, trade routes, harbours, and climate. The realization of the various potentialities of Palestine have been governed throughout its agrarian history by the presence (or, rarely, the absence) of outside powers and the complex interaction of external world events.

The most important feature of this synthesis for the present paper is that the emergence of Israel and the development of the monarchy, that is, the transition to statehood, must be seen as a continuum, within an imperial power vacancy, and not as a dialectical conflict, as is commonplace in other studies whether sociologically oriented or not. The common view, or rather the domain assumption, that the monarchy is some kind of aberration or "alien" institution foisted upon true Israel is partly due to the self-limiting perspective of specialization. The views of Bright and Noth (alien institution), Mendenhall (pagan reversion), and Gottwald (dialectically opposed) fail to explain how significant social change takes place. Buccellati, in his important study of Syria, had already emphasized the crucial point that such a notion denied the internal dynamics of Israelite society. The monarchy is rather an outgrowth, though not inevitable (contra Mayes 1977: 331), of the particular configuration of circumstances surrounding the emergence of Israel in Palestine.

Past and Present

It is the assumption of the uniqueness of Israel which has had the greatest distorting effect upon the study of Israel. This notion of uniqueness stems from Jewish and Christian ideologies which have developed from the Roman era to the present day. It is for this reason that it is essential to develop an analytical, interdisciplinary approach to the history of Israel. It is unreasonable to assume that Israel's social organization [[116]] differed from all other known human societies. The uniqueness of the Bible in Jewish and Christian culture stems from the developments that occurred long after the emergence of Israel. It is vital to ensure that the all-important dialogue between the past and the present is maintained rather than to abandon the past to the tyranny of the present.

It is inevitable that the historian approaches the past from the perspective of the present (Lewis 1968: ix). The ever-increasing pace of change over the past few centuries and particularly during the twentieth century means that our view of the past is subject to radical changes of perspective (cf. Renfrew 1973: 5). Comparative studies at least offer some hope that historians are not imprisoned by their own present. The perspective of *la longue durée* is able to readjust and balance our own view of the emergence of Israel.

The most fundamental question remaining touches ourselves as authors. How far are we as historians reshaping the past to suit our own present, to suit our own political and religious prejudices? Have we in undertaking this study reached back into the past and decreed that particular events did not take place, or at least that particular perceptions of those events are mistaken, because they do not conform to some present official (or unofficial) reality? It ought to be obvious that complete objectivity is not an attainable goal for the historian. That is surely one of the landmark perceptions of twentieth century historiography. All that is possible is to set out one's presuppositions and methods of working for critical gaze without turning the work into an extended treatise on the philosophy of history. It is hoped that this study will throw fresh light on the emergence of Israel onto the stage of history. The importance of the task is aptly summed up in the dictum of M. Bloch: "Misunderstanding of the present is the inevitable consequence of the past" (1954: 43). The opposite is of course also true, and we are aware that it is our understanding of the present that is to be tested here, as much as anything, as is the case with every other historian. It can only be hoped that the errors we have made will be corrected by others who find this approach of value.

The Emergence of Israel

Setting the Scene

Israel originated during the third and fourth quarters of the thirteenth century with the shift in the land use and settlement patterns of the Palestine highland and dry land margin. This shift occurred mainly in response to changes in the economy of the eastern Mediterranean area associated with a drop in trade during the thirteenth century. Such shifts are endemic to Palestine and are a major feature of its kaleidoscopic history. They differ in extent but are nearly always the result of economic and political forces from outside the region. The uniqueness of Israel that [[117]] makes it of such significance in world history lies less in its origin than in the persistence and adaptability of its ideologies as they functioned in various political and economic forms through history, along with the fact that the peoples of Palestine have, for geographical reasons, tended to play significant roles in the wider history of the world.

During the centuries prior to the emergence of Israel, the small highland population (Gonen 1984) concentrated by and large in and near cities, under urban organization and protection. In these areas, chiefly Shechem, Jerusalem, and Hebron, ruling military families headed by kings, governors, prefects and the like, frequently of non-local ethnic affiliation, held local arable land and much land planted in perennials in royal tenure under nominal Egyptian suzerainty. These lands provided part of the local grain requirements along with commodities for trade and commerce. These included wine, oil, fleece, salt, honey, wood, tar, and other locally available products.

Over the cultivators of the lands attached to these cities the urban military families exercised little control, and over tracts of uncultivated hilly and wooded hinterland none at all. The policing of the urban agricultural lands and their cultivators was subsidized by lowland and Egyptian contributions, as indicated for example by the appeals of Palestinian highland rulers for military reinforcements from Egypt in the Amarna texts. By turn these lands were secure and insecure. State control in the highlands was tenuous and competitive, as the Amarna texts demonstrate, with effective control in many areas non-existent. This fragmentation into local pockets was fostered by the imperial power of Egypt, which was interested in promoting political fragmentation and dependence rather than mutual interreliance conducive to independence.

With pastoralism and other avenues of withdrawal available, the integument enclosing the peasant cultivator in highland city regions was porous and friable at best. To simplify, if the peasant stayed to plant, it was as a beneficiary as much as a victim of the commerce of the city. Even when the peasant withdrew, there remained a close tie to the urban economy. This was perhaps less true for nomadic groups, a larger proportion of whose subsistence could perhaps be provided by their pastoralism. There is no questioning the participation and even integration of nomadic groups in agricultural society (see especially Rowton 1973a; 1973b; 1974; Gottwald 1979: 435–67). To the degree, however, that the nomadic tribe emphasized pastoralism, was a sociopolitically distinctive group, and was organized to maintain some domain, it functioned as "a paramilitary unit in a permanent state of partial mobilization" (Rowton 1973a: 255) and as such figured as an enemy or friend in the commercialized policing of urban agriculture and trade. The bandit or mercenary group, with little or no pastoral base, was more dependent on commerce [[118]] (Chaney 1983: 72–83; Horsley 1981: 409–32). The bandit either robs the rich or works for them, or both.

The Emergence of Israel

The dramatic change in highland settlement pattern, which witnessed a rapid expansion of agricultural settlements in the Palestinian highland and steppes during the 13th to the 11th centuries B.C.E., generally acknowledged by archaeologists and historians as evidence of the emergence of Israel, needs to be explained. At the same time Syro Palestinian archaeology has revealed a widespread destruction of many of the important urban centres as part of the upheaval experienced throughout the whole of the eastern Mediterranean. The causal connection between this wider movement and the emergence of Israel in Palestine is frequently overlooked or approached from the opposite perspective (with the exception of course of G. E. Mendenhall, who has campaigned for a long time for this view). Israel is seen to be largely or partly responsible for the destruction of urban Palestine either through conquest or revolt. If we are adequately to understand the processes we now label the origin of Israel and their implications for the rise of the monarchy, it is necessary to explain the connection between the break up of eastern Mediterranean civilisations and the emergence of the hillcountry settlements in Palestine.

The direct evidence for the period of the emergence of Israel in Palestine is limited. Nearly everyone agrees that the following pertain: (1) the mention of an "Israel" in the Merneptah stela about 1200 B.C.E.; (2) the expansion of mostly unwalled villages in the highlands; (3) a widespread destruction that affected nearly all the important urban centres of the region during the period of transition from LBA to the early Iron Age.

A comment about the last point might be instructive. Albright and his followers seized upon this destruction as ample testimony to the historicity of the biblical account of a planned campaign by Joshua. Yet the evidence is mute and ambiguous since there is no clear indication as to the agents of destruction. We know cities were destroyed. We do not know who destroyed them. It would appear to be the result of a combination of factors: internecine urban warfare, well attested in the Amarna texts; Egyptian imperial campaigns to the region, again well attested in the documentary evidence; the arrival of the Sea Peoples on the coast and inland lowlands; domestic fires; earthquakes; and conceivably immolation as a magical warding off of the contagion of disease. Furthermore, the fact that such cities as Jericho, Ai and Gibeon, key cities in the biblical account of the "conquest," provide no archaeological evidence of occupation during this period undermines the conquest model.

The whole of the eastern Mediterranean had become a vast nexus of international and interdependent trade. The imperial powers and petty

[[119]] kingships of the area were governed by highly centralized royal palace bureaucracies. The high degree of specialization demanded by such systems produced significant economies of scale that supported high concentrations of population. The interrelationships that evolved meant that even localized upheavals could resonate throughout the whole system and produce quite dramatic effects (see Renfrew 1979: 487–88; on "world" economies and trade, see Braudel 1984: 24; Curtin 1984). The direct causes of the traumatic upheaval of the 13th century B.C.E. in the eastern Mediterranean are hidden from our view. Whatever the causes, the Mycenaean and Hittite empires fell, Egypt was seriously weakened, and many city-states along the Levantine coast ceased to exist. This precipitated a dramatic decline in interregional trade during this period. The abrupt decline of this trade, which had sustained the power structures of the Palestinian cities and towns, crippled the urban elite and their means to power. It is these dramatic developments which provided the conditions for the emergence of Israel in the Palestinian highland.

As mentioned above, it is clear that it was not just the urban elite who depended upon interregional and regional trade for their livelihood, even though they might be described as the prime beneficiaries. Nomad, bandit and even peasant groups were also economically dependent upon such trade. As a result of the instability and material decline, such rural groups, particularly nomads and bandits, would have become increasingly politically independent as is the case in other periods of Palestine's history. The regional expansion of agricultural village settlements in the highlands, we suggest, was a means of risk reduction through a shift to and expansion of agriculture and pastoralism following the general economic collapse. The exploitation of more marginal areas away from the large urban centres seemingly became politically and economically viable as the close ties to and benefits from urban interregional trade disappeared. Tubb in fact describes a very similar process at the end of EBIV following the disruption of Palestinian trade. Approached from this perspective, then, Israel emerged in the Palestinian highlands as a result of a dramatic change in settlement and land use mainly in response to the reduction in East Mediterranean trade which had a seismic effect upon the material prosperity of Palestine.

The lack of state control in much of the highland was a major factor in the emergence of Israel. The drylands in the vicinity of Jerusalem were of prime importance in this respect as the domain of pastoral nomadism and the refuge for bandit groups. It is here we find the crucial mix of nomads, bandits and village communities in close proximity outside the reach of state power yet dependent on Jerusalemite commerce prior to its collapse in the Late Bronze Age. Pastoral nomads and bandits were in competition with the urban powers for much of the highland, or in their employ in the struggles for control. Such political instability meant the [[120]] highland was not exploited to its full agricultural potential. But clearly the unsettled areas were not to be thought of as empty wasteland awaiting a tidal wave of population to sweep over it from outside. The MBII period witnessed a similar, though not as extensive, expansion of settlement. The growing evidence for the view that the EBIV/MBI transition to MBII was due to internal factors rather than the result of some external Amorite invasion (Tubb 1982; Thompson 1978a, 1978b; de Geus 1976; Liverani 1973; and Dever 1980) provides the closest and most suggestive analogy to the emergence of Israel following the LBA collapse. The Early Iron extension of settlement in the highland should be viewed as a reopening and expansion of this move into the marginal areas rather than the opening up of virgin territory.

In the piedmont and lowland, the population was denser, the hinterland less extensive, and political and military control tighter. There the peasants had less of an option to stay in place and benefit from commerce at the same time. There too the integument fissured; yet once away, given the pervasive hinterland instability, the peasant, though less contained, became more not less dependent on the commercial sector of the socioeconomic system of his erstwhile containment.

In the highland hinterland, sparring bandit and nomad groups, allied to warring urban factions exercised over the various subregions a typically sporadic and alterable control. Although such interregional gang warfare, supplemented by inter-village gang warfare to judge from later evidence, was itself largely a result of severe depredation and extreme economic disadvantage; it was carried on largely by the means of weapons, resources, and influence acquired from or through the inter-urban network, as well as through raids on peasants. It was this rural political instability that prevented the establishment of village agriculture on any extensive or permanent basis beyond the lands within the bound of urban security, even though much of the uncultivated hinterland was fully suited to agriculture and had indeed in many areas at least once before been settled. And it was some change in this pattern of rural instability, rather than peasant unrest per se, that led to the emergence of Israel.

The change in the highland hinterland from political instability to political stability, and from hostility among bandit groups and nomad tribal bands to forbearance if not federation, was brought about not by a bandit victory, not to speak of a massive peasant revolt, but by a major economic change in the eastern Mediterranean area as a whole during the thirteenth century. The level of trade declined. Some would say it plunged. Within a generation, two of the three main trading states—the Mycenaean and Hittite empires—were destroyed. The third empire,

Egypt, came under attack by the invading Sea Peoples. Nevertheless Egypt at this time not only maintained its political presence in lowland [[121]] Palestine but even increased it. Egypt's presence continued to crescendo for a further two-thirds of a century or more, until the New Kingdom's collapse after the reign of Ramses III (1195–1164). Not until then did the Philistines assume sovereignty in the southern lowlands of Palestine in their place. According to Weinstein (1981), Egypt's presence in lower Palestine was greater just prior to its collapse than at any time in the entire LB period, even though its return on expenditure, due to the decline in trade, was ever less. The result is clear: for nearly a century Egypt's imperial budget, so to speak, ran a long-range and eventually catastrophic deficit.

The highland bandit leaders and tribal sheikhs (not necessarily always different persons) faced a choice: continue to choose sides in imperial or city-state conflicts whose economic basis—in terms of both support and purpose—was melting away, or find some alternative means of subsistence. Sufficient numbers chose the latter, and the means was subsistence agriculture. More precisely, it was a direct exploitation of an expanding subsistence agricultural base in place of an indirect exploitation of a shrinking commercial and commercial agricultural base. Again, the political condition for the exploitation of the highland hinterland land base for subsistence agriculture was stability. Under the circumstances, stability could only come about by an inter-subregional, inter-group, and inter-tribal (again not all mutually exclusive categories) stay of conflict. The political form—whatever it was—that achieved and maintained that stay was referred to by its adherents with the name Israel.

It is important to stress that the main event was not an agreement among usual and erstwhile hostile and aggressive opponents, but that the highlanders faced an economic choice. Their choice was individual and by groups, then eventually with a collective effect and finally some kind of collective political expression. But the economic choice was primary. When the urban arrangements of which they were a part decayed or collapsed, some alternative had to be found. Agriculture was at first a necessity, then an opportunity. The subregional peace—the switch from crime to crime watch, as it were—had to do with the lack of gain to motivate continued mutual hostility.

At the sociopolitical level at which this stay was carried through, it is difficult to choose between the alternative scenarios of mutual forbearance amongst a group of influential leaders or the dominance of a single leader. Band and tribal decision-making tends to be in terms of consensus conceived by and then imposed by the single dominant leader. A more realistic assessment might be that a "tacit" agreement came about simply because the problem of survival in such marginal areas was for a long time the dominant problem.

A stay in inter-subregional and inter-group conflict did not mean a stay in conflict altogether. The loose coalition of bandit and nomad groups [[122]] reinforced their truce, drew the political backing of some peasants, and attracted peasant support in the development of villages by exchanging subregional inter-group conflict for regional class conflict. The stay in inter-group conflict and the commitment to subsistence agriculture required among other things that the groups as a collective counteract any political advancement among themselves based on an individual's or group's commercial advantage. This tendency could be expressed, and corresponding strategies carried through, in dramatic class terms. One manifestation of this might be preserved in the anti-urban and anti-commercial bias of some laws, such as the prohibitions against man-stealing and household aggrandizement. Another might be the rooting of Israelite identity in a polemic against Egyptian corvée (particularly significant for the pastoralists of the Negeb and Sinai), of particular relevance in Palestine during the reigns of Ramses II and Ramses III. A third more general and important manifestation was the attack on local urban elites. These elites had of course been weakened by the same developments that had posed for bandits and nomads their crisis of subsistence: the drop in trade and Egypt's choice to exhaust its resources on its own presence in Palestine. Early Israel attacked the kings of its region under the leadership of erstwhile paramilitary leaders who had every reason to expect that they could bring that fighting to a successful resolution far more quickly than they could the fighting among themselves. And in the meantime, one had to eat.

Such a reconstruction calls for a different explanation of the population increase in the highlands from those usually advanced. It need not be denied that the settlement of the highland involved some external input as well as movement away (withdrawal) from the urban, especially lowland, areas. Perhaps some lowland peasants preferred to transfer their cultivation to lands under the aegis of some highland sheikh. The question remains how significant these factors were in the formation and growth of Israel. The statistical significance of any large-scale external nomadic invasion or infiltration has already been overturned by Mendenhall and Gottwald. However, as yet there is little archaeological evidence to suggest a large scale withdrawal from lowland areas corresponding to the increase in highland settlement. The major factor, we believe, in population increase may be postulated on the basis of comparative studies of agrarian societies. Harris shows how preindustrial societies regulate population through severe forms of psycho-biological violence and deprivation. The relaxation of such techniques allows a significant increase in

reproduction in a short time. This becomes possible when for some reason there is an increase in food production. The extension of agriculture
in the Palestine highland with the emergence of Israel allowed a relaxation of population controls. It is commonplace for ⟦123⟧ peasant populations to invest economic surpluses in population increase rather than
a higher standard of living. The increase in population led not to growth
in village size but to the proliferation of villages through fission. These
villages tended to increase in number faster than in size as the Iron Age
archaeological record shows. In Israel's case the increase was presumably
demand-induced through the need for labour vital to intensive activities
in the highlands as well as the need for defence (see Harris 1980: 68–70;
Meyers 1983).

Israel came into being when the highland hinterland population
shifted rather precipitously to agriculture. This hinterland population included not only peasants already involved in agriculture, but also nomad
and bandit groups. All three groups combined subsistence food producing and fighting skills in the same person, although in different degrees.
The increasingly extensive tilling of the hinterland was largely motivated
by short-term risk aversion and evasion. The formation of independent
villages in more marginal areas, in conjunction with bandits and nomads, would have enabled the population to hold off the already weakened urban threat. Israel thus designated a loose federation of highland
villages, small towns, pastoral nomad groups, and erstwhile bandits, to preserve and defend local village sovereignty over land and produce particularly against state encroachment. This was most probably an extension,
brought about by the economic crisis, of pre-Israelite decentralized alliances and agreements among hinterland groups.

Such an understanding of the emergence of Israel helps to explain
the lack of fortifications around highland towns and village, replicating
the lowland LBA pattern. This lack would appear to contradict models assuming widespread conflict in the emergence and establishment of early
Israel. We must reckon with a complex process, since there is evidence of
fortification at some sites, as for Giloh, and many of the highland sites
are inaccessible anyway and so have a kind of natural fortification. The
general political instability of these areas might help to explain such factors without appeal to invasion or the primacy of ideologically motivated
conflict. Most importantly it helps to explain why agriculture and settlement were extended in the highland *at precisely this time.* Other factors
such as appeal to technological innovations have at most considerably
less explanatory power.

We have characterized Israel as a loose confederation of various
groups, at times competitive or hostile with one another, held in equilibrium momentarily by a particular configuration of circumstances. The

inherent fragility of this configuration based on short-term objectives meant it was inevitable that the result of a change in circumstances would be either fission or fusion into a more centralized society. The gradual reestablishment of trade and an upturn in the interregional economy [[124]] provided the trigger which produced the fusion and the rise of the Israelite monarchy. Indeed one could say this process had begun with the very emergence of Israel.

A restatement of the main point made so far might be helpful. The settlement into villages in the hinterland was given political and incipient ethnic form in the loosely federated people calling themselves Israel. This shift and formation had as much to do with the economic losses suffered directly by trading, transporting, thieving, mercenary, and craft groups more or less dependent on the declining inter-urban economy as with the resultant shrinkage of urban military control over local lands and population. The latter—particularly in the highland—had already long been minimal. The main issue in the emergence of Israel was thus not the regional socioeconomic and political forces that led perennially to peasant unrest, though these obviously played a role in the equally perennial spawning of bandit and nomad groups. These forces were not distinctive for the thirteenth century, while the decline in trade was. Instead, the main issue was the supraregional economic forces and their political consequences that forced groups who held military control over separate pockets of the hinterland to turn to agriculture themselves, to supervise and to secure the extensive agricultural development of the hinterland by others for whom hinterland agriculture had at this point come to involve less risk than agriculture under city protection, and to settle for a more or less peaceable stand-off among themselves.

Although heirs to a history of mutual hostility among themselves or their heads, highly decentralized in their regional polity, and—if villages everywhere are any indication—parochial and even reclusive in their separate interests and identities, nevertheless these village groups collectively prevented, for several generation, the restoration of urban dominion over their newly developed lands. Although they did not themselves as a unity permanently dominate the highland region, they were able regularly, mostly within subregions, to fend off threats to local subregional autonomy, particularly during the twelfth century. Early Israel probably owed its collective security as much to its scattered production combined with expanding resources, production, and population as to its decentralized militia descended from the original hinterland armed bands and strengthened by the expression, through cult and otherwise, of its mutual self-interest. The unity of early Israel as seen in the Bible is the invention of state propaganda from a later period.

The consolidation of the political economical condition for the on-going development of highland agriculture—relative peace, order, and prosperity—was sustained on several interrelated fronts. From the beginning, the following factors were among the most important. Agricultural lands, and especially highland arable, expanded. Iron tools became increasingly available. The mortality slope flattened: a population largely [[125]] dispersed in villages away from the highways are less susceptible to epidemic diseases, and a more consistently maintained mixture of agriculture and pastoralism at the clan level made people less vulnerable to recurrent famine conditions. The birth rate rose in response to increased production. Early Israel adhered to an apparently sharpened male reproductive bias in order to favour fighters in defence of its political economy; yet Israel's overall reproductive success overrode this countervailing tendency. Greater population meant more labour for the expansion of agriculture. The villages retained the bulk of their product. Regional defence continued to be helped by geography and the low levels of production relative to the lowland. Lowland military elites were preoccupied with the shift from Egyptian to Philistine sovereignty. There was a continual migration of villagers from the lowland to the highland. Decentralized defence was particularly suited to support infrastructural expansion in the hinterland and to counteract the emergence of a more "expensive" military elite. Early Israel could not however prevent this development in the long run. Finally, as for domestic economy, early Israelite culture fostered an increase in peasant family size and perhaps favoured exogamy in order not to undercut the political basis of its federation.

To repeat, all these factors played a role in the emergence of Israel in that they contributed to its consolidation over a period of several generations. They were interrelated, cumulative, and in concert of gradual not immediate effect.

The Emergence of the State:
Some Theoretical Considerations

Factors in the Perception of a Dichotomy between
Premonarchic and Monarchic Israel

The standard perception is that the monarchy represented a decisive break with premonarchic Israel. S. Herrmann's treatment (1981: 132) is representative of this position: "All this confirms the common view that the monarchy was a later phenomenon in Israel, forced on it by historical circumstances and essentially alien to its original nature." The assumptions of this statement are widely shared, including the implication that

"Israel" should somehow exist beyond "historical circumstances," or that there is some essence of "Israel" quite apart from all but the first two hundred years or so, usually idealistically conceived, of its history.

Indicative of the strength of this notion that the monarchy is alien and due entirely to Philistine pressure is the striking agreement between the presentations of M. Noth and J. Bright. Their reconstructions of the premonarchic period represent antagonistic positions developed from widely differing methodological standpoints. However, these differences are almost completely resolved in their discussions of the rise of the monarchy. Noth (1960: 165) is of the opinion that "the idea of the monarchy [126] became effective so late and went so much against the grain in Israel," being due entirely to Philistine pressure which threatened the continuity and existence of Israel as a whole. A similar line of reasoning is pursued by Bright, who sees the cause as one and the same, the Philistines, concluding that the monarchy was "an institution totally foreign to Israel's tradition" (1981: 187), yet can go on to add "but Israel's monarchy was nevertheless unique. It was certainly not patterned on the feudal city-state system whether of Canaan or Philistia. While it may have borrowed features from the national kingdoms of Edom, Moab, and Ammon, it remained a phenomenon characteristically Israelite, at its beginning as little a change from the old order as possible" (p. 189). Bright's attempts to juggle the two conflicting notions that the monarchy is both foreign to Israel's traditions yet uniquely and characteristically Israelite points out a fundamental methodological problem common to these standard histories in their treatments of this period—namely, their inability to account for social change.

The disagreements between Noth and Bright over their reconstructions of the premonarchic period stemmed from different assessments of the value of the archaeological record in relation to the biblical text. With this methodological problem removed, due to lack of clear archaeological evidence for early monarchy, the biblical traditions assume a position of overwhelming importance as source material with the result that the events and characters which preoccupy these narratives have been magnified to such an extent that virtually all else has been obliterated from view. They offer accounts which are little more than a reiteration of the biblical text. As such they serve to perpetuate the theological world-view of these sources, be it the Deuteronomistic History or some other earlier or later document.

Although fresh stimulus has been given to the debate on Israel's emergence in Palestine, the main proponents of the so-called revolt model do not deviate significantly from the standard approach to the rise of the monarchy. Mendenhall's portrayal of the Israelite monarchy as a rapid reversion to LBA paganism, associated with what he describes as the typical Syro-Hittite monarchies of urban Canaan, draws the distinction with premonarchic Israel in even sharper relief. The same is true of Gottwald's contrast between egalitarian tribal Israel and its return to the exploitative social set up of the monarchy. The basic assumption remains that the Israelite monarchy represents a decisive break with what had gone before, being brought about entirely by external Philistine pressure (see Mendenhall 1983: 99; Gottwald 1979: 415). Mendenhall and Gottwald, like the proponents of the conquest and infiltration models of Israelite origins, are unable to explain significant social change embodied in the movement to statehood except by appeal to external forces.

If one begins with a formalistic definition of state, in essence what [[127]] the state became under David and Solomon, then it is natural that it appears to be diametrically opposed to emergent Israel. Premonarchic Israel defended itself on the basis of a decentralized village and sub-regional voluntary occasional militia supported by village production in order to preserve village sovereignty. Monarchic Israel, on the other hand, defended itself on the basis of a centralized palace standing army supported by village and state economic production designed to protect the royal family's sovereignty. If Israel is defined permanently and essentially in terms of its premonarchic arrangement thus categorically stated, then the monarchy will be viewed as an alien imposition, an excoriable departure, a morbid accretion, an awful violation of true Israel. The monarchy was, in a word, non-Israelite. It was the unlawful seizure of the nation by a minority who had forsaken their Israelite identity.

The whole question of the rise of the Israelite monarchy is in need of fundamental re-examination (cf. Flanagan 1981: 47). Whatever the reality of the Philistine threat—and we might characterize it as the catalyst to Israelite state formation—its portrayal as *the cause* of this transition, while concluding that the monarchy is alien to Israel, ignores the importance of internal developments and forces in combination with other external forces necessary for significant social change. It is commonplace for societies, or those in the positions of power who dictate and write history, to externalize crises and social change (see Adams 1974: 1). On the other hand, historians, social scientists and anthropologists are becoming ever more reluctant to attribute social change to catastrophic or major external events unless all internal stimuli have been discounted (see Kohl 1981: 103–104). More attention is being paid to the dynamic shifts and adaptations of internal patterns (Marfoe 1980: 34–35; Adams 1974: 1).

Clearly the state establishes the great economic advantage of a small class of urban elite officers, warriors, and land owners. In this respect the state represents a marked departure from the lesser degree of

stratification that may be posited for early Israel. The state of David and
Solomon turns Israel into a virtual imperium in its own right, with the
boundaries of its imperial influence extending many times over the earlier
heartland of Israel. The rapid amplification of the transition to monarchy,
from the modest court of Saul to the proverbial magnificence of Solomon
over a period of little more than a generation, magnifies the sense of the
state's departing from the "Israelite" norm. The tendency is to forget that
such amplification is itself the historical norm for emergent states. Finally,
much of the biblical literature with its "prophetic" point of view reinforces
the perception which indeed it introduces, that monarchy is an alien institution, "like the nations," not like Israel. As previously stated, if the question of the emergence of Israel has been too much determined by issues
of literary interpretation, then the question of the emergence of the monarchy has dealt too little with such issues in a truly critical way. [[128]] The
popular critique of the state that continues the prophetic analysis into our
own day and age, including the Marxian critique, is also valid. When ab-
solutized, however, its forms become less valid not more, and less analyt-
ically sharp. The prophetic literature of the Bible comes to us in the form
of state literature contained in the Scriptures of state churches: by itself
and in absolute form, its critique of the state lacks bite and is historically
superficial. The idealization of premonarchic Israel, furthermore, supports a wide spectrum of political and religious views today, both for and
against the state. There seems to be no single persuasive interpretation of
the current political meaning of premonarchic Israel.

All these factors and the perception of the dichotomy between Israel
the non-state and Israel the state which they support depend on limiting
the definition of the real Israel to a premonarchic static ideal with no reference to the inherent processive character of the emergence of the
monarchy and the points of continuity in the historical process that join
the monarchy not only with premonarchic Israel but also the very circumstances of its emergence. Such a limitation leaves many important
issues regarding early Israel's infrastructure and political economy unaddressed. We can scarcely make sense out of the development of the
monarchy in Israel without recognizing its continuities with early Israel.
Indeed, as already indicated, unless these continuities are recognized,
the origin of Israel itself is liable to be misunderstood.

Circumscription and the Limits on Early Israel

Before detailing the trends of early Israel's history that led relatively
directly to the monarchy, it will be useful to look briefly at the general
theory concerned with the emergence of states. The theory which is
most useful for conceptualizing the limits on early Israel's continuation

as a loose federation in the highlands of Palestine is Carneiro's theory of state origins which stresses the importance of environmental and social circumscription (cf. Hauer 1984).

Cohen (1978b: 35) claims that the decisive difference between pre-state polities, particularly chiefdoms, and states is the tendency to fission. Pre-state political systems have an inherent tendency to break up and form similar smaller units. Cohen (1978b: 56–57) goes on to show that such pre-state autonomies and chiefdoms can only tolerate a certain level of conflict before they either break up or fuse into new integrative institutions. One major question posed by Cohen's work is why pre-state polities that formed the basis of Israel fused rather than fissioned. It would seem that states emerge where such break-up is impossible or unacceptable, or where one chiefdom opens up new economic resources and thus acquires an advantage over all others.

There is considerable disagreement among political anthropologists [[129]] as to the specific causes or origins of the formation of the state (contrast Service 1978 and Fried 1978). The utilisation of the anthropological literature for the study of Israelite state origins is complicated by the fact that the major concentration is on the so-called "pristine" or "primitive" states, such as Egypt, Mesopotamia, China, the Indus Valley and Meso-America. Israel, by contrast, as Flanagan has already noted, was a secondary state formation. However, although the specific circumstances may differ, with the primary state acting upon the secondary state formation, both still appear to be in gradual process with discernible patterns (see Claessen and Skalník 1978: 620–21). Fried (1978: 37) also makes the point and adds the important observation that secondary states often use parts or all of the organisation of some prior state as a model for emulation and improvements. Similarly Kohl (1981: 112) points out that societies within historically interacting areas adopt basic organizational principles, not solely as a common solution to natural problems, but because they had been tried, tested and proven to work by earlier societies with which they were familiar.

The most important overall conclusion to be drawn from the extensive anthropological literature is that no one factor is sufficient or even consistently antecedent to state formation (Cohen 1978b: 30–70; Claessen and Skalník 1978: 629). This casts further upon the standard interpretation of the origin of the Israelite state as due entirely to Philistine pressure. Whatever triggers the process off sets in motion a multiple and complex feedback system involving and acting upon all forms of economic, social, political and religious organizations (Frick 1985; Cohen 1978a: 15; Claessen and Skalník 1978: 624–25). It is for this reason that, despite wide geographical and temporal differences, similar patterns of development can be discerned and strikingly similar end results occur. Examples include Egypt, Mesopotamia, China, Inca Peru, and pre-colonial West Africa (Cohen 1978b: 70).

A more developed approach would need to take account of other important environmental and social factors, rather than concentrating upon the Philistine threat, which on the basis of the anthropological literature must be viewed as a necessary, though not sufficient, cause of the Israelite state. Although pre-state polities appear to have an inherent tendency to fission or disintegrate, particularly through conflict, states develop where such disintegration is either impossible or unacceptable (Cohen 1978b: 57). The question remains: why did Israel not disintegrate or succumb to external force?

A modified version of Carneiro's argument that circumscription has an important role to play in state origins may help to illuminate this problem. Circumscription theory highlights the environmental and/or social factors which operate as a counterweight against the tendency of a society to disintegrate.

⟦130⟧ Carneiro took over the notion of "social circumscription" from N. A. Chagnon. Carneiro's original theory held that social and environmental circumscription intensified warfare and this acted as an impetus towards statehood. It is not simply a notion of warfare as the prime mover, as many have argued, since he notes (1970: 734) that warfare was a necessary, though not sufficient, condition for the rise of the state. His model is an attempt to explain why states arose where they did as a response to specific cultural, demographic and ecological conditions. Haas (1982: 135) cites some material which questions Carneiro's conclusion whereby the conflict was within valleys rather than between valleys. However, this might only be the first stage of the process of centralization within a valley before conflict spreads between valleys.

The geographical setting of Israel in the central highland of southern Palestine was effectively circumscribed by environmental factors, especially semi-arid steppe and desert regions. This was particularly true of the Judahite highlands, where the first stable state emerged and eventually took over the rest of the Israelite highland. The compact rock plateau that forms the Judahite highland was well provided with natural defences to the west, south and east. The soil distribution gives relatively shallow but fertile terra rossas throughout most of the highland. The deeper alluvial soils and pale rendzinas are also found on moderate slopes in the valleys. The Shephelah has the most easily workable pale rendzinas of moderate depth, with pockets of alluvium and grummsols in the wider valleys. The extreme south and southwest are adversely affected by aridity and form a semi-steppe zone (Thompson 1979: 49). An understanding of the environment is important, not as mere background to the picture, but in order to outline what kinds of possibilities or restrictions faced a community in adapting to its surroundings during several generations of agricultural and community development.

The loose federation of groups composing Israel was socially circumscribed by the network of lowland city-states, the incursions of hostile nomadic raiders (the Bible names the Midianites and Amalekites), and Philistine pressure from the Mediterranean littoral. It is the combination of environmental and social circumscription with other internal and external factors that provided the impetus to the formation of the Israelite state.

The standard interpretations of the rise of the monarchy, regardless of the position adopted on the origins of Israel, fail to pose or answer the major question of why it is this particular area and its population which centralizes and introduces an Israelite monarchy. Why is it the incorporation of the highlands which succeeds in subduing and incorporating into its own political structure the surrounding, especially lowland, areas despite the seeming military and economic advantages of urban Canaan or the Philistine pentapolis? The monarchy, far from representing some [[131]] alien cancer in the Israelite body politic, is fundamentally determined by the nature of the origins of Israel in the hillcountry and is the result of internal stimuli in response to social and environmental circumscription. It is not the case that there is a straight choice between two polar opposites but rather that pre-state societies and the state involve differing degrees of sharing, stratification and exploitation. For this reason, the origins of Israel in Palestine and the development of the monarchy need to be studied in tandem rather than in opposition. The emergence of an Israelite state also needs to be set in the wider context of the as yet little understood process which saw conflicting and almost simultaneous state formations in Edom, Moab and Ammon. The process culminating in an Israelite monarchy is inherent in the emergence of premonarchic Israel, though by no means inevitable, nor is it wholly unique in the patterns of Palestinian history (as the example of Dahir al-ʿUmar in the eighteenth century shows) or the even wider context of state origins.

The importance of understanding the formation of an Israelite state in terms of the preceding economic decline and systems collapse is borne out by Renfrew's general study of systems collapse: "The model propounded here suggests that increasing marginality, whether arising from an increased population, circumscription or whatever, may be one of the preconditions for the sudden catastrophic formation of a state society. Intriguingly it is likewise a necessary precondition for the catastrophic collapse of a highly centered political system" (1979: 499).

Trends toward Monarchy

How exactly did circumscription work in Israel's case? The history of Israel's decentralized, low production, and low military cost hinterland polity is the history of increasing production based more on expansion than intensification, increasing population, and increasing stratification. Gradually expansion became less cost-effective, growth depended more and more on intensification, the threat from urban based militaries in the lowland became greater and the cost of conquest more attractive to them. To survive, the hinterland polity of Israel was forced to shift to institutionalized intensification. This was the switch to the monarchy which when it occurred was a formal political redefinition of product distribution and labour arrangements carried through in order to regularize the intensification of productive relations and processes, to support increased defence costs. Though formally this shift occurred at a moment in time, through the establishment of royal sovereignty over arable, it was more generally one moment in a lengthy train of events and changing circumstances.

The reversal of some of the primary factors that led to the emergence of Israel set in immediately. If the emergence of the monarchy is in any sense a paradox, the paradox is to be located at Israel's birth rather than [[132]] in some premature death at the hands of a party of kingmakers. And in fact the monarchy was not a paradox, as has been intimated, but the result of the same major shift in highland infrastructure that marked the success of Israel's earliest years.

We can characterize this shift in the following way:

Economically, whereas Israel emerged in the midst of a shrinking economic base, from the beginning it grew steadily on an expanding economic base. In other words, the frontier, such that it was, gradually disappeared.

Socially, whereas Israel emerged in the midst of a diminished socioeconomic stratification, from the beginning it was characterized by increasing stratification.

Politically, whereas Israel emerged in the midst of a decentralized polity, from the beginning it included within it expanding groups whose interests lay in eventual centralization.

The tendency in histories of Israel has been to set the monarchy in opposition to the first set of tendencies, the ones that roughly identify the circumstances of Israel's emergence. Instead, or in addition, the monarchy ought to be seen as a continuation of the second set, which more accurately describe its growth. Of course, the opposed tendencies are not exactly equivalent, and thus do not contradict each other. The shrinking economic base refers primarily to trade and the expanding base primarily to agriculture. Diminished stratification refers to the exclusion of top and bottom in the highly fluid and mobile context of hinterland populations, and increasing stratification to the filling out of the vertical dimensions of the socioeconomic pyramid in the context of the relatively high commitment to settled, stationary village life.

One major factor that acts as a stimulus to this commitment, previously overlooked in favour of the all-encompassing Philistine threat, is the nature of highland farming strategies. Terracing was the most important technique for opening up marginal land in the highland, since this preserved shallow soils, removed rocks from the ground to provide terrace walls and prevented erosion on the steep slopes. Terracing demanded long-term investment. Terraces needed continual maintenance or they rapidly disintegrated. Tree crops like the vine, olive, and fig, furthermore, were one mainstay of highland agriculture. It required ten years for the olive to bear fruit and up to fifteen to twenty years for it to reach optimum production. Thus both terracing and tree crops, as Marfoe has pointed out, called for residential stability. This would have been a crucial factor in the complex forces which resisted disintegration and led to centralization under an Israelite monarchy. This process of compaction meant that "disintegration" was not possible (see also Frick 1985).

From its inception Israelite society and economy were committed to expansion and growth. We have already touched on a number of ways this [[133]] is so, but perhaps we should look at its economic, social and political development a bit more thoroughly in order to specify how precisely Israel did change over time in ways that led, intrinsically and through the process of circumscription, to the monarchy.

Expansion and Intensification of the Economic Base. The expansion of agriculture and the growth of population, supporting each other hand in hand, were the foundations of the adaptive success of early Israel. There existed powerful and uninhibited practical and ideological incentives for each. Systematic fallowing was weak or nonexistent. There is some evidence for alternate cropping with legumes, and the droppings from flocks were usable as manure. Enough land was apparently available that careful husbanding of cultivation was not required.

With respect to potential agricultural carrying capacity, Israel began with the capacity for major enlargement. The switch to agriculture by itself raised the carrying capacity of the highland, especially areas newly settled by the villagers of early Israel, far above what it had been. The premonarchic period is essentially a way to categorize the period it took for the growth in population to exceed the point of diminishing returns assuming a relatively higher standard of living. As J. K. Galbraith has written concerning poverty, "the law of secular diminishing returns can be indefinitely postponed in its operation in the rich (industrialized) country. It still works inexorably in the poor rural country" (1980: 53).

Eventually this law of diminishing returns set in and continued to work its disadvantageous effect. Arable was depleted, more marginal lands brought under cultivation, tougher forests attacked, and more labour was required to convert lands to production through terracing, provision of water in some cases, and similar tasks. Once the demographic faucet was turned on, furthermore, it was difficult to turn off. Although it is possible to point to traditions and institutions relating to Israel's need for demographic balance, these measures were limited in practice by the continued opportunities that existed for economic expansion and intensification and by the cultural expectations aroused by Israel's earliest experience.

It was only a matter of time before the effects of depletion and overpopulation would lead to the political forms created by landed interests for the furtherance of their power. Along with ecological pressure in favour of the cultivation of the vine and olives, richer people, those with more land, had less incentive to grow food and more to grow cash crops for market. It is impossible to understand early Israel without realizing that the market component of its product was continuously increasing, and that there was a probable correlation between expansion and market avoidance on the one hand and intensification and market acceptance on [[134]] the other hand, spurred on by the following factors which worked in combination: agglomeration of lands, an increase in *mulk*-like over *miri*-like holdings for a few, the shift from expansion to intensification, and from local consumption to urban marketing which hastened the social integration of wealthier Israelite farmers with residual urban elites in the highland cities. (The terms *mulk* and *miri* have been used in Palestine to refer respectively, to freehold land usually intensively cultivated, and to village lands nominally in state ownership and typically farmed as arable.) There was no way these trends could be halted given the decentralized forms which were Israel's initial advantage. The development of the monarchy shows that at most they may have been restrained. There is little likelihood that village arable was periodically redistributed, thus removing that brake on intensification, and the expendability of household *mulk* property gave a great potential for household improvement through intensification available to nearly every family.

Because an upswing in interregional trade throughout the eastern Mediterranean was one factor in the economic growth of Israel, why did the usually more dominant areas not benefit to a greater extent than Israel and engulf that newer political economy at the earliest opportunity? One answer is of course that in time they did. Whatever the degree of autonomy exercised by the highland Israelite monarchy—and autonomy in name might not always have meant autonomy in fact—with the death of the Israelite and Judahite states Palestine was again economically fully integrated into surrounding riverine regions. The answer for early Israel, however, has to do with certain features of circumscription as they worked themselves out in Israel. The lower level of interregional trade meant the higher value of what was traded, and this higher value had a correspondingly greater effect on Israel's lower overall economic level. Israel was of course well positioned to influence and benefit from trade. In the decades following the breakdown in trade, what traders who remained would have been looking for alternative trade routes, and Palestine's inland ways offered one possibility. As long as a deal could be struck with these less controlled people, goods could transit rather than being siphoned off (see Fritz 1981: 66; and Aharoni, Fritz, and Kempinski 1975: 108–9 for evidence of extensive trade relations in marginal areas).

The process of compaction was reinforced by the fact that the limits of the marginal areas available for agriculture were relatively quickly reached. With such tight environmental and growing social circumscription, the opportunities for the peasant agriculturalists to escape the increasing pressures of intensification and stratification were drastically reduced. Fried suggests that the potential for stratification was already present in egalitarian societies, simply waiting for the right conditions to make themselves felt. Once the population expanded to the limits of the land, there developed a chronically precarious balance between population [[135]] and food resources. Under these conditions, the rise of kingship may have been largely a self-generating process. Furthermore, the inherent fragility of the highland community based upon such short-term objectives increased the possibility that a change in circumstances would lead to greater centralization. The reintroduction of commercial trade throughout the eastern Mediterranean saw the re-emergence of Egyptian imperial power to the southwest as well as the development of more local regional political and economic centres such as Phoenicia, Edom, Ammon (cf. 1 Samuel 11) and the Aramaean kingdom of Syria (cf. Halpern 1981b: 84). The gradual development of such external pressures from urban Canaan, nomadic raiders, the Philistines and re-emerging or emerging regional and interregional political powers meant that there were numerous social and environmental factors acting and reacting in a multiple feedback process which gave impetus to centralization. The consequent strengthening of the position of various leaders or chiefs and the potential benefits of protection from external threat, along with the development of a system of economic redistribution, led Israel into chiefdom and ultimately to a centralized state. The largest effect of the gradual upswing in trade in the eleventh century however was not felt until the time when the monarchy actually did emerge.

Increasing Socioeconomic Stratification. Although the population of early Israel may be described correctly as more socioeconomically homogeneous than the typical population of a Palestinian city-state of the same period, it is essential not to overdraw such homogeneity. The concept is more relevant to contrasting Israel's emergent population with the highly class-stratified population of a city-state than to the internal constituency of early Israel. The idea that socioeconomic stratification increased in early Israel is based on nothing more than the assumption that over time, and in the midst of gradually expanding interregional trade, socioeconomic differences present at the outset would be magnified rather than erased or ameliorated. This is particularly true given the comparatively marginal level of Israel's town and village economy, in which even a slight advantage in land holdings or commercially based wealth would make a large difference. As mentioned above, furthermore, under circumstances where initially interregional trade was sparse, many items that a few Israelites would have access to would have that much more value.

The socioeconomic stratification of the monarchy, we would argue, was latent in an early Israelite stratification that had a number of interrelated facets. The subregional diversification and isolation in early Israel was greater than is nearly always suggested in the literature. Even within the subregions themselves, it is a reasonable guess that villages if not towns were isolated from one another. The ethnographic parallels hardly [[136]] allow any other construction. This social isolation permitted the ongoing economic diversification of the different subregions based on the varying degrees of contact with trading routes and centres and their own productive advantages. Proximity to urban centres and trade routes would give some Israelites more opportunity than others to sell some of their produce, or their labour or military service. The marginality of the Israelite heartland must not be thought of as automatically implying distance from whatever commerce there was. In many cases, such as the southern steppe, trade routes lay in the very midst of the marginal lands. A population along marginal routes, furthermore, under the circumstances stood to gain from the desire of traders to find alternate trade routes to the ones so recently shut down. This advantage holds whether the population uses its military readiness to intercept the trade or its marginal basis to convey it more efficiently. Distance from urban centres might reduce such commercial pressures, but the greater socioeconomic equilibrium within areas so removed from commerce would represent a long-term disadvantage as long as other segments of Israelite society were gradually expanding their participation in commerce.

The effect of subregional variability on the increase in stratification was compounded by other factors. Different families, groups, and areas had different relationships with nomadic groups, some of whom would have been particularly well-positioned to participate in what commerce there was. Some would benefit more than others from raiding along trade routes or controlling passes. It has been pointed out that this might be one of the reasons for the importance of the territory of Benjamin (cf. Halpern 1981b: 86). Some areas paid tribute to urban or nomad elites while others did not, so that different areas bore the burden of this kind of taxation, which did not cease with the formation of Israel, to different degrees. As villages fissioned, complex relations of dominance and subordination among them developed as a consequence of time and the vicissitudes of growth.

Each village would have its peculiar internal history of increasing stratification. Even slight initial differences would tend to be magnified over time by the random development of the economic careers of the different families, dependent on varying factors of production and economic relations. Years of hardship are known to have a particularly drastic effect in such situations. As long as there was work for more labour and little limit on fields for the taking, the success of a family was limited by their relative good fortune in reproduction. The bearing and raising of sons bestowed a disproportionate advantage. As richer farmers emerged, they grew increasingly for the market and thus improved their position as a creditor class within the town and village. This kind of opportunity was particularly present in the areas near the old highland cities, which [[137]] already combined traditionally more secure fields with the proximity of urban markets.

Halpern accurately describes the relationship among the different regional and socioeconomic sectors of early Israel as "loose, sectionally defined, and probably in constant flux" (1981b: 75). The agricultural heartland and foundation of early Israel benefitted least from this inherent socioeconomic variability. The basis of early Israel's general prosperity and therefore its prevailing ideology, namely its agricultural expansion, was quite distinct from the simultaneous basis of economic advantage in early Israel, namely agricultural intensification going hand in hand with some form of participation in commerce, conversely the targets of critical ideology. The inevitable search for economic advantage, of which the emergence of Israel was itself one consequence, in the context of circumscription led inevitably to the amplified stratification of the monarchic state.

Biblical indications of socioeconomic stratification include the stories of the premonarchic "judges," or subregional rulers. These figures are worth looking at for a moment, because they are not usually adduced in support of stratification in early Israel (cf. Whitelam 1979: 59–60). Not all the elements of these stories go back in origin to premonarchic times, but together these stories are consistent with the picture being suggested here. All these rulers were, in the end, rich. One group were established villagers or townsmen, another bandits.

The Deuteronomist gave notice but little elaboration to one group of "minor" rulers who were wealthy enough to have large families and were situated where they could take advantage of whatever trade was developing. In the context of early Israel they apparently represented a source of relative stability and so were of little interest to the Deuteronomist, who preferred to downplay traditions that did not illustrate the kind of social disruption that a strong centralized monarchy was good for preventing. Abdon is said to have had 40 sons, 30 grandsons and 70 asses (Judg 12:13–15). With that many asses he could transport a considerable quantity of goods and produce. Ibzan had 30 sons and 30 daughters, probably his sons wives, for each of whom he was able to provide a suitable bride price (Judg 12:8–10). He lived in Bethlehem, an Israelite town that no doubt prospered from its proximity to the erstwhile trading point Jerusalem. Jair of Gilead, a frontier area just off the main routes to Damascus, had 30 sons, 30 asses and 30 towns and villages (Judg 10:3–5). This clan head must have been one of the most powerful and influential individuals known to the greater Palestine region for a century or more. There is no reason to doubt that disproportionate wealth like his ramified throughout Gilead, and that most if not all Palestinian subregions contained such elite clan networks. Caleb of Hebron is pictured making grants of land [[138]] from his urban situation (Judg 1:11–15). Admittedly this tradition is as likely as any to have been edited by a monarchic scribe. Recent writers on Israelite history have been aware of the stratified nature of these rulers. Halpern speaks of "entrenched elites" (1918b: 63) and a "wealthy warrior class" (88). Bright himself describes Shamgar, albeit for slightly speculative reasons, as "presumably . . . a city king of Beth-Anath in Galilee." He could as likely have been a Galilean nomad sheikh, but the socioeconomic implications would be the same. We should perhaps think of Saul as belonging, at the beginning of his career, to this category of ruler.

Writers like Bright are equally aware of the bandit nature of the "major" rulers who for the Deuteronomist illustrate the kind of social disruption and subregional hostility kings were useful for preventing. Bright calls Jephthah a "bandit" (1981: 178) and a "Gileadite freebooter, an Apiru" (p. 181), and Samson a "rogue" (p. 178). These are the rulers who dominate the Deuteronomist's account of political turmoil prior to the institution of the state. The norm is for these to threaten to become king, and eventually one of them, David, does. They tend to be opposed, as David was opposed by Saul, by established leaders of the first type: the men of Gideon's town, the sons of Gideon in Schechem, the men of Succoth and Penuel, and the Judahites who turned Samson over to the Philistines in order to remove him as a source of friction between themselves and their Philistine neighbours. From the perspective of the Deuteronomist, the resistance of the good bandit David against Saul was an omen of Josiah's ascendancy over the established sheikhs, elders and other landed notables in his realm.

Among other indications in the biblical literature of stratification in early Israel are the traditions about town and village elders and the continued allowance of debt service. The elders would have been among the wealthier men of a town or village, whose influence was based upon, among other things, the ownership of greater amounts of land and capital than usual and the partial distribution of these in credit. Laws governing debt service, to the degree they refer to the premonarchic period, demonstrate the unequal distribution of capital (cf. 1 Sam 8:16 and 25:10).

It is important not to mistake the restraint of stratification which can be posited for early Israel for its successful suppression. The indications of an ideology of restraint are at the same time the clearest indications of the prevalence of its object, the existence of stratification. The monarchy that eventually emerged in Israel was based on a social structure whose stratification went back directly to Israel's beginnings.

Increasing Political Centralization. Political centralization increased at an accelerated pace during the [[139]] second century of Israel's existence. Centralization was the means by which an emergent landed class attempted to preserve the power and privilege created for them by their increasing wealth. Centralization was eventually perceived to serve the interests of these few rather than the many. There is evidence in the Davidic period texts, therefore, that centralization culminated in the monarchic redefinition of ultimate village tenure only after a struggle. This was a struggle within Israel between an increasingly dominant group of larger land owners whose primary social bonds had gradually shifted from the village to the regional level and a much larger subordinate group of non-wealthy villagers whose political economic integrity was being threatened by economic developments in Israel. The interests of the villages of Israel were represented at the regional level by the rural priesthood. Thus the struggle appears in the sources as between wealthier landowners and the priesthood. (Halpern 1981b, may be the best treatment of the emergence of kingship in such terms; see, e.g., pp. 76–79).

The priestly political representatives of the villages could not equal their landed opponents in solidarity. The villages with their priesthoods were intrinsically parochial, and the closest thing to a national priesthood had too many interests that coincided with those of the landed themselves. That the priesthood across the board was hereditary shows that it was based on some form of land tenure. The most likely situation is that the priestly families serving at shrines located in regional market and religious centres like Shiloh, who might have spearheaded a united villager movement, instead increased, through the advantages of their position, their land holdings disproportionately over time. If the traditions about the house of Eli are an accurate indication, the priests' espousal of villagers' rights was undercut by a tendency within their ranks for those who held hereditary offices at regional shrines to see their interests better served by the landowners than the villagers and their local priestly representatives. Bright's one-dimensional account is typical of historians who have not looked deeply into the socioeconomic tensions present: "Whatever Samuel thought of Saul, the remnants of the amphictyonic priesthood rallied round him and accompanied him in the field (1 Sam 14:3, 18)" (1981: 190). With the establishment of the house of Zadok by Solomon, however, all other priestly groups, whatever their allegiance had been in this struggle, were thrown into an opposing group representing rural and decentralizing values.

It would be inaccurate to describe this struggle simply as a class conflict. Superimposed upon the class-oriented grouping just outlined were the subregional clan, tribal, and party alliances endemic to Palestine. These find clearest expression in the sources in terms of the conflict between the houses of Saul and David, but this Davidic version of the situation no doubt schematized what in actuality was a complex [[140]] matrix of special interests and their realization in political groupings. The evidence is not available, however, for anything other than a theoretical statement of such complexities.

The pressures of circumscription contributed to political centralization in premonarchic Israel through two basic trends. First, as the increasing cost and burden of defence fell disproportionately upon the emergent landed class, they sought the means to shift these costs back down the socioeconomic scale. Second, highland participation in the interregional economy gradually came to be dominated by the few wealthiest families. These saw increasing advantage to themselves in integrating with the lowland political economies. The bulk of the emergent landed class, however, sought the means to prevent such a development. A single political economy ruled from the lowland would bring a considerable loss of power to the highland landed as a group. All but the wealthiest of the highland landed therefore sought the means to preserve control over their economy in the highland. The means to both these ends was for a sufficient number of highland landed to unite and appoint one of their number sovereign over the arable of Israel. With this crucial step—the climax of long-term trends—the monarchy came into existence.

Though these trends are theortical, they can be analyzed in slightly more detail. Basic to the political process of the creation of the monarchy was the relationship among the total product of Israel, the cost of defending Israelite control of that product, and the distribution of that cost amongst the people of Israel. These are the same prime factors used for analyzing Israel from its beginnings. We have already seen that the total product, though low in comparison to certain lowland areas, was increasing. There are reasons to believe that, as this product increased, the cost of defending control over it increased at a greater rate. In other words, as the total product increased, the percentage of it necessary for defence also increased. As the product increased, it became increasingly attractive to the lowland elites, apparently particularly the Philistines. As the standard histories note, over time the Philistines developed both the incentive and the means to undertake the conquest of the Israelite highland. With the gradual expansion in trade, moreover, the Philistines themselves became politically more centralized and enlarged their lowland dominion. Evidently for the first time in Israel's history they faced a militarily superior enemy on virtually all borders and deep within their highland heartland.

Both the regionalization of Israel's defence and its upgrading with whatever metal weaponry was available fell predominately to the emergent landed class with its superior regional ties and wealth. Moreover, although in one sense this class was better able to bear these costs and received the greater benefit from their expenditure, because defence in [[141]] Israel was traditionally conceived on the basis of clans and protective associations rather than the extent of land holdings—person power rather than wealth—the wealthier families who could contribute more sons to defence felt the greater burden. In sum, those in Israel who were increasingly called upon to bear the greater defence burden, and who in one sense were better positioned to do so, were at the same time increasingly able, through their power, to shift this burden back down to the village smallholders. Seen in this light, monarchy was a means of "redistributing" the cost of defence that increased along with but at a greater rate than the total product of Israel. The internal dynamics of this redistribution was veiled at the time, as it has been in the historiography of Israel, by the overwhelming consciousness of the Philistine threat.

The second trend saw the emergent landed class attempting to retain amongst themselves control of their participation in trade rather than allowing control to transfer, through the machinations of the wealthiest of them, to the lowland. There is little if any hint in written sources that the highland landed were involved in such trade in the first place. This bias of the sources, however, should occasion no surprise given the tendency of elites to externalize threat. The almost exclusive attention given to the Philistines in the sources, which come from the Davidic state, results from the same tendency. There is no reason not to take the comparative view and assume that the pattern of highland elite participation in interregional trade applies to the emergent elite of eleventh century B.C.E. Israel, whether they themselves conceived of such activity in this way or not.

The monarchy represented, therefore, the means by which a subgroup of emergent landed elite in Israel imposed greater costs of national defence upon village smallholders and retained political control over their participation in trade among themselves. The creation of the monarchy by a privileged subgroup of Israelites represented little threat to themselves. The right of the state to redistribute lands functioned to the advantage of those who already bore a larger share of defence. The threat posed by such a right was overwhelmingly greater for the more numerous village smallholders. Still, there was little incentive for the original kingmakers to give Saul a great deal of power. The expansion of the monarchy was mostly a result of internal forces let loose by the initial political transmutation.

The concentration of lands which the monarchy sealed produced a jump in the intensification of agriculture on the lands of the wealthier class dedicated to commercial viticulture and tree crops. Partly in response to this pressure, poorer farmers leaned further in the direction of pastoralism. This bifurcation of production set the stage for the emergence of David and his band as a force in Judahite and then Israelite politics. David gradually came to control the marginal pastoral lands [[142]] along the entire crescent of the southern border and to use this control for the benefit of southern farmers already furthest from the influence of the house of Saul.

Conclusion

The tentative reconstruction advanced above is an attempt to suggest some possible lines of inquiry in order to develop the discussion of the rise of the monarchy beyond the standard approaches. The reconstruction necessarily rests upon a number of broad generalizations. It is less concerned with what happened in the sense of a merely descriptive or chronological history, but rather with why it happened. In order to explain why social change takes place, it is necessary to search for broad patterns and generalizations within a theoretical framework. Only then is it possible to test the hypothesis more rigorously against all available data and to choose among competing reconstructions. This type of analytical, inter-disciplinary approach to the history of Israel is one way of ensuring that the all important dialogue between past and present is maintained.

Works Consulted

Adams, Robert McC.
    1974   The Mesopotamian Social Landscape: A View from the Frontier. Pp. 1–11 in *Reconstructing Complex Societies,* ed. C. B. Moore. Cambridge: ASOR.
Aharoni, Yohanan; Fritz, Volkmar; and Kempinski, Aaron
    1975   Excavations at Tel Masos (Kh. el-Meshah), Preliminary Report on the Second Season, 1974. *Tel Aviv* 2: 97–124.
Barr, James
    1980   Story and History in Biblical Theology. Pp. 1–17 in Explorations in Theology 7. London: SCM.
Blenkinsopp, Joseph
    1977   *Prophecy and Canon.* Notre Dame: University of Notre Dame Press.
Bloch, Marc
    1954   *The Historian's Craft.* Manchester: Manchester University Press.
Braudel, Fernand
    1972   *The Mediterranean and the Mediterranean World in the Age of Philip II.* Vols. 1–2. London: Collins.
    1980   *On History.* London: Weidenfeld and Nicholson.
    1984   *Civilization and Capitalism 15th–18th Century, Volume III: The Perspective of the World.* London: Collins.
Bright, John
    1981   *A History of Israel.* 3d ed. Philadelphia: Westminster.

Buccellati, Giorgio
    1967   *Cities and Nations of Ancient Syria.* Rome: Istituto di Studi del Vicino Oriente.
Carneiro, Robert L.
    1970   A Theory of the Origins of the State. *Science* 169: 733–38.
Chaney, Marvin L.
    1983   Ancient Palestinian Peasant Movements and the Formation of Pre-monarchic Israel. Pp. 39–90 in *Palestine in Transition,* ed. D. N. Freedman and D. F. Graf. Sheffield: Almond.
Childs, Brevard S.
    1979   *Introduction to the Old Testament as Scripture.* Philadelphia: Fortress.
Claessen, Henri
    1978   The Early State: A Structural Approach. Pp. 533–96 in *The Early State,* ed. H. Claessen and P. Skalník. The Hague: Mouton.
Claessen, Henri, and Skalník, Peter
    1978   Limits: Beginning and End of the Early State. Pp. 619–35 in *The Early State,* ed. H. Claessen and P. Skalník. The Hague: Mouton.
Cohen, Ronald
    1978a   Introduction. Pp. 1–20 in *Origins of the State,* ed. R. Cohen and E. R. Service. Philadelphia: Institute for the Study of Human Issues.
    1978b   State Origins: A Reappraisal. Pp. 31–75 in *The Early State,* ed. H. Claessen and P. Skalník. The Hague: Mouton.
Collins, John J.
    1982   The "Historical Character" of the Old Testament in Recent Biblical Theology. *CBQ* 41: 185–204.
Cutin, Philip D.
    1984   *Cross-Cultural Trade in World History.* Cambridge: Cambridge University Press.
Dever, William G.
    1980   New Vistas on the EBIV ("MBI") Horizon in Syria-Palestine. *BASOR* 237: 35–64.
Febvre, Lucien
    1973   *A New Kind of History and Other Essays.* New York: Harper.
Flanagan, James W.
    1981   Chiefs in Israel. *JSOT* 20: 47–73. [[Reprinted in this volume, pp. 311–34]]
Frick, Frank S.
    1985   *The Formation of the State in Ancient Israel: A Survey of Models and Theories.* Decatur, GA: Almond.
Frick, Frank S., and Gottwald, Norman K.
    1975   The Social World of Ancient Israel. Pp. 165–77 in *SBL 1975: Seminar Papers.* SBLSP 1. Missoula, Mont.: Scholars Press.
Fried, Morton H.
    1978   "The State, the Chicken, and the Egg; or, What Came First?" Pp. 35–47 in *Origins of the State,* ed. R. Cohen and E. R. Service. Philadelphia: Institute for the Study of Human Issues.

Fritz, Volkmar
1981   The Israelite "Conquest" in the Light of Recent Excavations at Khirbet el-Meshash. *BASOR* 241: 61–73.

Galbraith, John K.
1980   *The Nature of Mass Poverty.* Harmondsworth: Penguin.

Geus, C. H. J. de
1976   *The Tribes of Israel.* Assen/Amsterdam: Van Gorcum.

Gonen, Rivka
1984   Urban Canaan in the Late Bronze Period. *BASOR* 253: 61–73.

Gottwald, Norman K.
1979   *The Tribes of Yahweh.* Maryknoll: Orbis.

Haas, Jonathan
1982   *The Evolution of the Prehistoric State.* New York: Columbia University Press.

Halpern, Baruch
1981a   *The Constitution of the Monarchy.* Chico: Scholars Press.
1981b   The Uneasy Compromise: Israel between League and Monarchy. Pp. 59–96 in *Traditions in Transformation,* ed. B. Halpern and J. D. Levenson. Winona Lake: Eisenbrauns.
1983   *The Emergence of Israel.* Chico: Scholars Press.

Harris, Marvin
1980   *Cultural Materialism: The Struggle for a Science of Culture.* New York: Vintage.

Hauer, Chris, Jr.
1984   From Alt to Anthropology: The Rise of the Israelite State. Unpublished paper for the Society of Biblical Literature, Southeastern Regional Meeting, March.

Herion, Gary A.
1981   The Role of Historical Narrative in Biblical Thought: The Tendencies Underlying Old Testament Historiography. *JSOT* 21: 25–57.

Herrmann, Siegfried
1981   *A History of Israel in Old Testament Times.* 2d ed. Philadelphia: Fortress.

Hodder, Ian
1982   *The Present Past.* London: Batsford.

Horsley, Richard A.
1981   Ancient Jewish Banditry and the Revolt against Rome, A.D. 66–70 *CBQ* 43: 409–32.

Kohl, Philip D.
1981   Materialist Approaches in Prehistory. *Annual Review of Anthropology* 10: 89–118.

Lenski, Gerhard
1966   *Power and Privilege.* New York: McGraw-Hill.
1976   History and Social Change. *American Journal of Sociology* 82: 548–64.

Lenski, Gerhard, and Lenski, Jean
1982   *Human Societies: An Introduction to Macrosociology.* 4th ed. New York: McGraw-Hill.

Lewis, Ian M.
  1968   *History and Social Anthropology.* London: Tavistock.
Liverani, M.
  1973   The Amorites. Pp. 100–133 in *Peoples in Old Testament Times*, ed. D. J.
            Wiseman. Oxford: Clarendon.
Loyn, Henry R.
  1980   Marc Bloch. Pp. 121–35 in *The Historian at Work*, ed. J. Cannon. Lon-
            don: Allen and Unwin.
Marfoe, Leon
  1980   The Integrative Transformation: Patterns of Socio-Economic Organ-
            isation in Southern Syria. *BASOR* 234: 1–42.
Mayes, A. D. H.
  1977   The Period of the Judges and the Rise of the Monarchy. Pp. 285–331
            in *Israelite and Judaean History*, ed. J. Hayes and J. M. Miller. Philadel-
            phia: Westminster.
  1983   *The Story of Israel between the Settlement and Exile.* London: SCM.
Mazar, Benjamin
  1971   The Philistines and Their Wars with Israel. Pp. 164–79 in *The World
            History of the Jewish People. First Series: Ancient Times. Volume III Judges.*
            London: Allen.
Mendenhall, George E.
  1961   Biblical History in Transition. Pp. 32–53 in *The Bible and the Ancient
            Near East*, ed. G. E. Wright. Garden City: Doubleday.
  1975   The Monarchy. *Int* 29: 155–70.
  1976   "Change and Decay All around I See": Conquest, Covenant and *The
            Tenth Generation. BA* 39: 152–57.
  1983   Ancient Israel's Hyphenated History. Pp. 91–103 in *Palestine in Tran-
            sition*, ed. D. N. Freedman and D. F. Graf. Sheffield: Almond.
Meyers, Carol
  1983   Procreation, Production, and Protection: Male-Female Balance in Early
            Israel. *JAAR* 51: 569–93. [Reprinted in this volume, pp. 489–514]
Miller, J. Maxwell
  1977   The Israelite Occupation of Canaan. Pp. 213–84 in *Israelite and
            Judaean History*, ed. J. Hayes and J. M. Miller. Philadelphia: Westmin-
            ster.
  1982   Approaches to the Bible through History and Archaeology: Biblical
            History as a Discipline. *BA* 45: 211–16.
Noth, Martin
  1960   *The History of Israel.* London: Black.
Plumb, John Harold
  1969   *The Death of the Past.* London: Macmillan.
Price, Barbara J.
  1980   The Truth Is Not in Accounts but in Account Books: On the Episte-
            mological Status of History. Pp. 155–80 in *Beyond the Myths of Culture*,
            ed. E. Ross. New York: Academic.
Rainey, Anson F.
  1983   The Biblical Shephelah in Judah. *BASOR* 251: 1–22.

Ramsey, George
   1982   *The Quest for the Historical Israel.* London: SCM.

Renfrew, Colin
   1973   *Social Archaeology: An Inaugural Lecture.* Southampton: University of Southampton.
   1979   Systems Collapse as Social Transformation: Catastrophe and Anastrophe in Early State Societies. Pp. 481–506 in *Transformations: Mathematical Approaches to Culture Change*, ed. C. Renfrew and K. Cooke. New York: Academic.

Rowton, M. B.
   1973a   Autonomy and Nomadism in Western Asia. *Or* 42: 247–58.
   1973b   Urban Autonomy in a Nomadic Environment. *JNES* 32: 201–15.
   1974   Enclosed Nomadism. *Journal of the Economic and Social History of the Orient* 17: 1–30.
   1976   Dimorphic Structure and Topology. *OrAnt* 15: 17–31.

Sanders, James A.
   1972   *Torah and Canon.* Philadelphia: Fortress.

Sasson, Jack
   1981   On Choosing Models for Recreating Israelite Pre-monarchic History. *JSOT* 21: 3–24.

Service, Elman R.
   1978   Classical and Modern Theories of Government. Pp. 21–34 in *Origins of the State*, ed. R. Cohen and E. R. Service. Philadelphia: Institute for the Study of Human Issues.

Tadmor, Hayim
   1979   The Decline of Empires in Western Asia ca. 1200 B.C.E. Pp. 1–14 in *Symposia*, ed. F. Cross. Cambridge: ASOR.

Thompson, Thomas L.
   1978a   Historical Notes on "Israel's Conquest of Palestine: A Peasants' Rebellion?" *JSOT* 7: 20–27.
   1978b   The Background to the Patriarchs: A Reply to William Dever and Malcolm Clark. *JSOT* 9: 2–43.
   1979   *The Settlement of Palestine in the Bronze Age.* Wiesbaden: Reichert.
   1980   History and Tradition: A Response to J. B. Geyer. *JSOT* 15: 57–61.
   1982   Approaches to the Bible through History and Archaeology: Biblical History as a Discipline. *BA* 45: 211–16.

Tubb, J. N.
   1982   The MBIIA Period in Palestine: Its Relationship with Syria and Its Origin. *Levant* 15: 49–62.

Weinstein, James M.
   1981   The Egyptian Empire in Palestine: A Reassessment. *BASOR* 241: 1–128.

Weippert, Manfred
   1979   The Israelite "Conquest" and the Evidence from Transjordan. Pp. 15–34 in *Symposia* [[*Celebrating the Seventy-Fifth Anniversary of the Founding of the American Schools of Oriental Research (1900–1975)*]], ed. F. M. Cross. Cambridge: ASOR.

1982   Remarks on the History of Settlement in Southern Jordan dur-
           ing the Early Iron Age. Pp. 152–62 in *Studies in the History and
           Archaeology of Jordan*, ed. A. Hadidi. Amman, Jordan: Department of
           Antiquities.
Whitelam, Keith W.
  1979   *The Just King: Monarchial Judicial Authority in Ancient Israel.* Sheffield:
           JSOT Press.
  1984   The Defence of David. *JSOT* 29: 61–87.
Yoffee, Norman
  1982   Social History and Historical Methods in the Late Old Babylonian
           Period. *JAOS* 102: 347–53.

The Emergence of the Monarchy in Israel:
The Environmental and Socio-Economic Aspects

ISRAEL FINKELSTEIN

⟦43⟧ The emergence of the Israelite monarchy at the end of the eleventh century B.C.E. was one of the most crucial events in the history of Palestine. The political unification of the hill country under Saul, followed by David's conquests and the creation of one powerful state throughout most of the country, virtually changed the historical development of the entire region. For the first time a local independent political entity was established in Palestine—a national ethnic state with a distinctive ideological and religious identity.

This important period has attracted appropriate scholarly attention (although several studies on the reign of Saul and the beginning of the monarchy did not tackle the processes which brought about the emergence of the monarchy, e.g., Birch 1976; Gunn 1980; Bartal 1982). Historical discussions of the period have been based on the only available source—the biblical account. The contribution of archaeology has been surprisingly modest—focusing mainly on the finds from the Tell el-Fûl excavations, where a corner of a fortress was dated to the end of the eleventh century B.C.E. and attributed to Saul (Albright 1933: 8; Sinclair 1960: 6), or to the Philistines and in its later phase to Saul (Mazar 1954: 415; but see reservations on the fortress and its date in Finkelstein 1988a: 56–60).

Reprinted with permission from *Journal for the Study of the Old Testament* 44 (1989) 43–74.

Editors' note: Two illustrations that appeared in the original article have been deleted here: a map showing Iron Age II settlement patterns in Ephraim and a chart showing population estimates for Ephraim from the twelfth through eighth centuries B.C.E.

The most important archaeological dimension for tracing processes of this kind—the study of settlement patterns—was not used, since basic data were not available.

The significance of settlement patterns for detecting the stages of the state's emergence has been strongly emphasized in recent socio-political [[44]] works: "Probably the most powerful class of data to use in socio-cultural explanation is settlement pattern—the arrangement of population upon a landscape" (Price 1978: 165). Indeed, patterns of settlement have proved to be a pivotal tool in various works which evaluated the reasons for the emergence of ancient states (e.g., in southwestern Iran [Johnson 1973; Wright and Johnson 1975] and Adam's studies of urbanization in Mesopotamia [e.g., Adams and Nissen 1972: 9–33; Adams 1981: 27–129]).

Recent comprehensive archaeological surveys undertaken in the central hill country of Israel—the area where the processes which led to the emergence of the monarchy took place—permit a reliable and detailed reconstruction of Iron Age settlement patterns. But before dealing with these data, the generally accepted view concerning the emergence of the monarchy will be reviewed briefly, as well as the main socio-political theories used to explain the development of ancient states.

The Theory of Philistine Pressure

Almost all the scholars who have dealt with this period agree that an external element—the Philistine threat—brought about the emergence of the monarchy. The broadly accepted view since Alt's seminal article (1966, first published 1930; cf. already Wellhausen 1957: 248, 448–49, first published 1883) can be summarized as follows.

The idea of the monarchy was alien to Israelite society, which functioned in the period of the Judges under a tribal structure with charismatic leadership and only few central institutions. The revolutionary shift to the monarchy was not a result of a careful, well-planned policy; rather it was forced on Israel by external developments. The Israelite tribes were territorially separate and were organized in a social structure which preferred the smaller units of the nuclear or extended family. During most of the period, external threats were brief and geographically confined. Hence they could be handled locally. The Philistine threat was different, since it challenged all of Israelite society over an extended period of time. The Philistines were an economic, religious and political threat endangering the very existence of the Israelite entity. Their overwhelming advantage stemmed from their advanced military organization, which was as efficient in the hill country as on the plains. Furthermore, they [[45]] possessed technological superiority, especially in the field of metallurgy. Philistine pressure increased in the mid–eleventh century: the defeat of the Israelites at Eben-ezer, the destruction of their cultic and administrative centre at Shiloh and the deterioration of tribal leadership left the Israelites weakened, allowing the Philistines to establish garrisons in the heart of the hill country. Other enemies of Israel—Ammon and Amalek—took advantage of the situation and pressed the Israelites at the marginal areas of their settlement. The traditional local charismatic leadership could not cope with these new challenges. A strong central leader was now needed, to unify the tribes. Saul, the charismatic military chief with permanent power, who acted both as a Judge saving his people and as a king, marked the end of one era and the beginning of a new one. The monarchy emerged in the territory of Benjamin because this area was the focus of the Philistine threat (Noth 1960: 163–68; Malamat 1976: 88; Eissfeldt 1975: 570–72; Mayes 1977: 323–26; Aharoni 1979: 267–75; Gottwald 1979: 416–18; Halpern 1981: 61–63, 85–86; Bright 1981: 185–88; Herrmann 1981: 124–32; Mendenhall 1983: 99).

Almost all scholars pointed to Saul's leadership in the victory over Ammon as a crucial step in the shift to monarchy, and some argued that the struggle with Ammon and Amalek was a no less important factor in the process than the confrontation with the Philistines (Blenkinsopp 1975: 86–87; see also Herrmann 1981: 13; Halpern 1981: 62; 1983: 257; Gottwald 1986: 80).

As for the reasons which caused the clash between Israel and the Philistines, five main views have been presented: (1) Philistine expansion was an expression of their ambition to political domination in the entire country (Noth 1960: 166; Herrmann 1981: 131); (2) Philistine aggression aimed at preventing Israelite expansion to the coastal plain (Mayes 1977: 323, 325; Aharoni 1979: 274; Bright 1981: 185); (3) the Philistines reacted to Israelite raids on important trade-routes (Gottwald 1979: 416; see also Albright 1969: 162); (4) the Philistine expansion eastward was set off by population growth (Malamat 1976: 85–86); (5) the Philistine goal was economic exploitation of the hill country (Alt 1966: 180; Gottwald 1986: 88–93; Chaney 1986: 66–67; see also Frick 1985: 202, who sees the conflict as resulting from a combination of Philistine attempts to control the agricultural products of the hill country and Israelite hunger for land, caused by population growth).

[[46]] The above analysis of the emergence of the monarchy did not probe the internal processes within the hill country society of the eleventh century B.C.E. However, in recent years, as a result of the general tendency to adapt sociological theories to biblical research, there has been a trend to take these processes into account. New approaches have investigated the creation of the Israelite state from a socio-political point of view, i.e., with a special emphasis on internal social and economic factors (Frick

1985; 1986; Coote and Whitelam 1986 〚reprinted in this volume, pp. 335–
76〛; 1987; Whitelam 1986; Hauer 1986; Chaney 1986; Gottwald 1979:
655–58; 1986). But before surveying these new views, one should look at
the background of their development.

Socio-political Analysis

The socio-political research of recent years has dealt intensively with
the nature of the state, the reasons for its creation and the stages in
its development (see mainly Fried 1967; Flannery 1972; Service 1975;
Claessen and Skalník 1978a; 1981a; Cohen and Service 1978; Haas
1982). Two issues are basic to this research. The first is the difference between the *pristine state* and the *secondary state* (Fried 1967: 227–42; Price
1978; Sanders and Webster 1978: 274–75). Pristine states emerge in a
political vacuum, i.e., with no contemporaneous or previous developed
political entities in their vicinity. The best examples are ancient Egypt,
Mesopotamia, the Peruvian coast and the Indus valley. Secondary states
emerge from the collapse of other states or because of the influence
of a neighbouring state (sometime as a result of a confrontation with a
nearby state). It is clear that the Israelite monarchy was a secondary state
(Flanagan 1981; this is reflected in the elders' request for a king to judge
them "like all the nations"—1 Sam 8:5—Frick 1985: 32). But the relevant
literature is vague in respect to certain differences in the processes which
may lead to the creation of either type of state, and in any case, even if
external factors influence the creation of a secondary state, they are no
doubt deeply related to internal mechanisms (e.g., Claessen and Skalník
1981b: 485–86; Coote and Whitelam 1987: 145).

A second, even more important issue concerns the definition of
Israel's socio-political status at different stages leading up to the establishment of the monarchy. Service (1962) has described four phases of
development from a simple to a complex society: bands, 〚47〛 tribes, chiefdoms and states (see a similar classification by Flannery 1972: 401–3).
Fried (1967) uses slightly different terms: egalitarian society, ranked society, stratified society, and finally, state. Some divide the state stage into
two sub-phases—early state and mature state; others even subdivide the
early state stage into three phases (Claessen and Skalník 1978b: 637–50;
1978c: 22). The important stages for the study of the emergence of the
monarchy in Israel are the chiefdom and the state. The distinction between them in ancient societies is sometimes difficult (Service 1975: 304),
especially between a chiefdom and an early state, or, as the first phase of
an early state is called in the socio-political literature, an inchoate state
(Claessen and Skalník 1978c: 17–22; 1978d: 629; Cohen 1978: 32–36; Ser-

vice 1975: 16).[1] In a chiefdom offices are still only in the hands of those who are closely related to the ruler, mostly his family; the central government is not too strong and society still tends towards fragmentation. In contrast, in a state public positions are manned by specialists, some of whom do not necessarily belong to the leader's immediate circle; the economy of a state is more specialized and society more stratified (e.g., Flannery 1972: 403; Fried 1967: 229).

Because of difficulties in distinguishing between the above-mentioned socio-political systems, the few scholars who attempted to classify the first stages of the monarchy (solely on the basis of the biblical evidence) could not have reached consensus. Flanagan (1981), the first to deal with the subject, argued that Saul's leadership was typical of a chiefdom, that the reign of David reflects the transition from a chiefdom to a state and that only Solomon's kingdom can be classified as a fully developed state. Edelman categorized Saul as a "state builder" (probably referring to a transition from a chiefdom to a state), and his kingdom as a "territorial state" (Vikander-Edelman 1986: 9, 31).[2] In Hauer's (1986: 6–7) conception Saul's was a chiefdom, or a state, if one uses the military organization as a criterion. Following the model of Claessen and Skalník, Frick (1986: 21) divided the early days of the monarchy into three stages: Saul's reign and the early days of David were defined as the "inchoate state," the later days of David as a "typical state" and the reign of Solomon as a "transitional early state" on the threshold of a full-blown state. However, in his major work Frick (1985: 69) defined the kingdom of Saul and the early days of David as a chiefdom. Although this is not the place to discuss the [[48]] issue in detail, I wish to clarify my own view, based on the biblical source only, as archaeology does not permit socio-political distinctions within the short timespan of the monarchy's formative stage. Since the administration of Saul's kingdom was relatively undeveloped—there was no real central capital—and because Saul ruled over an ethnically homogeneous territory, his reign should probably be described as a chiefdom or an early stage of an early state. The reign of David, on the other hand, was characterized by territorial expansion, the rise of a heterogeneous, multi-ethnic state, the creation of a developed administration and the foundation of a real capital. It should therefore be classified as a full-blown state.

1. On the characteristics of a state see Sanders and Webster 1978: 274. See a detailed discussion of the early state in Claessen 1978 and different observations on the archaeological reflections of a chiefdom in Renfrew 1974: 73; Peebles and Kus 1977: 431–33.

2. On three types of a state from an ethno-territorial point of view—city state, territorial state and national state—see Buccellati 1967. In fact, according to Buccellati's classification, Saul's kingdom should be classified as a national rather than a territorial state—see already Alt 1966: 235.

Scholars have been interested since the last century in the processes which lead rural communities to establish states. Treatment of this topic has intensified in the last generation, being exemplified by attempts to present theoretical models based on observations of contemporary societies, or historical and archaeological ones. One of the main questions has been whether there is a "prime mover" which leads to the creation of a state (this question applies basically to the pristine state although many of the theories fit the development of a secondary state as well). The various "prime-mover" models were later divided into groups. Service (1978: 21–34; see also 1975: 266–308) classifies them as: (1) conflict theories, which describe how conflict between different population groups, sometimes against a social background, stimulate the creation of government and administration in order to terminate social unrest and the threat to the individual and his property; (2) integrative theories, which emphasize the environmental influence—both geographical and human. Claessen and Skalník (1978c) divide the models for the emergence of states according to internal and external factors. Wright (1978) recognizes four groups of theories: (1) managerial theories, in which various activities, like irrigation or trade, require a certain degree of management, leading to professional administration, social stratification and to the emergence of a state; (2) theories on internal conflict—where unequal resource accessibility causes social conflict resulting in the creation of the state as a governing and intermediary body; (3) theories of external conflicts, in which one society controls another's means of production and the elements which institutionalize this control become the nucleus of a state. (Or, according to a different approach, conflict between a state and a politically less developed [[49]] entity stimulates the political organization of the latter); (4) synthetic theories, describing the way different contemporaneous and related factors bring about the creation of the state. Four groups of models were also suggested by Cohen (1978: 32–36) but with different criteria: (1) demographic factors, primarily population growth; (2) external relations, like long-range trade or warfare (see below); (3) internal factors, e.g., the relations of nomads and sedentary groups in marginal zones; (4) cultural factors, like the role of irrigation in the rise of administration.

Models and Theories

In the following section, a few of these models, which may have implications for understanding the emergence of the monarchy and the state in ancient Israel, will be briefly mentioned.

1. *The Urbanization Model of V. G. Childe* (1950; 1951: 157ff.).   According to Childe, it is the production of agricultural surplus which leads to

urbanization. The intensification of agriculture directly creates surpluses which enable part of the population to engage in handicrafts. Agricultural surpluses create concentrations of wealth or property (usually in temples), around which rise the central settlements. These processes lead to specialized production of goods for trade and to a gradual development of stratified society with rulers, priests, craftsmen, merchants and farmers. Trade requires administration which, in turn, brings about the invention of writing, etc.

2. *Carneiro's Warfare or Environmental Circumscription Model* (1970). Carneiro argues that warfare is an essential, although not sufficient factor in the emergence of states. Carneiro describes fertile agricultural regions which are surrounded by geographical barriers like deserts seas or mountains. Constant population growth brings about utilization of all land available for agriculture, and results in an inevitable struggle between the local communities. The victorious take over the lands of the defeated and create a chiefdom. The continuation of the same process may create a state and finally, even an empire. At the same time changes within the society take place—administration in the conquered territories, land given to those who [50] distinguish themselves in the war, and other factors create social stratification, taxation and urban concentrations.

Webster (1975) had developed Carneiro's theory. In his opinion, warfare plays an especially important role in the emergence of a state under three conditions: (1) when a large area is inhabited by groups with different demographical potential, occupying sub-regions with different productivity; (2) when the agricultural potential is great enough to produce surpluses; (3) when population growth creates an outflux of people from core areas to peripheries. Under these circumstances, several stratified societies emerge, especially in the core area, and local chiefs react in response to pressures caused by competition for resources. The usual short term tendency will be to acquire additional resources by conquest, mainly in the direction of the less populated marginal areas. The outcome will be conflict between the prominent chiefdoms. Webster argues that there will be no clear military decision, but rather, an internal change— the creation of a stable military leadership which will manipulate available wealth, stimulating the growth of social stratification. The consequence is an intensification of agricultural production and economic specialization. Thus, according to Webster's model, warfare is a catalyst for internal processes which bring about the creation of governmental institutions.

3. *The Theory of the Role of Trade—Inter-regional or Intra-regional—in the Emergence of a State.* According to the inter-regional trade model, certain products are not available in a certain region. In order to obtain them via trade, the region must produce a surplus of its own products. This

brings about the development of administration, social stratification, etc.[3] According to the intra-regional version of this model, environmental and demographic variations in different parts of the same region engender specialization in sub-areas in order to produce surpluses to use for barter for the absent products (Wright and Johnson 1975; Johnson 1973).

4. *The Relations of Nomads and Sedentary Population.* An early version of this model was presented by Oppenheimer (1928: 51–55), who argued that energetic nomads who conquer agricultural areas with high-production potential may establish a state. Salzman (1978) described such a situation in Baluchistan: Occasional droughts [[51]] forced the nomads to raid the settled lands, making it difficult for the two groups to establish a peaceful symbiotic relationship. Finally with no alternative, one major nomadic group escalated the raids to a real conquest, and its leader became the lord of the agricultural lands. In this capacity, he then acted as a mediator between the rural communities—now under his protection—and the other nomads. At the same time he used the latter to suppress potential uprisings of the sedentary population, and in exchange, allotted them agricultural goods.

In recent years, the general approach to the causes behind the emergence of states has become more synthetic and less doctrinal—a combination of factors rather than one prime mover is now being sought. In other words, different reasons, conditions and circumstances relating to each other lead a rural society to statehood. Adams, in his studies of the urbanization processes in ancient Mesopotamia, was apparently the first to look for multivariant causality (1966), an approach which is now widely accepted (Flannery 1972: 408ff.; Service 1978: 31; Cohen 1978: 70).

Applying the Models to the Israelite Monarchy

Which of these models, if any, applies to the processes which took place in the central hill country of the land of Israel at the end of the eleventh century B.C.E.? Interestingly enough, the above-mentioned scholars, who dealt with models for the emergence of historical states, have not examined the Israelite monarchy as a case-study. Biblical scholars who saw the Philistine threat as the major factor in the emergence of the monarchy have described, without labeling it, the emergence of a secondary state according to an external conflict model. In any case, only in recent years have historians tried to explain the rising of the Israelite monarchy in light of modern socio-political theories.

---

3. On the application of this view for the study of the Maya culture of Central America see Rathje 1971.

Chaney (1986) postulated that two factors led to the rise of the monarchy—a Philistine threat to Israelite economy from the outside and the emergence of an economic elite from the inside. Technological innovations—terracing, plastered water cisterns and especially the use of iron, brought about the intensification of human activity in the hill country and the production of agricultural surpluses. This, in turn, facilitated the regions' economic independence. But the [[52]] prosperous hill country agriculture attracted Philistine aggression, which, in turn led to the emergence of the monarchy.

Gottwald (1979: 655–58) is of a similar opinion—the use of iron and plastered water cisterns enabled the expansion of hill country agriculture, production of surpluses and, consequently, population growth. The prosperous agriculture demanded advanced management and this led to social changes such as organization beyond the family unit. Chaney and Gottwald emphasize therefore Cohen's "cultural" factors in the emergence of states.

Hauer (1986) has adopted elements of Carneiro's warfare theory for explaining the rise of the Israelite state. The rising population density in the Iron I caused a growing struggle between different groups over limited resources; Philistine imperialism should be seen in this light. The Israelites faced two possibilities—either surrender or organize and fight back. They chose the second option.

Whitelam (1986: 61–62) argued that the monarchy emerged as a result of both external and internal pressures. As for the latter, the limiting ecological conditions of the hill country resulted in a competition for land when the population increased. This competition necessitated stabilizing institutions. This is in fact a theory in which internal conflict brings about the creation of the state as an intermediary institution (the second category in Wright's above-mentioned classification). Coote and Whitelam (1986: 127–41) claimed that the Philistine threat was the catalyst for the creation of the Israelite state, since it initiated complex internal economic, social, political and religious processes. The developing horticulture economy demanded long-term stability, which prevented the disintegration of Israelite society. It also created a class of land-owners and increased the importance of markets. The emergence of an elite of wealthy farmers and town dwellers (around the markets) was a major step in the stratification of Israelite society, but it was the external threat which led to the establishment of a chiefdom, and finally to a state. The first factor which resulted in the chiefdom was that defense expenses fell mainly on the wealthy class which wanted to share them with the rest of society; the second factor was the interest of the land owners in preventing political and economic integration with the lowlands (which was the goal of the rich merchants). Thereby, the landlords united to appoint a chief.

This explanation combined theories of external pressure (Carneiro) [[53]] and internal social strife. But in a later work Coote and Whitelam (1987) took a somewhat different course: early Israel was circumscribed both geographically (by steppelands) and socially (urban lowland people, nomads). Population growth led to the expansion of agriculture in the highlands; but soon, the limited arable areas required institutionalized intensification, which was an important factor in the rise of the monarchy.

Frick (1985: 26, 66, 81, 138, 191–204) has presented the most comprehensive reconstruction of the monarchy's emergence. He sees the Philistines as a necessary, albeit not sufficient, stimulator in the shift from chiefdom to state. Initially, what brought about the creation of the chiefdom was the intensification of agricultural production, which required solutions to problems such as integration and cooperation. These problems were caused, in turn, by the pressure of the growing population on the limited land resources. One of the solutions was terracing, the construction of which required investment and management. Frick paid special attention to agricultural risks, such as droughts, which also necessitated solutions beyond the family level; a better organization brings stability and better timing of agricultural activity, resulting in the production of a surplus. The economic advantages that the leader gives to his circle result in an unequal use of the resources, which in turn leads to social stratification headed by an agrarian elite. In effect, Frick has used a model framework called by Service (1978: 29) "redistributional economic systems."

The Archaeological Data

The views discussed so far are strong on the theoretical level. But some points taken from modern sociological and political theory seem to be out of context, because the most important for a realistic historical reconstruction—the archaeological data—were not available. I refer mainly to settlement patterns, which are of crucial importance for tracing any social, economic and political developments. For this reason, what follows makes use of the Iron I–II hill country settlement patterns for studying the processes under examination. I shall begin with the comprehensive archaeological survey which I have undertaken in the Land of Ephraim since 1980. The data collected from this region have made possible the construction of a [[54]] demographic-historical model, in light of which the data from other parts of the central hill country will be examined.[4]

---

4. The results of the survey have been discussed in detail elsewhere (Finkelstein 1988a: 121–204).

Six geographical sub-units can be discerned in the Land of Ephraim, each with specific ecological and economic features:

1. The desert fringe—the eastern, semi-arid strip. Parts of it, especially in the north, offer convenient agricultural plots. The subsistence economy of the population today, as in the past, is based on dry farming and animal husbandry (modern-day data are taken from Mandatorial sources and thus relate to the first half of this century).
2. The northern-central range. The most prominent feature of this part of the region is the small intermontane valley (such as the valleys of Shiloh, Lubban esh-Sharqiyyeh, Kabalan, Beit Dajan, etc.), which is the typical agro-economic unit of the area. The villagers' economy is based on dry farming with the addition of olive orchards. The inhabitants of the eastern part of the region enjoy good herding.
3. The southern central range—the continuation of the plateau of Benjamin. The economy here is based on both dry farming and horticulture, with the former somewhat more prevalent. Here too there are good conditions for animal husbandry in the eastern margins.
4. The northern slopes—the topography here is more dissected than in the central range but relatively moderate compared to the area to the south. The ridges have some flat areas and the wadis widen in certain places to create small valleys. Almost no permanent water sources are found here. The northern part of the area features rough rock formations. The subsistence economy is based on a balanced system of cereal growing and olive orchards. The area of Wadi Qanah in the north is suitable for herding.
5. The southern slopes. This is the largest (comprising one-third of the total area) and most rugged unit of the land of Ephraim. The landscape is composed of long and narrow ridges with flat tops but steep slopes, divided by deep and narrow wadis. The ridge is the typical economic unit of the area. There are abundant perennial springs, and olive orchards dominate the landscape (70% of the cultivable area).
6. The foothills. These are low and moderate hills, sloping down in [[55]] westward direction, with no stable water sources. Large parts of the area, especially in the west, are rocky and hence difficult for agricultural exploitation. The economy is based on cereal growing with the addition of some olive orchards. Good pasture exists in the western rocky terrain.

In summary, the land of Ephraim can be divided topographically into areas amenable to human activity—the desert fringe and the two units of the central range; areas of medium potential—the northern slopes and the foothills; and the harsher part—the southern slopes. Lithologically, the difficult areas for cultivation are the two units of the slopes and the foothills. From an agro-economic point of view, the area can be divided into the following categories: the strip of dry farming and animal husbandry—the desert fringe, the eastern sections of the central range and the western part of the foothills; areas with land use divided equally between dry farming and horticulture—the northern slopes and most parts of the southern central range; and the horticultural region (today comprising only olive orchards, but in historical periods olives and vines)—especially the southern slopes. Another factor which must be taken into consideration is the natural vegetation. Comparing the development of settlement patterns from the Middle Bronze Age to the Iron I, there is good reason to assume that in the western half of the central highlands the vegetation cover was still relatively dense.

One hundred fifteen Iron I sites have been found in the survey (for details see Finkelstein 1988a; forthcoming [a] [[1988–89]]).[5] The following table summarizes their distribution according to geographical subunits and size (large villages—5–6 dunams or more; small villages—3–4 dunams). It is important to note that the Iron I settlement pattern reflects the situation at the middle or the end of the eleventh century B.C.E.
Table 1 (see also Figure 1) shows a high density of sites in the desert fringe and northern central range (around the intermontane valleys) and substantial concentrations in the northern slopes, around Bethel in the south central range and near Rantis in the foothills. The activity in the southern slopes and most parts of the foothills was relatively limited. The large villages are found in the two units of the central range and in the northern slopes; the small villages are evenly scattered throughout the area and isolated houses (which may have been seasonal sites in certain cases) are relatively numerous in the desert fringe and foothills. The large villages are equidistant from each other, and in many cases a large village, one or two small villages and one or more house scatters are related to each other—a pattern of central sites surrounded by a peripheral population. This distribution of sites shows that the settlement process in the hill country was already in full swing at the end of

5. So far, about 80% of the 1050 square km designated for the study has been thoroughly combed. An initial survey of all sites marked on the maps has been conducted in the remaining area. The data is updated to the summer of 1987; six additional sites, including ᶜIzbet Ṣarṭah, were discovered in the 1970s by Kochavi and the Aphek expedition team on the western margins of the foothills (Finkelstein 1986: 202–3).

Table 1

	desert fringe	northern central range	southern central range	northern slopes	southern slopes	foothills	total
number of sites	14	43	9	18	19	12	115
percentage of total	(12)	(37)	(8)	(16)	(17)	(10)	
density (sq. km per site)	7.4	5.2	11.9	8.3	17	12.3	
large villages	2	11	4	5	3	1	26
small villages	4	12	1	4	7	4	32
few houses	8	20	4	9	9	7	57

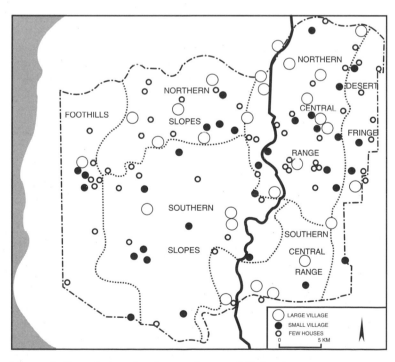

Figure 1. Iron I sites in the territory of Ephraim.

the eleventh century B.C.E. On the other hand, a settlement pattern with half of the sites classified as house scatters reflects a relatively early stage of agro-social organization. The distribution of the sites according to size probably reflects the social framework of the population, i.e., the division to clans, families, etc. (Stager 1985: 17–23). A large concentration of sites, some of them large villages, on the eastern strip of the two central range units—a location which offers obvious economic advantages (see below)—is worth mentioning. Looking at the region in two extended units—a western one (the slopes and foothills) and an eastern one (the desert fringe and the central range), we find that 57% of all sites and 65% of the large villages are located in the latter.

For a better understanding of the demographic processes which took place in the Land of Ephraim in Iron I, we should juxtapose the distribution of those sites occupied by the beginning of Iron I (twelfth and early eleventh centuries B.C.E.), with that of the sites established in the ⟦57⟧ eleventh century, and with the Iron II settlement pattern. These chronological classifications are based, of course, on ceramic observations. Table 2 (see also Figure 2) demonstrates the distribution of early and late Iron I sites (most early sites were evidently occupied also in the later phase of the period).

The results of this classification ⟦see table 2⟧ show that over 75% of the early Iron I sites are located in the eastern half of the Ephraim territory (90% with the slopes' sites bordering the central range). However, the settlement process in the western units intensified during the Iron I; 62% of the sites established in the later phase of the period are located in the slopes and foothills.

Table 3 presents population estimates for the different units of the Land of Ephraim in Iron I (on the method of calculation see Finkelstein 1988a: 193). The table indicates that in the beginning of the Iron I 76% of the population lived in the three eastern units (63% of the population of ⟦58⟧ all Iron I sites). But 46% of the inhabitants of sites established in late Iron I dwelt in the western units.

One hundred ninety Iron II sites were recorded in the survey (Figure 3 ⟦not reprinted in this volume⟧; this number reflects the peak of Iron II activity in the mid–eighth century B.C.E.). Now, for the first time in the demographic history of the land of Ephraim, the western units number more sites (51%) than the eastern. There is an increase of 95–100% in the number of sites of the western units (compared to the Iron I). Fifty-four % of the large villages are in the west and 53% of the estimated 31,000 inhabitants (Figure 4 ⟦not reprinted in this volume⟧; for a detailed discussion of the Iron II pattern of settlement see Finkelstein, forthcoming [a] ⟦1988–89⟧).

Table 2

	desert fringe	northern central range	southern central range	northern slopes	southern slopes	foothills	total
sites established in early Iron I	12	27	7	7	7	2	62
sites established in late Iron I	1	14	1	8	10	8	42
unclassified	1	2	1	3	2	2	11

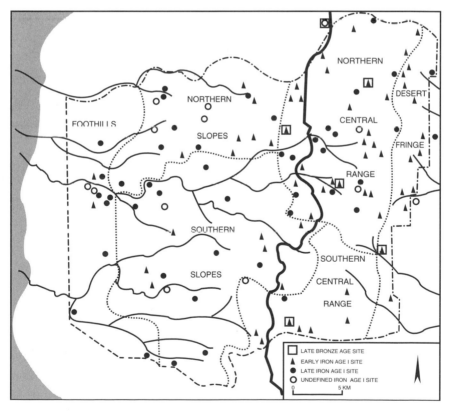

Figure 2. Division into early and late Iron I sites in the territory of Ephraim.

Table 3

	desert fringe	northern central range	southern central range	northern slopes	southern slopes	foothills	total
total Iron I	875	3825	1225	1600	1150	725	9400
early Iron I added in	450	1825	625	350	450	125	3825
late Iron I	425	2000	600	1250	700	600	5575

A study of the patterns of settlement from the beginning of Iron I to the eighth century B.C.E. demonstrates an ongoing process: in the early Iron I, the overwhelming majority of the population lived in the eastern units of the region, which are relatively amenable for habitation. During Iron I, with the increase of population (see below) and when the preferred areas became densely settled, a westward expansion into the slopes and foothills units began. This process intensified in the Iron II, so by the eighth century B.C.E. the demographic scale tilted toward the western units. It is possible that the growing use of iron in the eleventh and mainly in the tenth century B.C.E. (Waldbaum 1978: 27) facilitated the penetration into areas of dense coppice and difficult rock formations to the west.

What is the significance of this demographic process for the emergence of the Monarchy? The westward expansion meant a struggle with harsh topography, difficult rock formations and a dense vegetation cover. Furthermore, certain areas were devoid of stable water sources. Economically speaking, dwelling in the western units means practising an unbalanced economy, since this part of the region is suitable mainly for horticulture, while it is almost hostile to cereal growing and animal husbandry. The westward expansion required the clearing of rocky terrain and of forest, hewing water cisterns, and the terracing of slopes. It also necessitated contact with neighbouring areas—surplus orchard products were exchanged for the grain and animal products not easily raised in the western zone.

A similar demographic process was detected by Zertal in the hill country of Manasseh: the Iron I occupation began in the eastern part of the region, expanding in the second phase to the intermontane [[59]] valleys of central Manasseh. Penetration into the hilly and rocky areas in the west occurred only at a later stage (Zertal 1986: abstract, 327, 359). The 1968 survey in Judah and Benjamin revealed a similar pattern (Kochavi 1972): most Iron I sites are scattered in the eastern part of the area (in Judah also to the south), while by the Iron II the west was already densely settled.

In general, Iron I settlement patterns in the hill country and in neighbouring regions convey the following picture of Israelite expansion. Settlement process initially took place mostly on the desert fringes and in the central range between Jerusalem and the Jezreel valley. Only at later stages in the eleventh century, with the better lands already densely settled, did settlement on the ecological "frontier" of the hill country's western part intensify. The settlement process gathered its strength on the other ecological frontiers—the Judean hills and the Galilee, as well as in the arid zone of the Beer-sheba basin—at the same time (for details see Finkelstein 1988a). However, the ultimate "conquest," that of the ecological frontier of the central hill country—the western slopes of Samaria and the Judean hills—took place only in Iron II. The size of the "Israelite" population in the early Iron I sites west of the Jordan is estimated to have been ca. 20,000 souls (non-sedentary groups are not included), while the settled Israelite population at the end of the eleventh century B.C.E. is estimated at ca. 55,000 (Finkelstein 1988a: 330–35; for the use of the term "Israelite" for this period see Finkelstein 1988a: 27–33). It is important to note that the increase in the settled population in the Iron I stems from both natural growth (on growth rate increase in sedentarizing populations see Lee 1972: 339, 342), and from the increment derived from the ongoing process of sedentarization taking place amongst pastoral groups (on the origin of the Israelite population see Finkelstein 1988a: 336–48). In the eighth century B.C.E., the sites of the central hill country alone are estimated to have been settled by ca. 135,000 inhabitants.

The patterns of settlement described above explain, in my opinion, both the internal and the external conditions for the emergence of the Israelite monarchy. The expansion of Israelite Settlement in the eleventh century B.C.E. forced a relatively large number of people into the ecological frontier areas of Palestine, especially into the hill country (i.e., the western slopes of Samaria, the entire Judean hills, the upper Galilee) and also into the Beer-sheba basin. Settlement in [[60]] these regions required a bitter struggle with environmental obstacles. Obviously these tasks were easier to undertake in social frameworks larger than the local nuclear (or even extended) family. The need to become more efficient contributed to the collapse of barriers between the settling groups. Moreover, the settlement in the western part of the hill country and in the Galilee had far-reaching economic implications. Economically, it is not worthwhile to raise grain in these regions. They also lack pasture lands. On the other hand, these are the classic horticultural regions of the country; only orchard agriculture best exploits their potential. Hence the environmental conditions encouraged a specialized economy with important social implications. The population of the desert fringe and central range may subsist on a self-sufficient mixed economy, but the villages of the horticultural regions need the agricultural products of the neighbouring regions. They exchange some of their surplus (in products such as olives, oil, grapes, wine, etc.), for grain and animal products from the nearby areas. The existence of specialized agriculture in the horticulture regions now encouraged the villages of the desert fringe, eastern central range and parts of the foothills to specialize in grain growing and animal husbandry, and to intensify their efforts to produce greater surpluses.

This pattern of specialized economy and surplus production in different ecological niches of the hill country can be supported by data from recent times, and apparently demonstrated by the archaeological finds from Iron Age sites of western Ephraim.[6]

This situation, which developed mainly in the eleventh century, helped the population to overcome the geographical barriers between the various sub-regions of the hill country and to establish a strong intra-

6. Population and agricultural land use data from the Mandatorial period (see especially Government of Palestine 1938, 1945), make it possible to trace the flow of products between the various sub-regions of the hill country. Certain areas grew large surpluses of grain, while others could not produce the minimum necessary to be self-sufficient. For example, calculating an average annual yield of 60 kg wheat per dunam in traditional agriculture (e.g., Pinner 1931: 2), and an annual consumption of 200 kg grain per person (e.g., Clark and Haswell 1970: 54), we can, using the Mandatory data, illustrate sub-region exchange patterns: Deir Ghassana is a typical village in the southern slopes of the Ephraimite hill country, dependent mainly on olive orchards. The 880 people who lived in the village in 1945 grew grain on a limited area of 550 dunams. Therefore, the fields of Deir Ghassana could only supply enough grain for 165 people. On the other hand, the foothills village of Rantis, located only 7 km west of Deir Ghassana, produced 150 kg of surplus grain per person, per year! Another example: the village of Silwad, located on the eastern margin of the horticultural lands of the Ephraimite hills, produced in 1945 only enough grain for 750 of its 1910 inhabitants, but Kafr Malik, only 5 km to the east, produced a surplus of 400 kg grain per person.

An interesting example for the Iron II comes from a small site named Kli^c a, located near the village of Deir Ghassana. The site (which was established in Iron I), was surveyed and then excavated by Eitam (1980: 69–70; 1981: 16–17). The results of his study prove beyond any doubt that the inhabitants were occupied predominantly in olive oil and wine production. An opposite example, of a late Iron I site which produced mainly grain, comes from ^c Izbet Ṣarṭah. The most prominent element uncovered in Stratum II are the dozens of silos scattered around the central building. Rosen (1986) calculated the quantity of grain stored in the silos and consequently estimated the population of the site at around 190 people. But using three different methods of population estimation we came to the conclusion that the site was inhabited by only around 100 people (Finkelstein 1986: 114). In other words, instead of 190 inhabitants who consumed all the grain production of the site, there were probably only half of this number of people who produced a substantial surplus of grain. Indeed, it is interesting to note that Arab villages of the same geographical location (e.g., Majdal Yaba), produced in the 1930s and 1940s twice as much grain as that needed for their own consumption. The inhabitants of Iron II Kli^c a, like the people of Deir Ghassana in recent times, produced a surplus of oil and wine which they exchanged for grain and other goods. The people of eleventh-century ^c Izbet Ṣarṭah had a large quantity of grain surplus and were short of the products of the orchards.

regional flow of goods. An economic system of this type necessitated a certain level of organization, which served as the springboard for public administration. The fact that the population produced surpluses no doubt encouraged the development of an administrative social stratum—groups of people who were no longer occupied in the subsistence economy. At the same time, this process contributed to the stratification of the society— farmers and administrators, prosperous villages and poor ones, central sites with markets and merchants, etc. What occurred, therefore, was the crucial shift of the Israelite population from a rural society of small isolated groups to the beginning of organization into large socio-political systems.

[[61]] The external factor also made a contribution. The intensification of Israelite activity in the western part of the central hill country created friction with the inhabitants of the neighbouring coastal plain. Activity in the western margins of the foothills, on the border of the plain (in the vicinity of ʿIzbet Ṣarṭah), accelerated this conflict. The settlement in this latter area presumably stemmed not only from population growth in the hill country, but also from the demand for grain and animal products, which itself had been set into motion by increasing production in the horticultural areas of the western hill country. This was the chain of events which led to the inevitable confrontation with the Philistines. On the one hand Israelite expansion posed a threat to the lords of the plains. On the other hand, the developing horticulture economy of the hill country (the products of which were less available on the coastal plain, especially in its southern part), created economic temptation for the Philistines. This was the background for the clash between the two entities on the border of the foothills and the coastal plain the mid– eleventh century B.C.E. The Philistines, who had the upper hand, took advantage of the victory to pursue their political and economic plans; the Israelite center in Shiloh, which probably played an important role in the economy and political affairs of the hill country (Finkelstein 1985: 172– 73) was set ablaze. By this strategy the Philistines achieved a double goal—they crippled the ability of the Israelites to defend themselves and gained control over the Israelite economy. The next logical step in the Philistine effort was to garrison troops in the heart of the territory of Benjamin, an area which became the center of Israelite activity following the destruction of Shiloh.

The demand for grain apparently played an important role in the Israelite expansion to the southern Hebron hills and the Beer-sheba valley in the eleventh century as well (a process which is echoed in the biblical list of cities which received the booty of Amalek—1 Sam 30:26– 31). The Judean hills were still relatively sparsely settled at that time, hence the southward expansion could not possibly have been caused by population pressures from this direction (contra Kempinski et al. 1981: 176). But agricultural activity in the southern steppe brought the hill country groups into another confrontation—with the inhabitants of the Negev (Amalekites and other groups).

The economic *floruit* of the southern deserts in the Iron I (mainly [[62]] an outcome of prosperous Arabian trade—Finkelstein forthcoming [b] [[1988b]]), brought on major changes for the inhabitants of the Negev Highlands and the Beer-sheba basin. Their participation in this trade enabled groups of pastoral nomads in the Negev Highlands to sedentarize at the end of the eleventh century B.C.E. (Finkelstein 1984). The commercial center of the Beer-sheba basin in the Iron I, and especially in the eleventh century, was Tel Masos. The archaeological finds at that site have revealed close connections with the coastal plain and the southern deserts (see summary in Kempinski 1978). Most of the site's inhabitants were apparently local people who settled down, with the addition of coastal and possible hill country groups, who all concentrated at the site for economic reasons. The Negev Highlands and the Beer-sheba basin were the scene of interesting social changes, somewhat parallel to contemporaneous developments in the hill country: sedentarization, the emergence of an urban center and probably social stratification. These events may have led to political changes in this region as well. In fact, by the late eleventh century, the socio-political structure in the south could be described as a sort of a local chiefdom, developing in a direction of statehood.[7] A similar process which took place in the same area in a later period—the rise of the Nabataean kingdom—succeeded in achieving the ultimate political structure—the emergence of a strong desert state. The friction in the Beer-sheba basin between the Israelites and the local people was not only economic but also socio-political—it was a clash between two emerging entities who were both in a process of creating an advanced political and economic system. The Israelite penetration into the valley most probably threatened the monopoly of the desert dwellers over the southern trade. The victory of Saul over Amalek (1 Samuel 15), and David's southern policy (2 Sam 8:4), determined the outcome of this struggle. Subsequently, a reverse economic and social change took place—the decline of the southern trade (or more so, the decline of the southern peoples' role in that trade); a gradual abandonment of Tel Masos; a shift back to traditional

7. On the creation of a nomadic state on the fringe of the settled lands see Salzman 1978 and bibliography; Cohen 1978: 32–36. See also Khazanov 1981, despite the different geographical background, who describes a scenario in which nomads conquer sedentary lands in order to ensure permanent supply of agricultural products. See also Khazanov 1984: 228–302 for a summary of his observations on the topic of the nomads and the state.

pastoral nomadism in the Negev Highlands and finally, the desertion of the sedentary sites. By the tenth century we already find the young northern monarchy deeply rooted in the Beer-sheba basin (Amalek of this reconstruction is identified in the south, contra Edelman 1986).

At this point, part of the "classic" reconstruction of the monarchy's [[63]] incipience should be accepted. The stresses and strains with the Philistines to the west, Amalek to the south and Ammon to the east required a central (especially military) leadership. The above discussion shows that the change was not so drastic, since by the second half of the eleventh century B.C.E. early systems of administration were already operating in the Israelite hill country. The events which led to the rise of the monarchy took place in Benjamin because, following the destruction of Shiloh, the most important Israelite centers moved to this region, and because the population of this part of the country suffered most from the overt Philistine occupation. In this context one can claim that the actions of one strong personality were responsible for the emergence of the monarchy (Samuel or Saul)—what is known as the theory of the "Great Man" in human evolution. But even those who have considered this model, emphasized that a Great Man can only rise under suitable socio-historical circumstances (e.g., White 1969: 280–81).

Saul's military leadership rescued Israel from the dangers in the south and east, and pushed the Philistines from the heart of the hill country (on the role of warfare in the rise of leaders see Lewis 1981: 212–15). But it was only in the reign of David that the Philistine threat was completely eliminated. In his days the chiefdom or national state of Saul became a strong and large territorial state. The expansion of the monarchy into the coastal plain, the fertile northern valleys and the Galilee united most of the country for the first time in its history under one local rule. The conquest of the grain-growing lowlands brought agricultural specialization to its peak, since under one state it was now possible to exploit the various ecological niches optimally—the lowlands for dry farming and the hill country for horticulture.

Conclusions

The present reconstruction of the emergence of the monarchy includes several components of well-known theories on the rise of states: geographical and social circumscription; population increase creating pressure for the conquest of new frontiers for cultivation; intensification of agricultural activity which produces surpluses and creates social stratification; inter- and intra-regional trade between specializing groups in different ecological niches which leads to the [[64]] rise of advanced administration; and external conflict which unites the population under one military leadership. All this must be evaluated on the background of the specific geographical and historical conditions of ancient Israel at the end of the eleventh century B.C.E.

Bibliography

Adams, Robert McC.
    1966   *The Evolution of Urban Society.* Chicago: Aldine.
    1981   *Heartland of Cities.* Chicago: University of Chicago Press.
Adams, Robert McC., and Nissen, Hans J.
    1972   *The Uruk Countryside.* Chicago: University of Chicago Press.
⟦Aharoni, Yohanan
    1979   *The Land of the Bible: A Historical Geography.* 2d ed. Philadelphia: West-
             minster.⟧
Albright, William F.
    1933   A New Campaign of Excavation at Gibeah of Saul." *BASOR* 52: 6–12.
    1969   Samuel and the Beginning of the Prophetic Movement. Pp. 149–76
             in *Interpreting the Prophetic Tradition*, ed. H. M. Orlinsky. Cincinnati:
             Hebrew Union College Press.
Alt, Albrecht
    1966   The Formation of the Israelite State in Palestine. Pp. 171–237 in
    (1930)   *Essays on Old Testament History and Religion.* Oxford: Basil Blackwell.
Bartal, Arieh
    1982   *The Kingdom of Saul.* Tel Aviv: Hakibbutz Hameuchad [Hebrew].
Birch, Bruce
    1976   *The Rise of the Israelite Monarchy: The Growth and Development of I Samuel
             7–15.* SBLDS 27. Missoula: Scholars Press.
Blenkinsopp, Joseph
    1975   The Quest of the Historical Saul. Pp. 75–99 in *No Famine in the Land:
             Studies in Honor of John L. McKenzie*, ed. J. W. Flanagan and A. Weis-
             brod. Missoula: Scholars Press.
Bright, John
    1981   *A History of Israel.* Philadelphia: Westminster.
Buccellati, Giorgio
    1967   *Cities and Nations of Ancient Syria.* Studi Semitici 26. Rome: Instituto
             di Studi del Vicino Oriente.
Carneiro, Robert L.
    1970   A Theory of the Origin of the State. *Science* 169: 733–38.
Chaney, Marvin L.
    1986   Systemic Study of the Israelite Monarchy. Pp. 53–76 in *Social Scientific
             Criticism of the Hebrew Bible and Its Social World: The Israelite Monarchy*,
             ed. N. K. Gottwald. *Semeia* 37. Decatur, Georgia: Scholars Press.
Childe, V. Gordon
    1950   The Urban Revolution. *Town Planning Review* 21: 3–17.

1951 *Man Makes Himself.* New York: New American Library.

Claessen, Henri J. M.

1978 The Early State: A Structural Approach. Pp. 533–618 in *The Early State,* ed. H. Claessen and P. Skalník. The Hague: Mouton.

Claessen, Henri J. M., and Skalník, Peter

1978a *The Early State.* The Hague: Mouton.

1978b The Early State: Models and Reality. Pp. 637–50 in *The Early State,* ed. H. Claessen and P. Skalník.

1978c The Early State: Theories and Hypotheses. Pp. 3–29 in *The Early State,* ed. H. Claessen and P. Skalník.

1978d Limits: Beginning and End of the Early State. Pp. 619–35 in *The Early State,* ed. H. Claessen and P. Skalník.

1981a *The Study of the State.* The Hague: Mouton.

1981b *Ubi sumus?* The Study of the State Conference in Retrospect. Pp. 469–510 in *The Study of the State,* ed. H. Claessen and P. Skalník.

Clark, Colin, and Haswell, Margaret

1970 *The Economics of Subsistence Agriculture.* London: Macmillan.

Cohen, Ronald

1978 State Origins: A Reappraisal. Pp. 31–75 in *The Early State,* ed. H. Claessen and P. Skalník.

Cohen, Ronald, and Service, Elman R., eds.

1978 *Origins of the State.* Philadelphia: Institute for the Study of Human Issues.

Cootc, Robert B., and Whitelam, Keith W.

1986 The Emergence of Israel: Social Transformation and State Formation following the Decline in Late Bronze Age Trade. Pp. 107–47 in *Social Scientific Criticism of the Hebrew Bible and Its Social World: The Israelite Monarchy,* ed. N. K. Gottwald. *Semeia* 37. Decatur, Georgia: Scholars Press. [Reprinted in this volume, pp. 335–76]

1987 *The Emergence of Early Israel in Historical Perspective.* The Social World of Biblical Antiquity Series 5. Sheffield: Almond Press.

Edelman, Diana

1986 Saul's Battle against Amaleq (I Sam. 15). *JSOT* 35: 71–84.

Eissfeldt, Otto

1975 The Hebrew Kingdom. Pp. 537–605 in *CAH,* 2/2: *The Middle East and the Aegean Region c. 1380–1000 B.C.* Cambridge: Cambridge University Press.

Eitam, David

1980 Oil and Wine Production in Mt. Ephraim in the Iron Age. Unpublished M.A. thesis, Tel Aviv University [Hebrew].

1981 Klia. *Hadashot Archeologiot* 77: 16–17 [Hebrew].

Finkelstein, Israel

1984 The Iron Age "Fortresses" of the Negev Highlands: Sedentarization of the Nomads. *Tel Aviv* 11: 189–209.

1985 Summary and Conclusions: History of Shiloh from Middle Bronze Age II to Iron Age II. *Excavations at Shiloh 1981–1984: Preliminary Report,* ed. I. Finkelstein. *Tel Aviv* 12: 159–77.

1986 ᶜIzbet Ṣarṭah: *An Early Iron Age Site Near Rosh Haᶜayin, Israel.* BAR International Series 299. Oxford: B.A.R.

1988a *The Archaeology of the Israelite Settlement.* Jerusalem: Israel Exploration Society.

[1988b] Arabian Trade and Socio-Political Conditions in the Negev in the 12th–11th Centuries ʙᴄᴇ. *JNES* 47 [241–52].

[1988–89] The Land of Ephraim Survey 1980–1986: Preliminary Report. *Tel Aviv* [15–16: 117–83].

Flanagan, James W.

1981 Chiefs in Israel. *JSOT* 20: 47–73. [Reprinted in this volume, pp. 311–34].

Flannery, Kent V.

1972 The Cultural Evolution of Civilizations. *Annual Review of Ecology and Systematics* 3: 399–426.

Frick, Frank S.

1985 *The Formation of the State in Ancient Israel.* Sheffield: Almond.

1986 Social Science Methods and Theories of Significance for the Study of the Israelite Monarchy: A Critical Review Essay. Pp. 9–52 in *Social Scientific Criticism of the Hebrew Bible and Its Social World: The Israelite Monarchy,* ed. N. K. Gottwald. *Semeia* 37. Decatur, Georgia: Scholars Press.

Fried, Morton H.

1967 *The Evolution of Political Society.* New York: Random House.

Gottwald, Norman K.

1979 *The Tribes of Yahweh.* London: SCM.

1986 The Participation of Free Agrarians in the Introduction of Monarchy to Ancient Israel: An Application of H. A. Landsberger's Framework for the Analysis of Peasant Movements. Pp. 79–106 in *Social Scientific Criticism of the Hebrew Bible and Its Social World: The Israelite Monarchy,* ed. N. K. Gottwald. *Semeia* 37. Decatur, Georgia: Scholars Press.

Government of Palestine

1938, *Village Statistics.* Jerusalem.
1945

Gunn, David

1980 *The Fate of King Saul.* Sheffield: JSOT Press.

Haas, Jonathan

1982 *The Evolution of the Prehistoric State.* New York: Columbia University Press.

Halpern, Baruch

1981 The Uneasy Compromise: Israel between League and Monarchy. Pp. 59–96 in *Traditions in Transformation,* ed. B. Halpern and J. D. Levenson. Winona Lake, Indiana: Eisenbrauns.

1983 *The Emergence of Israel in Canaan.* Chico, California: Scholars Press.

Hauer, Chris

1986 From Alt to Anthropology: The Rise of the Israelite State. *JSOT* 36: 3–15.

Herrmann, Siegfried

1981 *A History of Israel in Old Testament Times.* Philadelphia: Westminster.

Johnson, Gregory A.
1973   *Local Exchange and Early State Development in Southwestern Iran.* Museum of Anthropology, University of Michigan Anthropological Papers 51. Ann Arbor: University of Michigan, Museum of Anthropology.

Kempinski, Aharon
1978   Tel Masos. *Expedition* 20(4): 29–37.

Kempinski, Aharon, et al.
1981   Excavations at Tel Masos: 1972, 1974, 1975. *Eretz-Israel* 15: 154–80 [Hebrew].

Khazanov, Anatoli M.
1981   The Early State among the Eurasian Nomads. Pp. 155–75 in *The Study of the State*, ed. H. Claessen and P. Skalník.
1984   *Nomads and the Outside World.* Cambridge: Cambridge University Press.

Kochavi, Moshe, ed.
1972   *Judea, Samaria and the Golan: Archaeological Survey 1967–1968.* Jerusalem: Carta [Hebrew].

Lee, Richard B.
1972   Population Growth and the Beginning of Sedentary Life among the Kung Bushmen. Pp. 329–42 in *Population Growth: Anthropological Implications*, ed. B. Spooner. Cambridge, Massachusetts: MIT Press.

Lewis, Herbert S.
1981   Warfare and the Origin of the State: Another Formulation. Pp. 201–21 in *The Study of the State*, ed. H. Claessen and P. Skalník.

Malamat, Abraham
1976   Origins and the Formative Period. Pp. 3–88 in *A History of the Jewish People*, ed. H. H. Ben-Sasson. Cambridge, Massachusetts: Harvard University Press.

Mayes, A. D. H.
1977   The Period of the Judges and the Rise of the Monarchy. Pp. 285–331 in *Israelite and Judean History*, ed. J. H. Hayes and J. M. Miller. London: SCM.

Mazar, Benjamin
1954   Gibeah. Pp. 412–16 in volume 2 of *Encyclopaedia Miqra[?]it* [Hebrew].

Mendenhall, George E.
1983   Ancient Israel's Hyphenated History. Pp. 91–103 in *Palestine in Transition*, ed. D. N. Freedman and D. F. Graf. The Social World of Biblical Antiquity Series 2. Sheffield: Almond.

Noth, Martin
1960   *The History of Israel.* London: A. and C. Black.

Oppenheimer, Franz
1928   *The State.* New York: Vanguard.

Peebles, Christopher S., and Kus, Susan M.
1977   Some Archaeological Correlates of Ranked Societies. *American Antiquity* 42: 421–48.

Pinner, L.
1931   *Wheat Culture in Palestine.* Tel Aviv: Palestine Economic Society.

Price, Barbara J.
  1978   Secondary State Formation: An Explanatory Model. Pp. 161–86 in
            Origins of the State, ed. Cohen and Service.
Rathje, W. L.
  1971   The Origin and Development of Lowland Maya Classic Civilization.
            American Antiquity 36: 275–85.
Renfrew, Colin
  1974   Beyond a Subsistence Economy: The Evolution of Social Organiza-
            tion in Prehistoric Europe. Pp. 69–85 in *Reconstructing Complex Socie-
            ties*, ed. C. B. Moore. Cambridge: ASOR.
Rosen, Baruch
  1986   Subsistence Economy of Stratum II. Pp. 156–85 in ʿIzbet Ṣarṭah, ed.
            I. Finkelstein.
Salzman, Philip C.
  1978   The Proto-state in Iranian Baluchistan. Pp. 125–40 in *Origins of the
            State*, ed. Cohen and Service.
Sanders, William T., and Webster, David
  1978   Unilinealism, Multilinealism and the Evolution of Complex Socie-
            ties. Pp. 249–302 in *Social Archaeology: Beyond Subsistence and Dating*,
            ed. C. L. Redman et al. New York: Academic Press.
Service, Elman R.
  1962   *Primitive Social Organization*. New York: Random House.
  1975   *Origins of the State and Civilization*. New York: W. W. Norton.
  1978   Classical and Modern Theories of the Origins of Government. Pp.
            21–34 in *Origins of the State*, ed. Cohen and Service.
Sinclair, Lawrence A.
  1960   An Archaeological Study of Gibeah (Tell el Ful). *AASOR* 34–35: 1–52.
Stager, Lawrence E.
  1985   The Archaeology of the Family in Ancient Israel. *BASOR* 260: 1–35.
Vikander-Edelman, Diana
  1986   *The Rise of the Israelite State under Saul*. Unpublished Ph.D. disserta-
            tion, The University of Chicago.
Waldbaum, Jane C.
  1978   *From Bronze to Iron*. Studies in Mediterranean Archaeology 54. Gothen-
            burg: P. Aström.
Webster, David
  1975   Warfare and the Evolution of the State: A Reconsideration. *American
            Antiquity* 40: 464–70.
Wellhausen, Julius
  1957   *Prolegomena to the History of Ancient Israel*. New York: Meridian.
  (1883)
White, Leslie A.
  1969   *The Science of Culture*. New York: Ferrar, Straus and Giroux.
Whitelam, Keith W.
  1986   Recreating the History of Israel. *JSOT* 35: 45–70.

Wright, Henry T.
   1978   Toward an Explanation of the Origin of the State. Pp. 49–68 in *Origins of the State*, ed. Cohen and Service.
Wright, Henry T., and Johnson, Gregory A.
   1975   Population Exchange and Early State Formation in Southwestern Iran. *American Anthropologist* 77: 267–89.
Zertal, Adam
   1986   *The Israelite Settlement in the Hill Country of Manasseh.* Unpublished Ph.D. Dissertation, Tel Aviv University [Hebrew with English abstract].

Prophecy and Ecstasy: A Reexamination

ROBERT R. WILSON

I

[[321]] In recent years form criticism has shed a great deal of light on the phenomenon of ancient Israelite prophecy. The method has been particularly successful in uncovering the structure and history of the prophetic literature. Since the pioneering work of Hermann Gunkel and Hugo Gressmann, form critics have produced a steady stream of increasingly sophisticated literary analyses of prophetic texts. Numerous prophetic speech forms have been isolated, and fruitful attempts have been made to trace the literary and social history of these forms. Their original settings have been explored, and scholars have described the ways in which the originally oral forms have been incorporated into their present biblical contexts. To be sure, scholarly disagreements still exist, and in particular the social matrix of prophetic language has proved difficult to analyze with any certainty. Nevertheless, it is fair to say that form criticism has made a major contribution to our understanding of the prophetic literature.[1]

To date, form critics have experienced difficulties in relating their literary analyses to certain known aspects of prophetic behavior. Particularly problematic has been the relationship between prophetic ecstasy and the relatively rational forms of prophetic action and speech that form critics have seen in the biblical literature. The existence of ecstasy in Israel cannot be questioned, for several biblical narratives describe ecstatic prophetic behavior. However, form critics have been unable to

Reprinted with permission from *Journal of Biblical Literature* 98 (1979) 321–37.

1. For convenient summaries of form-critical research on the prophets, see W. E. March, "Prophecy," *Old Testament Form Criticism* (ed. J. H. Hayes; San Antonio: Trinity University, 1974) 141–77; and G. M. Tucker, "Prophetic Speech," *Int* 32 (1978) 31–45.

agree on the role which ecstasy played in Israelite prophecy in general and have been uncertain about the relationship between ecstasy and the writing prophets in particular.

Although earlier treatments of Israelite prophecy had noted the existence of prophetic ecstasy, it became a major problem for form criticism after the work of Gustav Hölscher.[2] In contrast to the commonly held views of his day, Hölscher argued that ecstasy was characteristic of *all* Israelite prophecy, although he did try to distinguish between the ecstasy of the early *nĕbîʾîm* [['prophets']] and the ecstasy of the writing prophets. According to Hölscher, the prophets [[322]] actually delivered their oracles while in ecstasy and then later wrote them down. These original prophetic words were then edited and elaborated by later writers. By making this suggestion Hölscher posed for form criticism the problem of ecstasy in its sharpest form: How could Hölscher's picture of the ecstatic prophet be reconciled with the form-critical picture of prophets acting rationally and delivering coherent messages to the people? How could the ecstatic utterances of the prophets have resulted in the intelligible, highly structured oracles analyzed by the form critics?

Since the work of Hölscher, treatments of the problem of ecstasy have followed three major lines of development.[3] First, some scholars have simply denied that the writing prophets and those no-writing prophets whose words have been preserved were ecstatics. There are two major variations on this theme. Following the approach of scholars writing before the publication of Hölscher's work, some critics have admitted the existence of ecstasy early in the history of Israelite prophecy but have flatly denied the presence of ecstasy among the writing prophets.[4] In its extreme form, this approach is forced to overlook clear indications of ecstasy among the writing prophets, and most scholars following this line admit the occasional presence of "mild forms of ecstasy" in the writing prophets.[5] Taking a different tack, some scholars have argued that the

---

2. G. Hölscher, *Die Profeten* (Leipzig: J. C. Hinrichs, 1914) 1–358.

3. Very few scholars have accepted Hölscher's views without modification. For an overview of solutions to the problem of ecstasy, see H. H. Rowley, "The Nature of Old Testament Prophecy in the Light of Recent Study," *The Servant of the Lord* (2d ed.; Oxford: Blackwell, 1965) 95–134 (reprinted from *HTR* 38 [1945] 1–38).

4. W. Robertson Smith, *The Old Testament in the Jewish Church* (2d ed.; London: Adam and Charles Black, 1895) 282–308; M. Buttenwieser, *The Prophets of Israel* (New York: Macmillan, 1914) 138–63; I. P. Sierstad, *Die Offenbarungserlebnisse der Propheten Amos, Jesaja und Jeremia* (Oslo: Jacob Dybwad, 1946) 156–83; A. J. Heschel, *The Prophets* (New York: Harper & Row, 1962) 324–409; H. Junker, *Prophet und Seher in Israel* (Trier: Paulinus, 1927) 9–13, 49–60.

5. J. P. Hyatt, *Prophetic Religion* (New York: Abingdon-Cokesbury, 1947) 17; cf. J. Skinner, *Prophecy and Religion* (Cambridge: Cambridge University, 1922) 3–6; H. W. Robinson,

"true prophets" in Israel were not ecstatics, while the "false prophets" described in the prophetic literature were ecstatics.[6] By assuming that all of the writing prophets were true prophets, this view is able to dissociate them from ecstasy. However, this approach underestimates the problems involved in differentiating true and false prophets in Israel, and it also overlooks the fact that there is no good biblical evidence to indicate that all of the so-called false prophets were ecstatics.

A second major line of development has taken an approach followed by Gunkel before the publication of Hölscher's work.[7] In contrast to Hölscher, [[323]] who believed that the prophets delivered their oracles while in a state of ecstasy, Gunkel suggested that the prophets produced their oracles *after* their ecstatic experiences had ended. The oracles were thus the products of rational minds and were attempts to communicate what had transpired during the prophet's ecstasy. A number of scholars have accepted some form of Gunkel's position and have argued that the prophets composed their oracles either immediately after their ecstatic experiences or at a later date.[8] Although this view has the advantage of accounting for the more-or-less rational nature of the prophetic literature, it is based on very little evidence. In addition, there are clear indications that some prophets did deliver oracles while in a state of ecstasy. Jeremiah's oracle in 4:19 ("my anguish, my anguish, I writhe in pain") seems closely connected to ecstasy, and the fact that Jeremiah's speech could be described as that of a madman (Jer 29:26) suggests that at least some of the prophet's utterances were given while in ecstasy. Ecstasy is also indicated by Jer 23:9, where the prophet describes

---

"The Psychology and Metaphysic of 'Thus saith Yahweh,' " *ZAW* 41 (1923) 5–8; A. Causse, "Quelques remarques sur la psychologie des prophètes," *RHPR* 2 (1922) 349–56.

6. H. T. Obbink, "The Forms of Prophetism," *HUCA* 14 (1939) 25–28; S. Mowinckel, " 'The Spirit' and the 'Word' in the Pre-exilic Reforming Prophets," *JBL* 53 (1934) 199–227; O. Grether, *Name und Wort Gottes im Alten Testament* (Giessen: Alfred Töpelmann, 1934) 94–111; A. Jepsen, *Nabi* (Munich: C. H. Beck, 1934) 208–17.

7. H. Gunkel, "Die geheimen Erfahrungen der Propheten Israels," *Suchen der Zeit* 1 (1903) 112–53; cf. his later treatment in "Einleitungen," in H. Schmidt, *Die Schriften des Alten Testaments* 2/2: *Die grossen Propheten* (2d ed.; Göttingen: Vandenhoeck & Ruprecht, 1915) xxv–xxviii (= "The Secret Experiences of the Prophets," *The Expositor*, 9th series, 1 [1924] 427–32).

8. T. H. Robinson, *Prophecy and the Prophets in Ancient Israel* (London: Duckworth, 1923) 50–51; J. Hempel, *Die althebräische Literatur* (Wildpark-Potsdam: Akademische Verlagsgesellschaft Athenaion, 1930) 62–63; S. Mowinckel, "Ecstatic Experience and Rational Elaboration in Old Testament Prophecy," *AcOr* 13 (1935) 264–91; J. Lindblom, *Prophecy in Ancient Israel* (Philadelphia: Muhlenberg, 1962) 47–65, 105–8, 122–37, 177–82, 197–202, 216–19; G. Widengren, *Literary and Psychological Aspects of the Hebrew Prophets* (Uppsala: Lundequist, 1948) 98–120.

himself as shaking and like a drunken man because of the words of Yahweh.

The third approach to the problem of ecstasy has been taken by scholars who admit that even the writing prophets may have had ecstatic experiences of some type, although those experiences may have been mild and infrequent. These scholars argue, however, that the *content* of the prophets' words must be distinguished from the ecstatic *means* by which those words were received.[9] This argument has the effect of shifting the focus of scholarly inquiry away from the problem of ecstasy, but by doing so it leaves unanswered the form-critical question of the relationship between ecstasy and the prophetic literature.

II

This brief survey of attempts to deal with the problem of ecstasy indicates that there is much scholarly disagreement on the role which ecstasy played in shaping the prophetic literature. Not only are the three major approaches which we have outlined somewhat in conflict with each other, but no single approach is able to account satisfactorily for all of the biblical evidence. Clearly, then, if any progress is to be made on this problem, new approaches or new evidence must be employed.

[[324]] Any reexamination of the problem of ecstasy must begin with the observation that biblical scholars have been somewhat imprecise in their use of the term "ecstasy." Although few scholars actually define the term in their work, most seem to view ecstasy as the *means* by which divine-human communication takes place. In ecstasy the prophet becomes dissociated from his normal state and enters some sort of supranormal relationship with God. However, scholars also frequently use the term "ecstasy" to refer to the *observable behavioral characteristics* exhibited by a person in communication with the divine world. Thus the term is frequently thought to include such behavioral manifestations as loss of consciousness, physiological collapse, obsessive or compulsive actions, garbled speech, and visions or hallucinations.[10] Any new inquiry into the

---

9. Rowley, "Old Testament Prophecy," 128–31; cf. Mowinckel, "Ecstatic Experience," 279–80.

10. This vagueness in the use of the term "ecstasy" characterizes most of the scholarly discussion. However, Lindblom (*Prophecy*, 4–6, 216–17) recognizes different types of ecstasy, ranging from that caused by intense concentration on one idea or feeling to that involving absorption into the deity. The ecstasy of the early prophets tended to be of the former type, while the ecstasy of the classical prophets illustrates the latter type. According to Lindblom, the early prophets sought ecstasy as an end in itself, and their behavior was orgiastic. In contrast, for the classical prophets ecstasy was simply the means by which divine

nature and function of ecstasy in Israelite society must therefore have two foci: the nature of the process of divine-human communication and the behavioral characteristics arising from that process of communication. However, the history of scholarship on the problem of ecstasy suggests that the biblical evidence relating to these two areas of inquiry is difficult to interpret. It will therefore be helpful to supplement the biblical mate rial by examining some contemporary anthropological studies which have dealt with the social roles of divine-human intermediaries.

III

Anthropologists writing about divine-human intermediaries seldom use the term "ecstasy" in their work. When the term is employed, it is usually seen as a religious form of trance. "Trance" is a word used by anthro-pologists and psychologists to describe a psychological and physiological state, typically "marked by reduced sensitivity to stimuli, loss or alter-ation of knowledge of what is happening, [and] substitution of auto-matic for voluntary activity."[11] For our purposes, it is important to note that the word "trance" is usually used by anthropologists to refer to a *type of behavior.* The word is not used to [[325]] describe the *process* by which communication between the human and divine worlds takes place. For such descriptions, anthropologists usually rely on native explanations. In general, there are two major ways in which spirits are said to communi-cate directly with humans. First, the spirit may possess the intermediary. In this case the spirit physically enters the human body and takes control of the host's speech and physical actions. Second, the spirit or soul of the human may leave its body and travel to the world of the spirits.[12]

---

revelations were received. Thus Lindblom follows the common pattern by using the word "ecstasy" to refer both to a type of behavior and to a means of revelation, but unlike most scholars he *recognizes* that the word can be used in two ways. For another attempt to distin-guish different types of ecstasy on purely theoretical grounds, see J. Mauchline, "Ecstasy," *ExpTim* 49 (1937–38) 295–99.

11. E. Bourguignon, "The Self, the Behavioral Environment, and the Theory of Spirit Possession," *Context and Meaning in Cultural Anthropology* (ed. M. E. Spiro; New York: Free Press, 1965) 41. For a more thorough discussion of the characteristics of trance, see S. S. Walker, *Ceremonial Spirit Possession in Africa and Afro-America* (Leiden: Brill, 1972) 10–25.

12. For discussions of the general features of spirit possession, see Walker, *Ceremonial Spirit Possession,* 47–53; M. J. Field, "Spirit Possession in Ghana," *Spirit Mediumship and Society in Africa* (ed. J. Beattie and J. Middleton; New York: Africana, 1969) 3–5; and E. Bourgui-gnon and L. Pettay, "Spirit Possession, Trance, and Cross-Cultural Research," *Symposium on New Approaches to the Study of Religion* (ed. J. Helm; Seattle: American Ethnological Society, 1964) 39–46. Soul absence is discussed by S. M. Shirokogoroff, *Psychomental Complex of the Tungus* (London: Kegan Paul, Trench, Trubner, 1935) 317–22; and A. Balikci, "Shamanistic Behavior among the Netsilik Eskimos," *Southwestern Journal of Anthropology* 19 (1963) 384–92.

Although both of these descriptions of the process of divine-human communication appear in the Bible, in Israel Yahweh was usually thought to communicate with the prophets by means of possession. In our present text the existence of possession in Israel is indicated by expressions such as the following:

(1) "the hand of the Lord fell upon me" (Ezek 8:1; cf 1:3; 3:14, 22; 33:22; 37:1; 40:1; Isa 8:11; 1 Kgs 18:46; 2 Kgs 3:15; Jer 15:17)[13]
(2) "the spirit lifted me up" (Ezek 8:3; cf. 11:1, 24; 43:5)
(3) "the spirit entered into me" (Ezek 2:2; 3:24)
(4) "the word of the Lord was to me" (Jer 1:4 and often)
(5) "the spirit rested on them" (Num 11:25–26)
(6) "the spirit of the Lord is upon me" (Isa 61:1)
(7) "the spirit (of the Lord) clothed itself with Gideon/Amasai/Zechariah" (Judg 6:34; 1 Chr 12:19; 2 Chr 24:20)

It should be noted that these expressions indicate possession but do not necessarily imply trance or ecstasy. Because possession was the primary means of divine-human communication in Israel, from this point on, in the interests of brevity, we will confine our anthropological survey to studies of spirit possession.

When spirit possession is evaluated positively by a society—that is, when possession is not attributed to evil spirits or regarded as an illness— that possession may result in many different kinds of behavior. Trance may or may not be present. In the case of non-trance behavior, the intermediary may not exhibit any abnormal characteristics and may simply relay the message of the spirits or speak normally with the voice of the spirits. In the case of trance behavior, the intermediary's actions may range from apparently uncontrolled physical activity to completely normal physical activity. The speech of the intermediary may range from unintelligible nonsense syllables to perfectly coherent discourse.

[[326]] Although possessed individuals act in a wide variety of ways, it is important to note that within a given society possession behavior is almost always stereotypical. In many societies the onset of possession follows a standard pattern. For example, in many African possession cults potential cult members exhibit stereotypical symptoms which are easily recognizable by the society. In some societies a form of trance is included among these initial symptoms, while in other societies trance is absent. In many societies possessed persons are expected to perform certain prescribed actions. Thus, shamans in Asia, Africa, and America are

13. For a thorough discussion of this phrase, see J. J. M. Roberts, "The Hand of Yahweh," *VT* 21 (1971) 244–51.

expected to be able to carry out traditional rituals while in trance, and in some societies shamanic trance performances involve the coherent recitation of complicated lists of spirits. Deviation from the prescribed actions or failure to reproduce the traditional lists is usually taken as a sign of the failure of the shaman's powers.[14] Some of the most remarkable examples of this type of stereotypical behavior are to be found in Bali and Haiti. In Bali trance behavior sometimes takes the form of a highly complex dance, the pattern of which clearly indicates the identity of the spirit which is possessing the dancer. Each spirit has a characteristic dance which the dancer performs. In both Bali and Haiti trance behavior may take the form of traditional ritual dramas, in which each participant takes the part of the spirit by which he or she is possessed.[15]

Just as possessed intermediaries act in a stereotypical way, so they also use stereotypical speech patterns. In some cases the intermediaries speak in an unknown tongue that is not intelligible to bystanders. The unintelligible words are regarded as the secret language of the spirits, known only to their intermediaries, who translate after the spirits have spoken. In other cases, however, the language of the intermediaries is intelligible to normal individuals, although it may be slightly different from the language currently in general use. For example, mediums in the Ethiopian *zar* possession cult speak a form of Amharic—which, of course, is intelligible to the rest of the society—but the dialect of the spirits differs from normal speech in that the former makes use of only a few loanwords and uses a large number of paraphrastic expressions, metaphors, and comparisons. In this respect, the language seems almost formulaic, for it consistently uses the same unusual circumlocutions for common words and phrases. The morphology of the language is clearly Amharic, but occasionally unusual changes are made in the spelling of words, and some words are abnormally lengthened.

The stereotypical language of intermediaries sometimes even extends to their accounts of their revelatory dreams. Nuba shamans, for example, are usually drawn into their profession when they have strange dreams involving snakes, leopards, and red and white horses. These images are common in ⟦327⟧ shamanistic dreams and regularly appear in the shamans' accounts of their initial experiences with the spirits.[16]

---

14. Shirokogoroff, *Psychomental Complex*, 347–49, 353–58.

15. J. Belo, *Trance in Bali* (New York: Columbia University, 1960) 4, 52–66, 96–102, 200; Walker, *Ceremonial Spirit Possession*, 26–73.

16. W. Bogoras, *The Chukchee* (Leiden: Brill, 1904–1909) 416, 425, 437–39; Balikci, "Shamanistic Behavior," 384; W. Leslau, "An Ethiopian Argot of People Possessed by a Spirit," *Africa* 19 (1949) 204–12.

Not only do individual societies exhibit characteristic and stereotypical possession behavior, but sometimes within a single society different types of stereotypical behavior are connected with specific social situations and groups. Thus, for example, in some societies it is appropriate for participants in certain ritual activities to become possessed and to exhibit certain traditional types of behavior. However, outside of the context of the ritual, this possession behavior is viewed negatively and may even be suppressed. Similarly, in some societies members of certain social groups are allowed or even expected to become possessed, while people who are not members of these groups are not allowed to exhibit possession behavior. In some cases, professional intermediaries, such as shamans, priests, and diviners, are required to become possessed and to carry out certain professional functions, while this same possession behavior might be viewed as illness if it were to appear in non-professionals. Even when it is legitimate for two or more groups within the society to become possessed, each group may exhibit distinctive possession behavior, which is stereotypical within the group, and it may even happen that one group will view the possession behavior of other groups as illegitimate.[17]

The explanation for the stereotypical nature of possession behavior is probably to be found in the complex interaction between the possessed individuals and their societies. Several factors seem to be involved in this interaction. First, every society rigidly controls the type of public behavior which its members may exhibit, and for this reason certain types of possession behavior are evaluated negatively and suppressed. For example, a few groups allow extremely violent possession behavior, and many groups do not view completely uncontrolled trance as an acceptable manifestation of possession. Such behavior is usually considered an illness which must be cured or a sign of possession by demons that must be exorcised. For this reason, all successful intermediaries exhibit possession behavior that is controlled, even though it may appear to the outsider to be uncontrolled. Second, members of societies which believe in spirit possession face the problem of determining when possession is actually present. Because the external characteristics of valid possession are sometimes similar to those of illness, societies must develop some means of distinguishing the two. One way of solving this problem is to examine the behavior of people in the past who were known to have been [[328]] possessed and then to look for similar behavior in the present. In this way the society builds up a set of expectations about the behavior of possessed

17. M. J. Field, *Search for Security* (Evanston: Northwestern University, 1960) 56–57; E. Colson, "Spirit Possession among the Tonga of Zambia," *Spirit Mediumship and Society in Africa* (ed. J. Beattie and J. Middleton; New York: Africana, 1969) 82–85; A. J. N. Tremearne, *The Ban of the Bori* (London: Heath, Cranton & Ouseley [1914] 281–391.

persons, and these expectations serve as a guide for recognizing genuine possession. Finally, in societies where possession is evaluated positively and encouraged, people who, for various reasons, wish to be recognized as possessed respond consciously or subconsciously to social pressure to conform to expected possession behavior. To oversimplify the matter, we may say that potentially possessed individuals consciously or subconsciously learn from the society the sort of stereotypical behavior which is expected of them.[18]

IV

This brief survey of anthropological material dealing with spirit possession has two important implications for future studies of the behavior of prophets in Israel. When these implications are explored, then new light will be shed on the role of ecstasy in Israelite prophecy, and the relationship between ecstasy and prophetic speech can be better understood.

First, the fact that the anthropological literature records a multiplicity of behavioral characteristics associated with possession implies that biblical scholars should not be too quick to generalize about the nature of possession behavior in Israel. Prophets working in the context of one social or religious group may have exhibited behavior that differed from that exhibited by prophets in other groups. Even prophets within the same group may have behaved differently, and a single prophet may have varied his behavior according to his historical and social context. Simply because some prophets seem to have exhibited a type of trance behavior, it may not automatically be assumed that such behavior was characteristic of *all* biblical prophets. Similarly, it may not be assumed that all trance behavior was of the same type. The anthropological material indicates that many different kinds of *controlled* trance behavior exist, even though societies will not tolerate completely *uncontrolled* trance behavior. A person in trance may exhibit behavior that superficially resembles the symptoms of illness, or he may act and speak coherently, carrying on normal conversations with those around him. Therefore, it is not necessary to assume that while Israelite prophets were in trance they were only capable of unintelligible utterances that had to be translated and written down at a later time. There is no *theoretical* reason to deny Hölscher's suggestion that the Israelite prophets composed and delivered oracles while in trance. Ultimately, however, the question of the nature of prophetic

---

18. I. M. Lewis, *Ecstatic Religion* (Baltimore: Penguin, 1971) 34–35, 76–78, 176; Walker, *Ceremonial Spirit Possession*, 91; Belo, *Trance in Bali*, 3, 68–74; W. Mischel and F. Mischel, "Psychological Aspects of Spirit Possession," *American Anthropologist* 60 (1958) 254–60.

possession behavior must be answered with respect to each individual prophet and perhaps even with respect to each social situation in which the prophet worked.

[[329]] Second, the fact that the anthropological literature shows most possession behavior to be stereotypical within a particular group implies that stereotypical behavior may have been exhibited by the Israelite prophets as well. This possibility must be investigated in order to understand fully the relationship between ecstasy and prophetic speech, for both can be elements of possession behavior. Ecstasy itself may follow stereotypical patterns, and the use of stereotypical language may be a feature of possession behavior, whether ecstasy is involved or not. Form critics have long known that prophetic speech tends to follow certain set patterns, but it may be fruitful to try to determine whether or not these traditional prophetic speech forms are in reality simply manifestations of stereotypical prophetic possession behavior. Furthermore, the anthropological material also suggests that if stereotypical prophetic behavior, including ecstasy, existed in Israel, the various groups in Israelite society may have reacted to such behavior in different ways. Some groups must have at least tacitly supported the prophets' behavior, or they could not have continued to exist. On the other hand, some groups may have held less tolerant views and may have evaluated characteristic prophetic behavior negatively.

The question of the existence of stereotypical prophetic behavior in Israel can be answered only after a thorough examination of all of the Israelite prophets. However, there is at least one bit of evidence that suggests that such behavior did exist. This evidence has been used before in discussions of prophetic ecstasy, but to date the results have been inconclusive. To describe prophetic activity, the OT sometimes uses verbal forms of the root *nb* [['to prophesy']]. This root is used as a verb only in the niphal and hithpael, and both of these forms are assumed to be denominatives of the word *nābî*, the most common title given to Israel's prophets. However, the semantic distinction between these two verb forms is difficult to establish, for they often appear together and seem to carry the same meaning (for example, 1 Sam 10:5, 6, 10, 11, 13; Jer 26:20; Ezek 37:9–10). Therefore, most scholars assume that any original distinction between the two forms has been lost, and both are usually translated "to prophesy."[19] When scholars do try to reconstruct the original distinction between the two forms, some variation of the following semantic development is usually suggested: The hithpael forms, which predominate in the early texts, originally indicated ecstatic activity. The few niphal forms

---

19. See the survey of Rowley, "Old Testament Prophecy," 103–15.

occurring in early texts also seem to have had links to ecstasy, although this is not entirely certain. Soon, however, the niphal came to be associated only with intelligible prophetic speech, while the hithpael continued to be used to describe ecstatic prophetic activity. As the niphal forms became more common in the period of classical prophecy, the meaning of the hithpael gradually merged with that of the more common niphal until finally the two were used interchangeably.[20] There are several problems with this [[330]] hypothetical semantic development. First, it employs an oversimplified view of the nature of ecstasy, a view which cannot be supported from the anthropological material. Second, even when the common understanding of ecstasy is granted, the hithpael must sometimes be assumed to indicate ecstatic behavior in passages where in fact there are no clear indications of such behavior. Finally, this hypothetical semantic development cannot easily explain why the two verb forms finally merged. Scholars usually imply that the use of the niphal increased because Israel's classical prophets were more rational and coherent than their predecessors, while ecstatic behavior decreased, thus encouraging the hithpael to lose its original connotation. However, this scenario must make untested assumptions about the history of prophecy in Israel.

An alternative to this problematic reconstruction may be suggested on the basis of the anthropological evidence. On the analogy of forms such as *hithāl* ('pretend to be sick', 'act as if you were sick' [2 Sam 13:5; cf. 13:6]), *hit²abbĕlî* ('pretend to mourn', 'act like a mourner' [2 Sam 14:2]), and *lĕhištaggēaᶜ* ('to act like a madman' [1 Sam 21:16]), it may be suggested that *hitnabbē²* originally had the general meaning 'to act like a prophet', 'to exhibit the behavior characteristic of a *nābî²*'. This characteristic behavior may have varied, depending on the group in which the prophet was acting and the historical period involved, but the behavior would presumably have included both words and deeds. It would also have been recognized by the society as characteristic of prophets, although different groups may have held different opinions about the suitability of this characteristic behavior. In contrast, the niphal forms may have originally simply referred to prophetic speech. In groups where

---

20. For a defense of this argument, see R. Rendtorff, "*nābî²* in the Old Testament," *TDNT* 6 (1968) 797–99. Cf. the older treatments of F. Haeussermann, *Wortempfang und Symbol in der alttestamentlichen Prophetie* (Giessen: Töpelmann, 1932) 10–11; W. Jacobi, *Die Ekstase der alttestamentlichen Propheten* (Munich: Bergmann, 1920) 5–6; Jepsen, *Nabi*, 5–10; and W. F. Lofthouse, " 'Thus Hath Jahveh Said,' " *AJSL* 40 (1924) 243. Recently, S. B. Parker ("Possession, Trance and Prophecy in Pre-exilic Israel," *VT* 28 [1978] 271–75) has used anthropological evidence to argue that the niphal and hithpael forms of **nb²* both mean 'to be in, or to fall into, a possession trance'. This view is difficult to maintain, for, as we shall soon see, the passages in which these forms appear do not always describe trance behavior.

characteristic prophetic behavior was marked more by stereotypical speech than by stereotypical physiological conditions and actions, the hithpael and niphal forms would have merged, for 'to act like a prophet' would have been the equivalent of 'speaking prophetically'.

The various aspects of this developmental hypothesis can be tested by examining the texts in which the hithpael of *nb°occurs. One of the early occurrences of the hithpael is in Numbers 11. This chapter has a complex literary and tradition history, but the bulk of the material is usually attributed to E.[21] As a result of one of the murmuring incidents, Moses complains to Yahweh that Israel has become a burden that is too heavy for one person to [[331]] bear (Num 11:11–12). In response Yahweh instructs Moses to choose seventy elders and promises to take some of the divine spirit which is upon Moses and to distribute it to them so that they might share the burden of leadership (Num 11:16–17). Moses does as he has been commanded, and all but two of the seventy assemble with him at the Tent of Meeting. Yahweh then transfers some of Moses' spirit to the elders, and when the spirit rests upon them, they 'act like prophets' (*wayyitnabbe͗û* [Num 11:24–25]). Even the two who did not go to the tent receive the spirit and exhibiting characteristic prophetic behavior in the camp (*wayyitnabbe͗ bammaḥăneh* [Num 11:26–27]). The precise nature of this behavior is not clear, but it is recognized by the people as prophetic (Num 11:27). Furthermore, the behavior is evaluated positively. The possessing spirit comes from Yahweh and is not demonic. The appearance of the spirit is a mark of divine choice and serves to validate the elders' new authority. Joshua objects to the behavior of the elders not because of the behavior itself but precisely because he recognizes it as an indication of divine choice and therefore as a potential threat to the preeminence of Moses. In addition, he may not be sure that the behavior is actually caused by Yahweh's spirit and may be wary of attempts to usurp Moses' power. Moses reassures Joshua that Yahweh is indeed the source of the spirit and indicates that the sharing of leadership is the result of a divine command (Num 11:28–29).

A second early reference to characteristic prophetic behavior occurs in 1 Sam 10:1–13. Because this passage has played a crucial role in discussions of prophetic ecstasy, it must be treated in some detail. Although it is generally agreed that 1 Sam 10:1–13 reflects early tradition, the unity

---

21. The source analysis of Numbers 11 remains problematic. The units dealing with the prophetic activities of the elders (Num 11:16–17, 24–30) are usually regarded as editorial additions, but the origin of these units is uncertain. Nevertheless, the fact that the editor wove them, however loosely, into the remainder of the chapter indicates that they are to be interpreted in their present context. For a thorough discussion of the chapter's tradition history, see G. W. Coats, *Rebellion in the Wilderness* (Nashville: Abingdon, 1968) 96–101.

of the passage has recently been questioned. It has been suggested that the story of Saul's anointing originally involved an unnamed seer, who authenticated his act by predicting only two signs: Saul's meeting at Rachel's tomb with the men bringing news of his father's lost asses and the subsequent meeting at Bethel with the men carrying food (1 Sam 10.1–4). The third sign, the encounter with the prophetic band, is to be seen as a separate tradition, perhaps originally arising as an attempt to explain the origin of the saying, "Is Saul also among the prophets?"[22] This account of the tradition history of the passage is not without difficulties, but even if the account is accepted, the fact remains that editors attached the story of Saul among the prophets to the story of Saul's anointing, thus providing the context in which the prophetic story is to be [[332]] read. When seen in its context, the prophetic story gives some insight into the way in which a particular group viewed prophetic behavior, no matter whether that group originally created the whole text or was simply responsible for its editing.

The version of Saul's election found in 1 Sam 9:1–10:13 clearly places him in a favorable light, so much so that it has even been suggested that an early version of the narrative was used by Saul to justify his own rule. Even if this was not the original function of the story, the account reflects a positive view of Saul and of the manner in which he became ruler.[23] The narrative focuses on Saul, and the seer, whether originally Samuel or not, plays a subsidiary role. Saul is from an old, wealthy Benjaminite family and is the most handsome young man in Israel (1 Sam 9:1–2). He is zealous in pursuing the errand on which he has been sent, and when he is unable to locate the lost asses, he is concerned that his father will begin to worry (1 Sam 9:5). The visit to the man of God is initiated by a servant rather than by Saul, so there can be no suggestion that Saul was in any way responsible for engineering the events that were to follow (1 Sam 9:5–6). Before Saul's arrival, Yahweh gives Samuel instructions that imply no negative evaluation of Saul or his subsequent anointing. Saul is to be anointed as a leader (*nāgîd*), who will

22. Arguments against the unity of the passage are presented in detail by J. M. Miller, "Saul's Rise to Power: Some Observations concerning 1 Sam 9:1–10:16; 10:26–11:15 and 13:2–14:46," *CBQ* 36 (1974) 157–61. Counterarguments are presented by B. C. Birch, *The Rise of the Israelite Monarchy: The Growth and Development of 1 Samuel 7–15* (Missoula: Scholars Press, 1976) 29–42; cf. his "The Development of the Tradition on the Anointing of Saul in 1 Sam 9:1–10:16," *JBL* 90 (1971) 55–68; and T. N. D. Mettinger, *King and Messiah* (Lund: Gleerup, 1976) 64–78.

23. For a statement of the view that this unit reflects conditions during Saul's reign, see T. Ishida, *The Royal Dynasties in Ancient Israel* (Berlin: de Gruyter, 1977) 42–54. Although there is disagreement on the date and source of the narrative, its positive tone is generally acknowledged. See Birch, *Rise of the Israelite Monarchy*, 29, 42.

save Israel from the Philistines. There is no reference to anointing Saul as king. Furthermore, Yahweh's elevation of Saul is a gracious reply to the cries of oppressed Israel, and the language used to express this reply is reminiscent of the language used to describe Yahweh's deliverance of Israel from Egypt (1 Sam 9:16; cf. Exod 2:23; 3:7–9). When Saul arrives in Samuel's city, the young man reacts modestly to the seer's special treatment (1 Sam 9:21). Saul's reaction to the actual anointing is not even recorded, but his incredulity is implied by the fact that three signs are given to authenticate his election. The third of these signs, and the only one whose fulfillment is narrated in detail, is the meeting with the prophets. Saul is told that he will encounter a band of prophets exhibiting characteristic prophetic behavior (*mitnabbĕ³îm*). This behavior is not specifically described. However, the fact that the prophets are pictured playing musical instruments suggests that trance may have been involved, for music is frequently used to induce trance. Yet, apparently the prophets are still able to carry out normal human activities, such as walking and performing on musical instruments, and there is no suggestion that the trance state is incapacitating. When Saul encounters this group, the spirit of Yahweh will come upon Saul, and he will be changed. The positive nature of this experience is indicated by the fact that the possessing spirit comes from Yahweh and is an indication of divine election (1 Sam 10:5–6). The sign occurs just as Samuel had predicted. When Saul meets the prophetic band, he [[333]] exhibits its characteristic behavior (*wayyitnabbē³ bĕtôkām*). Again the precise nature of this behavior is unspecified, but no negative evaluation is given to it. However, the stereotypical character of Saul's behavior is clear from the fact that his acquaintances are able to recognize his behavior as prophetic. They are surprised at this turn of events, a fact that is said to explain the origin of the question, "Is Saul also among the prophets?" To the bystanders, the answer to this question seems to be, "Yes, it looks as if he is, but it is rather surprising." In fact, the reader knows that the answer to the question is "no." Saul's possession has to do with his election, not with his becoming a prophet.[24] The bystanders do not yet know this, however, and to settle the matter and to obtain an interpretation of Saul's behavior, one person inquires about the "father" or leader of the prophetic band of which Saul seems to be a member (1 Sam 10:10–13).[25] It is usually assumed that the "father" referred to in this inquiry is Samuel, although

---

24. For a grammatical analysis of the two possible answers to the question, see J. Sturdy, "The Original Meaning of 'Is Saul Also among the Prophets?'" *VT* 20 (1970) 210–11.

25. The question about the prophets' "father" is difficult to interpret in this context, but there is no doubt that *³āb* is the title of the leader of a prophetic group. See J. G. Williams, "The Prophetic 'Father'," *JBL* 85 (1966) 344–48; and A. Phillips, "The Ecstatics'

this passage never portrays him as the leader of a prophetic group.[26] In any case, Samuel would certainly be capable of answering the bystander's question. Saul's unusual behavior does not mean that he has become a prophet but that he has received Yahweh's spirit as a sign of election to Israel's leadership.

The story of Saul's election thus suggests that prophets in this period and in this place did exhibit stereotypical behavior which was evaluated positively, at least by the group responsible for this account. This behavior may have involved trance, although if so the trance behavior was controlled and not incapacitating.

[[334]] A very different picture of characteristic prophetic activity comes from the stories of David's rise to power. Although this material has a complex redactional history, it reflects Deuteronomic views and clearly supports David while opposing Saul.[27] The pro-Davidic outlook of the narrative is apparent already in 1 Sam 15:35, where Yahweh repents of having made Saul king. This is followed immediately by the election of David (1 Sam 16:1–13). As soon as David has been anointed, Yahweh's spirit departs from Saul, thus depriving him of his legitimacy, and Yahweh sends an evil spirit to torment Saul (1 Sam 16:14). It is therefore unlikely that this material came originally from the same group that produced the pro-Saul account in 1 Sam 9:1–10:13. If the two groups are the

---

Father," *Words and Meanings* (ed. P. R. Ackroyd and B. Lindars; Cambridge: Cambridge University, 1968) 183–94. Because there is no reference to any kind of prophetic speech in this passage, Phillips' theory that the prophetic "father" is sought to translate the incoherent ravings of the ecstatics cannot be supported in this instance. Rather, the "father" is probably sought in order to determine the real cause of Saul's behavior. Because in many societies the signs of genuine spirit possession and the symptoms of illness are virtually identical, a professional medium or diviner is frequently consulted for a diagnosis of the affected individual's condition (Belo, *Trance in Bali*, 1–3, 49–51; J. H. M. Beattie, "Initiation into the Cwezi Spirit Possession Cult in Bunyoro," *African Studies* 16 [1957] 150–61). Parker ("Possession Trance," 273–75) uses the absence of prophetic speech in this passage to argue that possession trance in Israel was not mediumistic and did not involve genuine communication between the divine and human worlds. In this particular passage Parker's argument is valid, but it cannot be generalized. The anthropological evidence that we have surveyed indicates that the presence or absence of intelligible speech cannot necessarily be correlated directly with the presence or absence of genuine divine-human communication. Some authentic mediums do not exhibit trance behavior that includes intelligible speech. Conversely, some individuals who speak intelligibly in trance are not recognized by their societies as genuine mediums. In the end it is the society that determines whether or not an individual's behavior indicates the presence of true divine-human communication, and many complex factors are taken into account in making this decision.

26. Williams, "The Prophetic 'Father'," 347–48.

27. For a summary of recent work on the accounts of David's rise to power, see Ishida, *Royal Dynasties*, 55–63. Cf. the more thorough treatment of Mettinger, *King and Messiah*, 33–47.

same, then the group must have undergone a radical shift in its evaluation of Saul's rule.

The first reference to characteristic prophetic behavior in this pro-Davidic narrative appears in 1 Sam 18:10–11. The evil spirit which Yahweh has sent possesses Saul and causes him to exhibit characteristic prophetic behavior (*wayyitnabbēʾ*). The precise nature of this behavior is unspecified, but it is apparently uncontrolled and violent, leading Saul to attack David with a spear. Saul's behavior is clearly evaluated negatively, a fact indicated not only by the description of its violence but also by its attribution to an evil spirit.

This negative view of characteristic prophetic behavior is further developed in 1 Sam 19:18–24. As a result of Saul's hostility, David is forced to take refuge in Ramah with Samuel, who is here clearly portrayed as the head of a group of prophets. When Saul sends messengers to capture David, they approach while the prophets are prophesying (*nibbēʾîm*), and the messengers too begin exhibiting characteristic prophetic behavior (*wayyitnabbēʾû*). Two more sets of messengers are sent, and each time the result is the same (1 Sam 19:20–21). The exact nature of the prophetic behavior is unspecified at this point in the narrative, but it is likely to have involved more than characteristic speech. The point of the story is that the messengers, through their contact with the prophets, are incapacitated and physically prevented from reaching David. This seems to suggest that the author of the story considers typical prophetic behavior to be a form of *uncontrolled* trance. This suggestion is confirmed by the conclusion of the story. Saul himself approaches, and he too begins to exhibit characteristic prophetic behavior (*wayyitnabbēʾ*). In this case the nature of the behavior is clear: Saul loses control of himself, tears off his clothes, and lies naked and helpless all day and night before Samuel. This incident, the narrator concludes, is the real origin of the saying, "Is Saul also among the prophets?" (1 Sam 19:22–24). Here there is no question that typical prophetic behavior is evaluated negatively. It is uncontrolled and incapacitating. Furthermore, in the overall context of these narratives, the traditional question, "Is Saul also among the prophets?" has a new answer. The reader already knows why Saul exhibits stereotypically uncontrolled, ⟦335⟧ violent prophetic behavior. He is possessed by an evil spirit which is driving him mad (1 Sam 18:10–11). The answer to the question is therefore, "No, Saul is no prophet; he is insane."[28] The group responsible for these narratives thus tends to evaluate

---

28. Sturdy ("'Is Saul Also among the Prophets?'" 211–13) is probably correct in suggesting that this saying originated in pro-Davidic circles and was used to denigrate Saul by calling attention to his "madness." If this was the original use of the saying, then its incorporation into the election narrative in 1 Sam 9:1–10:13 may represent an attempt by Saul's

possession behavior negatively and to consider it a potentially dangerous and uncontrollable type of activity.

A similar view is presented by a somewhat later text, one which again bears the stamp of the Deuteronomistic Historian. In the famous contest between Elijah and the prophets of Baal, the latter are said to have exhibited stereotypical prophetic behavior (*wayyitnabbĕʾû*). In this case the behavior seems to have been controlled, although it may have involved a form of trance. The prophets call on the name of Baal, "limp" around the altar, and slash themselves with knives (1 Kgs 18:26–29). The Deuteronomic writer evaluates this performance negatively, but not necessarily because trance itself is disparaged. Rather, for the Deuteronomist anyone who prophesies in the name of Baal is illegitimate by definition, even though the prophet otherwise speaks and acts like an orthodox prophet of Yahweh (Deut 13:1–5; 18:20–22).

After this description of the contest on Mt. Carmel, the occurrences of the hithpael of **nbʾ* increasingly focus on the speech of the prophets as the main characteristic of their behavior. In 1 Kgs 22:8, 10, 18 (= 2 Chr 18:7, 9, 17) both Micaiah ben Imlah and the four hundred Israelite court prophets are described by the hithpael of **nbʾ.* In both cases the focus of the narrative is on the conflicting prophetic oracles, and there is no suggestion of uncontrolled or violent behavior. Similarly, neither Micaiah nor the court prophets are evaluated negatively because of the form of their behavior. The king of Israel does not like Micaiah because he never delivers favorable oracles, but this objection is based on the content of his message rather than on its form. Similarly, the activities of the four hundred prophets are supported by the royal court, and the narrator uses no derogatory terms to describe their behavior. A negative note enters the narrative only when it is revealed that the *content* of the prophets' message is the result of possession by a lying spirit (1 Kgs 22:20–23).

In the same way Jeremiah uses the hithpael to describe the activities of Jerusalemite prophets who are misleading the people with false promises of [[336]] peace (Jer 14:14). Nothing further is known about the activities of these individuals, and they are condemned only because of

---

supporters to counter this pro-Davidic propaganda by providing an alternative explanation. This theory is not incompatible with Mettinger's suggestion (*King and Messiah*, 75–79) that prophetic groups were responsible for the present form of 1 Sam 9:1–10:13. For alternative interpretations see Parker, "Possession Trance," 278–79; J. Lindblom, "Saul inter Prophetas," *ASTI* 9 (1974) 30–41; and V. Eppstein, "Was Saul Also among the Prophets?" *ZAW* 81 (1969) 287–304. Parts of Eppstein's overall argument are problematic because they are based on unsupported assumptions about the history of prophecy in Israel.

the content of their message. Jeremiah later applies the hithpael to the prophets of Samaria who prophesied by Baal and misled the people (Jer 23:13). Again, there is no indication that Jeremiah opposed these prophets because of the form of their behavior. Rather he rejected them because of the source and content of their message. The hithpael is used in Jer 26:20 to describe Uriah the son of Shemaiah, who was killed because he proclaimed a message similar to that of Jeremiah (Jer 26:20–23). Finally, the hithpael is used to describe Jeremiah himself. After Jeremiah had written a prophetic letter to the exiles in Babylon, Shemaiah of Nehelam wrote to Zephaniah the priest saying that since he was in charge of 'every madman who acts like a prophet' (*kol-ʾîš mĕšuggāʿ ûmitnabbēʾ*) in the temple, he should discipline Jeremiah, who was prophesying (*hammitnabbēʾ*) and delivering inflammatory messages (Jer 29:24–28). Here it is clear that Shemaiah views Jeremiah's message negatively and perhaps also questions his authority, but there is no objection to the *form* of his behavior. In Ezekiel the hithpael of *ⁿbʾ* is used to refer both to the behavior of the Judahite women who prophesy (*hammitnabbēʾôt*) on their own authority (Ezek 13:17) and to the behavior of Ezekiel himself (Ezek 37:10). In both cases the focus is on the prophetic word, which is the sole basis of evaluation. The same is true in the latest use of the hithpael in 2 Chr 20:37, where the form is used to introduce a prophetic oracle.

This survey of the uses of the hithpael of *ⁿbʾ* suggests that this form was indeed used to describe characteristic prophetic behavior. However, this behavior seems to have varied from group to group within Israel and also changed over the course of Israelite history. The term sometimes designated types of ecstatic or trance behavior, but this was not always the case. Increasingly the term was used to describe characteristic prophetic speech, until finally the hithpael of *ⁿbʾ* became synonymous with the niphal.

V

Although we have examined only a small number of biblical passages during our survey of the meaning of the hithpael of *ⁿbʾ*, these passages indicate that at least some Israelite possession behavior did in fact follow patterns similar to those found in the possession behavior of modern prophets. We may summarize these similarities in the following way. First, the biblical evidence suggests that when Israelite prophets were possessed by Yahweh's spirit, they behaved in ways that were recognized by observers as indications of possession. Such recognition could have taken place only if the behavior followed stereotypical patterns that the observers associated with genuine prophetic behavior, so it is probably safe to assume that Israelite prophets, like their modern counterparts, acted and spoke in predictable ways during possession. When a prophet's normal possession behavior included ecstasy or trance, then the ecstasy itself presumably followed stereotypical ⟦337⟧ patterns. Second, the biblical descriptions of prophetic activity suggest that stereotypical prophetic behavior was not static. Just as modern prophets exhibit a wide variety of possession behaviors, so also the behavior of the Israelite prophets seems to have changed over the course of Israelite history and may have also varied according to the geographical, cultural, or social location of the prophet involved. Although during some periods and in certain groups ecstasy seems to have been part of a prophet's expected behavior, this was not always the case. Furthermore, even when ecstasy was present its characteristics were not always the same, and each prophet undoubtedly exhibited some deviations from the norm. In some cases ecstatic behavior included intelligible, although perhaps formulaic, speech, while in other cases there is no indication that the prophet spoke while in trance. Finally, the biblical evidence indicates that ecstasy was not viewed in the same way by all groups in Israel. As is also the case in modern societies, some groups in Israel considered ecstasy or trance an expected part of a prophet's behavior and a sign of genuine possession by Yahweh's spirit. However, other groups seem to have evaluated ecstasy negatively, and it was seen as a sign of mental illness.

The anthropological data and the small segment of biblical material that we have examined thus suggest that the question of prophecy and ecstasy is far more complex than earlier scholars had supposed. Many variables need to be considered in future research on the problem, and generalizations must be avoided. Only when each description of prophetic activity is examined individually will solutions to the problem begin to emerge.

Prophecy:
The Problem of Cross-Cultural Comparison

THOMAS W. OVERHOLT

[[55]] The phenomenon of prophecy has been widely distributed through-out human societies. We have recorded instances of prophetic activity from an impressive range of times and places, from the ancient Meso-potamian city-state of Mari, where in the 18th century B.C.E. prophets confronted royal administrators with the demands and promises of the god (Malamat 1966; Huffmon 1968; Hayes 1969; Moran 1969), to the New Yorker Joseph Smith, whose revelation and message have formed the basis for the development of Mormonism. The Saint-Simon movement of early 19th century France is another of the many instances of pro-phecy that have arisen within the Western stream of tradition (Talmon 1958), but prophetic activity has also been widespread outside that tradi-tion. Since the late 19th century the peoples of Melanesia have produced a whole series of cargo cult movements in most of which prophetic figures were of central importance (see Worsley 1968). There were Tokerua, the "prophet of Milne Bay" (Papua, 1893), Saibai, the prophet of the German Wislin movement (Torres Straits, 1913; see Chinnery and Haddon 1916–17; Eckert 1937), Evara and Biere of the Vailala Madness (Papua, 1919; see Williams 1923 and 1934), and Manehevi and his successors in the John Frum movement (Tanna, 1939–present; see Guiart 1951 and 1956; Barrow 1951), to name but a few. Prophets have [[56]] appeared in Africa (Lan-ternari 1963, Sundkler 1961), wartime Japan (May 1954), among various American Indian groups (see Mooney 1896: 657–763), and in other parts of the world as well.

Reprinted with permission from *Semeia* 21 (*Anthropological Perspectives on Old Testament Prophecy*; ed. R. C. Culley and T. W. Overholt; 1982) 55–78.

Nor has the appearance of prophets been confined to a particular kind of cultural adjustment. To be sure, the term "prophet" is likely first to call to mind the great high civilizations of the ancient Near East and figures like Isaiah, Jeremiah, and Muhammad. But Wovoka, the prophet of the Ghost Dance religion of 1890, was a Nevada Paiute, a tribe whose simple hunting and gathering culture had only recently come into close contact with European civilization. Navosavakadua, the first prophet of the new Tuka religion among Fijians, began his movement about 1885 in an interior region where there were as yet no white settlements (Sutherland 1910; Thomson 1895).

As one begins to explore the vast literature on prophecy, certain tendencies appear.[1] For one thing, data from primitive and higher cultures are usually dealt with separately. Studies of the Old Testament prophets, for example, normally make reference to extra-Israelite phenomena only to the extent that they bear directly on the development of Israelite prophecy. Much of the continuing discussion of the Mari prophets has centered on the question of the extent to which they were parallel in nature and function to the Israelite prophets, and one finds a similar concern mirrored in discussions of cult prophecy (Johnson 1962; Pedersen 1946), and other possible institutional analogues to Old Testament prophecy such as the royal messenger (Ross 1962) and royal vizier (Baltzer 1968). On the other hand, one finds studies of prophecy that are confined to its appearance within "lower cultures" (Schlosser 1950) or among "colonial peoples" (Fabian 1963; Lanternari 1963).

Another tendency of the literature is to discuss prophecy less for its own sake than as an element in some larger process. Studies of the Old Testament prophets have been very much preoccupied with the content of what these men proclaimed, and have found their message useful in helping to define the nature of Yahweh and his relationship to his people, as well as the general development of Israelite culture and religion. Thus we have discussions of "prophecy and covenant" (Clements 1965) and of the relationship of prophecy to certain specific aspects of Israelite culture (e.g., Donner 1963; Koch 1971). This inclination to be more interested in the theological content of the proclamation than in the prophetic pro-

---

1. The temporal vicissitudes of scholarly publishing make a note on chronology appropriate. This paper brings to completion a series of interconnected studies of the "prophetic process" which includes Overholt 1974 and 1977. In recent years there has been increasing interest in the "social location" of Israelite prophecy, and in the interval between the final revisions of this paper and its publication an important book-length study of the dynamic interrelationship between the Israelite prophets and their society has appeared which is limited by neither of the tendencies described in the following paragraphs (Wilson 1980).

cous itself is particularly evident in some of the well-known "theologies" of the Old Testament.[2]

When one turns to extra-Israelite phenomena, the situation is similar. The focus is not so much on prophecy itself as on the broader socio-cultural movements of which the prophets are a part, a concern which Anthony F. C. Wallace makes clear in his now-famous essay, when he defines a "revitalization movement" as "a deliberate, organized, conscious effort by members of a society to construct a more satisfying culture" [[57]] (1956: 265). Beginning with Ralph Linton's essay on "nativistic movements" (1943), there has been a continuing effort to classify these cults in terms of their beliefs and goals (Guariglia 1958; Koppers 1959; Köbben (1960), as well as numerous attempts to define their causes (in general see La Barre 1971). There have, of course, been many studies of individual movements, and these often take their departure from the kinds of theoretical analyses just mentioned (Zenner 1966, following Festinger 1956; Griffin 1970, following Wallace 1956). On the whole the same conditions persist in all these studies which led Jarvie to protest, with specific reference to theories of Cargo cults, that the prophetic leader himself has been unjustifiably neglected (1963: 131).

Now it must be acknowledged that there are good reasons for these two tendencies, for real stumbling-blocks to the comparison of prophets arise from at least three sources. The first has to do with the nature of the given group's cultural adjustment. There are obvious and striking differences, say, between stone age, tribal men of aboriginal New Guinea or North America and iron age, urban men of the ancient Near East, which complicate the task of comparison. And these differences do not stop with the material culture, but extend to world-views as well. One can think of the Judeo-Christian "historical" tradition as opposed to native mythological traditions and observe that persons who write about prophets tend to come out of the former and spend time discussing the "irrationality" of the latter. A second and closely related stumbling-block involves the content of the prophecies themselves, which in all cases is culturally conditioned. Separate movements may share a general hope for the eventual appearance or return of some valued person or thing, but to what extent are the specific objects of hope (e.g., Jesus, the buffalo, the ancestors bringing cargo) comparable? Finally, there is a real

2. W. Eichrodt's emphasis is on the covenant, the continuity through time of the Mosaic religion, and the personal quality of the divine-human relationship. G. von Rad is concerned with the larger process by which Israel's traditions underwent a series of reinterpretations, and I. Köhler mines the prophetic literature to construct a theological position conceived in Western categories.

danger that the investigator will fall prey to ethnocentricity and evaluate more highly what to him is more familiar or intelligible or "rational."

The difficulty of overcoming these barriers may be seen by glancing briefly at several attempts to do so. J. Lindblom, for example, approaches his study of ancient Israelite prophecy on the assumption that prophecy is a universal human phenomenon (1962). Early in the book he discusses extra-Israelite prophets and suggests what he considers to be the three defining characteristics of prophecy in general, namely that the prophet is a person who is conscious of having received a special call from his god, who has had revelatory experiences, and who proclaims to the people the message received through revelation. He then discusses the Old Testament materials with reference to these characteristics. But the extra-Israelite prophets are not again brought into the discussion for purposes of comparison, and it is clear that one of Lindblom's main interests, to which he devotes the last third of the book, is the specific theological content of the ancient Israelite prophetic messages.

[58] James Mooney's classic study of the Ghost Dance of 1890 is another case in point (1896). Mooney was not satisfied simply to describe the origin and development of this one prophetic movement, but attempted to set it in the context of a number of others which he took to be similar in character. Thus the first eight chapters of his book are devoted to descriptions of prophetic activity among various North American Indian groups, beginning with the Pueblo Revolt of 1680 and culminating with John Slocum and the Shakers of Puget Sound in the late 19th century. In addition a later chapter is devoted to "parallels in other systems" and discusses examples of such activity from the biblical period, Islam, and Christian sects and movements from the Middle Ages to the 19th century. Mooney does not elaborate any theoretical structure in terms of which he makes his comparisons, but one can find occasional statements that indicate he was using two general criteria in the selection of his materials. The first was the notion that messianic doctrines, wherever they are found, ". . . are essentially the same and have their origin in a hope and longing common to all humanity" (1896: 657). The second is a list of traits—inspiration via dreams, dancing, ecstasy, and trance—which are taken to ". . . have formed a part of every great religious development of which we have knowledge from the beginning of history" (1896: 928; see 719, 947). Because of its scope, Mooney's study is important and interesting, but it is more a listing of movements than a systematic comparison. It avoids the stumbling-blocks mentioned above by not acknowledging their presence, and throws little theoretical light on the nature of the prophetic process.

It is clear that the effort to compare prophecy cross-culturally would be greatly facilitated if one could arrive at some basis for comparison that was as much as possible free from culturally-conditioned content. With this in mind I want to propose a model of how the prophetic process works, apply this model to the discussion of two specific prophets, Jeremiah and Handsome Lake, and then suggest several implications that seem to me to follow from this approach to prophecy. The claim I wish to make is that although the specific *content* of their respective messages is culturally conditioned and, therefore, quite dissimilar, the prophetic *activity* of the two conforms to the same general pattern.

Before introducing the model itself, a word seems in order regarding its genesis. My own training has been in biblical studies, and my primary interest OT prophecy. I gradually became aware of and interested in what appeared to be prophetic movements among American Indians, and a post-doctoral fellowship which allowed me to spend a year studying anthropology afforded the opportunity for an extensive investigation of one such, the Ghost Dance of 1890. Though a formal cross-cultural comparison was not part of my original intention, it eventually became evident that the Ghost Dance as well as other prophetic movements and figures that I studied [[59]] had important features in common with OT prophecy. Reflection on this fact led to the development of the model, which I first proposed in a study of the Ghost Dance (Overholt 1974). I view the model, then, as the natural outgrowth of my study of Israelite and non-Israelite prophetic movements and of the important interpretive literature that has been generated by the scholarly investigation of both.[3]

Figure 1 states in the form of a diagram a way of understanding the nature of the prophetic process. The basic components of this model are two: a set of three actors and a pattern of interrelationships among them involving revelation (r), proclamation (p), feedback (f), and expectations of confirmation (e).

The focus on interrelationships that is evident here calls for some enlargement of traditional notions concerning a prophet's authority. Since the prophet functions as the messenger of the god, it seems justifiable to view his revelatory experiences as the primary source of his authority. In all instances of which I am aware it is simply assumed that a person who is truly functioning as a prophet has been the recipient of some such communication. These experiences are essentially private, and form the

---

3. A note on terminology is in order. In his recent work on the phenomenon Robert R. Wilson has chosen not to speak of "prophets," but rather of varieties of "intermediaries" who can be located with relation to each other along a continuum (Wilson 1980). The figures I have been studying under the rubric "prophet" are the OT prophets and leaders of non-Israelite "nativistic" movements. A millenarian component is often important in the proclamation of these persons, but that term alone does not provide a sufficient explanatory framework for understanding the process characteristic of their activity.

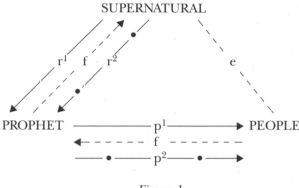

Figure 1

theological justification for his activity. They are also inevitably culturally conditioned, since both his perception and later articulation of them will be affected by the cultural and historical context in which he stands. In addition to this, however, there is a more public aspect of a prophet's authority which displays itself in various reactions to his message by the people to whom it is addressed. Since the act of prophecy must necessarily take place in a social context, these reactions are both inevitable and of critical importance. For the prophet seeks to move his audience to action, and his hearers may be [[60]] said to attribute authority to him insofar as they acknowledge and are prepared to act upon the "truth" of his formulation. In their response the hearers in effect judge the cultural "competence" of the prophet by deciding whether or not his message makes sense in the context of their cultural and religious traditions and is relevant to the current socio-political situation. As Peter Worsley has put it, "Charisma is thus a function of recognition: the prophet without honor cannot be a charismatic prophet" (1968: xii; cf. also Overholt 1977: 144f.). We will return to this point below.

Though most of the prophet's audience will be members of his own cultural community, we can expect that they will not all be of one mind in their evaluation of his message. But whether individuals accept, reject, or are indifferent to it, they will react to the prophet in some fashion, and it is this "feedback" and the prophet's response to it that defines the dynamic interrelationship between actors that is central to the model. Similarly, the prophet will assess his own message against his perception of the events going on around him and the feedback he gets from his audience. Since in his understanding the message he delivers is not strictly his own but is revealed to him by the god, we also need to assume the possibility of feedback from the prophet to god and an eventual new revelation either confirming or altering the original message.

Operating on the basis of this model, we can now list in a more systematic way the component elements that we would expect to find in any given example of the prophetic process. The minimum number of elements necessary for the operation and identification of the process are three: (1) The prophet's revelation. (2) A proclamation based on that revelation, which will have the following general characteristic: though it will inevitably contain innovative features, the message will nonetheless "make sense" in light of the cultural traditions of the prophet and his audience and the current social and historical situation in which they find themselves (cf. Barnett 1953: 181–266). (3) An audience to whom the proclamation is addressed and whose reactions to it—positive, negative, or indifferent—will be determined in large part by how well the message is perceived to meet the criterion suggested above. Additional components (prophetic feedback to the source of revelation; additional revelations; additional messages; certain experiences, here labeled "expectations of confirmation," which tend to independently confirm the god-given task of the prophet and strengthen the conviction of his authenticity) are possible, in fact even probable, although our ability to discover them will depend largely on the amount of data extant for any given instance of prophecy. Sometimes a fourth "actor," in the form of one or more disciples who serve as intermediaries between the prophet and his audience, may be added to the basic model sketched in Figure 1.

Because a prophet speaks in a concrete historical situation and elicits a response from his audience partly on the basis of their judgments [[61]] concerning what he says about it, it is necessary to preface the discussion of our two prophets with a brief sketch of the contexts within which they operated. The known public activity of the prophet Jeremiah spans approximately the last forty years of the existence of the Palestinian state of Judah (626–586 B.C.E.).[4] For the century prior to this period Judah had been an Assyrian vassal state, but by the time Jeremiah appeared on the scene the power of the Assyrians had begun to wane, particularly in the outlying regions of their empire. Under King Josiah (640–609 B.C.E.) Judah began to reassert her independence. Her political influence was extended northward into the Assyrian provinces of Samaria and Galilee, and accompanying this rebellion there was a major reform of the Yahweh cult. Based on an old lawbook found during the remodeling of the temple in 622, this reform sought to reassert the traditional form of the covenant relationship between Yahweh and his people.

---

4. This date has been disputed. For a discussion of the evidence cf. Overholt 1971. On the history of this period cf. 2 Kings 15–25; M. Noth 1958: 253–98, J. Bright 1959: 259–319, A. Malamat 1968: 137–56, and J. McKay 1973.

But though independent, Judah's geographical position placed her in the middle of an international struggle for power that made her situation precarious. Revolts in both Egypt and Babylon had contributed to the weakening of the Assyrian empire, but as the pressure on the Assyrians by Medes and Babylonians became more intense (614–610), Egypt, hopeful of preserving a buffer state between herself and these new threatening powers, came to the aid of her old enemy and joined Assyria in an abortive attempt to recapture the city of Haran near the headwaters of the Euphrates. It was while he was on his way to this rendezvous in 609 that Pharaoh Neco met and killed Josiah in battle, and on his return from the Euphrates three months later deposed Josiah's successor and placed a Judean of his own choice, Jehoiakim, on the throne in Jerusalem. Four years later in 605 the Babylonian king Nebuchadnezzar decisively defeated the Egyptian army at Carchemish on the Euphrates, and Judah again found herself squarely between two opposing powers.

As one might expect, there was considerable factionalism in Judah over how best to respond to this situation. During his reign, Jehoiakim and his supporters among the princes adhered to a pro-Egypt policy and came into open conflict with Jeremiah.[5] The king eventually revolted against Nebuchadnezzar, and the result of this action was the capture of Jerusalem and the deportation of persons and property to Babylon in the year 597. Under Zedekiah, the last kind of Judah, the same party dispute continued. The majority of the princes seemed to have been solidly pro-Egyptian, while the proclamations of Jeremiah became explicitly pro-Babylonian in the sense that he interpreted Nebuchadnezzar's conquest of Jerusalem as Yahweh's will and instructed the people to be obedient to their Babylonian overlord (cf. Jeremiah 27–29). The king wavered, but ultimately threw in with the former group. Judah revolted again, and Jerusalem was again besieged and captured. More of the population was exiled, and the city itself was destroyed and the temple of Yahweh burned. The prophet elected to stay in Judah, but shortly was carried away to Egypt against his will by a group of fleeing Judeans (cf. Jeremiah 37–44).

[[62]] This series of events presented the participants in them with a complex political and theological problem. Decisions were required concerning concrete and appropriate political and military actions, and in this critical time some looked to the religious traditions of the people for guidance. But prophets differed (cf. Jeremiah 28), and no single answer satisfactory to all emerged.

---

5. Cf. Jeremiah 26 and 36. In all of this Jeremiah, too, had his supporters in high places. Note particularly the references to members of the house of Shaphan in Jer 26:24; 29:3; 36:10–13, 25; 40:5f.; 41:2. Cf. Wilcoxen 1977.

Turning now to the New World, the Seneca tribe of North American Indians to which the prophet Handsome Lake belonged had been a member of the famed Iroquois League, a closely knit confederation of tribes whose origin predates the arrival of Columbus.[6] During much of the 18th century, this confederation was able, through a system of playing off the British against the French, both to maintain its territory and security and benefit from the material goods of European culture. But all that ended during the Revolution, which split the confederacy. Neutrality was abandoned, and most of the Iroquois gave their loyalty to the British. The ultimate result was that nearly all of their villages from the Mohawk River to the Ohio country were destroyed and they were cut off from their allies to the west, who established their own confederacy separate from the Iroquois.

The reservation system which was gradually imposed upon the Iroquois during the last decades of the century created what Wallace calls "slums in the wilderness, where no traditional Indian culture could long survive and where only the least useful aspects of white culture could easily penetrate" (1972: 184). The Cornplanter grant on the Allegheny River in northern Pennsylvania was somewhat unique among the reservations because of its relative isolation from white settlement. Though the influences of European material culture were considerable, many of the old social and political customs survived and the annual cycle of traditional religious ceremonials was still observed. It was there that Handsome Lake, Cornplanter's half-brother, resided. Of course, such isolation could only be relative, and the social pathologies that had been making inroads among the Iroquois for years were found also in Cornplanter's town. Drinking was a particularly serious problem.[7]

As in the case of Judah in Jeremiah's day, there was no unanimity of opinion among the Iroquois as to how to confront the problems inherent in their historical and cultural situation. Each reservation had its factions, the progressives "advocating the assimilation of white culture" and the conservatives "the preservation of Indian ways" (Wallace 1972: 202; Berkhofer 1965). Cornplanter may be reckoned with the former group, and by the time of Handsome Lake's vision his village had already come under the influence of Quaker missionaries. These men were nondogmatic in their approach to religion, and chose to concentrate on

6. This brief historical sketch depends mainly on Wallace 1972, especially pp. 21–236.

7. The followers of Handsome Lake recounted a legend of how the "evil one" enticed an unsuspecting young European to bring a bundle of "five things" (a flask of rum, a pack of playing cards, some coins, a violin, and a decaying leg bone) across the ocean to the Indians. This gift resulted in great misery and made necessary the "Good Message" or Gaiwiio (Parker 1913: 16–19). On drinking at Cornplanter's village cf. Parker 1913: 20–22, and Wallace 1972: 193f., 228–36.

offering positive assistance to the Cornplanter Seneca in such practical areas as farming, carpentry, and education. By May of 1799 they had also persuaded the council to ban the use of whiskey in the village (Deardorff 1951; Wallace 1972: 221–36).

⟦63⟧ The model outlined above assumes that for the prophetic process to occur there is required, first of all, a set of three actors designated the supernatural, the prophet, and the people. In the pages that follow we will be dealing with two such sets. The prophets are Jeremiah, a Judean of the late 7th and early 6th centuries B.C.E., and Handsome Lake, a Seneca who lived in the late 18th and early 19th centuries C.E. Jeremiah addressed his message to Judeans, primarily the inhabitants of the royal city of Jerusalem. Handsome Lake's message was directed to the Seneca of Cornplanter's band and, subsequently, other groups of Iroquois. The supernatural powers from whom each received his revelation were those familiar to the people: Yahweh, the ancestral God of Israel, and the Iroquois Creator.

The second basic component of the prophetic process is a pattern of inter-relationships among these actors. I have termed the modes of this interaction revelation, proclamation, expectations of confirmation and feedback. The latter is especially important, since it allows us to understand what has sometimes been conceived of as a one-way informational flow as a dynamic, two-way process. For the sake of brevity the following discussion will center mainly on two sequences of action involving revelation, proclamation and feedback.

The prophetic process involves what we might call a *revelation-feedback-revelation sequence*. The Book of Jeremiah opens with an account of an experience that Jeremiah understood to be a revelation from Yahweh commissioning him to be a prophet (1:4–10). Both from the style in which the various utterances of the prophet are framed and reports of other visionary or auditory experiences (1:11–12, 13–19; 13:1–11; 18:1–11; 19:1–15; 24:1–10), it seems clear that Jeremiah continued to receive revelations. But this communication with Yahweh was not all one-way. In the call vision itself Jeremiah is pictured as protesting against the role that was being put upon him (1:6), and these protests continued in a series of six "laments" or "complaints" in which he lashed out against his enemies (11:20, 12:1–4, 15:5, 17:18, 18:21–23), complained about the burdens of his office (20:7–9, 14–18), and accused Yahweh himself of acting unfaithfully (15:18, 20:7–9).[8]

It is important to point out that one of the factors in the mutual hostility between Jeremiah and some of his hearers was the question of

---

8. For a somewhat more detailed analysis of the Jeremiah materials from the point of view of this model cf. Overholt 1977.

the validity of his revelation and the message derived from it. Because he understood it to be part of what had been revealed to him, Jeremiah continually announced that disaster would befall the nation of Judah (cf. 1:10, 13–19; 17:16). But the people, who in any case would not have been overjoyed at such a message, at some point began to subject him to intense ridicule because the threatened calamity had failed to occur (17:15, 20:7f.). The prophet also seems to have had his doubts about the revelation (15:18, 20:7), and these formed one element in his feedback to Yahweh.

[[64]] The book also provides us with two examples of Yahweh's rejoinder to the prophet's feedback (12:5f., 15:19–23), and these can be considered "additional revelations" which in effect confirmed the prophet's original message. By implication we can assume that a similar feedback-response sequence lies behind that portion of the Hananiah episode (chap. 28) in which Jeremiah was temporarily unable to dispute the message of his opponent, but "sometime later" returned to condemn him as a liar. Further, it seems necessary to assume that, given the nature of prophecy, any alteration in message would be understood by the prophet to be grounded in an additional revelation from god, and therefore insofar as the announcement of a "new covenant" (31:31–34) and other passages of a more "positive" tone (e.g., 32:1–15) can be taken to reflect a genuine element of Jeremiah's message, they also imply further revelations.

The Gaiwiio ("Good Message"), a record of Handsome Lake's teachings which is still in use among followers of the "Longhouse way" (see Shimony 1961), begins by describing a "time of troubles" in Cornplanter village. The scene is at first community-wide. A party of Indians had just returned from Pittsburg, where they had traded skins and game for whiskey. A wild drinking party followed in which village life was disrupted and some families moved away for safety. The focus then shifts to a single sick man, who was held in the grip of "some strong power" and feared that he might die. Realizing that the cause of his illness was whiskey, he resolved never to use it again. Afraid that he would not have the strength to do this, he prayed to the "Great Ruler" and began to be confident that his prayer had been heard and he would live. The sick man was Handsome Lake (Parker 1913: 20–22).

On June 17, 1799, the sick man appeared to die. His body was prepared for burial and relatives summoned, but he revived and reported he had had a vision of three messengers who had been sent to reveal to him the Creator's will and instruct him to carry it to the people. The vision also contained a threat, for Handsome Lake was shown the steaming grave of a man who had formerly been commissioned "to proclaim that message to the world," but had "refused to obey." On August 7 of the same year the prophet received his second revelation in which he was guided on a journey through heaven and hell and given moral instruction. A third revelation occurred on February 5, 1800. Each of these visions was reported and discussed in a council of the people.[9]

Several passages in the Gaiwiio make it clear that Handsome Lake expected to receive further revelations. In his initial vision the three messengers promised, "We shall continually reveal things unto you," and this promise was repeated in 1809 when in the midst of a personal crisis the messengers came to the prophet and said, "We understand your thoughts. We will visit you more frequently and converse with you" (Parker 1913: 25, 47; Wallace 1972: 293f.). Although the present form of the Gaiwiio makes it difficult to date specific revelations, there is some internal evidence of such a ⟦65⟧ continuing sequence. Most conspicuous are the place names. The Gaiwiio specifically sets the initial vision in Cornplanter's village, but subsequent sections are said to derive from Cold Spring, Tonawanda, and Onondaga (all in New York; Parker 1913: 20, 46, 47, 57, 60–62, 76–80). These localities correspond to known periods of the prophet's activity. Furthermore, there are at least four sections of the Code that Wallace links to specific, dateable events: a derogatory reference to Chief Red Jacket arising out of a dispute over the sale of reservation land in 1801, a prophecy intended to discourage Iroquois participation in the "war in the west" (1811), and a composite section mentioning the people's reviling of Handsome Lake and his meeting with the Spirit of the Corn which seems to mirror events that took place in the years 1809 and 1815 (Parker 1913: 68, 65f., 47; Wallace 1972: 260, 293f., 318). The final sections of the Code deal with the revelations and events immediately preceding the prophet's death, which occurred on August 10, 1815, at Onondaga (Parker 1913: 76–80). It is clear that these revelations did not simply repeat what had gone before They arose out of Handsome Lake's attempt to deal with new situations, and were doubtless seen by him to be divine responses to his own quest for a solution.

The prophetic process involves as well a *proclamation-feedback-proclamation sequence.* Throughout his long career Jeremiah seems to have proclaimed a fairly consistent message, viz., that because of their actions and the "falsehood" that pervaded their existence the people were standing on the brink of a great national catastrophe (Overholt 1970). This message evoked both positive and negative responses from the people, though judging from the material available to us, the latter predomi-

9. This chronology was reconstructed by Wallace on the basis of the Simmons journal and other sources. The present form of the Code as represented in Parker has some of the revelations out of context. Cf. Wallace 1972: 359f., n. 5.

nated. The negative feedback was sometimes stated in terms of derision because the destruction he proclaimed had not yet come to pass (17:15, 20:7f.). In addition there are reports that he was at various times of his life threatened (11:18–23; 18:18, 22; 20:10), put in the stocks and beaten (20:1–6; cf. 29:26–28), brought to trial on a trumped-up charge (26:7–19), thrown into an abandoned cistern in hopes that he would die (38:1–6), charged with treason (37:13f., 38:1–4), and imprisoned (32:2f.; 37:15f., 20f.).

A further negative response to his proclamation can be seen in the numerous references to prophetic opponents whose message of "peace" contradicted that of Jeremiah (cf. 6:9–15, 23:9–40). A classic example because of its richness in narrative detail is the conflict with the prophet Hananiah recounted in chapter 28. We also have references to persons simply refusing to obey instructions conveyed to them by Jeremiah as the will of Yahweh (43:1–7, 44:15–19). On the other hand, there are instances of positive feedback. There are individuals and groups which supported the prophet (26:16–19, 24; 36:13–19; 39:11–14; 40:1–6), as well as occasions on which he was sought out by someone who wished to learn Yahweh's will for the current situation (21:1f., 38:14–16, 42:1–3).

[66] I have already suggested that the response of the people to a prophet will depend largely upon whether they perceive his message to be in continuity with their cultural and religious traditions and relevant to the current socio-political situation. But this is a rather flexible criterion, and not likely to lead to complete unanimity of opinion. It puts a tremendous burden upon the hearers, each of whom will be tempted to view the matter in terms of his own self-interests. It is evident that both Jeremiah and Hananiah had a following, and that the supporters of each could find some legitimate grounds for believing that their man's message was faithful to the tradition and relevant to the situation. I have dealt specifically with this problem in another place, and will not repeat that discussion here (1970: chaps. 2 and 5). It is sufficient for our present purposes to point out the intensity and significance of this feedback from the people to the prophet and suggest the mechanism by which it works.

As to whether the content of Jeremiah's message was affected by this feedback, the data are not so clear. In the Hananiah episode we have reference to a specific occasion on which the prophet was at least temporarily blocked and forced to retreat for some reconsideration and/or renewal of his message (28:11–16). Taken in conjunction with other passages in which he expresses doubts about his revelation (15:18, 20:7), it would seem reasonable to conclude that the intensity of the negative feedback Jeremiah experienced from time to time caused him to reconsider both the content of what he said and his own continuance in the prophetic office (cf. 20:9). Beyond that, the passages of more positive tone referred to above may indicate a response to a changing historical situation (looking beyond the destruction of Judah and Jerusalem) and mark the beginning of a substantive change in the prophet's long-standing proclamation of doom.

A summary of Handsome Lake's proclamation to the Iroquois has come down to us in the Gaiwiio. This narrative begins with an account of an episode of drunkenness and destruction in Cornplanter's village and of the prophet's sickness, death, and resurrection. It is in connection with the latter experience that the main themes of Handsome Lake's proclamation assert themselves, for the messengers revealed to him the four great wrongs by which "men spoil the laws the Great Ruler has made and thereby make him angry": drinking whiskey, using witchcraft, using "compelling charms," and practicing abortion. In the remaining sections considerable space is given to positive commands relating to social behavior (gossip, drunkenness, sharing, mourning customs, etc.), family life (the care of children, husband-wife relationships, the care of elders), and religion (the medicine societies were ordered to disband, but a number of the traditional ceremonies are specifically sanctioned and regulated). In addition the Code deals in several places with the relationship between Indians and whites (agriculture, schooling, and the Creator's protection of his people against extermination by the whites) and with the status of the prophet (disbelief is said to be due to the operation of an evil spirit, and ⟦67⟧ will be punished). A number of these themes are reinforced in the sections recounting the second revelation (the "sky journey"), where Handsome Lake witnessed the suffering of a variety of sinners (drunkard, wife-beater, gambler, etc.) in the house of the "punisher." Finally, there is reference to the apocalyptic themes of the sin of the world and the world's end and renewal.

Wallace understands the preaching of Handsome Lake to fall into two distinct phases. The first, covering the years 1799 to 1801, was characterized by an "apocalyptic gospel" in which the people were summoned to repentance and the recurring themes were world destruction, sin, and salvation. The second phase began in 1801 and featured a "social gospel" in which the main values that were stressed were "temperance, peace and unity, land retention, acculturation, and a revised domestic morality" (Wallace 1972: 278; cf. 239–302). As in the case of Jeremiah the response to this message was mixed. In the early years he as able to exercise both political and religious power, and the council at Buffalo Creek in 1801 prohibited the use of liquor and appointed him "High Priest, and principal Sachem in all things Civil and Religious." Over the next few years, however, his political influence declined. In 1807 the Iroquois confederacy was reorganized and the great council fire established at Buffalo Creek, where one of the prophet's chief rivals, Red Jacket, was influential. Handsome Lake and Cornplanter also quarreled, and factions developed in the Allegany band, causing the prophet to move out and locate first at Cold Spring and later at Tonawanda. But his religious influence remained strong. He made an annual circuit of visitations to other reservations preaching his gospel and winning converts (Wallace 1972: 260f., 286ff., 296ff.). As Wallace describes it, "these conversions were not casual matters. The Indians traversed the same mystic path to Gaiwiio as white converts to Christianity; the converts retained an intense devotion to the prophet who gave them strength to achieve salvation. "One of the Onondagas, when asked why they did not leave their drunken habits before, since they were often urged to do it, and saw the ruinous consequences of such conduct replied, they had no power; but when the Great Spirit forbid such conduct by their prophet, he gave them the power to comply with their request" (1972: 301).

What one notices about the Gaiwiio is how directly it spoke to the situation that plagued the Iroquois of Handsome Lake's day. Addressing a people debauched and demoralized by contact with white culture and the loss of their own traditional ways, the Gaiwiio accused them of wrongdoing,[10] laying heavy stress on evils disruptive of harmonious community life (strong drink, witchcraft, charms, and abortion, Parker 1913: 27–30). In its commandments great emphasis was placed on the strengthening of family relationships and the regulation of social behavior.[11] In response to the growing influence of white culture there was explicit approval of farming, house-building, animal husbandry, and, to a limited extent, education "in English schools" (Parker 1913: 38).

[[68]] In real life parts of this message evoked a negative response and caused the prophet trouble, particularly his determined attacks against witchcraft and supposed witch-inspired conspiracies. Reaction to the execution of one witch in 1809 caused him to have to leave Cold Spring, a situation reflected in the Gaiwiio: "Now it was that when the people

10. "The Creator is sad because of the sins of the beings that he created. He ordained that mankind should live as social beings in communities." Parker 1913: 36.

11. It is clear that Burke Long and I have been thinking about the problem of prophetic authority for several years now, and along similar lines. An earlier statement of the position taken here (Overholt 1977: 44–45) and the original draft of this paper were written before I had access to his 1976 study, but I want to acknowledge the influence of that study and of personal communications from Prof. Long on the final wording of these pages. One difference in our formulations is my suggestion that "perceived effectiveness" is likely to have been a general criterion for the hearers' attribution of authority to a prophet. Cf. also Overholt 1979.

reviled me, the proclaimer of the prophecy, the impression came to me that it would be well to depart and go to Tonawanda. In that place I had relatives and friends and thought that my bones might find a resting place there" (Parker 1913: 47; cf. Wallace 1972: 254–62, 291–94). Other sections which mirror responses to feedback in specific situations have been mentioned above.

The Gaiwiio spoke to the current situation, advocating such important cultural innovations as the involvement of men in farm labor, limited acceptance of white education, and the dissolution of the totem animal societies. But for all that, the Gaiwiio "made sense" in light of the traditions of the past. Social solidarity was stressed in the ethical commandments of the Code, and in particular the old religious values and ceremonies were for the most part retained. Its major new religious concept, the notion of judgment and afterlife in heaven or hell, was compatible with the old beliefs and was introduced "to insure the dedication of the people to conservative ritual." Handsome Lake "was in his own eyes as the messenger of God, necessarily the defender of the faith" (Wallace 1972: 318; cf. 251–54, 315–18). As Parker puts it, "Handsome Lake sought to destroy the ancient folk-ways of the people and to substitute a new system, *built of course upon the framework of the old*" (114; emphasis added). Eventually, a myth even developed to account for the origin of the conditions that made the Gaiwiio necessary and fix its place in the overall order of things (see note 7).

The position taken in this paper is that feedback from the people to the prophet is important both because of its potential for helping to shape the latter's message and because their acceptance forms one of the bases of his prophetic authority. That the message of Handsome Lake gained such wide acceptance among the Iroquois in his own day would seem to be due largely to the skill with which he utilized the old traditions of the people in addressing himself to the crucial problems of the present. And when after his death (1815) some of the traditional Iroquois leaders sought a way to counter the threats of both sectarian Christian and disruptive nativists, they found it convenient to call upon the memory of Handsome Lake in attempting to define the form and spirit of the old religion. At the religious council at Tonawanda in the summer of 1818 John Sky repeated a version Handsome Lake's teaching and a minor prophet recounted a vision confirming it. Similar incidents occurred over the next two decades, and by the 1840s the text of the Code, which continues to this day to be an important force in Iroquois life, was fixed (Wallace 1972: 330–37).

In discussing specific instances of prophecy we are always dependent upon the vicissitudes of historical reporting for our information. This is

[[69]] especially evident in the case of the final interactive element of the model, *expectations of confirmation*. We are dealing here largely with beliefs based upon circulating reports of individual experiences of a "supernatural" character, and such pious tales easily escape the attention of the chroniclers of prophetic movements. Nevertheless, enough examples are available to suggest that this element was of importance in the people's response to a prophet. Faith in Wovoka, the prophet of the Ghost Dance of 1890, was certainly enhanced by Indians returning from visits to his camp with tales of how he could control the weather and miraculously "shorten" the homeward journey of those who made the long trip from the northern Plains to western Nevada to visit him (Overholt 1974: 47–48). With respect to Handsome Lake the same dynamics can be seen at work in the Onondagas crediting the Great Spirit with giving them the power to give up alcohol and follow the Gaiwiio, as well as in the visions of other prophets confirming his message. If it is difficult to find such clear examples as this in Jeremiah (20:7–8 and 44:16–19 rather seem to echo disconfirming experiences), that is perhaps because the book as we have it is preoccupied with the negative reactions of Jeremiah's audience to him.

It seems fair to conclude on the basis of the foregoing summary of evidence that the model which I have proposed for understanding the nature of the prophetic process "works" cross-culturally. That is to say, it provides us with categories in terms of which to compare the activity of two such culturally disparate holy men as Jeremiah and Handsome Lake in a fashion not unduly prejudiced by the obvious differences in their respective messages. This is an important conclusion in several respects. In the first place it has been pointed out above that the processes of interaction which lie at the heart of the prophetic act have for the most part not been given their due by students of prophetic movements. Moreover, it would seem that adopting this view of prophecy enables us to put into satisfactory perspective three interrelated problems which are important for any attempt to understand prophecy: the nature of the situation in which the prophet operates, the nature of prophetic authority, and the problem of how the content of a prophet's proclamation relates to the cultural tradition in which he stands.

The prophetic process has its locus in a specific situation. This means that any discussion of a prophet's activity will need to be informed by details of the cultural context and historical moment in which he operated. The question is whether in comparing situations which gave rise to prophecy one can say anything beyond the widely recognized fact that they are invariably times of "crisis." Let me briefly suggest, with the aid of concepts borrowed from Kenelm Burridge and Clifford Geertz, that it is possible to understand these situations more fully.

Burridge's view of the prophet situation derives from his notion that religion is "the redemptive process indicated by the activities, moral 〚70〛 rules, and assumptions about power which, pertinent to the moral order and taken on faith, not only enable a people to perceive the truth of things, but guarantee that they are indeed perceiving the truth of things" (1969: 6–7). Religion thus establishes a prestige system in which the criteria of one's integrity within the social order are well known and consistent with everyday experience. The crisis of the prophetic situation resides specifically in the fact that events have taken place (usually involving contact with another culture) which have posed a serious challenge to these assumptions. The result is that the experience of a loss of prestige and integrity and the need for regeneration are widely felt among the populace. In a similar fashion Geertz speaks of a religious system as a cluster of sacred symbols woven into an ordered whole which supports a certain view of morality "by picturing a world in which such conduct is only common sense" (1973: 129). Religion creates a synthesis of ethos (the moral and aesthetic tone of a culture) and world view (a culture's picture of the way things are in sheer actuality). Either of these elements taken by itself "is arbitrary, but taken together they form a gestalt with a peculiar kind of inevitability" (1973: 130). Above all, such symbolic activities are "attempts to provide orientation for an organism which cannot live in a world it is unable to understand" (1973: 140–41). The prophetic situation, then, is one in which the basic religio-cultural understanding has been undermined. In what did the integrity of the Seneca male reside, now that the game animals were depleted and he could no longer go to war? To be able to subsist more emphasis had to be put on farming, but that was woman's work! And what could be more damaging to the system of beliefs about Yahweh's election and protection of his people Israel than the death of "good king Josiah" and the first Babylonian conquest of Jerusalem (597 B.C.E.) and exiling of its inhabitants? In these situations men found chaos breaking in upon them (cf. Geertz 1966: 12–24), but heard as well prophets like Jeremiah and Handsome Lake proclaiming an interpretation which promised a new order.

This leads to a second problem, viz., how one is to understand the basis or source of a prophet's authority. My main concern here has been to avoid a one-way interpretation of the prophet's activity, that is to say, an interpretation of the power of the prophet over others which dwells too exclusively on the presumed divine source of his message. The divine revelation which the prophet claims is, of course, important to his understanding of himself (cf. Amos 3:8), and can be used to justify his utterances (Jer 26:12–15) and condemn his opponents (Jer 28:15–16). It is also an important element in the people's understanding of a prophet. But despite this fact the prophet's exercise of his role cannot be effective unless his message is met with a positive response on the part of at least some of his hearers.

Thus there are two aspects to the prophet's authority. On the one hand, the prophet makes the claim that the deity has authorized the proclamation of a certain message. The basis of this claim is usually a religious [[71]] experience which is private and therefore essentially intangible and unverifiable by the members of his audience, who nevertheless assume that a genuine prophet will have had such an experience. I wish to be emphatic about this, since the "call" of a deity is an absolutely crucial element in the constitution of a given occurrence of prophecy, not only in the OT but in other cultures as well. On the other hand, the prophet cannot be effective, cannot function as a prophet, unless the people acknowledge his claim to authority by their reaction to his words, and the social reality of prophecy depends upon this act. The brute fact behind the words of Peter Worsley quoted above is that the members of the prophet's audience are free to choose whom they will follow. Burke Long has summarized the matter in this way:

> The authority of a prophet was a vulnerable, shifting social reality—closely tied to acceptance and belief. It was supported by concrete deeds of power.... But the authority rested upon acceptance of those appeals (1977: 19).

To speak of authority in terms of acceptance is to acknowledge that, from the point of view of the hearers, a particular instance of prophecy will be deemed "authoritative" on the basis of certain tangible marks. One such mark is the prophet's ability to clarify and articulate what the people who follow him have themselves begun to feel about their particular situation. His utterances are experienced as having explanatory power. Burridge in fact sees the task of the prophet as one of organizing and articulating a new set of assumptions which suggest a way of making sense out of the chaos of the present situation (1969: 11–14). In doing so he concentrates in himself the people's own probings, and his revelation usually "echoes the theorizing and experimentation that has gone before" (1969: 111). The prophet is thus a transitional figure in a redemptive process the goal of which is the regeneration of the people as a group, i.e., the creation of new assumptions about power in the broad sense, a new politico-economic framework, a new mode of measuring man, new criteria of integrity, a new community. The people choose their prophets, that is they attribute authority to them, because they perceive in their proclamation continuity with the cultural traditions sufficient to make what they say intelligible and at the same time innovations sufficient to offer the possibility of a new interpretation that will bring order out of chaos. Thus, a second and closely-related mark of a prophet's authority is the effectiveness, real or imagined, which seems to characterize his activities. This effectiveness is perhaps most often experienced in the form of rhetorical skill (to his followers the prophet's message "makes sense" out of the current crisis situation), but marvelous acts, including instances of fulfilled prophecy, may also play a role (cf. Long 1977: 13–16). Such seemingly supernatural occurrences help to confirm the authenticity of the prophet. They are accounted for in the model under the rubric "expectations of confirmation."

From the point of view of audience reaction, then, the general criterion for the attribution of authority to a prophet might be expressed as [[72]] "perceived effectiveness." The hearers do not by their act of attributing authority to a prophet confer his powers on him, since, from one point of view, the claim to supernatural designation means that he already has or is perceived to have these powers. What they do, in effect, is confirm him in his role. Their affirmative response, necessary for his exercise of that role, is an act of commitment based on their recognition of that power. It must be stressed, however, that while some positive response to his message appears to be necessary for the operation of prophecy, large numbers are not. Crenshaw has shown with respect to the OT prophets that conflict with perhaps the great majority of those who heard them (even other prophets) was "inevitable" and that on the whole they had little impact upon their contemporaries. That they had some support, however, is shown both by references to specific instances (Isaiah's mention of his disciples, 8:16; the aid Jeremiah received from various members of the house of Shaphan, 26:4, chap. 36) and by the very fact that their utterances were preserved, collected, and eventually committed to writing.

Perhaps one of the most striking examples of this role of the people is the case of Yali, a native leader in post–World War II New Guinea. Though he made no supernatural claims for himself, his audience began to attribute prophetic authority to him, in effect making him a prophet even in the absence of any claims to revelatory experience. Without their reaction he would neither have claimed to be nor functioned as a prophet (Lawrence 1964). Since prophecy is always situation-bound and public, private revelation alone is insufficient to establish its authority.[12]

12. On the matter of the prophet's authority cf. also Overholt 1979.

This leads, finally, to the problem of how much "old" and how much "new" we might expect to find in a prophet's message. There can, of course, be no neat formula. Clearly, the message must have enough recognizable roots in the traditional but now threatened cultural synthesis for it to be understood and acceptable. In Burridge's scheme the millennial prophet is central to a process by which a people moves from a time when the "old rules" of the society remained intact, through an interim time of "no rules," and to a final synthesis of a set of "new rules" (1969: 165–69). Thus a consistent theme in Handsome Lake's preaching was condemnation of the individual autonomy and glorification that had been characteristic of the old Iroquois way, lately fallen into the chaos of social pathology, while advocating in its place restraint in social affairs. Elizabeth Tooker has suggested that what the prophet was trying to do was "to introduce a value system . . . consistent with the economic system that was also introduced at the same time" (1968: 187). With the collapse of the old hunting-trading system the Iroquois were forced into more intensive agriculture, but plow agriculture is a man's work and the yearly agricultural schedule demands a stable social order. Therefore, the values he selected emphasized communal order over individual gratification. If these values were similar to those of the white society, it was primarily because both were agrarian.

[[73]] That the message of the OT prophets arises out of and is in dialogue with the religious traditions of their people is well known (cf. Clements 1965, 1975). For his part Jeremiah stood within the old exodus-election tradition of Judah (cf. for example, 2:1–8). His accusations against the people make it clear that from his viewpoint (i.e., that of a "pure" Yahwist; one wonders how many such there were among his compatriots) the present period was one of "no" rules, at least in the sense that the people had chosen to ignore important aspects of their covenant with Yahweh. Put differently, we might say that he was interpreting the fruits of a long process of acculturation in the land of Canaan as apostasy. Yet in the future he saw the institution of a "new covenant," one recognizable in terms of the old but operating on the basis of new assumptions about the nature of the relationship between Yahweh and Israel (31:31–34).

Almost inevitably when we look at a prophet we consider first the content of his proclamation, and having adopted this approach we are likely to be most impressed by his differences from all other prophets about whom we know. The argument of this paper has been that when we go beneath the level of content to that of process significant similarities begin to emerge. And having learned something about the underlying similarities of two specific prophets, Jeremiah and Handsome Lake, we have, I believe, gained at least some understanding of all other prophets as well.

Works Consulted

Baltzer, K.
1968 Considerations Regarding the Office and Calling of the Prophet. *HTR* 61: 567–81.

Barnett, Homer G.
1953 *Innovation: The Basis of Cultural Change.* New York: McGraw-Hill.

Barrow, G. L.
1951 The Story of Jonfrum. *Corona* 3: 379–82.

Berkhofer, Robert F.
1965 Faith and Factionalism among the Seneca. *Ethnohistory* 12: 99–112.

Bright, John
1959 *A History of Israel.* Philadelphia: Westminster.

Burridge, Kenelm O. L.
1969 *New Heaven, New Earth.* New York: Schocken.

Chinnery, F. W. P., and Haddon, A. C.
1916– Five New Religious Cults in British New Guinea. *HibJ* 15: 448–63.
1917

Clements, R. E.
1965 *Prophecy and Covenant.* London, SCM.
1975 *Prophecy and Tradition.* Oxford: Blackwell.

Crenshaw, James L.
1971 *Prophetic Conflict: Its Effect upon Israelite Religion.* BZAW 124. Berlin: de Gruyter.

Deardorff, M. H.
1951 The Religion of Handsome Lake: Its Origin and Development. Pp. 79–107 in *Symposium on Local Diversity in Iroquois Culture,* ed. W. N. Fenton. Bureau of American Ethnology, Bulletin 149. Washington: Government Printing Office.

Donner, H.
1963 Die soziale Botschaft der Propheten in Lichte der Gesellschaftsordnung in Israel. *OrAnt* 2: 229–45.

Eckert, Georg
1937 Prophetentum in Melanesian. *Zeitschrift für Ethnologie* 69: 135–40.

Eichrodt, Walter
1961 *Theology of the Old Testament,* volume 1. London: SCM.

Fabian, J.
1963 Führer und Führung in den prophetisch-messianischen Bewegungen der (ehemaligen) Kolonialvölker. *Anthropos* 58: 773–809.

Festinger, Leon; Riecken, Henry W.; and Schachter, Stanley
1956 *When Prophecy Fails.* Minneapolis: University of Minnesota.

Geertz, Clifford
1966   Religion as a Cultural System. Pp. 1–46 in *Anthropological Approaches to the Study of Religion*, ed. M. Barton. London: Tavistock.
1973   Ethos, World-View, and the Analysis of Sacred Symbols. Pp. 126–41 in *The Interpretation of Cultures*. New York: Basic Books. (Originally published in 1957.)
Griffin, William B.
1970   A North Mexican Nativistic Movement. *Ethnohistory* 17: 95–116.
Guariglia, G.
1958   Prophetismus and Heilserwartungsbewegungen in niedern Kulturen. *Numen* 5: 180–98.
Guiart, Jean
1951   John Frum Movement in Tanna. *Oceania* 22: 165–75.
1956   Culture Contact and the "John Frum" Movement in Tanna. *Southwestern Journal of Anthropology* 12: 105–16.
Hayes, John H.
1969   Prophetism at Mari and Old Testament Parallels. *Trinity University Studies in Religion* 9: 31–41.
Huffmon, H. B.
1968   Prophecy in the Mari Letters. *Biblical Archaeologist* 31: 101–24.
Jarvie, I. C.
1963   Theories of Cargo Cults: A Critical Analysis. *Oceania* 34: 1–31, 108–36.
Johnson, A. R.
1962   *The Cultic Prophet in Ancient Israel*. 2d ed. Cardiff: University of Wales.
Köbben, A. J. F.
1960   Prophetic Movements as an Expression of Social Protest. *International Archives of Ethnography* 44: 117–64.
Koch, Klaus
1971   Die Entstehund der sozialen Kritik bei den Profeten. Pp. 236–57 in *Probleme Biblischer Theologie: Gerhard von Rad zum 70. Geburtstag am 21.10.1971*, ed. H. W. Wolf. Munich: Kaiser.
Köhler, L.
1957   *Old Testament Theology*. London: Lutterworth.
Koppers, W.
1959   Prophetismus und Messianismus als völkerkundliches und universalgeschichtliches Problem. *Saeculum* 10: 38–47.
La Barre, Weston
1971   Materials for a History of Studies of Crisis Cults: A Bibliographic Essay. *Current Anthropology* 12: 3–44.
Lanternari, Vittorio
1963   *The Religions of the Oppressed*. New York: Knopf.
Lawrence, Peter
1964   *Road Belong Cargo: A Study of the Cargo Movement in the Southern Madang District, New Guinea*. Manchester: Manchester University Press.
Lindblom, J.
1962   *Prophecy in Ancient Israel*. Oxford: Blackwell.

Linton, Ralph
1943 Nativistic Movements. *American Anthropologist* 45: 230–40.
Long, Burke O.
1977 Prophetic Authority as Social Reality. Pp. 3–20 in *Canon and Authority*, ed. G. W. Coats and B. O. Long. Philadelphia: Fortress.
McKay, John
1973 *Religion in Judah under the Assyrians.* London: SCM.
Malamat, A.
1966 Prophetic Revelations in New Documents from Mari and the Bible. Pp. 207–27 in *Volume du Congrès International pour l'étude de l'Ancien Testament: Genève 1965.* VTSup 15. Leiden: Brill.
1968 The Last Kings of Judah and the Fall of Jerusalem: An Historical-Chronological Study. *IEJ* 18: 137–56.
May, L. Carlyle
1954 The Dancing Religion: A Japanese Messianic Sect. *Southwestern Journal of Anthropology* 10: 119–37.
Mooney, James
1896 The Ghost-Dance Religion and the Sioux Outbreak of 1890. *Annual Report of the Bureau of American Ethnology* 14. Washington: Government Printing Office.
Moran, W. L.
1969 New Evidence from Mari on the History of Prophecy. *Bib* 50: 15–56.
Noth, Martin
1958 *The History of Israel.* New York: Harper.
Overholt, Thomas W.
1970 *The Threat of Falsehood: A Study in the Theology of the Book of Jeremiah.* London: SCM.
1971 Some Reflections on the Date of Jeremiah's Call. *CBQ* 33: 165–84.
1974 The Ghost Dance of 1890 and the Nature of the Prophetic Process. *Ethnohistory* 21: 37–63.
1977 Jeremiah and the Nature of the Prophetic Process. Pp. 129–50 in *Scripture in History and Theology: Essays in Honor of J. Coert Rylaarsdam*, ed. Arthur L. Merrill and Thomas W. Overholt. Pittsburgh: Pickwick.
1979 Commanding the Prophets: Amos and the Problem of Prophetic Authority. *CBQ* 41: 517–32.
Parker, Arthur C.
1913 The Code of Handsome Lake, the Seneca Prophet. *New York State Museum Bulletin.* No. 163. Albany: University of the State of New York Press. Reprinted in W. N. Fenton, ed. *Parker on the Iroquois.* Syracuse: Syracuse University, 1968.
Pedersen, J.
1946 The Role Played by Inspired Persons among the Israelites and the Arabs. Pp. 127–42 in *Studies in Old Testament Prophecy*, ed. H. H. Rowley. Edinburgh: T. & T. Clark.
Rad, Gerhard von
1965 *Old Testament Theology*, volume 2. New York: Harper and Row.

Ross, J. R.
   1962   The Prophet as Yahweh's Messenger. Pp. 89–107 in *Israel's Prophetic Heritage*, ed. B. W. Anderson and W. Harrelson. New York: Harper.
Schlosser, K.
   1950   Prophetismus in niederen Kulturen. *Zeitschrift für Ethnologie* 75: 60–72.
Shimony, Annemarie
   1961   *Conservatism among the Iroquois at the Six Nations Reserve.* Yale University Publications in Anthropology 65. New Haven: Department of Anthropology, Yale University.
Sundkler, B. G. M.
   1961   *Bantu Prophets in South Africa.* 2d ed. Oxford: Oxford University Press.
Sutherland, W.
   1910   The "Tuka" Religion. *Transactions of the Fijan Society, 1908–1910*: 51–57.
Talmon, J. I.
   1958   Social Prophetism in 19th Century France. *Commentary* 26: 158–72.
Thomson, Basil
   1895   The Kalou-Vu (Ancestor-Gods) of the Fijans and A New Religion: The Tuka Cult. *Journal of the Anthropological Institute of Great Britain and Ireland* 24: 340–59.
Tooker, Elizabeth
   1968   On the New Religion of Handsome Lake. *Anthropological Quarterly* 41: 187–200.
Wallace, Anthony F. C.
   1956   Revitalization Movements. *American Anthropologist* 58: 264–81.
   1972   *The Death and Rebirth of the Seneca.* New York: Vintage.
Wilcoxen, Jay A.
   1977   The Political Background of Jeremiah's Temple Sermon. Pp. 151–66 in *Scripture in History and Theology: Essays in Honor of J. Coert Rylaarsdam*, ed. Arthur L. Merrill and Thomas W. Overholt. Pittsburgh: Pickwick.
Williams, F. E.
   1923   *The Vailala Madness and the Destruction of Native Ceremonies in the Gulf Division.* Port Moresby: Papuan Anthropology Reports, No. 4.
   1934   The Vailala Madness in Retrospect. Pp. 369–79 in *Essays Presented to C. G. Seligman*, ed. E. E. Evans-Pritchard, Raymond Firth, Bronislaw Malinowski, and Isaac Schapera. London: Routledge & Kegan Paul.
Wilson, Robert R.
   1980   *Prophecy and Society.* Philadelphia: Fortress.
Worsley, Peter
   1968   *The Trumpet Shall Sound.* 2d ed. New York: Schocken.
Zenner, Walter P.
   1966   The Case of the Apostate Messiah: A Reconsideration of the "Failure of Prophecy." *Archives de Sociologie des Religions* 21: 111–18.

Religion and Socio-Political Structure in Early Israel:

An Ethno-Archaeological Approach

FRANK S. FRICK

[233] With the progressive and increasingly convincing critique of the amphictyonic and bedouin analogy models as heuristic devices for an understanding of the place of religious ideology and practice in early Israel (ca. 1250–1000 B.C.), the need has become more pressing for the development of new models. De Geus (1976) and others have succeeded in pointing out the numerous and weighty problems in accepting the amphictyonic thesis as definitive, or even worse, as being the Procrustean bed to which all future studies must be made to conform. Consider this partial list of difficulties: the dominance of linguistic and textual studies; the unstated assumptions concerning the relationships between biblical texts and archaeological data; the often simplistic assertions about the identity of the particular culture which is responsible for supposed remains (Franken 1976); the uncertainties and disagreements about what constitutes cultic remains; and especially the lack of adequate comprehensive research designs to permit the systematic use of the data coming from the excavations.

Revised and reprinted with permission from *Society of Biblical Literature, 1979: Seminar Papers, Volume 2* (Society of Biblical Literature Seminar Papers 17; Missoula, Montana: Scholars Press, 1979) 233–53.

In the light of these and other difficulties, it would appear that what is needed is a rather thoroughgoing reassessment of much of the available data based on different starting points. At the very minimum it would seem desirable to sort out as many as possible of those items in our treatment of early Israelite religion as we can, in order to straighten out some of the circular reasoning which has become entrenched in our thinking and writing due to the dominance of the amphictyonic theory. As one step in this direction, it is the intention of this paper to focus on some suggestions from what is happening in processual archaeology as providing some useful heuristic models for the continuing study of the religion of early Israel. In particular, emphasis will be placed on the necessity of bringing more closely together the "ecological approach" employed by anthropological archaeologists and other social scientists with the "humanistic approach" of historians of religion. Kent Flannery (1972: 399–400) has aptly described the limitations of either approach when pursued in isolation from the other:

> The limited success of so-called "ecological approaches" to complex societies has led to understandable criticism from humanists. . . . Up until now, it has mainly been the humanists who have studied the informational aspects of complex societies—art, religion, ritual, writing systems, and so on. The "ecologists" have largely contented themselves with studying exchanges of matter and energy. . . . Humanists must cease thinking that ecology "dehumanizes" history, and ecologists must cease to regard art, [234] religion, and ideology as mere "epiphenomena" without causal significance. In an ecosystem approach to the analysis of human societies, everything which transmits information is within the province of ecology.

Flannery and other American and British processual archaeologists clearly operate within a systemic framework, specifically, general systems theory. The variant adopted is an ecosystemic approach which concentrates on the relations which exist between the various societal subsystems and their environment. These archaeologists also tend to accept the premise that the given system is basically in equilibrium and that most aspects of the system work to maintain that equilibrium, encouraging negative feedback and homeostasis.

Following such a lead, this paper will set forth at least a partial outline for an ecosystem approach to the analysis of early Israel in which the data deriving from archaeology, textual studies, and ethnographic analogies will be utilized in the explanation of the pre-state sociopolitical organization of Israel, and in particular, the place of religion in that society. In such an explanation, religion will be seen as but one aspect of the culture of early Israel, so that a particular sociopolitical organization is its necessary presupposition. In other words, the religion of early Israel is rather the expression (albeit a very important one) of a particular cultural identity rather than its sole foundation.

Certainly it goes without saying that one's definition of religion is determinative of how one reads the material remains. In this regard it has been rather common practice to follow the program of Hawkes (1954) who orders the information available from the archaeological record into four levels of increasingly more difficult inference. He maintains that techniques and then subsistence economies are fairly easy to infer, but to infer to the sociopolitical institutions is considerably harder, and to infer to the religious institutions and spiritual life is the most difficult inference of all. One of the most important contributions of the "new" archaeology for those who are concerned with the religious dimensions of a people's life, is the development of research designs and methods in which attention is explicitly given to the widest possible range of religious impact on the material remains of a culture. No longer need there be a religious interpretation of archaeological remains as a kind of court of last resort. As an aside at this point, it is assumed that even the novice would recognize that field archaeology has priority here in terms of providing the basic data for all other archaeological endeavors; all other archaeology is of the arm-chair variety, trying to interpret the data, seeking correlative data, etc. But as soon as the archaeologist goes beyond the acquisition of a data base, he or she has entered into a different realm of archaeology in which inductive logic and analogy play crucial roles and from which one can generate testable hypotheses which can then feed back into the acquisition process. In that light, field archaeology by itself has no relevance for the study of religion; but without it there could be no such study in relation to archaeology at all. So, the assumption is made here that religion, when viewed in dynamic and holistic terms, does ⟦235⟧ make a discernible imprint on material culture. The ancient human community resembles the modern one in that both are organismic, i.e., living systems. Religion functioned and had meaning within a whole ideological-behavioural network of mutual adaptations, or symbiotic situations.

In our attempts to understand a society such as early Israel, in which religious ideology and practice seem to have operated as the functional equivalents to political power, more attention needs to be given to the work of Roy Rappaport, one of the most influential contemporary American anthropologists who is working on religious function and meaning in such a context. Unfortunately, much of his work has been published in sources which are often difficult to obtain, so he has not received the attention he deserves (Rappaport 1968; 1970; 1971a; 1971b). Rappaport's work begins with the assumption that the form and structure of the subsystems responsible for regulation and control in non-state societies are not as clearly defined as are those operating in states. Generations of anthropologists have asserted that such institutions are "embedded" within the wider social organization of the society. Rappaport's principal contribution, for our present purposes, is that he shows that in many societies homeostatic mechanisms are part and parcel of sanctified ritual activity:

> In technologically simple societies—whose authorities, in the complete or relative absence of power, stand upon their sanctity—the sacred and the numinous form part of an encompassing cybernetic loop which maintains homeostasis among variables critical to the group's survival (Rappaport 1971a: 39).

In Rappaport's work, the role of religion (or, as he prefers, "the sacred") in human communities and in the regulation of social and ecological systems is approached through ritual as the public expression of religious ideology. Operating out of a "systems model," he sees religious ritual as a powerful force in the homeostasis of a system:

> Rituals, arranged in protracted cycles . . . articulate the local and regional systems, and, furthermore, regulate relations within each of the subsystems, and in the larger systems as a whole (1971b: 60).

Religious activities are thus primarily seen as part of the informational processes of human societies. What then are the particular aspects of religious rituals that uniquely suit them to function as homeostats and communication devices? Rappaport stresses both *content* and *occurrence.* Content is particularly important in the transmission of quantitative or more-less information, and is of significance mainly within single systems or subsystems. Occurrence, on the other hand, is particularly important in the transmission of qualitative yes-no information across the border of separate systems or subsystems. The content aspect of ritual is well illustrated by Rappaport's own field work among the Maring of New Guinea. The Maring transmit information concerning the amount of military support that may be expected from a friendly group in future warlike endeavors *via* ritual. Calendric ceremonies occurring at the same [[236]] time every year, as well as longer-term ritual cycles can help to maintain undergraded environments, limit intergroup raiding, adjust man-land ratios, facilitate trade, redistribute natural resources, and "level" differences in wealth (Rappaport 1970: 55–56). Some rituals are thus public counting devices and as such they can play an important role in regulation by revealing the states, not otherwise apparent, of important systemic variables. On the basis of such information, corrective action may

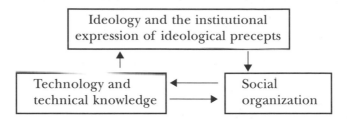

be taken if necessary or possible. Calendric rituals are of chief importance with respect to the content dimension, while non-calendric rituals
communicate information by their very occurrence. A non-calendric ritual occurrence may thus be a "yes-no" signal which may have been trig-
gered by the achievement or violation of a particular state or range of
states of a "more-less" variable and, because of the sanctity associated
with it, is a statement free of ambiguity.

In essence, therefore, the acts and interactions of ritual are seen as
rendering complex, fluctuating data into a form on which concrete decisions and action can be taken. Ritual *content*, e.g., including meaning,
might be used as a "program" to keep the agricultural cycle on the right
track; ritual *occurrence* might be used as an unambiguous signal to neighbors that the society is ready for warfare (cf. Judg 19:29–30; 1 Sam 11:7).
Finally, because of the sacred nature of these ritually transformed pro-
nouncements or proclaimed consensuses, the information and decisions
are assigned truth value by their sacred context (Rappaport 1971a: 69).
The act and interactions encompassed by ritual transform the ambiguous and indeterminate into the unambiguous and believable.

In the assessment of this author, Rappaport's work provides a most
important starting point for the construction of a more comprehensive
theory for explaining the ways in which religion can contribute to the
formation of social units which transcend local kin groups. In some societies religion plays a much more important part in such a process than
it does in others. This point might seem so obvious as to be not worth
mentioning were it not for the fact that since Durkheim and Weber, one
scholar after another has put forward a theory of the impact of religion
upon social structure. Many of these have made little advance over a
simple Radcliffe-Brown sense that religious rites aid social integration by
inculcating and strengthening the proper sentiments of loyalty and
identification with the collectivity, or by stating and resolving conflicts
within the group. Rappaport's work is valuable because it takes seriously
the relationship between ideology, social organization, and subsistence
technology, a relationship which might be diagrammed as [above] (cf.
Smith 1976: 496).

[[237]] As such relationships are taken into consideration, the question arises of how to understand the particular pre-state or non-state form of sociopolitical organization found in early Israel, a form in which the sacred could and did function in ways similar to those outlined by Rappaport. If we choose from those non-state types of societies which have been described in the literature of social anthropology, it would seem that there are two possible choices: tribe or chiefdom. In making the choice, Mendenhall's advice should be taken:

> The point of the historical and religious problem is to understand, not merely label, the functioning of a surprisingly large social solidarity that seemingly had a minimum of permanent political structures or military organization and resources (1976: 133).

Or, as Gottwald has said in commenting on the distinctiveness of early Israel:

> . . . the Israelite tribes were not so much unique in their basic form of segmented organization by extended families, protective associations and tribes, but decisively different in constituting a very broad alliance of such units that managed to throw off the central authority and take over its entrepreneurial socio-economic, military and religious functions at the village and tribal levels (1976: 149).

Our problem is thus how to explain the way in which religion functioned within a given form of sociopolitical organization to maintain a non-state alliance of basically independent villages over a space of about 200 years. Can such an alliance best be understood operating from a model of tribalism or of chiefdom?

The very concept of "tribe" or "tribal society" is not one subject to ready definition in anthropological circles. In an essay, which provided the occasion for an extended discussion on the problem of tribe, Morton Fried said:

> Unfortunately, if I had to select one word in the vocabulary of anthropology as the single most egregious case of meaninglessness, I would have to pass over "tribe" in favor of "race." I am sure, however, that "tribe" figures prominently on the list of putative technical terms ranked in order of degree of ambiguity as reflected in multifarious definitions (1968: 4–5).

Certainly there is little agreement on what constitutes a "tribe" in the essays contained in the above-mentioned volume. If agreement cannot be reached on such a cross-cultural level, what kind of situation presents itself when the referent is limited to the "tribe" in early Israel? Probably the most thoroughgoing recent discussion of the Israelite "tribe" is that of C. H. J. de Geus, in which he concludes:

> One may conclude therefore that an Israelite tribe was always a "branch" of the whole people, and had no meaning without that whole. At the same time the tribes expressed [[238]] the inevitable territorial, linguistic, and historical differentiation. The tribe was for the Israelite the manner in which the people functioned for him in his region, though he remained aware that the people was more than the tribe. That the contours of the concept "tribe" remain more vague than those of the clan, is due to the nature of the Israelite tribe. This vagueness is increased by the way the concepts *mišpāḥā* [['family']] and *šēbeṭ* [['tribe']] are used. . . . That the "tribe" remains so vague, therefore requires a structural and not a historical explanation. Israelite tribes were regional alliances of essentially independent clans. Real power resided with the clans, or a few of them, but not at a tribal level (1976: 150, 156).

What is particularly telling about de Geus' conclusion is that the tribe appears to be an unsatisfactory starting point in the search for the development of those federations or alliance networks which made up early Israel. If, in fact, tribal names functioned primarily as territorial indications and tribes were regional alliances of essentially independent clans which were the fully functional social and political units, the explanation of the development of the larger unit must begin with the clan. If, furthermore, clan and village often coincide, archaeological tests can be proposed which can support a developmental model. While such archaeological tests can show developing linkages and alliance networks on the village level, such tests have so far proved unsuccessful on the tribal level.

Certainly one of the most prominent examples of a tribal confederacy cited in ethnographic literature is that of the Iroquois, a seventeenth-century political organization in what is now New York state, composed of the Seneca, Cayuga, Onondaga, Oneida, and Mohawk tribes. William Engelbrecht has made the attempt to infer the existence of the League of the Iroquois on the basis of ceramic patterning within and between Iroquois village sites (1974). In his study Engelbrecht used two different coefficients. One was a measure of ceramic homogeneity (Whallon 1968). The assumption is that the greater the heterogeneity of ceramic designs within any site, the greater the contact with other sites. The other measure used to infer degree of contact between sites was the Brainerd-Robinson coefficient of agreement (Brainerd 1951; Robinson 1951). In this case it is assumed that if a pair of contemporaneous sites shares a higher coefficient of agreement than another contemporaneous pair, there has been greater contact between the former pair. Engelbrecht thus assumed that if the formation of the League is reflected in ceramic production, one would expect to see an increase in similarity between sites in different tribal territories within the area of the League and an increase in heterogeneity of ceramics within the sites in the area but not included in the League itself. For the latter, sites in the Niagra frontier, outside the area of the League, were examined for control. Engelbrecht's conclusion was that the existence of the League of the Iroquois was not reflected in the ceramic evidence.

This author knows of no similar test which has been devised and applied to early Israel in order to infer the existence of tribes as such or of a tribal league. For a later [[239]] period and on a different level of sociopolitical organization, Holladay (1976) has convincingly demonstrated that even the commonly held "northern"/"southern" dichotomy of ceramic forms, in fact represents a chronological rather than geopolitical distinction. Studies such as McClellan's (1975) might be utilized in developing an archaeological test along the lines of Engelbrecht's which could contribute significantly to the discussion of the nature of the formation of early Israel and of the level at which alliance networks developed.

De Geus' assertion that the clan/village is the basic sociopolitical unit, and the one around which alliance networks are formed, has considerable support in ethnographic literature. E.g., Gluckman's observations of the Lozi in northwest Rhodesia demonstrate the central significance of the clan/village (1959). Among the Lozi, villages are the only corporate groups of kindred. The Lozi family is thus both a political unit and a kinship group. In land-holding the village is the largest and the ultimate political unit. Inter-village linkages among the Lozi are called "vicinages" (Gluckman 1959: 71). One's vicinage is constituted by those villages close enough to his own for there to be frequent contact.

Likewise, among the Shona of southern Rhodesia, as reported by Holleman (1959), the village is primary and the next unit above the village is the *dunhu*, which comprises a varying number of separate and mutually independent villages. The *dunhu* is well defined territorially and has a nuclear body of agnatic kinsmen who are spread over more than one village. It is the *dunhu* which holds the communal right over all the territory within its borders. It is also the head of the *dunhu* who initiates the non-calendric rituals. Holleman observes that rituals on the *dunhu* level are the most important ones, and that "Tribal rituals are . . . singularly few in number. The thanksgiving celebrations at the end of a good season do not appear ever to have been held . . . on behalf of the whole tribe" (1959: 377).

Edward Winter's work among the Iraqw is most valuable for our purposes, concentrating as it does on the relationship existing between ritual and social integration (Winter 1966). The three levels of organization among the Iraqw below that of "people" are those of the household, village, and "county" (an area of ca. 30–40 square miles). Social cohesion at the level of the household is obviously provided by kinship, so Winter concentrates on the villages and "county." The village performs services for the households which they cannot provide for themselves and its existence is thus necessary for practical reasons of subsistence. Such practical reasons, however, do not seem to account for the existence of "counties." Why, e.g., are some rites carried out at the level of the "county" when they could be done at the village level or at one place for the Iraqw people as a whole? Winter's conclusion is that the organization of communal ritual on a "county" basis makes sense in terms of the patterns of rainfall variation (1966: 169–70). This variation causes a group of people who see themselves as facing similar rainfall conditions to cooperate ritually to solve the problem, as they visualize it, and since a group of this sort invariably involves an area larger than a village and [[240]] yet smaller than the entire people, this cooperation takes place on an intermediate level. Thus the widest territorial group which acts in a unitary fashion, the "county," is defined and organized in purely ritual terms. Might the "tribe" in early Israel have been similarly defined and organized?

Turning to work more directly related to the Near East, a recent study by Diakonoff (1975) has dealt with the rural community in the ancient Near East. His observations are particularly relevant when viewed in the context of the peasant revolt model, for he insists that peasants outside of the state sector inevitably create their own organization, a communal organization:

> Communal organization was the only organization inside which a free-man could exercise the maximum of civic liberties. Among them were the liberty to possess movables, to take part in the communal proprietorship in land, and to participate in the self-government of a rural, city, or "nome" community (Diakonoff 1975: 123).

In the several forms of such communal organization cited by Diakonoff, two are relevant for our purposes—the "clan," extended family, or lineage community; and the rural community consisting of related or non-related families settling in one neighborhood. Both Jankowska (1969) and Heltzer (1976) also have dealt with communal organization in Arrapḫa and Ugarit respectively. In both cases the strength of the village as the base of the social and economic structure is evident. In both, the communal character of the village is stressed, a character which "having been formed by thousands of years of the kinship system of economics, could withstand the most powerful king, owing to its traditional regimentation of all aspects of economic and social life" (Jankowska 1969: 282).

Bringing together these examples from ethnographic studies and Near Eastern archival material, and applying them to early Israel's sociopolitical development, we might conclude that the "tribe" did not exist as a ready-made unit to provide the necessary communal organization in the face of the defection of Israelite villages from the domination of the city-states. One should not conclude, however, that early Israel consisted of an anarchical mass of individuals, but of rural communities which already possessed many of the mechanisms for self-defense and cooperation of a now free rural population which could continue to exist and prosper outside of the state sector.

Beginning then with the village community as the sociopolitical base upon which early Israel was formed, we have yet to examine the particular forms and institutions through which the sacred could operate as a functional alternative to political power. In other words, what was the nature of and locus of authority? If authorities are taken to be loci in communications networks from which directives emanate, then human societies can be placed on a continuum, from societies that are regulated in the near absence of human authorities through societies in which highly sanctified authorities have little actual power, to societies in which authorities have great power but less sanctity (Rappaport 1971b: 72). In such a context we [[241]] are interested in exploring the ways in which sanctity permitted the progressive centralization of regulatory hierarchies. How did the sanctity of the leaders of early Israel make it possible for them to command the men and control the resources that eventually provided their successors with the kind of power known in the state? What kind of leaders were the *šōpheṭîm* [['judges']] and what was the concept of Israel in which they exercised their leadership? In what follows, it will be suggested that the social type "chiefdom" provides a useful explanatory model for understanding both the *šōpheṭîm* as religious and political leaders, and the form of society in which they functioned. Some possible archaeological tests for such a model will also be suggested.

The great merit of the work of Elman Service (1962, 1971, 1975) has been, as pointed out by Renfrew (1972: 71–72), the recognition of the failure to look closely at societies which range somewhere between the egalitarian tribal and state, and to discuss their functioning without assuming that they are only intermediate. Service has singled out "chiefdom" as a society with an identifiable degree of social integration and has presented several features which are sometimes seen in such societies but are generally lacking in those tribal societies sometimes called "egalitarian." Sahlins (1958, [[1962]]) has observed that there is a wide variety of sociopolitical complexity within the class of societies that can be designated chiefdoms, and Goldman (1970), who examined the same group of societies as Sahlins, set forth three "types" in a sequence which can be measured by increases in power and authority—the "traditional," "open," and "stratified" (Goldman 1970: 20). Renfrew differentiates between group-oriented and individualizing chiefdoms (1972: 74). Given this variety of subtypes, what do chiefdoms have in common that differentiates them from the egalitarian society? In egalitarian societies ritual activities are usually organized as a network of acts and interactions for the transmission of information which *all* members of the society enter into as equals, except where age, sex, and achieved status are imposed as barriers. That is, at least for the duration of the ritual activity the flow of information is from all to all, and there is complete interaction among the human components of the system. In chiefdoms, on the other hand, there is a sanctified ritual separation between the chief and the remainder of the population, and ritual interaction reflects this separation. The flow of information is from all to the chief and from the chief to all. Chiefdoms, like egalitarian societies, rely on sanctified authority rather than power for regulation and control. But, unlike egalitarian societies, chiefdoms are marked by a higher level ritually-sanctioned homeostat— the chief. The complete interaction of segmentary societies has been replaced in chiefdoms by a loosely coupled two-level hierarchy (Earle 1978). Rappaport points out some of the benefits of such a shift:

> While . . . ritual regulation benefits from its very simplicity it must be recognized that it also suffers from simplicity's limitations. Consensus concerning deviations from acceptable conditions forms slowly, and corrective programs are both inflexible and unlikely to be proportional to deviations. . . . Novel challenges . . . might require [[242]] more flexible regulatory mechanisms, such as discrete human authorities. . . . Chiefs, for instance, are more expensive to keep than ritual cycles and can make more mistakes. But they can respond to system-endangering changes in the environment with much more sensitivity, speed, precision, and flexibility than ritual cycles (1971b: 66).

Furthermore, Peebles and Kus (1977) have suggested a number of other consequences which can be realized in the change from a network to a loosely coupled hierarchy of ritual control. Among these are: (1) an increase in the quantity and complexity of information that can be processed by the cultural system as a whole; (2) more numerous and larger residential groups can be integrated into a single cultural system; (3) production can be rationalized and part-time craft specialization can be in-corporated and supported; and (4) buffering against environmental fluctuation can be centralized (Peebles and Kus 1977: 430).

Archaeologists are now beginning to be able to identify a number of the features of a chiefdom in the archaeological record. Renfrew, who admittedly is one of the more optimistic, cites some twenty fea-tures and asserts that there is not one of them which cannot be identified in favorable circumstances from the archaeological record (1972: 73). Peebles and Kus (1977) argue for the removal of redistribution and eco-logical specialization as necessary and sufficient determinants of a chief-dom, but still contend for a number of direct implications for the recognition of this form of organization of regulation and control. The demonstration of ranking, the form of regulation and control, and the spatial arrangement of settlements are all variables cited as significantly diagnostic of chiefdoms. They go on to propose five major areas of vari-ability distinctive of chiefdoms for which hypotheses can be presented and tested with archaeological materials (Peebles and Kus 1977: 431–33). These chief variables are: (1) clear evidence of non-volitional, ascribed ranking of persons; (2) hierarchy of settlement types and sizes; (3) settle-ments located in areas which assure a high degree of local subsistence sufficiency; (4) evidence of organized productive activities which tran-scend the basic household group; and (5) correlation between those ele-ments of the cultural system's environment which are of a frequency, amplitude, and duration to be dealt with but which are least predictable, and evidence of society-wide organizational activity to buffer or otherwise deal with these perturbations. In the archaeological record, (1) can be most effectively demonstrated through the analysis of mortuary practices, (2) and (3) can be seen in settlement patterns, and for (4) there are two areas in which the organization of tasks leaves archaeologically visible traces—public works and organized part-time craft specialization, usually coupled with intersocietal trade. (5) is evidenced in defensive organiza-tion, a mixed strategy of storage and distribution of foodstuffs, and the "management" of intersocietal trade.

For the purposes of initiating discussion, I have chosen the site of Tel Masos (*Ḥirbet el-Mšaš*) in the eastern Negev as an early Iron I site to be used in testing the above propositions. The treatment which follows is necessarily incomplete due to the fact that it is based on preliminary reports and [[243]] private communications with the excavators, and be-cause of the limitations of space. A monograph by this author on "The Israelite Village" is now in preparation and will treat items more fully than can only be suggested here [[unfinished]].

The site of Tel Masos is most important for any reconstruction of early Israel for a number of reasons. First of all, it is a site whose excavation was uncomplicated by earlier or later remains. There was no Late Bronze settlement in the eastern Negev, and because the low hills of Tel Masos were unsuitable for the erection of a well-fortified city, the settlement pattern shifted away from this site to the adjoining mountain slopes during the monarchy, leaving the remains of the Iron I village undisturbed by subsequent building activity. Secondly, Tel Masos provides us with one of the best preserved and most extensive examples of an unwalled Israelite village of the early Iron I period yet excavated. As such it provides telling evidence against both the conquest theory and that of the seminomadic origins of early Israel. As Aharoni has commented:

> Instead of the conquest of Canaanite cities we find the new settlement in an unoccupied area. Instead of the poor settlement of a semi-nomadic tribe we have the relatively massive settlement in a well-to-do village (Aharoni, Fritz, and Kempinski 1975: 119).

Thirdly, while early Iron I is represented in this region at both Tel Arad and Tel Beer-sheba, both of which became important central sites later during the monarchy, during the period in question, Tel Masos seems to have been *the* central, large settlement in the area. The settlement from the period of the Judges covered an area of about fifty dunams. It was established in the late thirteenth century B.C. and terminated late in the eleventh or early tenth century B.C. (Aharoni, Fritz, and Kempinski 1974: 7). In Tel Masos we thus have an unfortified settlement, a village, which endured for at least 200 years. The final reason for our selection of this site for the purpose of testing propositions is that it is in a region which has been rather extensively surveyed and/or excavated in recent months and years, and thus some observations can be made about settlement patterns and subsistence arrangements in its immediate environs. In particular, another contemporary Iron I site at Tel Esdar, some five kilometers south of Tel Masos, presents some interesting data with regard to settlement hierarchies and village relationships in the period.

With regard to the first of the variables cited by Peebles and Kus, there does appear to be evidence for non-volitional ascribed ranking in the early Iron I society of Tel Masos. In the northeastern sector of the site (Area A), which has been thoroughly excavated, remains of about ten houses have been uncovered. These domestic structures form a chain of units which encompasses a central courtyard which has been only partially excavated. The houses are joined together to form a protective belt which, in the judgment of the excavators could seal off the settlement from desert marauders, but was not capable of defending it against military attack (Kempinski and Fritz 1977: 140). These houses are remarkably uniform in plan and [[244]] size. In plan they are of the one-story "four-room" house type which Shiloh maintains was an original Israelite concept (Shiloh 1970, 1973, 1978). The examples at Tel Masos are certainly among the earliest of this house type yet discovered in Palestine. In the first phase of stratum II (mid–twelfth century B.C.) the four houses whose plans are most complete (1065, 88, 2 and 42) range from about seventy-two to ninety-six square meters in area. Applying the formula which suggests that the number of inhabitants can be very roughly estimated as of the order of one-tenth the floor area in square meters (Naroll 1962), these houses would house on the order of six or seven persons. In no case was there more than one hearth per dwelling, nor are the individual dwellings interconnected, which suggests that there were not large extended families. There is also a remarkable uniformity in the artifactual finds in these houses, consisting almost entirely of locally-made typical Iron I pottery with only very small quantities of Philistine ware.

While the above might suggest a planned settlement made up of egalitarian small extended families, it is house 314 in Area H in the southern part of the settlement which would seem to point rather clearly to a ranked society. In terms of size alone, house 314 is about 160 square meters, or about twice the size of the typical "four-room" house in Area A. Size alone, however, is not a reliable indicator of the wealth or status of a household since wealthier households do not, as a rule, have more square meters per person (Kramer 1978). House 314 is also distinctive in plan, showing an arrangement of rooms on three sides around an almost square courtyard, a throwback to Canaanite structural traditions (Kempinski and Fritz 1977: 150). The inventory of finds from this structure includes hand-burnished bowls, jugs with two-color decoration (bichrome style), and red-slipped black-decorated flasks (Aharoni, Fritz, and Kempinski 1975: 107), none of which was present in the "four-room" houses. This pottery is thus entirely different from the undecorated, unburnished ware found elsewhere on the site in stratum II and is certainly not made locally, but imported. Some locally made pottery was found in house 314, including jugs, storage jars, and lamps. A carved ivory lion's head was also found in this structure. Given the distinctive size and plan of this house together with the sumptuary goods found within it, the occupants of this structure would seem to be especially wealthy, having far-reaching connections with Phoenician cities and Midianite settlements in the Arabian desert (Kempinski and Fritz 1977: 150). The existence of such a dwelling in an otherwise rather uniform settlement, would seem to constitute evidence for ascribed ranking, especially so since the status of this house seems to remain unchanged throughout the early Iron I period. Unfortunately there are no further confirming data available through the analysis of mortuary practices, since the search for the cemetery was not successful (Fritz 1979). A large cemetery of the Israelite period, the first of its kind in the Negev, has recently been discovered on the eastern slope of Tel ᶜIra, some three kilometers northeast of Tel Masos. This cemetery might be related to Tel Masos even though Tel ᶜIra as an urban site was only developed later in the monarchy.

[[245]] The second of the areas of variability mentioned above maintains that in a chiefdom there should be a hierarchy of settlement types and sizes, and that the position of settlements in the hierarchy should reflect their position in the regulatory and ritual network (Peebles and Kus 1977: 432–33). While the evidence for the area under consideration is far from complete, a two-level settlement hierarchy, which is evidenced in chiefdoms (Johnson 1973: 10ff.; Earle 1978: 2ff.; Taylor 1979), might be suggested on the basis of the relationship of Tel Masos to other sites in the area, especially to Tel Esdar. It seems clear that Tel Masos was a central site in the area in the period just preceding the monarchy. Tel Masos, e.g., covered about sixty dunams, while no other site was larger than the twenty dunams of Tel Esdar. In the excavation of Tel Esdar stratum III (second half of the eleventh century B.C.) revealed houses built on the summit of the hill in a circle of about 100 meters in diameter. Some eight houses were excavated and the remains of another two were distinguished on the surface (Kochavi 1969). All of these houses were of about the same size and plan and the pottery found in them was typical Iron I ware, locally made and showing no signs of decoration, slip, or burnish. Unlike Tel Masos, there was no distinctive structure which might indicate ranking, and the ceramic evidence confirms this judgment. The excavators have suggested that at least two ceramic types (the chalice and the storage jar) found at Tel Esdar and Tel Masos are from a single potter's workshop (Aharoni, Fritz, and Kempinski 1975: 103–4). It is thus suggested that Tel Esdar was linked with Tel Masos in a two-level hierarchy of settlement types characteristic of chiefdoms.

Data for the third and fourth variables—location so as to assure a high degree of local subsistence sufficiency and evidence of organized productive activities which transcend the basic household group—are only partial, and thus our suggestions in this area should be taken as quite tentative. It does seem clear, nevertheless, that the size of Tel Masos was not selected for its defensibility, and that it was this factor which probably contributed to its abandonment in favor of a more readily defensible site in the monarchy. The location of this site, like that of many of the new Israelite sites in early Iron I, must have been made with subsistence sufficiency in mind, as suggested on a general level by Ron:

> Settlements were established in sites less suitable for cultivation and terracing, near, but never on, the arable land itself. In all cases, preservation of cultivable area overrode in each case all other considerations in choosing the site of settlement. . . . This is the reason for the location of most sites at the margin of the mountain plateaus and crests of ridges adjoining it. . . . The site of settlements, the direction of their expansion and their pattern is dependent on and adapted to the feasibility of terracing, to a great extent (1966: 120–21).

In a growing number of studies of ancient agriculture in the Negev and elsewhere (Kedar 1957a, 1957b; Golomb and Kedar 1971; Evenari, Shaman, and Tadmor 1971; de Geus 1975), the variety of methods used to extend cultivation in this difficult and agriculturally unpromising region rests fundamentally on two factors: [[246]] physio-geography (topography, lithology, exposition of the slopes, soil and the presence or lack of water sources) and the social and administrative factor (land tenure, land-tax laws, and the general economic welfare). The combination of these two basic factors has determined the specific types of land-use patterns, which is the clue to a better understanding of the economic-geographic background of a rural society (Golomb and Kedar 1971).

A detailed aerial survey of the area in question has only been completed in the last several months and the data from it are not yet available. This survey has revealed, however, that an area about one kilometer east and southeast of Tel Masos is scattered with farm houses of Iron I (Kempinski 1979). There is also evidence of at least one dam in the wadi bed of Nahal Beersheba, which was not investigated by the excavators under the assumption that it belonged to a much later period (Fritz 1979. This dam is clearly visible on Plate 16B in *ZDPV* 89, 1973.) Those structures belonging to runoff agriculture are, however, notoriously difficult to date. De Geus maintains that agriculture on terraces in wadi beds was introduced into the Negev only in the tenth century B.C. as an extension of the techniques in the North. He does so apparently on the assumption that the state is a necessary presupposition for the planning and execution of such public works:

> One must assume that such valuable and vulnerable institutions as the terraces, which often extend for more than a kilometer from the village, with crops left at considerable distance, presupposes political units

of some significance, if not the territorial state of the Iron Age (de Geus 1975: 69).

On such an assumption, however, it is difficult to account for the local subsistence sufficiency of a settlement the size of Tel Masos in the mid-twelfth–mid-eleventh centuries B.C. If, according to the model of a peasant revolt, the establishment of a site such as Tel Masos in this period represents an attempt by the settlers to maintain a subsistence cereal agriculture free from the Canaanite and Philistine spheres, then we must assume that its establishment and maintenance for nearly 200 years outside of the state sphere implies a form of sociopolitical organization which, while not relying on the kind of external compulsion associated with the state, could provide the necessary coordination between family groups such as that in evidence in chiefdoms which are "redistributional societies with a permanent central agency of coordination" (Service 1971: 134). The contradictions inherent in an agricultural society could be resolved by appointing a person or lineage to collect, store, and redistribute surpluses on an equitable basis. Such persons would oversee other productive and ceremonial activities as well. Thus, the potential of surplus production which would become possible with the resource drain of the city-state system eliminated, could be realized without inordinate social conflict and dislocation between the domestic producing units. Furthermore, professional specialization of productive tasks from administration through to actual food production could be organized without fears of a similar nature. The chief ruled by nature of the kinship [247] system and not by fiat supported by police-military specialists. It is our contention that what took place during the period of the Judges was that there developed a unifying ideology which both satisfied the needs of farmers for retaining a portion of the egalitarian structure of the chiefdom, and gave over to priest-bureaucrats additional powers to organize production and enforce laws. Perhaps these "theocrats" could even call upon a citizen's army of volunteers to enforce decisions from time to time. Perhaps they also had limited authority to enforce labor corvées in the construction of socially-sanctioned projects.

Although the real divisive factor in agricultural villages may more likely be increasing professional specialization than sheer village size, it is certainly true that the growth of a village's population, such as is indicated in additions to several houses in a later phase of stratum II at Tel Masos, produces sociopolitical change. Trigger has demonstrated that where settlements do not exceed a few hundred people no authoritative officials are needed, but where such villages exceed 500, as Tel Masos undoubtedly did, they are necessary.

In the initial instance, the authority seems to take the form of a council of chiefs recognizing a paramount headman as their spokesman. Where local groups exceed 1,500 (which would seem unlikely in the case of Tel Masos) officials must be able to exercise police functions (Trigger 1974: 97).

The mechanism that maintained social solidarity and law and order on the village and inter-village level, and made possible multi-community groupings may very well have been a unifying religious ideology. Such groupings do not require the political integration of the state

Multi-community groupings require less political integration since, especially if the technology remains simple, local groups can manage most of their own affairs. Tribal governments are largely concerned with suppressing internal blood feuds and regulating relations with other groups. Because of this, larger numbers of people may come together as members of a single political entity without developing a state than can remain together in similar conditions in a single community (Trigger 1974: 97).

The fifth and last of the variables maintains that there should be a correlation between those elements of a cultural system's environment which are of a frequency, amplitude, and duration to be dealt with but which are least predictable, and evidence of society-wide organizational activity to buffer or otherwise deal with these perturbations (Peebles and Kus 1977: 432–33). At least three aspects of the environment can be explored as causal factors in the rise and maintenance of a chiefdom: the demands of agriculture, interregional exchange and alliance, and warfare. The very brief sketch which follows is only meant to suggest linkages rather than to prove them, and is thus intended as a heuristic guide for further research in this area.

[[248]] One of the crucial agricultural decisions in a society such as that of early Israel would have been when and how much to plant. One would expect, therefore, that one of the duties of the chiefly establishment would include the maintenance of a calendar. In this connection, it is perhaps noteworthy that the Covenant Code (Exod 20:22–23:33) is largely neutral in regard to the Israelite faith, yet clearly sets forth a cultic calendar (23:10–19) which contains provisions for a fallow year and three pilgrimage festivals geared to agricultural events. Since these festivals called for the presence of all adult males, and thus had a census function, perhaps it was at these festivals that decisions were made about when and how much to plant in the context of the ritual cycle. The Gezer calendar may also reflect the connection of calendrics and cult at another level. The periodic adjustments of agricultural allotments within and among the clans may also have been associated with the pilgrimage festivals. Ideologically, of course, Yahweh, as the one who succeeded to the city-state kings as owner of the territory, was seen as the one who allotted fields to the various clans/villages, not as a possession but as a fief to be enjoyed in perpetuity so long as the vassal obeyed his obligations under the covenant (Mendenhall 1976: 138). Having said this, however, there still remains the question of the mechanics of administration. As Mendenhall has observed, the one specialization well attested in the archaic narratives is the priest/Levite:

> It is assumed that the *functions* of prophet or "judge" are not occupational specializations. From the story of Micah and the Danites in Judges 18 we can infer beyond doubt that religious specialists were in some demand in Palestinian culture of the twelfth century. The "Levite" in question was merely a specialist in religious ritual (1976: 149–50).

We would add that at least one of the reasons that they were in such demand may well have been because of their importance in agricultural decision-making.

Evidence for interregional trade has been mentioned above. As we pointed out, the items of non-local materials and craftsmanship are clearly associated with the elite residence at Tel Masos.

The relationship of the "judges" to warfare has been the subject of extended treatment in recent years (Mendenhall 1958; Bess 1963; Malamat 1967; Richter 1965; Glock 1968, 1970; Ishida 1973; Hauser 1975; and Reid 1975). The consensus seems to be that along with the ritual involvement of the *šōfēṭ* [['judge']] or *nāśî* [['prince']] the other main function which he performed was a military one, and certainly this function was one which could make possible some type of regional authority over a coalition of clans on the part of one who began as a purely local chief (Hauser 1975: 195ff.).

Conclusion

In an effort to clarify the role of religious ideology and practice in the sociopolitical structure of early Israel, a [[249]] refined model of chiefdom is suggested which has utility for the analysis of the archaeological remains of that society. Suggestions have also been made as to ways in which ideology and environment are correlated. It is suggested, furthermore, that the situation which favors the selection for a chiefdom form of organization—i.e., which selects for a higher level homeostat—is one in which the information processing capabilities of a single-level network are transcended, and higher level controls are necessary for the maintenance and survival of the system. Following Rappaport (1971a; 1971b) it is suggested that the locus of this differentiation is in the organization of ritual within the cultural system.

Sources Consulted

Aharoni, Yohanan; Fritz, Volkmar; and Kempinski, Aharon
    1974   Excavations at Tel Masos (*Khirbet El-Meshash*): Preliminary Report on the First Season, 1972. *Tel Aviv* 1: 64–74.
    1975   Excavations at Tel Masos: Second Season, 1974. *Tel Aviv* 2: 97–124.
Bess, Stephen H.
    1963   *Systems of Land Tenure in Ancient Israel.* Unpublished Ph.D. Dissertation, University of Michigan.
Brainerd, G. W.
    1951   The Place of Chronological Ordering in Archaeological Analysis. *American Antiquity* 16: 301–13.
Diakonoff, I. M.
    1975   The Rural Community in the Ancient Near East. *JESHO* 17: 121–33.
Earle, Timothy
    1978   *Economic and Social Organization of a Complex Chiefdom: The Halelea District, Kahua'i, Hawaii.* Anthropology Paper 63. Ann Arbor: Museum of Anthropology, University of Michigan.
Engelbrecht, William
    1974   The Iroquois: Archaeological Patterning on the Tribal Level. *World Archaeology* 6/1: 52–65.
Evenari, Michael; Shaman, Leslie; and Tadmor, Naphtali
    1971   *The Negev: The Challenge of a Desert.* Cambridge: Harvard University Press.
Flannery, Kent V.
    1972   The Cultural Evolution of Civilizations. *Annual Review of Ecology and Systematics* 3: 399–426.
Franken, H. J.
    1976   The Problem of Identification in Biblical Archaeology. *PEQ* 108: 3–11.
Fried, Morton H.
    1968   On the Concepts of "Tribe" and "Tribal Society." Pp. 3–20 in *Essays on the Problem of Tribe*, ed. June Helm. Seattle: American Ethnological Society.
Fritz, Volkmar
    1979   Personal communication.
Geus, C. H. J. de
    1975   The Importance of Archaeological Research into the Palestinian Agricultural Terraces . . . , *PEQ* 107: 65–74.
    1976   *The Tribes of Israel.* Amsterdam: Van Gorcum.

Glock, Albert E.
1968   *Warfare in Mari and Early Israel.* Unpublished Ph.D. Dissertation, University of Michigan.
1970   Early Israel as the Kingdom of Yahweh. *Concordia Theological Monthly* 41: 558–605.
Gluckman, Max
1959   The Lozi of Barotseland. Pp. 60–74 in *Seven Tribes of Central Africa,* ed. Elizabeth Colson and Max Gluckman. Manchester: Manchester University Press.
Goldman, Irving
1970   *Ancient Polynesian Society.* Chicago: University of Chicago Press.
Golomb, B., and Kedar, Yehuda
1971   Ancient Agriculture in the Galilean Mountains. *IEJ* 21: 136–40.
Gottwald, Norman K.
1976   Early Israel and the "Asiatic Mode of Production" in Canaan. Pp. 145–54 in *Society of Biblical Literature 1976: Seminar Papers.* SBLSP 15; Missoula, Montana: Scholars Press.
Hauser, Alan J.
1975   The "Minor Judges": A Re-evaluation. *JBL* 94: 190–200.
Hawkes, C. F. C.
1954   Archaeological Theory and Method: Some Suggestions from the Old World. *American Anthropologist* 56/1: 155–68.
Heltzer, Michael
1976   *The Rural Community in Ancient Ugarit.* Wiesbaden: Reichert.
Holladay, John S., Jr.
1976   Of Sherds and Strata: Contributions toward an Understanding of the Archaeology of the Divided Monarchy. Pp. 253–93 in *Magnalia Dei: The Mighty Acts of God,* ed. Frank M. Cross, W. E. Lemke, and P. D. Miller. Garden City, New York: Doubleday.
Holleman, J. F.
1959   Some "Shona" Tribes of Southern Rhodesia. Pp. 354–95 in *Seven Tribes of Central Africa,* ed. Elizabeth Colson and Max Gluckman. Manchester: Manchester University Press.
Ishida, T.
1973   The Leaders of the Tribal League in the Pre-Monarchic Period. *RB* 80: 514–30.
Jankowska, N. B.
1969   Communal Self-Government and the King of the State of Arrapḫa. *JESHO* 12: 233–82.
Johnson, G. A.
1973   *Local Exchange and Early State Development in Southwestern Iran.* Anthropology Paper 51. Ann Arbor: Museum of Anthropology, University of Michigan.
Kedar, Yehuda
1957a   Ancient Agriculture at Shivtah in the Negev. *IEJ* 7: 178–89.

1957b   Water and Soil from the Desert: Some Ancient Agricultural Achievements in the Central Negev. *Geographical Journal* 123: 179–87.

Kempinski, Aharon, and Fritz, Volkmar
1977   Excavations at Tel Masos: Third Season, 1975. *Tel Aviv* 3–4: 136–58.

Kempinski, Aharon
1979   Personal communication.

Kochavi, Moshe
1969   Excavations at Tel Esdar. *ʿAtiqot* 5: 14–48 [Hebrew, with English summary, pp. 2*–5*].

Kramer, Carol
1978   Estimating Prehistoric Populations· An Ethnoarchaeological Approach. A paper presented at the Colloque international C.N.R S. No. 580 (13–15 June 1978): "L'Archacologie de l'Iraq du début de l'Époque Néolithique à 333 avant notre ère: Perspectives et limites de l'interpretation anthropologiques des documents."

McClellan, Thomas L.
1975   *Quantitative Studies in the Iron Age Pottery of Palestine.* Unpublished Ph.D. Dissertation, University of Pennsylvania.

Malamat, A.
1967   Aspects of Tribal Societies in Mari and Israel. *XVᵉ Rencontre Assyriologique Internationale: La Civilisation de Mari.* Liège: Université de Liège.

Mendenhall, George E.
1958   The Census Lists of Numbers 1 and 26. *JBL* 77: 52–66.
1976   Social Organization in Early Israel. Pp. 132–51 in *Magnalia Dei: The Mighty Acts of God*, ed. Frank M. Cross, W. E. Lemke, and P. D. Miller. Garden City, New York: Doubleday.

Naroll, R.
1962   Floor Area and Settlement Population. *American Antiquity* 27: 587–89.

Peebles, Christopher S., and Kus, Susan M.
1977   Some Archaeological Correlates of Ranked Societies. *American Antiquity* 42/3: 421–47.

Rappaport, Roy A.
1968   *Pigs for the Ancestors.* New Haven: Yale University Press.
1970   Sanctity and Adaptation. *Io* 7: 46–71.
1971a   The Sacred in Human Evolution. *Annual Review of Ecology and Systematics* 2: 23–44.
1971b   Ritual, Sanctity and Cybernetics. *American Anthropologist* 73: 59–76.

Reid, Patrick V.
1975   *šbty* in 2 Sam. 7:7. *CBQ* 37: 17–20.

Renfrew, Colin
1972   Beyond a Subsistence Economy: The Evolution of Social Organization in Prehistoric Europe. Pp. 69–85 in *Reconstructing Complex Societies*, ed. Charlotte B. Moore. Cambridge, Massachusetts: American Schools of Oriental Research.

Richter, W.
1965   Zu den "Richtern Israel." *ZAW* 77: 40–72.
Robinson, W. S.
1951   A Method for Chronologically Ordering Archaeological Deposits. *American Antiquity* 16: 293–301.
Ron, Z.
1966   Agricultural Terraces in the Judean Mountains *IEJ* 16: 33–49, 111–122.
Sahlins, Marshall D.
1958   *Social Stratification in Polynesia.* Seattle: University of Washington Press.
⟦1962   The segmentary Lineage: An Organization of Predatory Expansion. Pp. 89–119 in *Comparative Political Systems,* ed. R. Cohen and J. Middleton. Garden City, N.Y.: American Museum of Natural History.⟧
Service, Elman R.
1962   *Primitive Social Organization.* 2d ed. New York: Random House.
1971   *Cultural Evolutionism: Theory in Practice.* New York: Holt, Rinehart, and Winston.
1975   *Origins of the State and Civilization.* New York: Norton.
Shiloh, Yigal
1970   The Four-Room House: Its Situation and Function in the Israelite City. *IEJ* 20: 180–90.
1973   The Four-Space House: The Israelite Type House. *Eretz-Israel* 11: 277–85 [Hebrew, with English summary, p. 32*].
1978   Elements in the Development of Town Planning in the Israelite City. *IEJ* 28: 36–51.
Smith, Jason W.
1976   *Foundations of Archaeology.* Beverly Hills: Glencoe.
Taylor, Donna
1979   Some Settlement Pattern Correlates of Chieftaincies and Simpler States. Unpublished typescript on file at the Museum of Anthropology, University of Michigan.
Trigger, Bruce
1974   The Archaeology of Government. *World Archaeology* 6/1: 95–105.
Whallon, Robert, Jr.
1968   Investigations of Late Prehistoric Social Organization in New York State. Pp. 223–44 in *New Perspectives in Archaeology,* ed. S. R. Binford and L. R. Binford. Chicago: Aldine.
Winter, Edward H.
1966   Territorial Groupings and Religion among the Iraqw. Pp. 155–74 in *Anthropological Approaches to the Study of Religion,* ed. Michael Benton. London: Tavistock.

Life on the Land:

The Subsistence Struggles of Early Israel

DAVID C. HOPKINS

But they shall sit every person under his vine and his fig tree,
and none shall make them afraid (Mic 4:4).

⟦179⟧ In the early Iron Age, beginning around 1200 B.C.E., the highlands
of Canaan were the heartland of what would become the Israelite nation-
state. What was life like for the first Israelite settlers in this region? Until
recently, the debate about the character of the settlement process—
whether it occurred by means of conquest, infiltration, or a peasant revolt (see Fritz 1987)—has usually diverted attention from this question.
Now, however, a few portraits of the life of these settlers have begun to
appear (Callaway 1983; Stager 1985; Ben-Tor 1979). Yet our understanding of the struggle for agricultural subsistence, the most basic level of life
for the settlers of the highlands, remains largely indistinct. What were the
challenges that faced the ancient Israelite farming families? How did they
grow enough food to survive? Answering such questions will provide a
new perspective from which to view issues surrounding the emergence of
Israel.

To conjure up the world of the Israelite farmers of the early Iron
Age, one must recognize the complexity of agricultural systems, even
among the preindustrial communities of the ancient world. Agriculture
is affected by many variables: crop types, length of growing season, water

Reprinted with permission from *Biblical Archaeologist* 50 (1987) 178–91.

Editors' note: The original article contained several charts, photos, and drawings that
illustrated Hopkins' general viewpoint. Only two of them are reprinted here.

resources, kinds of implements, types of land use, and forms of economic organization, to name but a few. In general, these can be classified as environmental, demographic, and technological factors.

The interrelatedness of these factors bears emphasizing. For instance, it is clear that farming in the highlands of Canaan was limited by certain environmental constraints, especially the availability of water. But this limitation was offset by the presence of certain technologies, such as techniques of cistern construction, terrace building, and the knowledge of surface-water properties. These technologies, however, depended in turn on economic feasibility. In Iron Age Israel this economic feasibility was mostly a matter of labor supply, and thus we arrive at the demographic factor. The relationship between population and labor supply is clear but not straightforward. All sorts of factors can influence how much work a given population will accept, so that even the simplest measure of how many hands might be available to hew cisterns and construct terraces is elusive. Students of the period are left wondering whether at one time there were enough hands to keep the growing number of mouths fed and whether at another time there were enough lands to keep the growing number of hands occupied. This interrelatedness can be daunting, but it is only by interpreting the emerging data on the environment, population, and technology in a holistic fashion that the world of the early Iron Age settlers of the highlands becomes clear.

Environment

What was the nature of the environment that faced the settlers of the early Iron Age? Archaeologists are using a variety of scientific analyses of data unearthed in their excavations to answer this question. These analyses include the studies of sediments (geology), of tree and plant [[180]] remains (paleobotany), and of pollen grains (palynology). Even with these new methods, however, any reconstruction we may wish to make must remain tentative. For example, only limited areas of Palestine are suited for pollen preservation; thus palynological studies have offered only minimal help. The data do record, though, the decline of tree-pollen percentages—which presumably parallels the expansion of settlement—from even before the historical period (Horowitz 1971; Van Ziest and Bottema 1982: 283–84).

Other studies have proved more fruitful. Liphschitz and Waisel (1980, and previous articles cited there) have identified plant remains recovered from stratified contexts from a variety of sites. These plant species invariably occupy the same regions today, albeit in greatly reduced numbers. In this way, their study has provided further evidence for the conti-

Early Iron Age

Excavated Site	Size in Hectares
Izbet Ṣarṭa	0.40
Tel Harashim	0.45–0.50
Giloh	0.50–0.70
Tel Isdar	0.78
Khirbet Raddana	0.80
Beth-zur	0.85
Tell Qiri	1.00
Ai	1.00
Shiloh	1.20
Tel en-Naṣbeh	1.80[a]
Tell Beit Mirsim	3.00
Tel Masos	4.50
Hazor	6.10[b]

Notes: [a]Estimate based on Iron II size.
      [b]Estimate.

nuity of of the composition of vegetation of the highlands. By inference, this paleobotanical work also testifies to a continuity of the climate. This conclusion in turn grants authority to the use of present-day climatological data to portray the ancient situation. Thus, farmers of the highlands could probably count on the same propitious temperatures known today in Palestine but would also have to contend with the same desiccating seasonality and variable precipitation patterns. Some analysts offer more dramatic conclusions, such as a greatly expanded winter wet season for early historical times. These ideas, however, are too tenuous to play a part in historical reconstruction.

Progress in the study of paleosediments, especially in the drier valleys of the south, may allow a more reliable reconstruction of the relative humidity and aridity of particular periods (Rosen 1986). Yet even this data cannot be used in a heavy-handed manner. Means for recovering the absolute state of the ancient environment do not exist, and the role of humans in altering the landscape cannot be neglected.

Until the potential of paleobotanical, palynological, and geomorphological study is fulfilled, more exacting determinations of the state of the climate and vegetational cover of the highlands during the early Iron Age will not be possible. Yet enough is known to correct the more-or-less romantic portraits of settlement life that have often pictured Israel's

ancestors as woodsmen wielding axes to open up life-space for themselves in previously unoccupied areas. While this picture of a densely forested landscape serves well in overcoming our images of today's barren, denuded landscape, forest clearing was not a key activity in the settlement of the highlands. The original vegetation of the area was never the dense forest with little underbrush in the mold of the Grimm's fairy tales. Rather, evergreen oaks and deciduous terebinths were scattered among an often dense thicket of tall shrubs known as maquis. By the early Iron Age the forest and maquis were already declining as a result of both previous sedentary occupation (in [[181]] the Early Bronze Age) and the activities of nonsedentary exploiters who wielded fire as a tool to improve pastures and flush game. In the hands of the early Iron Age settlers of the highlands, fire probably also played a much more significant landclearing role than the ax. In any case, in preparing the predominantly terra rossa fields of the highlands for farming, the settlers faced a more arduous task than felling trees: removing stumps and roots. A field opened to the sun and rain through burning or other methods of deadening trees, however, would have initially been planted around the denuded trunks. The readily plowable field only emerged over a period of time among these technologically simpler farming communities.

Demographics

Demography is perhaps the most neglected area of the historical study of the biblical world. Evidence is limited and, as applied to the ancient highlands, demographic science remains rudimentary. That the highlands of the early Iron Age experienced a massive increase in population and a radical alteration of settlement patterns stands, nevertheless, as a fact unquestioned by any side in the debate about the settlement period. As the mapping and excavation of these settlements proceed, more precise demographic calculations will be possible. Already, several highlights of the changing population landscape stand out. The dominant feature of this landscape is the dispersed pattern of small settlements, variously situated in environments that span the scale of agricultural feasibility. Stager (1985: 3) has calculated that the average size of the early Iron age site was less than 2 hectares (approximately 5 acres). That the median size rests below this figure is readily apparent in the survey data (Stager 1985: table 1) and is further suggested by the clustering of the sizes of excavated sites at the low end of the scale. From the geological and ecological standpoint, the locations of these sites lack the homogeneity often attributed to them (see, for example, Callaway 1985:33). Their locations are diverse with respect to agricultural conditions, defensive possibilities, and communications routes. Most of these sites were newly founded in the early Iron Age, but many were resettlements. Thus the early Iron Age settlement boom involved both opening new areas and reclaiming previously settled villages. Recognizing this fact helps to brighten the portrait of the environmental conditions of the early Iron Age expansion of settlement.

Many of the sites of this dramatic surge of occupation were at marginal locations where previous highlanders had chosen not to settle. They are sites with a limited access to fresh water and a rugged topography offering little bottomland. The zone of human occupation was expanded at Giloh, Tell Isdar, and Izbet Ṣarṭa, all newly founded sites with limited subsistence potential. Settlement was renewed at sites—such as Ai—that offered essentially unfavorable agricultural conditions. But a large percentage of sites offered much better agricultural circumstances; these were close to springs, situated on slopes at the edge of basins of colluvial soils, or nestled on hills astride fairly level small plateaus. On this side of the ledger renewed settlement at Khirbet Sasa, Hazor, Tell en-Naṣbeh, and Shiloh found good environmental conditions. The founding settlers of Tel Masos and Tel Harashim (at the end of the Peqiᶜin valley, which runs southeasterly) also encountered favorable circumstances for farming. Four unexcavated sites from the central highlands, at which surveyors found pottery of the earliest phase of the Iron Age (Kochavi 1972: 154), are worthy [[182]] of notice in this respect: Khirbet Ibn Naṣir, sitting above the valleys east of Shechem; Tel Abu Zarad, a renewed occupation of a well-watered tell situated equidistant from Shechem and Shiloh, about 10 kilometers west of the north–south highway; Khirbet er-Rafid, at the southern edge of the Shiloh valley; and Ras eṭ-Ṭaḥuneh, near Khirbet Raddana on the north–south highway that runs across one of the least dissected portions of the Bethel Hills. These sites provided settlers with agricultural opportunities markedly better than those often associated with early Iron Age settlements.

The domestic architecture of these small sites offers a dramatic indicator of the nature of the life led by their inhabitants. The familiar four-room house is a strikingly small structure, one that could only have been occupied by a nuclear family. Based upon a cross-culturally derived estimate of per person space allotments, houses at Ai and Raddana furnished room for 3 or 4 occupants, while the households at Tel Masos were somewhat larger. The small size of these families is conspicuous and testifies to the settlers' demographic dilemma. What few demographic statistics are available for the ancient eastern Mediterranean confirm this perception of instability. In analyzing cemetery populations from Greece in the early Iron Age, Angel found 4.1 births, but only 1.9 survivors, per female (1972: 94–95, 97). Under these conditions even the extended family (*bet ᵓab*), such as might be evidenced archaeologically by the house clusters at Ai and Raddana (Stager 1985: 18), would be hard-pressed to achieve stability through increased household size. How many extended families reached the proportions of the ancestral family of Jacob is difficult to say (Gen 46:8–27); presumably, high mortality rates often kept their numbers low. Thus, periodically, a thriving *bet ʾab* would lose its breadth and be returned, de facto, to a nuclear family, probably unable to fend for itself agriculturally.

Composed of such small and inherently unstable units, the populations of the small sites that peppered the landscape of the early Iron Age highlands never mounted very high. If Ai with its densely packed houses is taken as typical, then early Iron Age villages boasted no more than 200 to 300 individuals. This fact gives rise to an important paradox of the highlands settlement boom. Communities that were collectively part of a tremendous surge in population were beset by many problems arising from not having enough people. The demographic realities faced by individual families and villages are easily overlooked in contemplating the transformation of the settlement landscape of the highlands, but they likely constituted the most severe constraint faced by the settlers themselves. The facts of domestic demographics and the small sizes of the early Iron Age villages make it easy to understand why so many failed to develop. Coupled with the growing centralization and urbanization associated with the emergence of the monarchy, the dismal realities of reproduction help to explain the abandonment of so many sites after a few generations (Mazar 1981: 33).

Technology

In outlining the technological level in the highlands during the early Iron Age, scholars have ordinarily focused on tools and the processes for making them, as well as on various agricultural and construction techniques. [[183]] This has unfortunately ignored a whole range of vital knowledge, organizational abilities, and skills (especially social skills). Moreover, the role of individual innovations in material technology has been greatly exaggerated both from the standpoint of substantive evidence and with respect to their impact on highlands subsistence as a whole. To take a widely recognized example, William F. Albright (1971: 113) suggested that the discovery of a waterproof lining for cisterns was a key for Israelite settlement. Yet this claim has had to be abandoned because of the discovery of lime-plastered cisterns from much earlier contexts, as well as of cisterns hewn in naturally impermeable limestone. In addition, water cisterns do not stand out as an integral feature of most of the occupation sites of the early Iron Age (Callaway 1985: 40 offers the opposing view). The settlers of sites that offer no evidence for cisterns, such as Izbet Ṣarṭa, Tel Masos, and Giloh, must have found another way to meet their water needs, one that better fit their total subsistence situation. Similarly, the widely disseminated idea that the development of iron metallurgy was the decisive material basis for the expansion of highland settlement has not been proven. Statistical studies of archaeologically recovered metals have undercut this notion by chronicling the drawn-out, centuries-long rise of iron to common use. Metallurgical studies have shown the slow and haphazard appearance of an iron (steeled iron) that was actually superior to bronze (Stech-Wheeler and others 1981: 255; Waldbaum 1978: 41). The effect of the introduction of a new make of tool (rather than a new type) has also been greatly overestimated; we have often not considered what can actually be accomplished by the iron ax or iron plowpoint within an agricultural system where land-clearing and plowing are only two crucial operations among many. In fact, neither of these so-called advances in technology played a decisive role in the achievement of agricultural subsistence in the highlands of Canaan during the early Iron Age.

The technique of agricultural terracing also fails to fill the role of the prime mover of the expansion of settlement in the highlands during this period. Terraced hillsides were doubtless a feature of the agricultural landscape of the early Iron Age (see Stager 1985: 5–9), but a systemic investigation also raises real questions about how prominent they were. It must be asked, for example, what labor force built and maintained these terribly costly, long-term investments? Evidence for widespread terracing in this period is at best thin and the practice apparently did not become widespread until the eighth century B.C.E. Historical reconstructions of the settlement period that have granted determining roles to terrace construction, iron metallurgy, or plastered water-cisterns all show the dangers of [[184]] abstracting tool technology from the farming world in which it functioned.

Agricultural Objectives

With my preceding comments serving as an orientation, we can now consider the three basic objectives around which highlands agriculture shaped itself and how each fit within the environmental, demographic, and technological scene of early Israel.

Water Conservation and Control

Water availability was the decisive environmental constraint under which village agricultural systems of the highlands operated. Rainfall in Palestine is concentrated in a few winter months and is highly intensive. (When it rains, it pours.) The same amount of rainfall that London sees spread over three hundred raindays falls onto Jerusalem in only fifty. This high-intensity rainfall means high rates of runoff; precious water is thus lost to agriculture. When it is not raining, it is sunny, and the climate is marked by world-class insolation rates. During the summer months this extreme insolation drains the soil of whatever small quantity of moisture remains from the wet season. Unlike the middle latitudes, where the dead season (winter) is wet, the crops of the highlands' planting season are completely dependent upon the rains of the planting season for their germination and growth. Thus the winter plantings are highly vulnerable to any hiatus of precipitation after germination. Sowing of the fields cannot even begin until sufficient moisture has accumulated in the soil left hard-baked by the summer heat.

In addition to its frustrating seasonality, rainfall is also highly variable, both with respect to its distribution throughout the year and the achievement of average annual accumulation. This variability is such that three years out of ten might not follow the expected pattern—for example, it might be very wet in the beginning of the season and very dry towards the end—so that there could be an agricultural drought even though the absolute total rainfall reaches the average. What's more, one or two years out of ten might show more than a 25 percent deviation from the mean annual rainfall. Drought years are known historically to bunch up, adding to the difficulties of subsistence. There is no mistaking that this is a very high-risk environment.

Very limited possibilities for irrigation from springs or streams leave farming villages with no choice but to face the difficult facts of water availability head-on. What strategies of water conservation and control did the highlanders of the early Iron Age pursue? The primary strategy for water conservation is terracing. Though the motivation for terracing has often been seen as the desire to protect soils against erosion, it was more important in early Israel as a water-conservation measure. Farming communities cannot change the patterns of precipitation, but through terracing they can reduce the losses of water due to runoff. Its benefits include drought resistance as well as higher yields for any village able to apply this kind of special treatment to surrounding slopes. But here was the problem for the small and demographically unstable communities of the early Iron Age. Terrace agriculture is highly intensive and demands a great deal of labor for construction and maintenance. It may well be that [[185]] the labor-strapped villages would be willing to bear the high labor costs of terracing in order to enjoy its clear-cut advantages, especially the reduction of the risk to crops that enhanced water accumulation would present. Evidence for terracing around early Iron Age villages it not compelling, however. It is more reasonable to picture terrace systems of the time not as a dominating feature of the landscape but as an occasional phenomenon, the result of variable local conditions and site histories. Unable to take advantage of terracing, and lacking conditions for other strategies for water conservation and control, such as irrigation and drainage works, most villages would have been hard-pressed to do much about the agriculturally frustrating pattern of water availability.

Soil Conservation and Fertility Maintenance

At most of the highland sites that were settled in the early Iron Age, soil profiles offered a fairly productive environment, one not yet stripped of its mantle of soil by radical deforestation. Nevertheless, the relative scarcity of bottomland meant that hillside slopes (which are easily eroded) were cultivated. Furthermore, no agricultural community can forever neglect the task of conserving the plant nutrients of its soil environment, nutrients that are depleted with each season's cropping. But how much energy did early Israelites expend in conserving and protecting their soil environment? Despite some romantic projections of contemporary ecological concerns onto the record of the past, the answer to this question is: very little. Terraces would best protect hillside slopes, but these were too costly. In their struggle for agricultural subsistence, the early settlers had to devote their energies to the short term and could ill afford to take long-term viability into consideration. Farming is possible on unterraced slopes, and "soil mining," the consumption of the soil base, is a regular feature of incipient agricultural communities.

With regard to fertility maintenance, however, early Israel undoubtedly practiced a form of agricultural fallowing, as well as fertilization. Based upon literary sources and on the practices of contemporary traditional farming communities of the Mediterranean region, it is most probable that the highland settlers used a type of short-term fallowing in which a year of cultivation was followed by a year of bare-ground fallow (Hopkins 1985: 194–95). The practice aided in the recovery of fertility and also broke the natural cycle of noxious plant pests and diseases. Bare-ground fallowing, however, is a most inadequate means of restoring plant nutrients, and some kind of fertilization is usually associated with it. In the highlands during the early Iron Age this amounted to nothing more than the grazing of flocks and herds on fallow ground, harvested fields, and orchards as the means of applying manure. This is not the most efficacious system either, but, for various reasons, it well suits the demographic and environmental situation.

The outcome of such a system of fallowing and fertilization was that these communities had to be satisfied with fairly low crop yields that they could do little to enhance on a broad scale. Precisely what these yields were is not easy to say. Because there are no economic records on the yielding characteristics of early Iron Age crops and cultivation techniques, evidence comes only indirectly. From later talmudic reports, Roman literary sources, and calculations made by Mayerson (1960: 18–19) based on papyri of the seventh century C.E. recovered at Nessana in the Negeb, it is clear that a seemingly meager ten- to fifteen-fold harvest would have been welcomed by any framing family. Falling yields would have provided incentive to put more land into production as villages "mined" the soil in their environs. Migration would also suggest itself, as distances from village homes to newly opened fields became intolerable.

Risk-Spreading and the Optimization of Labor

⟦187⟧ The first two objectives of highland agriculture that I have discussed here—water conservation and control, and soil conservation and fertility maintenance—aimed to lower the risk of farming by producing larger and more reliable harvests. Initial attempts to lower the risks of farming in the highlands through terracing, replenishing soil nutrients, and protecting the soil environment could not have been very successful. This negative conclusion adds considerable importance to the third objective of highland agriculture. It sought not to lower the risk (by manipulating the environment) but to spread it out (by distributing the community's energies across a broad spectrum of pursuits). Thus, a natural concomitant of risk-spreading is the optimization of labor, where an attempt is made to balance labor demand and availability throughout the agricultural year.

How was labor organized to spread the risk of farming? In the crucial grainfields, the farming families adopted staggered patterns of sowing their wheat and barley. This procedure was well suited to the limited availability of labor and draft animals for plowing. It also hedged against the variability of rainfall mentioned above. As the first lines of the Gezer calendar indicate, with their reference to two periods (four months) of planting, the sowing of the seed was spread out over the first months of winter in order to avoid depending upon any particular pattern of rainfall. Sown all at once, an entire crop could be lost to an unpredictable, but not surprising, dry spell.

Grains were by no means the sole focus of the agricultural effort. Farming communities planted a variety of crops in a wide selection of environmental niches. The natural diversity of the highlands' environment aided in this endeavor. The crop mix included not just the staple cereals and vegetables but also tree and vine crops, as the "seven species" list of Deut 8:8 makes plain. Thus, the tree and vine crops spread the risk by diversifying the subsistence base. And this could be done without their competing for the labor needed for field crops, because grapes, olives, and figs do not require attention at the same time as field crops. The repertoire of highlands crops also included other fruit and nut trees (for instance, the pomegranate and almond), as well as many important vegetables such as broad beans, lentils, chick-peas, and common peas, all of which have been attested archaeologically (Borowski 1987: 93–97).

Agriculture was also mixed with pastoral pursuits. The rich and specific vocabulary of the Hebrew Bible is ample testimony to the importance of pastoralism in the economy, [[188]] and archaeological attention to the recovery of animal bones more than supports this conclusion (Hesse 1986; Hesse and Wapnish 1986; LaBianca 1987). The exact nature of the pastoral-agricultural mix remains to be clearly defined, but the indispensability of livestock husbandry and its complementarity to farming are without question. The grazing of livestock—sheep, goats, cattle— added greatly to the resiliency of communities struck by agricultural failure. Animals are a mobile resource subject to a different set of environmental constraints than fixed fields of crops.

The dietary contribution of herd animals was significant, with milk and milk foods (cheese and curds) the most important products. Animals could also be used directly for food (though never incautiously, for they constituted a capital investment) and otherwise contributed wool to home and commercial industry. Livestock husbandry also made use of marginal land, provided needed fertilizer, and did not compete for agricultural labor, because shepherding could be carried out by youths (recall that David, the youngest of Jesse's sons, nearly missed Samuel's visit because he was out pasturing the flock—1 Sam 16:11).

The settlers of the early Iron Age highlands also developed ways to preserve produce from a year of plenty for a year of want. Much of the produce yielded by various trees and crops could be stored, such as fruits, processed juices, and oil. Large storage jars (the collared-rim pithoi and the Galilean pithoi) and household grain pits that have been found at the sites of the period are concrete and nearly ubiquitous manifestations of this strategy. Perhaps the crucial attribute of flocks and herds is their ability to act as a kind of storage—"a disaster bank on the hoof"—subject to a different set of constraints than agriculture and capable of receiving deposits in good years and withstanding withdrawals in years when crops do not suffice. That this need to store foods found communal expression has now been demonstrated by the discovery of an unambiguous storage building at Shiloh dating to the early Iron Age (Finkelstein 1986). The building has offered up more than forty collared-rim pithoi. Its existence at a site with strong cultic connections cannot be a coincidence and testifies to the role played by the religious institutions of early Israel in structuring the emerging society.

Some highlands' communities may have become involved in inter-regional trade, either as predators, transit agents, or trading partners (Coote and Whitelam 1986: 133–35 [[reprinted in this volume, pp. 335–76]]). Though the historical circumstances are highly suggestive, actual evidence for this participation is almost entirely lacking. The sites of the period have not yielded, for example, any kind of commercial containers.

The collared-rim pithoi are clearly too heavy to be involved in transport. Nevertheless, they may themselves have been items of trade (Mazar 1981: 30). Trade in deerskins is evidenced at Tel Masos by the discovery of fallow deer remains (foot [[189]] bones; see Hesse and Wapnish 1986). Some sites were also well positioned to take advantage of trade as a nonsubsistence-related means of diversifying. Har Adir is the most striking example. Its location vis-à-vis Phoenicia is suggestive, as is the remarkably well-worked pick—an item of trade?—discovered by its excavators (Muhly 1982: 45; Kochavi 1985: 57).

Finally, risks were spread through the development of interhousehold and intervillage systems of cooperation and networks of exchange. These were especially important for sharing food when, as was often the case, proximate villages experienced concomitant crop success and failure. Further, they provided the means for regular labor exchange to cope with the great seasonal fluctuations in labor demand and to provide the greater quantity of labor needed for large-scale projects.

The Demographic Challenge and the Social Dimension of Subsistence

This review of the major objectives and strategies of highlands agriculture reveals how crucial risk-spreading and labor-optimizing strategies were for securing agricultural subsistence in the early Iron Age. Other events and activities that are often taken to be determinative of the struggles of the period—developing iron metallurgy, clearing forests, hewing cisterns, and building terraces—certainly shaped aspects of the settlers' lives. Yet these did not spell the difference between survival and failure, as did diversifying crops, mixing farming and husbandry, investing in means of storage, and developing reciprocal interfamily and intercomunity networks. It is on these goals that the highlanders concentrated.

The key to securing subsistence through risk-spreading and labor-optimizing (and, indeed, to laying the groundwork for further highland development) rested in the second term of this dual objective. The importance of mustering sufficient labor can be read in the population landscape. The small and demographically unstable villages composed of small and demographically unstable families constantly faced crises of insufficient hands. While the tension was in part a consequence of the demands on pioneer settlements, it was primarily the result of the pressures on conducting agricultural operations. In addition to its importance for the short term, labor-optimizing is essential for moving beyond mere coping with risk to risk-reduction through terracing and other special treatments of the environment. Because no technological quick fix, such as a more efficient iron plow, solved the labor problem for highlanders of the early Iron Age, these settlers relied upon other means of adding to the quantity of available labor. Among these, the most obvious was enlarged population. As a rule, village cultivators the world over invest farming surpluses in increased family size rather than in increased standard of living.

Though reproductive success could hardly be controlled in the ancient world, literature from the early Israelite period clearly indicates the desire of the farming family for great size (see, for instance, the wish expressed by the witnesses to the marriage of Ruth and Boaz in Ruth 4:11–12). Furthermore, the prominence of regulations of sexual morality in the Hebrew Bible has been related to the unstable conditions of the settlement period (Meyers 1978: 98–99); the stipulations would have assured that sexual energies were directed toward the crucial task of replenishing the family. One thing is clear: burgeoning family and community size would fuel greater investments in risk-reduction and risk-spreading. These would lead to more stable agriculture, better nutrition, lower infant and mother mortality rates and, thus, further increases in population size. Many of the prominent families in the narratives of the book of Judges are depicted—in symbolic terms—as having attained considerable size and may reflect just this process. Gideon is reported to have had "seventy" sons, all his own children (Judg 8:30); Jair and Ibzan each had "thirty" sons (10:3 and 12:9); while Abdon sired a total of "forty" (12:14).

Another means of enlarging the labor supply is to provide inducements to larger individual contributions of labor—longer days in the field, more arduous types of work. The high view of work that is part of the creation epic of Genesis 2 and 3 (the human creature is placed in the garden to till it and keep it) makes good sense in such a context, as does the encouragement of the Joseph tribe by Joshua to undertake difficult land-clearing operations (Josh 17:14–15). The way that the Sabbath commandment is phrased in the early legal collection of Exodus— "Six days you must do your work, but on the seventh day you must rest" (23:12; compare also 20:9)—stands as a reminder that the indirect force of a single day of rest is six days of work. This represents a strikingly intense commitment to labor when compared to most preindustrial agricultural societies.

A third means of meeting the labor requirement of highland agriculture may have been the formation of communal work groups. Presumably, these groups would cooperate at times of peak labor demand when many households were unable to supply their total needs. The group may also have made collective investments in the agricultural economy beyond the domain of individual households. Similarly, reciprocal exchange networks linking proximate villages may have come into existence; such an exchange would have taken advantage of variable harvest times by sharing labor. The advantages of regular cooperation and incentives for sharing in times of want suggest that the highlands of the early Iron [[190]] Age were crisscrossed by social relations that contributed to securing subsistence.

Here is where the study of farming contributes most to our understanding of the emergence of Israel. The social dimension of subsistence, in particular the risk-spreading and labor-optimizing, can help us reconstruct more accurately some of the reasons for the transitions and changes in Palestine in the early Iron Age. Robert Coote and Keith Whitelam (1986: 118–21) have emphasized how dramatically the decline in trade and commerce during the Late Bronze Age affected those nonsedentary groups that were in large measure dependent upon that economy. With the decline of trade, pastoral nomadic groups and bandits, among others, were forced to seek alternative sources of income; many adopted agriculture and village life in order to secure their subsistence. As Late Bronze society ended, so did the incessant conflict between city-states that is so pervasively portrayed in the Amarna correspondence. The calming of the rural instability that had been inspired by the urbanized political environment of the Late Bronze Age permitted the expansion of village agricultural life beyond the limits of urban control and protection. Finally, the movement towards more intensive, sedentary agriculture was propelled by the gradual increase in the population of the highlands. Fed by the dispersion of city centers and immigration from the lowlands, and stimulated by decline in warfare (and, perhaps, the distance from epidemic disease that may have been prevalent in urban centers), the overall increasing population of highland regions could not be supported by the predominantly pastoral economy of the Late Bronze Age. Agricultural intensification ensued. Thus, the transformation of the population landscape that took place after the breakdown of society in the Late Bronze Age can be viewed as representing the movement from a more pastoral and less sedentary economy to a primarily agricultural economy dominated by small settlements.

It is precisely within the context of such a shift that the new social relations that set the foundation for the emergence of Israel were forged. In place of their reliance upon the broader economic framework of the Late Bronze Age and the autonomy and resiliency afforded by the predominantly pastoral mode of production, the diverse highlander groups of the early Iron Age were impelled towards cooperation. The abatement of conflict instigated by the city-states played a role in creating conditions conducive to such cooperation. But the sheer necessities of short-term survival contributed even more fundamentally to the creation of intercommunity networks. These networks could be relied upon both for the exchange of vital commodities in times of need and for the provision of labor to carry out the various special strategies necessary to increase the stability of production. Though it would be easy to overstate the role played by the daily subsistence struggle of households and villages, there can be no doubt that the perception of shared concerns and the development of institutions to express and put into effect this mutuality contributed significantly in shaping the emerging Israelite identity.

The material evidence for the emergence of the village-dominated landscape that would become the heartland of Israel suggests that the process of agricultural intensification was a gradual one that took an extremely uneven course. As noted above, many sites were occupied for only short periods and were victims of subsistence failure, demographic difficulties, and ecological deterioration of the village life-space, among other agents. But the picture was not everywhere so dismal. Some communities were able to meet the challenges of this demanding highland environment. The towns of Tell en-Naṣbeh and Shiloh, though the latter met an untimely military destruction, offer ready evidence of growing stability and subsistence security. Throughout the countryside as well, villages prospered and families put down roots. The whole highland region experienced a tremendous growth in rural stability, wealth, commerce, and, also, stratification as various communities experienced different rates of development. With the success in the early Iron Age struggle for agricultural subsistence came the conditions and tensions that led to a second and more durable transformation of the highlands: the emergence of the monarchy and the nation-states of Israel and Judah.

Bibliography

Albright, W. F.
   1971   *The Archaeology of Palestine.* Reprint edition. Gloucester, Mass.: Peter Smith.
Angel, J. L.
   1972   Ecology and Population in the Eastern Mediterranean. *World Archaeology* 4: 88–105.
Ben-Tor, A.
   1979   Tell Qiri: A Look at Village Life. *Biblical Archaeologist* 42: 105–13.
Borowski, O.
   1987   *Agriculture in Iron Age Israel.* Winona Lake, Ind.: Eisenbrauns.
Callaway, J. A.
   1983   A Visit with Ahilud: A Revealing Look at Village Life When Israel Settled the Promised Land. *Biblical Archaeology Review* 9/5: 42–53.
   1985   A New Perspective on the Hill Country Settlement of Canaan in Iron Age I. Pp. 31–49 in *Palestine in the Bronze and Iron Ages: Papers in Honor of Olga Tufnell,* edited by J. N. Tubb. Institute of Archaeology Occasional Publication, 11. London: Institute of Archaeology.

Coote, R. B., and Whitelam, K. W.
1986   The Emergence of Israel: Social Transformation and State Formation following the Decline in Late Bronze Age Trade. *Semeia Supplements* 37: 107–47. [[Reprinted in this volume, pp. 335–76]]

Finkelstein, I.
1986   Shiloh Yields Some, but Not All, of Its Secrets. *Biblical Archaeology Review* 12/1. 22–41.

Fritz, V.
1987   Conquest or Settlement? The Early Iron Age in Palestine. *Biblical Archaeologist* 50: 84–100.

Harmon, G. E.
1983   *Floor Area and Population Determination: A Method for Estimating Village Population in the Central Hill Country during the Period of the Judges (Iron I)*. Unpublished Ph.D. Dissertation, Southeastern Baptist Theological Seminary.

Hesse, B.
1986   Animal Use at Tel Mine Ekron in the Bronze Age and Iron Age. *Bulletin of the American Schools of Oriental Research* 264: 17–27.

Hesse, B., and Wapnish, P.
1986   The Contribution and Organization of Pastoral Systems. Paper presented at the Ancient Mediterranean Food Systems Symposium at the annual meeting of the American Schools of Oriental Research in Atlanta, November 1986.

Hopkins, D. C.
1985   *The Highlands of Canaan: Agricultural Life in the Early Iron Age*. Social World of Biblical Antiquity 3. Decatur, Ga.: Almond.

Horowitz, A.
1971   Climatic and Vegetational Development in Northeastern Israel during Upper Pleistocene Times. *Pollen et Spores* 13: 255–78.

Kochavi, M.
1985   The Israelite Settlement in Canaan in the Light of Archaeological Surveys. Pp. 54–60 in *Biblical Archaeology Today: Proceedings of the International Congress on Biblical Archaeology, Jerusalem, April 1984*. Jerusalem: Israel Exploration Society.

Kochavi, M., editor
1972   *Judea, Samaria, and the Golan: Archaeological Survey, 1967–1968*. Archaeological Survey of Israel 1. Jerusalem: Keter. [Hebrew]

LaBianca, Ø. S.
1987   *Sedentarization and Nomadization: A Study of Food System Transitions at Hesban and Vicinity in Transjordan. Hesban I*, edited by L. T. Geraty. Berrien Springs, Mich.: Andrews University Press.

Liphschitz, N., and Waisel, Y.
1980   Dendroarchaeological Investigations in Israel (Taanach). *Israel Exploration Journal* 30: 132–36.

Mayerson, P.
1960   *The Ancient Agricultural Regime of Nessana and the Central Negeb*. London: Colt Archaeological Institute.

Mazar, A.
  1981   Giloh: An Early Israelite Settlement Site near Jerusalem. *Israel Exploration Journal* 13: 1–36.
Meyers, C.
  1978   The Roots of Restriction: Women in Early Israel. *Biblical Archaeologist* 41: 91–103.
Muhly, J.
  1982   How Iron Technology Changed the Ancient World and Gave the Philistines a Military Edge. *Biblical Archaeology Review* 8/6: 42–54.
Rosen, A. M.
  1986   Environmental Change and Settlement at Tel Lachish, Israel. *Bulletin of the American Schools of Oriental Research* 263: 55–60.
Stager, L. E.
  1985   The Archaeology of the Family in Ancient Israel. *Bulletin of the American Schools of Oriental Research* 260: 1–35.
Stech-Wheeler, T., et al.
  1981   Iron at Taanach and Early Iron Metallurgy in the Eastern Mediterranean. *American Journal of Archaeology* 85: 245–68.
Van Ziest, W., and Bottema, S.
  1982   Vegetational History of the Eastern Mediterranean and the Near East during the Last 20,000 Years. Pp. 277–95, in *Palaeoclimates, Palaeoenvironments and Human Communities in the Eastern Mediterranean Region in Later Prehistory,* edited by J. L. Bintliff and W. Van Ziest. British Archaeological Reports International Series 133. Oxford: British Archaeological Reports.
Waldbaum, J. C.
  1978   *From Bronze to Iron: The Transition from the Bronze Age to the Iron Age in the Eastern Mediterranean.* Studies in Mediterranean Archaeology 54. Gothenburg: Åström.

Procreation, Production, and Protection: Male-Female Balance in Early Israel

CAROL L. MEYERS

[[569]] In recent years there has been a growing reawakening to the necessity for dealing with ancient Israel as a community, as a social entity the concerns of which are reflected—sometimes dimly and other times sharply—in the writings of the Hebrew Bible. Decades have passed since Max Weber first established the value of a social history of Israel with its accompanying insights into the socio-economic factors affecting various aspects of Israel's emergence and development. While political and literary factors continue to be seen as important in understanding the biblical period, patterns of social organization and of economic realities have become accentuated in the search for a comprehensive picture of Israelite life and beliefs (e.g., Mendenhall 1962; Gottwald and Frick 1976; Gottwald 1979).[1]

Reprinted with permission from *Journal of the American Academy of Religion* 51(1983) 569–93.

1. As a result of the social scientific analyses of early Israel, the conquest, nomadic, and amphictyonic models of Israelite beginnings which have dominated biblical studies in this century have now been challenged by a social revolutionary model. The fullest articulation to date of this way of comprehending early Israel is to be found in Gottwald's *Tribes of Yahweh* (1979). The social revolutionary model, it should be emphasized, does not claim to eliminate the older formulations but rather seeks to deal with their weaknesses and also to set their contributions into a fuller and more plausible social context. The social revolutionary model itself is certainly subject to modification and amplification, as witness the plethora of comments in the various reviews of *Tribes of Yahweh* as well as in the subsequent refinements that Gottwald himself has offered (1983; forthcoming [[1983b]]), in which he

Emerging from the absorbing but limiting concerns of theological
or historical or literary studies, the quest for penetration into the mystery
of Israelite beginnings and survivals has benefited from a great variety of
twentieth-century scholarship produced by the social sciences, sociology
and anthropology in particular. Descriptions of groups such as tribes,
with their class and family subdivisions and their characteristic uses of
leadership and available resources, have been enormously helpful in allowing [570] contemporary scholars to enter the social world of ancient Israel.
Furthermore, the sensitive relationship between ecological-economic variables and the nature of group behavior, organization and environmental
consciousness has received considerable attention.

The social unrest of the sixties and seventies perhaps stimulated this
renewed search for insight into biblical social structures. Similarly, one
particular aspect of such social structures—the relationship of the roles
of male and female—has emerged as a concern of biblical studies no
doubt under the stimulus of the women's movements of the same decades. The interest in sexual roles and in evaluation of those roles for the
biblical period has become heightened. Yet the growing number of publications on this subject often exhibits a subjective preoccupation with the
needs of the present world and tends therefore to obscure the scholarly
task. It is fascinating to see how both the upholders and the opposers of
the androcentric order deal with certain biblical texts, sometimes even
drawing similar conclusions but rarely overcoming *a priori* positions in order to achieve the critical understanding of the biblical materials which
should precede hermeneutical evaluations and homiletical applications.

This rather chaotic situation, which perhaps should have been anticipated, given the nature of the emotional fervor involved, is slowly being
tempered by the emergence of an approach which attempts first and
foremost to analyze what is there in the ancient documents and which is
willing, sometimes at the risk of great existential distress for those committed to the sanctity of the canon, to accept what is to be found. This
growing attention to an investigation of the relationship between the
sexes in ancient Israel, characteristically and with some justification focusing on the far more elusive female role and experience, has paralleled
to a certain extent the increasing utilization of sociological considerations in the study of Israelite origins. Ironically, however, there has yet to
be any substantive interaction between these two areas or modes of
investigation. The validity of sociological methodology in biblical stu-

---

takes into account such matters as the "frontier hypothesis" and the specific mode of agrarian production in ancient Canaan.

dies in and of itself would warrant its application to such an area as the place of women in the biblical world. The usage of social scientific approaches becomes even more compelling, given the dilemma of trying to extract a balanced view of women's status from a biblical corpus overwhelmingly patriarchal in its stance and scope. Thus the possibilities arising from an application of the fruits of sociological and anthropological labors in this field relatively barren of hard data encourage such a venture.

The necessity for an approach which can utilize materials and paradigms from outside the Bible itself derives not only from the fact of the patriarchal nature of the scriptural record but also from the existence within such a record of texts which do seem to place men and women on an equal footing. The most obvious biblical passages that deal with the concept of sexual balance are the creation narratives of Genesis. Although the [[571]] verse in the first chapter of the Bible recounting creation of humanity in God's image ("Male and female he created them") has often been understood (e.g., Vos n.d.: 15) as implying sexual equality, by which females partake of God's image no less than do males, it actually is concerned with the biological pairing of the sexes rather than with shared roles (Bird 1981). However, recent scholarship involving literary analysis of Genesis 2 (Trible 1973: 35–38 and 1977: 72–105) has called into question the traditional interpretation, in which woman is viewed as the secondary or derivative sex and hence an inferior segment of humanity, of the second creation account. Rather, woman may be equal in creation with man in the full composition—and perhaps even elevated in position according to the message of the story. Further, the archaic poem and the narrative summation of this account underscore the essential sameness of male and female. The marriage bond is exalted over the powerful Semitic filial bond (Terrien 1973: 326–28).

The solidarity and equality between man and woman in the ancient Yahwist creation account presents a situation which hardly seems to fit the patriarchal pattern readily discernible in the rest of the Bible. The very ideal nature of this material, particularly since no society, let alone ancient biblical society, has ever actualized such an ideology of sexual equality (Rosaldo and Lamphere 1974: 2–4; Rosaldo 1974: 17; Ortner 1974: 57–71), makes them inadmissible as direct evidence for reconstructing the sexual balance in biblical antiquity. This is not to suggest that such texts should be ignored; rather, their utilization must be in cognizance of their ideological character rather than their direct reflection of a social reality. The fact of their existence as ideological statements is not irrelevant. It is part of the stimulus for investigating the sexual balance which existed within the Israelite society which produced those very texts. If the nature of relative gender roles and status can be clarified, then perhaps the relationship of such realities to idealized texts can be comprehended.

What follows is an exploration of a way in which models and hypotheses formulated in the social sciences can be brought to bear upon the search for information about sex roles in the biblical period. In particular, the role of women and its relationship to the role of men in early Israel, in the formative trial period, will be the focus of this discussion. Precisely because this premonarchic period represents a transitional era in the larger cultural sense in Palestine, a transition from Bronze Age political structures with their particular economic bases to Iron Age (Israelite) ones, the availability of information extracted from the archaeological record adds an invaluable source of data which can provide the framework for utilizing sociological-anthropological models in an analysis of gender roles and relative sexual status. Furthermore, the premonarchic period produced the situation of the unquestioned leadership of Miriam and Deborah, a society [[572]] which a generation later sought counsel from the wise women of Tekoa and Abel Beth Ma^cacah (Camp 1981), and a tradition which lauded the heroic deeds of Rahab and Yael. The period of Israel's origins thus emerges as a significant era with respect to the formation of sex roles and the ideological formulation reflecting those roles.

Conceptual Models

The relevant propositions and variables that determine the relationships between men and women in pre-modern societies[2] must first be delineated:

(1) To begin with, it is axiomatic, perhaps to the point of seeming irrelevant, that the specific roles and activities that characterize male and female behavior vary enormously from group to group (Rosaldo 1974: 19). What is female behavior or responsibility in one society may be typical of male behavior and responsibility in another society. Hence attempts to arrive at some universal characteristics of sex roles or behaviors, aside from the obvious exception of the physiologically based activities of the bearing and nursing of children, have uniformly run

---

2. Analysis of these dynamics can be found in many of the articles from the social sciences, particularly anthropology, cited in the list of references. Many of these sources, as well as others not listed and also additional bibliography, can be found in an anthology, *Women, Culture and Society*, edited by M. Z. Rosaldo and L. Lamphere. Another good introduction, with glossary and references, to the topic of sex roles and relationships is E. Friedl's *Women and Men: An Anthropologist's View.*

into dead ends. With the burgeoning of twentieth-century anthropological investigations of a wide variety of cultures, a concomitant variety in the balance and nature of sex roles is continually observed, although the proper understanding of these roles is still in its infancy, partly at least because of the analytical and technical problems of dealing ethnographically with women (Ardener 1975).

(2) The next point to be considered is another seemingly self-evident fact, namely, that there is division of labor, or of contributive roles, in any society (Brown 1970: 1073). While some tasks can be performed by either male or female, normally a set of clearly defined and traditionally re-inforced responsibilities which are divided along gender lines is operant within any given community. Just as the existence of great variety in possible sex roles can be said to be axiomatic, the division of labor along sexual lines can be viewed as universal. However, except for the biologically determined roles of childbearing and suckling, there is virtually no universal assignation of any specific societal role to one particular sex. This striking plasticity of gender behavior has, in fact, been the basis of arguments for nonbiological determination of sex-role behaviors (Hamburg 1974: 374). [[573]]

(3) The relative contributions, not only the type of contributions, of male and female vary greatly from society to society (Brown 1970: 1075; Sanday 1974). The disproportionate expenditures of energy by men and women in the basic survival tasks of a society (see below) constitute the male-female division of labor within a society and determine to a great extent the relative status of the members of that society. While the concept of "female status" is in fact frustratingly vague and resistant to measurement and thus to analysis (Whyte 1978), several patterns of the relationship between status and the assignment of tasks by sex can be recognized. At one extreme are situations in which women may contribute very little beyond biological reproduction and its immediate demands. In such cases, the status of women within the society tends to be low. At the other extreme are examples of social organization in which women may support a society almost completely, bearing children and also carrying out subsistence activities. Strangely, in such societies the status of women also tends to be low, perhaps because this arrangement usually obtains in situations in which men have had to withdraw into another crucial task such as defense, thus increasing female dependence upon males and consequently reducing female status. Between these two extremes, there is a continuum of various proportions of male-female contributions to society with corresponding variation in the status of each. The greater the relative contribution of females to subsistence tasks, the higher their status tends to be.

(4) Despite the intersocietal variations in division of labor, by type and by amount, within any given society there is a universal evaluation of sex roles whereby prestige is attached to at least some male activities while female activities are at least partially devalued (Friedl 1975: 5; Ortner 1974; Rosaldo and Lamphere 1974: 3). Even when male-female roles *approach* some kind of balance or equality in their relative contributions, and where social stratification by sex is least pronounced, at least some male activities are always recognized as predominantly important. Women seem always to be considered in some way inferior to men (but cf. Leacock 1981), though the ways in which societies express this, implicitly or explicitly, may vary greatly.

(5) The balance of sexual dimorphism and thus of the relative status of males and females is not necessarily fixed within a society (Sanday 1974: 194ff.; Rosaldo and Lamphere 1974: 6). External factors can exert influence upon the relative contribution of each sex, with the result that the contributive role of the female can shift and her relative status and power within the society can thereby change.

This last point is particularly germane to our topic and needs elaboration. The survival and hopefully the prosperity of any group is dependent upon three major activities: (1) procreation (reproduction), (2) production (subsistence), and (3) protection (defense). The asymmetry of gender roles arises from the disproportionate amount of energy expended by males and [[574]] females in these three activities. The first activity is biologically based and thus lies within the realm of female responsibility, and the third activity is characteristically almost entirely dependent on male activity. The regular demands of the reproductive and the attendant nurturing tasks tend to usurp much of the female's energy, which is thus concentrated in the domestic sphere. This fact among others (Murdock and Provost 1973) tends to limit the range of the female's participation in the second activity, subsistence tasks. In addition, it normally precludes the same kind of participation in the extra-domestic public domain and consequent exercise of power available to males. On the other hand, the irregular demands of defense activities allows for surpluses of male energy. Hence the subsistence or production category normally draws more heavily on male energy. Thus, both the nature of defense and warfare activities and the economic controls growing out of primary involvement in production contribute to male status and power.

In assessing the male-female balance in a society, the critical activity to be evaluated is the second, or subsistence area. It is important to recognize in this connection that, under certain conditions, females are called upon to shoulder sometimes a larger or sometimes a smaller portion of the subsistence activities. The former shift, that is the assumption

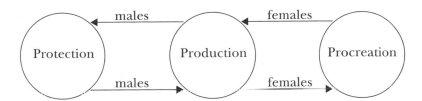

Flow Chart. Shifting concentrations of male and female energy in the three basic societal activities (adapted from Sanday 1974: 195, fig. 2).

of a larger portion of the subsistence tasks, has demonstrable implications for an increase in female status. As women move into the subsistence sphere, a condition nearing equalization of critical responsibilities ensues and female status increases. The more balanced the division of labor in this sphere, the higher regard for the female, the more authority she possesses in the domestic and even in the public domain, and the more she is respected in both the public and private domains. Therefore, the possible conditions which can bring about this kind of shift, whereby the subsistence contributions and hence the status of women both increase, must be considered. The dynamics of this situation are illustrated in the chart [see above].

Several major sets of circumstances which would draw males away from the performance of subsistence tasks, and thus increase the female role in such tasks, can be enumerated. Perhaps the most obvious condition [575] is the involvement of men in defensive or offensive activities during periods or episodes of warfare. Even if men are not called into formalized standing armies, and instead a kind of militia system is operative, the uncertainty of sufficient, dependable male labor at all seasons of the year would necessitate female expertise and participation in many aspects of agrarian activity. In other words, a certain basic amount of female involvement in subsistence activities insures that sporadic male absence would not be disastrous to the economic survival of the family.

Another circumstance contributing to an inability of males alone to cope with the demands of subsistence and an accompanying increase in female participation arises under shifts in a group's environment. Prolonged drought or extensive flooding or enemy conquest can remove normal sources or modes of food procurement and thus necessitate augmented compensatory energy in the production of adequate food supplies. Finally, the movement of a group from one ecosystem to another can require adaptive shifts, involving increased female labor especially at the initial stage of such a move. Usually such movements entail increases in the kinds of tasks associated with building new homes, clearing plots of land, etc. These initial tasks typically constitute a male monopoly (Friedl

1975: 53–57), partly perhaps because of their intensely arduous nature. That is, men alone clear the land and perform the concomitant tasks demanded by the establishment of a new settlement; and thus women are drawn into the regular and ongoing subsistence activities to compensate for male energy directed elsewhere.

In short, there is a large range of more or less exogenous factors which, singly or in combination, can be operant in effecting larger female contributions to the subsistence sphere. Demographic variations have been offered as another or separate possible source of change in the balance of labor, for in a sense they permeate the conditions already described. Let it be recognized, however, that popular declines, whether because of epidemic disease or ecological disasters or military defeats, can operate in competing ways for female energies. Recovery of food supplies or compensation for slain armies can bring women into enlarged subsistence roles while at the same time decreased population can bring about an emphasis on reproductive activities which might exert limitations on extensive female contributions to subsistence. The interrelatedness of many of the conditions enumerated above with the matter of demography makes that latter factor one of high variability in its consequences for sexual balance.

A possible quantitative factor can be introduced into the discussion at this point. Characteristically, the most balanced societies, those in which men and women share nearly equally in the tasks not dictated by their particular female or male responsibilities in reproduction or defense, are ones in which females contribute a maximum of 40% of the subsistence effort (Sanday 1974: 199). When such a ratio exists, female status reaches [[576]] its highest level. If the female contribution exceeds such proportions, there is often a negative effect (see above) and female status diminishes. In any event, this 40–60 figure seems to be a reasonable deviation from an equal or 50–50 division of labor, given the fixed datum of the reproductive role for women. The theoretical existence of such a ratio in early Israel and its implications for sexual attitudes and beliefs will become clear below.

This presentation of empirically achieved descriptions of various aspects of the male-female balance has been schematic and so lacks the enrichment of illustrative examples, drawn from ethnographic research, that are found in the literature of the social sciences. Still, it provides a set of cross-culturally determined and widely accepted models for approaching the question of male-female balance and the corollary matter of female status in ancient Israel. If a description of the exogenous features affecting the basic village setting of early Israelite society can be provided and then related to these anthropologically determined concepts, a fresh avenue of insight into the character of the sexual asymmetry in formative Israel can be opened.

The ensuing investigation will be based upon the proposition that the organization of the subsistence strategies of a society has crucial meaning for the relationship between men and women with regard to both pragmatic and ideological expression. Examination of subsistence participation therefore becomes a key for dealing with sex roles and valuations. Since the biological characteristics of men and women with respect to reproduction remain constant in all societies, and since the discharge of military responsibilities is nearly always constant with respect to sex, the specific way in which men and women relate to each other in any individual society can be seen as a function of their roles in that variable aspect of human life, the nature of their respective contributions to the range of tasks involved in the subsistence technology (Friedl 1975: 7–9).

Exogenous Factors and Effects in Iron I Israel

Fortunately, for the particular period under consideration—the early Iron Age in Palestine—environmental and demographic changes of the sort which are known to bring about shifts in the male-female balance can be documented from the results of archaeological excavations and surveys. Perhaps the archaeological contribution is far less than what it potentially could have been by this time for Syria–Palestine because of the relative insensitivity of Palestinologists until the sixties towards the recovery of the ancient ecosystem of a given site. Nonetheless, there is an emerging complex of data which can inform the task at hand. The biblical record likewise is a source of information for delineating the features affecting the division of labor and hence the male-female balance in the nascent Yahwistic community.

[577] The clearest picture of the demands on human energy for each of the three areas of human activity emerges in the realm of military participation for the males. Palestine, during the end of the preceding Late Bronze Age and during the period of Israelite formation, was beset by a persistent state of petty warfare. The Amarna letters reveal a period of continued hostilities; the archaeological record shows widespread destruction of fortifications and cities (Chaney 1983); and the art historical material shows the introduction of military themes in a way that reflects incessant warfare (Liebowitz 1980). The military factor, which was perhaps most intense at the onset of Israelite occupation of the hill country and which resumed intensity several generations later under the pressure of the Philistine encroachment, was never entirely absent from life in the tribal period. The Book of Judges makes it clear that both defensive

maneuvering and offensive operations were recurring necessities during this period (Malamat 1978; Meyers 1983b).

The Israelite military response, however, was distinguishable from the military organization of the enemies in two ways which are relevant to the internal effects of warfare on Israelite society. First, the Canaanite cities of Palestine seem to have supported a warrior class which, because of the nature of the terrain and the utilization of the chariot and cross-bow, developed into a professional group which held a privileged position in Canaanite society (Mendelsohn 1971: 42). This position may have eroded somewhat by the end of the Late Bronze Age (Reviv 1972), but continuation of a professional if not always an elite group of warriors would have been sustained. Second, this warrior class and its support groups would have represented a rather small proportion of the population; and in general the size of the armies needed for defensive purposes in the Canaanite city-states as well as for the offense in the case of chariot warfare was relatively small (Campbell 1960: 20). In contrast, the episodes in Judges would indicate that the largely unwalled Israelite villages supported no such independent control sphere as a military class. Yet the absence of professional soldiers and sophisticated equipment created a vulnerability which could be met only by commitment of substantial numbers of foot soldiers who could be called up at a moment's notice.

Therefore, defensive tactics within the tribal groups of Israel meant the sporadic withdrawal of some males from ongoing participation in subsistence activities. Even in war time some cultivation chores of planting, tending, or harvesting would have to continue. Women typically provide a greater portion of the cultivative labor under such conditions.

In addition to the possible military factor, there were present several environmental aspects of life in nascent tribal Israel which would in themselves call for a shift of the male-female ratio in subsistence responsibilities. The establishment of new settlements in the Palestinian hill country, which had previously been sparsely settled and large uncleared, placed [[578]] extraordinary demands on human labor as well as inventiveness. Marginally arable land had to be made productive by means of energy intensive labors which would have been carried out on a wide scale only during the period of initial settlement and population growth. Forest wilderness had to be cleared (cf. Josh 17:18) since the open spaces of coastal and Jezreel plains were unavailable. Cisterns had to be excavated for the storage of rain water (Davis 1982), since the more easily attained spring waters lay largely across the springline of the piedmont and hence were also unavailable to the tribal settlers (Baly 1963: 62). Further, the rocky and mountainous terrain demanded that the hills not only be cleared of natural forestation but also that terraces be constructed on the hillside to make them suitable for dry farming (Stager

1976: 13; de Geus 1975: 67). These kinds of activities, which accompany the transition of a marginal territory into an expanding frontier with a frontier or pioneer society, are efforts that are mandatory for settlements in a new ecosystem or in the expansion of previously developed systems. Further, the labor involved is precisely the kind which falls within the male domain. The degree to which these tasks need to be done affects the degree to which women assume responsibility for a portion of the cultivation chores.

Therefore, perhaps because of demands in the military sphere—protection—but surely in light of the requisite pioneer tasks, the division of labor in early Israel would have required a shift encompassing increased female participation in the subsistence—or production—sphere. The necessity for such a shift, mandated by the military and land-use situation described above, would have been further heightened by the presence of another factor affecting the nature and distribution of cultivation chores.

This other factor derives from early Israel's need to be economically independent. The new Israelite settlements situated atop the highland ridge of Cisjordan consisted of small villages seeking to establish or being forced to establish self-sufficient economic viability. The earliest Iron Age sites in the hill country are notably lacking in imported pottery or any other artifacts which would imply an exchange of goods or services with neighboring regions of the country, let alone with more distant lands (Albright 1974: 104). The material culture in general seems to have been impoverished, with little or no labor being expended upon other than the struggle to achieve the basic necessities of shelter, sustenance, and safety.

The new inhabitants of the hill country appear to have come from an agrarian background, bringing with them the agricultural techniques and tools—grinders, mortars, pestles, querns, and flint blades—usually associated with cereal food production (Callaway 1969: 59 and 1976: 29). This must be contrasted with the fact that the rocky hills, which constituted the core of the settlement during the premonarchic period, were hardly the most desirable locus for extensive grain cultivation. The growing of cereals [[579]] is an agricultural process which is more suited to the heavy or semiheavy soils and broad expanses of the eastern and southern parts of the Coastal Plain and of the Jezreel Valley, to the lava fields of northern Trans-Jordan (the Golan Heights), and to a lesser extent to the loess soils of the northern Negev around Beersheba in rainy years (Orni and Efrat 1964: 274–75). However, those regions were precisely the area of Canaanite or Philistine or Syrian-Aramean hegemony. It was thus incumbent upon the settlers of the hills to develop their territorial acquisitions as independent economic units isolated from the material, technical, or agricultural resources of the dwellers of the plains (Aharoni 1967: 220).

The hill country was best suited to viticulture, particularly in the south (as well as in the Gileadite area of Trans-Jordan) and also to horticulture, which consisted chiefly of olive orchards. Although other fruit trees were also grown, the importance of the olive as a source of oil led to the predominance of that tree in the horticultural spectrum. The basic agrarian economy as depicted in the Bible and as still found in Palestine consisted of a threefold system: the "grain and wine and oil."[3] The latter two were gradually brought within the grasp of the Iron Age settlers, once the trees were cut back and the terraces and cisterns were established. Grain remained a problem for as long as the cereal-producing lands remained outside Israelite control.

The archaeological record has preserved a glimpse of the strenuous attempts of the highlanders to produce grains in an environment lacking in suitable terrain or soils (Davis 1981). At least at several sites (Ai and Radanna) in Benjamin, excavation of agricultural terraces has shown that the early Iron Age Palestinians grew cereals (Callaway 1969: 59). This was probably true at other hilltop campsites as well (Callaway 1976: 29). Additional evidence comes from the increased presence of cylindrical, flat-bottomed pits or silos, lined with gypsum plaster (*huwwar*) and in some places still preserving traces of carbonized grain (Albright 1936–37: 54–65 and 1941–43: 1; Kelso 1968: 10–17). These characteristic installations of the early Iron Age attest to large-scale efforts at grain storage not duplicated in the preceding or succeeding periods. The implication is that grain in this era was locally produced and stored rather than brought in as an exchange commodity, as needed, from adjacent grain-producing regions where the growing of cereals was easier. This evidence for extensive local grain storage constitutes another view of the archaeological picture which depicts a dearth of imported wares in this period. The full image is one of little or no [[580]] exchange of goods, of a condition of economic isolation.

Perhaps "isolation" with its possible negative overtones expresses the situation better than does the notion of self-sufficiency. The establishment of an independent economic unit in the hill country, without the benefits of a larger regional economy drawing upon the primary "bread baskets" of the coast or the Jezreel or Bashan, was not economically de-

3. The importance of animal husbandry in this scheme is not to be minimized, as the use of animal protein not only provided important nutritional elements in normal years but also could partially compensate for decreased production of field, tree, or vine in years of drought or crop disease (see Dever and Clark 1977: 102–17; Mariottini 1981). Herds of livestock were an important resource for providing at least partial subsistence in times of need (Adams 1974: 6–7).

sirable, given the great difficulty in carrying out the tripartite cultivational scheme in the hilly regions by themselves. The inefficiency of cereal cultivation in the hill country is to be stressed (Stager 1976: 13). The upland farmers were in the position of having to produce their own cereals, an enterprise requiring large efforts for relatively small gains in the rocky hills. As if this weren't hardship enough, the military factor impinged directly upon the agricultural efforts of the mountain dwellers: the raiding Amalakites or Midianites characteristically destroyed produce in hand or threatened the planted crops (Judg 6:3–5, 11). Indeed, the fragility of the Iron I settlements under such conditions is underscored by the apparent inability of some of them to become viable and enduring communities (e.g., Giloh; see Mazar 1981).

The cumulative evidence leads to the conclusion that the combination of environmental factors affecting the needs for human expenditure of energy in the subsistence sphere was particularly intense for those involved in the settlement of the mountainous core of Palestine in the early Iron Age. Under the best conditions, Palestine is not a country where crops grow easily. Under the demands of the pioneer period, the necessity for an enlarged effort in the subsistence sphere could hardly have avoided intensifying the utilization of the labor resources of the female members of the community. This is particularly true in light of the fact that the solution to the environmental crisis of food production lay within the efforts and designs of the smallest units of society, within the steady advances in clearing and planting made by each family group within the village community.[4] In short, a situation mandating substantial and essential female entry into the subsistence sphere had clearly developed, not only for reasons of military exigencies and of pioneering tasks, but also because of the agricultural/environmental reality of the need to produce cereals as well as olives and fruits in the hill country.

The archaeologically retrieved contrast between the living conditions [[581]] evident in the hilltop villages and those discernible in the cities of the plains and valleys further substantiates this understanding of the strain on the limits of human resources. The domestic structures of the small unfortified villages throughout the Cisjordanian highlands were consistently small and crudely built in comparison with those of contemporary

---

4. Contrast the situation in the riverine areas of Egypt and especially Mesopotamia, where the family group is not the basic productive unit since there is need for a larger social unit which could cope with regional problems of land and water management (i.e., irrigation, fallow system) that affect all the inhabitants of an area. Without such a larger managerial unit, maintenance of subsistence as well as the possibility for growth are severely curtailed. See Adams 1974: 4–7 and Frankfort et al. 1946: 128. The adverse effects of such crucial centralized control in its transference to the rainfall agriculture of Syria and Palestine are noted by Mendenhall (1976: 142).

Canaanite centers, even if a relative homogeneity of ground plans be recognized (Braemer 1982; Stager 1968: 7–9). Comparable lowland sites built *de novo* in the Iron Age, the Philistine city at Tel Qasile, for example, reveal a diversified economy and a standard of living (Stager 1968: 1–7) indicative of a prosperous and balanced economy. The natural and commercial resources for developing a similar level of material stability and security were unavailable to the hill country sites in this period. Hence a compensatory surge in human labor could, for the beginning period of settlement in the hills, do no more than meet basic subsistence requirements. Only in subsequent phases of the Iron I villages can larger homes, the beginnings of defense walls, and other signs of economic advance be discerned (e.g., Callaway 1976: 30 and fig. 13). At their inception, the Iron Age settlements in the hill country would have depended upon the combined efforts of their inhabitants, male and female alike, for their very survival. Progress beyond that critical initial stage, it is hardly necessary to suggest, would have been inextricably bound up with the continuation of the joint contributions of males and females to the fulfillment of basic societal needs.

The discussion thus far has dealt with sex roles in relation to defense and subsistence, where historical developments as exogenous conditions could be identified and related to a shifting balance of gender roles. The reproductive process, however, should not be omitted from consideration. There is some evidence (Meyers 1978: 96–100) that earliest Israel was suffering from a demographic problem of serious proportions. The strenuous tasks of a pioneer society called for large families just as Palestine was emerging from a period of famine, disease, and warfare, which contributed to what was probably a significant decrease in population. Hence the procreative role of women would have been underscored with a concomitant enhancement of female status with respect to that role.

What has been established up to this point can be summarized as follows. Several particular conditions influencing the three basic areas—protection, production, and procreation—of the Israelite experience in the formative period have been identified. These factors have been set against the conceptual propositions described at the outset. In this way, some conclusions concerning the male-female balance in early Israel can be reached.

First, there existed on the one hand an extraordinary intensification of the sort of conditions which would have tended to draw men away from the basic cultivation tasks of the subsistence sphere. Military demands and pioneering needs simultaneously contributed to this situation.

[582] Second, the resolution of the heightened demands upon men in their domains of primary involvement, defense and land-clearing, could be met, according to the conceptual paradigms, by a nearly equal

involvement of men and women in the critical production sphere. Within that area, a division of labor approaching the nearly equal 40–60 balance would have been established. A kind of double duty for women, in the reproductive and in the subsistence areas, would have balanced the expanded male responsibilities in securing and preparing new agricultural lands, in growing cereal crops in unsuitable terrains, and in defending the community as a whole.

Third, the maximizing of the potential for female participation in the societal tasks would have meant, according to the theoretical models, an increase in the status accorded to females. If a nearly equal balance in the division of labor had been reached, with males dependent upon female contributions to subsistence chores, a concomitant high evaluation of females and an accordance to them of considerable power would have been established. Similarly, the need for population growth would have enhanced the female's reproductive role.

At this point, it is legitimate to ask whether any of these conclusions, reached largely through consideration of extrabiblical materials and concepts, can find corroboration in the scriptural legacy of Israel. At the very least, one can imagine that an ideology promoting a work effort such as would have been required to meet the full spectrum of the community's needs would have arisen and left some trace in the cultural document produced by that community.

Male-Female Balance: The Biblical Record

The first of the conclusions stated above has been reached with repeated reference to biblical information. The military, the pioneering, the agricultural, and the demographic factors all do indeed find support and confirmation in the Bible. This is particularly true in the biblical books ostensibly dealing with the chronological period, the Iron I Age, under consideration. In Numbers, Joshua, and Judges, the hardships and crises of early Israel are documented, albeit in stylized or hyperbolic fashion.

Yet these help chiefly in corroborating the military and technological demands that the historical and archaeological record would suggest. The effects of these demands on the male-female balance within early Israel seem to be far less apparent. Yet perhaps the data are actually there but we have not learned to recognize them or to ask the questions which will elicit recognition of them. Hopefully, the other conclusions stated above will have stimulated a sensitivity towards seeing in the biblical record an echo of these reconstructions as well.

The existence of a wide variety of texts which reinforce the notion of [[583]] biblical society as patriarchal and which appear to devalue women must not be taken as evidence against the kind of conclusions about near parity in the male-female division of labor just described. It is to be recalled that whatever the balance of labor in any society, there always exists an area or areas of exclusively male activity to which prestige adheres and/or a devaluation of at least certain aspects of types of female behavior. Since this is true even in societies that most approach a balanced arrangement, the presence of biblical texts devaluing females, limiting their options, or exhibiting some kind of double standard does not in and of itself constitute evidence that a ratio of male-female participation conducive to a relatively high female status could not have been in effect.

The existence of general woman's status is far too complex and elusive a phenomenon to permit characterization by such texts, which deal only with individual subsystems of sexual roles, such as institutions of cult or land tenure, and which cannot alone represent the full and intricate fabric of female status. The asymmetrical location of legal authority of men over women in Israelite society with respect to certain formal transactions, such as those involved in marriage, inheritance, and the like, does not automatically indicate either the existence of an equally asymmetrical preponderance of power or influence of male over female or of a lopsided positive evaluation of male over female. Men everywhere appear to have some authority over women (Rosaldo 1974: 21), yet there is an important distinction to be made between authority (an abstract or legal right to make decisions affecting other humans) and power (an ability to act effectively on persons or things, to sustain influence). Furthermore, many of the legal texts dealing with the circumscribed rights of women may not have been operant in the earliest Israelite community but rather may have arisen or become applicable in a later stage of Israelite existence. For all these reasons, the biblical texts that seem to devalue women and that limit their authority do not interfere with the possibility that a nearly equal situation existed with respect to contributive roles in the earliest period of Israel's existence.

What texts, then, can provide suitable insights? This is not meant to be a comprehensive answer to that question. Many passages may indeed come to mind and provide information that supports the schema that has been delineated. Rather, the focus here[5] will be on one biblical chapter, Leviticus 27, which may seem remote or irrelevant at first glance. However, it does contain quantitative information which, if examined in relationship to social scientific data, can be shown to be remarkably pertinent.

---

5. See also my study (Meyers 1983a) of Gen 3:16 in light of an anthropologically informed sensitivity to gender roles. The contribution of Wright (1979) in raising the issue of the Decalogue as it is related to family integrity and is thus rooted in Israelite social, economic, and political circumstances, is also to be noted.

[[584]] The division of labor within early Israel, as can be understood from the exogenous factors in relation to the conceptual models, approached near parity proportions in the subsistence sphere. Those proportions, it is to be recalled, have been quantified by social scientists (Sanday 1974: 198; Coppinger and Rosenblatt 1968: 310–13). A ratio of 3:2, with women bearing nearly 40% of the workload, is taken as a balanced division of labor, given the nature of the biological demands upon women in reproduction. Biblical evidence bearing upon that quantitative dimension can be found in Leviticus.

The last chapter of the book of Leviticus comes after the long section known as the Holiness Code (chapters 17–25) and stands as a kind of appendix or supplement to the book as a whole. Its relationship to the rest of Leviticus is not clear, since there is little connection in terms of content and since it is a relatively self-contained unit (Noth 1977²: 203–4). Its appendage status would seem to indicate a late date (de Vaux 1961: 466). Yet there are other indications that the language and provisions of that chapter are rooted in archaic and conservative cultic practices. An early date for this chapter in its overall form and content, if not all its specific details, cannot be ruled out.

For example, the troublesome verse (27:12) dealing with an animal exchange transaction has been shown to be part of an authentic and old economic procedure with analogues at Nuzi (Speiser 1960). Similarly, the critical term 'your valuation' (ʿerĕkĕkā), which occurs some twenty-one times in chapter 27 as well as elsewhere in Leviticus, poses a grammatical difficulty. This can be resolved only by viewing the final pronominal ending as a fossilized suffix that has been inactivated and absorbed into the nominal stem (ibid.). Again, an archaic origin for this Leviticus passage is indicated.

Another possible analogue to the notion of the disposition of persons has been suggested, in support of the antiquity of Leviticus 27, namely, an Egyptian-Hittite treaty in which the extradition of persons follows treaty terms (Vonk 1963: 722ff. [cited in Vos n.d.: 115 n. 138]). The thirteenth-century date of this treaty is attractive, but the validity of relating international political arrangements to what seems in Leviticus to be a regularized economic exchange function is to be seriously questioned.

A more relevant kind of information comes from the Middle Babylonian period in the work rosters drawn up by the bureaucracy to deal with servile laborers (Brinkman 1979). The categories of age and sex which constitute the classificatory principles of these texts are remarkably similar to the Leviticus categories. While the absolute figures would not be expected to correspond, since the Babylonian texts deal with a servile and/or slave population, the classification system itself can be compared with that of Leviticus. Thus these Babylonian socio-economic documents of the fourteenth and thirteenth centuries are a source of demographic statistics [[585]] that are similar in arrangement to the Leviticus listings.

In relation to extrabiblical materials, therefore, Leviticus 27 would seem to contain archaic materials. On internal grounds as well, the passage appears to predate the late (exilic?) compilation of Leviticus. Leviticus 27 concerns the commutation of gifts—people, property, animals, and so on—vowed to Yahweh. The concept of the vowing or consecration of persons to the sanctuary or to the deity is very old, as the dedication of Samuel by Hannah (1 Sam 1:11) and the Nazirite status of Samson (cf. Num 6:2, which uses language similar to Lev 27:1) indicate. These narratives dealing with the premonarchic period indicate the existence at that time of the practice of vows and consequently provide indirect evidence for a system of regulation that would have accompanied it. For in the event that a vow should prove unworkable or become an undue hardship, a mechanism would have to exist whereby the thing or person vowed could be released from consecrated status.

Leviticus 27 sets forth a series of valuations to allow for such redemption. The valuations are expressed in monetary units ("shekels of silver, according to the shekel of the sanctuary"), which would seem to indicate the existence of a developed economy. Yet *šeqel* can mean 'weight' and not money *per se* (de Vaux 1961: 203–7). Furthermore, the Levitical text even as it stands does not represent a complete or consistent conversion of votive gifts into monetary equivalents (Noth 1977[2]: 204). Thus the principle of dedicating persons and the values placed thereon represent an ancient tradition, even if the absolute evaluations or the priestly computational framework is not original to the framework.

The scale of money payments, therefore, while meaningless in an absolute sense, appears to preserve an authentic ancient assessment of human worth according to age and sex in a relative sense. Further, the notion of human worth is clearly in terms of value in the "labor pool" since the overall orientation of this chapter is one of economic and legal transactions (Graham 1979). The table below conveys the information concerning human valuation, by age and sex, contained in the appendix to Leviticus:

Age	Male/Shekels	Female/Shekels	Combined Value	Female Percentage
0–5	5	3	8	38%
5–20	20	10	30	33%
20–60	50	30	80	38%
60–	15	10	25	40%

Since the critical variables in this scale are age and sex, the assessments can be understood as a reflection of the actual and/or potential contribution of males and females of various ages to societal tasks. Obviously, children below the age of five can contribute very little in terms of actual work to the activities of a community and the absolute values set upon them are low, whether for males or females. Moreover, as a ⟦586⟧ potential source of productivity, the high mortality rate of youngsters up to the age of five—35% being a suggested figure (Meyers 1978: 95)—would keep the valuation low. Thereafter, the absolute level for both sexes rises, with highest levels being reached for the adult population over the age of twenty.

With respect to relative valuations, in three of the four age groups represented in this table, the female percentage of the combined value of a male and a female at a given age hovers at or near the 40% level. The only departure from this pattern is the 5–20 year old bracket, in which twice as much is required to redeem males as opposed to females. In absolute values, the category as a whole is still lower than the next age group. One would expect this in light of the continued existence of high mortality in preadult groups whereby roughly half of a population would not live beyond 20 (Genovés 1969: 442, Table B). Thus the significant shift is the relative one, seen in the lower percentage of the female valuation. This fact doubtlessly derives from the inclusion of the major segment of a woman's childbearing years within the 5–20 year span.

The Bible gives us no indication as to the age of marriage for women, which would not be appreciably different from the age at which childbearing begins. However, based on the tenuous calculations of the marriage age of certain Judean kings (e.g., Josiah: age 14; Amon: 14) and the rabbinic stipulation of twelve as the minimum age of marriage for girls and thirteen for boys, an early age for marriage can be presumed (de Vaux 1961: 29). Similarly, the relatively short life spans of the ancient world, particularly in plague epochs, would lead to the conclusion that marriage took place soon after puberty, with betrothal preceding marriage perhaps by many years. In any case, a girl marrying near the age of fifteen would be bearing at least several if not most of her children before the age of twenty. Her potential during that period for contribution to subsistence would thus decrease because of her greater procreative responsibilities and the concomitant increase in her own mortality risks.

Male-Female Balance and Female Status

The Leviticus passage has thus enriched and corroborated the kinds of conclusions drawn above, using social scientific models in conjunction with an analysis of the socio-economic realities of early Israel. The balance of labor operant in the formative stages would have represented a female contribution of nearly 40%, which is considered a balanced situation given the childbearing component of a woman's contributive potential. This optimal balance of labor between men and women is related, as has already been indicated, to the establishment of a relatively high status for women. While this hardly indicates equality for women in matters of property control or regularized leadership roles, it does represent a condition of [587] near mutual dependence which affords women considerable power in domestic matters and which also gives men the experience of accepting female power when it is exercised in other capacities, including in extra-domestic situations.

The oft-mentioned biblical heroines may in fact reflect such a social context. The unquestioned deference to the leadership of Miriam and Deborah and to the wise women of Tekoa and Abel Beth Ma^cacah, to cite again the notable few, are not really exceptions that prove the patriarchal rule but are rather examples of how, even within a male-dominated society, a balanced division of labor means a relatively high status for women. Female status is usually measured by power in domestic and/or extra-domestic contexts and also by deferential and respectful treatment in either or both of those contexts. Therefore, these few examples preserved in the Bible of women's actions in public contexts indeed reflect the kind of positive status that ensues when women are contributing significantly to productive labor.

A further insight into biblical gender status may derive from another result of anthropological research on sex roles. In many of the social contexts that ethnographers have investigated as they have sought to comprehend labor balance and relative gender status, a relationship can be shown to exist between female roles and female goddesses. That is, there is a high correlation between the number of deities who are female in a given society and the female contributions to the essential tasks of that society (Sanday 1974: 204–6, table I and fig. 3). The theoretical explanation of this correlation suggests that the belief system is a reflection and legitimization of vital female contributions to subsistence or production activities. The existence of female deities with general or specific cosmic powers can be seen as a means for males to accept female status and power. The variables that determine the number of goddesses in a pantheon, the kinds of powers attributed to them, and their benevolence or malevolence in their mythologies are complex and cannot be easily evaluated. Yet a belief system involving female deities evidently can reflect, in its shifting patterns of male and female deities, the active and crucial participation of females in the important tasks of a society. The goddesses thus affirm in the powerful mechanisms of religious sanction the legitimacy and beneficence of the female role within a balanced society (Christ 1979: 274–78).

The direct applicability of this correlation between goddesses and female status to Israelite society is obviously ruled out insofar as Israelite religion was a monotheistic system lacking a pattern of sexuality other than a metaphorical one associated with Yahweh. However, the functional equivalent of an increase in goddesses where female roles and thus status are enlarged may nonetheless be identified in biblical materials, such as the ideological statement of Genesis 2, which seems to defy the overwhelming [[588]] patriarchality of Israelite society. If in early Israel there existed a male-female balance of labor approaching parity, a balance which can in some societies give rise to an amplification of female deities, then perhaps the second creation account represents an ideological and functional equivalent.[6] A situation in which females have entered the subsistence sphere in significant ways and have gained status thereby is not expressed in equal legal rights, which could hardly be expected amidst the realities of the ancient world and the emerging social system of the Israelites, but rather in a theoretical (or Edenic) equality. With no provisions for goddesses to provide such legitimization in the monotheistic or at least monolatrous Yahwistic system, a beginnings account in which women and men were created equal supplied a phenomenologically equivalent religious response to the social reality of a near equal participation of men and women in basic societal tasks.

Seen in this way, the symbolic value of an ideology of equality becomes apparent in both sociological and psychological terms (Geertz 1972: 167–72). Socially, it would create an ethos or "motivation" for carrying out the social arrangements and societal tasks most beneficial to the group. The impetus for and acceptance of the woman's expanded and necessary role would be culturally reinforced. On the psychological level, the ideological value of an equality formulation would fulfill the need for a mood which could tolerate a psychically difficult life situation. The threat to patriarchal male authority when female power rises would be diffused by a symbolic or religious statement that God has ordained a mutual effort in the critical tasks of society and that a two-way dependency has divine sanction. For a community which had eschewed divine sexuality in the forms of binary pairs of gods and goddesses, biblical materials portraying an idealized sexual equality apart from the actual formation of patterns of inequality within the society would have sustained a high

6. An analogous situation perhaps exists for the postexilic period, during which the repatriation of Judah constituted a replication albeit in a reduced way of the exigencies of the premonarchic pioneer period. A doctoral work by C. Camp at Duke University has investigated the relationship between the role of women in wisdom literature in general and the hypostatization of Wisdom as a woman in Proverbs in particular to the socio-economic conditions of the Persian period.

status for women commensurate with their contributive roles within the patriarchal framework. Indeed, the actual societal patterns should not be expected to be mirrored in either ideological statements on the one hand or legal proscriptions on the other hand. Social reality hardly provides a one-to-one correlation with either its conceptual framework or its regulatory mechanisms.

The overall approach followed here suggests that a full understanding of the sex roles and attitudes of biblical Israel, even for the formative period alone, cannot be achieved without a diachronic perspective. What we have begun here remains incomplete without following it through into the ⟦589⟧ Iron II period. The legal and historical texts which so strongly suggest male dominance emerge from the monarchic period. Such sources must be carefully investigated with an eye towards the continuities or shifts in the nature of gender activities and roles. The pioneer villages became transformed into walled settlements, the population increased, conscription was established, and centralized distributive mechanisms emerged with the monarchy. All those factors of internal development, along with a new array of exogenous factors, would be expected to have influenced the sensitive configuration of sex roles. Yet these roles would also have been affected by the traditional, Yahweh-sanctioned values that accompanied the balanced pattern established in the period of Israel's origin.

Bibliography

Adams, R. M.
  1974   The Mesopotamian Social Landscape. Pp. 1–11 in *Reconstructing Complex Societies: Archaeological Colloquium*, ed. C. B. Moore. Cambridge: American Schools of Oriental Research.
Aharoni, Y.
  1967   *The Land of the Bible*, trans. A. F. Rainey. Philadelphia: Westminster.
Albright, W. F.
  1936–37 *The Excavation of Tell Beit Mirsim*, volume 2: *The Bronze Age*. Annual of the American Schools of Oriental Research 17. New Haven: Yale University Press.
  1941–43 *The Excavation of Tell Beit Mirsim*, volume 3: *The Iron Age*. Annual of the American Schools of Oriental Research 21–22. New Haven: Yale University Press.
  1974   *The Archaeology of Palestine and the Bible*. 3d ed. Cambridge: American Schools of Oriental Research.
Ardener, E.
  1975   Belief and the Problem of Woman. Pp. 1–28 in *Perceiving Women*, ed. S. Ardener. London: Dent.

Baly, D.
1963   *Geographical Companion to the Bible.* London: Lutterworth.
Bird, P. A.
1981   "Male and Female He Created Them": Gen 1:27b in the Context of the Priestly Account of Creation. *Harvard Theological Review* 74: 129–59. ⟦Reprinted 1994. Pp. 329–61 in *"I Studied Inscriptions from before the Flood": Ancient Near Eastern, Literary, and Linguistic Approaches to Genesis 1–11.* SBTS 4. Winona Lake, Ind.: Eisenbrauns.⟧
Braemer, F.
1982   *L'architecture domestique du Levant à l'âge du Fer.* Éditions Recherche sur les civilizations 8. Paris: Association pour la Diffusion de la Pensée Française.
Brinkman, J.
1979   Forced Laborers in the Middle Babylonian Period. Paper given at the American Oriental Society Meeting, St. Louis.
Brown, J.
1970   A Note on the Division of Labor. *American Anthropologist* 72: 1073–78.
Callaway, J.
1969   The Significance of the Iron Age Village at "Ai (et-Tell)." Pp. 56–61 in *Proceedings of the Fifth World Congress of Jewish Studies* 1. Jerusalem: World Union of Jewish Studies.
1976   Excavating Ai (et-Tell). *Biblical Archaeologist* 39: 18–30.
Camp, C. V.
1981   The Wise Women of 2 Samuel: A Role Model for Women in Early Israel. *Catholic Biblical Quarterly* 43: 14–29.
Campbell, E. F., Jr.
1960   The Amarna Letters and the Amarna Period. *Biblical Archaeologist* 23: 2–22.
Chaney, M.
1983   Ancient Palestinian Peasant Movements and the Formation of Premonarchic Israel. *Biblical Archaeologist* Supplement. Philadelphia: American Schools of Oriental Research. ⟦Ancient Palestinian Peasant Movements and the Formation of Premonarchic Israel. Pp. 39–90 in *Palestine in Transition: The Emergence of Ancient Israel,* ed. David Noel Freedman and David F. Graf. Social World of Biblical Antiquity Series 2. Sheffield: Almond.⟧
Christ, C.
1979   Why Women Need the Goddess: Phenomenological, Psychological, and Political Reflections. Pp. 273–87 in *Womanspirit Rising,* ed. C. P. Christ and J. Plaskow. San Francisco: Harper & Row.
Coppinger, R. M., and Rosenblatt, P. C.
1968   Romantic Love and Subsistence Dependence of Spouses. *Southwestern Journal of Anthropology* 24: 310–19.
Davis, J. B.
1981   Hill Country Dry Farming: A Revolutionary Development of Iron Age I. Paper given at the Society of Biblical Literature Southeastern Region meeting.

1982 Availability and Use of Water Resources in Hill Country Villages in Iron Age I. Paper given at the Society of Biblical Literature Southeastern Region meeting.

Dever, W. G., and Clark, W. M.
1977 The Patriarchal Traditions. Pp. 70–148 in *Israelite and Judean History*, ed. J. H. Hayes and J. M. Miller. Philadelphia: Westminster.

Frankfort, H., et al.
1946 *Intellectual Adventure of Ancient Man.* Chicago: University of Chicago Press.

Friedl, E.
1975 *Women and Men: An Anthropologist's View.* New York: Rinehart and Winston.

Geertz, C.
1972 Religion as a Cultural System. Pp. 157–78 in *Reader in Comparative Religion*, ed. W. A. Lessa and E. Z. Vogt. 3d ed. New York: Harper & Row.

Genovés, S.
1969 Estimation of Age and Mortality. Pp. 400–452 in *Science and Archaeology*, ed. S. Brothwell and E. Higgs. London: Thames and Hudson.

Geus, C. J. de
1975 The Importance of Archaeological Researches into the Palestinian Agricultural Terraces. *Palestine Exploration Quarterly* 107: 65–74.

Gottwald, N. K.
1979 *Tribes of Yahweh.* Maryknoll, N.Y.: Orbis.
1983a Early Israel and the Canaanite Socioeconomic System. *Biblical Archaeologist* Supplement. Philadelphia: American Schools of Oriental Research.
forth- Two Models for the Origins of Ancient Israel: Social Revolution or coming Frontier Development? ⟦Pp. 5–24 in *The Quest for the Kingdom of God:* ⟦1983b⟧ *Studies in Honor of George Mendenhall*, ed. H. B. Huffmon, F. H. Spina, and A. R. W. Green.⟧ Winona Lake, Ind.: Eisenbrauns.

Gottwald, N. K., and Frick, F. S.
1976 The Social World of Ancient Israel. Pp. 110–19 in *The Bible and Liberation*, ed. N. K. Gottwald and A. C. Wise. Berkeley: Community for Religious Research and Education.

Graham, P.
1979 The Perspectives of Leviticus 25 and 27 on Real Property: A Comparative Study. Paper given at the Society of Biblical Literature Southeastern Region meeting.

Hamburg, B. A.
1974 The Psychobiology of Sex Differences: An Evolutionary Perspective. Pp. 373–90 in *Sex Differences in Behavior*, ed. R. C. Friedman et al. New York: Wiley.

Kelso, J. L.
1968 *The Excavation of Bethel (1934–60).* Annual of the American Schools of Oriental Research 39. Cambridge: American Schools of Oriental Research.

Leacock, E. B.
   1981   *Myths of Male Dominance.* New York: Monthly Review Press.
Liebowitz, H.
   1980   Military and Feast Scenes on Late Bronze Palestinian Ivories. *Israel Exploration Journal* 30: 162–69.
Malamat, A.
   1978   *Early Israelite Warfare and the Conquest of Canaan.* Oxford: Centre for Postgraduate Hebrew Studies.
Mariottini, C. F.
   1981   The Village Pastoral-Agrarian Economy in the Period of the Judges. Paper given at the Society of Biblical Literature Southeastern Region meeting.
Mazar, A.
   1981   Giloh: An Early Israelite Settlement Site near Jerusalem. *Israel Exploration Journal* 31: 1–36.
Mendenhall, G. E.
   1962   The Hebrew Conquest of Palestine. *Biblical Archaeologist* 25: 66–87.
   1976   Social Organization in Early Israel. Pp. 132–51 in *Magnalia Dei,* ed. F. M. Cross, W. E. Lemke, and P. D. Miller Jr. New York: Doubleday.
Mendelsohn, I.
   1971   Society and Economic Conditions. Pp. 39–51 in *World History of the Jewish People,* volume 3: *Judges,* ed. B. Mazar. Tel Aviv: Massada.
Meyers, C.
   1978   Roots of Restriction: Women in Early Israel. *Biblical Archaeologist* 41: 91–103.
   1983a   Gender Roles and Genesis 3:16 Revisited. Pp. 337–54 in *The Word of the Lord Shall Go Forth,* ed. C. Meyers and M. O'Connor. Philadelphia: American Schools of Oriental Research / Winona Lake, Ind.: Eisenbrauns.
   1983b   Of Seasons and Soldiers: A Topological Appraisal of the Pre-Monarchic Tribes of Galilee." *Bulletin of the American Schools of Oriental Research,* forthcoming [[252: 47–59]].
Murdock, G. P., and Provost, C.
   1973   Factors in the Division of Labor by Sex: A Cross-Cultural Analysis. *Ethnology* 12: 203–25.
Noth, M.
   1977[2]   *Leviticus,* trans. J. E. Anderson. Philadelphia: Westminster.
Orni, E., and Efrat, E.
   1964   *Geography of Israel.* Jerusalem: Israel Program for Scientific Translations.
Ortner, S. B.
   1974   Is Male to Female as Nature Is to Culture? Pp. 67–80 in *Women, Culture, and Society,* ed. Rosaldo and Lamphere. Stanford: Stanford University Press.
Reviv, H.
   1972   Some Comments on the Maryannu. *Israel Exploration Journal* 22: 218–28.

Rosaldo, M. Z.
  1974   Women, Culture, and Society: A Theoretical Overview. Pp. 17–42 in
          Women, Culture, and Society, ed. Rosaldo and Lamphere.
Rosaldo, M. Z., and Lamphere, L.
  1974   Introduction. Pp. 1–16 in *Women, Culture, and Society*, ed. Rosaldo
          and Lamphere. Stanford: Stanford University Press.
Rosaldo, M. Z., and Lamphere, L., eds.
  1974   *Women, Culture, and Society*. Stanford: Stanford University Press.
Sanday, P. R.
  1974   Female Status in the Public Domain. Pp. 189–206 in *Women, Culture,
          and Society*, ed. Rosaldo and Lamphere.
Speiser, E.
  1960   Leviticus and the Critics. Pp. 29–46 in *Yehezkel Kaufmann Jubilee Volume*,
          ed. M. Haran. Jerusalem: Magnes.
Stager, L.
  1968   The Archaeology of Palestine in the Eleventh Century. Seminar paper,
          Harvard University (unpublished).
  1976   Agriculture. Pp. 11–13 in *The Interpreter's Dictionary of the Bible Supple-
          mentary Volume*, ed. K. Crim. Nashville: Abingdon.
Terrien, Samuel
  1973   Toward a Biblical Theology of Womanhood. *Religion in Life* 42: 322–33.
Trible, P.
  1973   Depatriarchalizing in Biblical Interpretation. *Journal of the American
          Academy of Religion* 41: 30–48.
  1978   *God and the Rhetoric of Sexuality*. Philadelphia: Fortress.
Vaux, R. de
  1961   *Ancient Israel*, trans. J. McHugh. New York: McGraw Hill.
Vonk, C.
  1963   *De Voorzeide Leer*. Barendrecht.
Vos, C. J.
  n.d.   *Women in Old Testament Worship*. Delft: Judels and Brinkerman.
Whyte, M.
  1978   *The Status of Women in Preindustrial Societies*. Princeton: Princeton
          University Press.
Wright, C. J. H.
  1979   The Israelite Household and the Decalogue: The Social Background
          and Significance of Some Commandments. *Tyndale Bulletin* 30: 101–24.

The Place of Women in the Israelite Cultus

PHYLLIS BIRD

[[397]] Despite the timeliness of the question posed in the title of this essay, it is not a new one in the history of Old Testament scholarship.[1] It occasioned lively debate at the turn of the century, in terms remarkably similar to arguments heard today. A key figure in that early debate was J. Wellhausen, whose analysis of Israelite religion emphasized its masculine, martial, and aristocratic nature, positing an original coincidence of military, politicolegal, and religious assemblies, in which males alone had full rights and duties of membership.[2] Others argued that women were disqualified from cultic service by reference to an original ancestral cult of the dead which could be maintained only by a male heir.[3] A further argument associated women's disability or disinterest in the Yahweh cult with a special attraction to foreign cults or pre-Yahwistic beliefs and practices involving local numina.[4]

Underlying these arguments and assumptions concerning the marginal or subordinate status of women in the Israelite cultus was a common understanding of early Israel as a kinship-structured society of nomadic

Reprinted with permission from *Ancient Israelite Religion: Essays in Honor of Frank Moore Cross* (ed. P. D. Miller, P. D. Hanson, and S. D. McBride; Philadelphia: Fortress, 1987) 397–419.

1. This chapter is a preliminary and highly abbreviated form of the introduction to a book-length work (in preparation) on women in the Israelite religion.

2. J. Wellhausen, *Israelitische und jüdische Geschichte* (3d ed.; Berlin: Georg Reimer, 1897) 89–90.

3. I. Benzinger, *Hebräische Archäologie* (Freiburg im Breisgau and Leipzig: J. C. B. Mohr, 1894) 140, and W. Nowack, *Lehrbuch der hebräischen Archäologie* (Frieburg im Breisgau and Leipzig: J. C. B. Mohr, 1894) 154, 348.

4. See, e. g., B. Stade, *Biblische Theologie des Alten Testaments* (Tübingen: J. C. B. Mohr, 1905) 1.40. Cf. E. König, *Geschichte der alttestamentlichen Religion* (Gütersloh: Bertelsmann, 1912) 216 n. 1.

origin, whose basic social and religious unit was the patrilineal and patriarchal family.[5] Though it was the agricultural village with its assembly of free landowners that Wellhausen had in mind when he correlated political and religious status, the principle he articulated had broader applicability: "Wer politisch nicht vollberechtigt war, war es auch religiös nicht."[6] Women, who were disenfranchised in the political realm, were disenfranchised in the religious realm as well.

Stated in such terms of disability—or disinterest and disaffection—the widely held view of women's inferior status in the Israelite cultus, exhibited in the critical historiography of the period, elicited vigorous rebuttal in a series of studies aimed at clarifying, and defending, women's position in ancient Israelite religion and society.[7] While the arguments and conclusions of these studies differed, the general outcome was to demonstrate [[398]] that women's participation in the religious life of ancient Israel was in fact broader and more significant than commonly depicted.[8]

Today many of the same arguments and much of the same evidence put forward in the earlier discussion are being employed once more in a renewed debate over the androcentric and patriarchal character of Israelite religion.[9] This time, however, the discussion appearing in scholarly publications, or in works by biblical scholars, is fueled by a debate arising outside the academy and borne by a literature that is primarily lay-oriented and largely lay-authored, a literature marked by the anger and urgency of profound existential and institutional conflict.[10] Modern

5. See, e.g., Benzinger, *Archäoligie* (1907), 102; Nowack, *Lehrbuch*, 153–54.

6. Wellhausen, *Geschichte*, 94.

7. The earliest (1898) and most positive in its assessment was that of I. Peritz, "Women in the Ancient Hebrew Cult," *JBL* 17 (1898) 111–48. Other major studies include the following: M. Lohr, *Die Stellung des Weibes zur Jahwe-Religion und Kult* (Leipzig: Hinrichs, 1908); G. Beer, *Die soziale und religiöse Stellung der Frau im israelitischen Altertum* (Tübingen: J. C. B. Mohr [Paul Siebeck], 1919); and E. M. McDonald, *The Position of Women as Reflected in Semitic Codes of Law* (Toronto: University of Toronto Press, 1931).

8. For an excellent review and assessment of the history of scholarship on women in Israelite religion, see chap. 1 of U. Winter's *Frau und Göttin. Exegetische und ikonographische Studien zum weiblichen Gottesbild im alten Israel und in dessen Umwelt* (Freiburg and Göttingen: Universitäts / Vandenhoeck & Ruprecht, 1983). Winter's work, which became available to me only after the completion of my initial draft, exhibits substantial parallels to my own approach and significant accord with my analysis.

9. See, e.g., C. J. Vox, *Woman in Old Testament Worship* (Delft: Judels & Brinkman, 1968); J. Otwell, *And Sarah Laughed: The Status of Women in the Old Testament* (Philadelphia: Westminster Press, 1977); and Winter, *Frau und Göttin*.

10. By "lay" I mean nonbiblical specialist. This literature, which is a product of, or response to, the modern women's movement, is largely, though by no means exclusively, written by women and is characterized by a high degree of existential involvement and political intention (protest and advocacy). In the three decades since the appearance of S. de Beauvoir's *The Second Sex* (New York: Alfred A. Knopf, 1953; French orig., 1949), it has swelled to

feminist critique of the Bible as male-centered and male-dominated has elicited widely differing historiographical and hermeneutical responses, ranging from denial of the fact or intent of female subordination to rejection of the authority of the Scriptures as fundamentally and irredeemably sexist.

In the current debate, with its heavy charge of personal and theological interest, the biblical historian has a limited but essential contribution to make by isolating and clarifying the historical question. The task of Old Testament historiography must be to determine as accurately as possible the actual roles and activities of women in Israelite religion throughout the Old Testament period and the meaning of those roles and activities in their ancient socioreligious contexts. The question for the historian today is the same as that addressed to earlier scholars, but it must be answered in a new way—because of new data, new methods of analysis, and a new understanding of history. The following is an attempt to set forth a rationale and a plan for that new answer.

The question about the place of women in the Israelite cultus exposes a defect in traditional historiography—beginning already in Israelite times. It is a question about a forgotten or neglected element in traditional conceptions and presentations of Israelite religion, which typically focus on the activities and offices of males. Where women appear at all in the standard works, it is in incidental references, as exceptional figures, or in limited discussions of practices or customs relating especially to women. This skewed presentation may be explained by the limits of the available sources and may even be understood as an accurate representation of the Israelite cultus as a male-constituted or male-dominated institution. But it can no longer be viewed as an adequate portrait of Israelite religion. The religion of Israel was the religion of men and women, whose distinctive roles and experience require critical attention, as well as their common activities and obligations. To comprehend Israelite religion as the religion of a people, rather than the religion of males, women's roles, activities, and experience must be fully represented and fully integrated ⟦399⟧ into the discussion. What is needed is a new reconstruction of the history of Israelite religion, not a new chapter on women. Until that is done, the place of women in the

---

a flood, establishing itself as a major new category in both religious and secular publishing—and affecting the entire field of publishing in its attention to gendered language and images. While this literature treats a broad range of social, psychological, and historical issues, a recurring theme, in secular as well as religious writings, is the legacy of biblical tradition in Western understanding of the nature and status of women. Recent scholarly attention to women in the biblical world has arisen, in part at least, as an effort to correct and inform the "popular" discussion (cf. Winter, *Frau und Göttin*, 17).

Israelite cultus will remain incomprehensible and inconsequential in its isolation, and our understanding of Israelite religion will remain partial, distorted, and finally unintelligible.

A first step toward this integrated reconstruction must be an attempt to recover the hidden history of women and to view the religion through their eyes, so that women's viewpoint as well as their presence is represented in the final account.[11] The obstacles to that effort are immense, but, I shall argue, not insurmountable. They do, however, require that critical attention be given to methodology before any reconstruction can proceed. That being the case, this chapter can offer no more than a highly provisional sketch of the assigned subject, prefaced by a summary of the methodological study that forms the essential introduction.

Preliminary Methodological Considerations

1. Two fundamental shifts in focus or perspective are necessary to the reconstruction I have proposed: (a) The cultus must be understood in relation to the total religious life in all of its various forms and expressions, "private" as well as public; heterodox, sectarian, and "foreign" as well as officially sanctioned;[12] and (b) religious institutions and activities must be viewed in relation to other social institutions, such as the family, and in the context of the total social, economic, and political life. While both of these shifts are essential to an understanding of Israelite religion as a total complex, they have particular consequence for the understanding of women's place and roles.

2. The information needed to give a fully adequate account of the place of women in Israelite religion, including the cultus, is in large measure unavailable—and unrecoverable—from either biblical or extrabiblical sources. We have at best isolated fragments of evidence, often

11. Cf. E. Schüssler Fiorenza's groundbreaking work for the New Testament, *In Memory of Her: A Feminist Theological Reconstruction of Christian Origins* (New York: Crossroad Publishing Co., 1983).

12. By cultus I understand the organized, usually public, aspects of religious life centered in a temple, shrine, or other sacred site, maintained by a priesthood and/or other specialized offices and roles, and finding expression in sacrifices, offerings, teaching and oracular pronouncement, feasts, fasts, and other ceremonies and ritual actions. Since our knowledge of Israelite religion is limited almost entirely to the "national" cultus and its several schools of theology or streams of tradition, it is easy to slip from analysis of the cultus to generalizations about the religion. This tendency has been qualified to some extent by the recognition that we have no direct evidence for North Israelite theology and practice and by attempts to cover and reconstruct it from elements surviving within Judean compositions. It is also being qualified by new attention to local or folk traditions of Israelite Yahwism evidenced in extrabiblical texts. The question about women in the cultus, I shall argue, raises the question about the role of the cultus in the total religious life of Israel in an even broader and more radical way.

without clues to context. As a consequence, any reconstruction must be tentative and qualified. The same, however, is true, though in less extreme degree, of our knowledge of men's roles, and demands similar caution and qualification. Our fullest and best information is partial and skewed.

3. A comprehensive and coherent account of Israelite religion and of women's place in it requires the use of an interpretive model, not only to comprehend the available evidence but also to locate, identify, and interpret missing information—which is often the most important.[13] The blanks in the construct are as essential to the final portrait as the areas described by known data. They must be held open (as the boxes in an organizational chart)—or imaginatively filled—if the structure is not to [[400]] collapse or the picture is not to be rendered inaccurate or unintelligible. The primary means of filling the blanks is imaginative reconstruction informed by analogy.

4. The closest analogies may be found in other ancient Near Eastern societies. They are limited, however, by dependence on written documents, most of which come from the spheres of men's activities and reflect male perspectives.

5. Modern ethnographic studies of individual societies and institutions and cross-cultural studies of women's roles in contemporary non-Western societies can aid the Old Testament historian in formulating questions and constructing models.[14] Such studies are especially valuable for their attempts to view societies as total systems as well as for their attention to features that native historians and lay members of the society may overlook or deem unimportant. Because they do not depend

---

13. The need for consciously articulated interpretive models has been convincingly argued in recent decades and needs no further defense. It does need reiteration, however, as paucity of evidence intensifies the need. For example, if we assume that the Israelite congregation was composed of all adults, we will picture women as a silent constituent even where no reference is made to their presence. But if we construe the congregation as a body of males, we must give a different account of the missing women—and of the role of the cultus in the society.

14. This is an exceedingly rich and suggestive literature combining descriptive and theoretical interests. It is also expanding so rapidly that it is impossible to list even the most important works. The following is a sample of works I have found useful: M. K. Whyte, *The Status of Women in Preindustrial Societies* (Princeton: Princeton University Press, 1978); M. K. Martin and B. Voorhies, *Female of the Species* (New York: Columbia University Press, 1975); M. Rosaldo and L. Lamphere, eds., *Woman, Culture, and Society* (Stanford: Stanford University Press, 1974); N. A. Falk and R. M. Gross, eds., *Unspoken Worlds: Women's Religious Lives in Non-Western Cultures* (San Francisco: Harper & Row, 1980); E. W. Fernea, *Guests of the Sheik: An Ethnography of an Iraqi Village* (Garden City, N. Y.: Doubleday & Co., 1969); E. Bourguignon et al., *A World of Women: Anthropological Studies of Women in the Societies of the World* (New York: Praeger Publishers, 1980); and S. W. Tiffany, ed., *Women and Society: An Anthropological Reader* (Montreal: Eden Press Women's Publications, 1979).

on written records but are based on observation and interview of participants, they give us access to women's roles and experience that is otherwise unavailable.

6. Androcentric bias is a pervasive feature of the ancient sources,
their subjects, and their interpreters. It has also characterized most anthropological research and writing until recently.[15]

Summary of Findings of Cross-Cultural Studies

The most important finding of cross-cultural studies for a reconstruction of women's religious roles in ancient Israel is the universal phenomenon of sexual division of labor, which is particularly pronounced
in preindustrial agricultural societies.[16] Basic to this division of labor is
an understanding of women's primary work as reproductive work, including care of children and associated household tasks, with a consequent identification of the domestic sphere as the female sphere, to
which women's activities may be restricted in varying degrees.[17] This
fundamental sexual division of labor has far-reaching consequences for
the status and roles of women in the society as a whole as well as their
patterns of activity and participation in the major social institutions. In
all of the primary institutions of the public sphere, which is the male
sphere, women have limited or marginal roles, if any. Thus leadership

15. For efforts to identify and counter this bias and an introduction to the study of gender as a major new field of anthropological theory, see especially J. Shapiro, "Anthropology
and the Study of Gender," *A Feminist Perspective in the Academy: The Difference It Makes* (ed.
E. Langland and W. Gove; Chicago: University of Chicago Press, 1981) 110–29; N. Quinn,
"Anthropological Studies on Women's Status," *Annual Review of Anthropology* 6 (1977) 182–
222; and S. Ortner and H. Whitehead, eds., *Sexual Meanings* (Cambridge: Cambridge University Press, 1981).

16. M. Rosaldo, "Woman, Culture, and Society: A Theoretical Overview," Rosaldo and
Lamphere, *Women,* 18, and J. K. Brown, "A Note on the Division of Labor by Sex," *American
Anthropologist* 72 (1970) 1074–78. Cf. Martin and Voorhies, *Female of the Species,* 276–332,
and Whyte, *Status of Women,* esp. 156–73.

17. Rosaldo, "Woman, Culture, and Society," 26–27. See further H. Papanek and
G. Minault, eds., *Separate Worlds: Studies of Purdah in South Asia* (Delhi: Chanakya Publications, 1982) esp. 3–53 and 54–78; Fernea, *Guests;* and Martin and Voorhies, *Female of the Species,* 290–95. Women's activities are never completely confined to the home, but sexual
division is the rule in both work and play wherever mixed groups are found. See Brown, "A
Note"; P. R. Sanday, "Female Status in the Public Domain," Rosaldo and Lamphere, *Woman,*
189–206; and E. Friedl, *Women and Men: An Anthropologist's View* (New York: Holt, Rinehart
& Winston, 1975) 8. For Old Testament examples, cf. the young women (*nĕʿārôt*) as distinct
from the young men (*nĕʿārîm*) working in Boaz's field (Ruth 2:8, 9; cf. 2:22, 23). Note the
sexual division of labor described in 1 Sam 8:11–13. Cf. also Old Testament references to
women drawing water (Gen 24:11; 1 Sam 9:11), grinding grain (Job 31:10; cf. Matt 24:41),
cooking and baking (1 Sam 8:13; Lev 26:26), and dancing and singing (Exod 15:20; 1 Sam
18:6–7).

roles in the official cultus are rarely women's roles or occupied by women.[18]

Conversely, however, women's religious activities—and needs—tend to center in the domestic realm and relate to women's sexually determined work. As a consequence, those institutions and activities which appear from public records or male perspective as central may be viewed quite differently by women, who may see them as inaccessible, restricting, [[401]] irrelevant, or censuring. Local shrines, saints and spirits, home rituals in the company of other women (often with women ritual leaders), the making and paying of vows (often by holding feasts), life-cycle rites, especially those related to birth and death—these widely attested elements of women's religious practice appear better suited to women's spiritual and emotional needs and the patterns of their lives than the rituals of the central sanctuary, the great pilgrimages and assemblies, and the liturgical calendar of the agricultural year.[19] But the public sphere with its male-oriented and male-controlled institutions dominates and governs the domestic sphere, with the result that women's activities and beliefs are often viewed by "official" opinion as frivolous, superstitious, subversive, or foreign.[20]

Women in Israelite Religion and Cultus: Observations and Hypotheses

We have argued that an adequate understanding of the place of women in the Israelite cultus requires attention both to the place of the cultus in the total religious and social life of the society and to the place of women in the society—including consideration of the society's understanding of male and female nature, capacities, and inclinations and its organization and assignment of male and female roles, activities, rights, and duties. Despite the efforts of the Israelite cultus to exert a controlling influence over the total life of the society and despite its significant stamp on the culture, the cultus must still be seen as one institution among others, influenced by general social and cultural norms, especially as they define appropriate male and female roles and activities. Consequently, we should expect significant correspondence between women's roles and status in the cultus and in the society as a whole.

18. Rosaldo, "Woman, Culture, and Society," 17, 19–21. Cf. Ortner and Whitehead, *Sexual Meanings,* 4 and passim; P. R. Sanday, *Female Power and Male Dominance* (Cambridge: Cambridge University Press, 1981); and Shapiro, "Anthropology," 118–22.

19. These generalizations summarize an extensive review of descriptive literature and case studies, which cannot be documented here. For a fuller analysis with examples and references, see my forthcoming work.

20. Cf. I. M. Lewis, *Ecstatic Religion* (New York: Penguin Books, 1971) 86–88, 96–97, 101.

Three prominent elements of that general understanding of women's nature and duty have direct bearing on women's place in the cultus: (1) the periodic impurity of women during their reproductive years;[21] (2) the legal subordination of women within the family, which places a woman under the male authority of father, husband, or brother, together with a corresponding subordination in the public sphere in which the community is represented by its male members; and (3) an understanding of women's primary work and social duty as family-centered reproductive work in the role of wife-mother.

The effect of each of these determinants is to restrict the sphere of women's activities—spatially, temporally, and functionally. Only roles that were compatible with women's primary domestic-reproductive role and could be exercised in periods or situations free from ritual taboo, or [[402]] from the requirement of ritual purity, were open to women. While restrictions also existed on men's ability to participate in particular cultic roles and activities (e.g., economic constraints on offering vows and sacrifices and restriction of priestly office to members of priestly families), these did not affect all males as a class. A significant distinction between male and female relationships to the cultus may be seen in the fact that for women, but not for men, conflict between social and cultic obligation is a recurring phenomenon—which is resolved by giving priority to social demands. Examples may be seen in the annulment of a woman's vows by her father or husband (Num 30:1–15)[22] and in the "exemption" of women from the requirement of the annual pilgrim feasts (Exod 23:17; 34:23; Deut 16:16). In both of these cases one may argue that responsibility to the family is the underlying principle and that it is understood as a religious, not merely a social, obligation; but a contrast remains between the understanding of a male and a female religious obligation.[23]

This explanation assumes a conflict of duty or interest (defined socially, not individually) as grounds for women's limited role in the Israelite cultus, but the limitation might also be explained by an understanding of the cultus as an originally, or essentially, male institution or association. The evidence suggests that there is truth in both views.

---

21. While the menstrual taboo is cultically defined and regulated, it is so universal a factor of human culture that it may be viewed as a general social concept apart from its specific interpretation and institutionalization in the Israelite cultus.

22. The divorced woman and the widow alone are free of overriding male authority.

23. The consequences and implications of this conflict in ordering, or contrast in defining, the religious priorities for women are far-reaching. In a society in which cultic service is accorded highest value, women are disadvantaged when they are excepted from that obligation. The various attempts within the Old Testament to extend to women obligations and options that were originally formulated with males in mind leave unaddressed the tension between the requirement and the ability to fulfill it.

Wellhausen was surely right in recognizing behind the generic language of many texts and translations a cultus conceived and operated as a male association to which women were related, if at all, in a marginal and mediated way. Evidence for an understanding of the cultic community as fundamentally a body of males is substantial. While the best examples relate to the early period, they are not confined to it: for example, the prescription for the pilgrim feasts ("Three times in the year shall all your males appear before the Lord God," Exod 23:17; cf. Deut 16:16); the instructions to the "people" at the mountain of God ("Be ready by the third day; do not go near a woman," Exod 19:15); the tenth commandment ("You shall not covet your neighbor's wife," Exod 20:17); and other injunctions, exhortations, blessings, and so forth, that address the cultic community as male ("Blessed is everyone who fears the Lord. . . . Your wife will be like a fruitful vine," Ps 128:1–3; "Jeremiah said to all the people and all the women," Jer 44:24).

Further evidence may be seen in the Hebrew onomasticon, where theophoric names describing the individual as a worshiper or votary of the deity (names compounded with *ᶜebed/ᶜōbēd*, i.e., 'servant of ') are reserved to males and have no female counterpart—in contrast to Akkadian and Phoenician practice.[24]

Objections to Wellhausen's view that seek to show broad participation [[403]] of women in religious and cultic activities fail to challenge his basic argument, which is not that women were prohibited from participation, but rather that their participation was not essential and that it played a less central or less important role in women's lives than in men's. Wellhausen's insight was also sound in positing an "original" coincidence or congruence of military, legal, and cultic assemblies; the three represent the primary institutions of the public sphere, which is everywhere the sphere of male activity. His understanding of the correspondence of rights and duties in these overlapping realms can also be substantially affirmed, though areas of divergence require greater attention together with cases of status incongruity. A further modification is required by the extension of both the cultic and the legal spheres beyond the circle of males to encompass the broader community.[25] As a

---

24. Old Babylonian *amat*-DN names, i.e., 'handmaid of [divine name]', exceed *warad*- ('servant-') names proportionally, even when the names of *nadītu* women are excluded as cloister names. The data for these comparisons together with a full analysis of sexual distinction in naming are found in my unpublished study, "Sexual Distinction in Israelite Personal Names: A Socio-religious Investigation."

25. The cultic assembly is not, I believe, to be understood as a male sect or society (though the early cultus has many of the features of a men's religious organization) but rather as a male-constituted and directed institution at the center of Israelite society, representing the community as a whole and directing and controlling its life. The way in which

consequence, women, who were excluded from the governing or representative institutions of both (namely, the priesthood and the cultic assembly, and the council of elders and the assembly of landholders), were nevertheless brought within their spheres of interest and authority.[26] Thus women possessed dual status in the legal and cultic realm, being members of the outer circle governed by the community's norms but restricted in varying degree from the inner circle where the norms were formulated, inculcated, and rationalized.

In the cultic realm, differentiation of roles is associated with a hierarchy of offices and prerogatives ordered according to a concept of graduated degrees of holiness (represented spatially, e.g., in the plan of the Temple and its courts). At the center, which is also the apex of authority, stands the priest or high priest, surrounded by other members of the priesthood and/or other orders of cultic personnel (the local shrine represents the simplest form of cultic leadership, invested in a resident priest—and his family—while the Temple cultus occupies the other end of the spectrum, with its elaborate, graded system of special orders and offices). Beyond the priesthood stand members of the community (more specifically, the free citizens), bound by duty of pilgrimage, addressed directly by the cultic proclamation and having limited rights of sacrifice (varying according to period). The outer circle is represented by women, dependents, and resident aliens. They are also addressed by the cultic proclamation, but usually indirectly; both their hearing and their response is commonly mediated by a male guardian.

While this scheme gives a general picture of the relationship of women to the Israelite cultus, it must be qualified in a number of ways, especially with regard to changes or variations in internal and external relationships over the Old Testament period, some of which appear to have significant consequence for the nature and extent of women's participation. Factors [[404]] requiring consideration include the number of cultic centers, the types of activities associated with them, and the rela-

---

it related to the larger community and the understanding of its own constitution seem to have changed over time in the direction of greater openness and inclusiveness, in respect not only to women but also to slaves, dependents, and resident aliens (cf. Deut 16:10–11, 13–14). See Conclusion.

26. Thus women shared many of the same rights and duties as men, made use of the same aid provided or mediated by the institutions, and, as men, were held accountable by them. Women, in common with men, prayed, consulted oracles, attended festivals and sought justice in the courts, received theophanies and divine commissions, sought oracular judgments and legal redress for wrongs suffered and received punishment for wrongs committed. It appears that they were not as a rule prohibited from general religious practices but rather were hindered from fuller participation by competing interest or duty (see below) or attracted by their own particular circumstances to make use of some means of religious expression more than others.

tionships among them; the status and affiliation of the cultic personnel, the degree of centralization, and the extent of professionalization or specialization of cultic maintenance roles; and the relationship of the central cultus to other institutions and spheres of life.

While this chapter does not permit detailed study of the complex assortment of data embedded in the Old Testament text, a summary review of the more prominent features of the major periods may help to provide a context for a series of concluding hypotheses concerning patterns of participation and changes in women's relationship to the cultus.

The fullest and richest evidence for women's religious activity is found in literature pertaining to the premonarchic period, which also provides the richest portrait of women in leadership roles. We see Miriam leading the Israelites in a song of victory at the sea (Exod 15:20–21), punished for claiming equality with Moses as one through whom the Lord had also spoken (Num 12:2), and ranked with Aaron and Moses as leaders of the people (Num 12:2–8; Mic 6:4);[27] women "ministering" at the tent of meeting (Exod 38:8; 1 Sam 2:22); Deborah honored as a "mother in Israel" (Judg 5:7), as a judge and a prophet summoning the forces of Israel to holy war at Yahweh's command and accompanying them into battle (Judg 4:4–10; 5:7, 12–15), and as a singer of Israel's victory through Yahweh (Judg 5:1); Jephthah's virgin daughter "initiating" an annual ritual of mourning by the daughters of Israel (Judg 11:34–40);[28] Micah's mother commissioning an image for the family shrine established by her son (Judg 17:1–13, esp. v. 4); women dancing at the yearly feast at Shiloh (Judg 21:19–21); Hannah and Peninnah accompanying their husband on his annual pilgrimage to Shiloh and sharing the portions of the sacrifice (1 Sam 1:1–4); and Hannah, weeping, praying, vowing at the sanctuary, and finally paying her vow with the dedication of the child (1 Sam 1:9–28). In these images we see most of the roles attested in the later period.

Sources pertaining to the period of the monarchy and to the postexilic period expand the references to heterodox practices and sharpen the distinction between legitimate and illegitimate roles and activities. Two female prophets, Huldah (2 Kgs 22:14–20) and the unnamed *nĕbîʾâ* ⟦'prophetess'⟧ of Isa 8:3, are the only women portrayed in approved cultic roles.[29] The rest are viewed as illegitimate. These include references to

27. Miriam's historical role is impossible to reconstruct, but her ranking alongside Moses and Aaron suggests a position of considerable importance—and a cultic role. She is not identified by a husband but by her "brothers," the priest and the prophet. The roles of cultic singer and prophet are suggested.

28. The mythic and aetiological character of the narrative does not limit its value as evidence for a women's ritual.

29. The meaning of *nĕbîʾâ* in the latter case is disputed. It is clear, however, that the term in Isa 8:3 is used as a role designation ('*the* prophetess', not 'my wife') whether or not

qĕdēšôt ⟦'female cult prostitutes'⟧ (Hos 4:14; Deut 23:18);[30] to queens and queen mothers who introduced foreign cults and cult objects (Maacah—1 Kgs 15:13; Jezebel—1 Kgs 18:19 [cf. 16:31–32]; Athaliah—2 Kgs 11:18; cf. Solomon—1 Kgs 11:1–8); to women weaving vestments for Asherah (2 Kgs 23:7); and to women ⟦405⟧ baking cakes / burning incense for the Queen of Heaven (Jer 7:17–18; 44:15–25), weeping for Tammuz (Ezek 8:14), and engaging in sorcery ("prophecying"—Ezek 13:17–23). Postexilic literature yields only a prophet opponent of Nehemiah (Noadiah—Neh 6:14), showing a continuation of women in the class of prophets.[31] The number and nature of references to women's religious roles and activities during the monarchy appear to reflect the consequences of the centralization of the cultus under royal control and a tendency, culminating in the Deuteronomic reform, to brand all worship at the local sanctuaries idolatrous/promiscuous.[32]

Evidence from patriarchal traditions depicts a family-centered or clan type of cultus in which the patriarchs perform all of the roles of sacrifice and blessing and are portrayed as founders of various local shrines or cults (Gen 22:9–14; 26:23–25; 28:18–19; 35:6–7, 14–15).[33] Rachel's stealing of the teraphim (as cultic objects belonging to her father) is further witness to clan-based religious practice, but it tells us nothing about women's religious roles. Her audacious and amusing act of theft and coverup in which she "protects" the sacred objects by professing defilement does not describe the institutionalization of an action. Rachel remains a dependent as she cleverly assists her husband in robbing her father.

Summary Generalizations

The following is an attempt to summarize the evidence in a series of preliminary generalizations.

---

it designates Isaiah's wife, and that it designates one who is to assist in the symbolic act that will complete Isaiah's sign.

30. The term used in Gen 38:21–22 is intended to describe a Canaanite practitioner in a Canaanite (and pre-Israelite) setting. Cf. n. 41, below.

31. Here opponents of Nehemiah. The Greek and Syriac apparently understood the name as masculine.

32. The narrowing of acceptable roles for women is correlated with a general narrowing of options in religious practice. The greater variety of roles and the fuller or more candid descriptions of practice in the premonarchic period in comparison with the later period raise the question whether the earlier practices disappeared or were simply reinterpreted (as heterodox) and/or suppressed. What is allowed to stand in the tradition of the earlier period was interpreted, in part at least, as evidence of the low moral state of the time—a judgment made explicit in the final editing of the Book of Judges (19:1, 30; etc.).

33. Use of patriarchal traditions as sources for social reconstruction requires particular caution; they depict individuals or families with little attention to social context and treat them as representative or symbolic figures.

Women in Cultic Service

1. Leadership of the cultus appears at all times to have been in the hands of males (though with differing patterns and sources of recruitment into the leadership group). Women, however, were not excluded absolutely from cultic service or sacred space, though increasing restriction is suggested, correlated with increasing centralization, specialization, and power (at least in Judah) under a royally sanctioned Zadokite priesthood. Persistence of women in cultic roles in the later period is identified in the canonical texts with heterodox practice.

2. The attested roles of men and women in the service of the cultus appear to exhibit a sexual division of labor corresponding closely to that discernible in the society as a whole.

a. Males occupy the positions of greatest authority, sanctity, and honor and perform tasks requiring technical skill and training. They preside over the presentation of sacrifices and offerings,[34] have charge of the sacred lots, interpret the sacred law and instruct the congregation, pronounce [[406]] blessing and curse, declare absolution and pardon, and guard the purity of the sanctuary and the worshipers; that is, they perform the priestly service in both sacrificial and oracular functions. Priestly office in Israel, as in the rest of the ancient Near East, was reserved to males. Contrary to popular opinion, Israelite Yahwism was not distinguished from the surrounding religions by its rejection of women in priestly office, but conformed to common practice.[35] The Israelite cultus in its basic institutional forms appears to have shared the essential features of the cultus known in surrounding cultures.

---

34. The one religious activity from which women appear to have been excluded by principle rather than circumstances was the offering of sacrifices, which eventually became the sole prerogative of the priest. The exclusion may ultimately be connected with the menstrual taboo, but it is not confined to periods of menstrual impurity. It appears, rather, to have been common practice elevated to a principle (cf. Winter, *Frau und Göttin*, 38–40) or to have been understood more in symbolic than in practical terms. Efforts to show that women offered sacrifices fail, I believe, in the case of biblical evidence. Presenting a sacrificial offering to the priest is not itself a sacrificial action (contra Peritz, "Women," 126–27) but an act of offering to which all are bound. In the case of the offering required for a woman's purification (Lev 12:6–7), a clear distinction is made between the woman's presentation of the animal to the priest ("she shall bring a lamb . . . to the priest," v. 6) and the offering made *by* the priest *for* the woman ("and he shall offer it . . . and make atonement for her," v. 7) (cf. Lev 15:19–33). Nor is the sharing of a sacrificial meal an act of sacrifice, though it is an important form of cultic participation, as Peritz insists ("Women in the Ancient Hebrew Cult," 123–25). Manoah prepares and offers the sacrifice on behalf of his nameless wife to whom the angel has appeared (Judg 13:19), and Elkanah sacrifices (*way-yizbaḥ*) at the shrine of Shiloh, distributing portions to his wives and children (1 Sam 1:4).

35. J. Renger's study of the Old Babylonian "priesthood" based on the *lú = amēlu* list shows only one among the nineteen classes identified as *Kultpriester* [['cultic priest']] in which men and women are identified by a common term, namely, the *en* [['high priest']],

b. Women's cultic service seems to have been confined largely to maintenance and support roles, essential to the operation of the cultus but not requiring clergy status—or prescription in texts concerned with the proper performance of the required rituals. Since these roles are poorly documented in the biblical sources, we can only speculate based on chance clues, parallels in domestic life, and the suggestions afforded by comparative studies of cultic organization and maintenance elsewhere in the ancient Near East. The following tasks appear likely (further suggestions must await a fuller study of comparative materials): the weaving and sewing of vestments, hangings, and other textiles for cultic use;[36] the

---

the highest ranked and earliest attested office in the list ("Untersuchungen zum Priestertum in der altbabylonischen Zeit" [*ZA* n.s. 24 (1967) 110–88] 113). The sex of the *en* appears to have been complementary to that of the deity, suggesting that the *en* was understood to represent the divine spouse. The rest of the classes are distinguished by gender and nomenclature and grouped (with the exception of the *entum*, the later Akkadian designation of the female *en*) in the typical hierarchical order of male-female, strongly suggesting sexual division of labor within the cultus rather than shared roles. Despite Renger's use of the term *Priesterinnen* [['priestesses']] to describe the female classes, they do not appear to have performed activities that would properly be described as "priestly." Use of the term "priestess" to describe such women is misleading, since it suggests comparable, if not identical, roles and equal status with priests.

The third group in the *lú = amēlu* list, exorcists, consists of five classes, all male—as we might expect, since these represent offices requiring technical skills and mastery of a body of esoteric knowledge, like the *bārû* diviners in the second group. It is only in the second group, comprising the oracular speakers, that we find professional classes with both male and female members, namely, the *šāʾiltum/(šāʾilum)*, *maḫḫûm/maḫḫūtum*, and *āpilum/āpiltum* [['asker; ecstatic; answerer', respectively]]. The pattern presented in the Old Babylonian sources corresponds exactly to that which the more meager, and less specialized, Old Testament data suggest: priestly roles involving technical expertise and leadership in the sacrificial cult or other cultic ritual were male, as well as other roles demanding specialized knowledge, while the more charismatic forms of divination open to lay as well as professional practitioners involved women as well as men, just as their Old Testament prophetic counterpart. Cf. R. Harris: "Except for the religious functions of royal women and dream interpretation and divination, women played a minor role in cultic life. Only in the lower echelons of the 'clergy' did female singers, dancers, and musicians participate in the cult" ("Woman in the Ancient Near East," *IDBSup*, 960–63, esp. 962).

Syrian and Canaanite sources are too meager to confirm a pattern. The Ugaritic texts contain no reference to any class of female cultic personnel as a recognizable group. Phoenician and Punic sources contain the only known ancient feminine form of *khn* ('priest'). In the Eshmunazar sarcophagus inscription (*KAI*, 14:15) it is applied to the queen of Sidon as royal patron, and hence chief official, of the city god Ashtart. I would interpret this as evidence of a royal cultus in which the king/queen, qua ruler, assumed the title and role of priest/presider in the official cultus, not as evidence for a class of female priests. The status and function of the women bearing this title in several Punic inscriptions (*KAI*, 70:1; 93:1; 145:45[?]; 140:2) cannot be determined. See now J. A. Hackett, *The Balaam Text from Deir ʿAllā* (Chico: Scholars Press, 1984) 25.

36. While the women weavers expelled from the Temple by Josiah were associated with the service of a "foreign" deity or cult object, the Yahweh cultus also had need of such

preparation of cultic meals or foods used in the ritual;[37] and the cleaning of cultic vessels, furniture, and quarters.[38]

c. Some reference to women associated with the cultus point to more public and representative or symbolic roles, suggesting a need to include within the cultus activities or attributes specifically identified with women,

---

service. According to Exod 34:25–26, the material for the tabernacle hangings was spun by women. The weaving of the hangings, however, was supervised by the master craftsman Bezalel or his male assistant (Exod 34:35), an example of the male professionalization of female crafts observed in cross-cultural studies of gender roles. It is not certain who actually did the work; the *kol ḥakam-leb bĕʿōśeh hammĕlāʾkāh* ('everyone able to do the work') with its masculine plural verb could be a generic use of the masculine to describe a group of workers of mixed gender.

37. This is suggested on the analogy of work in the domestic sphere, though cultic specialization might well make cooking and baking male activities. Nevertheless it is worth speculating who prepared the sacrificial victims for the communion meals eaten at the sanctuary and who baked the shewbread. In the report of the "priests' custom with the people" in 1 Sam 2:13–17, it is clear that neither the priest nor the priest's servant is involved in boiling the meat, since the priest's servant takes or demands the portion desired by the priest. The man sacrificing is addressed in 1 Sam 2:15, but did he cook as well as slaughter the animal? Might not his accompanying wife have performed her usual work for the family feast? Or when the sacrifice later became a priestly prerogative, might not women of priestly families have performed this service?

Ezekiel's provisions for the restored Temple include designation of areas for cooking and baking within the Temple complex, carefully separating the place where the priests were to boil the *ʾāšām* [['guilt offering']] and the *ḥaṭṭāʾt* [['sin offering']] offerings and bake the *minḥâ* [['cereal offering']]—which was to be within the inner court (Ezek 46:20)—and the 'kitchens' (*bêt hamĕbaššĕlîm*) where 'those who minister at the Temple' (*mĕšārĕtê habbayit*) were to boil the 'sacrifices of the people' (*zebaḥ hāʿam*)—which were located in the outer court (Ezek 46:21–24). This late scheme clearly assigns all actions related to the sanctuary to priests, guarding this sphere from that in which the preparation of meals for the people took place. Hearths are provided for the latter purpose and the activity was supervised by a lower class of Temple personnel (not priests). This stage of prescription for the cultus has professionalized actions earlier performed by the worshiper, including the slaughter of the sacrificial victims, which is now assigned to the Levites (Ezek 44:12; cf. Lev 2:4–7 and 3:1–17).

The mention of women as cooks and bakers in the palace service (1 Sam 8:13) may also provide a clue, at least for the earlier period, since the administration of the Temple was similar in many ways to the administration of the palace. A third type of female work mentioned in 1 Sam 8:13, that of "perfumers," has a counterpart in the cultus in the preparation of the holy anointing oil, a special skill described by the use of the same verb (*raqqāḥôt* [['perfumers']]; *rōqēaḥ* [['anointing oil']], Exod 30:25). However, the distinction in the use of the aromatic oils produced for the cultus may make this a male specialty in the cultic setting.

38. The suggestion is again by analogy to the almost universal assignment of housecleaning to women—or slaves. In large public buildings, palaces, etc., such work is usually done by slaves or low-caste groups, with tasks divided by sex, and that may have been the case in the Temple, too. But at local shrines presided over by a single priest, the housekeeping chores of the deity's house might well have fallen to the female members of the priest's family.

for example, as singers and dancers[39] or as attendants in the sanctuary. Both the *ṣōbĕʾôt* ⟦'ministering women'⟧ (Exod 38:8; 1 Sam 2:22)[40] and the

39. Women are widely identified with singing and dancing as well as instrumental musicmaking in both biblical and extrabiblical texts and in pictorial representations (see, e.g., *ANEP*, 63–66, 111, 346; I. Seibert, *Woman in Ancient Near East* [Leipzig: Fortschritt Erfuhrt, 1974], pls. 10, 34, 99; O. Keel, *The Symbolism of the Biblical World* [New York: Seabury/Crossroad, 1978] 336–39). None of these activities was restricted to women (cf. *ANEP*, 63–66, David's reputation as a singer, and his dance before the Ark, 2 Sam 6:14, 16), though some types of instruments and performance may have been regarded as peculiarly or typically female. The "timbrel" (*top*), e.g., appears to have been a preferred instrument of women (cf. Winter, *Frau und Göttin*, 33 n. 164; E. Werner, "Musical Instruments" [*IDB* 3.469–76] 474); women musicians and dancers are widely attested as professional entertainers of men (cf. the Arabic *shayka* ⟦'matron'⟧, the Japanese geisha, and the Old Testament image of the prostitute as a troubadour, singing to the tune of her harp [Isa 23:14–15]); and women typically formed a welcoming chorus line to greet warriors returning from battle (Exod 15:20; 1 Sam 18:6). The disputed question is whether women participated as musicians or dancers in cultic celebrations and whether they belonged to the personnel of the sanctuary.

The question is too complex for adequate treatment here. It may be that references to cultic dancing should be eliminated altogether, or at least those described by *māḥōl/mĕḥōlâ* ⟦'dance, dancing'⟧ and verbal forms of *ḥwl* ⟦'dance', 'whirl'⟧, which appear always to designate actions of the congregation or groups of lay women, not a professional activity, and may refer to antiphonal singing rather than dance (see J. M. Sasson, "The Worship of the Golden Calf," *Orient and Occident: Essays Presented to Cyrus H. Gordon*, AOAT 22 [1973] 151–59, esp. 157; cf. Winter, *Frau und Göttin*, 32–33). The function of the three daughters of Heman, mentioned in a parenthetical note in 1 Chr 25:5, is unclear, though the sons constituted a major Levitical guild of musicians in the Second Temple. The *mĕšōrĕrîm ûmĕšōrĕrôt* ⟦'male and female singers'⟧ of Ezra 2:65 clearly represent a different class from the Temple singers described by the same term (masculine plural) in Ezra 2:41; Neh 7:44. Their place in the list following male and female servants and preceding the horses suggests a menial class of entertainers.

It seems likely that the public, professional roles of musicians in the Temple service were assigned to males, at least in the later period of the monarchy and the Second Temple period, while women's specialized musical activity was limited to secular entertainment and funeral dirges (a "home" ritual). The earlier period, however, suggests a different picture in the attribution of two important songs of praise to women, both called prophets (Exod 15:20–21; Judg 4:4; 5:1; cf. 1 Chr 25:1, which describes the function of the Temple musicians as "prophesying" with lyres, harps, and cymbals). While the narrative contexts point to a traditional secular role of women in greeting returning warriors (cf. Winter, *Frau und Göttin*, 33), both texts may also be understood to describe cultic actions, whose setting is the celebration of Yahweh's victories, not simply as one-time historical acts, but as repeated cultic actions recalling the great victories (or does the shift in attribution of the Song at the Sea from Miriam to Moses reflect a cultic institutionalization of the victory song in which the secular/lay role of the woman leader is transformed into a cultic/professional male role?). Ps 68:26 ⟦25⟧ suggests that in the Temple period at least women formed a recognized group among the Temple musicians (*ʿălāmôt tōpēpôt* ⟦'young women playing timbrels'⟧, mentioned between *šārîm* ⟦'singers'⟧ and *nōgĕnîm* ⟦'players (of stringed instruments)'⟧ in the procession to the sanctuary; cf. Winter, *Frau und Göttin*, 34–35).

40. The many questions about these women cannot be explored adequately here, much less resolved. For the most recent discussion and review of literature, see Winter, *Frau und Göttin*, 58–65. Both the Samuel and the Exodus passages suggest the persistence of the office

qĕdēšôt [['female cult prostitutes']] (Gen 38:21–22; Deut 23:17; Hos 4:14) [41]
are associated with the service of the sanctuary, though the exact nature
and form of their respective service remains unclear. Both represent
classes rejected or superseded by the normative cultus that preserved the
record of their existence, suggesting that they played a larger role (for a
longer period of time) than the meager references would at first intimate.
The identifying symbol or implement of the former group (a mirror) and
the innuendo in references to the latter suggest that in both cases female
sexuality was a significant aspect of the role.

   d. If we posit any specialized service of women within the cultus, we
must also consider the social organization that would enable permanent
or continuous (short-term or long-term) cultic activity. Since women's
place in society is determined by their place within the family, women are
not normally free to operate for extended periods outside this sphere.
The well-known exceptions are the widow, the prostitute, and the hiero-
dule. Two possible arrangements may be suggested to account for women's
[[407]] service in the Israelite cultus. One would see the women as members of priestly families, hence resident at or near the sanctuary and sharing in some degree the special sanctity of the priest, which would give

---

or institution after the initiation of the Yahwistic cultus and its tent shrine in the desert.
Winter has seen rightly, I believe, that the significant information in the archaic Exodus
tradition is the reference to the mirrors (*Frau und Göttin*, 60). For a critique of his interpretation, which views the mirror as the symbol of a female deity associated with fertility and
the women as *Hofdamen* [['ladies in waiting']] visiting the sanctuary, rather than cultic personnel, see my forthcoming work. Cf. J. Morgenstern, "The Ark, the Ephod, and the Tent,"
HUCA 17 (1942–43) 153–265, *HUCA* 18 (1943–44) 1–52, for an interpretation of the
women as shrine attendants based on pre-Islamic Arabic parallels.

   41. This is not the place to review the evidence and arguments concerning the *qĕdēšâ*
[['female cult prostitute']]. The literature is far larger than that on the women at the entrance to the tent of meeting and the presence of cognates and of presumed parallel institutions in other ancient Near Eastern cultures requires a more thorough investigation and
report than the chapter in this present volume permits. Of the three Old Testament references, two suggest a foreign origin or, at least, a non–Yahwistic institution (Deut 23:17 and
Gen 38:21–22), while all three parallel the term with *zônâ* ('prostitute'). The cultic nature
of the office or role is clear from the etymology and from the one text that describes an activity (Hos 4:14): "[The men] sacrifice with *qĕdēšôt*." Since the term is paired in Deut 23:17
with the masculine *qādēš* [['male prostitute']]—in the reverse of the normal male-female order—any judgment about the *qĕdēšâ* must involve consideration of the whole class of cognate terms. In overview, it appears that the Old Testament usage is so generalized and
polemical that it may serve more as a cover term for proscribed cultic roles rather than as
the precise designation of a particular office or function. Since all of the masculine references (all apparently collective, except Deut 23:17, and therefore presumably inclusive) are
in Deuteronomic contexts, the possibility must be considered that the term was used in
Deuteronomistic circles to describe roles or offices, such as that of the *ṣōbĕʾôt* [['ministering
women']] of the Tent of Meeting, that were at one time considered a legitimate part of the
Israelite cultus.

them access to the sacred space. The other would assume that they are women without families (whether widows, virgins, or women separated from their families by a vow). In the latter case we may expect, as in the case of the various classes of Babylonian hierodules, that the cultus will assume the authority and control of father or husband and that restrictions, comparable to those applying within the family, will be placed on the woman's sexual activity for the duration of her service (whether as a prohibition of sexual activity or of having or keeping children).

e. Women might also on occasion play a role in the royal cultus through their roles in the ruling house. A queen, in the absence of a male ruler (or in the presence of a weak one), might assume the role of titular head and patron of the state cult. Since our best Old Testament example is provided by a foreign queen (Jezebel), presiding over a foreign cult, the cultic role of the king's wife or mother may not have been as fully developed in Israel as elsewhere—or it may have been rejected. This specialized cultic role is in any case dependent upon a secular role and the particular politicoreligious relationship of the royal cultus.

3. The most important and best-documented religious office occupied by women in ancient Israel, that of prophet, stands in an ambiguous relationship to the cultus. Whatever the role of the prophet within the cultus, it was clearly not a priestly office. Since recruitment was by divine designation (charismatic gift) and not dependent upon family or status, it was the one religious office with broad power that was not mediated or directly controlled by the cultic or civil hierarchy and the one religious office open to women. Because recruitment to and exercise of the role did not depend on socially or sexually defined status but on personal attributes, it was also the one role shared by men and women, a pattern attested in Mesopotamia and in cross-cultural studies.

The lack of formal restrictions to women's assumption of the office does not mean, however, that women were equally free to exercise it. Here, as in the case of other extrafamilial roles, women were confronted with a dual vocation, which was normally—and perhaps always—resolved in favor of the domestic obligation. Women prophets probably exercised their charismatic vocation alongside their family responsibilities or after their child-rearing duties were past. As a consequence of this complementary or sequential pattern of women's prophetic activity—and as a consequence of the normal patterns of social organization, which placed women as dependents in family-centered units—one would not expect to find women organized in prophetic guilds (the professional [[408]] guild is a male form of organization). Nor would one expect to find women prophets as heads of schools or having the freedom of action and access to political and cultic power that is apparent in the case of their most prominent male counterparts. It is therefore not unexpected that no prophetic books carry the names of women, and it requires no explanation of prejudice or conspiratorial silence—but rather conflict of duty, which made every woman a mother before she would exercise another vocation.

4. Some forms of cultic service by women associated with the central Yahwistic cultus were judged heterodox or foreign by the canonical sources. In addition to these reference the Old Testament contains frequent references to local cults of alien gods and to foreign cults brought into the central cultus. These references, which are always polemical and usually formulated in very general terms, do not supply us with adequate information about the related cultic personnel, but presumably some of these were women (e.g., *qĕdēsîm* [['cult prostitutes']] in 1 Kgs 15:12; 2 Kgs 23:7 may be understood as an inclusive use of the generic plural). It is impossible on the basis of our sources, however, to determine whether women played a larger role in the service of non-Yahwistic cults. Evidence for a female deity or female aspect of deity as a persistent and at times, perhaps legitimate element of the Yahwistic cultus requires reassessment of the terms "foreign" and "syncretistic" as descriptions of discredited worship as well as a reassessment of the ritual and personnel of such cults. The sources suggest that disavowal, rather than discontinuance, of the practices and beliefs is what is indicated in the increasing and increasingly polemical attention to "foreign" cults and cultic practices in late source.

Women as Worshipers

1. Since women rarely emerge in the text from behind the facade of generic male terminology, it is impossible to determine with certainty the extent of their participation in prescribed or reported activities. Isolated clues suggest, however, that women attended the major communal feasts and rituals, insofar as personal and domestic circumstances permitted, and presumably contributed to the preparation of meals and of food (especially grain) offerings. Animal slaughter and sacrifice, as an action of the worshiper, was reserved to males—as elsewhere generally—but this appears to have been the sole specific exclusion or reservation. In the major pilgrim feasts and other festivals at local shrines, as well as in family-based ritual meals, the woman participates as a member of a family unit. But she may also exercise her role in "the great congregation" and as "a daughter of Israel" bound by covenant law in individual acts of [[409]] devotion and duty: in songs of praise (1 Sam 2:1–10) and prayers of petition (1 Sam 1:10–16), in the making and performing of vows (1 Sam 1:11, 24–28; Num 30:3–15), in seeking oracles (2 Kgs 4:22–23; cf. 1 Kgs 14:2–5), in bringing offerings, and in performing the rituals prescribed for ritual cleansing, absolution, and so forth (Lev 12:1–8;

13:29–39; 15:19–29). The locus of these activities might be the central shrine (on occasions of pilgrimage) but was surely most commonly a local shrine or holy place or simply the place of daily activity. That women's communion with the deity was common and that women were recipients of divine communications is indicated by a number of theophany traditions—though where the response to the appearing deity takes cultic form, as in the case of Manoah's wife, the action shifts to the male (Manoah presents the offering and questions the angel, cf. Judg 13:2–7 and 8–20).

2. Of family-centered ritual we know even less, except in the case of the Passover. We may expect in this and in other cases that the normal male and female roles in the family will be reflected in the ritual, with food preparation belonging to the women and the presiding role, reading and recitation, assumed by males. The alternative practice of segregated dining and ritual, common in Islamic custom, was more likely the rule in cultic meals of larger groups or societies formed for such purposes.

3. Peculiarly or predominantly female forms of ritual and worship are suggested in the canonical sources only in reference to heterodox cults, the clearest examples of which are the women weeping for Tammuz (Ezek 8:14) and making offerings to the Queen of Heaven (Jer 7:17–18; 44:19). Though the whole population is explicitly implicated in the latter case, the women seem to have a special role. Prophetic use of the metaphor of the promiscuous bride to describe Israel's apostasy may reflect a special proclivity of Israelite women for "foreign" cults, but the sin that is condemned is the sin of the people, and this usage alone is insufficient to demonstrate a pattern. Of possible greater significance for an understanding of women's religious participation and the total religious life of the community is the hidden realm of women's rituals and devotions that take place entirely within the domestic sphere and/or in the company of other women. Cross-cultural studies show that these often constitute the emotional center of women's religious life as well as the bulk of their religious activity, especially where their participation in the central cultus is limited. For such practices, however, we have little or no direct testimony, as this order of religious practice is generally seen as unworthy of note unless it challenges or undermines the central cultus. (Women's rites may even be unknown to men, who have no part in them.) Ceremonies and practices that belong to this category might include birth [[410]] and mourning rites and other rituals of the life cycle performed in the home or the village, especially with a woman as ritual specialist; prayers; vows and their performance in such actions as holding a feast, endowing a shrine, or dedicating some prized possession; making pilgrimages; consulting mediums and seers; and participa-

tion in spirit-possession cults or rituals. The line between religion and magic or orthodox and heterodox is more difficult to draw in this realm of practice and belief since the controls of the central cultus, its priesthood and theology, are largely absent. Like folk religion everywhere, it is typically seen as debased or corrupted and often as syncretistic.

The freedom to engage in such actions may vary considerably, relating in part to the degree to which they may be seen as convergent with or contrary to cultically prescribed duties. For example, ritual prescriptions governing the state of impurity associated with childbirth draw the otherwise private birth event into the sphere of the central cultus in its attempt to maintain the purity of the people as a cultically defined community. But the satisfaction of the cultic requirement does not exhaust the ritual need associated with the birth, which may be supplied by a naming ceremony, circumcision feast, and/or special rituals to assist the mother in the birth—rituals in which a female specialist such as a midwife may play a role closely analogous to the role of a priest in other situations of crisis. Women's private rituals or actions favored by women may also be opposed by male authorities as frivolous, superstitious, costly, and unnecessary. But opposition does not always mean compliance. Women may take vows that are costly and undertake forbidden pilgrimages as actions of rebellion or flight from oppressive household responsibilities and restrictions. As religiously sanctioned actions they may offer limited relief to women whose options for action were often severely circumscribed.

4. On the boundary of the sacred sphere that is organized by the central cultus or claimed by rival cults, a sphere extended in the name of the principal deity, or deities, to the rituals of daily life, there exists a quasi-religious sphere of spirits, demons, and various malevolent or amoral forces that trouble people and over which they attempt to gain control by special knowledge and defensive action. Those skilled in discerning and controlling these forces, by sorcery, witchcraft, necromancy, medicine, or other means, may be acknowledged by the cultus as practitioners of valuable practical arts or proscribed as challenging the fundamental claims of the deity to embody or control all forms of superhuman power. While some religions might incorporate such beliefs and practices into their belief systems, Israelite Yahwism, from the time of Saul, proscribed the practices and banned the practitioners (1 Sam 23:3, 8). ⟦411⟧ It has often been suggested that women had a special attraction to these quasi-religious practices, both as clients and as practitioners, and it makes sense that women should prefer to seek help for their problems from a local specialist than from a general practitioner or ritual specialist serving a remote God. That women should also constitute a significant proportion of the mediums and other specialists in spirit manipulation is

also understandable. However, the Old Testament evidence is insufficient to confirm such a pattern of preference and contains more references to male than to female classes of occult practitioners.

Conclusion

During the period reflected in the Old Testament sources there appear to have been a number of changes within the cultus and in its relationship to the population as a whole that had significance for women's participation. The progressive movement from multiple cultic centers to a central site that finally claimed sole legitimacy and control over certain ritual events necessarily restricted the participation of women in pilgrim feasts and limited opportunities for women to seek guidance, release, and consolation at local shrines, which were declared illegitimate or demolished. At the same time, increased specialization and hierarchal ordering of priestly/levitical ranks within the royal/national cultus deprived males in general (as well as Levites) of earlier priestly prerogatives, increasing the distance or sharpening the boundary between the professional guardians of the cultus and the large circle of male Israelites who comprised the religious assembly. Reorganization of the cultus under the monarchy and again in the postexilic period appears to have limited or eliminated roles earlier assigned to women. On the other hand, there appears to have been a move (most clearly evident in the Deuteronomic legislation) to bring women more fully and directly into the religious assembly, so that the congregation is redefined as a body of lay men and women. As the priesthood becomes more powerful and specialized, the primary cultic distinction or boundary within the community becomes that between priest and laity rather than between male and female.

The Politics of Ezra:
Sociological Indicators of Postexilic Judaean Society

DANIEL L. SMITH

〚73〛 It is the purpose of this paper to survey briefly some textual and archaeological evidence from exilic–postexilic sources that can be subjected to sociological or anthropological analysis. It is hoped that sociological analysis may remove some of the mystery surrounding the Persian period of Jewish history. But before I consider some of the texts and arguments, let me clarify that I am limiting my comments to biblical texts whose chronological locations in the exilic period have been determined with a reasonable amount of scholarly consensus. That being the case, I have not considered the otherwise very provocative suggestions by Schmid, Thompson, and Van Seters that major sections of the "J" narrative of the Pentateuch (Hexateuch?) are in fact postexilic.[1] I can say, however, that some of my own brief investigations on, for example, the history and provenance of institutions of confinement in the ancient Near East have also led me to have questions about the appearance of houses of confinement or bondage (בית אסרים ,בית משמר ,בית אסרים; Gen 40:3; 42:19; Judg 16:21; etc.) in the stories of Joseph and Samson. There is little evidence before the exilic period that such forms of punishment existed in the monarchical period.[2] There are also the clearly impressive lexical parallels that were already noted by Rosenthal in 1895 with regard to the

Reprinted with permission from *Second Temple Studies 1: Persion Period* (ed. P. R. Davies; Journal for the Study of the Old Testament Supplement Series 117; Sheffield Academic Press, 1991).

1. On this, see John Van Seters, *Abraham in History and Tradition* (Yale, 1975); H. H. Schmid, *Der sogenannte Jahwist* (Zurich, 1976); T. L. Thompson, *The Historicity of the Patriarchal Narratives* (Berlin, 1974). I have a brief discussion of this matter in my *The Religion of the Landless: A Sociology of the Babylonian Exile* (Bloomington, 1989) 42–43.

2. See *The Religion of the Landless*, 171–74.

stories of [[74]] Daniel, Esther, and Joseph.[3] The evidence marshalled by Van Seters and Schmid of a literary nature, and by Thompson of a historical nature, is more substantial and convincing.

I also refrain from extensive reference to the recent work on archaeological material, specifically coins and clay seals, from the Persian period. This material has been subject to very important analyses by Avigad, Meshorer and most recently (to my knowledge) by Betylon.[4] These scholars are trying to reconstruct lists of leaders in the postexilic community up to the Hellenistic period. Finally, R. Zadok, N. Cohen, and M. D. Coogan have attempted to apply a more sophisticated methodology to the study of Hebrew onomastica in the "Murashu Archives"—a line of investigation first suggested by S. Daiches in 1912.[5] Onomastic studies may be able to suggest social indicators of ethnicity by observing, for example, how frequently the "pious" names of Haggai and Sabbtai appear. Porten, in his studies of the Elephantine Documents, has even made similar arguments about another foreign colony of Jews. But it seems a risky business to conclude, as Coogan attempts, that the frequency of names created, for example, from the root *šlm* is a possible reflection of the desire of the exilic/postexilic community for peace.[6] Sociological analysis is under enough suspicion for building castles out of [[75]] sand, so I shall not add these observations to the ramparts.

Background to a Sociology of the Exilic Community

The most sociologically significant event is precisely the military defeat and mass deportation of Judaeans to a foreign environment composed of a dominant Babylonian population and other conquered peoples. In his

3. L. Rosenthal, "Die Josephgeschichte mit den Büchern Ester und Daniel verglichen," *ZAW* 15 (1895) 274–84 and "Nochmals der Vergleich Ester, Joseph-Daniel," *ZAW* 17 (1897) 125–28. See also D. Redford, *A Study of the Biblical Story of Joseph (Gen. 37–50)* (Leiden: Brill, 1970).

4. See N. Avigad, "Bullae and Seals from a Post-Exilic Judean Archive," *Qedem* 4 (1976) 1–36, and "A New Class of Yehud Stamps," *IEJ* 7 (1957) 146–53; Y. Meshorer, *Ancient Jewish Coinage. 1. Persian Period through Hasmoneans* (New York, 1982); idem, "Yehud, A Preliminary Study of the Provincial Coinage of Judea," in *Greek Numismatics and Archaeology. Essays in Honor of Margaret Thompson* (ed. O. Markholm and N. Waggoner; Wetteren, 1979); J. W. Betylon, "The Provincial Government of Persian Period Judea and the Yehud Coins," *JBL* 105 (1986) 633–42.

5. S. Daiches, *The Jews in Babylonia in the Time of Ezra and Nehemiah according to Babylonian Inscriptions* (London, 1912); cf. R. Zadok, *The Jews in Babylonia during the Chaldean and Achaemenid Periods* (Haifa, 1979); N. Cohen, "Jewish Names as Cultural Indicators in Antiquity," *JSJ* 7 (1976–77) 97–128; M. D. Coogan, *West Semitic Personal Names in the Murashu Documents* (Chico, CA, 1976).

6. Coogan, *Personal Names*, 85.

very important study of mass deportation in the neo-Assyrian Empire
(which includes observations about neo-Babylonian practice as well),
Oded estimated that four and a half million people were forcibly moved
by the neo-Assyrian war machine. The single largest deportation comprised some 208,000 taken from the Babylonian heartland to Assyrian
territory in northern Mesopotamia.[7] Clearly, these numbers dwarf even
the highest figures for the Judaean exile at the hand of the Babylonians,
and caution us against hasty conclusions about what numbers could be
"too large to be credible." According to 2 Kgs 24:14, 10,000 captives were
taken, but in v. 16 the numbers of 'men of valour' (גבורי החיל) and 'craftsmen and smiths' (החרש והמסגר) are given as 7,000 and 1,000 respectively.
Jeremiah gives three figures, usually considered to be more reliable, although the most common reason I have seen for this conclusion is simply
that they do not appear to be rounded off, and look like accurately cop-
ied figures. Jer 52:28 lists 3,023 in Nebuchadnezzar's seventh year, 832 in
his eighteenth year and 745 in his twenty-third year (the last date and
figure is a deportation not referred to elsewhere in the Bible). The total,
4,600, probably comprises mature men only, and perhaps only the most
important men. So, if we multiply the figure of 4,600 by four, to take account of family members, we are already approaching a total of 20,000
exiles as a minimum number. Albright had estimated that Judah's population in the 8th century was approximately 250,000 and fell to "roughly
half that number" between 597 and 586.[8] In an unpublished doctoral dissertation on the exile, Heinrich Wurz suggested that Jeremiah's first figure of 3,023 represented exile from outside Jerusalem ("cities of Judah"),
while the 7,000 of 2 Kgs 24:16 ⟦76⟧ represent exiles from Jerusalem. The
two figures together, suggests Wurz, may be the basis for the figure of
10,000 given in 2 Kgs 24:14.[9] Finally, let us keep in mind that the "Golah
List" ⟦'exiles' or 'diaspora' list⟧ of Ezra 2 / Nehemiah 7 numbers the returning exiles at 42,360, again most likely only mature males of the *bêt*
ʾabôt ⟦'house of fathers', 'clan'⟧—a social structure that we will consider below. The numbers in the "Golah List" obviously do not include
those Jewish exiles who apparently liked the Persian political climate and
remained behind.[10] But sociologically speaking, the only point that we

---

7. B. Oded, *Mass Deportations and Deportees in the Neo-Assyrian Empire* (Wiesbaden: Otto
Harrassowitz, 1979) 20–21.

8. Quoted in S. S. Weinberg, "Post-Exilic Palestine: An Archaeological Report," *Proceedings of the Israel Academy of Science and Humanities* 4 (1971) 78ff.

9. H. Wurz, "Die Wegführung der Juden durch König Nebukadnezzar II" (Th.D.
dissertation, University of Vienna, 1958).

10. This reluctance of many Jews to return may have been connected with the political
intentions of the Persians in authorizing the "return." If Jewish subjects loyal to the Persian crown were sent to provide a "buffer" against the Greeks, then the less hearty may have

need to make is that the exile community was certainly numerous enough to be settled in communities large enough to maintain a clear communal identity, and to have sufficient numbers to reproduce such traditional forms of self-governance as elders, heads of families, and gatherings of elders to hear, and in the case of Ezekiel 5 to watch, the prophets who continued to deliver their messages from God. On this evidence alone, a sociological picture begins to emerge of the exilic community; yet it is far from complete without further consideration of the actual circumstances of exile.

The exilic community survived both military defeat and mass deportation. The significance of both aspects is partially explained by what we now understand about the importance that ancient Near Eastern generals and rulers attached to the psychology, and indeed spirituality, of dominance.[11] This was clearly a major element in neo-Assyrian and neo-Babylonian warfare. Neo-Assyrian tactics are famous for including the terrorism of public executions,[12] and public ⟦77⟧ addresses like the speech before the city gates during the siege of Jerusalem in Hezekiah's reign. Renaming captives or client rulers, as Nebuchadnezzar did in the case of Zedekiah (which recalls details in the stories of Daniel), erecting stone tributes to military prowess in the conquered territories, and displaying power in the home country, as well as publicly humiliating the gods and temples of conquered peoples, were all tactics familiar to neo-Babylonian rulers. The act of carrying away Temple furniture and treasures, but not destroying the objects (in cases of non-Jewish conquests including the act of carrying away cult statues[13]) reveals a psychological intention beyond simply looting. The spiritual morale of the exiles in the light of such daily reminders that they are not home, and that "their god" appeared to have failed them, are theological problems to which the exilic prophets Deutero-Isaiah and Ezekiel clearly address themselves. Speculation on the time of deliverance is clearly an issue between Jeremiah and Hananiah (Jeremiah 26–29), a prophetic struggle that was

---

chosen to avoid the assignment. See O. Margalith, "The Political Role of Ezra as Persian Governor," *ZAW* 98 (1986) 110–12 and J. Blenkinsopp, "The Mission of Udjahorresnet and Those of Ezra and Nehemiah," *JBL* 106 (1987) 409–21.

11. See the following: M. Liverani, "The Ideology of the Assyrian Empire," in *Power and Propaganda: A Symposium on Ancient Empires* (Mesopotamia 7; Copenhagen, 1979) 297–318; H. Spieckerman, *Juda unter Assur in der Sargonidenzeit* (Göttingen: Vandenhoeck & Ruprecht, 1982).

12. See H. W. F. Saggs, "Assyrian Warfare in the Sargonid Period," *Iraq* 25 (1963) 145–54.

13. See D. L. Weisberg, *Guild Structure and Political Allegiance in Early Achaemenid Mesopotamia* (Yale, 1967); M. Cogan, *Imperialism and Religion* (Chico, CA: Scholars Press, 1974) 34–40.

known to the first exiles as well as those still in the land before the second major deportation.

Oded, on the basis of cuneiform texts, reliefs and administrative texts, suggested that in the neo-Assyrian practice the use of chains was rare, but also cited warnings to soldiers to protect the exiles from abuse. Exiles are depicted in Assyrian reliefs accompanied by animals and family members as well as carrying supplies. There is clear evidence that neo-Babylonian practice was similar. The Weidner Text, the only cuneiform document we have from Babylon that explicitly mentions Jehoiachin,[14] is a ration list that refers to the king's sons which (according to 2 Kings) he did not have when he first left Jerusalem. Secondly, we know that Jeremiah advised the exiles in the famous "letter" of chap. 29, to let their sons and daughters marry, and we presume that he was not advocating mixed marriages. But Jer 40:1 *does* refer to chains (cf. Nah 3:10) and the oracles against Babylon in Jeremiah 50–51 condemn severity. This lends [[78]] some credibility to Josephus's later reference to exiles in chains.[15] J. M. Wilkie believes that the treatment of the exiles was increasingly severe, noting the references in Deutero-Isaiah, especially 42:22, but including 40:2; 41:11–12; 42:7; 47:6; 49:9, 13, 24–26, which all seem to refer to serious suffering and confinement.[16] Finally, one can consider the term for 'yoke' על. In only a minority of cases does על refer to working animals. In Isa 10:27; 14:25 and notably 9:4, all probably exilic–postexilic, there is a clear reference to forced labour or confinement. In any case, על as a reference to the conditions of exile becomes common, in connection with "those that have enslaved you" in Ezek 34:27, in Jer 28:48, and Isa 47:6. And certainly, one must keep in mind the canonical legacy of Babylon as the archetypal symbol for the oppressor, a symbol that remained viable even for early Christian radicals who intended a reference to Rome (as in the book of Revelation). Dandamaev has admittedly concluded that there is no evidence for chattel slavery in this period,[17] but while this may certainly be the case, there is other evidence that the need for the concentration of captive populations in the Babylonian heartland was as much for labour as for discouraging revolt in the defeated territories. In short, deportees may not have become slaves in the technical or conceptual sense that we understand this term, especially under the

14. E. F. Weidner, "Jojachin, König von Juda, in Babylonischen Keilschrifttexten," in *Mélanges Syriens offerts à monsieur René Dussaud* (Paris: Geuthner, 1939) 2.923–35.

15. Josephus, *Ant.* 10.100–103 (p. 212 in Loeb 6).

16. J. M. Wilkie, "Nabonidus and the Later Jewish Exiles," *JTS* ns 2 (1951) 36–44.

17. M. Dandamaev, "Social Stratification in Babylonia, 7th to 4th Century B.C.," in J. Harmatta and G. Komoroczy (eds.), *Wirtschaft und Gesellschaft im alten Vorderasien* (Budapest: Akademiai Kiado, 1976) 433–44.

influence of images of post–Civil War American slavery, but centralized work forces are another matter.

. . . .

⟦79⟧ The cumulative force of this evidence is that the Babylonian exile was no holiday as long as the Chaldaean rulers were in charge, however much conditions changed with the arrival of the Persians.[18] This background information, then, allows us to appreciate more fully the sociological factors in the formation of exilic–postexilic society.

The Formation of a "Culture of Resistance"

⟦80⟧ Survival of a disaster (as the exile was) requires the achievement of social solidarity. We need therefore to ask: are there indications of such a solidarity in the exilic community during and after the exile?[19] To begin with, the presence of elders gathering to consult the prophet Ezekiel is, as I have mentioned, significant. Elders acting as communal leaders are a very old institution in ancient Israelite society, although Rost has suggested that they grew less prominent with the increasing bureaucratic divisions associated with the Solomonic and post-Solomonic monarchy.[20] Their presence in Ezekiel, and their prominence in Ezra–Nehemiah, suggests self-government. The gathering at the city gate to hear cases was apparently replaced by gatherings in homes, as we find in Ezekiel. But beyond the presence of elders, there is considerable uncertainty about the precise nature of the communal leadership attested in the exilic literature. Among his fascinating studies of postexilic Judaean society, Weinberg has pointed out that the *bêt ʾābôt* ⟦'house of fathers', 'clan'⟧ emerged as one of the central characteristic components of the postexilic community.[21] Weinberg has shown that *bêt ʾābôt*, or simply *ʾābôt*, are characteristic of the postexilic literature, and further elucidates this social constituent of the postexilic, as opposed to pre-exilic, social formation. The most intriguing problem in relation to the *bêt ʾābôt* is the numbers of its members indicated by the "Golah ⟦'diaspora'⟧ List." This text, which appears in Ezra 2 / Nehemiah 7 (as well as in 1 Esdras 5) is considered by many scholars to be a genuine indication of the exilic communal structure in the decades after the liberation by Cyrus. In his

18. This would be against opinions such as the following: "Once settled, however, it appears that they enjoyed considerable economic well-being. This may be gathered from Jeremiah's letter . . ." (I. Zeitlin, *Ancient Judaism* [Oxford: Polity Press, 1984] 259).

19. See I. Ephᶜal, "The Western Minorities in Babylonia in the 6th to 5th Centuries BC: Maintenance and Cohesion," *Orientalia* ns 47 (1978) 74–90.

20. L. Rost, *Vorstufen zur Kirche und Synagoge im Alten Testament* (Stuttgart, 1938).

21. J. Weinberg, "Das Beit-ʾAbot im 6-4 Jh. v.u.Z.," *VT* 23 (1973) 400–414.

commentary on Ezra–Nehemiah, Rudolph argues for an early date for the list, based on his observations of the internal evidence in the list itself.[22] It appears to have a clear beginning and ending as a separate document, it is associated most clearly with Zerubbabel, and it refers to the banning of the family of Hakkoz from priestly functions, while elsewhere in Ezra–Nehemiah (Neh 3:4, 21 [[81]] and Ezra 8:33) Uriah, a son of Hakkoz, is clearly restored. Alt, and more recently Galling, have associated the list with the rebuilding of the Temple, which they date to approximately 525–520 or 18 years after the traditional date for the liberation by Cyrus in 538.[23] But what we are specifically interested in is the *bôt ʾābôt* in the Golah List, and most specifically, the numbers associated with them. Batten doubted the authenticity of the list, owing in part to his doubts about the large numbers for families when compared to the pre-exilic *bêt ʾāb*. Agreeing with Meyer, who wrote before the turn of the century, Batten speculated that the confusion of the numbers may be associated with an apparent confusion between family names, and names of places of residence, indicated by the variation between the terms 'sons of' and 'residents of' (בני and אנשי).[24] But let us review briefly why the numbers of the constituent units appear to present a problem by considering work on pre-exilic forms. The classic exposition of pre-exilic Judaean society is given in Joshua 7. J. Scharbert,[25] considering this and other textual references to the 'House of the Father', believes that the *bêt ʾāb*, a blood-related family of a living eldest male, could conceivably consist of four generations. On the basis of Judges 9, Scharbert calculated that Gideon's family could have been composed of as many as seventy adult males (although the Judges passage is problematic, since there is a clear emphasis on unusual circumstances and epic-sized events). Gottwald concluded that a single *bêt ʾāb* [['father's house']] could consist of 150 persons or more.[26] Finally, Stager's interesting archaeological contributions to this debate resulted in his postulation [[82]] of a dwelling unit that was conceivably based on the *bêt ʾāb*:

22. W. Rudolph, *Ezra und Nehemiah* (Tübingen: Mohr, 1949) 7–17.

23. See K. Galling, "The 'Gola-List' according to Ezra 2 / Neh 7," *JBL* 70 (1971) 149–58 and *Studien zur Geschichte Israels im persischen Zeitalter* (Tübingen: Mohr, 1964). Alt wanted to date the return to the era of Cambyses' invasion of Egypt, while Galling prefers a time when Darius had successfully put down the revolt of the self-proclaimed "Nebuchadnezzar III." At this time Zerubbabel could go to Darius and point out that the Jews remained loyal and deserved to be allowed to rebuild in Palestine.

24. L. Batten, *Ezra and Nehemiah* (ICC; Edinburgh: T. & T. Clark, 1913) 71–81.

25. J. Scharbert, "Beyt Ab als soziologische Grösse im Alten Testament," in W. Delsman, J. Peters and W. Romer (eds.), *Von Kanaan bis Kerala* (FS J. van der Ploeg; Berlin, 1972) 213–38.

26. N. K. Gottwald, *The Tribes of Yahweh. A Sociology of Liberated Israel* (Maryknoll, N.Y.: Orbis, 1979) 285ff.

it is likely that the spatially isolated clusters of dwellings—the compounds—housed the minimal *bêt ʾāb*. . . if we assume that a honeycomb
pattern prevailed at Raddana, i.e., an even distribution of contiguous,
multiple family compounds throughout the settlement, there might have
been 20 or more such households in the village, totalling ca. 200 persons
under high fertility—low mortality conditions. But this projection may
be too high. . . . These upper estimates do not take into account the various phases of the family cycle within established multiple family households, the establishment of new nuclear households, and the dissolution
of others. . . .[27]

In any case, it is a long stretch between the numbers of the *bêt ʾāb*
familial unit in either Gottwald, Stager or Scharbert's estimates, and
the numbers given for the postexilic *bêt ʾābôt* [['house of fathers', 'clan']].
As I have indicated, many scholars have suggested that the List itself is of
dubious authority. Others have suggested that the *bêt ʾābôt* is simply a
continuation of the pre-exilic *mišpāḥôt* [['families']], rather than of the
bêt ʾāb.[28] But I think that Mowinckel was on the right track when he suggested that what we have are, in fact, fictionalized family units.[29] More
recently, Robert Wilson suggested that genealogical reformation often
reflects changed social circumstances,[30] and this is further illustrated in
the anthropological work of Tait and Middleton.[31] If we follow this line
of reasoning, then we must ask what kind of social circumstances would
give rise to such a suggested "rearrangement" of the basic familial unit
in the exile?

I would like to submit three interrelated possibilities that are suggested by biblical texts. They are: (1) the creation of social solidarity in
order to preserve the integrity of the social unit under [[83]] pressure,
reflected in (2) the creation of a minority group consciousness characterized by social borders delimiting the "inside" and "outside" of the
group, and also by concerns for purity and group integrity, and (3) the
possible results of adaptation to organizational units imposed from outside the social group, perhaps in order to facilitate centrally assigned work
duties. The last point is the most speculative, and I must admit that I am

27. L. Stager, "The Archaeology of the Family in Ancient Israel," *BASOR* 260 (1985) 1–
36 (22–23).

28. There is, however, a rather stubborn insistence in Numbers (P) to associate *bêt ʾāb*
with larger social units, and never with the *mišpāḥôt*. The point is that the term *bêt ʾābôt* was
coined to equate the solidarity of the smaller unit with the size of the larger unit.

29. S. Mowinckel, "Die Listen," in *Studien zu dem Buche Esra–Nehemia*, vol. 1 (Oslo:
Universitetsforlaget, 1964) 62–162.

30. R. Wilson, *Genealogy and History in the Biblical World* (New Haven: Yale University
Press, 1977).

31. D. Tait and J. Middleton, *Tribes without Rulers* (London: Routledge & Kegan Paul,
1958).

still in the process of formulating it. In outline, what I want to suggest is that a possible explanation of who ended up with what group among the exiles in a settlement or neighbourhood (which was then fictionalized into a familial unit) may have been partially determined by a central authority whose main interest was the organization of groups to provide work crews. This possibility was suggested to me not only by the evidence I have already cited for work among the neo-Babylonian captive populations, but also on at least two biblical precedents. First, Solomon's building programme required strict bureaucratic social organization (see 2 Chr 7:17, relating Solomon's census to David's earlier census). Even though 1 Kgs 9:22 claims that Hebrews were not made workers (but cf. 1 Kgs 5:13), part of the revolt of Jeroboam after Solomon's death was fuelled by the complaints of Northerners with regard to the severity of the yoke imposed upon them by Solomon. Secondly, Nehemiah's work assignments (Nehemiah 3) in Jerusalem were centrally directed by crews provided by strictly recorded units, some of whom appeared to resemble the units of the Golah [['di-aspora']] List while others were apparently guilds of specialized workers—although those two features may not have been exclusive. The frequency of the "yoke" image, in relation to the exile itself, as well as Solomon's work assignments (1 Kgs 12:4), has already been alluded to. Finally, we have the (admittedly very late) passage from Josephus that the Jews were "settled" by the Babylonians according to "allotments."[32]

We know, at any rate, that there was a tendency among the exiles to identify themselves as a special community, a kind of "hibakusha" community (borrowing the term used by Japanese survivors of the atom bomb) with a marked particularism. Still in the time of Ezra, probably 70–90 years after the liberation of Cyrus, the community was using terms like 'children of the Golah', and 'the holy seed' (בני הגלה, זרע קרש, Ezra 9:2). The break-up of mixed marriages is [[84]] only the most dramatic example among many others that we could cite, of a community very much concerned with what the Norwegian anthropologist Frederick Barth has called "boundary maintenance" and Bernard Siegel refers to as "defense structuring."[33] The break-up of mixed marriages, as a sociological as well as theological phenomenon, has caused a great deal of anxiety among scholars who anguish over the theological implications of exclusivity.[34] This is to miss the point, however. From the socio-psychological

32. *Apion* 1.128–42 (Loeb 1), quoting Berossus.

33. F. Barth, *Ethnic Groups and Boundaries. The Social Organization of Cultural Difference* (Bergen: Universitetsforlaget, 1969); B. Siegel, "Defense Structuring and Environmental Stress," *AJS* 76 (1970–71) 11–32.

34. J. G. Vink bends over backwards to make Ezra "ecumenical," but in doing so must deny the historicity of the break-up of marriages. See "The Date and Origin of the Priestly Code in the Old Testament," *OS* 15 (1969) 30–33.

and anthropological work that has been done on the sociology of refugee behaviour and the survival of disaster, we know that the ability of a group to reconstruct its identity is essential to its survival in a foreign cultural environment. One can cite, for example, the work of Elise Brenner, Richard Clemmer, and Edward Spicer on American Indian cultural strategies for survival. The wider anthropological work of Frederick Barth and Nelson Graburn on strategies of boundary maintenance mechanisms allows us to see that the social forms that a minority, exiled, or refugee community creates can be the result not of a desperate attempt to cling to pointless and antiquated traditions from a previous era or homeland, but rather a creative construction of a "culture of resistance" that preserves group solidarity and cultural identity.[35]

Seen in this way, the work of the priests (the Priestly revisers of the Pentateuch, the prophet-priest Ezekiel and Ezra) is to be understood in a new light. Indeed, Weinberg's argument that the priests emerged as the leaders of the postexilic community would tend to be supported [[85]] in this way.[36] A sociological analysis would challenge the Wellhausean prejudice of a sacerdotal decline from prophetic majesty, by pointing to the creation of a culture of resistance by priests who faced very real political and social threats in a massive disaster like the Babylonian exile. Part of this culture, as Mary Douglas has so helpfully illustrated in her analysis of Leviticus,[37] is a concern for ritual purity that expresses, symbolically, the concern to preserve the integrity of the social group:

> When rituals express anxiety about the body's orifices, the sociological counterpart of this anxiety is a care to protect the political and cultural unity of a minority group . . .
> . . . pollution behavior is the reaction which condemns any object or idea likely to confuse or contradict cherished classifications (pp. 36, 124).

The revision of the older priestly laws, wherein we see the main concern with the transfer of pollution, becomes a characteristic concern of the exilic period. This can be illustrated briefly by a consideration of the re-

35. As a beginning see M. Barkun, *Disaster and the Millennium* (New Haven: Yale University Press, 1974); A. Wallace, "Revitalization Movements," *American Anthropologist* 58 (1956) 264–81; W. Peterson, "A General Typology of Migration," *American Sociological Review* 23 (1958) 256–65; E. Kunz, "Exile and Resettlement: Refugee Theory," *International Migration Review* 15 (1981) 42–51; H. B. M. Murphy, "Flight and Resettlement: The Camps" (Geneva: UNESCO, 1955); L. Baskauskas, "The Lithuanian Refugee Experience and Grief," *International Migration Review* 15 (1981) 276–91; N. Graburn, *Ethnic and Tourist Arts: Cultural Expressions from the Fourth World* (Berkeley: University of California Press, 1976) especially the Introduction.

36. Weinberg, "Das Beit-ʾAbot," n. 4.

37. M. Douglas, *Purity and Danger* (New York: Praeger, 1966) [[for an excerpt from Douglas's book, see pp. 119–34 in this volume]].

dactional history of a passage like Leviticus 11, and a brief consideration of the term בדל. In their form-critical studies of levitical priestly law, Elliger, Reventlow, Koch, and Rendtorff have proved that the priestly redactors of the exilic–postexilic period reworked older cultic traditions.[38] An example is Lev 11:2–23, which appears in Deut 14:1–20, suggesting an earlier source. But only Leviticus continues with detailed passages on the *transfer* of pollution in vv. 24–47. According to Elliger, vv. 46–47 are the final additions to this passage, a summary of the concerns of the entire passage.[39] The key term here is בדל 'make a separation'. Apart from its strictly cultic uses, P employs this term to refer to separation between *peoples* (Num 16:21; Lev 20:24, 26). In Ezra–Nehemiah it applies always to the separation of the "holy community" (Neh 13:3)—from foreign [[86]] wives (Ezra 10:11), the ʿam hāʾāretz [['people of the land']] (Ezra 9:1; Neh 10:31) and the gōyē hāʾāretz [['peoples of the land']] (Ezra 6:21). This use of בדל is a key to discovering the Priestly theology of a "culture of resistance" (or a "spirituality of resistance") which uses a religious term to accomplish social ends, namely the avoidance of social "pollution."

To return to the *bêt ʾābôt*, and conclude this section on communal formation, I want to suggest that what has occurred in the expansion of the basic familial unit for pre-exilic society (the *bêt ʾāb*) is a fictionalized family unit. Thus far I follow Mowinckel. But I want to argue further that this expansion is yet another example of creating a "culture of resistance" by increasing the level of social solidarity and communal protection: the drawing inward in a fictionalized familial unit in response to the pressures of a hostile foreign environment, and the teaching of a theology of separation to protect boundaries. It is important to note that Frederick Barth's research revealed that the creation of "boundary maintenance" social responses was not in any way mitigated by the mutual intelligibility of spoken languages or similarity of cultures.

The Return from Exile and Social Conflict with "Outsiders"

One final area of investigation remains. If such a "hibakusha" group as suggested above was created, we would expect to see evidence of that group's interaction with, or tensions with, those outside the group. There

---

38. See K. Elliger, "Sinn und Ursprung der priesterlichen Geschichtserzahlung," *Kleine Schriften* (München, 1966); H. G. Reventlow, *Das Heiligkeitsgesetz formgeschichtliche Untersucht* (WMANT; Berlin, 1961); K. Koch, *Die Priesterschrift von Ex. 25 bis Lev. 16. Eine überlieferungsgeschichtliche und literarkritische Untersuchung* (Göttingen: Vandenhoeck & Ruprecht, 1959); R. Rendtorff, *Die Gesetz in der Priesterschrift* (Göttingen: Vandenhoeck & Ruprecht, 1963).

39. "Sinn und Ursprung," 148ff.

are a number of theories about just such tensions in the postexilic community, which we can briefly summarize. It is here that we bring into our analysis an important sociological element which we have not mentioned before, namely those Jews who were not taken into exile and remained in the land.

As a starting point, I take Hag 2:10–14. The debate surrounding this passage reveals many related issues. Inequality between those who were in an advantaged position at the restoration and those who were disadvantaged, conflict with the Samaritans, and the dispute about the rebuilding of the Temple, all rise from this particular passage. The final phrase is crucial:

> Haggai then spoke out, It is the same with this people, he said, the same with this nation as I see it—it is Yahweh who speaks— the same with everything they turn their hands to, and what they offer there is unclean. . . .

⟦87⟧ The LXX adds the following curious phrase, part of which echoes Amos 5:10:

> because of their quickly won gains, they will suffer for their labours and you hated those dispensing justice at the city gate. . . .

The context of Amos 5 is an oracle against economic injustice that is detrimental to the poor. Could this addition be here because of an early interpretation of this passage as referring to those repressing the poor of the "Return"?

Rothstein had already argued in 1908[40] that this passage represents yet another example of the break between the postexilic Judaic community and the Samaritans, that is, those who began their syncretistic religion because of the exchange of populations by the Assyrian conquerors, as particularly reported in the annals of Sargon (*ANET*, p. 284). This view has many supporters including Rudolph, Koch, Elliger and Bowman.

Rothstein's original assumption that Hag 2:10–14 refers to the Samaritan split is open to question. Coggins has convincingly shown that the identification of the group theoretically opposed to the Jerusalem Temple community as Samaritans involves a significant assumption about the Samaritan community itself. That is, Samaritanism could hardly be consid-

---

40. J. W. Rothstein, *Juden und Samaritaner* (Leipzig: Hinrichs, 1908).

ered heathen or syncretistic if their main trait came to be precisely their *conservatism*:

> the basic features of Samaritan belief and practice have been seen to be very closely akin to those of Judaism, the differences being only of a kind which mark out the Samaritans as more conservative than Rabbinic Judaism came to be. One might well feel compelled to ask why Samaritans and Jews ever parted, and what distinguished them from each other. . . .[41]

Commentators such as Morton Smith[42] still maintain that such an evolution is possible, although I think Coggins has given good reason to believe that this is unlikely. As Coggins concludes:

> [[88]] The simple truth is . . . that there is no reference to the Samaritans in the Hebrew Old Testament . . . Samaritanism is part of that larger complex which constitutes the Judaism of the last pre-Christian centuries . . . (p. 163).

Another scholarly tradition, seen especially in the work of Mitchell, Bloomhardt, Welch, Ackroyd and May[43] sees Hag 2:10–14 as a condemnation of the returning Jewish community itself in the same vein as the first chapter, and for the same reason: the building of the Temple. Ackroyd states: "if their offerings are unclean—that is, unacceptable—then so is their whole life and condition."[44] May has argued that there are many prophetic analogies both to the arguments of the prophets that the people can be unclean, and to the double use of the reference "nation" and "people," and thus does not accept that Haggai himself made any references to the separation of communities in Palestine by using the term "remnant" (which he would say belongs to a later redactor under the influence of the Chronicler[45]). He continues, "the burden of proof

---

41. R. J. Coggins, *Samaritans and Jews. The Origins of Samaritanism Reconsidered* (Oxford: Blackwell, 1975) 138.

42. Morton Smith, *Palestinian Parties and Politics That Shaped the Old Testament* (New York: Columbia University Press, 1971) 92: "the Samaritan cult on Mt. Gerizim is probably a survival of one practiced during the Israelite monarchy. . . ."

43. H. G. Mitchell, *Haggai and Zechariah* (ICC; Edinburgh: T. & T. Clark, 1912); P. Bloomhardt, "The Poems of Haggai," *HUCA* 5 (1928) 153–95; A. C. Welch, *Post-Exilic Judaism* (Edinburgh: T. & T. Clark, 1935); P. R. Ackroyd, *Exile and Restoration* (London: SCM Press, 1968); H. G. May, "'This People' and 'This Nation' in Haggai," *VT* 18 (1968) 190–97.

44. *Exile and Restoration*, 168. As we shall see, the claim that Israel was not yet holy without its Temple is an assumption based largely on Haggai, but even Haggai's earlier warning about the absence of the Temple was based on misfortunes such as drought and not fear of unatoned "impurity." Where, then, is this idea corroborated?

45. "'This People' and 'This Nation,'" 192.

lies on those who presume [the reference to another people in 2:14] and would therefore make a distinction between 'the people' in 2:14 and 'this people' in 1:2, which refers to the Judean community." . . .

[[89]] The symbolic logic of the metaphor is not usually given attention. The metaphor does *not* deal with a single entity that is in a particular "state of being," that is, "pure" or "impure" (such as the passage quoted by May in Isa 64:56). One would have expected a single substance or people in the metaphor if *one body* of people is meant here. The prophet, however, refers to two substances in relation to each other, *transferring purity or impurity from one to the other.* The metaphor refers to groups of actual people, for the text plainly makes the transition from v. 14: "so it is with this people. . . ." There is a strain in the logic of the argument if one does not make this transition from "relations between substances" to "relations between peoples." A separation between pure and impure groups (food or bodies) implies a schism between those that are addressed by Haggai, and those that are referred to as עם [['people']] and גוי [['nation']].

We have already made reference to the work of Mary Douglas, and her arguments are relevant here also, especially her assertion that purity fears relate to ritualistic anxiety about classification and protection of boundaries. Douglas's theory that pollution fears are related to societal strains, I submit, is strikingly confirmed by the passage we are considering, where the two themes of purity and group integrity are explicitly integrated. We must recall that the exile itself [[90]] was frequently considered by Ezekiel to be the result of the "pure" Jewish people allowing themselves to be defiled by "Gentiles," thus again emphasizing the dangers of social intercourse—which is indeed often compared to sexual intercourse in the graphic language of prophecy. In Ezekiel 20, which highlights the theme of God's action "for the sake of my name," defilement is declared a result of contact with enemy nations. The theme of exile as punishment for defilement is found in chap. 22 as well.

I thus believe that the grounds for seeing Hag 2:10–14 as reflecting social conflict are strong, for whenever defilement was discussed in the context of defilement by inanimate and living things and enemy nations, these discussions were exilic or postexilic. But even if Haggai *is* referring to the Jewish community itself as those who are defiled, surely the reason cannot be that the Temple had not yet been built so as to remove pollution—which would have meant that pollution was unalterably universal at the destruction of the Temple! In Leviticus 18 and 20, where clear references to the exile are also contained in the postexilic punishment clauses, we find again warnings against defilement (Lev 18:28;

20:22). Without a sociological analysis, such warnings seem to be foreign to the subjects of the chapters themselves, dealing as they do with familial relations.

However, if, as I believe, Haggai is referring to pollution from some group outside the community he is addressing, who is this group? A number of possibilities have already been suggested in the literature.

Religious Conflict after the Exile

This first view comes from those scholars who are a part of what E. W. Nicholson has referred to as the "back-to-Wellhausen" movement. This tendency is seen in Morton Smith's *Palestinian Parties and Politics That Shaped the Old Testament* and Bernhard Lang's *Der einzige Gott*.[46] Lang and Smith believe that Hosea is the most significant early exponent of the monotheistic theology of the "Yahweh Alone Movement." The significance of this background becomes clear when both Smith and Lang refer to a conflict between "parties." The "Yahweh Alone Movement" continued as a minority which struggled [[91]] against the continued syncretism all around, and among, the Jewish people. Citing the constant anti-idolatry messages of the prophets (Jer 44:15ff.) through the exile (Ezek 14:1ff.) and even into the Persian period (Zech 10:2; 13:2), Smith points out that it was a constant struggle in all periods. Lang, largely agreeing with this reading of "monolatry" arising from a "Yahweh Alone" sect, uses more direct sociological terms in describing it: "Yahweh Alone worship can be understood as a crisis cult which continued beyond the actual crisis situation. Or, rather, the crisis situation is perceived as permanent . . ." (p. 23).

Thus, one can talk about a conflict between "Yahweh Alonists" and "Syncretists." But does this line follow the division between "exiles" and those left in Palestine during the exile? Smith does not think the matter is so simple. Syncretists were clearly among the exiles, if one interprets intermarriage of the priests in Ezra 10:18–28 as motivated by such a syncretistic mood (or at least not prevented by a monotheistic one). That economic interests were involved between the exiles as former landlords, and those *dallat hā-ʾāretz* [['poor of the land']] left behind, is also suggested by Smith.[47] But Smith believes that the main lines of the religious conflict, noted in Hag 2:10–19, refer to the religious community of those left in the land; namely, a large number of people who represent the

---

46. Translated into English as *Monotheism and the Prophetic Minority* (Sheffield: Almond Press, 1983).

47. *Palestinian Parties and Politics*, 55ff.

kind of syncretistic worship which so horrified Ezekiel in his vision of his return to the Temple (Ezek 8:1ff.).

Religious/Class Conflict in the Restoration

Paul Hanson's *The Dawn of Apocalyptic*[48] approaches the problems of the beginning of apocalyptic literature in our period by positing social tensions between two groups during and after the exile. Early in Hanson's work, we see that he is drawing a distinction between those who dream visions and those who face the pragmatic decisions of power and control, especially with regard to the cult. This opposition, Hanson believes, continues from even earlier struggles between Zadokites and Levites, and Isa 63:18 suggests that this conflict was "internal" and therefore between rivals within the community of Israelites, not between Israelites and non-Israelites or "syncretists."

[[92]] As far as the conflict between Zadokites and Levites is concerned, there is little doubt that the two groups fell out. But the evidence, especially the chronological evidence, can be interpreted in different ways. In his recent history of the priesthood, for example, Cody points out that, contrary to Hanson's interpretation, Ezekiel's restoration programme represents an important compromise between the two groups, with Levites gaining some advantages they did not previously have.[49] Furthermore, contrary to supporting exclusive claims of either Levite or Zadokite, Trito-Isaiah shows signs of a profound *generalization* of the priesthood; in 61:6 *all Israelites are priests to the rest of the world.* Moreover, 66:21 states that even some from foreign nations will be taken to be priests and levites. Cody notes that by the time of Ezra 8:2, both groups are called "sons of Aaron."

A different theory along similar lines, but with more attention to the formative nature of the exile itself, is provided by Hugo Mantel.[50] Mantel believes that the conflicts of the Hellenistic era between the Pharisees and Sadducees can be traced to the 6th and 5th centuries in conflicts along similar sociopolitical lines, and thus he works backwards into the time we are concerned with. Mantel's main sources are Ezra and Nehemiah. Ezra 7:25–26 interestingly implies that the law which Ezra metes out applies only to those who "know the law" (having been taught?) and punishment also applies only to them. Who, then, are those to whom

---

48. P. D. Hanson, *The Dawn of Apocalyptic* (Philadelphia: Fortress Press, 1975).

49. A. Cody, *A History of the Old Testament Priesthood* (Rome: Pontifical Biblical Institute, 1969) 166.

50. H. Mantel, "The Dichotomy of Judaism during the Second Temple," *HUCA* 44 (1973) 56–87.

Ezra speaks? Precisely to that community, states Mantel, which called itself, again and again, the "sons of the Golah [['diaspora']]." Mantel thus
develops the very interesting theory that the returned exiles formed an
autonomous community on the strength of the social bonds created during the exile. . . .

Class Conflict: Materialist Theories

[[93]] An important aspect of this argument is the potential conflict between the large population that remained behind, and the returning, old
"aristocracy," which provides the material for a "class"-aligned conflict,
as suggested by Janssen.[51] Janssen points to the cordial relationships between Jeremiah and the Babylonians, the latter apparently well aware of
Jeremiah's implicitly pro-Babylonian stand. The possibility of a Jerusalemite "fifth column" within the late pre-exilic community may have had
some influence on the redistribution of the land among those left behind on the land (Jeremiah 40), although as "workers" and not owners,
a view taken also by Alt.[52] Janssen makes the interesting point that the
threat of "foreigners" possessing the lands and fields of Israelites is a
common warning used by the prophets (Amos 5:11; Mic 6:15; Jer 5:17).
In the situation of the exile, one might imagine the foreigners to be
Babylonians, but Janssen refers to the internal conflict of Trito-Isaiah to
suggest that the "foreigners" were other Israelites, who were the "new
ᶜam-hāᵃāretz" [['people of the land']] since they now possessed the land
and enjoyed its fruit. This replacement policy is reflected in passages
such as 1 Kgs 8:33 and Deut 28:43 (which warns of others "in your land").
Thus Hag 2:10–14, 19, with its impure people, and the mention of robbers in Zech 4:1–5; 5:11, all reflect the problem of loss of land by those
in exile.

In selected biblical texts, we can see what a significant issue land
possession was for the exiles [Ezek 11:14–18, 33:23–27]. . . . [[94]] These
sentiments should also be seen in the context of Jeremiah's redemption
of family lands, after which he states, "Fields and vineyards will once
again be bought in this land" (32:6–15). On the basis of these texts, and
the reported redistribution of lands of the people among the *dallat hā-
ᵃāretz* [['poor of the land']], it is obvious that one must consider the possible implications of land dispossession in relation to the return of the

51. E. Janssen, *Juda in der Exilszeit. Ein Beitrag zur Frage der Entstehung des Judentums*
(FRLANT 69; Göttingen: Vandenhoeck & Ruprecht, 1956), especially chap. 1, "Die Bevor-
zugung der *Dallath HaᵃAretz* durch die Babylonier."

52. A. Alt, "Die Rolle Samarias bei der Entstehund des Judentums," in *Kleine Schriften
zur Geschichte des Volkes Israel* 2 (Munich: Beck, 1953) 316–37.

exiles. The most important theorists of class conflict working on this period are Joel Weinberg and Heinz Kreissig.[53] Kreissig's ⟦95⟧ monograph is more concerned with the Achaemenid period, but his ideas about formation and struggle in the Jewish community depend on his analysis of the pre-exilic period, specifically in relation to the monarchy. Kreissig's view is that monarchy in Israel approached a kind of despotic control by the king over massive proportions of the land, which was previously held in the ownership of the *mišpāḥôt* ⟦'families'⟧.[54] If this was the case, as Kreissig states, "In terms of the agricultural forms of production in Judah, there could hardly have been a greater change from the Monarchical period" (p. 26).

Thus, the population of Judah may have struggled on as best they could after the conquest, in small settlements rather than the destroyed cities, as suggested by archaeological evidence, and others may have formed new main population centres, as implied by the movement of Gedaliah to Mizpah (Jeremiah 40). One could easily assume that many of these people did very well, creating a new "upper class" on its own terms. Nehemiah's later efforts to repopulate Jerusalem as a centre of power may well reflect the diversified settlement pattern as a result of the destruction on exile. The rise of a new upper class answerable to the Babylonians is furthermore proved by the neo-Babylonian involvement in Gedaliah's resettlement, and Zedekiah's earlier appointment. In other words, *contra* Alt, there does not seem to be a need to posit a foreign aristocracy, in order for an "upper class" to exist in the area of Palestine after the exile.

Kreissig raises two important points in his analysis. One is that an internal aristocracy existed within Palestine, and even possibly within the Golah community itself, as indicated by Ezra–Nehemiah. The other is that there is also a presence of an external aristocracy, indicated not only

---

53. J. Weinberg, "Probleme der sozialökonomischen Struktur Judäas vom 6. Jahrhundert v.u.Z. bis zum 1. Jahrhundert v.u.Z. (Zu einigen wirtschaftshistorischen Untersuchungen von Heinz Kreissig)," *Jahrbuch für Wirtschaftsgeschichte* 1 (1973) 237–51; H. Kreissig, *Die sozialökonomische Situation in Juda zur Achämenidenzeit* (Schriften zur Geschichte und Kultur des alten Orients 7; Berlin: Akademie, 1973) (see also B. Funck's review of Kreissig, "Zur Bürger-Tempel Gemeinde im nachexilischen Juda," *Klio* 59 [1977] 491–96); H. Kippenberg, *Religion und Klassenbildung im antiken Judäa. Eine religionssoziologische Studie zum Verhältnis von Tradition und gesellschaftlicher Entwicklung* (Göttingen: Vandenhoeck & Ruprecht, 1973). In a recent article comparing the reforms of Solon to Nehemiah, Yamauchi claims that this comparison was "to his knowledge" suggested by Morton Smith. In fact, these three, Weinberg, Kippenberg, and Kreissig, as well as Eisenstadt, have considered such a comparison. See E. Yamauchi, "Two Reformers Compared: Solon of Athens, and Nehemiah of Jerusalem," in G. Rendsburg (ed.), *The Bible World* (FS Cyrus Gordon; ed. G. Rendsburg et al.; New York: Ktav, 1980) 269–92.

54. See Gottwald's helpful analysis of social structure and function in *The Tribes of Yahweh*, 237–344.

by the "Samaritans" and their interest in Judaean affairs, but also implied by the intermarriage of the "chief men and priests" (Ezra 9:1–3). Kreissig supposes that material motivation to regain land was high among the returning Jews from Mesopotamia, and fuelled the class conflict. There may be further hints about the [[96]] economic domination of an internal hierarchy or aristocracy. Kippenberg suggests that the Darian innovation of silver currency throughout the Persian empire, as reported by Herodotus (*Hist.* 111:89), may have brought about a growing impoverishment of farmers, who had to produce more surplus to exchange for silver (explicitly mentioned in Nehemiah 5) to pay taxes, and thus encouraged the independence of small families who could produce more surplus rather than be responsible for more mouths to feed. The failure of some families would then lead to debt-bondage, also reported in Nehemiah 5. Nehemiah's reforms thus sought to deal with this growing economic problem among the Golah community.

We see that there are many lines that inter-communal conflict could follow, and there is greater or lesser evidence for each of them. But the majority of arguments support the suggestion that the Sons of the Golah returned to Palestine only to find their land in the hands of a new *ʿam-hāʾāretz* [['people of the land']] which may have included some of the Samaritan upper-class, or the previous "fifth column" supported by Jeremiah and Gedaliah, or former debtors and even slaves. Some of the families were able to re-establish themselves quickly, by intermarriage or by independent means, such as those whom Haggai scolds for building their own homes before attending to the Temple. But the larger group created, whether intentionally or as a result of their ideology, a separate community with an independent ethos. This community also found itself engaged in a largely class-oriented conflict with both the aristocracy from the "return," and those who were able to intermarry and regain their former status. Attention to social mechanisms for survival, however, cautions against a predominantly materialist basis for postexilic conflict. I would argue that the separate religious, social and structural development of the exiles, apart from those that stayed behind, was antagonized by the arguments over property and finances, but that such conflicts had many other causes as well. In any case, all the evidence, as we have seen, does not lead to an exclusively religious explanation, either.[55]

---

55. I am now working on the problem of intermarriage in the Ezra–Nehemiah material. After consulting some of the contemporary literature on the sociology of cross-cultural, cross-racial and cross-class marriage, I again see that new questions must be asked about the implications of this problem for the self-consciousness of the postexilic "Sons of the Golah," and the economic complications of intermarriage.

Summary

⟦97⟧ There is little doubt that Ezra's constant use of the exclusive terms regarding these "Sons of the Golah," the frequent exhortations against intermarriage with the impure of the land, thus possibly corrupting the "pure seed," the priestly reforms (as seen in Leviticus 11 and the discussion of בדל ⟦'separate'⟧), and Nehemiah 5, all add up to a self-conscious community that is occupied with self-preservation, both as a pure community in a religious sense, and also in a material sense, a self-consciousness that continued at least two generations after the liberation of ca. 520 B.C.E. Haggai's use of the term "remnant of the people" has its sociological-theological parallel in Ezra's use of "holy seed"—both terms that are important not only for those they include, but also for those they exclude. Social boundaries erected as a mechanism for survival led to conflicts upon returning to Palestine. The exiles formed a community not only self-consciously defined—a "Hibakusha" community—a community of "survivors" who returned to Palestine, but who also formulated a theology of innocence and purity against the defilement of those who remained behind complete with social structures to accommodate the communal solidarity requirements. To be troubled by what appears to be "exclusivism" on the part of Haggai, or to feel a need to put an acceptable face on the separation of the marriages in Ezra–Nehemiah, is to misunderstand profoundly the nature of group solidarity and survival of minorities. Sociological literature, as we have seen, alerts the biblical exegete towards a possibility of a creative response to the threat of domination and minority existence. We are invited to look at Ezra–Nehemiah, Haggai, and others from an "exilic consciousness," from the perspective of their worries and experiences in order to understand fully the "politics of Ezra."

INDEX OF AUTHORITIES

INDEX OF SCRIPTURE

Scripture is indexed according to Hebrew chapter and verse divisions; where the Hebrew versification differs, English chapter and verse are supplied in brackets.

Hebrew Bible

567

New Testament and Deuterocanonical Books